BEHOLD!
THE
POLISH-AMERICANS

Also by Dr. Joseph A. Wytrwal

AMERICA'S POLISH HERITAGE

POLES IN AMERICA

POLES IN AMERICAN HISTORY AND TRADITION

Books Edited by Dr. Joseph A. Wytrwal

POLAND—THE CAPTIVE SATELLITE
by John W. Zurawski

KOSCIUSZKO
by Dr. Joseph Johns

AN AMERICAN IN POLAND
by Anne J. Pawelek

TALES OF EARLY POLAND
by Sigmund H. Uminski

GIRYS I BIRUTA
by Dr. Joseph Lukaszewicz

KOPERNIK THE GREAT HUMANIST
by Benedict Markowski

Behold!
the
Polish-Americans

by

JOSEPH A. WYTRWAL

ENDURANCE PRESS
Detroit, Michigan

ISBN 910552-01-7

Library of Congress Catalog Card Number: 77-84476

First Edition

BEHOLD! THE POLISH-AMERICANS
Copyright © 1977 by Joseph A. Wytrwal

All rights in this book are reserved. No part of the book may be used or reproduced in any manner whatsoever without written permission except in the case of brief quotations embodied in critical articles and reviews. For information address Endurance Press, 5695 Lumley Street, Detroit, Michigan 48210.

Printed in the United States of America

To
NELLIE KADLOF WYTRWAL
My Mother

ACKNOWLEDGMENTS

During the process of research and composition, a number of individuals gave the author valued and liberal assistance which is hereby gratefully acknowledged.

Unlimited assistance was given by Benedict Markowski, who critically read the entire manuscript, and subjected it to his characteristically exacting and perceptive analysis. His meticulous and shrewd criticism and detailed suggestions were of inestimable benefit. For this time-consuming and highly important task I am especially grateful. In addition, I am also grateful for the Foreword written by Benedict Markowski.

Over the years, John Kowalski, Vice-President of the Association of Sons of Poland, consistently sent information on past and contemporary Polish-Americans in the New York area. For this material as well as for his continuing interest, I am most grateful. John Kowalski by example emulates Jakub Bojko's dictum—"Zbierzcie te okruszyny, aby nie zginely."

Henry Polowniak, librarian, Orchard Lake Schools, gave freely of his time in locating useful material for this study.

Dolores E. Mulcahy and Don Fucinari prepared the index.

Henry Archacki prepared the maps.

J.A.W.

July 14, 1977
Detroit, Michigan

Table of Contents

Foreword by Benedict Markowski ix

1. THE POLISH INHERITANCE 1
2. PRELUDE TO THE POLISH PEASANT IMMIGRATION 33
3. POLISH PEASANT IMMIGRANTS 88
4. RISE OF NATIONAL FRATERNAL ORGANIZATIONS 138
5. THE POLISH-IRISH ENCOUNTER 174
6. WORLD WAR I 197
7. DISSOLUTION AND ASSEVERATION 233
8. THE SECOND GENERATION 265
9. POLISH CULTURAL HERITAGE IN AMERICA 288
10. POLISH-AMERICAN CULTURAL ORGANIZATIONS 302
11. THE VALIANT YEARS (1939-1945) 335
12. IN THE SERVICE OF THEIR COUNTRY 365
13. YALTA 399
14. THE PAX AMERICANA (1945-1950) 419
15. WAR IN KOREA 431
16. WAR IN VIETNAM 436
17. POLISH-BLACK RELATIONS IN AMERICA 457
18. POLISH-JEWISH RELATIONS IN AMERICA 497
19. POLISH-INDIAN RELATIONS IN AMERICA 524
20. POLES AND THE AMERICAN LABOR MOVEMENT 533
21. THE CATHOLIC CHURCH VS. POLONIA 554
22. THE THIRD GENERATION 579
23. AMERICA IN THE BICENTENNIAL 600

Bibliography 609

Index 625

Appendix 667

FOREWORD

Behold! The Polish-Americans is Dr. Wytrwal's third major attempt to write a history of an indefatigable ethnic group which emigrated from Europe many centuries ago. Their history has been recorded in books, periodicals, monographs, pamphlets, etc., in many different languages, but never so thoroughly in English under one cover.

Although Dr. Wytrwal returns to some of the same topics which appeared in his two previous histories: *America's Polish Heritage* (published in 1961) and *Poles in American History and Tradition* (published in 1969), here again, eight years later, Dr. Wytrwal has produced a new title which has almost double the number of pages of his previous histories. He has not only amplified the information previously covered (wherever necessary), but he has also added several new chapters which offer an additional dimension to his work: notably a sociological comparative study of the Poles as they relate to Blacks, Jews, Indians, and the Irish during their American encounter. This reveals new facets of their positive democratic character; unlike the image that has been unfairly disseminated by some of these groups for anti-propaganda purposes.

The Poles are also treated in chapters involving them in the Labor movement during the oppressive years from the mid-nineteenth century to the present.

Dr. Wytrwal also considers, how the third and later generations of Polish-Americans, unlike the second, have returned to a self-awareness of their Polish heritage with a fierce pride that has been exhibited at such popular Polish festivals (which are a continuation of the picnics and gatherings they held during the valiant World War II years) or commemorative parades. Even new classes in Polish language and culture, at different institutions of higher learning, convey more of this latent aggressive search for the unique identity and heritage. The establishment of a variety of Polish cultural organizations have enabled their people to preserve some semblance of Polish culture and traditions.

The entire history is prefaced by a summary, albeit a lengthy one, of Poland's 1000 years in order to convey gleanings about their distinctive character which recurs over the centuries as they were confronted with numerous obstacles. It enables the reader to comprehend the Polish character which appears noblest under stress. All of this information must preface the various migrations, especially the largest one comprising of Polish peasants from the southern region or earlier from the Baltic Coast (Kaszuby) or Poznan region who pioneered in Michigan and established numerous Polish communities: among the earliest is an historic hamlet called Parisville which now vies with Panna Maria, Texas as the earliest Polish permanent settlement in the United States.

Dr. Wytrwal fully discusses the rise of national fraternal organizations, which phenomenon arose during a time when social needs of immigrants were not considered by the Land of Plenty. Out of desperation and a new feeling of isolation these divergent Poles congregated to form new societies, organizations, pressure groups in America. They continued their philosophy of self-reliance in many ways which often provided as many solutions as new differences and rivalries. The clash became more apparent on religious grounds. The Poles were reverent Catholics throughout the centuries and continued their support of the Church even though the Church displayed callousness, lack of appreciation and a denial of representation towards them. This led to the fourth major national schism against the Catholic Church, after the Orthodox, Lutheran and Anglican Churches, with the establishment of the Polish National Catholic Church. Others reacted anti-clerically, who envisioned a national organization established on broader and more democratic interests which would benefit the Polish citizens living in the United States.

Their heroism and patriotism is best displayed in the chapters which cover the great wars of the 20th century, including the interim after World War I when Poland regained its independence. The Valiant Years depicts how Poland struggled to preserve its hard-won independence after the German and Russian onslaught to reconquer it; and during the post war era when the struggle against Communist captivity ensued to little avail because of a myopic foreign policy of our democratic presidents. Other chapters reveal the Rolls of Honor of Polish-American combatants from private to commissioned officers from World War II, to Korea and later Vietnam.

The closing chapter brings us to the present with the celebration of the American Bicentennial, a milestone in our history which this book notably proves the contributions of these forebearing and distinctive Slavs.

Working closely with the author during the last two years has been a time-consuming task. But the final product brings personal satisfaction that a good work has been accomplished which now can be utilized by all interested in the subject as a reference work, for casual perusal or self-identification.

BENEDICT MARKOWSKI

July 10, 1977
Detroit, Michigan

Ja kocham caly narod!—objalem w ramiona
Wszystkie przeszle i przyszle jego pokolenia,
Przycisnalem do lona
Jak przyjaciel, kochanek, malzonek
Jak ojciec.

Chce go dzwignac, uszczesliwic
Chce nim caly swiat zadziwic.

—*Adam Mickiewicz*

No man may love the beauty of his race
Unless he knows the path by which he came,
Unless he knows that blood-soaked, hallowed place
Where histories of the ages call his name;
Where footsteps of his fathers traced the soil
From sun's arising to the last moon's wane,
With hieroglyphics attesting the toil
Of harvesting and sowing of the grain.

O knowledge born of beauty, bearing love,
O threefold, priceless heritage of man,
Man fit to arm and wear the bright shield of
Wisdom—and walk among her royal clan!
Unless he touch his fingers to the plain
Can man have knowledge—nor be born again.

—Victoria Janda: *The Heritage*

BEHOLD!
THE
POLISH-AMERICANS

CHAPTER ONE

The Polish Inheritance*

"La Pologne est la clef de voute de l'Europe."
—Napoleon I

Poland is one of the few countries with a national image strong enough not only to have survived political upheavals, wars, partitions, and persecutions, but even thrived through these ordeals. The national history of Poland is long and glorious. Poland had been not only one of the great powers of Europe, but geographically it was one of the largest nations of Europe. For centuries Poland withstood the Teutonic threat from the west, north and south. During the period of the Counter-Reformation in the North, Poland had been an island of refuge for dissenters despite the fact it was a Catholic country. And for a whole century Poland had been a warden of Europe against the Turks. Under King Jan Sobieski Poland had rolled back the Turkish tide from the very walls of Vienna and eliminated the possibility of the Ottoman Empire to extend its western frontier to the Rhine, or even Paris. Had the Turks succeeded, the Moslem religion would predominate in Europe today instead of Catholicism. That was the significance of Sobieski's victory!

During a reign of a thousand years, the boundaries and extent of the Polish state have changed several times. As late as 1770, Poland was a vast country extending from the Baltic Sea almost to

---

* Racial qualities are not only inherited, but all people have a history and common culture with an awareness which goes far toward shaping their outlook on life. A brief backward glance at Polish history clarifies much about the Poles and the national traits which they brought to America. The non-Polish reader may find it useful to glance at a brief or summarized history of Poland in order to have a point of reference.

the Black Sea, lying between Russia and Germany with an area of about 280,000 square miles and a population roughly estimated at eleven-and-a-half million. It stood third in rank among European nations as regards extent, and fifth in population. Between 1772 and 1795, Russia, Prussia and Austria had partitioned Poland after many centuries of stable, national and progressive government. An independent Poland ceased to exist until its rebirth following World War I, although there were brief periods when the Duchy of Warsaw and the Congress Kingdom of Poland did unsuccessfully attempt to regain its freedom.[1] At best, they were semi-autonomous states set up to appease the valiant Polish spirit.

Today, as a result of the international agreement—reached without Poland's participation at the Yalta Conference with the "Big Three Powers"—Poland's geographical area comprises approximately 121,000 square miles. This is a twenty percent reduction prior to its invasion in 1939, and its fourth partition by Germany and the Soviet Union. Along Poland's eastern border a swath of land from 50 to 150 miles wide was annexed by the Soviet Union with the callous and expedient approval of the United States and Great Britain.

Today, Poland is not one of the world's "great" competing powers. However, her size, population, natural resources and past contributions throughout the centuries can number her among the leading states of the world. Approximately the size of the state of New Mexico, Poland is more than twice the area of Czechoslovakia; and, excluding the Soviet Union, Poland is surpassed, in Europe, only by France, Spain and Sweden. Neither West Germany nor East Germany is larger than Poland. Its gross national product surpasses all the states of South America and Africa, most of the states of North America, and all the states of Asia, with the exception of China and Japan.

Poland is in the same latitude as England, and extends some 400 miles south from the Baltic Sea and approximately 428 miles east of the Oder and Neisse Rivers. The territory is a varied ter-

---

[1] Of the three partitioning powers, Prussia had formerly been in a state of vassalage to Poland; Russia once saw her capital and throne possessed by Polish forces; and Austria was indebted to King Sobieski for the preservation of Vienna.

rain which slopes gently from the Carpathian Mountains to the shores of the Baltic Sea. Before World War II Poland was primarily an agricultural country (65.5 percent); in comparison with today, the ratio is about 45 percent. Poland has over 34,000,000 people. Close to 14,000,000 Polish citizens were born after the cessation of World War II. In contrast to the pre-war period, it is ethnically almost homogeneous, being approximately 96 percent Polish.

The traditional Polish national emblem is a spread white eagle, looking westward against a scarlet field. One source claims that the white eagle originated with the captured insignia of the Roman legionnaires by the Sarmatians, the immediate ancestors of the Poles. The legendary claim to the origin of the national emblem is simpler and more romantic. In the legend, King Lech I—who lived about the middle of the sixth century A.D.—was one day clearing away the ground to mark out the site for his fortified castle, when he uncovered an eagle's nest. Hereafter, it was called *Gniezno*, from the Polish word *Gniazdo*, a nest, thereby adopting the representation of a white eagle for the royal symbol. The white eagle was later crowned by the Jagiellonian kings and became the Polish royal coat-of-arms. Except for the crown, the white eagle remains the official coat-of-arms by the present state. The traditional colors, white and red, also have been retained in the national flag.

Polish history can be divided into six periods, each characterized by a different structure: the Piast period of the national state resisting the German *"Drang nach Osten"*; the Jagiellonian period of the multi-national commonwealth; the period of elective kings and of ultimate political decay; the period of the partitions; the recent interwar period of the rebuilt First Polish Republic; and finally, the present Polish People's Democratic Republic.

In racial classification the Poles are Slavs.[2] They form the westernmost branch of the Slavic race, the so-called Nordic group, which is characterized by tallness, an oblong shape of the skull and face, fair hair, and blue eyes. Following the legendary disintegration of the old Slavonic family into distinct tribes, one was situated in central Europe since prehistoric times: a vast land as

---

[2] See chart on page 667.

far west as Berlin and reaching eastward into the depths of central Russia between the Baltic and the Carpathian mountains. The Sarmatians, a tribe located on both banks of the Vistula, revolted against the Roman legions under the leadership of Varus. The earliest information about the Slavonic tribes of that area is to be found in the first and second century writings of Pliny and Ptolemy, who mention such geographic names as Calisia (known as Kalisz today) and the Vistula River.[3] Sixth-century records also locate Slavonic tribes along the banks of the Elbe, Oder, Vistula, Dniester, and Dnieper rivers.

By virtue of Poland's position, the Poles came in contact with both the Byzantine and the Roman civilizations, which have greatly influenced the formation and development of the Polish character and national life. The wealth of the people at that time is demonstrated by the considerable quantity of silver objects found at excavation sites. In greater Poland (or the region of Western Poland), over a hundred such treasures (sixteen to twenty pounds of silver) have been unearthed; in Pomerania (near the Baltic Sea) ninety sites were excavated; while in Podlesie (northeastern Poland) a treasure of Roman gold coins from the third century A.D. were unearthed.

The agricultural character of the Polish tribes is implied in their name, which is derived from the Polish word *pole* meaning fields or plains. The Polanie (later Polacy) or dwellers in the fields, have left their name to the whole Polish nation. Their territory was centered in Western Poland around Gniezno, the first capital, and Poznan, the seat of the first archbishop, which comprised the nucleus of the early Polish State. Among other tribes, which were annexed by the Polonians, were the Silesians and the Mazovians. Eventually the tribes of the upper Vistula, around Krakow, were absorbed by the Polanie tribes, who were stronger and politically better organized.

Poland asserted its national identity in the tenth century. A legendary chieftain, named Piast, was the first ruler of Poland. He lived in the 9th century, and his son, Ziemowit was crowned

---

[3] Calisia (Kalisz) was mentioned in Ptolemy's map as one of the principal cities of the north where the Roman merchant caravans passed through to the Baltic Sea in search of amber and other prized objects. Many recent archeological excavations of primitive burial mounds have uncovered Roman coins, glass objects and jewelry.

a prince in Gniezno. There are no facts about his rulership, but according to persistent legend, it must have occurred after the demise of Popiel, who was eaten up by vengeful rats in his castle tower at Kruszwica, about the 7th century. The Piast dynasty, which became the first national dynasty of Poland, governed the whole of Poland until 1370. The Piast rule was characterized by free peasant proprietorship with an extension of Polish territory through which runs the Vistula River. Piast's grandson, Mieszko I, in 962, married Dabrowka, a Bohemian princess, who had been a Christian for some time. Through her influence, Mieszko introduced Christianity into Poland. St. Adalbert (Wojciech) was a member of the royal Bohemian family. He attempted to convert the Prussians, who later murdered him, and offered his corpse in ransom of its weight in gold to the Polish people.

Mieszko left no doubt as to his sincerity in his new faith. Having dismissed his seven concubines, he issued an order for the destruction of all the idols throughout the country. In a large measure, he did receive support from his nobles. They once demonstrated their sincerity while present at a public worship: half of the nobles drew their sables at the intonation of *Gloria tibi, Domine,* which showed that they were ready to defend their new creed with their blood—a custom which survived in Poland for seven whole centuries. In 980, Mieszko issued his edict that every Pole who had not already submitted to the rite, should forthwith repair to the waters for baptism. He was obeyed without a murmur. For all his measures on behalf of the Roman Catholic Church, Pope Benedict V nevertheless refused to transform the Polish state into a kingdom, although this honor was conferred upon Hungary about this time.

After conversion to Christianity, the Polish church was brought under the jurisdiction of the Holy See. Thereafter, primarily Franciscan and Dominican monks came from Italy to proselyte the Poles. Jan, the first bishop of Wroclaw, was an Italian. The Cistercians (outstanding in building churches and agriculture), as well as the Benedictines, who provided several bishops, came to Poland from France. Gallus Anonymous, attributed to be a Frenchman (or Belgian), was the first chronicler on Polish history. He resided at the royal court during the beginning of the twelfth century. Ireland and Spain also furnished Poland with monks. In his acceptance of Christianity from Bohemia, Mieszko deprived the Germans of the religious pretext of converting the Slavs. The Roman Catholic religion brought Poland again into the orbit of Rome; for in ancient times there was active trade with the earlier Slavs, the Venedi or Wends. The eastern Slavs embraced the Greek rite, the Cyrillic alphabet, and Byzantine culture. This division became a permanent factor which deeply influenced the history of central Europe.

The rule of the early Piasts coincided with continuous struggles along the western border in defense of Polish suzerainity. Boleslaw Chrobry, surnamed the Brave (crowned King of Poland in 1025), was one of the greatest Polish monarchs; he united the Poles, Czechs, Slovaks, and Lusatians into one state. Also, after sixteen years of war with Emperor Henry II, he managed to establish the Polish western boundary along the Elbe and Elster rivers, the Danube in the south, and along the Baltic Sea in the north. Boleslaw also incorporated into the Polish state Red Ruthenia, the Lwow region as far as Kiev; he also retained Moravia throughout his reign. In addition, Boleslaw secured an autonomous ecclesiastical hierarchy in the archbishop of Gniezno. And under his direction, a powerful permanent army was organized for the Polish State. In the international field, his power was acknowledged through the marriage of his sister to Sven, King of Denmark, who used Polish troops in the invasion of England, in 1013. Boleslaw's sister won Sven over to Christianity; their son Canute became King of Denmark, Norway, and England. Boleslaw's daughter married the grand duke of Kiev. Adelaida, sister to Mieszko and aunt of Boleslaw, was also the mother of St. Stephen, King of Hungary. She married the Hungarian Geza, and influenced his conversion to Catholicism.

Boleslaw left his inheritance to his son, Mieszko II. He was followed by Kazimierz I, the younger son of Mieszko II, who resumed his great-grandfather's work of unification. He left a well consolidated state to his eldest son, Boleslaw II, called the Bold. Like his glorious ancestor, Boleslaw the Bold made Poland completely independent of the Empire, and like Boleslaw the

Brave, had himself crowned King of Poland during Christmas 1076.

The reign of Wladyslaw Herman, who followed Boleslaw II, lasted twenty-three years. He was followed by Boleslaw III, whose reign is memorable for his heroic defense of Silesia. The imperial army suffered such severe defeats under the walls of

Glogow and before Wroclaw that it was forced to rereat, leaving Boleslaw III, the Wrymouth, master of the entire Polish region. The Polish border along the Oder, Bober and Quels rivers marked the limits of the Polish tribes which formed, at that time an

almost impenetrable defense line running twenty miles east of the western Niesse River.

Boleslaw III established, in his testament, the rule of seniority in order to regulate the succession in the Piast dynasty, by which the eldest sons were to preside over the brothers, all of whom had hereditary provinces. His eldest son, Wladyslaw, received Silesia; the second, Boleslaw received Mazowia; the third, Mieszko, inherited the principal part of Greater Poland; while the fourth, Henry, received the region of Sandomierz to the east of Krakow, which eventually Kazimierz inherited, for whom no portion had been provided. After the death of Boleslaw II, in 1138, his son Boleslaw IV succeeded to the throne. He was followed, in 1173, by young Kazimierz, son of Boleslaw, the Wrymouth.

Surnamed the Just, Kazimierz united all of central and eastern Poland. He also reestablished the Polish influence in the borderland principalities of Wolynia and Halicz. In 1180, Kazimierz convoked at Leczyca the lords of his territories, as well as the bishops of the whole of Poland; here he made them recognize that Krakow held supreme power and was to be henceforth hereditary from his lineage. This reform was sanctioned by the pope as well as the emperor. After the death of Kazimierz the Just, in 1194, his eldest son, Prince Leszek, surnamed the White, inherited the throne. He was followed by Boleslaw V, surnamed the Chaste.

The brilliant efflorescence of medieval culture in the thirteenth century of St. Louis, was an epoch of struggles and hardships in Polish history. The following disasters oppressed the development of the Polish state: wars with jealous neighbors; internal political and religious reaction and disorganization; struggle for supremacy among the princes, resulting in the decrease of monarchical power; Tartar invasions from the east; Teutonic ravages—which under the pretext of converting Poland to Christianity—had been responsible for great outrages, murders, and destruction of life and property. These ill-fated disruptions coincided with the destruction of the Slavs of the Elbe: the Slavonic Branibor became Brandenburg; and Barlin, Berlin; thus, the German frontier ran along the Oder instead of the Elbe, and the German Empire acquired a common frontier with Poland. Due to the heavy losses inflicted on towns by the Tartars, Polish princes promoted the migrations of Germans and Jews to Poland. Also, as the weak principalities were unable to defend their borders against the heathen Prussians, a tribe akin to Lithuanians and Latvians, the prince of Mazowia brought Teutonic Knights to Poland to assist him in converting the Prussians. The knights ruthlessly destroyed the Prussians, took over their lands, and over the years built the powerful state which captured Pomerania and Gdansk that ultimately threatened the very existence of the Polish state.

During this period, Poland was ruled by Henryk IV of Wroclaw, Przemysl II, and Wladyslaw the Short, who united Poland in 1320. Under his rule and that of his son Kazimierz the Great, Poland achieved internal stability and prosperity, thereby regaining her power.

The reign of Kazimierz the Great ushered in the dawn of a new era. His merits were so remarkable that of all the numerous Polish kings, he was the only one who won the title of "Great." He expanded the Polish borders in the southeast, created a central administration, and established a currency. He incorporated mercenaries into the army and imposed military duty on every landowner. He established a uniform law for the entire kingdom, and extended his protection to the Polish towns, for which he created a special tribunal whose commercial interests he carefully safeguarded. He protected the peasants against ill treatment, and succored them during famines. He gave special protection to the Jews. In addition, he covered the country with new villages to which he granted extensive liberties. A great constructor, he built—besides numerous churches—approximately forty fortified towns to protect the Polish frontiers; hence, the popular saying: "that the king had found Poland built of wood, but he left it in stone." But his crowning achievement was the establishment of a university in Krakow, in 1364, which was organized on the model of Italian universities.[4] With the death of Kazimierz the Great, the four-hundred year old Piast dynasty came to a close.

---

[4] Before the establishment of a university in Krakow, Poles had to go abroad to study; the majority went to Bologna and Padua, some to Paris, and others to Prague.

During this period, the economic, social and political development of the nation was apparently progressive in character, mainly because the peasants possessed a large measure of freedom. This was a remarkable contrast to the feudalism and serfdom which prevailed throughout Europe. The knights—engaged in military service—did not concern themselves with agriculture; they depended for their livelihood chiefly on the rents from their peasants, which were paid in kind as well as money. This form of rental facilitated the development of trade and growth of of towns where the knights and peasants exchanged their agricultural surplus for the wares made by craftsmen of various guilds or numerous imports brought by merchants.[5]

Until the discovery of America, two world trade routes crossed Polish soil: one was the south-north route from the Mediterranean, the center of medieval world trade, to the Baltic Sea called the "amber route"; the other was the west-east route from Western Europe to the Black Sea, Turkey, and lands beyond as far as India. These routes carried a highly profitable trade, both in export

---

where a university had existed since 1348. During the first thirty years of the existence of the Jagiellonian University, 4,300 students enrolled in it, of whom 800 were from abroad—Hungarians, Silesians, Germans, and Swiss. Within the fifteenth century the number of students exceeded 18,000, among them 8,000 foreigners. Among the professors there were several outstanding scholars, while counted among the student body were such famous men as Mikolaj Kopernik (Copernicus), the Polish historian, Jan Dlugosz, and the German humanist Konrad Celtes.

The cleverness of Kazimierz the Great in establishing the University cannot be underestimated. Permission for such action was first required from the Pope or Holy Roman Emperor. King Kazimierz appealed to the emperor. The Papacy feared overeducating the populace thereby restricting opportunities for more extensive education. In this manner the stigma of the term "Dark Ages" applies to the Church, since these early centuries did advance in enlightenment and material achievement.

During this period many cathedral schools and academies existed in various cities throughout Poland. Great enlightenment was also centered at the various monasteries where 1,000 monks lived together praising their Lord through their good works: illuminating, copying ancient manuscripts of Greek and Latin, composing sacred music and building libraries. Their achievements in agriculture and animal husbandry, and herbs as medicines, were great. They also built magnificent churches during the thirteenth century. Cistersians were especially conspicuous with their activities.

[5] From the fifteenth century, however, the role of the knights and their relationship to the state was altered. In consequence of the invention and application of gunpowder, methods of warfare were fundamentally changed and the famous Polish Hussars became useless. From then on, there was a general levy of knights only in case of emergency and gradually having hitherto despised agricultural occupations, the knights returned to their manors and began to organize their estates.

and import, except for the Polish nobles whose castles were situated strategically along the amber route demanding tribute from the merchants for safe passage. The trade continued to flourish for many centuries. Krakow—situated at the crossroads on the southern Vistula River—became a very important center for this trade

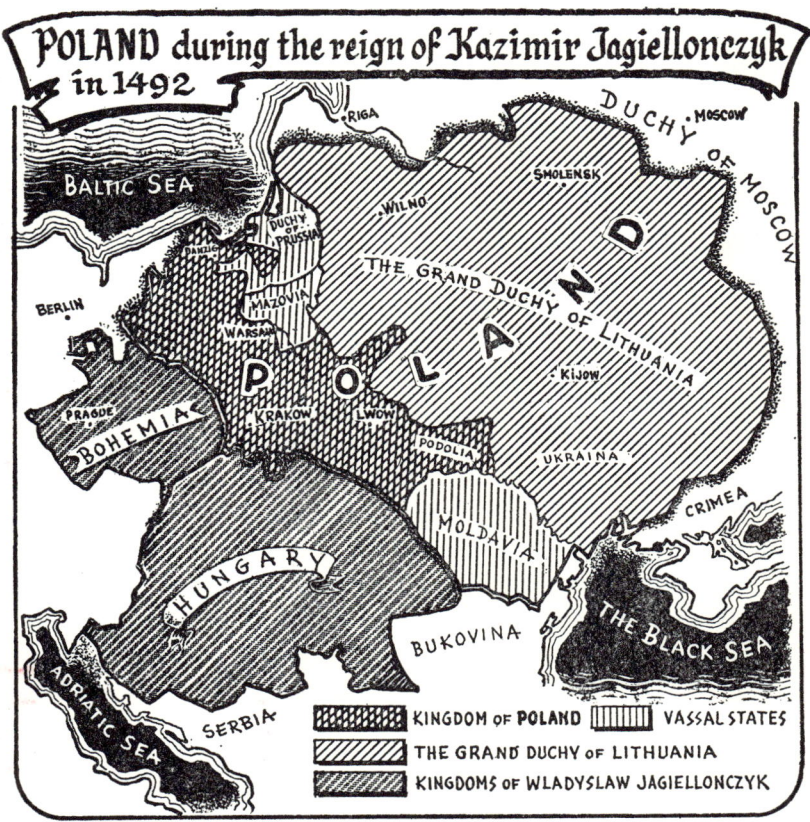

and a member of the Hanseatic League. Although far from the sea, by means of the Vistula River, it was connected with Torun and Gdansk, also prosperous mercantile cities on the Vistula River. There was a steady flow of goods by highway and by water to and from Krakow, along the Vistula River to Gdansk on the Baltic Sea, whence Polish ships sailed to all parts of Europe.

The Jagiellonian dynasty (1386-1572) introduced into Poland

the Eastern element, which subsequently was to play an important role in the history of Poland. The Jagiellonian period opens with the union of Poland and Lithuania through the marriage of the Polish queen Jadwiga (the younger daughter of King Louis of Anjou, who, in Hungary, was regarded as Louis the Great) to the great duke of Lithuania, Jagiello, in 1385.[6] Lithuanians, in 1253, formed a vast principality by conquest which expanded immensely southward toward the Black Sea, including Ruthenia.

Since Lithuania remained heathen, the Teutonic Knights raided her territory under the pretext of spreading Christianity. The Polish-Lithuanian union was established primarily to defend both states against German rampage and conquest. Lithuania accepted Christianity through Poland in the person of the queen, Jadwiga. The first bishopric, at Wilno, at once received similar privileges to those of the church in Poland. The first chapter of privileges was simultaneously granted to the Lithuanian boyars; it proclaimed the principle by which the boyars were to obtain all the rights enjoyed by the Polish nobility. The Polish-Lithuanian Commonwealth became the strongest, largest, and most progressive state in Eastern Europe, spreading from the Baltic to the Black Sea, and from Silesia to the vicinity of Moscow. When the commonwealth was at its height, it included among its cities Poznan, Torun, Warsaw, Gdansk, Riga, Krakow, Lwow, Wilno, Minsk, Kiev, and Smolensk, and nearly all the province drained by the Dnieper River. The University of Kazimierz the Great, in Krakow (under Queen Jadwiga's patronage) was re-founded through a bequest it received of her jewels. The Sorbonne with its brilliant theological department was taken as a model. At the battle of Grunwald (also known as Tannenberg), on July 15, 1410, the Teutonic Order was utterly defeated and its power shaken by the combined Polish-Lithuanian army in one of the great decisive battles of the Middle Ages.[7]

---

[6] King Ludwik I and Jadwiga belonged to the House of Anjou which followed the Piast dynasty. The Poles did not enjoy the dual monarchy of Hungary and Poland under Ludwik and insisted, after his death, on separate states and monarchs. An interegnum followed for two years without a ruler. Some proposed his eldest daughter Marie, while others hoped to restore the Piast dynasty through Siemowit IV or Semka of Mazowia. The second attendance of the Sejm decided on the younger daughter of Ludwik, Princess Jadwiga and she was quickly crowned.

Jagiello's son, Wladyslaw, also became the King of Hungary; he tried to crush the Turkish power and remove that danger to Christendom, but he lost his life at Warna, in 1444, at the head of a combined Polish-Hungarian army. Under his brother, Kazimierz, the Commonwealth achieved prosperity. The gentry, which at that time constituted ten per cent of the nation, was accorded voting privileges. In the war with the Teutonic Knights, Poland regained Gdansk and Pomerania, incorporated part of East Prussia, and extended her suzerainity over the remainder of the country, which became her fief. Kazimierz also secured the crowns of Bohemia and Hungary for his son. The Jagiellonian dynasty then ruled over all eastern and central Europe, playing a major role in building from the fourteenth century to the sixteenth century a federation which linked Poles, Lithuanians, Ruthenians, Tartars and White Russians into a Polish-Lithuanian Commonwealth.

The rule of the Jagiellonian dynasty is also characterized by religious tolerance, quite unknown in the remainder of Europe. While Europe was torn by religious wars, Catholics, Protestants, Jews and Orthodox Christians, lived in peace and tranquility. Some of the brightest chapters in the development of Unitarianism (also called Arians or the Polish Brethren) were written in this tolerant Polish climate. In addition, Poland gave asylum to many Scotch Calvinists, Huguenots, Germans, Jews and Gypsies —even though Poland was more than 90% Roman Catholic. As for the Jews, Polish tolerance proved to be so attractive that in time, nine out of every ten Jews in the world lived within the confines of the Polish-Lithuanian Commonwealth.

This period in Polish history is also characterized by the introduction of humanism, the glory of its Renaissance, the spread of the Hussite movement, and the secularization of the State or its supremacy over the Church. Poland also recommended in the early 15th century, under Pawel Wlodkowicz, such modern concepts as a United Nations of Europe and an International

---

[7] The Teutonic hordes continued their raids on Polish soil until 1525 when they were finally defeated. Kopernik witnessed the final subjugation of the Teutonic Knights. Their subsequent history is ironic, for in Germany they converted into Protestants.

Court to settle disputes between nations without wars. Wlodkowicz was the true "Father of International Law and Peace."[8]

Because there were no natural boundaries to separate the Polish-Lithuanian Commonwealth from her neighbors, Poland often mediated between two empires, two races, two cultures. In her early centuries, she had to repel Mongol invasions from the east and to battle against the incessant border raids of the Order of the Teutonic Knights from the west. Poland has also fulfilled a similar office between the rival religious faiths of Christianity and Islam. Repeatedly Poland repulsed the assaults of Turks and Tartars, who coveted its land and accumulated wealth. To Poland goes the credit of checking the Moslem drive westward and rescuing Vienna from the Turks under the excellent campaign conducted by King Jan III Sobieski in 1683. Poland was often referred to as the spiritual bulwark of Christian Europe.[9] She was also a buffer state against eastern influences to the west and against all pagan invasions from the east throughout the centuries.

---

[8] When the Teutonic Order of Knights broke the peace of 1410 after the great victory of Grunwald (or Tannenberg), one year later Wlodkiewicz was sent to Buda, Hungary to present the Polish side against the Teutonic Order. Sigismund of Luxemburg, King of Hungary and later elected Holy Roman Emperor, was chosen as an impartial arbiter in hearing the charge. Wlodkowicz accused these Catholic Crusader knights of conducting wars against the pagans—the Lithuanians and Samagotians—by which they grew prosperous. He regarded these religious wars as unjust and demanded that not only they cease their campaigns, but also that they return their loot.

In 1415-18, Wlodkowicz again presented his case at the Council of Constance in his *Tract on the Power of the Pope and the Holy Roman Emperor in Relation to the Unbelievers*. Wlodkowicz, a priest, had the courage to declare the action of the Catholic Knights of the Cross as more sinful than heresy, for theirs was a sin of hypocrisy, a sin against love. He stood alone in this theory. He even went further, that not only was it permissible for Christians to fight with heretics against a common evil, but that it was also their duty to defend the pagans against the crimes of others, namely, the religious order of Teutonic Knights. In this concept he preceded Francisco deVittoria, notable theorist on international law by a hundred years and also Bartolome de las Casas, the great defender of the Indians in Mexico.

Wlodkowicz proposed the establishment of an International Court to settle all international controversies for war never settles any grievances and is a crime against mankind. He also opposed compromises which only benefited the evil-doer and enhanced the nation to commit future evil. His prophetic ideas preceded the League of Nations, the Hague and International Court of Justice and the present United Nations by more than five hundred years.

[9] Another factor which affected Polish European history was the animosity, throughout the centuries, between France and Great Britain, which Germany skillfully played up. If these two countries were united by friendship, Germany would never dare to play an aggressive role and would have been checked. Because of

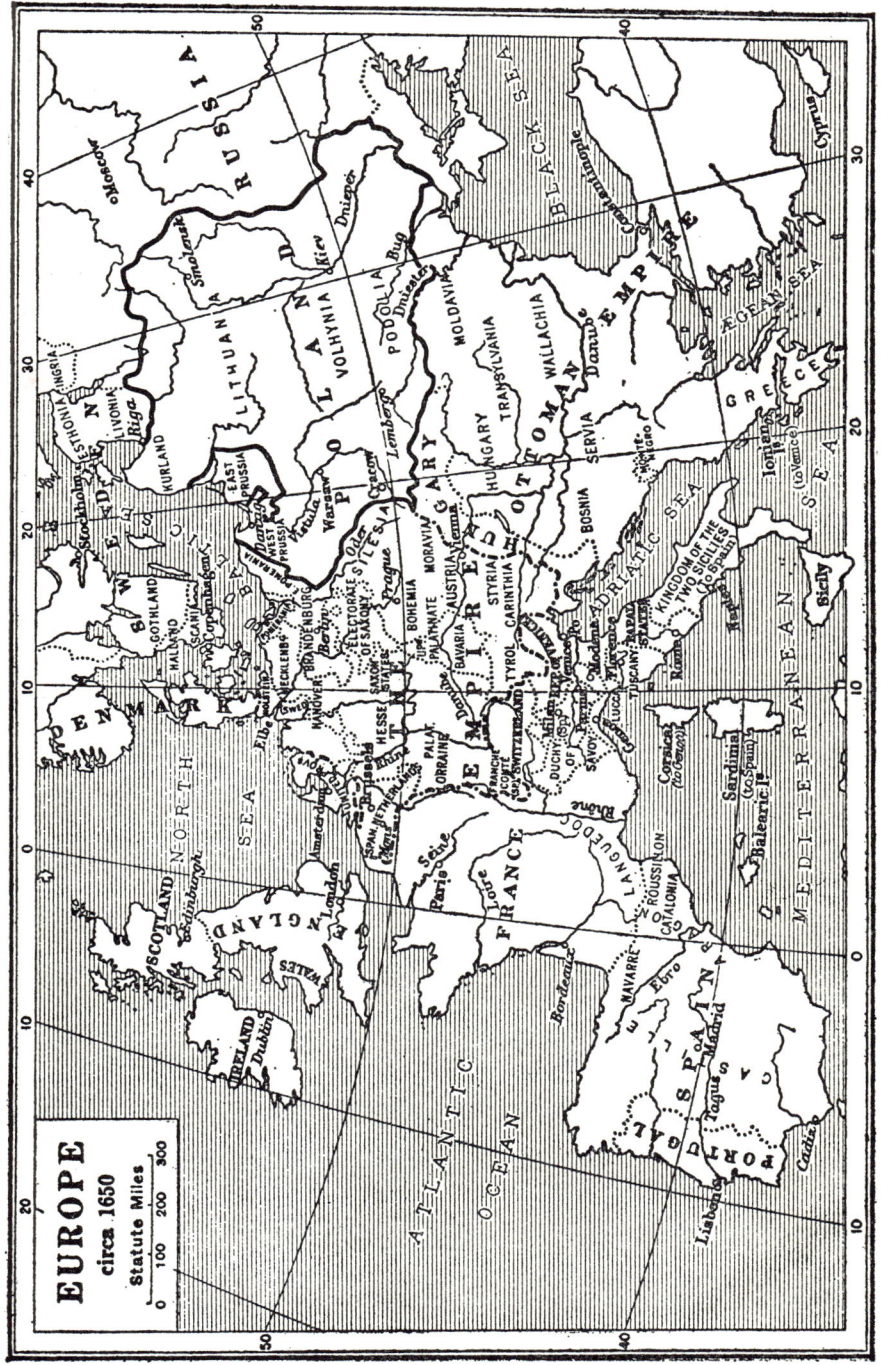

The beginning of the sixteenth century was marked by the introduction of the parliamentary system, in which the Sejm (Parliament) had to approve all important decisions of the kings.[10] Nevertheless, in the sixteenth century, the Commonwealth achieved such prosperity and cultural progress that the reign of the last two Jagiellonians is called the "Golden Age" of Poland. On the political scene, Poland successfully checked the Duchy of Muscovy; agreed to the secularization of the Teutonic Order; and extended her borders in Livonia, as that province sought Polish protection against the Duchy of Moscovy and Sweden. In 1569, Poland and Lithuania entered into a close union, at Lublin, which unified both nations under one king and one parliament.[11] The rule of the last Jagiellonian, Zygmunt August, is also characterized by a religious tolerance almost unknown in other parts of Europe, which was torn by religious wars. Not only did Poland reach, in that century, the climax of its political development,

---

them the world had to suffer two World Wars. They were also never reliable in their commitments. If France was politically sincere, she was wholly ineffectual and without the capacity to fulfill its promises. On the other hand Great Britain always pursued an expedient policy in foreign affairs and even was envious of any ally to become more powerful or greater than herself. Her policies were consistently selfish and egoistic, not pragmatic or conservative. She relied little on allies; it was best to reign throughout the world where her influence and control was felt benevolently. Both Great Britain and France must share the guilt in the partition of Poland for they allowed it to happen. If Great Britain had sent an army against Prussia, the latter would have retreated from her aggressive policy, Austria would have remained neutral and Poland would have been able to defeat the Prussians. Poland's ideals and high principles were a devastating threat to the autocracy of Europe which should not be allowed to be put into practice for fear of toppling the thrones of Europe. England's treacherous policies were diabolically Machiavellian in practice, especially since the reign of Elizabeth I until World War II and afterwards. Great Britain had mellowed only after the gradual disintegration of her once glorious empire. It was an empire in contrast to Poland's federation or commonwealth.

[10] The evaluation of the Polish Parliament (Sejm) is a long and interesting one. The first Senate (Magnates and Prelates) met at Łęczyca in 1180. The first gathering of the Lower House (the Gentry or Knights) met in Piotrków, in 1468. The English institution of a King in Parliament (King's Council under the presidency of the King with Lower House) found its earliest analogy in 15th century Poland. Knights already convened together as early as 1404 to exercise their rights of influence over the treasury. According to traditional Polish Constitutional theory, the king proposed, the Senate discussed and the Chamber of Deputies (Lower House) gave consent. Poland had the most advanced constitution in Europe giving full political rights to a very large body of citizens. The protection of the English *habeas corpus* act, in 1685, was already a guarantee to the Polish citizen since 1430.

[11] Under the previous Union of Horodlo, in 1413, after the spectacular **victory of Grunwald**, whereby forty-three clans adopted a similar number of Lithuanian chief-

but also it experienced material prosperity, scholasticism, scientific progress, artistic glory, and international influence.[12]

Polish prosperity was directly influenced by events which were taking place at that time in Western Europe. The discovery of America, and the sea route around the Cape to India, brought about a complete transformation of world trade by making the Mediterranean basin less important with the rise of British and Dutch trading. The rise of towns and cities, with the increase in population, led to a large demand for agricultural products. English and Dutch merchants went to seek grain in Eastern Europe. Gdansk became a flourishing center for the export of grain, livestock, and timber; and the peasants and merchants of Poland began to draw large profits. This resulted in an increase for luxury, decorative arts and greater comforts. In Krakow, Torun and Gdansk, additional stories were added to town houses. This increased the number and sizes of their windows which were added to their front elevations, by which they were taxed accordingly. The entrance hall was abandoned as a sleeping area. Beds replaced pallets, while plates, wall hangings and furniture accumulated. The usual contentment with primitive simplicity gave way to the quest for opulence.

Seeing the possibility of wealth in the export of agricultural products, the magnates—who lived in castles and palaces on several estates that formed a *klucz*, as well as townhouses—secured the dominant position in the grain trade.[13] Faced with an almost insurmountable difficulty—the scarcity of cheap labor—they secured the limitation of personal freedom of the peasants to leave their tenant farms where they worked. Opportunities to secure free land in eastern and northern Poland threatened their pros-

---

tains allowing the latter to use their respective Polish family crests. Likewise they were granted the same fiscal and judicial privileges as were granted the Poles.

[12] Krakow was the sixth city in the world to print a book. Printed in 1472 it was the work of the Italian cardinal Torrecremata. Aleksander Bochenski, "Polish Bibliophiles," *Poland* (December, 1972), p. 22.

[13] When the magnates acquired the monopoly of the grain export, the share of the towns in trade dwindled to nothing. It consisted of the import of luxury goods for the nobles and the export of goods manufactured in the towns, enough to maintain the population, but not enough to bring any prosperity to the towns. In 1493, the magnates acquired the right to import goods, duty free, for their own consumption. This privilege of exemption from import and export duties is *almost* unique in the history of Europe.

perity.¹⁴ As land without the peasant's labor became worthless, it was in the interest of the nobles to keep him bound to the land, thus making the peasant virtually a part of the real property, depriving him of the opportunities available through migration.

The struggle of the gentry against the peasants and burghers, as well as the king, for complete supremacy in the state was the turning point in Polish history. The aims of the nobles were threefold: (1) concentration of all land in their hands with the creation of large estates for the production and export of grain;

---

¹⁴ In 1466, the nobles acquired the right to expropriate the peasants from their holdings on payment of a compensation according to the value of the land. Later, in the process of consolidating their estates, they frequently exercised this right without any compensation. In 1633, a law was passed which transformed colonists into serfs if they lived at least one year on the nobleman's land.

(2) the commuting of the rent system into serfdom in order to obtain sufficient labor; and (3) the direction and control of the state.

With the death of Zygmunt August, in 1570, the Jagiellonian dynasty ceased; all future kings of the Polish Commonwealth would be elected for life by an assembly of magnates and the higher dignitaries of the Church. Each elected king was required to sign the "Pacta Conventa," a pledge to maintain the liberties of the Commonwealth. Every attempt to limit the influence of the magnates and nobles was doomed to failure, especially since any power exercised by the king was discontinued during the interregnum following his death, during which the nobles (especially the magnates) controlled the destiny of the Commonwealth. Since it was easier to impose the terms of the "Pacta Conventa" on foreigners, the great majority of Polish kings, after the sixteenth century, were of foreign blood.[15]

In the year 1573, the throne of Poland was offered to Henri of Valois, Duke of Anjou, afterwards King Henry III of France.[16] His brief reign was followed by Stefan Batory (1576-86) from

---

[15] The Polish magnates were seeking foreign alliances, especially after the success of the Jagiellonian dynasty which expanded the realm and brought security to the eastern border. This was workable with good foreign kings who were sincerely interested in the welfare of Poland. Unfortunately the shallow and egotistical Henri de Valois abdicated a year later when the French throne was made vacant. The Vasa dynasty brought to Poland foreign dynastic problems which led to war. The Saxon kings were also poor examples of wise and good rulers: August I was preoccupied with every pretty woman at court resulting in about 300 bastard children, besides his legitimate fifteen.

A greater self-reliance on raising her own magnates to the throne would have proven more successful. Kings Jan Sobieski, Stanislaw Leszczynski and Stanislaw August Poniatowski were all kings of great stature. If Chancellor Jan Zamoyski had agreed to accept the throne instead of supporting Zygmund III Vasa, Poland would have experienced the second renaissance since he was one of Europe's most cultivated and cultured gentlemen with a proper instinct for economic reform. He even built his own city of Zamosc with a castle, cathedral, academy, printing press and extensive fortifications. Poland had many outstanding persons to draw on, but Polish nobles were often envious of each other and didn't wish to support one another for a common good except in a crisis. The Czartoryski and Potocki families produced many eminent men who could have ruled Poland more ably than most monarchs throughout Europe.

[16] When the throne of Poland was offered to Henri of Valois, twelve Polish ambassadors accompanied by 150 young nobles arrived in Paris on August 19th, overwhelming the French inhabitants with the splendor of their appeal. They occupied fifty carriages, each drawn by four or six richly harnessed horses, and wore loose flowing roles in an oriental style, caps trimmed with fur and scimitars studded with

Transylvania, who turned out to be one of the wisest and bravest of Polish kings. He strengthened Polish authority in Gdansk, and conducted three victorious campaigns against Ivan the Terrible, thus winning back Polock, and insuring Poland's rule over the whole of Livonia. In internal affairs, his greatest deeds were the creation of courts of appeal, which made the organization of jurisdiction more efficient, and the founding, in 1579, of a university in Wilno. Stefan Batory also struggled against the autocracy of the gentry, though generally without success. On one occasion he said to a gentleman named Kazimierski: "Silence, you clown!" He received the following answer: "I am not a clown, but I elect kings and I do away with tyrants!"[17] What would have been the fate of a French or Spanish gentleman of the time, had he dared to answer his king in this manner?[18]

Stefan Batory was succeeded by the members of the Swedish House of Vasa, who were, in turn, followed by Michael Wisniowiecki, Jan III Sobieski, August I, Stanislaw Leszczynski,[19] August II, and Stanislaw August Poniatowski.

During the Vasa period, Poland fought long and bloody wars against the Duchy of Muscovy, Sweden, Turks, Tartars, and Cossacks, who rebelled against the Polish magnates in the Ukraine.[20]

---

precious stones. When they were presented to Prince Henri in the Louvre Palace, they wore robes of golden cloth. What amazed the French was that they were able to converse in Latin, French, German, and Italian as well as in their own language. John Murray Gibbon, *Canadian Mosaic* (New York: 1939), p. 267.

[17] Manfred Kridl, *A Survey of Polish Literature and Culture* (New York: 1956), p. 41.

[18] This liberal and democratic principle, unfortunately, concerned only one social class, which consistently and stubbornly refused to grant rights to the burghers and peasants. The Polish gentry were the freest men in Europe, and were proud of the fact that they owed nothing to the king except a realty tax, war duty, and the use of the royal name in court summons. The concept of divine right, of the king anointed by God, which still prevailed in Europe, had disappeared in Poland a long time before. Together, with the fall of monarchical power, worship of the king (who was only a nominal ruler) also disappeared.

[19] The daughter of King Stanislaw Leszczynski, Marie Leszczynska, married King Louis XV of France in 1725. King Stanislaw, after he lost his throne in Poland, became the beloved and wise Duke of Lorraine, in France. His memory is still revered in France.

[20] In the Perejslaw Treaty of 1654, the Cossacks submitted themselves to the Duchy of Muscovy. In the following period, known in Polish history as "the Deluge," Poland was attacked by Sweden, the Duchy of Muscovy and Transylvania. Polish territory was almost completely occupied. Soon, however, Poland regained her

In 1596, a religious union was concluded between the Catholic and Orthodox churches in Poland, as a result of which the Orthodox population became Catholics of the Greek rite. The fanatic Catholicism of Sigismund III not only prevented his son from being elected Czar of Russia, which prevented the union of Poland with Russia and deprived the Russian people of an advanced humanistic government free of despotic rule, but also involved Poland in a war with Sweden.

Polish-Turkish wars during the reign of Jan III Sobieski culminated with his victory over a vast Turkish army which besieged Vienna in 1683. His victory, inspired by the defense of Christendom, brought the liberation of Hungary, and marked the beginning of Turkish decline in Europe. With the death of Sobieski, in 1696, the power and glory of the old Commonwealth also vanished. Nothing was effected to improve the status and condition of the peasantry. As the seventeenth century wore on, their situation grew worse. The following conversation quoted by a writer gives a witty idea of their lot.

> A gentleman said to a peasant: "You poor thing, you work so hard in this world; surely you will go to Heaven after you die." The peasant replied: "And who would chop the wood for the Lord and make his fire in hell? There is no other way, I must follow him there too."[21]

In the eighteenth century, Poland declined steadily under the rule of the Saxon kings. Culture and learning reached its nadir. The degeneration of the parliamentary system was brought about by the "*Liberum Veto,*" a privilege exercised by the gentry. All laws had to be passed unanimously by the nobles in assembly. If anyone disagreed with a measure he could dissolve the Sejm—a very powerful weapon. Financial mismanagement caused the reduction of the standing army. Religious intolerance, which was previously unknown, was introduced by the Jesuits. The decline of towns, the supremacy of the magnates, and the impoverish-

---

position and the army led by Hetman Czarnecki drove out the enemies. The Ukraine was to become, through the Union of Hadziacz, in 1658, the third autonomous part of the Commonwealth, but the agreement was cancelled by the Ukrainian-Turkish alliance.

[21] Kridl, *op. cit.*, p. 98.

ment of the country for the sake of the vain foreign kings and aristocrats, characterize this period. The decline of education brought indifference and apathy to the gentry. Suffering from these and other defects, the Commonwealth could not long resist the invasion and interference in the internal Polish affairs of foreign powers who excelled each other in aggressiveness and in their territorial greed. However, the first partition of 1772, brought a revival on a greater scale as the spirit of indifference was shaken.

The revival began when educational reforms were instituted under the last Polish king, Stanislaw August Poniatowski. Among the reforms was the first establishment in Europe of an official Ministry of Education, in 1772, along with the first public and later national library in Europe.[22]

---

[22] Apart from other political consequences, this fact had an influence on the history of Polish libraries. The royal libraries, like the Frederick II Royal Library in Berlin or the Bibliotheque Nationale in Paris, could not become national libraries.

The beautiful and fine *ex libris,* that have survived since Mieszko II (1026-1035) testify that nearly every Polish king owned a library. The book collection of Queen Bona Sforza was bequeathed in her last will to various relatives or monasteries and churches.

In 1747 Bishop Jozef Andrzej Zaluski and his brother opened officially his library to the public in Warsaw. The largest collection in Europe which was nationalized in 1772. It was the first national library in Europe. The sum has been estimated at closer to 300,000 books and 10,000 manuscripts. By the time of the death of Bishop Zaluski in 1774, it had doubled in size. The family collection of books that had belonged to King Jan Sobieski and to the 17th century Primate Olszowski were later added to the Zaluski library. However, most of the library was amassed by Bishop Zaluski while in exile abroad for supporting King Stanislaw Leszczynski, who was deposed by the Saxons. Besides the books and manuscripts, the collection contained a huge collection of maps and illustrations and a nearly complete collection of all Polish publications since 1473. The library was arranged by languages, subjects and format size. Fifty hand written catalogs (destroyed in 1944) comprised the record of the library.

In 1761, Bishop Zaluski gave his library to the care of the Jesuit College. After his death, and the termination of the Jesuit influence in Poland, in 1774, it was turned over to the nation and called the Zaluski Government Library and placed under the care of the Commission of National Education whose director was Count Ignacy Potocki. In spite of the lack of funds, the Commission completed the collection and planned to expand the building.

In 1780, the Sejm passed a law that made it compulsory for each Polish publisher to send a free copy to the library. After the death of Janocki, the ex-Jesuit, Jerzy Kozminski, became its director and undertook a thorough re-organization of the collection. From 1787-1794, a Piarist father, O. Kopczynski became its director.

After the third partition of Poland, Catherine II confiscated the entire Zaluski Library and had it sent to St. Petersburg in order to become the foundation of the Imperial Library. Part of it was lost in transport because of the lack of care. After

THE POLISH INHERITANCE

Also a stronger government was established and greater privileges were extended to the towns. The Four-Year Parliament also enacted a progressive Constitution on May 3, 1791, which was adopted without bloodshed. Based on the American and French democratic ideas, the Constitution aimed at the revival of Poland and reformed her political structure. As those challenged the foreign interference and influence, they brought on the second partition of Poland, in 1793, between Prussia and Russia. When the partition reduced Poland to the status of a protectorate, a national uprising began in 1794. In spite of the many valiant attempts and struggles of individuals like Kosciuszko and others, Poland was overrun by its hostile neighbors, and the third partition—which erased Poland from the map of Europe—followed in 1795.[23]

What had alarmed the three despots of Europe was the threat to their autocracy. Voltaire's liberal teachings during the Age of Enlightenment were mere toys to flirt with in theory, but never to dare to put to practice, for it would destroy their power. Poland, in her continuing spirit of daring experimentation and her pursuit of humanitarian ideals, had to be punished and humiliated.

Even England and France stood by and watched Poland being raped without protest. Poland was a danger to Europe, long after the third partition. That is also why Napoleon never dared to restore her, which he could as he had promised. Poland continued to remain the threat throughout the entire 19th century,

---

1921, the Peace Treaty of Riga, a great portion of the library returned to Poland between 1922-34, which became part of the Polish National Library.

In 1939, a large part of the library was destroyed by bombs or burnt by the Germans, in 1944. Only 30,000 books and 2,000 manuscripts of the original collection were saved.

[23] There were individuals among the upper ranks of the nobility who, motivated by fear of losing their estates and of the French Revolution, readily accepted their new masters. Stanislaw Szczesny Potocki, the pro-Russian marshal of the notorious Targowica Confederation, declared: "I no longer speak of Polishness and the Poles. This state, this name, have vanished, as have many others in the history of the world. I am already a Russian forever." Stanislaw A. Blejwas, "The Origins and Practice of 'Organic Work' in Poland: 1795-1863," *The Polish Review* (Autumn, 1970), p. 25. For every such selfish fool as Stanislaw Szczesny Potocki, there were a dozen more noble Polish patriots: Emilia Plater, Countess Klaudyna nee Dzialynski Potocka, Prince Adam Jerzy Czartoryski, Zygmunt Krasicki, the Sanguszkos, Sapiehas and others.

and from the seeds of its heroes and poets germinated the new spirit of nationalism and independence which rang the death knell to all empires too ambitious for their own good. Poland was sacrificed for her glory, her virtue, her humanity, her progressiveness, her liberality, her uniqueness in all world history. But her spirit never perished.

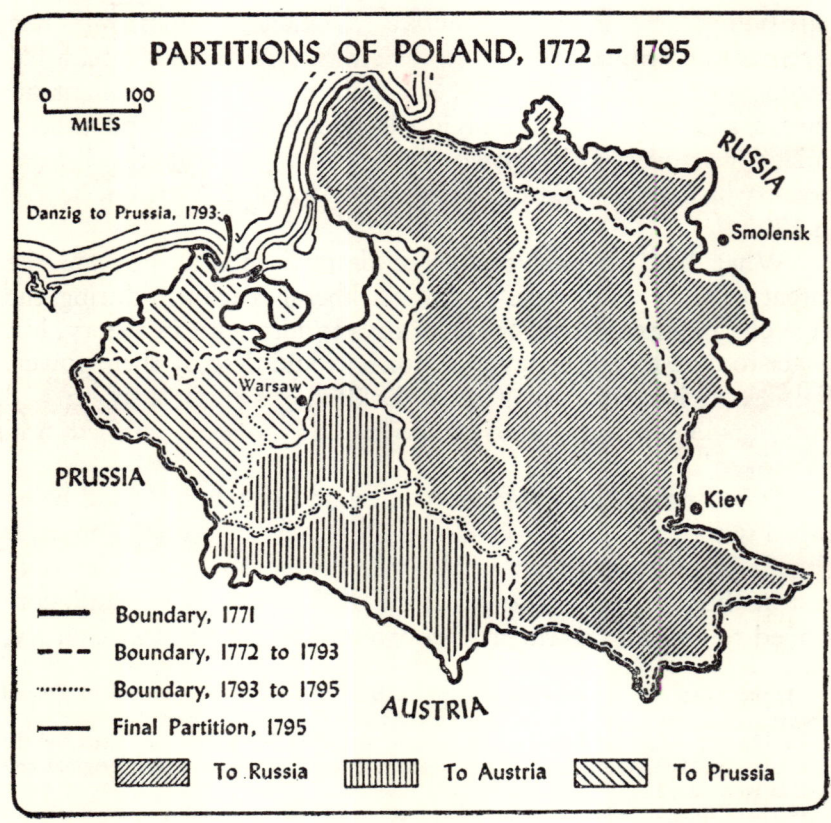

The reform of the Constitution of 1791 inspired future generations in their struggle for Polish independence. The hopes of the partitioned Polish nation were tied to the emerging military power of France under Napoleon Bonaparte. In the course of Napoleon's war with Prussia and Austria, Poland was recreated as a small duchy of Warsaw. The 1812 disaster of the French army in Russia, supported by a Polish army of 80,000 shattered all hopes of the Polish nationals for the rebuilding of the Polish state. The Congress of Vienna of 1815 formed a small Kingdom of Poland in a personal union with Russia out of parts of the duchy of Warsaw, while the residue of Poland was annexed by Russia, Prussia, and Austria. The material and social progress of

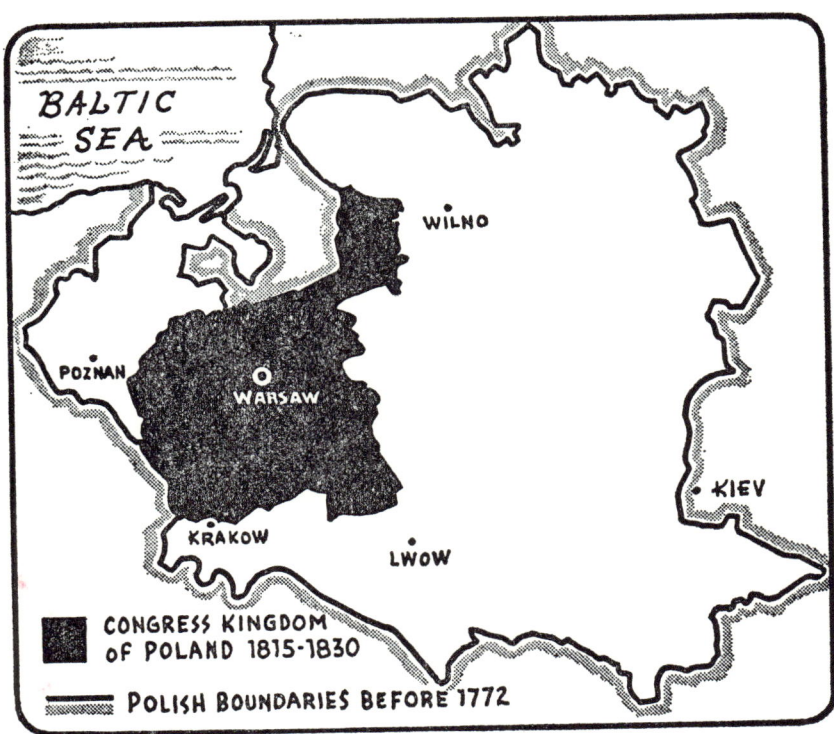

the Kingdom was, however, marred by the tyranny of the Grand Duke Constantine, brother of Czar Alexander I. The ascent of an absolute and reactionary Nicholas I to the Russian and Polish thrones resulted in political tensions which chafed for an early independence. While Polish leaders abroad tried to tie the Polish cause to all major international conflicts, the patriotic elements in Poland prepared the 1830, 1848 and 1863 insurrections, besides a host of numerous riots, protests and civil demonstrations at the cost of great human life. After each insurrection to regain independence, thousands of despondent Poles took refuge in exile to escape further repression. Even the Polish language was prohibited in the Russian sector of Poland. If observed, one could be deported to Siberia.

Abroad these men continued to struggle as exiled revolutionaries and apostles of Polish nationalism. Many fired by idealistic proposals, had aspired to achieve it for Poland and extend it to others. Thus, Poles participated in every revolution during the period from 1800 to 1871. Polish Legions assisted the French during their revolutionary wars, in the cause of Liberty, Fraternity, and Equality. General Jan Skrzynecki was for a time Commander-in-Chief of the Belgian forces which led to its independence, and later even organized the army of the young Belgian state. Another Pole, General Jozef Bem, commanded the Hungarian armies struggling for the freedom of Hungary, in the years 1848-1849, referred to frequently as "The Spring of Nations." General Chrzanowski organized the Sardinian army with Polish volunteers who also served under Garibaldi. Ludwik Mierowslawski—between leading uprisings in 1848 and 1863—directed revolutionary forces in Sicily and the German duchy of Baden. General Peter Zaraza fought for Simon Bolivar in the war for South American independence.

Polish literature during this period reached new heights producing four chief poet-dramatists: Adam Mickiewicz, Juliusz Slowacki, Zygmunt Krasinski and Cyprian Kamil Norwid. Each championed world liberty and urged all nations suffering under the yoke of some empire, to assert their right to a free identity.

This longing for a free Poland affected all the arts producing giants like Chopin, great painters like Matejko, and Wyspianski, the birth of the national opera under Moniuszko, continually inspiring Poles to persist in their hopes of a free Poland once again. Sienkiewicz, the author of *Quo Vadis* and winner of the Nobel Prize, retold Poland's glorious past in his many fine historical novels.[24]

For this reason, the French poet Jean Cocteau, called Poland

---

[24] Joseph A. Wytrwal, *Poles in American History and Tradition* (Detroit: 1969), pp. 291-303.

"a poet among nations," for the very principles she has constantly defended: and if not her realm, other nations at great cost to herself. Poland's politics never followed a plan of deception or treachery; her history is not marred by broken treaties for the sake of expediency.

Great Polish scientists and engineers found themselves in Latin America and Russia. Ignatius Domeyko labored in Chile as a geologist and mineralogist for fifty years. The modern wealth of Chile, all of her rich mines, were discovered through Domeyko's lifetime research in that country. Domeyko founded meteorological stations, an ethnographical museum, many technical schools, and reorganized the University of Santiago on the basis of his alma mater, the University of Wilno. His memory is greatly honored in Chile to this day.

Another Pole, Ernest Malinowski, submitted to the Peruvian Government the most daring project: to build a railway across the Andes Mountains from the seashore to the tablelands of the interior. Ten years later that project was being realized through the help of a number of Polish engineers and mathematicians. To this day the world admires the Andes Railway as one of the great engineering wonders of the world.

Konstantin Ciolkowski, the Father of Modern Rocketry, claimed by Russia, was born of Polish parents during the time when Poland lost her independence.

The oppression of the Russians and the Prussians and the heavy losses sustained in armed efforts to regain independence, resulted in the spread of positivistic theories which stressed improvement through education of economic and social conditions.

The turn of the nineteenth century brought the development of political organizations which, although united in the final goal, approached it in different ways. Two political organizations emerged during World War I. The majority of the Galician parties—led by Jozef Pilsudski and the Socialists—advocated action against Russia; the National Democrats, led by Roman Dmowski, wanted to achieve independence with Russian support against Germany. The Western powers, allied with Russia, could not openly support the Polish claims for independence.

After World War I, all three empires, which had shared

Poland, were defeated, and during the throes of their own revolutions, the Poles succeeded in regaining its own independence. Another irony of fate: How the mighty have fallen! The Polish Republic was established in Warsaw with General Jozef Pilsudski, as temporary chief of state. After the course of World War I, the new Polish state was called upon to defend the Western way of life once again, as Russian imperialism, found in communism, a new pretext for expanding into the heart of Europe. Without outside support, Poland met the onslaught of the Russian armies and successfully defeated them on the banks of the Vistula River, in what Count d'Abernon has called the eighteenth decisive battle of World History. The victory delayed Russia's expansion into the heart of Europe for another twenty years.

While the western frontiers of Poland were delimited by the Treaty of Versailles, and the Silesian plebiscite, the eastern frontiers were fixed only after the Soviet-Polish War of 1919-21. Polish borders were recognized by the Council of Ambassadors,

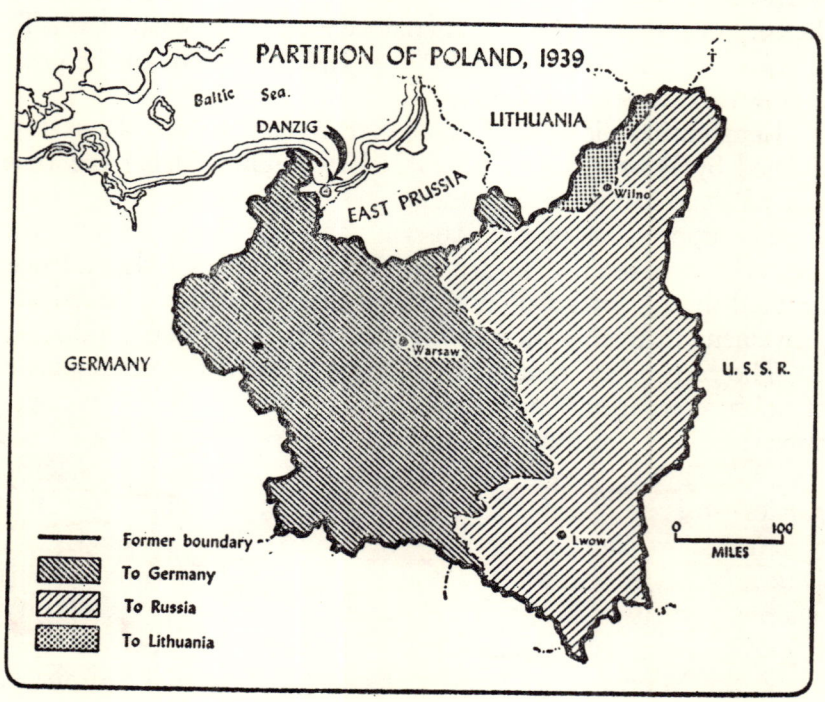

in 1923, and thus, Poland was able to concentrate on her internal problems.

During the twenty years of independence, Poland modernized and expanded her industry, and achieved marked progress especially in removing the effects of the uneven economic development of the country as a result of over a century of occupation. That progress, however, was checked by the German invasion of Poland which precipitated World War II and abruptly terminated the independent life of Poland.

Between 1939 and 1949 Poland lost nearly a third of its population through death, expulsion and repatriation. The Nazi policy of extermination eliminated 6,000,000 Poles. Countless number of Poles lost their lives in defending their Jewish neighbors.[25] In fact, more Poles lost their lives in aiding and assisting Jews during World War II than did any other people in Europe. Recent studies have revealed that some 300,000 Jews were able to survive the Nazi holocaust thanks to the assistance given by Poles who risked their own lives in aiding the Jews. The penalty for assisting Jews in Poland was immediate execution.

In vain, Nazi leaders used every effort to persuade Poles of stature to accept office and to collaborate with them in the hope of creating a satellite state. They could have saved themselves much trouble and worry. In these hopes they were completely disappointed, since there were no quislings to be found who would betray the national honor.[26] Largely, on this account, they vented their indignation especially on teachers, civil servants and other cultural leaders—the most conspicuous example was the arrest, early in November 1939, of almost the entire body of professors of the Jagiellonian University in Krakow, who were then removed

---

[25] Stanislaw Wronski and Maria Zwolakowa, *Polacy Zydzi 1939-1945* (Warszawa: 1971).

[26] When the German general staff, in the early days of World War II, pulled up in front of the castle of 85-year-old Princess Sapieha, to commandeer it, the Colonel-General declared that he held her personally responsible for the safety of his officers while they were quartered there. "Herr Colonel-General," said the Princess, "I am alone in this castle with my four-year-old grandson. But he is a Polish male, and I am therefore unable to guarantee the personal safety of the General or general staff under these eaves." Ernest Cuneo, "No Joking Matter," *The Polish American World* (June 1, 1968), p. 2.

and detained, for nearly a year, in a concentration camp, where many of them perished.

After World War II, as a result of the Big Three agreement, Poland was transplanted bodily westward, losing 75,000 square miles in the east and gaining half of that area in the west and north. A Polish provisional Government of National Unity was

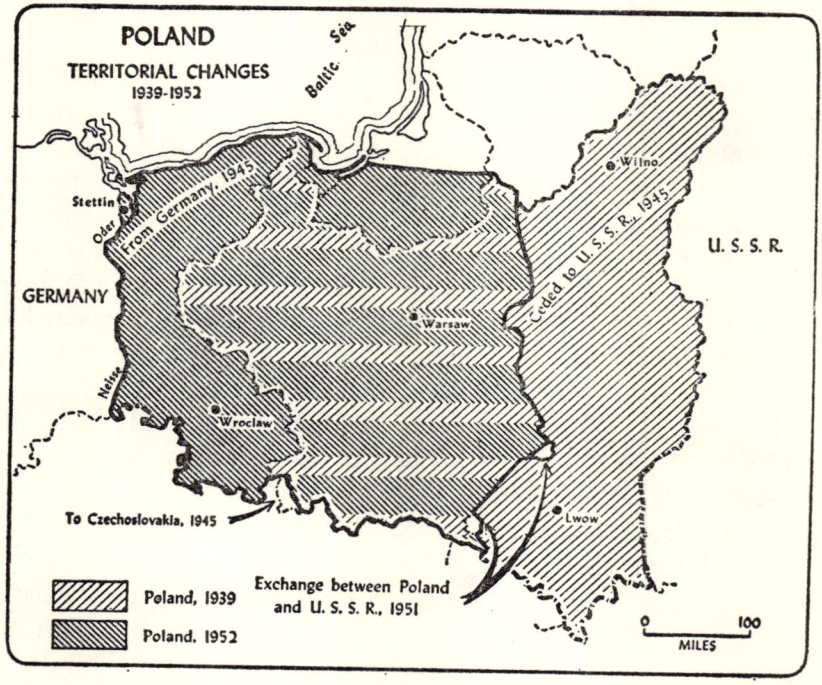

formed in 1945. It took office on June 28, 1945, and was recognized by the United States on July 5, 1945. Stanislaw Mikolajczyk was the principal non-Communist participant. The Yalta agreement called for free elections. However, those held on January 19, 1947, were controlled by the Communist Party, in violation of the Yalta provisions. The Communist, then, established a regime entirely under their domination. Mikolajczyk fled the country in October, 1947. Thus Poland, in its restricted boundaries, became a Russian satellite and the Polish people found themselves under the terrible yoke of Communism.

THE POLISH INHERITANCE

In October 1956, following the 20th Soviet Party Congress in Moscow, and after the serious "bread and freedom" riots in Poznan during June, a shakeup in the Communist regime brought to power Wladyslaw Gomulka, a former head of the Polish Communist Party, who had been ousted in 1948, and later imprisoned for refusing to support certain policies of Stalin. Although retaining traditional Communist economic and social aims, the Gomulka regime has liberalized Polish internal life to some extent.

Wladyslaw Gomulka was turned out of office after a series of bloody pre-Christmas food riots in December, 1970. He was replaced by Edward Gierek, an ex-miner. Not a liberal, but Gierek does have the reputation of being just, pragmatic and closely in touch with the working class of Poland from which he sprang. Gierek—more than any Soviet-bloc country ever has—borrowed money as though thrift has gone out of style. The inflow of hard currency raised the living standards and made Gierek popular.

Secure in power now and regarded by Poles with respect, if not affection, Gierek rarely has engaged in either anti-Catholic or anti-Semitic activities. Under his leadership the church was granted a series of long-sought concessions that so far have set the tone for the more relaxed atmosphere. The Polish government among other things granted the first meeting in more than ten years between a Polish prime minister and the conservative primate, Cardinal Stefan Wyszynski. Church-state talks also were resumed on a regular basis. The government also repealed a law requiring the church to maintain detailed inventories of all its property for inspection by the state. The government also permitted construction of a limited number of new churches, although far fewer than what the church says it needs to accommodate population shifts.

Cardinal Wyszynski, who was arrested in the Stalinist 1950s and has been an outspoken critic of past regimes, acknowledged the government's concessions in an unusually warmly worded sermon June 18, 1972. "There are new lights on the horizon of Polish life," he told a congregation in Radom, "We have to recognize them and praise them. One should be joyful of this."[27]

---

[27] Howard A. Tyner, "Church-State tensions appear easing in Communist Poland," *Long Island Press* (August 20, 1972), p. 15.

For many years after World War II the Polish Americans were quite skeptical about relations with Communist Poland. There was a fear that any overtures or contacts might allow a "Trojan horse" to be introduced in the Polish-American communities.

Now many bridges are being built, including scholarship programs for students from this country to study in Poland. The tourist traffic is quite brisk. Some of the best scenography in the world is done in Poland and students from abroad study the unique accomplishments in this art form.[28]

The present attitude is to separate the "real Poland" from the current Communist regime. However, relations are good enough that Polish Americans welcome even representatives from the Warsaw government.[29] Recently, Poland's leadership, in a move apparently without precedent in Communist Eastern Europe, has decided to permit outside private investment in the country—but only by people of Polish origin now living in the West.[30]

Despite repeated affirmations of binding ties to the Soviet Union, Poland increasingly is conducting its own search for the Communist millennium. Experts believe that if detente continues to provide the umbrella for flourishing Western trade contacts, Poland could become a markedly more open society, continuing its drift from the Moscow model.[31]

---

[28] Poland was a pioneer in innovating many new stage designs. The latest foreign plays are quickly translated into Polish and appear there sooner than on Broadway. Arthur Miller was very pleased with the Polish version of his *After the Fall*, and Durrenmatt's plays enjoyed tremendous popularity, and according to the author, performed better in Polish than in the original German in Berlin. Six of George Bernard Shaw's plays had their world premieres in Poland. Shaw felt that the Poles understood his wit better than the English did. Polish films have also won many awards at various film festivals.

[29] Some of the strongest resentment remains among the displaced persons who fled Poland. Many have unpleasant memories of the Communist ways.

[30] "Poles Woo Emigrant Cash," *The Detroit News* (April 15, 1976), p. 5-B.

[31] "Gierek Puts Poland on a Red Tightrope," *The Detroit News* (December 17, 1975), p. 14-A.

CHAPTER TWO

Prelude to the Polish Peasant Immigration

Once I thought to write a history of the immigrants in America. Then I discovered that the immigrants were American History.

—OSCAR HANDLIN

The Poles are not strangers to America, even though there never was a "New Poland" on the map of America to match the New Spain, New England, or New France claimed for those countries.[1] Nevertheless, Polish roots were established considerably prior to the establishment of the American republic, for in one way or another, Poles were in every major stream of migration which made its confluence in the New World, thereby contributing to its diversified character.

Traditionally, Polish history, in America, is founded upon three principal waves of migration. The first of these—the smallest in size and the longest in duration—was the colonial migration: it extended from 1608 to 1783. These immigrants were the fore-

---

[1] Poland's two and only colonies in the American hemisphere, were purchased by Duke Jacob of Courland (1610-1687) from Holland and settled in 1652. These were the Islands of Tobago and St. Andrew in the Caribbean which remained in Poland's possession until 1737. The Duke's fleet—built at Mitau and Libau shipyards—numbered seventy-nine commercial vessels and forty-four ships.

In 1652, Jacob, Duke of Courland, sent out two shiploads of Courlanders. These were followed by Dutch colonists. A dispute arose between the two groups, and in 1658, the Courlanders were completely overpowered by the Dutch. In 1664, the grant of the Island to the Duke of Courland was renewed, but the Dutch refused to recognize his title. Louis XIV restored the Island to the Duke of Courland in 1662, but he transferred his title to a company of London merchants. Courland River and Great Courland are names of places on the Island of Tobago.

runners of millions of Polish men and women who reached America's shores after the colonies became a nation. The second wave began in 1783 and lasted until 1870. This wave was larger than its predecessor. It was also more conscious of its role as a cultural entity within American civilization and more influential upon its environment. By far the largest and the most obvious of the waves of Polish immigrants to the United States began after the Civil War when the last opportunities disappeared in partitioned Poland, while they grew more promising in America. It was made up almost entirely of Polish peasants who joined their predecessors, mostly titled or military exiles. The new immigrants had to create their own community, evolve their own tradition, and produce their own leaders. It lasted from 1870 until 1924, and had the strongest impact upon American civilization at large.

The decade, from 1870 to 1880, added nearly 35,000 Poles to the population of the United States. The decade, ending in 1890 added nearly 99,000; and the last decade, 1890-1900, nearly 236,000.[2] Between 1855 and 1870, the Poles founded twenty churches in the United States. Eight churches were located in Texas, five in Wisconsin, four in Missouri, and one each in Michigan, Illinois and Pennsylvania.[3] In 1900, the natives of Poland in the United States numbered 383,407, or twenty-six times as many as a generation earlier, in 1870.[4] The 1900 census reveals that of the total foreign-born Poles in America, who numbered over a third of a million, thirty-nine percent came from Prussian Poland, forty percent came from Russian Poland, and fifteen percent came from Austrian Poland. In the six years, between 1899 and 1904, the arrivals from Prussian Poland made up only five percent of the total Polish immigration, while those from Austrian Poland and Russian Poland comprised the other forty-six and forty-nine percent respectively. More significant was the surprisingly high literacy rate: seventy-one percent of the Poles could read and write. For the period 1899 to 1909 the Polish literacy rate was eleventh of thirty immigrant nationalities.[5]

[2] Emily Greene Balch, *Our Slavic Fellow Citizens* (New York: 1910), p. 132.
[3] Emily Greene Balch, "Our Slavic Fellow Citizens, History or Settlement Previous to 1880," *Charities and the Commons* (April 20, 1907), p. 20.
[4] Balch, *Our Slavic Fellow Citizens*, p. 132.

From 1900 to 1910, the total immigration nearly reached 875,000. The Russian economic crisis of 1901-1903, and the effects of the revolutionary troubles of 1905, increased the immigration from the Polish lands of Russia. This optimistic wave of humanity, searching for success, continued to rise until World War I, reaching its zenith in 1912-1913, when 174,365 Poles entered the United States. This inflow concentrated in the new industrial cities, along the Great Lakes, in the mining and industrial districts of Pennsylvania, and on the northeastern coast of the United States. By 1920, cities whose Polish population had been insignificant in 1890, had become Polish centers: Chicago had a Polish population of 350,000; New York had 250,000; Buffalo had 80,000; Milwaukee had 75,000; and Pittsburgh totalled 200,000. In Detroit, the Polish population reached 300,000 in 1930. The Poles of Jewish descent went mostly into the sweat-shop industries in their homes, and especially the tailoring business in New York. Most of the Jews in New York are of Polish origin. Immigrant Poles came to these cities because they were growing commercial and manufacturing centers; Poles followed general population trends. The free and cheap land in the United States did not attract them, partly because they came too late when the frontier was closing. After 1885, many Poles, who had been engaged in industrial pursuits in the cities, were attracted by advertisements of cheap land and settled on farms in Wisconsin and the Dakotas. The 1930 census listed 1,268,583 foreign-born Poles in the United States and determined the total Polish stock with one or both parent Poles to be 3,342,198. The most serious causes for emigration were the unfortunate economic, political and social conditions in partitioned Poland.[6] Those leaving Poland certainly were not destitute. Besides the relatively high degree of literacy, many actually owned land or else their families did; and some, at least, were able to pay the expenses of making the long passage to America. Thus, sheer grinding poverty did not compel Poles to emigrate as was the case

---

[5] U.S. Senate, 61st Congress, 3rd Session, *Report of the Immigration Commission: Emigration Conditions in Europe* (Washington, D. C., 1911), p. 30.
[6] Joseph A. Wytrwal, *America's Polish Heritage. A Social History of the Poles in America* (Detroit: 1961), pp. 106-148.

for Irish settlers. The real cause was probably the hope of acquiring income in order to re-establish the peasant in his own position in the village. Reymont, in his saga, *The Peasants*, observed the importance of land ownership:

> A man without land is like a man without legs: he crawls about and cannot get anywhere.[7]

Bernault also noticed the importance of land ownership:

> Such is the nature of a peasant that even if it should mean untimely digging, his own grave, he would still strive to buy a piece of his holy earth.[8]

Posner also confirmed this observation:

> The peasant eager for land, attached passionately to the earth, makes all possible sacrifices for it. He goes to find money in America in the crushing labor of the mines and factories.[9]

For Poles to remain in their native land meant to accept a present and a future without hope of fulfillment for either themselves or their children. Poland during the nineteenth century had been partitioned by Russia, Prussia and Austria, thereby depriving the Poles totally of their political, economic and social rights. Although gallant Poles dared to place the quest for freedom above life itself, and to challenge superior forces, in rebellion after rebellion, they failed to shake off their foreign occupation and oppression. Failing to achieve independence, they continued to resist extinction at great cost. They clung to their religion because it was a mark of difference between them and their conquerors; because they cherished liberty, they raised their language to literary significance in Europe, producing great Romantic poetry and dramas eschewing their idealistic philosophy.

Poland is a land rich in natural resources. Yet, the Poles remained paupers under the partition. They occupied the lowest

---

[7] Ladislaus Reymont, *The Peasants* (New York: 1925), II, p. 77.
[8] Elsa Bernault, *Polish Peasant Autobiographies* (unpublished Ph.D. dissertation, Columbia University, 1950), p. 81.
[9] Posner, *Les Forces Sociales de la Pologne*, p. 238. Quoted in Victor R. Greene, *The Slavic Community on Strike* (Notre Dame: 1968), p. 222.

PRELUDE TO THE POLISH PEASANT IMMIGRATION 37

levels of the social structure: either the industrial proletariat or as agricultural toilers. Abused and persecuted, they were permitted to exist as an alien group in their own country. A high birth rate, longer life expectancy, overdependence on agriculture, too little industrialization and decline of Polish ownership of land created a serious problem.[10] There were few industries in Poland to absorb this large surplus population. The population of Austrian, Prussian and Russian Poland rose from 11.4 millions in 1857 to 24.3 millions by 1900. This increase was not equal in each of the three partitions; it was highest in Russian Poland (179.4%), followed by Austrian Poland (77.7%) and Prussian Poland (52%).

> This increase in numbers can be attributed in the first place to the abolition of serfdom, which took place in all parts of Poland between 1815 and 1864. Secondly—as in Western Europe—there was a definite improvement in communications and an increase in productivity due to technological progress. Finally, there was a marked fall in mortality. In the Congress Kingdom the death rate fell from 27.5 per 1000 in the decade 1871-1880 to 19.3 for 1910-11; in Poznania the fall was even more striking, from 30.0 per 1000 in 1871-1880, to 24.1 per 100 in 1910-1911. Since 1889 there has been in Poland no major epidemic which resulted in an annual excess of deaths over births.[11]

All of these factors led to a pronounced increase in population. To make matters worse, between 1846 and 1885, almost 1,250,000 acres passed from the Polish landed gentry to German ownership in Prussian Poland. As more German estate owners appeared in Prussian Poland, they were attracted and forced to rely on the poorer, lower class, which comprised of Polish seasonal laborers from Austrian and Russian Poland. Entire villages of dependent peasants in Prussian Poland found their own condition increasingly more difficult with the appearance of the labor force from Austrian and Russian Poland. The result was

---

[10] The prolific Pole, in the 1890's, had a birth rate one-sixth above the European average (43.5 per 1,000); and by World War I, it was the highest on the continent. Poland, Chief Bureau of Statistics, *Concise Statistical Yearbook of Poland, 1937* (Warsaw: 1937), pp. 40, 43.

[11] Jerzy Zubrzycki, *Polish Immigrants in Britain* (The Hague: 1956), p. 13.

mass migration from Prussian Poland. In Austrian Poland, many regions (especially Podhale) were plagued with droughts, repeated crop failures and a general decline in prices.

Although the economic conditions were bad—and the political conditions were even worse—the majority of the Poles chose to remain in the land of their fathers. But thousands of other rural Poles—often with hope and concern for their own and their children's future—started searching for a new, larger, and more inviting world which would not disappoint them. They left behind the familiar landscape, the language spoken since birth, and the security of the village where their people had lived for generations, when they risked the fearful and difficult voyage to an unknown shore.

For most, the new shore, which they selected to expand their horizons and opportunities, was America. And the promise of the new place was contagious, for it was a land where all that was denied to them in Poland might be achieved, including liberty, opportunity and fulfillment. These three words, used frequently in letters from America, conjured up the brightest imaginings in the minds of Poles and provided ideas as to what life in America would be like, where mobility had no parallel anywhere in the world. America was a land of promising opportunity where one could enter society on his own merits, to go from one income level to a higher one, to travel from one place to another without interference, and to rise from one economic and social class to a greater one.

Poles are not strangers to America, for they knew it by reputation. A recent investigation has uncovered at least sixty references to America in thirty-nine Polish books and manuscripts of the sixteenth and seventeenth centuries.[12] The New World constantly reappears in a limited number of contexts—either as a symbol of the exotic, or as a testimonial to the achievement of the church triumphant. Although enthusiastic about the discoveries of the Spanish and Portuguese explorers, Polish authors and

---

[12] J. H. Elliott, *The Old World and the New 1492-1650* (Cambridge: 1970) p. 13. See also Janusz Tazbir, "La Coquete de l'Amerique a la Lumiere de l'Opinion Polonaise," *Acta Polonaie Historica*, XVII, 1968, pp. 5-22.

travelers advocated colonizing eastern Europe instead of America.[13]

Poles were not unknown in America, for many of their kinfolk had come here since the early seventeenth century. Peter Stuyvesant, recognizing Poles as valuable farming and fighting colonists, induced them to settle in New Holland. Poles had been in Delaware as early as 1650, and William Penn numbered them among his loyal settlers. Some Poles had come to America as indentured servants, bound to a master for a number of years, after which they would be free in the new land to make their own fortunes.[14] Hundreds had come to America in the years prior to the Revolutionary War.[15] Many joined the army of George Washington, and suffered casualties and continuously underwent privations to free the country from British domination.[16] Generals Pulaski and Kosciuszko were magnificent heroes, among the finest representatives of Polish-American friendship.[17]

When the cannons had ceased their destruction, America had achieved her independence and inaugurated her first president; simultaneously, Poles continued to make their presence known. Many were already a second or third generation removed from Poland. Again, Poles were among the explorers who crossed the old trails of Spanish adventurers and French priests, and confirmed the 200-year-old accounts of their discoveries; they were among the cowboys riding lonely trails and herding cattle in waterless wastes; they were the railsplitters who constructed a network of railroad lines against the seeming insurmountable difficulties of nature's awesome wonders; they were among the gold-

---

[13] Joseph A. Wytrwal, *Poles in American History and Tradition* (Detroit: 1969), pp. 1-3.
[14] Miecislaus Haiman, *Polish Pioneers of Virginia and Kentucky* (Chicago: 1937), p. 51. See also James Curtis Ballagh, *White Servitude in the Colony of Virginia*, XIII Serial, Volumes VI-VII, p. 40.
[15] Wytrwal, *Poles in American History and Tradition*, pp. 1-29.
[16] *Ibid.*, pp. 30-88.
[17] The National Lancers, a volunteer, ceremonial group in Boston, was organized in 1836 by Governor Edward Everett as his personal militia to escort him to the Harvard Commencement. The ceremony he established remains today. The Lancers wore bright red and blue uniforms with plumed helmets, after the original Polish Lancers under General Thaddeus Kosciuszko. The Lancers' basic weapon for ceremonial purposes is the lance, and they boast that the only other organization in the world still equipped with the lance as a weapon is the Swiss Guard at the Vatican.

seekers with their faithful burros carrying equipment and sharing their solitude and privations amidst the evanescent glimmer of shadow and sunlight which gives the desert its color; Poles were resolute homesteaders living in sod houses on the high, dry, lonesome land, so long possessed by the buffalo, the Indian, and the cattlemen who broke the vast prairies and converted them into fields of corn and wheat; they were the miners who mined coal, copper and iron to make steel; they were among the post-Civil War New England pioneers who demonstrated that abandoned farms could be made productive once more as a fine legacy for their children; Poles were among the army of employees in the automobile and steel industries which revolutionized American life; and also among the officers and soldiers who fought, and sometimes died, in order to make other men free during the wars involving the United States.

As the great mass of Polish immigration increased, they spread across the country, moving to various cities, state after state. The advance of Polish settlement can usually be traced by the establishment of Roman Catholic parishes; for more than three-fourths of the Poles were devout members of the church. Polish surnames and place names such as: Sobieski, Opole, Wilno, Tarnow, Chojnice, Polishville, Warsaw and Gniezno, dot the map of the United States in profusion. There are Krakows in Missouri and Nebraska; there is a Poznan in Illinois, and a Posen in Michigan. There are Pulaskis in Alabama, Arkansas, Georgia, Illinois, Indiana, Iowa, Kentucky, Virginia and Wisconsin.[18] Kos-

---

[18] Joseph A. Wytrwal, "Memories to General Pulaski in the United States," *The Georgia Historical Quarterly*, XLIV (September, 1960), pp. 245-262. Recently New York City's Board of Education named Public School 304, General Pulaski School. The school, costing $2,500,000 is located on Pulaski Street in the Bedford-Stuyvesant section of Brooklyn. *Polish American Historical Association Bulletin*, Dr. Joseph A. Wytrwal, Editor, Number 189 (May, 1960), p. 1. Most recently an equestrian statue of Count Casimir Pulaski, costing some $125,000 was erected at the Main Street entrance to Pulaski Plaza, adjacent to the Federal Building in Hartford, Connecticut. This was one of the most expensive bicentennial ethnic projects of any U.S. group. The statue is cast in bronze on a granite pedestal and steps with overall dimensions: height 12 feet, 2 inches; 18 feet 6 inches long; 13 feet two inches long.

History records that General Casimir Pulaski was a thirty-second degree Mason. He was a member of a Masonic Lodge in Savannah, Georgia, where the Masons erected a statue in his memory. There are twelve Masonic lodges in the United States named after General Casimir Pulaski.

ciuszko appears in Mississippi and Texas.[19] Even a Panna Maria in Texas! The Polish immigrant made an impact on America through his skills and ingenuity throughout the United States. As a people the Polish immigrants differed from other nationals by their unique presence, manner of life, industriousness and self-reliance. The Portuguese were fishermen exclusively, the Swedes were lumbermen and farmers, the Italians were urban people who sought protection under the cloak of the Mafia.

Among the most common Polish surnames in the United States (according to a machine count made by the Social Security Administration) are: Kowalski—21,220 persons; Nowak—18,062 persons; Kaminski—16,274 persons; and Wisniewski—15,017.[20] Stevens Point is a city of 25,000 in northern Wisconsin. More

---

[19] Jacques Kosciuszko-Morizet, the current French ambassador to the United States, is not related to General Thaddeus Kosciuszko. One of his ancestors adopted this family name in honor of the American and Polish hero. In the city of Poznan, Poland, there are 500 individuals whose surname is Kosciuszko.

[20] There are some Americans of Polish descent who change their "difficult" to pronounce Polish names for business reasons. This is not true of Franciszek Joseph Bojanowski, Hotpoint executive in Chicago. When one of Bojanowski's business associates said to him that "it seems that since you're now so successful, it would be much easier for everyone concerned if you would change your name so that we could pronounce it with less difficulty." Bojanowski replied: "I did change it once before—it used to be Smith." *Polish American Journal* (May 25, 1957), p. 2.

Ann Landers who deals with various love and domestic problems in her popular column, which is published in numerous newspapers throughout the country, received this letter: "I am going out with a wonderful man. We are talking seriously about getting married. For several months I've been thinking about asking him to shorten his name. Finally, last night I broke the ice. He went into a rage and said he'd change girls before he'd change his name. I told him I didn't want to change it. I just want him to leave off the 'yowski.' He made it plain that he has no intention of doing so, and if I want him I'll have to take his name. What is your opinion—is he being arbitrary? I just can't see myself going through life with a name that is unpronounceable." Miss Landers answered Miss Smith as follows: "Dear Miss Smith: How would you like to be Miss Smith forever? It could happen—and it would serve you right. No name is unpronounceable. Some names require a little more effort than others. This young man is proud of his name and you should be happy to have it." *Polish American Journal* (August 1, 1959), p. 2.

Herman Borleske was a refugee who had skipped out of Eastern Germany to escape conscription into the iron army Bismarck was building to bind the provinces of the German Empire. Somewhere in Herman's journey to America he had been told to link the word "poor" with his name, possibly by a practical joker; more probably by some misguided friend who thought America, the land of the great heart, should know right off its newest arrival was flat broke. Thus, when he was asked his name, Herman would point a finger at his chest and smile as he said "poor Lesky." Herman couldn't spell it in English and an immigration official wrote

than half of the population is of Polish origin. Jan Siedlak in surveying the city's telephone directory made the following observations:

> Right under the first letter of the alphabet you will see 7 Adamczaks and 15 Adamskis. There are also 15 Adam's and no one knows how many of these are only abbreviated Adamskis.
>
> Under B we have 13 Banachs, which doesn't sound truly Polish, but they are of Polish origin, and some of them speak Polish. Brylowski changed the spelling to Brillowski and there are 18 of them. Ciszewskis number 25 in such variations as Ciseski and Cisewski.
>
> Under F there are 10 Falkaviges which sounds quite near as Falkiewicz, and 35 Firkuses which also doesn't sound Polish but nevertheless are. Then we have 19 Grosheks, and one of them is a member of the Wisconsin Legislature. We also have 23 Jakuszes, 15 Kieliszewskis and 39 Klucks. These Klucks' ancestors had such Polish names as Klukowski, Kluczkowski or Kluczynski.
>
> Some names were not only simplified in spelling, but literally translated: I know two brothers, one named Krol, and the other King, and the other two brothers with names Fox and Lis, and their close relative with two s's, Liss. Fourteen Miesiewiczes simplified their spelling to Mansavage! Lukaszewices to Lukasavige, and there are 19 of the first and 14 of the latter.[21]

---

him off as Herman Borleske, which bothered neither of them the least bit. Jack Hewins, *Borleske. Never Far From Hope* (Seattle: 1966), p. 13.

There is a Chinese restaurant in San Francisco named Kowallske's. It is operated by a full blooded Chinese, who gave the following explanation: "I came through immigration, stand in line. They ask man ahead of me what name. He say "Kowallske." Then my turn. They ask my name. I say Sam Ting. So-O-O, ever since." *Polish American Journal* (July 17, 1971), p. 1.

Cesar Enrique Sanchez, a native of Ecuador, became an American citizen recently. He selected a new name to go with his new citizenship. He selected Krzywonski Dennis Savatski. He gave "personal reasons" for the name change. *Polish American Journal* (December, 1972), p. 1.

Mary Martin is so proud of her Polish heritage that she has changed her name back to its original Polish form. Monroe County Judge George Ogden has given Miss Martin permission to change her name to Mary Strzyzewski. Miss Martin said her father had changed the family name of Strzyzewski to Martin after he emigrated from Poland to America. In a statement to the court, she said, "the mores of the community are changing . . . it is no longer inconvenient and embarrassing to have a foreign-sounding name." "As a matter of fact," she added, she "would carry such a name as Strzyzewski with a great deal of pride." *Polish American Journal* (June, 1973), p. 1.

[21] Jan Siedlak, " 'Gzibas' and 'Rybas' in Stevens Point," *Gwiazda Polarna* (January 1, 1972), p. 5.

Polish American Cultural Activities

Prior to 1870, the Polish immigration into the United States was composed chiefly of soldiers and political exiles. In 1802, there was a revolt in Santo Domingo, a French colony. To help suppress the rebellion Napoleon Bonaparte sent three battalions of Polish Legions in 1802 and a Polish brigade in 1803. Commanders of the Legionnaires were Brigadier General Francis C. Jablonowski (1769-1802) and General Casimir Malachowski (1765-1851). The French lost, and with them the Poles, who fought unwillingly.[22] Some Poles went over to the Negroes and settled among them. Two-hundred-and-forty Polish legionnaires were permitted to sail for the United States. Another group became stranded in Florida and planned a colony there.[23]

After Napoleon's downfall, in 1815, numerous Polish soldiers from his army emigrated to the New World. Several joined a group of French colonists who gathered at Philadelphia under General Charles Lallemand. In 1817, they sailed, 400 strong, for the Spanish province of Texas, where they planned to build a fortified colony—Champ d'Asile—then rescue the Emperor Napoleon from imprisonment on Saint Helena.[24] They settled near the present town of Liberty, Texas. Food shortages and reports of an advancing Spanish army caused abandonment of the project within eight months. Most of the refugees made their way to Louisiana. The United States Congress in 1817 granted 92,000 acres of land in Alabama to French and Polish exiles of the Napoleonic Wars "for the culture of vine and olive."

An undetermined number of Polish-born fighting men came

---

[22] The British, who had been helping the native rebellion against the French, forced many captured Poles into the English armies. During the 1811-1812 campaign against the United States, the 500 Poles taken prisoner in Santo Domingo were forced to fight on the side of Britain, in a unit known as the de Wateville Regiment. The Poles took part in the attack on Fort Barrie, south of the Niagara Falls. The survivors deserted their unit and crossed to the American side and settled in Dakota. For names of the Poles who served in the De Wateville Regiment see Mieczyslaw Haiman, *Slady Polskie w Ameryce* (Chicago: 1938), pp. 57-95.

[23] Wytrwal, *Poles in American History and Tradition*, pp. 113-114.

[24] Construction of the fortifications at Champ d'Asile was under the direction of several artillerymen who had served with Napoleon. One was Constantin Malczewski, brother of the famous Polish poet, Anthony Malczewski. After Champ d'Asile collapsed Malczewski emigrated to Mexico, where he became a general of artillery in the Mexican Army from 1834 to 1837.

to Texas during the winter of 1835-1836 to aid in the war for independence. Few lived to claim their reward of bounty in lands in the new Texas Republic. When disaster overtook Colonel James Fannin's little army at Goliad, there were Polish exiles in the ranks as engineers and artillerymen. Michael Debicki, who had been a major in the Polish Army, served as an engineer in Captain Peyton S. Wyatt's company at Goliad. Some of the volunteers in Fannin's artillery were the brothers Francis and Adolph Petrussewicz and John Kornicky, all three of whom were members of the Huntsville (Alabama) Volunteers. Joseph Schrusnecki also helped to man the howitzers. The artillery commander, Francis Petrussewicz, was killed at the disastrous battle of Goleto. Felix Wardzinski enlisted in Captain Amada Turner's company for the duration of the Texas Revolution.[25]

Well-educated, accomplished and sober, aware of the scheming forces for political power, the Polish immigration of this period belonged for the most part to the intellectual elite—exiled gentlemen deprived of their estates in Poland, because of patriotic zeal. Many of them had great energy and drive, while some of them possessed marked ability. Living in a strange country, and under new conditions, the political exiles strove to help each other by organizing their own societies.

The first Polish organized body in the United States was the Polish Committee, elected by 234 Poles, who had been exiled

---

[25] Felix Andrew Wardzinski saw action in the famous battle of San Jacinto, which sealed the triumph of the Texan War of Independence against Santa Anna and the Mexicans. In the battle at the Buffalo and Vince Rivers, Lieutenant Wardzinski encircled the Mexican army of General Antonio Lopez, destroyed the bridge on Vince River and won the victory over General Lopez. On the next day Wardzinski appeared before General Houston with a very valuable prisoner: this was no other than President and dictator of Mexico himself, General Santa Anna. The dictator bowed and signed peace.

When General Houston was elected president of the Texan Republic, Wardzinski retired from the army on August 5th, 1837. Wounded and weak, he became a farmer in Harris County, Texas, where he received 320 acres of land. In 1845, he joined the American army against Mexico and served until the end of the war February 2, 1848. After the war, he retired to his farm in Harris County, where he died. Texas Centennial Exposition bulletin of January, 1936 writes: "In the Hall of Heroes in that Million dollar Texas Hall of State at the Centennial Exposition opening in Dallas, June 6, Felix Wardzinski's name will be inscribed along with that of Sam Houston, liberator, and Stephen F. Austin, colonizer and father of the Lone Star Empire."

from Austrian Poland. The official journal of the Committee stated that the Poles who had been deported to the United States by the Austrian government, wished to remain as one body with the rest of the nation, Poland. Following a conference, they decided to form a committee which would represent the entire group. The Polish Committee was formed on April 1, 1834, in New York. All 234 Polish exiles signed the agreement. Half of the exiles were officers; fifty of whom had served in the Polish Army before the November Insurrection. Only one exile, Kwiatkowski, was accompanied by his wife. Most of the exiles were between twenty-six and forty. However, the existence of the Polish Committee lasted a very short while.

This assembly of wayfarers submitted a plea to Congress which, in part, said: "Although pilgrims in a foreign land, with nothing but the sad recollection of the past and hopes for the future, we wish to live a life of active industry, and become useful to the country of our adoption. . . ."[26] Their unhappy circumstances and those of their fellow countrymen prompted strong emotional sympathy in the United States.[27] Appeals to help the exiles and the cause of an independent Poland came from various prominent Americans: among them, the author, James Fenimore Cooper. He described Poland as "an heroic nation that should excite our esteem."

Although the American Aid Committee dispersed a considerable number of the Polish exiles to various states, nevertheless, a large number remained in New York City. In March 1842, upon the initiative of Henryk Kalussowski, they established, in New York City, the Association of Poles in America. The first meeting held under the presidency of the Rev. Ludwik Jerzykiewicz elected Bazyli Jaroszynski, Izydor Czarnomski, Wladyslaw Lange, and Henryk Kalussowski to serve as officers of the Association. It was resolved that every Pole, regardless of position, race or religion, had the right to become a member of the Association: the first aim being brotherhood and mutual aid. The association

---

[26] Laura Pilarski, *They Came From Poland. The Stories of Famous Polish Americans* (New York: 1969), p. 7.
[27] Mieczyslaw Haiman, *Polacy Wsrod Pionierow Ameryki* (Chicago: 1930), pp. 187-215.

was active until 1848, the year of the revolt called the "Spring of Nations," when Kalussowski, its main leader, returned to Europe to participate in the Revolution.[28]

Another active Polish exile in the United States, who arrived from France, in 1836, was Major Kaspar Tochman.[29] Endowed with sound common sense, energy and unflagging idealism, Tochman felt it was the duty of every exile to uphold the prestige of Poland among the American people and to gain as many friends for the Polish cause as possible. To counteract the Russian propaganda—especially to offset the pro-Russian articles in the *National Intelligencer*, which tried to convince the Americans that "to expect the resuscitation of Poland is to expect the tide of human affairs to roll backward, and about as rational as to hope for the resurrection of the Roman Empire"—Tochman travelled and lectured in the eastern part of the United States.[30] Tochman's arguments combined deftly a presentation of Poland as "the morning star of conscience and tolerance."[31] On a more practical level he pointed out that the existence of an independent Poland would be beneficial to the interests of England, France and the United States. Tochman was ahead of many Americans in understanding that "the ocean is no longer a barrier."

Tochman delivered over a hundred lectures on Poland's plight during the period from 1840 to 1844.[32] A fiery orator, he justly gained the reputation of being a stout champion for the cause of freedom. More than 250,000 people attended his well organized meetings. He was frequently welcomed as an honored guest in many state legislatures.

> Thus the Legislature of the State of New York declared on March 3, 1842, that nothing could justify the partition of Poland, "the unoffending nation among rapacious neighbors," and that no citizen of the free republic of America "can ever be indifferent to the fate of a

---

[28] Krystyna Murzynowska, "Henryk Korwin-Kalussowski (1806-1894)," *Problemy Polonii Zagranicznej*, Volume V (Warszawa: 1964-1965), pp. 117-128.

[29] Wytrwal, *Poles in American History and Tradition*, pp. 192-197.

[30] Mieczyslaw Haiman, *Z Przeszlosci Polskiej w Ameryce* (Buffalo: 1927), p. 244.

[31] *Ibid.*, p. 244.

[32] *Ibid.*, pp. 244-260.

nation whose annals shine with some many a bright record of her love of liberty, of religious toleration, and of scientific culture. . . ." The legislature of Connecticut resolved on May 12, 1842, "that in all conflicts between the tyrant and the oppressed, our best wishes are due to the latter, and especially extended to the Polish nation." The New Hampshire legislature expressed its ardent sympathy by resolving that the cause of Poland was the common cause of all friends of freedom throughout the world, and that even though Poland is "now humbled, dismembered and trampled under the iron heel of military despotism, we trust in the God of Justice, that the time will ere long come when she will rise, break her fetters and be free."[33]

Tochman also addressed seven other state legislatures. His subject matter invariably was the "Social, Political and Literary condition of Poland and her future prospects, conjointly with the policy of Russia towards these United States.[34] When first published in 1844, it was a scathing denunciation of the alleged friendship of the czarist regime towards the American Republic.

In 1846, Tochman, with the aid of other exiles, organized the Polish Slavonian Literary Association. He secured an official charter by an act of the New York legislature on March 26, 1846, which enabled him to incorporate the association in order "to promote the diffusion of knowledge on the History, Science, and Literature of the nations of the Slavonic race."[35]

Kaspar Tochman and Henryk Kalussowski were not the only individuals in America active in promoting a favorable opinion in the cause of Poland. Major Joseph Hordynski published, in Boston, his *History of the Late Polish Revolution*. The composer, Adam Kurek, also published, in Boston, in 1842, his "Twelve Admired Quick Steps to the Memory of Lost Poland."[36] In New

---

[33] Jerzy Jan Lerski, *A Polish Chapter in Jacksonian America* (Madison: 1958), pp. 157-158. Haiman Z *Przeszlosci Polskiej w Ameryce*, p. 250.

[34] Haiman, Z *Przeszlosci Polskiej w Ameryce*, p. 244.

[35] The society included among its members such prominent Americans as historian Jared Sparks, Harvard College President Josiah Quincy, Albert Gallatin, Jefferson's Secretary of the Treasury, and William H. Seward, a New York Senator.

[36] A talented musician, he organized itinerant bands in America. Since he changed American orchestras entirely by replacing the old drums and pipes with wind instruments, he is often called the "Father of the touring brass band in America." A prolific composer, he often named his compositions after leaders of the Polish November Uprising. For titles of his compositions see Wytrwal, *America's Polish Heritage*, p. 58.

York, J. K. Salmonski published his biography of the heroic lady colonel of the November 1830 Uprising under the title *The Life of Countess Emily Plater*. Jan N. Kryczynski, in collaboration with A. Wasilewski, published *The Recovery of Poland: By a Polish Exile*. The subject of the book was "a short history in vindication of a fallen nation." Much later, in 1854, another more detailed account of the history of Poland was published, written by an exile in New York, Julian Allen. It was entitled *Autocracy in Poland: Or a Description of Russian Misrule in Poland and an Account of the Surveillance of Russian Spies at Home and Abroad, Including "The Experience of an Exile."*

In 1842, the first Polish orientated periodical in America, an illustrated monthly magazine, *Poland, Historical, Literary, Monumental*, appeared in English. It was published by Paul Sobolewski in collaboration with a designer-illustrator, Eustachy Wyszynski. The magazine endeavored to present the greatest possible variety of subjects which would be of special interest to Poles in the United States. "Coronation of Boleslaus the Great," "Thaddeus Kosciuszko," "Castle of Ojców," and "Customs of the Polish Peasantry," are samples of the periodical's content. A recognition of *Poland, Historical, Literary, Monumental* as an outstanding publication was not slow in coming. As early as May 1942, *The New World* published an article in which the following remark appeared concerning this new publication: "Three numbers of this popular and interesting work already appeared. Each number is embellished with engravings, and contains well written and authentic articles on various subjects relating to unfortunate Poland. This work is worthy of patronage, and we hope that the American public will extend to it a liberal support. It is published at the low price of fifty cents a number."

The unfortunate experiences of the veterans of the 1848 Revolution seem to repeat those of the earlier Polish exiles. Many veterans emigrated to America. Bohdan Zaleski in his letter to Jan Kozmian, dated September 1849, reported that many exiles are leaving for America.[37] In his November letter, he reported that approximately one hundred Poles, among them several fam-

---

[37] Wiktor Weintraub, "Czy Ameryka byla dla Norwida infernem?" *Kultura* (April 1963), p. 42.

ilies, emigrated to the United States.[38] Correspondent Klaczko in the *Gazeta Polska* on December 6, 1850, reported that thirty emigrants sailed for America. They were helped by Count Wladyslaw Zamojski who worked closely with Lord Dudley and the Literary Association of Friends of Poland. Located in England, the association financed the departure of many Poles to America.[39]

Some of the exiles, after 1848, surpassed in prestige those of the 1834 exiles to the United States. Some taught school in the United States, especially French and mathematics. Outstanding examples of the emigres from the 1848 Revolutionary movement known as the "Springtime of Nations" were the following: Vladimir Krzyzanowski and Joseph Karge were breveted brigadier generals after the Civil war by the United States Senate. Joseph Karge, Leopold J. Boeck and Emil D'Alfonse became important educational leaders. John Tyssowski, who had been the dictator of Kraków during the rebellion, advertised for a teaching position on arrival in New York and joined Karl Heinzen, a German refugee, in editing the *Deutsche Schnellpost*. In this newspaper, Tyssowski propagated the ideals of freedom, democracy and progress, believing that only through the victory of those ideals in the world is there hope for Polish independence. He stayed in close contact with the Polish political emigres in Europe and America. In January 1849, Tyssowski found work as a draftsman in the Congressional Committee on Public Lands and moved to Washington. After two years he began working for the Treasury Department. In 1853, he was given an important post in the Patent Office, a post which he held until his death on April 5, 1857.

On September 17, 1852, there appeared in the *New York Daily Tribune*, under the heading of "The Poles in America," a manifesto of a newly formed group of Poles (sixty in number), who decided to organize under the name of the "Association of Polish Exiles in America." This was later changed to the "Democratic Society of Polish Exiles." As with the previous organization, the Association of Poles in America, incorporated into its

---
[38] *Ibid.*, p. 42.
[39] *Ibid.*, p. 43.

by-laws the provision that every Polish immigrant is eligible for membership without regard to social status or religion. The organization had branches in several cities, and it endured longer than all of the previous Polish organizations in America. The organization had no officers, and in an interesting democratic fashion each member presided, in turn, at its meetings. It paid small benefits to members, and even to non-members in cases of need; and it organized the first Polish library, at the headquarters, in New York City. The organization also strongly condemned slavery.

In 1853, on the occasion of the 23rd anniversary of the Polish rebellion of 1830, it celebrated in New York City with Polish, German and Italian speeches. Eight years earlier, a similar celebration was described in the *New York Weekly News*, with representatives of all the important immigrant groups appearing on the program. In 1859, Polish exiles, in Cincinnati, arranged a banquet to commemorate the Warsaw Uprising of 1830, at which two actual participants were present as honored guests. In August 1869, the 300th anniversary of the Union of Lublin was celebrated in New York and Chicago with 900 people in attendance.[40]

The Democratic Society of Polish Exiles continued until February 27, 1860, the date of the last recorded minutes which abruptly ended without a record of its dissolution or any further information about it. The dissolution of the Democratic Society of Polish Exiles was most likely due to the outbreak of the Civil War. Many of its members served as officers of various ranks in the Union Army, while others served in the lower ranks.

Cyprian Norwid left Liverpool, England on December 12, 1852. He arrived in America in February, 1853. He returned to Europe with Marceli Lubomirski in 1854. Ludwick Bulewski, known as the Polish Mazzini, visited the United States in February 1866. During his stay, he met with some members of Congress, and was instrumental in organizing the European Revolutionary Committee under the chairmanship of E. A. Stansbury. Likewise, he was instrumental in organizing the Fraternal of

---

[40] Jerzy W. Borejsza, *Emigracja Polska Po Powstaniu Styczniowym* (Warszawa: 1966), p. 36.

Slavs in the United States, which had as an honorary member the president of the United States.[41]

In the post-Civil War period a group of Polish intellectuals came to California to establish an utopian community on the style of Brook Farm or New Harmony. When the venture collapsed and the participants were forced to earn their daily bread, Helena Modjeska began to study English and became one of America's leading Shakespearean actresses.[42] Henryk Sienkiewicz was one of its members, and later gained the Nobel Prize for Literature with his novel, *Quo Vadis*.

Nevadans were unquestionably interested, amused, and impressed by the Polish born residents who commanded special favors and elicited special attention. The Nevada newspapers reveal a constant procession of bogus aristocrats like Count Mitkiewicz of Poland.

> Mitkiewicz charmed Virginia City society during the first part of 1872, while he was searching for a rich heiress to marry. Later in the year, he found and married a wealthy lady in Rochester, New York, only a few days before he was exposed as a charlatan.[43]

Not all would-be aristocrats were as lucky.

> On February 8, 1873, the *Gold Hill Daily News* revealed that Albert Sobieski, a Polish nobleman, had died penniless in the county hospital. Before his death Sobieski had explained to a local bartender that although he was heir to great estates, he had chosen exile rather than the trammels of Europe and had spent his life wandering throughout the world. The reporter remembered the Pole as intelligent, cultivated, a master of languages, a brilliant conversationalist, and a good athlete. He was often seen waiting at the Virginia City post office for money that was to have been dispatched from Europe. But the funds did not arrive and Sobieski sat up in saloons because he could no longer pay for lodgings. Whether nobleman or peasant, he finally died, a public charge, at the county hospital.[44]

Frank Schollata, "the counterfeit Pole of Humboldt," had no wish to become famous or share in the picturesque Nevada immigrant traditions.

---
[41] *Ibid.*, p. 146.
[42] Wytrwal, *Poles in American History and Tradition*, pp. 242-246.
[43] Wilbur S. Shepperson, *Restless Strangers. Nevada's Immigrants and Their Interpreters* (Reno: 1970), p. 98.
[44] *Ibid.*, pp. 98-99.

In early June, 1879, Frank Scholatta was arrested in Winnemucca for counterfeiting half dollars. The authorities seized the plaster of Paris molds, lead, babbit metal, antimony, ladles, and other equipment. But while being transported to Carson City, Schollata jumped off the train near Lovelock and for over a week eluded a sheriff's posse of nearly a hundred white men and a band of Indian scouts. Eventually captured on the Oregon border, Schollata was taken to Carson City and brought to trial in November, 1879. To the dismay of the federal officers, the Pole was acquitted by a jury who seemed to agree with the defense attorney's arguments that Winnewucca needed a mint, that Nevada needed more coins, and that no one had proved that Schollata planned to use the newly minted money illegally.[45]

Interest in Americans of Polish descent continued to our own day.[46]

Many Polish exiles were also active in journalism. From June 10, 1863 until April 22, 1865, they published, in New York, a Polish language newspaper, *Echo z Polski,* which on October 8, 1864, changed its banner to *Echo Polskie.* Schriftgiesser, a political refugee, published it along with Romuald J. Jaworowski.[47] The paper contained very few original articles. Most of its material consisted of reprints from the European papers: *Czas, Gazeta Narodowa,* and *Niepodleglosc.* During the Civil War it supported the North because the North, according to its editorial, "does not attack, rob, conquer, and did not cause the war and it does not murder."[48] The motto of the paper was, first, to know the history of the fatherland: her glories and her defeats.[49]

---

[45] *Ibid.,* p. 105. See also a series of articles in the Nevada *Morning Appeal* published between June 10, 1879 and November 21, 1879.
[46] Nora Linger Bowman in *Only the Mountains Remain* (1958) developed the character of a Polish gardener who lived with the family on their ranch in eastern Elko County, Nevada. Recently Mary Ellen Chase in *A Journey to Boston* described the Polish Americans in Massachusetts.
[47] Schriftgiesser was a Polish patriot of Jewish origin. After the Polish Uprising of 1863, many Polish patriots of Jewish descent left Russian-occupied Poland and settled in New York. Before 1870, more than 15,000 Poles of Jewish descent were living in New York City. They participated actively in many of the Polish liberation activities. Many were among the leaders of the *Związek Ludu Polskiego.* Borejsza, *Emigracja Polska Po Powstaniu Styczniowym,* p. 47.
[48] Borejsza, *Emigracja Polska Po Powstaniu Styczniowym,* p. 89.
[49] *Ibid.,* p. 88.

PRELUDE TO THE POLISH PEASANT IMMIGRATION

In 1870, in the little town of Washington, Missouri, the second Polish newspaper appeared: *Orzel Bialy*. The history of its struggle to survive, in a community of scarcely a dozen families, is an interesting commentary on the hardships and sacrifices entailed in the founding of the Polish press in America.

Because of the paucity of their numbers, and because they were widely scattered, they could not afford the luxury of subdividing into several organized groups. Also the culturally centripetal homogenizing forces of American life proved to be too formidable in order to resist or overcome individually. In France, the Polish exiles established roots in their exiled soil and they did form intimate relations with French society.[50] In America, the exiles did adapt themselves to their new conditions. They mixed freely with the native community and blended into American society as individuals. And despite their valiant attempts to preserve their language and literature, they rapidly adjusted to living conditions in America. They left a few documents referring to the first Polish association which they established in this country. Their education and intellectual attainments did not hinder them; in fact they enhanced their adjustment. And it was this very group of statesmen and soldiers, writers and scholars, journalists and artists, who fostered the Polish spirit of independence and who acquainted Americans with the Polish problem. They succeeded in personally influencing and recasting many of the distorted images of the old Polish state previously held by Americans.

---

[50] The first Polish publication in France appeared on July 1, 1832, entitled *Pamietnik Emigracji Polskiej*; it was published by Michal Podczaszynski.

The first Polish library was established, in 1835, in Paris. There was much intermarriage with French nobility. Adam Mickiewicz taught at the College de France. Leonard Chodzko published a four volume history *Memoires sur la Pologne et les Polonais depuis 1778 jusqu's la fin de 1815* (1826-1827). Chodzko also contributed material on Poland and Poles to *Le Constitutionel, Le Courrier Francais, Revue Encyclopedique,* and *Biographie universelle portative des contemporains*. Chodzko also organized an assembly to honor the anniversary of Kosciuszko's death. At the event General Lafayette gave the main address. In the audience was also Victor Hugo. Chodzko also organized an exhibit on Polish art which was well received. The exiles also influenced many French writers and dramatists to write on Polish topics. See Maria Straszewska, *Zycie literackie Wielkiej Emigracji we Francji 1831-1840* (Warszawa: 1970).

The European Exiles

The Polish exiles also maintained their contacts with Polish revolutionary leaders in France and Italy. The Polish emigration in Paris, after 1831, was politically divided into two main groups. The Aristocrats professed monarchism and considered its spokesman, Prince Adam Jerzy Czartoryski, as their "uncrowned King of Poland." They saw hope for Poland through diplomatic intervention by various European governments, and accordingly, assailed their offices with visits and memorandum, articles and pamphlets. The Aristocrats became an organ of protest before the bar of public opinion throughout Europe. They believed they had only to convince the people of Europe of the justice of the Polish cause and they would rise in arms to help at once. The Aristocrats made use of well-known friendships in all the courts of Europe. Under the leadership of Prince Czartoryski, the most experienced diplomat of his generation, the Aristocrats worked for two objectives: the first, an immediate one, to force the English House of Commons to debate the Polish question openly; the second, less immediate, but ultimately more important: to compel British statesmanship to recognize the Polish question as an integral and inseparable part of the greater question of the whole Near East.[51]

The democratic group was represented by Joachim Lelewel, a notable historian.[52] The democratic group blamed the egoism of

---

[51] Every variety of enterprise which governments normally sponsor, Prince Czartoryski undertook, carrying them out with funds supplied by himself, his wife, and secret sympathizers in Poland, and by friends in England. Schools were established, scholarships were provided, posts were found for the exiles, journals were published, philanthropic work including every branch of charity was organized, and a complete diplomatic service was established. Prince Czartoryski's agents were in every country, gathering information to use in his negotiations with friendly governments and watching for propaganda likely to harm the Polish cause. Thus, Prince Czartoryski was able to keep the Vatican informed as to the treatment of Poles in the Russian partition of Poland and also to supply the British government with a special investigator of the conditions in Asia Minor in the person of General Chrzanowski.

[52] Joachim Lelewel (1786-1861) was born in Warsaw, where he received his secondary education at the Piarist Fathers' School. He then travelled to Wilno for further study. Upon completing his studies he taught ancient history and geography at the Lyceum in Krzemieniec, the University of Wilno, and at the University of Warsaw. The 1831 Insurrection compelled him to flee to France; but he settled in Belgium, in 1833, where he remained to the end of his life.

His life-long interest in geography and numismatics proved to be more than of

the aristocracy, gentry and church hierarchy for the principle failure of the November 1830 Insurrection, which failed to secure the confidence of the peasant farmers and the insignificant urban proletariat. Realizing this error, the democratic group endeavored to make the next insurrection a social, as well as a national revolution; and they believed that their hopes of success lay in the prospects of a European revolution. Thus, they directed their appeal, not to governments, but to liberal groups in France, Italy, Spain, Belgium, Portugal and Germany, to whom they issued manifestos as busily as the aristocratic group addressed diplomatic notes to ministers. There was certainly more response from popular sentiment, in Europe, to the democratic group's appeal than there was from the official quarters to the representatives of the aristocratic group. There was also wider support for the democratic group among the rank and file of the immigrants themselves. Mickiewicz and Slowacki, while deploring or despising the strife among the two groups, distinctly sympathized with the revolutionary ideals of popular freedom and international brotherhood.[53]

The democratic group believed in the possibilities of renewed armed movement in Poland itself, and continually stirred up the spirits of active resistance there. Full enfranchisement of the peasant and the free ownership of land that he tilled, were proclaimed as the principal slogans of the democratic group. To acquaint the peasants with their objectives, they sent emissaries from abroad to Poland. These emissaries became familiar figures in all parts of Poland and the object of intense, but mostly vain

---

casual interest, for he wrote two monumental works on these subjects, which introduced him to Belgian scholarly circles. Soon he received a position at the University of Brussels which allowed him to devote himself to his works on Polish history.

Because Lelewel was the first to give Polish historical research a solid methodological basis, he is called the "Father of Modern Historical Research." He also made use of subsidiary disciplines and divided Polish history into scholarly periods. *Poland: Her History and Her Affairs* (in twenty volumes) and his history of *Poland Told Colloquially*, are among his best known works. He also published *Bibliograficznych Ksiąg Dwoje*.

His political activities are equally as significant as his efforts in scholarly research. He organized the Zjednoczenie Emigracji Polski, was the chairman of Komitet Narodu Polski and also active in Towarzystwo Patriotyczne. His ideas and efforts influenced political thinkers in exile as well as in Poland for many generations to come.

[53] In the pure Romantic spirit Mickiewicz believed that the Poles must discipline themselves so as to live nobly for their country; Slowacki believed that the Poles must discipline themselves so as to die nobly for it.

pursuit by the police of the partitioning powers. The work of the emissaries was supported by secret democratic societies in Poland —formed by enthusiastic university students composed of men and women from all ranks of the intelligentsia—and anxious to make contact with the popular masses. Against the endeavors of these democrats, the partitioning governments—through a calculated system of police persecution based on a conscious and persistent policy of sowing discord among the Polish gentry and peasants, and posing as the protectors of the Polish peasant against his landlord—undermined all of the good efforts of the democrats. Eventually four schools of political thought, apparently irreconcilable with each other, developed in partitioned Poland and abroad: the idealism of revolt and protest embodied in the democratic group; diametrically opposite to it, the realistic view of cooperation with the partitioning powers as personified by Margrabia Aleksander Wielopolski in Russian Poland, by Prince Antoni Radziwill in Prussian Poland and by the Counts Potocki in Austrian Poland. Midway between these two divergent schools stood the school represented by Andrzej Zamojski, who combined the idealism of day-to-day economic activities. The fourth school represented by Prince Adam Czartoryski—with his headquarters in Paris, at Hotel Lambert—utilized diplomacy to make the Polish question a central issue of the two main problems agitating Europe, namely, the Near Eastern question and the rise of Liberalism. Prince Czartoryski hoped, through diplomacy, not only to keep the Polish question alive, but to regain the independence of Poland.[54] The four schools of political thought did not bring about the independence of Poland, but they kept the idea of a resurrection of Poland alive by revealing to the world that the settlement of 1815 was not accepted by the Poles any more than the partitions of the eighteenth century.

Threefold Loyalty

After 1863, throughout the three partitions of Poland, there was an universal violent revulsion, in the national mind, to all

---

[54] To his chateau in Paris, Hotel Lambert, he attracted the notable Polish artists, poets and musicians, as well as other nobles at evening soirees or other benefits. His residence was one of the most prominent centers of Polish culture, in Europe, during his long life.

romantic and heroic dreams of political change through revolution, since this program had disastrously failed and brought about only greater repression and humiliation. Furthermore, participants were considered rebels: just targets for the rifles of the firing parties when the day of wrath came. There was also a reaction against all tendencies to seek national comfort in the glories of the past. Wlodzimierz Zagorski stated this explicitly in his poem *Lojalnosc* published in 1868.

Miałem sen straszny! okropny!
Zbrodniczy! grzeszny! fatalny!
Śniłem, że jestem Polakiem,
Ja—Galilejczyk lojalny!

Jak mogłem śnić coś takiego,
Ja? powiatowy marszałek?
Kiedym się ze snu obudził,
Dałbym był sobie sto pałek!

I dotąd biedzę się jeszcze
Rady nie mogąc dać sobie!
Ach, przebacz Wysoki Rządzie!
Już nigdy tego nie zrobię!

The heroic Insurrection of 1863 was viewed as a vast piece of tragic national folly. It depressed the nation profoundly. Conspiracy and violent methods were almost entirely abandoned, and replaced by a policy of so-called "organic work" which implied political resignation and patience endeavoring to strengthen the nation through economic and educational progress. The economic success of the individual came to be regarded as the most acceptable measure of patriotism, and as an indication of the growing welfare of the nation. This necessitated cooperation with foreign rule; or if counteraction was necessary, at least it would be achieved through legal methods only. Father Kalinka, a rising historian, expressed this view in 1857, in the columns of the *Polish News*, a journal founded by Prince Czartoryski.

> War with Russia is indeed the goal of our hope, and it must also be the crown of our striving. But it is not only war that counts in history. Achievements won in times of peace are no less honourable. They are also no less lasting and decisive.[55]

---

[55] Quoted in William John Rose, *The Rise of Polish Democracy* (London: 1944), p. 17.

Aleksander Glowacki, in a striking metaphor from natural science, made the following observation:

> When a bullet strikes a wall, it halts and generates heat. In mechanics this process is called the transforming of mass motion into molecular, of what was an outward into an inner force. Something like this happened in Poland after the cruel quelling of the insurrection. The nation as a whole woke up, ceased to fight, and to conspire, and began to think and work.[56]

The daily *Czas*, the organ of the aristocratic Conservative Party in Austrian Poland, made the following comment in the late seventies:

> We have said to ourselves: no organism can live long in a fever. New ways must be found; for if we follow the old ones, our devotion will inevitably be burned up, at least every fifteen years in a conflict of blood. It will be exhausted in useless adventures, and the toil of the interval be wasted at the very time when it might bear fruit.[57]

Such tendencies albeit realistic, stressed the material aspects of life with a lesser concern towards incorporating all of the high and noble principles of a democratic constitution.

International considerations also influenced this view. Although Russia was probably the most oppressive of the occupying powers, few Poles wished to take action which might lead to the increased power of Prussia or Austria. After the alliance between France and Russia, in 1894, there was no encouragement from France. Besides, Russian industrialization offered a profitable market to the rapidly growing Polish industries. To workers and capitalists alike, insurrection threatened a new way of life which seemed to offer a comfortable future.

The adaptability of the Poles to the partitions produced in Poland a strange spirit, which has been mockingly described as "threefold loyalty." Reinforcement and support for this triple loyalty was preached and practiced by the school of Warsaw "Positivists," the Krakow Historical Schools, and by the group known as "Stanczyk." They all stressed that the romantic enthusi-

---

[56] *Ibid.*, p. 17.
[57] *Ibid.*, p. 37.

asm of the past decades should give way to cold logic; no longer armed uprisings or military revolutionary plots, but a general economic, cultural, and national uplifting of the masses of Polish people should become their goal and patriotic duty.

The school of Warsaw Positivists, prevalent in Russian Poland after the 1863 Uprising, implied an acceptance of the existing political authorities by the middle class or bourgeoisie of Polish society.[58] Polish Positivism also insisted that nationality should be divorced from statehood, and that the Polish nation should accommodate itself to foreign rule or try to circumvent this oppression by concentrating on the cultural development of its people—its primary criterion for existence. Polish Positivism, which developed after the tragic defeat of the 1863 Insurrection, was an ideological as well as a literary movement. It abandoned its former romantic and heroic concepts, as well as all obscurantism in philosophy. It asserted a positive outlook on the future based on a pursuit of the exact sciences. Its motto, "Organic Work," referred to raising the cultural, as well as the economic level of the nation through useful means. This could be attained through a thorough education which was highly restricted in Russian Poland. In particular, women could not aspire to an higher education in Poland. It compelled them (if they had Marie Sklodowska-Curie's determination) to seek a university education in a foreign land. In this manner, the "Underground University" was formed at great risk to those in attendance. The Czarist regime feared and suppressed all Polish intellectual activities, and strictly forbade the use of the Polish language on penalty of deportation to Siberia. The indomitable will of the Polish people could not be crushed, even under the severe threat to their life and property. The spirit of the Polish people was best kept alive through its literature and periodicals. Among its most significant exponents

---

[58] Its philosophy was adopted from Auguste Le Comte (1798-1857), who abandoned metaphysics for a strict limitation of philosophy to factual or non-abstract matters with a fundamental practical acquisition of knowledge that would be useful to mankind. Speculations by philosophers on non-material matters, like the soul, being, power, etc., were irrelevant. Other positivists were John Stuart Hill (1806-73), and Herbert Spencer (1820-1903). A later school of Neo-Positivist from Vienna consisted of Rudolph Carnap and Moritz Schleck. *Mala Encyclopedia Powszechna* (Warszawa: 1959), p. 763.

were: Eliza Orzeszkowa, Aleksander Prus, Aleksander Swietochowski and Piotr Chmielewski. They were both creative writers as well as literary historians and essayists.

Polish Positivism was responsible for raising the intellectual and cultural level of Polish society. Having a basic respect for education, they expanded their own horizons, which resulted in becoming more self-reliant. (It was the basic ideology of the middle classes or bourgeoisie in Poland.) One aspect of Polish Positivism took expression in Slavophilism.[59] In Austria, after 1867, the cultural rights of the Poles were finally attained and respected. The Poles meanwhile also had gained provincial self-government. As a result, the Polish conservatives became the staunchest supporters of the Dual-Monarchy. And even in Russian and Prussian Poland, the conservative class, which consisted of the great landowners and industrialists, proclaimed the gospel of loyalty to the State, fondly hoping that as a reward for this loyalty, they might obtain a reversal of the policy of forcible Russification or Germanization. Jozef Ignacy Kraszewski, in Russian Poland, also preached the gospel of "organic work" with its corollary of conciliation (*ugoda*) towards the Russian Empire.

Polish Positivism thrived until the middle 1880's when the proletariat class arose with its socialist banner. Some Polish socialists were nationalists before they were socialists; others like Rosa Luxemburg, believed that nationalism was an outmoded creed, and that Poland was destined to become a part of a larger multi-national workers' state.

Roman Dmowski, the leader of the non-socialists Polish radicals, advised his countrymen to seek an alliance with Russia. He thought that Prussia was the main enemy of Polish national-

---

[59] This movement had, as its objective, the unification of all Slavic peoples. The Pan-Slavism of this period sought the preservation and development of a Slavic civilization through the union of all Slavic peoples in a strongly centralized autocratic and orthodox state ruled by the Russian Czar as the head of the largest group of Slavs. The Poles opposed Pan-Slavism as it would have meant giving up their nationalism and their Catholicism. Excluded from Germany by Prussia, Austria felt obliged to become a constitutional state, and to rely upon the Slavic subjects for the support of its Empire. This made the Poles valuable to Austria. Not only were they one of the largest Slavic groups, but they were also the only group to definitely oppose Pan-Slavism which was a real menace to the Austrian Hungarian Empire with its numerous nationalities (Slavic and non-Slavic) chafing for independence.

ism. The growing rift between the three occupying powers was a key factor in Polish thought. Independence, it was thought, would come as a result of an international war, that is, so long as the Polish nationalists place themselves on the winning side. Insurrection would merely serve to reunite Russia, Austria and Prussia.

The Krakow Historical School, under the leadership of the influential historian and political activist, Jozef Szujski, embarked on a review of the nation's past and ended by reversing the accepted views of the Polish partitions.[60] Jozef Szujski became a professor of the more than 500-year-old Jagiellonian University, in 1869.[61] His thesis of Polish history was the Polish partitions were not caused by external factors, but internal ones, which brought Poland to its catastrophic end.[62] The prolonged immuta-

---

[60] Jozef Szujski (1835-83) was a historian (*Dzieje Polski*), publicist, political activist, dramatist, and poet. He participated in the 1863 Insurrection. At first a liberal, but later a conservative and one of the founders of *Przeglad Polski* (*Polish Review*) and a co-author of *Teki Stanczyka* (*Stanczyk's Portfolio*). From 1869, he was a professor at the Jagiellonian University.

[61] As an historian Szujski made some of the most ridiculous and illogical statements. To be an historian one must absorb all history and see it in a panoramic view simultaneously. Szujski makes one charge, and gives an excuse for it. Not at all examining where other procedures, according to his argument failed. He gives the wrong reasons for Poland's downfall and reveals how little he was equipped to write history.

[62] The fate of Poland was brought about by no one particular factor upon which the historian of nationality can, metaphorically, lay his finger. Poland's collapse was due to a combination of causes, reacting one upon the other. Generally speaking, these predisposing factors can be classed as political, religious, geographical or fortuitous.

As for the political causes the monarchical system of Poland made for instability. In the earlier days, the succession was to all intents and purposes in the families of the Piasts and Jagiellons. The elective system often resulted in the choice of foreign princelings, lacking any real knowledge of Polish conditions, and without any sense of permanency in their succession. These sovereigns were incapable of devising a foreign policy suitable for the development of the country. Prior to the partitions, the monarchical principle was in other countries being strengthened and centralized; and wider powers were conferred upon the king, as representing the people, in order to ensure consistency and stability to the State. This was not true in Poland. Another unfortunate political factor was the legislative dead-weight known as the *liberum veto*.

The strong political power of the nobles was gained at the expense of the throne, and unfortunately for Poland, a want of patriotism prevailed amongst them. They had no ideals; their views were parochial; and most of them preferred their own local and family interests to that of the nation at large. Unfortunately, the order of nobles abrogated to itself two of the most important privileges of a citizen. They supplied the fighting force of the nation, and they alone voted at the elections for

bility of economic conditions in Poland kept Poland at a very low economic level up to the final partition. Poland's premature parliamentarism reduced the monarchial power, thereby taking away from the nation its influential guide and leader, especially in the domain of foreign policy, which resulted in fractionalism and

members of the Sejm. A lack of national cohesion also grew out of the system by which the more powerful nobles were allowed to maintain in their own lands bands of retainers and to indulge in private warfare; and the existence of these private armies enabled discontented nobles to flout the legal Sejm and to assemble rival confederations. Among the most important and valued rights in Poland was that of being free from taxation. No danger, however great, no calamities, however threatening, no perils, however overwhelming, could induce the nobles to submit to the smallest present burden to ward off future disaster. They preferred any load of infamy, however great, to any burden of taxation, however light.

The failure to replace feudalism with a strong middle class was also a decided misfortune for Poland. During the last two centuries of the Polish Commonwealth, the burghers declined and came to have alien interests. The arrogance of the nobles and the suppression of the burgher element effectively choked any real patriotism. The burghers had lost the right of holding landed property, except in the immediate vicinity of towns; they were not permitted to send deputies to the Sejm; and were excluded from all share of legislative authority. Also since the burghers were not obliged to march against the enemy, they incurred the contempt of the war-like gentry.

The condition of the Polish peasants during the eighteenth century was a difficult lot. They toiled on the land. Of personal liberty they had little. They were forbidden to leave their villages if vassals on the lord's estates, but as tenant farmers they were left scanty leisure to cultivate their own diminutive plots. Exalted patriotism from the unfortunate peasants was hardly to be expected. The Russian peasants had it worst of all, for they were human chattel—worse than the Negroes in the United States. They were on par with the livestock.

Poland was ahead of all Europe in the matter of religious toleration. However, the influence of the Jesuits was particularly strong, and they were responsible for the persecution of non-Catholics, and to their exclusion from the service to the Crown. While Russia strove to identify the interests of the Slavs with those of the Greek Church, Prussian kings became the champions of North German Protestantism. Thus, they were naturally hostile to Poland which had long been the center of militant Roman Catholicism.

The geographical drawbacks of Poland were serious. Except for the protection it had from the Tatra mountains to the South and the Baltic Sea to the North, Poland had no natural frontiers to the east and west. Nevertheless Poland had much rolling country, many impenetrable forests and dotted with many lakes. But its interior was open to incursions by highways, rivers, the Baltic Sea and much open terrain.

Another misfortune was the lack of some vigorous rulers, such as Boleslaw the Brave and Kazimierz the Great. King Stanislaw August Poniatowski and Stanislaw Leszczynski were culturally and intellectually advanced of any contemporary European monarchs. Frederick the Great and Catherine the Great were despots. Because of the backwardness of each country they ruled, they could retain their thrones, but in Poland they could never reign.

Poland was divided by too much factionalism. Furthermore, Poland encouraged it rather than try to suppress it. Too much of a good thing spoils it for others.

internal disorder.⁶³ Also Poland's colonizing mission in Lithuania and the Ukraine was an ambitious enterprise which exceeded the strength of the nation.⁶⁴ This Polish eastward expansion absorbed too many forces which should have been devoted to reforming the nation. The best, most active and creative elements of the nation were lost or absorbed by the immense territories united to the Republic; and the Republic was devastated.⁶⁵

Humanism and the Reformation likewise weakened Poland, having decimated the homogeneous force of organization through Catholicism.⁶⁶ In accomplishing its civilizing mission in the East,

---

⁶³ Not necessarily so, the English monarchy endures to this day. But the English monarchy suppressed all nationalism through the assimilation of its people. It was Great Britain with no emphasis on England or Wales, or Scotland, or Ireland. It survived through pomp and ceremony, the panoply of power displayed at the expense of frequent foreign conquests. It also had a great navy and extensive mercantile influence. When this disappeared, the trappings also disappeared.

⁶⁴ Poland's expansion into a Commonwealth was not beyond her means or strength for it would have failed in the first century of its attempt, not 300 years later. The Commonwealth was most workable, practical, sensible and good in that Polish influence extended so far. If Poland's boundaries were smaller she might have been absorbed sooner by the larger imperial powers.

⁶⁵ The expansion of Poland eastward was inspired by protective measures to confederate against the encroachments of Prussia. It was never a ruthless armed conquest of Lithuania and Russia. Lithuanians inherited a Polish throne and they mutually accepted the terms, in 1569, at the Treaty of Lublin. Once Poland was secure in the east, she would never be threatened by Prussia or Austria.

Poland profited from the eastward expansion; but she also suffered because of it. She had lost her homogeneity. Poles were never oriented towards the East in any regard but toward the West. Necessity caused this. However, the confederative East was civilized through Poland. Magnates were rewarded with vast estates or latifundia, in the east, for great and meritorious service to the king and the nation.

It was the Cossacks and the Ruthenians that partially depleted the strength of Poland. Another contributing factor was the election of Zygmund III with his bigoted views that engaged Poland in a protracted war with Sweden for sixty years. Two fronts depleted her strength. And this effort was a northern one. Likewise the Vasas intermarried with the Habsburgs which was even another direction for an alliance.

Ivan the Terrible coveted Katarzyna Jagiellon, who spurned him for a Swedish prince. If Poland was only easterly oriented, she would have leaped at this marriage alliance. Poland's astute politicians sought a more westerly direction: the second wife of Wladyslaw IV was a Frenchwoman, Sobieski's granddaughter, Clementine, married a James Stuart, the "Old Pretender" to the British throne. And Zygmunt I took an Italian princess. Likewise all of the non-Polish kings, Henri de Valois, August I and II, Stefan Batory as well as other candidates, emanated from Western Europe.

It was the idealism of Sobieski that eventually undermined the Polish State when he defeated the Turks at Vienna, thereby removing the one enemy of Russia and

Poland gradually lost or at least attenuated its occidental characteristics; it underwent the contagion of oriental and Muscovite barbarity. In *Some Truths About Our History,* published in 1867, Szujski had argued that Poland ceased to be a sovereign state through her own merit. The year 1791, had put an end to the old vice of *liberum veto;* the events of 1863-1864 had closed once and for all the epoch of *liberum conspiro.*[67] He argued that to carry on revolutionary tactics then, in whatever form, would only lead the nation to destruction.[68]

Where scholarship demanded it, the Krakow Historical School, which was presided by Szujski's disciple, Michal Bobrzynski, sometime Galician governor, had no qualms about assigning the dismemberment of Poland to the grievous incompetence and blindness of the Polish gentry. In his book, *Historia Polski,* which was published after the Franco-Prussian War, Bobrzynski accuses the Polish gentry of having produced no men sufficiently ardent or powerful, passionate or decisive, or to have had the courage to

---

Austria that always checked their aggression. Poland's greatest contribution to the world was a moral principle.

Poland also sought to extend her liberal doctrines to the backward and primitive lands of eastern Europe in the name of democracy and religion. Had Wladyslaw IV succeeded to the Russian throne, all European history would have changed. It was the last and only opportunity Russia ever had to experience true democracy. Its loss meant autocracy, backwardness for its people and repression for centuries. The strong habit of despotic rule did not change with the Communist revolution.

[66] Poland was the only nation that avoided religious wars and allowed the Protestant Reformation to run its natural course. It did not engage in any wars that raged over Europe. As a sanctuary for the Arians, Poland benefited by intellectual stimulation the Arians offered.

[67] The *Liberum veto* permitted any deputy to dissolve the Sejm, even annulling the decisions taken before his intervention. This absurd democratic principle of unanimity had developed as time went on. Its significance to Poland was total agreement based on the theory that through open discussion a conciliatory point of view could be reached which would benefit the whole state.

[68] Szujski recommends the apathy of nationalism. Revolutions are costly in human life, but rarely are governments altered peacefully without the spilling of blood. Without the Romantic fervor and the undying will to become an independent nation, Poland would have been absorbed. Poles are highly developed people which must be contrasted with other nationalities. They have gone through every test of fire, water, steel and survived. There are many other peoples—but how many survived 100 years of statehood There are three nationalities in Czechoslovakia, seven in Yugoslavia and over 200 in 16 national republics of the Soviet Union, but Poland is supremely Polish even when it was a Confederation. Its greatness was always apparent even surviving 125 years of partitions and during this period producing an era of great literature and art. What other nationality that has been subjected to such direful conditions can claim the same achievement?

push history into drama, into great conflicts of passions or political crises. He completely ignores such great leaders as Rejtan, Kosciuszko, Bem, Czartoryski or the Potockis. Polish toleration seemed to him a proof of weakness, not strength; and the struggle against powerful and resolute monarchical power appeared to him one of Poland's greatest historical sins. In an age when kings throughout Europe boasted of reigning by Divine Right, one could not but look down upon a king who reigned by the vote of the nobility. The civil liberties of the Polish nobility were to him the source of all Polish calamities. The fact that the rights of the individual were never sacrificed to the needs of the state, led Poland to ruin. Bobrzynski also lauds the influence of Byzantium, among the orthodox Slavic states, where the Church was subjugated to the laity. Bobrzynski was the advocate of absolute power and the admirer of great sovereigns who had had the strength to impose their will on the nation. Under his ferociously brave and bold pen, Polish parliamentarism was the cause of Poland's annihilation. "Our fall could come only after a whole series of faults, after a long period of violations of the higher laws of God assigned to the life and development of nations."

The *Stanczyks*, supporters of the pro-Habsburg policies, repudiated the revolutionary past of the Polish nation, and urged "down to earth" practical work for the welfare of both their own class and the nation as a whole.

Another school of history flourished at Lwow University under Professor Ks. Xavier Liske (1838-1891), a scholar of vast erudition.[69] Historians at Lwow extolled the constructive achievement of Poland in the past and, in contrast to their fellows at the Krakow Historical School, attributed chief responsibility for Polands' downfall in the eighteenth century to the rapacity of predatory neighbors. Intellectual warfare between the Krakow "realist" and the Lwow "romantics" enlivened Polish historical learning and infused it with a dynamic character that brought to

---

[69] At his seminars, many of the leading Polish historians of the next generation received their professional training. His brilliant colleague, Szymon Askenazy, who was educated in the Russian University of Warsaw, concerned himself with polemical researches in modern history, in particular with the Napoleonic period and its diplomacy. See Wytrwal, *Poles in American History and Tradition*, pp. 298-299.

light a wealth of new evidence on the antecedents of Poland's spoilation. But after 1900, the realistic interpreters were reluctantly obliged to acknowledge the victory of the Lwow scholars.[70]

Poles, in partitioned Poland, if not loyal to foreign rule, began in their mentality, to resemble the nations they were subject to. The three partitions of Poland were drifting apart, and each going its separate way. Although it seemed as if Poles were voluntarily moving along a road where Polish national history must cease and become merged in the different histories of the three empires, this was not the case. A revival of interest in national history among the general population appeared some twenty years after the last insurrection. Developments in the middle eighties showed the antithesis between the heroism of the past and the spirit of conformity; the practiced accommodation of the present was more imaginary than real.

Against the voices of the Positivists, the church and the nobility—which urged the renunciation of all Polish national conceptions and aspirations—now stirred the voices of the peasants, who followed the ideas developed by Joachim Lelewel. He called upon the Poles to arouse their dormant national energies and to direct them toward their own spiritual regeneration: the rebuilding of their historic homeland. Lelewel saw the source of real strength in the common people. He found the roots of weakness

---

[70] The Krakow Historical School was replaced at the beginning of the 20th century by an "optimistic" approach. Warsaw historians, writing at the beginning of World War I, were convinced that Poland had produced a superior type of state (compared with the European West and East), a morally superior historic type, preceding other countries in this field, and there lay the principal cause of Poland's fall.

Tadeusz Korzon in his *Listy otwarte, Mowy, Rozprawy, Rozbiory* demonstrated the value and importance that must be attached to the federative and republican institutions of ancient Poland. Wladyslaw Smolenski, in *Przewrot Umyslowy w Polsce wieku XVII*, gave a detailed description of the moral revolution produced in Poland at the end of the eighteenth century, immediately before the catastrophe, which had bequeathed to the nation regenerative and renovative principles. R. Rembowski in *Konfederacja i Rozkosz* proved, in a plan of comparative history, that all the "anarchies" and all the risings of the *szlachta* in Poland represented nothing exceptional in Europe. Finally, Szymon Askenazy devoted himself to the task of demonstrating that the Partitions had been the result of entirely exterior factors. His rich archival researches, his great knowledge of diplomatic documents and persons, his penchant for biography, and his Polish nationalistic spirit, facilitated for him the execution of this enterprise. It was Russia, Prussia and Austria that had dismembered Poland, and not Poland herself.

in the gentry, who had fallen victim to foreign influence and class egoism.

The collapse of the Polish State did undoubtedly contribute to the birth of the nation in the modern sense of the word: a nation composed of men and women from all social classes, speaking the same tongue, for the most part holding the same religious creed, and cherishing common traditions and aspirations. Henceforth, society became fluid, as never before. Social barriers crumbled steadily, the *ancient regime* was fast disappearing. A new order, no longer static, but dynamic, was replacing it. The growing political awareness of the Polish people, which coincided with economic growth and social differentiation, was fundamentally affected by the loss of a political focus after 1863.

For over a century, the Poles—torn apart and divided between three empires—struggled desperately to maintain their spiritual unity. So long as it was nourished by the common spirit of revolt, the Polish nation, despite internal conflicts, seemed to remain intact. When the idea of violent resistance was abandoned, and the Polish people replaced their swords with political arguments, elements of disunity—derived from long years of separation—began to appear. Moreover, considerations of political tactics forced the Poles to pursue different policies in each of the three empires. As patriots or opportunists in Poznan, Warsaw or Krakow, they had to use their own methods of resistance or conciliation when faced with specific dangers, or when taking account of specific advantages.

THE CATHOLIC CHURCH

The Catholic Church was also a great obstacle in the path of achieving equality and independence in Poland. It was a conservative force: not on the basis of preserving Catholic doctrine, or preventing the corruption of her children, but simply to ward off threats which would erode its own security and influence. Many Poles were sorely troubled by the role of the Holy See during the partitions.

> It did not pass unremarked, either in Poland or outside, that the Vatican made no protest at any of the three courts, Habsburgh, Hohen-

zollern or Romanov, against the violence done to the recognized laws of civilized society by the Partitions; nor did it escape the notice of observers that ways and means were found by the Church of adjusting itself to the new situation. There were even found men of high position in the hierarchy who put the orders laid on them by the conqueror before the demands of patriotism; men whose conduct was regarded by many as betrayal of the cause of their country and of freedom. Fortunately, they were few in number, and for every one a dozen were found ready to endure any hardship rather than compromise with despotism.[71]

For many Poles, Rome's behavior was a serious offense, one of omission which they could not forgive. The Catholic Church—although it did not seek to impose any specific position or take a public stand—quietly urged the Poles to reconcile themselves to the partitions. In serving the ruling class, the dominant theme of the Catholic Church, during the partitions, was not to help the Poles to become rich and blessed with this world's goods, but to help the Poles to become spiritually content in this life and happy in an afterlife. Aside from building churches with funds extracted from peasants and nobles and stationing peasant priests in Polish-speaking parishes, the Catholic Church did little to aid materially or socially the rural, untraveled and poorly educated Poles. Nevertheless, after the partition of Poland, Polish Catholicism became patriotic as well as religious in character; having a form of worship different from that of their Russian, and German—if not of their Austrian oppression—Poles were able to keep alive a sense of national identity.

The Catholic Church, with its cosmopolitan bishops, who were members of the upper classes along with the better educated village parish priests, became very influential. The Church was more powerful in Austrian Poland than in Russian or Prussian Poland. In Galicia, or Austrian Poland, the Catholic Church was obviously part of the Establishment, and it would never support a class against the government. Likewise, in Russian Poland, the Catholic Church should have campaigned for the

---

[71] William John Rose, *Poland Old and New* (London: 1948), p. 190. For the role of the Catholic Church during the partitions of Poland see Witold Lukaszewicz, *Targowica i Powstanie Kosciuszkowskie* (Warszawa: 1953), pp. 274-288.

dignity of its people many decades ago which it failed to do. To maintain its presence there—regardless of who held political power—the Catholic Church was obliging in accepting any foreign regime, provided that she had the right to express her theological views freely without any restrictions. While in Prussian Poland, the Catholic Church should have made some effort to break down religious sectarianism. It also made no effort in this regard. Very few sermons were ever preached on political or ethnic tolerance. Occasionally, there was a sermon stating that, whether the peasant agreed or not, he should respect the legally established authorities and not complain about the manner in which the authorities treated their subjects. They admonished the Biblical phrase: "Render unto Caesar what is Caesar's and unto God what belongs to God." Unwilling to trust the liberal Catholics, the Catholic Church never hesitated to stifle any initiative for change, and constantly urged the faithful to abstain from participating in liberal movements. Thus, liberal Catholics had to struggle to be heard. It is, therefore, not strange that bitterness, along with a good share of apathy and disillusionment toward the Catholic Church, had developed.[72]

THE JEWS IN POLAND AND THE CATHOLIC CHURCH

From the beginning of its political history, the Polish State practiced tolerance:

> Jews began to settle in Poland before Christianity had found general acceptance in Eastern Europe. References to Jewry are found on

---

[72] The Vatican rarely showed any outward appreciation to Poland for her staunch faith, or ever rewarded her for Polish valor. If King Jan Sobieski had not defeated the Turks at Vienna, in 1683, the Moslem faith would have replaced all of the Catholic and Protestant churches in Europe. Ironically, France, a Catholic nation with a penchant for intrigue, deceit, expediency and intolerance, urged the Turks to overrun Europe, but especially to destroy her rival, the Holy Roman Empire. The Vatican did no more than protest and the Holy Roman Emperor fled without attempting to defend Austria against the Turkish invasion. The great nobility of King Jan Sobieski's victory—albeit not wise for his sacrifice in depleting the Polish treasury in order to save a continent—was never appreciated. The Battle of Vienna was truly one of the most decisive battles in Western European history, yet historians are reluctant to discuss the matter for it calls to mind so much ignobility on the part of European nations. Poland never had to fear the Turks, who always respected her. Ironically, the defeated nation championed Poland's independence for over a century when Poland was partitioned by Russia, Prussia and Austria. Even at this time, Austria failed to pay her debt to Poland.

coins of Mieszko I, first king of Poland who reigned in the mid-tenth century, and it is known that in the year 933 the Jewish community of Wronki built itself a synagogue. Even etymologically the Jews associated themselves closely with their new homeland, and its name was interpreted in Hebrew either as *Polin,* "Here ye shall dwell," or *Polaniah,* "Here dwelleth the Lord."[73]

Already in the late tenth century, in the newly-found Kingdom of Poland, the city of Poznan had a sizeable Jewish community whose members enjoyed all liberties. The Kings of Poland were especially tolerant. As early as 1264, Boleslaw the Pious of Greater Poland (1247-1279) granted the Jews inviolability of person and property when he signed the Statute of Kalisz. For the first time in the history of Christian civilization a government granted equal protection under the law to Jews. These rights and privileges were confirmed by all the Polish kings which later became part of Poland's common law.

> It reached its climax under Casimir the Great (1333-1370), the most energetic of all Polish sovereigns, under whom the country became, to some extent, a "Western" Power. A determined opponent of the lawlessness of the nobility, his policy was such as to win him the spiteful sobriquet "King of the serfs and the Jews." In 1354, he ratified and extended the provisions of the Charter of Boleslaw the Pious of a century earlier.[74]

Kazimierz the Great even dared to equate the Jews with the nobility, in case of injury or murder, and imposed identical punishment upon the guilty.

> Just as in the Carolingian Empire four or five centuries earlier, such preferential treatment provoked the resentment and vehement protests of the clergy, probably with reason.[75]

Still, it is certain that the Jews lived on excellent terms with the Christians.[76]

Kazimierz III had bestowed on the Jews social privileges such as they enjoyed nowhere else.

---

[73] Harry M. Rabinowicz, *The Legacy of Polish Jewry. A History of Polish Jews in the Inter-War Years 1919-1939* (New York: 1965), p. 17.
[74] Cecil Roth, *A Short History of the Jewish People* (London: 1953), p. 290.
[75] Leon Poliakòw, *The History of Anti-Semitism.* Translated from the French by Richard Howard (New York: 1965), p. 247.
[76] *Ibid.,* p. 246.

Among minor points, Jews might bathe together in the same river with Christians—a right frequently denied them. Further, any Christian who brought the baseless charge of ritual murder against a Jew, and was unable to substantiate his charge on credible testimony, was held punishable with death.[77]

In Poland, indeed, in the reign of Zygmunt I (1506-1548) the Rabbi was confirmed by the king, and was, in a sense, an agent of the crown, collecting the poll-tax, and enjoying large powers of civil and criminal jurisdiction.[78]

The economic life in Poland, when left to flow in its own channels, developed broadly and more amply than elsewhere. While in other lands, Jews were confined to money-lending and petty trading, Jews in Poland participated in all branches of industrial endeavor. They imported from the East and exported to the West. Every facility was given to the Jews for carrying on their business activities. They were allowed unrestricted domicile throughout the realm, as well as the right of transit and access to the municipal bathing establishments. The Jews were allowed to lend money on interest. They were authorized to rent estates, even from the nobility and the priesthood, or to hold them in mortgage. Both person and property were protected by law. In order to secure impartiality—the verdict over disputes in which they were concerned—was determined by the Crown. Violation of a Jewish cemetery was punishable by forfeiture of all estates; desecration of a synagogue warranted the imposition of a high fine. A special addendum to the charter rendered Christians liable to fines if they withheld help from Jewish neighbors in distress.[79] No wonder Rabbi Mosses Isserles wrote in poignant phrases of Poland's hospitality.

> Had not the Lord left this land as a refuge, the fate of Israel would indeed have been unbearable. By the grace of God, both the kings

---

[77] Israel Abrahams, *Jewish Life in the Middle Ages* (New York: 1969), pp. 402-403.
[78] Ibid., p. 39.
[79] Rabinowicz, *The Legacy of Polish Jewry. A History of Polish Jews in the Inter-War Years 1919-1939*, p. 19.

and the nobles are favourably disposed toward us. In this country there is no fierce hatred as there is in Germany.[80]

The papal legate, Commendori, also confirmed this view.

"In these regions, masses of Jews are to be found, who are not subject to the scorn they meet with elsewhere. They do not live in abasement and are not reduced to menial trades thereby. They own land, engage in commerce, study medicine and astronomy. They possess great wealth and are not only counted among respectable people but sometimes even dominate them. They wore no distinctive insignia, and are even permitted to bear arms. In short, they have all the rights of citizens." In these terms the papal legate, Commendori, described the status of the Polish Jews about 1565. Indeed, there was no possible comparison between the condition of the Polish Jews and that of their less fortunate co-religionists in the other European nations.[81]

The Jews were expelled from England in 1290, from France in 1306, and from a number of cities in Germany and Austria in the fourteenth and fifteenth centuries. In 1492, all Jews were expelled from Spain, except those who accepted baptism; and among these were the Marranos (as they were called) whom the Inquisition persecuted grievously. In 1498, all Jews from Portugal were compulsorily baptized, unless they preferred martyrdom; and after a few decades (1531), they, too, were handed over to the Inquisition.[82] The Jews, who were expelled from Germany, were well received in Poland, where, together with the contemporary Germany immigrants, they fulfilled most of the functions of a non-existent middle class.[83]

For long generations Poland continued to appear in the light of a land of promise for the Jews of northern Europe, and to receive a perpetual accession of new settlers: refugees escaping massacre; young men seeking opportunity; merchants from distant Italy or the Balkans, hoping for gain.

In time, many new towns and villages sprang up with an

---

[80] *Ibid.*, p. 19.
[81] Poliakov, *The History of Anti-Semitism. From the Time of Christ to the Court Jews*, I, p. 249.
[82] Hugo Valentin, *Antisemitism Historically and Critically Examined* (London: 1936), pp. 34-36.
[83] *Ibid.*, p. 34.

entirely Jewish population. Since the new communities—as provided by the royal charters—were virtually self-governing city-states, Jews were able to preserve in full vigor their own institutions and mores, their own culture and language (Yiddish); these conditions proved to be a decisive barrier to Jewish integration with the Polish community at large. In 1500, the number of Jews in the country was estimated to have been only fifty-thousand souls, a century and a half later, it had risen to half a million.[84] The first systematic census, taken about 1765, revealed that the Jews constituted ten percent of the country's population.[85]

Nothing was more characteristic of Polish-Jewish life than the remarkable degree of self-government which it attained. In 1551, Zygmunt August III, the last king of the Jagiellonian dynasty, issued an edict permitting the Jews of Poland to elect their own Chief Rabbi and lawful judges, with authority to exercise jurisdiction in all matters concerning Jewish law, and answerable to the Crown. All individuals were commanded to comply with their decisions and rulings under extreme penalties. This measure has justly been described as the Magna Carta of Jewish self-government in Poland; for it set the seal of the royal approval upon the natural urge of the Jew to govern himself according to his traditional jurisprudence.

By slow degrees the Council became omnipotent in Polish-Jewish life. It ultimately became known as the Council of the Four Lands (or provinces) comprising Greater Poland, Lesser Poland, Podolia, and Wolynia, which together comprised the Kingdom. In its prime, the Council was virtually the Parliament of Polish Jewry, with power nearly as absolute as that of any legislature. It was composed of thirty delegates: twenty-four of them were laymen, and the remainder outstanding Rabbis. No-

---

[84] Just as the expulsion from Spain concentrated the majority of Sephardic Jewry in Turkey and its dependencies, so, from the beginning of the sixteenth century, the main body of Ashkenazy Jewry—the remnants of the communities of medieval England, France and Germany, with others from farther afield—were concentrated in Poland and among the surrounding Slavonic territories. It is from the latter group that the overwhelming mass of Jews, in the world today, are descended.

[85] Poliakov, *The History of Anti-Semitism. From the Time of Christ to the Court Jews,* I, p. 249.

where, ever since the decay of the Jewish center in Palestine, had so complete an approach to autonomy existed.[86]

> One measure of this autonomy was that Jewish learning and scholarship were very quickly organized. Every Jewish town of any pretension boasted its own academy and distinguished scholars, and Polish Jews characteristically prided themselves on the number of their young men who devoted themselves "to prayer and study." Here, as always, the hero-type was the scholar and not the merchant. Thus, the well-to-do merchant would maneuver to fashion a match for his daughter with some promising young scholar—poverty-stricken though he may have been—rather than with the scion of some commercial magnate.[87]

Anti-Semitism was introduced to Poland when the Polish cause and the Catholic faith became indissolubly linked. Towards the end of the eleventh century, at the Council of Clermont, on November 26, 1095, Pope Urban II called upon sovereigns and knights to liberate Jerusalem, "the center of the earth and second paradise," from the heathens. All who would take part in the Crusade were promised forgiveness for their sins. Whole nations were seized by the frenzy. The First Crusade was a bloody overture of terror and persecution that pilloried and persecuted the European Jews for centuries.

The Crusader bands moved into Bohemia, their trail marked by murders, pillaging, and forced baptisms. The Jews of Prague were dragged to baptism, and all who resisted were killed. When the baptized Jews of the Prague community began emigrating to Poland and Hungary, so that they could return openly to their religion, the Bohemian Prince Vratislav II ordered that they be stripped of all their possessions. "You brought no riches with you from Jerusalem to

---

[86] This nation-wide apparatus of government guarded Jewish civil interests, in Poland, by acting as the intermediary between the Jews and the Polish diet and courts. It apportioned the taxes due the state among the various provinces and collected them. It attempted too, with rather less success, to govern the inner life of Polish Jewry by regulating the economic, religious, judicial, and administrative activities of the individual provinces. The Council of the Four lands never reached maximum efficiency; nevertheless, it did perform useful functions as spokesman and defender of Jewish rights before the Polish court, and as guardian of Jewish honor when attempts were made to assail it. It might have survived, with some modifications, had Poland itself not been on the verge of political and economic collapse.

[87] Frederick M. Schweitzer, *A History of the Jews Since the First Century A.D.* (New York: 1971), p. 148.

Bohemia," he declared. "Naked you came into the land, and naked you must leave it."[88]

The Fourth Lateran Council of 1215, during the reign of Innocent III, prepared the way for the downfall of Jewish communities throughout Europe. It forbade Jews to practice Christian occupations. One cannon prescribed that Jews, "whether men or women, must in all Christian countries distinguish themselves from the rest of the population in public places by a special kind of clothing." In November 1215, a papal bull gave these decisions, formulated by the Council, the force of Canon law. England chose a badge depicting two stone tablets inscribed with the Ten Commandments. In France, St. Louis ordered a badge to be made of red felt or saffron yellow cloth, cut in the shape of a wheel, to be worn on the upper garment: one each in front and back, "so that those thus branded may be recognized from both sides."

The effects of the Council's decisions were felt in Poland as well. The protection accorded to the Jews by the Polish kings and princes, displeased the Catholic clergy, who were under instructions from Rome to oppress and humiliate the Jews wherever they could.

An ecclesiastical council, in Breslau (1266), decided that the proximity of Jews was particularly dangerous to the Christians, in Poland, where the people had but recently been converted to Catholicism. The council therefore ruled that in all cities, the Jews should live apart from the Christians. In a separate quarter, surrounded by a wall or trench. It was further provided that they should be made to shut themselves inside their homes whenever a religious procession was passing their streets; that they should have no more than one synagogue in each city; and "in order to distinguish them from Christians" they should be made to wear a special headgear, in the form of a hornshaped hat, and whosoever should be seen in the street without it, would be liable to punishment according to the customs of the country. Christians were forbidden to eat or drink with Jews, dancing and merrymaking together, at weddings or other festivities, was also forbidden. Neither might Christians buy meat or other foodstuffs from Jews lest, in some guileful manner, the vendors should seek to poison

---

[88] Werner Keller, *Diaspora; the Post-Biblical History of the Jews*. Translated from the German by Richard and Clara Winston. (New York: 1969), p. 205.

them. Rulings made by the church in former times were reiterated, viz., forbidding Jews to keep Christian servants, nurses or wet-nurses; and debarring them from office as tax-collectors or holders of any other public charge.[89]

The Catholic Church, from the very beginning, saw danger in overly peaceful and neighborly relations between Poles and Jews. "In consideration of the fact that Poland represents a new planting in the soil of Christianity," a declaration of the Polish clergy, as early as 1267, read, "it may be feared that the Christian population here, where the Christian religion has not yet been able to strike from roots in the hearts of believers, may all the more easily be swayed by the false religion and the wicked customs of Jews living in their midst." In 1279, the Buda synod decreed a badge consisting of a wheel of red cloth for Hungary and southern Poland.

Had these cruel, church-oriented laws been exercised in Poland, the life of the Polish Jews would have been almost as intolerable as that of the German Jews who were oppressed and treated as an inferior caste without any human rights.[90] Fortunately, even though the clerical synods clamoured for the enforcement of the repressive legislation of the Lateran Councils, the Polish king and the secular princes of that time (as well as most of the populace) paid no attention to the recommendations of the fanatical priests, the jealous merchants of German origin—who resented the privileges extended to the Jews, or the Christian immigrants from Germany—who wanted to introduce their

---

[89] S. Doubnow, *An Outline of Jewish History*, III (New York: 1929), pp. 166-167.

[90] The Rindfleish massacres, in 1348, sent more and more Jews fleeing into Poland. The persecution of Jews among German principalities was also felt in Poland, particularly in the cities near the German border where lurid libels against Jews raised their heads and claimed their victims. Thus, in 1399, the rabbi of Poznan and thirteen community notables perished at the stake on the charge of "bleeding the host." In Krakow, a priest, in 1407, accused the Jews with slaying a Christian child, and many of them were murdered by the mob which attacked the Jewish quarter. In 1454, the rabid inquisitor, John Capistrano, who gloried in the title "scourge of the Jews," was invited by the Archbishop of Krakow to come to Poland in order to help the gentry to pare the powers of King Kazimierz Jagiellonczyk (who reigned from 1447 until 1492) and thereby terminate the charter of Jewish rights. Rufus Learsi, *Israel: A History of the Jewish People* (New York: 1949), pp. 347-348.

own intolerant standards. Poland remained a haven where the Jews lived on in peace and friendship with the Christians, enjoying several centuries of affluence free from most restrictions.[91]

Polish Jewry was not, by any means, confined to the menial occupations pursued by their forefathers, or by their contemporaries in adjacent countries. Some were indeed money-lenders, whose activities were regulated by law; but these did not constitute a high proportion of the whole. There was a very large mercantile class engaged in every branch of commercial activity. Many were interested in handicrafts and the manufacture of products. The Guilds sometimes tried to limit their activities or to prevent them from opening shops in Christian neighborhoods; but it was long before they met with any real success. Wealthy Jews were found as tax-farmers; they administered the excise and tolls; and were frequently employed as financial agents for the sovereign and other nobles. Some leased and exploited the landed property of the nobles, or of the Crown domains. They were apparent, all over the country, as stewards and administrators of great estates of Polish magnates, looking after, in some instances, the aristocrats' interest in relation to the peasants. Often they operated flour mills and taverns. They, also, worked in salt-mines, purchased standing timber, traded in furs, exported surplus agricultural produce to Germany. The Jewish innkeeper-tax collector, was a familiar and influential person in village life. Jewish apothecaries as well as Jewish physicians were highly esteemed and were frequently in the employ of noblemen. More than one Polish sovereign had a Jewish private physician. Among poorer ones, they were itinerant peddlers, craftsmen, and sometimes even agricultural workers. Communities, or isolated individuals were to be found in almost every hamlet, as well as in the great towns.

The sixteenth century was the Golden Age for Jews in Poland and Lithuania. Poland inherited the supremacy in Jewry that Spain had lost, for the horrors of inquisitions and pogroms in Western Europe drove multitudes of Jews into Poland where they influenced its economic development.

---

[91] Doubnow, *An Outline of Jewish History*, III, p. 166.

Thus, sixteenth-century Poland saw, not the ferocious repression and disabilities of Jews that characterized Christendom elsewhere, but rather the high point in Jewish autonomy and parliamentary self-government throughout the whole history of the Diaspora.[92]

For a century and a half, before 1648 (the tragic year of Polish Jewry), the number of Jews in Poland grew from 50,000 to 500,000. Here, they attained a rich inner life, enjoyed wealth and power, and had exercised a larger measure of internal autonomy than in any other community of dispersed Jews.

In Poland, however, where they had settled in vast numbers during the XVIth century, they lived in peace and freedom within their autonomous communities. Poland thus became to the Jews of this period what Babylonia had been in ancient times and Spain in medieval times, the center of the spiritual life of the race towards which all outlying sections of the dispersed people naturally gravitated.[93]

For Polish Jewry, the sixteenth century was no less splendid than the golden age of the Jews of Spain (900-1200), or the Talmudic period in Babylon. The royal charters permitted Jews to preserve to the full their own way of life and to govern themselves according to the Torah and Talmud. One measure of this autonomy was that Jewish learning and scholarship were very quickly organized. Every Jewish town of any pretension boasted its own academy. There were innumerable men, equally in learning as in piety. Such *Halachic* luminaries included Rabbi Jacob Pollak (1470-1541), Rabbi Shalom Shachna (1510-1559), Rabbi Solomon Luria (1510-1573), and Rabbi Mordecai ben Abraham Jaffa (1530-1612).

It was in Poland that Yiddish was reared to rich maturity. The German dialect (middle German), uprooted from its source, absorbed Hebraic and Slavic elements as time went by. This friendly familiar amalgam of many languages became known as Yiddish, the mother tongue of successive generations, a unique form of international

---

[92] Frederick M. Schweitzer, *A History of the Jews Since the First Century A.D.* (New York: 1971), p. 148.
[93] Doubnow, *An Outline of Jewish History*, III, p. 177.

Esperanto, second only to Hebrew in its influence on the Jewish masses of Eastern Europe.[94]

Jewish learning continued to flourish in Poland during the XVII century as it had done in Babylonia during the era of the Amoraim. A great many works of scholarship were printed by Jewish printers in Krakow and Lublin. Talmudic and rabbinical studies held undisputed sway throughout the country.

The excellent circumstances of the Jews often aroused the envy of the Catholic clergy, whose influence had suffered a great diminution with the spread of religious reforms from Western Europe. The Protestant movement, which went back to the Bible for its source, inclined many Catholics toward Judaism, and a number of voluntary conversions ensued.

During the reign of Zygmunt I (1506-1548), the Protestant Reformation began to make inroads into Poland, and the clergy, more watchful than ever, accused the Jews of proselyting Poles to Judaism.

> One Polish woman, Catherine Zeleszovska, accused of "Jewish tendencies" was burned at the stake by order of the local bishop; the execution took place in the market place of Cracow, in 1539. The clergy accused the Jews of seeking conversions, particularly in Lithuania, and discussed repressive measures against them. But the good King Sigismund saw that nothing came of their attempts to interfere with the people he had taken under his special protection.[95]

In the sixteenth century, the Catholic Church did not yet have sufficient influence upon the government. Kings Zygmunt I and Zygmunt II (1548-1572) were more interested in the economic benefits accrued from the Jews who had migrated to Poland, and thus protected them against exclusions, expulsions, and persecutions.

The Jews had unquestionably lived as a people isolated from others, with their own religion, their own customs, dress, language, reckoning of time, their own self-government and laws of marriage and inheritance. Their contracts and wills, their account-

---

[94] Rabinowicz, *The Legacy of Polish Jewry. A History of Polish Jews in the Inter-War Years 1919-1939*, p. 22.
[95] Doubnow, *An Outline of Jewish History*, III, p. 236.

books and private letters were written in cursive Hebrew characters. They associated and married only among themselves. They still constituted a unity, more or less independent of national frontiers.

Not until the middle of the seventeenth century did misfortune come to the Jewish communities in Eastern Europe. The inroads of the Jesuits changed all this. During this period—referred to as the Counter-Reformation—the Jesuits were rising to immense power throughout Poland and the world. Using every conceivable means, the Jesuits fought with equal frenzy all non-Catholics in the Polish commonwealth. Victims of the Jesuits efforts of extermination included the Protestants, Greek Orthodox Catholics, as well as the Jews.

> The attack on the Jewish quarter of Posen, in 1618, was led by the teachers and students of the local Jesuit academy. With suppression of the Protestant Reformation as their primary objective, the Polish Jesuits, in the reign of Stefan Batory (1572-1586) acquired control of the schools, and Stefan's successor, Sigismund III (1586-1632), surrounded himself with Jesuit advisors. The Jesuits taught their pupils to hate Jews and Protestants, and their pious hostility extended to members of the Greek Orthodox Church, many of whom lived under Polish rule, for as far back as 1320 the Russian principality of Kiev had been conquered by Lithuania, which later became part of Poland.[96]

Graduates of Jesuit schools were not oriented to practice tolerance.

> The pupils of the Jesuit schools specially distinguished themselves in attacking and ill-treating the Jews. The Jews were blamed for all the misfortunes of Poland. They were described as sympathizing with the Turks, the Swedes, the Protestants, and when the Diets broke up and were unable to agree, that of course was also the fault of the Jews.[97]

The Jesuit pupils grew to occupy positions of importance in every walk of life, and their influence soon permeated the government.[98]

---

[96] Learsi, *Israel: A History of the Jewish People*, pp. 349-350.
[97] Valentin, *Antisemitism Historically and Critically Examined*, p. 40.
[98] The greatest misfortune that befell Poland was the election of Zygmunt III as

PRELUDE TO THE POLISH PEASANT IMMIGRATION   81

The spirit of the Polish heretics had to be crushed, and the Jesuits utilized the trade jealousies of the German dealers in Poland to rouse animosities against the Jews, which culminated in the cruelties which they suffered during the revolt of the Cossacks.[99]

As craftsmen and merchants, the only rivals the Jews faced were immigrant Germans, who found it profitable to incite the Poles to persecute their Jewish competitors. They found willing allies in the Catholic clergy, whose primary objective was to suppress the non-Catholic religions in Poland, or at least to hold them in subjection.

In 1720, a synod of the clergy demanded that the Jews be forbidden to build new synagogues or repair old ones. By their degradation and misery the Jews must bear witness to the "tortures of Christ," and to their "unbelief and stubbornness"; such was the solemn pronouncement of another synod held in 1733. The clergy, moreover, gave willing support to the Catholic merchants in their crusade to destroy their Jewish competitors; the sordid purpose was dressed up in the vestments of religion, and it became popular with the Polish masses. And not only the merchants, but the artisans also could always count on the support of the priests, as well as the city councils and courts, in their warfare against Jewish competitors.[100]

Neither persecution, nor prejudice, could separate the Jews and Poles in the Polish Commonwealth, for their hearts beat together in sympathetic aspiration towards that which strengthened the bonds of a common brotherhood. Instances of this mutual personal regard were very common in the sixteenth and seven-

---

joint king of Poland and Sweden. With his accession the troubles began. Because of his bigotry and pro-Jesuit support, religious tolerance was lost in Poland, but because he lost the throne of Sweden, he and his sons involved Poland in wars for seventy years. His foreign policy was disastrous for Poland. Ironically, Zygmunt III's folly and prejudice interfered in the accession of his son, Wladyslaw, as Czar of Muscowy which was the last opportunity Russia ever had to observe democratic government and thereby unite three realms into the greatest confederation Europe would have witnessed. His ego prevented this epochal change that would have altered European history and would have prevented the later partitions of Poland. Yet his beloved sister, Princess Anna, accepted her father's Lutheran faith and had a protestant chapel erected in the royal castle of Warsaw, which was quite inconsistent with his bigotry.

[99] Abrahams, *Jewish Life in the Middle Ages*, p. 403.
[100] Learsi, *Israel: A History of the Jewish People*, p. 375.

teenth centuries. But the continuous action of forces, devised against free intercourse with the Jews, eventually made itself quite obviously and broadly felt. The establishment of the ghettos, the garb's insignia of disgrace, and the activities of the Catholic Church, all helped to deny fellowship to the Polish-Jewish inhabitants.[101] The extraordinary fact is not that Jews and Christians so rarely formed friendships in the seventeenth and eighteenth centuries; the marvel is that they formed such friendships at all.

After Poland's final dismemberment as a sovereign state, Polish Jews found themselves at the mercy of three absolutist monarchies, that of Prussia, Austria and Russia.[102] All three monarchies subscribed to the notion that the Jews represented an alien, harmful and unenlightened element.[103] They prepared Draconian "rehabilitation" programs by purging the group of its "antisocial ways" and preparing it for a "fusion" with the native

---

[101] The *ghetto* strengthened Jewish seclusion. They were walled and had gates that closed each evening at curfew, by which time Jews had to be inside or suffer various penalties. The last ghetto in western Europe, that of Rome, was abolished only in 1870, when Italian unification was completed.

[102] On the eve of Poland's impending demise, a large number of Jews participated in General Kosciuszko's abortive uprising of 1794. Thousands of Jews contributed food, clothing, and money to the insurgent forces. Under the direction of Berek Joselevitch, the Jewish estate manager of a Catholic bishop, a Jewish legion was organized to fight at the ramparts of Warsaw. Like Joselevitch, most of the Jewish volunteers were convinced that national liberty was one of the indispensable prerequisites for Jewish emancipation. Nearly every member of this Jewish legion was cut down by the Russian cavalry. Joselevitch himself survived the assault.

Later, as a member of a Polish uhlan regiment, he was killed in battle by the Austrians. This display of Jewish loyalty to his fatherland made a great impression on the Poles. Joselevitch became the hero of Polish songs and fables; during the nineteenth century his name was enshrined in Polish folklore as the man who "resuscitated the image of those men of valor over whom, in the days gone by, wept the daughters of Zion."

[103] During the eighteenth century, the imperial Russian Court at St. Petersburg sternly denied the petitions of Polish-Jewish merchants who sought the right of temporary domicile in Russia. Peter I, who imported thousands of non-Russian nationals for the sake of modernizing his empire, refused to admit Jews. He said: "I prefer to see in our midst nations professing Islam and paganism rather than Jews. ... It is my endeavor to eradicate evil, not to multiply it." Czarina Catherine II expressed the same hostility in denying entrance to a group of Jewish tradesmen. "From the enemies of Christ," she explained to the mercantilists in her Council, "I desire neither gain nor profit." In 1762, Catherine permitted all foreigners to travel and settle in Russia "except the Jews" (*kromye Zhydov*). This phrase would reappear continually in subsequent ukases and statutes. Before the century ended,

population.[104] Consequently, the Polish-Jewish communities—confronted by centralized, bureaucratic powers, brutal in their methods, and bent upon reordering, if not eliminating Jewish life—responded by closing ranks and treating external innovations and influences as stratagems and heresies.

After 1881, few Jews could be safe or prosperous in Russian Poland, a legacy of the first and second Polish partitions. Whole settlements were often ordered out of villages where they lived for generations, and were driven to cities where they had no homes and no means of livelihood. This great mass of immigration from Russian Poland eventually emigrated to America. They came not as individuals, nor as family groups. They represented the transplantation of practically entire communities: rich and poor, learned and ignorant, together. They possessed a great deal of Jewish culture, as their rabbis, and also many laymen, were learned in the Bible and Talmud. Because of their overwhelming numbers, they exerted a great influence on the development of Jewish life in America.[105]

POLISH SOCIALIST PARTIES

The political growth of the Polish nation was marked by the emergence of many political parties, divided in their tactics, and

---

Czarina Catherine II inherited nearly a million Jews as a result of the Polish partitions.

In 1794, Czarina Catherine II issued an ukase that was destined, in the century to come, to have far-reaching and momentous consequences for Polish-Jewish life. The ukase confined Jews to a "Pale of settlement," an area delimited by the boundaries of the former Polish kingdom. No Jew henceforth dared venture beyond the tightly quarantined territory. It is doubtful if any decree in history, even the Spanish expulsion edict of 1492, or the establishment of the Western ghetto in the sixteenth century, imposed a more burdensome political, economic, or intellectual strait jacket on an ethnic group.

[104] Fusion hopefully would lead to conversion.

[105] Having been exploited and mistreated, in Russian Poland, for over a hundred years, the Jews acquired certain unattractive characteristics which frequently enabled them to survive persecution and massacre. In America, they were frequently accused of being secretive, mistrustful, deceptive, clannish and exclusive—so tightly knit that no outsider was admitted amongst them. Difficult times, danger, and persecution placed a premium on such modes and attitudes. In Russian Poland, especially in the ghetto, it became a sheer necessity to distrust strangers and outsiders, or even neighbors; to band together, and to mislead Russian officials. The capacity to deceive, trick, bribe, cajole S.S. officials and informers saved many Jews from the Nazi gas chambers during World War II, in eastern Europe.

to a certain degree, even in their ultimate aims. Two of these political parties—operating in all the territories inhabited by Poles—became the most important, and eventually came to represent the two major political choices (both socialistic) in the years prior to the First World War. The first party embraced the workers and socialists, originating in the late 1880's. It was at first a small, conspirational group: small, because of a lack of economic development; and revolutionary, because of the necessity to operate underground.

The increased tempo of industrial growth in the eighties, as well as the renewed trend towards political resistance among the Poles, provided a more favorable ground for the growth of the Socialist movement. The first two Socialist organizations to emerge marked also the beginnings of a significant split within the Socialist ranks. *Lud Polski* (The Polish People) was founded by Boleslaw Limanowski, in 1880. He combined aid for the exploited with a warm patriotism. For Limanowski, it was an axiom that every nation had the right to be free. In contributions to *The Clarion,* a socialist journal appearing in Paris under the editorship of exiled Poles, he expressed firmly this opinion and was soon regarded as an authority.

The second organization, the Socialist Revolutionary Party, referred to as the "first" *Proletariat,* was founded, in 1882, by Ludwik Warynski. It accepted a program of class struggle, emphasizing the principle of solidarity with the workers of other nations and with the Russian revolutionaries. It was this group which, following the example of the Russian "People's Will," committed acts of violence and terrorism which led ultimately to its forceful suppression.

In the last decade of the nineteenth century, the increased class-consciousness of the Polish workers led to the emergence of mass socialist parties. Of these, by far the most important was the *Polska Partia Socijalistyczna* (Polish Socialist Party). It owed its origin to a meeting of eighteen socialist leaders, in Paris, in 1892, for the purpose of creating an all-Polish socialist party. Its program, worked out by the Union of Polish Socialists Abroad, combined the idea of Polish nationalism and independence with that

PRELUDE TO THE POLISH PEASANT IMMIGRATION 85

of socialism which, they believed, could be achieved gradually, and even through legal means.¹⁰⁶

As early as 1893, under the leadership of Julian Marchlewski and Rosa Luxemberg, a group of internationally-minded socialists seceded from the Polish Socialist Party. Fascinated by the idea of a proletariat "without country or nationality," and rejecting the demands for Polish independence, these followers of Karl Marx, founded the Social Democratic Party in 1896. By 1900, after being joined by the Polish noble, Feliks Dzierzynski, it assumed the name *Socjal-demokracja Krolewstwa Polskiego i Litwy* (Social Democracy of the Kingdom of Poland and Lithuania).¹⁰⁷

The Polish League was founded in Switzerland, in 1887. This body returned to the democratic ideology of the Polish Democratic Society, founded, in Paris, after 1830. The composition of the League was sufficiently broad to combine the veterans of 1863 with men who followed the example of the Russian Populists, yet also sought to renew national self-confidence by relying on the peasants. Among these men was Zygmunt Balicki, remembered as the author of a pamphlet, *National Egoism*, with ideas

---

¹⁰⁶ The Polish Socialist Party was not a single unified party. In Russian Poland the Party was restricted to illegal activities, where it managed to elect an underground Central Workers' Committee in which Jozef Pilsudski, the successful organizer of the Wilno district, assumed a leading role. In Austrian Poland, the Social Democratic Party of Galicia and Silesia operated openly and legally from 1893, and greatly profited from the able leadership of Ignacy Daszynski. In Prussian Silesia and Poznan, the Polish Socialist Party worked in close cooperation with the German Social Democrats.

¹⁰⁷ One thesis propounded by a Detroit scholar, Benedict Markowski, believes that Communism was definitely a Jewish calculated revenge against the aristocracy of Europe whose class they could never attain above a baronetcy. Marx and Engels were both Jews. Communism was inspired by the plight of the Jews who could never be recognized by polite society, no matter how much wealth they acquired. Furthermore, they could never attain titles in Europe. The Rothschild banking family could only become barons. The only other notable exception was Benjamin Disraeli, who became the Earl of Beaconsfield.

In destroying the class system, they did away with the privileged society which they disdained the most, yet ironically benefited most from because they were the employees and managers of the noble's estates to whom they offered loans at usurious rates. The Jews had contempt for the aristocracy. They were made to feel inferior, yet were obliged to manage their affairs which they were either incapable of or found beneath their station in life. A majority of the socialists and communists were Jews. This pattern continued to the present day. That is why, until the present expulsion, so many Poles of Jewish descent had top positions in the Polish government.

based largely on the work of Herbert Spencer. The program of the Polish League was broad, embracing both revolutionary ideas and diplomatic action with educational work among its people. In 1894, the organization changed its name to the National League and extended its activities to all three partitions of Poland. Its original leadership was replaced by members of the younger generation, among whom Roman Dmowski was its most notable representative.[108] The idea of a militant resistance to the partitioning powers was not abandoned by the National League. The lack of active uprisings was due to a number of factors. Perhaps the most important factor was the change which had occurred on the international scene which became unfavorable to Polish national aspirations. Likewise, the developments in military science rendered any attempt to armed insurrection hopeless.

The National League organized a series of revolutionary acts, the purpose of which was to force the Russian government to make significant concessions to the Poles. The result was that it incurred the hostility of the Russian authorities. There were mass arrests, but Dmowski and a few other members of the League, managed to escape to Lwow where, in 1897 they founded the *Stronnictwo Narodowo-Demokratyczne* (the National Democratic Direction).

The end of the century saw the emergence of other political parties in Austrian Poland. The *Polskie Stronnictwo Ludowe* (Polish People's Direction), represented the peasants and found able leaders in Wincenty Witos and Jakub Bojko.[109]

---

[108] When Dmowski settled in Lwow, he began to publish the *All Polish Review*. He agreed with Jan Poplawski, who founded a weekly, *The Voice*, in 1887. Poplawski had no faith in the tenet of Triple Loyalty as a solution to the Polish problem. *The Voice* broke new ground by taking an interest in the lot of small towns, and it set about educating the readers in civic, economic and cultural issues in the spirit of Positivism. Refusing to recognize the boundaries that cut right through Polish lands, Poplawski nurtured thoughts and feelings of common interest to the whole nation.

[109] In 1913, the Polish People's Direction split into two groups: the majority, which was headed by Witos, adopted the symbolic title of "Piast," thus associating itself with the first ruler of the Polish State; the other, much smaller group, chose the name of the Polish People's Direction—the "Left."

Wincenty Witos, who was the son of a peasant, viewed the shame and weakness of his peasant class as a national calamity. Born in 1874, he was a correspondent for a newspaper managed by reformers. He wrote on a variety of themes. Although a loyal churchman, he was wary of clerical interference in political matters.

He was determined to see the peasants represented in the councils of the nation. In 1908, he won a place as county councillor in the provincial Diet in Lwow. When the principle of manhood suffrage had been accepted in the Dual Monarchy, Witos was to become the first Polish peasant to represent his nation in the Viennese Reichsrath. After Poland regained her independence, Witos became prime minister.

In his speeches and writings, Witos sought to enlighten the world of the virtual illiteracy of the masses in Austrian Poland. He was also unhappy with the schools that did exist. He wanted the schools to teach the children about their Polish heritage, so that the children would be mindful both of their origin and their identity. He believed that only the education of the masses and participation in political life would correct the situation. He believed that the ruling classes exercised little responsibility towards their constituents. If they did not accept persuasion, then he advocated sterner methods with the ruling classes.

CHAPTER THREE

Polish Peasant Immigrants

The home we first knew on this beautiful earth,
  The friends of our childhood, the place of our birth,
 In the heart's inner chamber sung always will be,
  As the shell ever sings of its home in the sea.[1]

No one can live in a Polish environment and not feel there is something more to man than the mere life in his body. The indignity of belonging nowhere, and the great need of belonging somewhere, experienced by the peasants, at this time, was in great part responsible for the awakening of the Polish national movement. Nationalism is not a normal condition of mind; it is called into being by injustice and the thwarting of healthy patriotism. Europe suffered from it, in modern times, because men and nations wanted to dominate each other, while the victims found in it a weapon of defense. Polish nationalism was not normal because it was subjective: it was a spirit without a body, or a family group without a home to dwell in. Independent nations have nurtured patriotism on both invisible and visible levels: on both the interior front of common traditions and aspirations, and on the external front of a territory which it inhabits as well as the free institutions which it rules and exploits. Poland had only common traditions and aspirations. At this time, she possessed no territory or national institutions.

Nationalistic sentiment was further stimulated by the philosophy and literature during the first decades of the nineteenth century, called the Age of Romanticism. In reaction to the ration-

---

[1] Stanley R. Pliska, *Polish Independence and the Polish Americans* (unpublished Ph.D. dissertation, Columbia University, 1955), p. 38.

alism of the eighteenth century, Romanticism extolled emotion in preference to reason; it idealized the noble attributes of mankind and glorified the past. This romantic attitude towards the past fostered a reverence for history which awakened national loyalties among European peoples that resulted in an intensified study of their own respective spiritual and cultural heritages. Scholars were busily engaged studying the language, folk-customs, music, and history of their particular regions or nationalities. The Romanticists believed that only through the cultivation of that intrinsic culture—which is a product of its own national genius and deeply rooted in its historic traditions—can a people discover true self-realization. Herder in his writings stated:

> "The best culture of a people is not hastily acquired; it does not permit itself to be forced through a foreign language. That culture flourishes most beautifully upon its native soil, or I might say thrives only through the dialect which a people inherits and passes on to posterity. . . . Truly as God tolerates all languages in the world, so should also a ruler not only tolerate but honor the various languages of the people he rules.[2]

The emancipation of the serfs, in 1861, by Russia under Czar Alexander II, produced a profound change in Poland during the late nineteenth century when compared with Poland of an earlier period. The nobles and the clergy were no longer the spokesmen of the nation. The parcelling of the vast estates owned by the magnates brought increased wealth and comfort to the peasant class which led, not only to a class of thrifty cultivators, but also it tended to increase the population. The surplus of this population helped to expand the class of artisans, and to increase the growth of the cities and villages in Poland.

It was this class that brooded upon such topics as Polish nationalism and sufferance which they learned from the operas of Moniuszko, the writings of Lelewel, the paintings of Matejko and the dramas of Wyspianski.[3] They saw not only the kinship

---

[2] Quoted in Louis Greenberg, *The Jews in Russia. The Struggle for Emancipation* (New Haven: 1944), I, p. 131.
[3] The Congress Kingdom of Poland was a territory which had been incorporated into Russia proper, only after the Uprising of 1863. Thereafter, the full scheme of

between Poland and the peasants, but a kinship and identity between the Polish peasant and his regional culture.[4]

Thus, on the eve of the peasant migration to America, the Polish peasants were very conscious of their ethnic identity and mission. Though not yet recognized as partners in a society, the peasants had long since proved their worth for the national cause. They mustered their aggressiveness, rolled and twisted their anger into a knot, and tried to hold on to what was theirs: their rights in the land, their family identity, their memories, their pattern of speech, their way of looking at the world.

Very possibly, the movement of peasant Poles, from 1870 to 1920, has no parallel in the history of Poland. Even the eastward surge in Poland was not equal to it; and while larger masses of people have moved, it was never under conditions that resembled the great trek of the Poles out of partitioned Poland into a *terra incognita*. For these were not the erudite, sophisticated, cosmopolitan city dwellers, nor were they men of wealth or influence.

These were poor, indeed destitute peasants, whose lives were circumscribed by the tiny villages they inhabited. The villages held the peasants in the grip of the customary and the familiar. There had been no drastic change in the relations between lord and

---

czarist anti-Jewish persecutions were made thoroughly operative. Here 400,000 Jews lived. During this time a comfortable Jewish bourgeoisie developed. Jews with sufficient leisure familiarized themselves with the Polish language and Polish cultural traditions. Accordingly, the Jewish middle class provided a base for a significant Polish-Jewish intelligentsia, which made its appearance during the 1860's. Jews found employment in banks, commission houses, export concerns, and in the liberal professions. Jews, too, were often the patrons of the most important Polish journals and newspapers. The Natanson family, for example, owned the largest Polish publishing house. The Jews played a significant role in the book trade and the theatrical and concert booking offices. Until the Polish Uprising of 1863, the Jews of the Congress Kingdom of Poland made outstanding contributions to Polish cultural life: their sons were writers, doctors, scientists, philologists, musicians, actors, painters and sculptors. Indeed, the rate of Jewish acculturation in the Congress Kingdom of Poland was much faster than in the remainder of partitioned Poland. Both in the remainder of Poland and in the Congress Kingdom of Poland the passion to adopt non-Jewish mores was responsible for conversion to Christianity of a significant minority of Jews.

[4] On the initiative of the poet, Adam Asnyk (1838-97), the peasants decided to commemorate the centenary of the Constitution of May 1791 by securing an endowment of a million francs for the Common Schools Society. This was only one of the many projects which they initiated. See Wytrwal, *Poles in American History and Tradition*, pp. 291-301.

peasant for centuries. However galling, the village maintained a stable course where the peasant knew what was expected of him, no matter how difficult his life. His family and ancestors were rooted in the soil and bound by customs that had been handed down for generations.

The fundamental economic and social unit of the rural community was the family, a relationship in which the peasant and his sons performed most of the heavier outdoor tasks, while his wife and daughters, not only cared for the house, but made butter, preserved the fruit and vegetables, and fabricated at least part of the clothing. Women also looked after the livestock and helped in harvesting the grain. Thus, the personality of the Polish peasant was not warped by a narrow specialty nor dwarfed by slavery to a machine. The peasant was a self-reliant man: he was a producer of crops and a breeder of animals which he later slaughtered, carved and sold the meat. He was a mechanic, who could mend a wagon, shoe a horse, or fashion iron runners for sleds and spokes for wheels. He was an entrepreneur, who understood that the conditions of survival compelled him to develop the shrewdness of the trader and the foresight of the wise investor. He was an empiricist whose common-sense materialism was softened by his ideals of love of God, land, home and sheer hard work.

Fixed in one place for centuries, most of the peasants barely managed to live from subsistence farming; the peasants thought of themselves mostly in the simple terms of their own village circle, within which they were at home and outside of which they were only strangers. Always their interests had been local, limited to the area within the shadow of their own church tower, so that even a man from only a few miles away was distinguishable in dialect and costume. As the honest and hard-working peasants gathered in the meadows for their summer feasts, in those days, their light-heartedness was not diminished by too much knowledge of the outer world. The sphere of social contact for the peasant in Poland was very small, limited to the village, or nearby provincial capital, where he journeyed few times during the year on regular market days, or on a pilgrimage to a church or monastery that was known for its miraculous image celebrated on special feast days. Such was the peasants' limited knowledge of Poland where rebellion had failed, social movement was blocked, individual talent brought no recognition, social wrongs continued, and appeals for understanding brought no quarter. Lives centered, even to the smallest detail, around work and worship, which became the stabilizing influences; but they discouraged deviation from the customary pattern which seemed never to have an end.

The majority of the uneducated Polish peasants, who had never known anything but poverty, carried this background with them as they went into the unknown, yet eager to put their hands to work. Some had little money, but the majority were modestly equipped with the world's goods, and likewise limited in the way of skills. They filled their pockets with what food they had, tied up their few portable possessions into trunks, quilts or bags, and with a myriad variety of dreams, they sailed for America. The vast, wide, deep and terrible ocean with its destructive power and brooding lonely emptiness—provided the test necessary to overcome in order to realize their dreams. As they recalled the thatched old white-washed cottages (sometimes leaning precariously on makeshift foundations, or the outdoor privies left behind) many dreamed of becoming rich. Some dreamed of becoming richer than they were. In many, the formation of national characteristics which are ordinarily formed unconsciously resulted in a silent guerrilla war between memory and desire. In the land across the ocean they knew that life could not be more bleak than it was in partitioned Poland. Looking forward to reunions with relatives or neighbors, they hoped for a better life.

When they arrived, they were bewildered by the buzzing large American cities or fast growing farm communities. These immigrants from the quaint, rural and familiar villages—where they lived in a simple but dignified universe—were confronted with new customs and mores. In some instances, with their exotic dress and language—which was either unfamiliar or bizarrely accented, along with the other retained traits—they became objects of derision, caught within the forces over which they had no mastery. The Polish immigrants, who reached the United States, found themselves cut adrift from the stratified rural environment of the Polish villages where many previous generations lived. In their new country, their poverty was compounded by the agony of feeling like undesirable aliens. To ward off loneliness, they were drawn to their own people, sharing, working together, and enjoying that which was familiar, in no less a common language with reversed traditions. Without the security of their former life, many found it enormously difficult, despite their sturdiness and resourcefulness—to adjust to their new economic, social, religious and cultural surroundings.

The nature and severity of the immigrant struggle made it difficult for the immigrant to tell which aspect of his life he found most distressing: whether the rapid tempo of work in his new home, a contrast to the former leisurely manner of working in the fields; or the all-pervading, unashamed acquisitiveness with its rewards for success entailing a complete reversal of social status; or the apparent necessity of giving up his old cultural and religious values and customs in order to attain a degree of apparent comfort and security.

The Polish immigrants were creatures of their environment and they found it difficult, if not impossible, to cut themselves entirely from their old moorings. This national consciousness, with a distinct Polish identity, was formed amidst huge populations and vast reaches of territory: the different languages and customs, the complex and ever-changing technologies, the great emphasis on specialization, the complicated literate symbol systems, the labyrinthian social structures, the self-consciousness among other alien groups which were frequently hostile—the fears of social annihilation, and the realization of the differences between Poles and other immigrants or natives.

Native Americans did not regard the recent ethnic arrivals as their equal; and national consciousness increased under the impact of the recent immigration. This prejudice was codified in the school books of nineteenth-century America. The ideal American is of a white race emanating from a northern European background. He is Protestant, self-made—if not a farmer—at least retaining the virtues of his yeoman ancestors. The textbook exalted the English to a position just below the Americans. Americanism was synonymous with Anglo-Saxon Americanism which apparently did not speak another language. Unless they attended parochial schools, immigrant children were taught these prejudicial views in school.

Americanization, in this form, was a powerful influence in encouraging the development of ethnic patriotism among all the immigrant groups. The Germans, the Irish, and the Jews, had been fully imbued with cultural self-awareness upon their arrival in America. But for the majority of the new immigrants, ethnic patriotism was mainly a product of the American ghettos where the immigrants found not only the strength and fortitude to endure, but a spiritual reserve that made them flourish. It was here that these Italian, Polish, Hungarian, or Greek immigrants became conscious of themselves as belonging to any distinctive social group at all beyond the family and the village of their home country. They became hyphenated-Americans all at once by simultaneously discovering their identity as citizens of their adopted country and their identity as representatives of an ethnic group in Europe.

No human sympathy closed the breach between the native American and Polish immigrants. Americans might honor General Kosciuszko, founder of West Point, or admire General Pulaski, the hero of Savannah; but they did not associate them meaningfully with the bewildered newcomer, recently disembarked, or the exploited laborer on a city street. Whatever intercourse existed between the Polish peasants and Americans was of a commercial or political nature. It was not social. The native American population did not stay in the neighborhoods invaded by immigrants, but moved to uptown districts or suburbs. This naturally left the immigrant settlement solidly foreign, and quite to themselves, where they lived in anonymity amidst, but apart, from the thousands around them. Small wonder that one Greek humorously remarked:

> We have been in America for six months. . . . We had neither heard English nor become acquainted with Americans. In the mill there worked Polish men and women and only Polish was spoken in the factory and in the streets of the small town.[5]

---

[5] Theodore Saloutos, *They Remember America: The Story of the Repatriated Greek-Americans* (Berkeley: 1956), p. 19.

And his friend added.

> I believe the captain of our ship made a mistake and instead of bringing us to America brought us to Poland.[6]

Learning English was not only a desire but a necessity. Without some understanding of it, the immigrant was limited in his attempts to better himself in his work or living conditions. In an English-speaking country the first demand was that he learn to speak English and to read and write it, at least a little. It was also a measure of achievement. But the learning was not easy for a man isolated in a foreign neighborhood, whose associations at work and at home were mainly with those who knew no more English than he did. In some neighborhoods there were night classes in English that he could go to; but he had little leisure for study and often little enough time just to sleep or eat. For those who had never learned to read or write in any language, attempting to learn one that was strange to their tongues was more baffling than most foreign languages were to Americans.

The immigrant settlements were an aggregate of individuals concentrated in several areas, but they were not a community whose lot was secure, peaceful or untroubled with cares and worries. Life was not simple, but difficult. However, there was a certain felicitous atmosphere created by good fellowship between neighbors.

Among the relatively few American social workers and intellectuals, who defended the new immigrants, were Jane Addams, Jacob Riis, Horace Kallen and Hutchins Hapgood. They were not motivated by faith in the "melting pot" theory. They were cultural pluralists, who argued that America was being culturally enriched by the new elements in the population. This was a line of argument that was a practical one in the context of settlement work; but it was not calculated to appeal widely to the American public.

Here, in the massive, sprawling, dirty, amazing and freewheeling cities of America, it was expected that the Germans in their German neighborhoods, would speak German, just as the

---

[6] *Ibid.*, p. 19.

Italians would speak Italian, and the Jews would speak Yiddish. It was natural and obvious, just as natural as the Greeks—in their neighborhoods—spoke Greek, or the Hungarians spoke Hungarian. In the American cities, you could also expect to find newspapers in every language imaginable. There was no common religion: Baptists, Episcopalians, Presbyterians, Methodists, Lutherans and Catholics, joined all of the exotic faiths of the world. There were few common historical traditions; the early immigrants to America came from lands of varying backgrounds and traditions. There were originally no common myths connected with the past, or linked, as in Poland, to such legendary figures as Wanda and Krakus. There was, in early America, no common cultural pattern. Above all, there was no common descent or lineage stretching backward in time to the earliest beginnings of American civilization. Teeming tenements with inadequate sanitation and crowded streets made for mutual helpfulness and an interdependence. On the other hand, there were also social differences within the new neighborhoods. Men and women, coming from different parts of Europe, discovered that they were, after all, not exactly alike. Each group regarded the other as inferior, almost as much as the descendants of earlier settlers disdained others who could not trace their ancestry. The intimacy and fellowship to which the immigrants had been accustomed to in the towns and villages, from whence they came, was apparently lacking.

American religious discrimination within the Catholic Church was also decisive in the formation of a Polish identity. In the American Catholic Churches, the evidences of their foreignness confronted the Polish immigrants. For the most part, the Polish immigrants found the Church already established in the cities where they chose to settle. But the Church was unfamiliar. Built by other worshippers, the priests, saints, and other names, even the very language, was foreign. Even though they were Catholic, the faith shared with the Italians was, least of all, a common bond which united them.

Thus, the cultural mold, in which the Polish identity was fashioned, was a composite of certain unique and inextricably intertwined religious, economic, and political experiences which were to shape their destiny for generations after they had settled in America. The common language, common religion, political subjugation, economic destitution, religious discrimination within the Catholic Church, and the mutual recollection of old experiences, were decisive factors in the formation of a Polish identity that was responsible for the unique and intense commitment of the Poles to Polish nationalism and culture. Religious discrimination against the Polish clergy was also a major reason for the emergence of the Polish priests as the authoritative voice among the Poles. Upward mobility for the Polish clergy was proscribed. Unable to enter the dominant Catholic hierarchy, the Polish priests felt constrained, but united amongst themselves as well as with the Polish community where they created a remarkable solidarity among the Poles and with whom they shared closely their triumphs, their disappointments, their accomplishments and setbacks. The impact of these events led to the emergence of a cohesive social structure which gave rise to the fundamental cultural values upon which it rested.

While in old Poland—weighted down with history, protracted by wars and insurrections, and endlessly vacillating between greatness and decline—many of the immigrants rarely imagined themselves in anything more than local or regional terms. But the impact of events, in America, brought this about; the Polish immigrant who had not been politically deeply committed to the Polish cause, or greatly involved in the struggle for independence, suddenly became aware of Poland's calamity and identified with the cause of freedom proclaimed by Mickiewicz, Kosciuszko, Pulaski, Slowacki, Sienkiewicz, Zeromski and countless others. As an active patriot, the immigrant manifested a great desire (almost a need) to write on behalf of Poland which he idealized as the home of suffering heroes and glorious causes, as well as the splendid repository of all those treasures which American society stripped from his heritage. The peasants were stirred by the rebirth of Poland; sharing in it, drew them closer to one another, which gave many a deeper appreciation of their Polish identity and feeling. Many assumed responsibilities which, in Poland, they would ordinarily have abstained as if it were beyond their physical powers. They not only contributed money but dedicated countless hours of work to the Polish cause.

To the end of their days, many peasants still referred to themselves in village terms, or continued to call themselves Germans, Austrians or Russians; nevertheless, a cohesive Polish group steadily evolved which identified with a particular nation, not quite restored, but decidedly characterized by a common language, culture and spirit. It was the Polish language which served to cement their ties to one another. Polish gave them more than an affiliation to a personal past, more than a personal identity; it became the bond that united them into cohesive social units bearing a proud identity. In 1900, a million foreign born and 700,000 native born, identified themselves as Polish-Americans. Nurtured in the warmth of an ethnic family life, the children of these immigrants learned to speak their parents' native tongue and to sing Polish songs and carols before they learned English. They also acquired the games and dances known to their parents. Yet, the second generation could not share entirely the ethnic life of their parents because their experiences were also American. Though their love and loyalty for their parents were genuine, many were also keenly aware that their ethnic status was a source of deprivation and humiliation. Theo Lippman and Donald C. Hansen, in their book *Muskie* relate the experiences of Senator Edmund S. Muskie in the public schools of Maine.

> The son of the tailor was greeted at school by cries of "dumb Polack." His ancestry and his religion were held up to ridicule. The taunting of the Muskie children at school continued for about five years. He had no friends. Irene and Lucy, who also faced the jeers, came home crying and told their parents. "I felt so awful and ashamed," Lucy said. But the proud tailor told the girls, "Let them call you all the names they want. The names aren't going to hurt you. Be proud to be Polish."[7]

The general lot of the Poles in the cities was extraordinarily depressing. They usually learned English and tried to adopt American manners and customs; but they never entirely shed the influence of their earlier life. A great deal of this sentiment was

---

[7] Theo Lippman, Jr., and Donald C. Hansen, *Muskie* (New York: 1971), p. 35.

caused by nostalgia: the memory of a place that seemed better in most instances, than it really was; a life they wished they had never left. This was reinforced by hardships, homesickness, loneliness and attachment to the family and friends left in Poland. The peasants, thousands of miles from native roots, never forgot their memories of a happy childhood among their family and friends, or the recollection of poverty and want in their youthful days.

Although the peasants did find greater material prosperity and ease, they were happiest when they gathered around each other's tables. Always the extended family consisted of active, visiting aunts and uncles, cousins, relatives by association, or distant relatives for whom a family pooled the hard-earned passage money, or arranged for entry into the United States. Almost all of the immigrants came to the United States as individuals. Parents sent for children, husbands for wives, siblings for each other or their parents. This person-by-person family exodus created the basic immigrant fabric typical of first generation family groups.

In these gatherings, the children were excluded from the magic circle, for the familiar snatches of table talk had continuity only for the adults, whose words spun out their memories and created a link, even though fragile, with the homeland. As the conversation flitted from one topic to another—rising and falling with the emotion of the moment—the staid Polish demeanor of daily life would often dissolve into Polish merriment when someone would laughingly recall an immigrant who had pastured geese as a girl in Poland, and now displayed the airs of a countess when, during church services, she tossed coins with her bediamonded hands. The sound of "folk-style Polish" enhanced their memories and alleviated their homesickness and loneliness which continued to haunt them. Always in the center of the table, amid the generous array of newer and lighter American dishes, stood the Polish platter which held the familiar Polish foods such as pierogi (dumplings), kielbasy (sausages) and other typically Polish dishes well seasoned and cooked in red wine with dill and other herbs. There were also paczki (jelly doughnuts) and chrusciki (a light, powdered pastry sometimes called angel's wings). Sometimes the meal would include steaming Polish vegetable soups served with sour cream, while in the summer cold fruit and vegetable soups called chlodniki.

In addition, various obligations toward others in Poland made the sentiment constant. Nostalgic memories of home usually manifested itself in a readiness to do something to alleviate the misery of those still remaining in partitioned Poland. The modest wages, which they earned, were often drained by purchasing passage tickets to America for the relatives that remained in Poland. The most important kind of material help was gifts of money sent to support parents or a wife and family, to help discharge family debts, or to maintain, improve, or purchase additional land. They also contributed toward village improvements, and subscribed to national liberation projects. Often funds were solicited in America for political prisoners deported from Poland into the mines and frozen wastelands of Siberia. They contributed generously to the Common Schools Society Endowment Fund. Funds were also raised for the unsuccessful revolution of 1905. It is therefore not surprising that even though abstract national ideas did not appeal to the peasant masses, incidents in the native country caused considerable excitement in America to form meetings, collections or protests.

Besides the social barriers, in the beginning, their meager incomes forced them to live in squalid slums and tenements; and with taverns at every turn, which became constant inducements to them, here they sought escape from their misery, or commiseration, in drink. Many Poles succumbed to excessive drinking: despite whatever temporary release it may have afforded them from the duress of life, it effectively helped blot out realistic hopes and possibilities for a better life which they wanted so desperately for themselves and their children.

Only after the initial shock of contact with American conditions had worn off, and after they had withstood the storms and tides of years, did the bulk of the peasant immigrants—without name or influence to help them, often with no money save what they had gained by their own efforts—set about constructing a life for themselves on the social frontier. The difficulties of adjustment during the early years were enormous. All at once, it seems, they had to adjust to the discipline of the industrial society, to become acquainted with the customs and traditions of the land, to overcome homesickness, to endure native opposition, and acclimate themselves to a society composed of diverse ethnic and religious groups.

In this environment, the Polish immigrants discarded their old world habits and acquired concepts. Although there was much activity in America to distract ethnic minority groups from distant concerns, the Polish immigrants—sensitive to the emptiness which so often followed the great adventure of coming to America and grappling constantly with the American environment—slowly moulded their environment to their needs and purposes. Eventually they formed the Polish-American Community, *Polonia Amerykanska*, a marginal society with institutions which embodied their new needs and ideas. While their roots were in the soil of Poland, its structure and content was gradually modified by adaptations to each new situation which arose.

Due to a lack of perception, many Americans mistakenly assumed that the ethnic communities and institutions had only one dimension. They believed that the communities and institutions simulated surroundings of their fatherland and perpetuated isolated group life; hence, through churches and schools, as well as through social, fraternal and national organizations, immigrants worked to retain the speech, the ideals and, to some extent, the manner of Polish life. Exploring beneath the facade of the Polish community, one discovers that its communities and organizations possessed two dimensions. They represented an important step away from old world patterns. Because the city prevented isolation, neither the community, nor its institutions, was fully Polish in character; nor was it wholly American. They served an interim group, the immigrant with his old-world traditions amidst new world surroundings.

In the isolated and tightly knit Polish villages, it was an accepted standard that the primary group remained responsible for its own members: all of whom were expected to live up to their obligations. The good peasants in Poland were the men who shared the little they had with their neighbors in time of need. They helped relatives and neighbors bring in their hay before the rains came. They knew their appointed place in the community and kept it; likewise, they respected their fellows who did the same. America, they learned, was not the haven for the good peasant. It was the first of many sad disillusionments: in this new homeland, the ruthless fellow—the mean, tight-fisted man, who grabbed what he could and shared nothing—made out the best. Their previous exposure to status had little relevance. The peasants could not keep their place, because they could not find it. They had to go forth and strive to find whatever place they could.

Mutual Aid Societies and Political Clubs

In a time of need, rather than to turn to the established "charities," with their searching and degrading investigations, the Polish immigrants preferred to turn for assistance to their own group. During the early stages of the evolving Polish-American community mutual help was exercised sporadically: from case to case, by means of collections made for the benefit of the sick, the poor individual or a particular family in distress, a transient, or the departed, who needed burial. For many years the brunt of social welfare fell on the more settled, or financially solvent members of the community. However, when the vast stream of immigrants, which poured in incessantly, increased the need for charitable donations, the financially solvent were eager to substitute this unregulated voluntary assistance with a regular system of death and sickness insurance. Thus, they favored the establishment of mutual aid societies which would diminish their risks and contributions.

The mutual aid society usually took the name of a patron saint or an American Revolutionary War hero, in order for the group to identify with. The first Polish-American mutual aid society was the St. Stanislaus Kostka Society of Chicago, established in 1864. According to its constitution of 1866, the following were the objectives of the society: to visit and help the sick, to bury the dead, to help widows and orphans, and to encourage peace and morality in the community. The initiation fee was between $5.00 and $10.00; and the monthly dues were 50¢. In case of death of any member, a special fee of $1.00 was charged.

In a highly mobile country, such as America, vast numbers of immigrants found themselves uprooted from familiar surroundings, and life patterns and also separated from their loved ones. For them the society fulfilled a great social void. To join a society was to become a member of an identifiable group; and most important, they saw that their lives were enhanced through cooperation with others. Few immigrants would have denied John Donne's quotation: "No man is an island."

In order to attract and hold membership, the mutual aid society expanded its services from the basic named functions to include other social ones as well: among them, providing provision for recreational facilities with special annual events, such as picnics, dances and religious celebrations. In addition, many societies required all members to attend funeral services, or pay a fine as a penalty for nonattendance. In this manner, the organization assured each member a proper burial and a well-attended service, with the result that funerals tended to become social events. Over the years, the burial service developed into an occasion for old acquaintances to gather at irregular intervals, and to reminisce about old days. Since young and vigorous members predominated, more deaths resulted from accidents or disease which grew out of hazardous working conditions.

In time, the mutual aid society became a kind of social club and community center after working hours. Because the immigrant peasant dreaded boredom, he shunned anonymity and sought to dispel his anxieties. For these reasons the community center prospered. Here, they discovered new friends with whom they could share ideas, preferences and gossip, and ambitions, and empathize with their vulnerabilities and vices.

The center was usually a large hall filled with tables and chairs. Here, Polish songs, rhythmic folk dances, lively music, stirring declamations and moving dramas of Polish heroes with their exploits, were presented; gems of Polish literature were read and reread, just as many episodes from Polish history were related. The walls of the center were adorned with portraits of Polish revolutionary heroes, or pictures illustrating a decisive battle in which the Poles emerged victorious against the Turk, Russian or Prussian or other foreign campaigns.

The rooms were also occupied with newspapers which could be read at leisure. In these newspapers, the immigrants might read the typical news of the day, besides poems, moral advice, recipes, editorials, biographical sketches, some history, the necrology, and bits of curious, useful or entertaining information. More important, the newspapers carried shrewd political articles on current political issues in the United States and Europe written by some of the best writers on the scene in Polish. Reading the daily and weekly newspapers with their stories, editorials and advertisements led many immigrants to discover that such reading was in itself a liberal education which expanded their knowledge. If the immigrant was sufficiently ambitious and gifted, he could find in these newspapers an opportunity to express his own thoughts, since the newspaper became—by printing contributor's letters—a public forum.

The atmosphere of the community center—clouded with foul cigarette or cigar smoke—was hardly inviting or comfortable. But this was the place to hear local gossip; who had died or was getting married; who was leaving for partitioned Poland, or returning to America; job openings; as well as the inevitable evaluation of the competence or incompetence of the club officers.

The need for identity is one of the basic factors which psychologically motivates the behavior of all human beings. The need for stimulation is not distant. The mutual aid societies were useful in that they supplied identity through membership, and stimulation through the competitions between groups and individuals. They also provided stability within the security of the group. The formal ritual of the meetings gave flair to the otherwise drab existence of its members; the benefits paid to the sick and bereaved tided many a family over a difficult period; the discussions at the meetings answered the needs of its members. Through the celebration of American holidays (which were usually part of the societies' program) and through the speeches of the local politicians (who found a useful forum in the lodge) the members were introduced to the political life of the country and given a deeper understanding of the role and opportunity for them within it.

Much later, in addition to the mutual aid societies, political clubs were formed. The first political club, organized in Philadelphia, in 1871, was the "Kosciuszko Club." The first meetings were held in the home of one of its members. Monthly dues were modest and the membership increased rapidly. Each member was required to obtain citizenship; when he received his final papers, the members of the club presented him with a gift of three dollars. As the club expanded, larger quarters were needed. It was then that a large room was secured at the corner of Front and Green Streets. The club possessed a few books, but at each meeting the members were required to visit the "library" and sign their names. Books were not plentiful in those days, and the club was a haven for many new immigrants, who spent many happy hours there. In Detroit, the Polish collection at the Detroit Public Library was the most active during these years, far more popular in usage than the earlier and larger established collections: French and German. The members were urged to be good Americans. The club used the following motto: "A good Pole is a good American citizen."[8]

Saloons as Community Centers

Accompanying the growth of American Polish communities was the appearance of many saloons, most of which were owned by Poles. The saloon was the "poor man's club," where the immigrants could learn the important news about employment, politics and Poland. The saloon was a congenial, lively place where people could indulge themselves in idle gossip and discussion, or find respite from the drudgery of work, as well as from the duress of life and its onerous responsibilities.

The saloon proprietors were very important figures in the Polish American community. Their status as entrepreneurs, along with their business acumen, elevated them to positions as officers in the mutual aid societies and political clubs, marshals in church processions and chairmen at church meetings. Some became actively engaged in politics and organized the Poles into clubs

---

[8] Sister M. Theodosetta, H.F.N., "The Polish Immigrant in Philadelphia to 1914," *Records of the American Catholic Historical Society in Philadelphia*, LXV (June, 1954), No. 2, pp. 83-84.

that provided them with a local base from which to launch their political careers. Others used their influence in the community to win favors from officials at city hall. American politicians instinctively recognized how helpful saloon proprietors could be for supporting their candidates. With the general improvement in living conditions, the saloon became a tavern, and then a bar, and only gradually ceased to serve as the place where party workers and politicians gathered to exchange information about local politics.

As the vast, constantly growing immigrant population increased, a concentrated effort was made to regain Poland's independence. All of these political strategies and pressures were clearly devised to realize this goal. Eventually the mutual aid societies, political clubs and saloons assumed other functions and activities. They became centers of information for recent immigrants, recent visitors and travelers. Their leaders released to the local and national press news or information about opportunities which the locality could offer to the Polish immigrants. They also appeared publicly at Divine Service on national or religious holidays. They also acted as the representatives of the community in its relation with American institutions and agencies which tried to reach the Polish community for social purposes. Politically conscious, they were frequently sensitive to the need of reconciling the conflicts between the immigrant group and its surrounding community. Along with concern for preserving tradition, they also demonstrated a great eagerness to adapt to the new. Since they were usually interested in delivering the vote, they encouraged attendance at evening classes where English and the concepts of democratic government could be learned. As a result of their activities, the evening classes were crowded with men and women who had recently arrived from Europe.

Polish-American Parishes and Schools

Eventually the leaders of the Polish-American community, who desired more recognition, prestige and security, adopted as one of their objectives the establishment of Polish-American parishes based on the churches they had known in Poland. They well realized that a Polish-American parish, with Polish priests, would assure permanence to the social cohesion in the Polish-American community. Furthermore, the parish would not only provide better social cooperation, but it would stimulate interest in new lay activities which had little or no religious significance: musical clubs, insurance funds, cooperative merchandising groups, literary associations and cultural societies whose avowed purpose was to maintain a familiarity with the Polish language and its culture.

Three saloons were partially responsible for the establishment of the Polish parish in Polonia, Wisconsin. When the early Polish settlers arrived in Wisconsin, they joined the Germans to establish a church, dedicated to St. Martin. Father Jan Polak, a Polish immigrant, came to Stevens Point to celebrate mass. But the differences in language and customs between the Germans and Poles prevented the growth of a unified community. By 1864, forty-four Polish families wanted a church of their own. With the blessing of Milwaukee's Bishop John Henri, the Polish community built a new church dedicated to St. Joseph and welcomed Father Bonaventura Buczynski as their pastor.

The presence of two national parishes, within a short distance of each other, did nothing to cement community spirit. Rival groups soon developed into feuding groups. The three saloons, built near St. Joseph's Church, were frequently the scenes of brawls, assaults and petty riots. Even on Sunday, the congregation itself was interrupted during the celebration of the mass. The violence and rioting became so uncontrolled that Bishop Melcher, of Green Bay, placed the parish under interdict from 1868 to 1870. Eventually he sent Father Dabrowski to bring peace to the parish. Unable to exert any influence on the saloon keepers, who encouraged gambling and other vices and waged a constant war on his efforts, Father Dabrowski proposed the following remedy:

> One Sunday morning, Father Dabrowski assembled his parishioners after Mass and proposed transplanting the church to a more suitable site. He won enthusiastic approval for this drastic scheme, and many volunteers pledged their help.
> Early the next day, farmers from all parts of Portage county rode into the parish square bearing axes, picks, hammers, horses, wagons

and carts. They dismantled the building in sections, stacked them on wagons and formed a unique cavalcade to a hilltop two miles east of the old site.

On 20 acres of land bought from an Irish farmer, Hannah McGreer, for $50, they began rebuilding their church piece by piece in the spirit of the medieval cathedral builders. Willing hands quickly completed the church, then built a rectory for their pastor.

Bishop Melcher blessed the church on September 12, 1872, and placed it under the patronage of the Annunciation of the Blessed Virgin. Father Dabrowski symbolically named the site Polonia—the Latin name for Poland.[9]

Although Polish immigration to Milwaukee had begun in 1848, with the arrival of Anthony Kochanek, a shoemaker, it was not until 1866, that the first Polish parish in Wisconsin, St. Stanislaus, was established. The Polish immigrants bought a small Lutheran church building at Grove (South 5th) and Mineral Streets. This was used until 1872, when the present fine brick twin towered church was built at Grove and Mitchell Streets. The Kaszuba fishermen, so called for their Kaszubian dialect, were the most picturesque of the early Polish settlers. They contributed greatly to the building of St. Stanislaus.

There was such a marked increase in the Polish immigration to Michigan during the 1860's that in the early 1870's there were enough Poles in the city of Detroit to establish a Polish parish, called St. Albertus, after the first Polish saint, a Bohemian Prince. Founded in 1871, it was located at East Canfield near St. Aubin, in the heart of the earliest Polish-American community. At this time there were approximately 300 Polish families living in Detroit. The area they occupied was bounded by Canfield, Garfield, Orleans and St. Aubin Streets.[10]

St. Albertus, rich in Polish lore, was completed in 1885. The church is noted for its imposing marble altars, the glass crypts holding life-size recumbent statues of two of the Polish Catholic saints: St. Hedwig, the consort of Henry the Pious, dressed in robes of velvet suitable for a queen, and St. Stanislaus Kostka,

---

[9] "Polonia Wisconsin—Cradle of Two Polish American Institutions," *Zwiazkowiec* (June 8, 1972), p. 6.
[10] Wincenty Smolczynski, *Historya Osady i Parafij Polskich w Detroit, Michigan. Ksiazka Pamiatkowa z zycia Polakow na obczyznie* (Detroit: 1907), pp. 67-73.

the son of a 16th century Polish noble family. As a youth, Stanislaus thwarted his father's efforts to keep him from joining a Jesuit seminary, and eschewed the political career his family desired for a life of humility and service to his church. The church of St. Albertus is one of the churches that has the most exquisite stained glass windows in Michigan. Sunlight and moonlight, filter its jeweled rays through the windows that line both sides of the church's walls, the upper reaches in back of the main altar, and even at the entrance to the church. The Detroit Historical Society arranges tours to visit this historic church. The visitors invariably pause in silent admiration before the imposing three-paneled stained glass window showing Poland's King Mieszko being baptized by a priest. A gift of Father A. Guzicki, it is called the Millennium Window because it was installed in 1966, a thousand years after the king made possible the conversion of Poland to Christianity. The magnificent stained glass windows of Sweetest Heart of Mary Church in Detroit are the largest and the finest probably in North America. Coincidentally, father Dominik Kolasinski was the builder of both churches.

The east side was not the only area settled by the Poles. Eventually a second group settled at 20th Street and spread through 23rd Street. Eventually, in 1881, St. Casimir's parish was built for this group on Detroit's west side. Father Pawel Gutowski became its first pastor.[11]

By 1870, a few Polish families were established in Buffalo.[12] As their numbers increased, a special Mass was said for them each Sunday in a chapel adjoining St. Michael's Church. Near Christmastime, in 1872, at the advice of a visiting Bohemian priest, Father Ivannef M. Gartner, this small group of Poles organized their first association, the St. Stanislaus Society. The following year, John Pitass, a 29-year-old theological student arrived from Rome.[13] He was ordained at Niagara University, in June, 1873,

---

[11] *Ibid.*, pp. 74-77.
[12] Martin Stephanowski, his wife Barbara, and their four children arrived in Buffalo around 1864. Stephanowski was the first Polish Catholic to settle in Buffalo. Of peasant stock, he could neither read nor write, but he became a cooper, and bought a frame house valued at $1100. He was the forerunner of scores of other Poles, who arrived in Buffalo, but did not stay. Most Poles pushed on farther west to Chicago, Detroit, Toledo and Milwaukee.

and said his first Mass in St. Michael's Chapel the next day. That afternoon, St. Stanislaus Parish was organized. A frame, 300-seat church was built on remote land donated by the City Treasurer, Joseph Bork (today, it is situated at the corners of Peckham and Townsend Streets). It opened on a fiercely cold day, January 25, 1874. By 1886, the present two-story St. Stanislaus Church was erected since the old one parishioners had outgrown. Father Pitass, a pastor, contributed considerable leadership with physical labor.[14]

> Seeing four men struggling to carry the bell from the old church to the new one, Father Pitass stepped in and carried it alone, to the hoist where it was raised to call a congregation of 28,000 parishioners to worship.[15]

The establishment of the parish marked the second phase in the development of the Polish-American community. As envisioned, it became the center of all social and cultural activities. Now, the tendency to congregate grew stronger. At the turn of the twentieth century, for example, two Polish-American parishes were larger in size than most dioceses. Under the leadership of the Rev. Vincent Barzynski, C. R. (1838-1899), St. Stanislaus Parish, in Chicago, grew into the largest Catholic parish in the world. At one time it numbered approximately fifty different church societies, some of which contained as many as four thousand members. By 1899, St. Stanislaus parish alone numbered

---

[13] John Pitass was born in Piekary, a village in the province of Silesia. He received his secondary education at Gliwice and Racibor. In December, 1868, he went to Rome to study.

[14] It is a unique case in Church history that a priest would become a pastor immediately after ordination and remain in the same duty in the same place for forty years. In 1894, Father John Pitass was the recipient of an unusual distinction. Bishop Stephen Ryan appointed him dean of all the Polish parishes in the diocese. Although Bishop Quigley in 1896, revoked this privilege, yet to the end of his life he was "Dziekan Pitass," to the Polish people. In 1901, he was named an "irremovable rector." He died December 11, 1913. Father Pitass conceived of the idea of the Polish Catholic Congress whose meetings were held at St. Stanislaus in 1896 and 1901 with delegates coming from all over the country.

[15] Ellen Taussig, "The Polish Community Part I: '. . . We've Come a Long Way. . . ,'" *Buffalo Evening News* (November 13, 1971), p. B-3.

50,000 members.¹⁶ In 1889, the Buffalo parish of St. Stanislaus, Bishop and Martyr, numbered 30,000 parishioners.

The rise of the second Polish parish in Buffalo, St. Adalbert's is unique and most interesting. In 1884, construction of a church on Broadway and Beck was started. Bishop Ryan refused to give, at that time, permission for a second Polish parish. A severe storm destroyed the structure well advanced, and the project was terminated temporarily. In 1886 it was resumed again. After a petition was presented to the Sacred Congregation at Rome, permission was granted, and Bishop Ryan appointed Rev. Anthony Klawiter as its first pastor.

After the fire of 1889, a larger church was planned which was brought to completion with a solemn dedication on July 12, 1891. In 1895, Rev. Thomas Flaczek was appointed pastor. During the summer of 1895, many discontented members of St. Adalbert's left and organized the Polish National parish under the name of Holy Mother of the Rosary, on Sobieski Street. The year 1907 was marked with a distinctive event. Acquiescing to Bishop Colton's petition, presented by Father Flaczek, Pope Pius X (by an authenticated document) had adjoined the Church of St. Adalbert's to St. Peter's basilica in Rome, thereby granting "in perpetuo" the privilege of enjoying all the spiritual favors which the Vatican basilica enjoys. St. Adalbert's is the only basilica in the city of Buffalo. In 1924, the basilica was decorated by a young artist, Joseph Mazur, with beautiful inspirational paintings. Father Thomas Flaczek died August 23, 1926.¹⁷

The oldest church of the Polish community in Pittsburgh is also named St. Stanislaus. It was founded in 1875.¹⁸

---

¹⁶ Miecislaw Haiman, "Poles in Chicago," *Poles of Chicago 1837-1937* (Chicago: 1937), p. 4.

¹⁷ The last great event in the parish was the golden anniversary observance in December of 1961 under the guidance of the present pastor, Msgr. Joseph Stelmach. St. Adalbert's parish has its own cemetery on Walden Avenue near Harlem in Cheektowaga. In 1890, Father Mozejewski bought ten acres of land; in 1913, Father Flaczek bought eleven more. There is a beautiful monument called Calvary in the cemetery. Lately the parish bought the third part of its cemetery. The chapel, where final prayers are said instead of at the gravesite, and the modern mausoleum for forty crypts are an asset to St. Adalbert's cemetery.

¹⁸ In the 1960's, the Polish-Americans fought a long battle with the City and with the U.S. Government to save the church from being razed for the site of a regional post office complex. Today in the Pittsburgh, Erie, Altoona-Johnston and

112 BEHOLD! THE POLISH-AMERICANS

Whenever Poles concentrated in considerable numbers, they organized parish churches. The progress of the Polish settlement in Brooklyn, New York can be charted by taking note of the Roman Catholic parishes established by the Poles. The first church, St. Casimir's was established in December, 1875. The second church, Our Lady of Czestochowa, was organized in 1897. St. Stanislaus Kostka Church, located on Driggs Avenue and Humboldt Street, was the third parish organized in Brooklyn. It grew to be the largest Polish parish in Brooklyn.[19]

As their wealth increased, so their desire to praise God more exuberantly and more ostentatiously developed correspondingly. Among the 899 churches built for the greater glory of God, in the United States, by American Catholics of Polish descent, the largest and most imposing was the landmark of the Polish settlement in Milwaukee, St. Josaphath's basilica, at South 6th Street and West Lincoln Avenue, whose jade-green dome rises in impressive grandeur from the clustering of small homes and stores surrounding the parish. It is one of the five basilicas in the United States. This distinction is bestowed by the pope on churches of distinctive beauty and nobility which are also granted ceremonial privileges. It became the first Polish basilica in America on November 18, 1928. With its green dome dominating the South side of the city, it has been called "the Polish Cathedral" and "the Chartres of America."

Its history is as interesting as its size is impressive. The edifice was erected partly through the piety and accumulated pennies from Polish immigrants as well as through the vision, fortitude and bold imagination of its pastor, Father Wilhelm Grutza.

Greenburgh dioceses there are fifty-seven Catholic churches listed as Polish with 80,000 souls. St. Adalbert's on Pittsburgh's southside with a membership of 4,100 is the largest, and St. Mary of Czestochowa of New Kensington is next with 4,000. According to studies by John Bodnar, of the Ethnic Studies Program of the Pennsylvania Historical and Museum Commission, there are 1.1 million persons of Polish descent in Pennsylvania. Of these an estimated 175,000 live in the western part of Pennsylvania. Clarke M. Thomas, "Pittsburgh's Polonia—Weddings, Yes, and Much More," *Pittsburgh Post Gazette* (April 25, 1973), p. 49.

[19] In 1898, the three original parishes—St. Casimir's, Our Lady of Czestochowa, and St. Stanislaus Kostka—organized more than three hundred volunteers for the Spanish-American War. Ralph Foster Weld, *Brooklyn in America* (New York: 1950), p. 210.

St. Josephat's congregation was organized in 1888 under the Rev. William J. Grutza, "the blacksmith priest." Fire destroyed the first church and school building in 1889, and a larger brick church was built at S. 1st and W. Lincoln.

By 1896 the congregation had outgrown this building, and Father Grutza started raising money for a new one. Reading that the old Chicago post office was being razed, he exclaimed "I need that!" and immediately contracted for the dismantled materials. It took 500 railroad flatcars to haul the carved stone, granite pillars, iron scroll-work and copper sheating here, and the cost was beyond the wildest fears of the modest congregation. They were $300,000 in debt by the time the building was finished, in 1898, and Father Grutza was broken in health. The archdiocese eventually shared the cost, and, in 1928, Pope Pius XI fulfilled the dream of the early parishioners by making the edifice a basilica.[20]

Completed in 1898, it was dedicated in 1901 by the second Apostolic Delegate to the United States, Archbishop Sebastian Martinelli.

Under the Rev. Felix Baran, O.F.M., the church became an artistic Shrine as well as the repository of Polish religious culture and traditions. As one parish historian put it: "The greatness and history of Poland with its Saints and Polish eagle find reflection therein and will ever stand as a monument to the great mind of the beloved Father Baran."

The jade dome—204 feet high and eighty feet in diameter—comparable to that of St. Peter's in Rome, was decorated with scenes and figures representing the Catholic religion in its historical development. Scenes from the Old Testament vie with groups of Apostles and theologians of the Church. The windows of the church depict the many aspirations of the Blessed Mother represented in Poland. Beginning from the center of the basilica to the right are: Our Lady of Czestochowa; Our Lady of Ostrobrama; Our Lady of Mercy—found above the main altar in the Cathedral of Lwow; Our Lady of Zebrzydowa near Krakow; the Coronation of the Blessed Virgin in Heaven; Our Lady of Pinsk; Our Lady of the Sands of Krakow; and Our Lady of Gilda.

---

[20] H. Russell Austin, *The Milwaukee Story. The Making of an American City* (Milwaukee: 1946), p. 152.

On the Epistle side, above the side exit, can be found a mural of Thaddeus Kosciuszko at the Battle of Raclawice, taking the pledge to defend Poland against invaders and receiving a blessing before going to battle. Above the Gospel side exits is a painting of Father Piotr Skarga, Poland's famous Jesuit delivering his jeremiads, and foretelling the future partitions of Poland. Also on the Gospel side, in the gallery, is a painting symbolizing the historic times of Poland during the first partition. The Venerable Jadwiga, Queen of Poland, is seen sitting on the throne in an allegory of the Spirit of National Unity. Above her crown is the Polish flag.

In the vestibule are five striking murals of Polish saints: St. Josaphat dressed in the garb of the Orthodox Church, St. John Cantius (Jan Kanty), St. Adalbert (Sw. Wojciech), St. Stanislaus Kostka (Sw. Stanislaw Kostka), and St. Casimir (Sw. Kazimierz).

Dedicated in a special manner to the service of God, St. Josaphat's Basilica was built for the ages, and dominates not only the skyline of Milwaukee's South Side, but also the religious horizon of the Polish-American community in the United States. Like all great churches, it speaks to us in the artistic language of its time. It soars and glows with resplendence conveying its message in Christian and poignantly Polish terms. A truly great monument to the spirituality and reverence of the Poles living in the United States.

The parish church in America took on for the Polish immigrant the form of a "Poland in miniature"—the embodiment of Polish culture. The Polish immigrant regarded his American parish as both a religious and community center. Through its activities, the parish provided the immigrant, and other parishioners, with articles of faith; it also offered the immigrant the opportunity for common religious worship, along with spiritual guidance in his own language. In addition to faith and morals, the sermons were concerned with the problems of daily life. The funeral sermon repeated and interpreted news of shipwrecks and other calamities. The ordination sermon was weighted with theological learning, while the election-day sermon aimed to advance political understanding. The sermons also introduced a belief in the equality of opportunity for all to rise to higher levels of society. Each social strata is open to properly qualified people below it. By applying himself, by utilizing his talents, by acquiring the necessary skills, the immigrant could advance himself and his family. During the sermon, the priests sometimes offered consolation, with helpful advice on how to shoulder their tribulations. They also exalted poverty, prescribing it for all suffering humanity with the Kingdom of Heaven as their reward. In addition, they admonished the community to care for the poor and welcome the stranger as a matter of course, not as charity. The weekly sermon provided the stimulus for household discussions and enlarged the mental horizons of many immigrants, who found an intellectual interest in Christianity, as well as comfort and support. After the sermon, notices of meetings and social activities were read off by the priest.

Priests enjoyed a pre-eminent status among the people. To the Polish immigrants, the priests, who had emigrated to America, served as confessors, teachers, counselors, social directors, almsgivers, and even political leaders. They reminded their parishioners that only through faith and the use of the Polish language could they maintain their national identity. They warned the immigrants against succumbing to the teachings of Protestants and non-canonical priests, who were capitalizing on their spiritual needs, often misleading and seducing them into acceptance of strange and heretical creeds. They issued endless warnings against mixed marriages and any deviations from the traditional path. A genuine Pole was faithful to his Catholic religion and to Poland. The church, with its appeal to divine sanctions, was an effective weapon against the struggle for cultural survival.

The parish provided the immigrants with an additional incentive for congenial social life, with a focal point around which to develop it, since activities of a wider scope, outside the parish, interested the immigrants only slightly. With the establishment of Polish parishes, emphasis was placed on establishing Polish-American parochial schools. The rationale for such schools has been training in the traditional faith and language was a *sine qua non* for Polish survival; that the study of Polish history and civilization—its sources, values and practices—makes one a better

Pole, hence a better person as well as a better American.

The clergy, with their increasing duties and complex roles, became the leading representatives of intellectual interests. This was especially evident in the support they gave to elementary education. In 1887, there were as many as fifty Polish-American schools with 14,150 pupils; by 1914, the number had reached 395 schools, bringing the number of pupils to 128,540.[21] Most of them were in Pennsylvania, Illinois, Wisconsin, New York, Michigan and Ohio.

For various reasons, the clergy placed less emphasis on secondary education. They were principally concerned to mold the mind of the child and imbue it with the early responsibilities required of it as a good Polish-American. Another reason for this philosophy is because education in Poland was aimed at achieving early social competence, for the child was a member of a society which believed in early economic maturity, early social adulthood and very early social conformity.

> All in all, a very small fraction of children attended Polish secondary schools—in 1914, for instance, there were only five hundred of them. This was largely due to high fees. The number of Polish youth studying in public secondary schools was also rather modest. In Buffalo they constituted only 1.6 percent of all pupils, while the Poles made up one-fifth of all the inhabitants. In 1911, in Chicago, among the twelve hundred secondary school graduates there were only 10 youths of Polish descent.[22]

Like the church, the Polish-American parochial school brought the Polish-American immigrants together, and created a bond between the old and new generations by preserving the Polish language. The Polish-American school aimed at the spiritual growth of both the individual and society. Concerning the children in school, it endeavored to develop a sensitivity and an appreciation of ethical, social and spiritual values revered by the Poles. It also imparted a knowledge of the Polish heritage which is necessary for meaningful and intelligent Polish living.

---

[21] Jozef Miaso, *Dzieje Oswiaty Polonijnej w Stanach Zjednoczonych* (Warszawa: 1970), p. 291.
[22] *Ibid.*, p. 294.

It further created a desire to observe the Polish traditions, and to identify with and become an active member in the Polish community. It also helped Polish children become good Americans through an understanding and appreciation of the essential harmony between the ideals and traditions of America and Poland.[23]

The teaching corps—thoroughly American in thought and speech and thoroughly Polish in sympathies with the incoming immigrants—made for a healthy conservatism and precluded violent ruptures with traditions of the past.[24] The Felician Sisters came to Polonia, Wisconsin from Krakow, Poland, at the request of the congregation and invitation of Father Dabrowski, to minister to the education of the parish children. The first five Felicians who arrived on November 20, 1874, were Sisters Monica, superior, Wenceslaus, Cajetan, Vincent, and Raphael. By December, one classroom was available for them to teach. This was the cradle in America of the Felician congregation which was to become a dynamic force in Catholic education in many states.[25]

---

[23] The school's purpose was not only to impart Christian education but to acquaint the child with its Polish heritage. From its first day in school the child was taught the prayers and catechism in Polish. In the higher grades, reading and writing in Polish, Polish history and Polish literature formed part of the grade school curriculum. To insure this religious and national education, the Poles sought the aid of the Polish Sisterhoods, urging them, for that purpose, to establish or transfer their homes from Poland to America or else establish new religious communities. Their members were recruited among the Poles in America. In 1942, the Polish teaching sisterhood numbered 4,822 members, in charge of 553 elementary schools. Rev. S. Targosz, *Polonja Katolicka w Stanach Zjednoczonych w Przekroju* (Detroit: 1943), p. 5.

[24] The children were taught by the Bernadine Sisters of Saint Francis, Reading, Pennsylvania; Sisters of the Third Order of Saint Francis, Chicago; Polish Franciscan School Sisters, St. Louis, Missouri; Felician Sisters, Order of St. Felix; Sisters of the Holy Family of Nazareth, Chicago; Polish Sisters of Saint Joseph, Stephens Point, Wisconsin; Sisters of the Resurrection, Chicago; and Sisters of Notre Dame.

Today, ninety-five percent of the teachers in the Polish-American Schools are American by birth. The older religious communities, several of which have reached a high degree of efficiency, cannot supply the increasing demand in the schools already under their charge. New parishes must content themselves with such as the more recently established communities can afford. The presence of lay teachers in the Polish schools is evidence of the inadequacy in the number of Polish nuns.

[25] The Felicians were soon an integral part of the community. By 1876, three girls became candidates in the order, and made their first vows the following year. The same year, the Felicians felt confident enough to accept a mission outside the state. They accepted an invitation to staff a school in LaSalle, Illinois. The next year, they took on two new schools, one in Bay City, the other in Detroit, Michigan. By

The Polish-American parochial schools prospered in the congenial atmosphere of the Polish-American communities, because parents frequently took the position that children grew away from them and from the stabilizing influences of Polish customs too rapidly when they entered public schools, where an exposition of Anglo-Saxon origins and culture were most preferred.

> The children who attend school here, and many of them who came here within school age or who are born here are attending public schools, learn new things which baffle them and surprise them indefinitely. They don't hear any more about Poland, and if it is being referred to by the teachers it is usually with an air of superiority. The Polish heroes, except Kosciuszko and Pulaski, are not recognized, not worshipped in this country. America and not Poland is being constantly eulogized by the teachers and set as an example of national and spiritual superiority, and the Polish boy or girl soon does not know what to make of it. Has he not already a definite fatherland in Poland? Has he not learned to identify himself with Polish people which in the opinion of his father and mother are the best people in the world? How should he take the deprecatory remarks about his old country, and the light making or overlooking of his Polish heroes? Have his parents been wrong in their teachings and ideas?[26]

Polish parents were left untouched and outside the life of the public school. Parents learned about America through their children, but their contacts with the school were almost nil. Not being able to speak English well, if at all, ignorant of the mechanisms of the system, possessing little understanding of what transpired within the walls of the school, the parents stayed away. The public educators seem to accept and prefer this state of affairs, and so it prevailed. The general attitude prevalent at the time, which permeated the schools, was that if the children received a good education, the parents would be assimilated through their children.[27]

Sometimes the parents kept their children at home and out of

1880, they had members in Indiana, Buffalo, New York and Shamokin, Pennsylvania. In the first 25 years of their apostolate in the United States, they were staffing forty schools. The fast growth of the Felician Sisters forced them, in 1882, to move their provincial headquarters from Polonia, Wisconsin to Detroit, Michigan.

[26] Joseph S. Schneiweis, *Certain Aspects of Polish Assimilation in the State of New York* (unpublished Master's thesis, Columbia University, 1930), pp. 25-26.

[27] Unfortunately what was not grasped was that the formal education of the child

school as long as possible; or they would have them taught the first element in Polish, in the Polish spirit. Sometimes the child learned so much about Polish culture and the noble courage of the Poles that he attributed—especially during the formative years—everything great to Poland and her people. Thus, it was not strange that a little boy once asked his mother, in the presence of Brandes: "Is it possible that Columbus was not a Pole?"[28]

> The fear of losing the children haunts the older generation. It is not merely the natural desire of parent to retain influence over child. Nor is it simply the dread that the wayward offspring will mar the good name of the immigrant group by abuse of his newly found freedom. It is a vague uneasiness that a delicate network of precious traditions is being ruthlessly torn asunder, that a whole world of ideals is crashing into ruins; and amidst this desolation the fathers and mothers picture themselves wandering about lonely in vain search of their lost children.[29]

Desiring for some means of cushioning the sudden cultural shock administered to the younger generation, parents and clergy made certain that the Polish language was taught as well as some Polish history and culture.[30] The training in the Polish-American parochial schools was different from that of the public schools. It was more demanding and severe; it punished physical aggression, but encouraged the discharge of such energies in social achievement. Ideally, it trained for individual responsibility and

---

would not prove successful if his parents were neglected. Essentially, assimilation is a spiritual, emotional, psychological and social transmutation; it is not primarily an intellectual one. To assimilate the children, as well as the adults, both had to be adjusted to the new environment. Evidence seems to indicate that the educational process did not ameliorate the plight of the immigrant parent, who remained very much in ignorance of what the schools were trying to do, and who had little opportunity, or incentive, to obtain information about the purpose and aims of the type of instruction the children were receiving.

[28] George Brandes, *Poland, A Study of the Land, People and Literature* (London: 1903), pp. 67-68.

[29] Julius Drachsler, *Democracy and Assimilation* (New York: 1920), p. 80.

[30] When the Polish newspaper, *Kuryer Polski*, proposed, in 1910, that the Polish language be taught in the public schools of Milwaukee, along with German, Catholic leaders regarded this step as a program to destroy the parochial school system and bitterly resisted it. In 1912, Archbishop Messner of the Milwaukee Archdiocese issued a decree forbidding all Catholics to read the *Kuryer Polski*. The newspaper rejoined with a damage suit for $100,000 which was thrown out of courts. Since then the Polish parochial school system has not been successfully challenged.

autonomy. It frowned on the free expression of impulses and rewarded restraint, foresight and the acceptance of superior, but more remote goals. When such training was successful, individuals were produced who were often candidates for social mobility.³¹

Dr. Francis E. Fronczak, Buffalo City Health Commissioner, from 1910 to 1946, wrote the following comment on his experiences with the Polish-American Catholic schools.

> At the rear of the Church there were two school classes arranged. I remember them well, for it was there I received the foundation of what knowledge I may have today.³²

Kasimir I. Kozakiewicz, who served as president of the Polish Roman Catholic Union, made the following observation about the Polish-American school:

> I remember my grammar school days, and perhaps you do too; our almost entire school day was conducted in the Polish language, only

---

³¹ Dr. Francis E. Fronczak brought stature to the Buffalo Polish-American community. The son of a soldier during the Polish insurrections of 1848 and 1863, who had emigrated to the United States in 1870, he attended St. Stanislaus School, Canisius High School and Canisius College, where he received both his bachelor and master's degrees, and later, obtained doctorates in medicine and law at the University of Buffalo.

Dr. Fronczak was Buffalo City Health Commissioner for thirty-six years, the longest period anyone has held this post. He was recognized as one of the country's foremost public health authorities. A lieutenant colonel in the Medical Corp during World War I, he was a member of top-level national and international relief and military councils. In World War I, he was president of the Central Relief Committee to Poland, and a member of the Polish National Committee which represented Poland in the Council of the Allies, and director of its Department of Public Welfare, where he supervised 97,000 troops, 57,000 Polish war prisoners and thousands of Polish refugees. He also was a member of the three-man Council of War of the Polish Forces in France, and a member of the first American Red Cross Commission to Poland.

After World War II, he was medical advisor, observer and coordinator of the Polish Mission of the United Nations Relief and Rehabilitation Administration. Dr. Fronczak was also an Assistant Collaborating Epidemiologist in the U.S. Health Service and served his country by representing the United States at International Health Conferences by appointment from every president from President McKinley to President Roosevelt.

On December 12, 1965, the City of Buffalo honored the memory of Dr. Fronczak by naming the public library on Broadway in his honor. Dr. Wytrwal delivered the main address. "Dr. Wytrwal Leads Host of Speakers Eulogizing Dr. Fronczak as Library Opens," *Am-Pol Eagle* (December 16, 1965), p. 1.

³² Ellen Taussig, "The Polish Community Part I: '. . . We've Come A Long Way. . . ,'" *Buffalo Evening News* (November 13, 1971), p. B-3.

some of the time was devoted to English reading, writing, spelling, history, and geography. If my memory serves me right we even studied arithmetic in both Polish and English.[33]

Dr. Joseph Kij, son of Polish immigrants and a graduate of St. Barbara's School in Lackawanna, New York, made the following observation.

> A graduate of St. Barbara's school admitted that many of the first teachers knew only Polish. Until third grade most of the teachers spoke Polish in the classroom, and until the 1920's all students studied Polish culture, songs and poetry, and recited their school prayers in Polish. However, Polish was used as a bridge, since English was taught, and American History, Mathematics and the Sciences were always taught in English. The graduate of St. Barbara's insisted that some Polish language in the schools did not hinder learning of English. He believed that "Americanization" did not have to involve forgetting all one's ethnic background, since America is made up of all ethnic groups.[34]

Anna G. Tremaine, a teacher in the Buffalo public school system, who had the son of Health Commissioner Franczak in her class, made the following comment:

> The boy was very slow, no slower than his Polish companions, but slower than we thought he should be, judged by his father's position. The father could not understand his son's lack of progress. With a good deal of hesitation he finally confessed his difficulty to us. He did not understand much of what was said. Up to the time he entered high school he attended Polish schools and the family talked Polish at home entirely, because the father feared the children would forget their Mother tongue.[35]

Peter A. Speek, in the early twenties, visited an old, comparatively large Polish colony in Posen, Michigan. His field notes supply the following information on the Polish school in that area.

---

[33] Kasimir I. Kozakiewicz, "The President's Pad," *Narod Polski* (May 19, 1955), p. 15.

[34] Richard S. Sorrell, "Life, Work and Acculturation Patterns of Eastern European Immigrants in Lackawanna, New York: 1900-1922," *The Polish Review* (Autumn, 1969), XIV, pp. 82-83.

[35] Anna G. Tremaine, *The Effect of Polish Immigration on Buffalo Politics* (unpublished Master's thesis, Columbia University, 1928), p. 56.

There is, at the church, a four-room parochial school housed in a substantial brick building, with five teachers including a priest. The school lasts ten months. Teaching is in English, except that an hour each day is devoted to the Polish language and Polish history. The priest admitted that the teaching of religion is in Polish. The school program is the same as in the standard public schools of eight grades. The same textbooks are used. Although the law does not require examination of the children, nevertheless to appease the county officials and show the efficiency and value of their school, they send the children to the county board of education for examination, and the county board has always expressed great satisfaction with the advancement in education of the children of the Polish school. The teachers are all Poles, appointed by the bishop, candidates being presented by the priest.[36]

The priest explained, as follows, the need for this school:

It Americanizes the children more quickly than the American school—that is, it is more efficient in teaching the children the American way of life and American history than the American public school, for the teachers are all Poles, know their people and their psychology better than do the teachers in the public schools. During a later discussion, the priest admitted that the Church service is in the Polish language and that the Polish school exists rather for sentimental reasons of a racial character than for practical reasons. The settlers also claimed that the Polish school and the Church service in the Polish language are needed for the reason that they like this better; they complained that the expenses are too high; they would have the county or state help them. Sometimes a few adults come to the school, but they are irregular in attendance.[37]

In several of the rural communities, visited by Speek, there were successful bilingual churches:

In the Polish colony at Posen, Michigan, the sermon in the Catholic Church is offered in two languages: Polish and English. The priest explained that the Polish language is needed, as the people, especially the older people, understand it better and the priest is able to penetrate their souls more intimately in their mother tongue. The English language is needed for two reasons: among the colonists are a few American farmers, who belong to the same church and do not speak

---

[36] Peter A. Speek, *A Stake in the Land* (New York: 1921), pp. 168-169.
[37] *Ibid.*, p. 169.

Polish; and a few of the younger generation understand English better than Polish, especially those newcomers who have been born outside of the colony among Americans.[38]

Why the Poles sacrificed so much in order to build schools where their Polish language would be perpetuated was ably expounded by the Rt. Rev. Dr. Valerian Jasinski with the following reasons why Americans of Polish descent should study the Polish language and culture:

> You study because you love and respect your parents. Only he who values highly what is dear and sacred to his parents, loves and respects them. The Polish language is the language they used—and still use—in prayers for the many graces granted to you and to themselves. It is, moreover, the reflection of the culture and the spirit of the nation. It is one of the richest languages from the point of view of grammar and expression, which is evidence of the high culture and the intelligence of your forefathers. Does one who does not care to study the language of his parents really love them? On the contrary, he who neither knows nor understands the language of his parents, does not know or understand either his parents or what is dear to them. Is one who has little interest in his parents, who are God's greatest gift to him, a good child?—Son, you love and respect your parents; therefore do not stay that you do not want to study the language of your forefathers.[39]

In his second exposition of the spirit behind the study of the Polish language and culture, Monsignor Jasinski stated:

> You want to study the Polish language and the culture of Poland because you want to be a useful citizen of the United States. You are an American citizen. This privilege, from the point of view of the Decalogue, imposes upon you a responsibility. What are you willing to render to America in return for the benefits you receive as a citizen? Is he not a thief, who takes, but does not give? You don't want to be a parasite; you must, therefore, enrich America's culture in some way. You have much to give her. Your heritage is rich with a thousand years of Polish culture. You may draw from that treasure plentifully. A glimpse into the histories of America and Poland will convince you that the educational, religious, and pedagogical culture

---

[38] *Ibid.*, pp. 187-188.
[39] Rev. Walery Jasinski, Ph.D., *Po Co Sie Uczyc Jezyka Polskiego i Kultury Polskiej w Ameryce* (Plymouth: 1941), p. 5.

of Poland is older and wealthier than the American culture. The history of European culture is aware of Poland's five-hundred years of university tradition. Poland was so much in the lead in Physics that within twenty years' time two International Physics Congresses were held in Warsaw. Her achievement in the arts and other sciences: astronomy, chemistry, engineering, theology, literature, music, art and architecture—is equally praiseworthy. Is one, I ask, a useful American citizen who has such gigantic treasures, but who does not want to share them with America? How can one who does not know the treasures of Polish culture himself, because he does not care to study, enrich America without them?[40]

With an extensive knowledge of Polish culture and language, Monsignor Jasinski expected that the children, as useful citizens, would contribute to an enrichment of the intricate and complex culture of America:

> The children in the majority of cases, become accustomed to speak and to think in English; this language becomes their daily language, while the Polish language and Polonism are the synonyms of the festal celebrations during the Polish holidays. Hence, we see children that on the platform have just sung Polish songs or declaimed Polish verses, speaking familiarly with one another in English as they are descending from the platform. These children, later, when they grow up, will speak familiarly with one another, likewise in English, carrying on at the same time a conversation with guests in Polish. Many of them will remain in the mob, but many of them will graduate from universities. In this way there arises the Polish-American intelligent class.[41]

Besides elementary and secondary parochial schools, the Polish immigrants also established institutions of higher learning: Saints Cyril and Methodius Seminary and St. Mary's College at Orchard Lake, Michigan—founded by the Rev. Joseph Dabrowski; Saint Bonaventure College at Pulaski, Wisconsin; Saint John Cantius College at Erie, Pennsylvania; the Academy of the Holy Family of Nazareth at Chicago; and Alliance College at Cambridge Springs, Pennsylvania—founded by the Polish National Alliance.[42]

---

[40] *Ibid.*, p. 6.
[41] Rev. Walery J. Jasinski, *Teksty Dotyczace Asymilacji Polakow w Ameryce* (Detroit: 1944), p. 14.
[42] Joseph A. Wytrwal, *America's Polish Heritage. A Social History of the Poles in America*, pp. 203-209.

Besides these institutions, there was Saint John's College in Philadelphia—founded by Rev. J. A. Godrych, which for eight years, prepared students for universities.[43] In Washington, D.C., the Rev. J. Lehard—founder of the "Congregation of the Fathers of Divine Love"—established Saint John's College for students of Polish descent. It continued for about five or six years, until the death of Father Lehard, when it was discontinued. In Schenectady, New York, the Rev. J. Bobolewski founded a Polish college, but after five years it was closed due to a lack of funds. In 1891, Rev. Vincent Barzynski, C. R., founded St. Stanislaus Kostka College in Chicago.[44]

Soon after the emergence of the Polish National Catholic Church, the need for a seminary to train its priesthood became the foremost concern of the founder, Bishop Francis Hodur. With a modest faculty Bishop Hodur provided the early theological studies in the rectory and hall of the Cathedral. From 1914 to 1917 a modest building generously provided by the Good Shepherd parish in Plymouth, Pennsylvania, served as the Savonarola Theological Seminary.

In 1917, Savonarola Theological Seminary was transferred to the *Straz* building of the Polish National Union located in Scranton, Pennsylvania. The third floor provided ample room for study and lecture halls, with easy access to the ample library of the Polish National Union. With the continued progress of the Polish National Catholic Church, and increased applications of young students, the Seminary administration saw the need for more spacious facilities. A large brick building at the corner of Cedar Avenue and Elm Street, in South Scranton, was purchased in 1926. After extensive remodeling, the building served as the resident seminary of the Polish National Catholic Church. In time it became obvious other facilities were necessary, and an addition was constructed which was dedicated by the Rt. Rev. J. Misiaszek on November 23, 1950.

Savonarola Seminary offers men an opportunity, in a Catholic

---

[43] During World War I, so many were called to the United States Army, or to the Polish army, that the college was discontinued and the courses reduced to agricultural, engineering and mechanical drawing.
[44] Now known as Weber High School.

atmosphere, to achieve for themselves a higher education in the liberal arts, philosophy, the Bible and theology, as well as guidance in their vocations to become priests of the Polish National Catholic Church.

The lack of Polish-Americans in the professions, in the late nineteenth and early twentieth centuries, was principally caused by the pastors of the Polish Roman Catholic parishes, as well as by the isolation of the Polish-American communities. Pastors—who represented privilege, wealth and intelligence under the influence of the feudalistic society of the old world—remained in effect feudal lords.[45] They were concerned with preserving their authority, while insisting on retaining the Polish customs and language without simultaneously integrating them into the American society. They did not stress higher education, and if they had, it was merely in terms of preparing for the religious orders, or skilled trades.[46] They did not encourage the parents to make innumerable sacrifices to save their dollars and deny themselves the necessities and luxuries which would provide their children the opportunity to grasp the golden key of higher education. The Polish-American clergy failed miserably in inculcating the value of a higher education to the cautious and thrifty parents of their parishes, still anxious about surviving future economic depressions.[47] Despite this, a number of Polish-Americans did attain a higher education.

---

[45] The modern terms, "pastor" and "bishop" are derived from the ancient words for shepherds and overseer-guardian; to this day the bishop's staff is a shepherd's crook.

[46] If the number of vocations to the priesthood and sisterhood is any indicator, learning was linked inextricably with the inner life; it provided strength and dignity and a superiority to ephemeral, demeaning externals. By the same token, if the number of professionals is another indicator, the schools produced an astonishingly small number of intellectuals—and even pseudo-intellectuals. The very small number was totally out of all proportion to the size of the Polish immigration.

Many members of the judiciary and attorneys accused the Polish clergy of actually retarding the entry of Polish-Americans into the professions. Ellen Taussig, "The Polish Community Part I: 'We've Come A Long Way. . . ,'" *Buffalo Evening News* (November 13, 1971), p. B-4.

[47] Cut off from the school life of their children—not having an appreciation of education because of a lack of opportunity, and a peasant background at the same time, imbued with the concept that the family was the transmitter of knowledge and that a person succeeded through hard work—the Polish peasant saw no additional value in an advanced education. High schools were viewed as college preparatory schools. If properly informed, the parents would have responded and cooperated for they were most ambitious for their children. Inefficient teaching, large

Dennis F. Pawlak, a winner of a dental scholarship awarded by the Professional and Businessmen's Association of Buffalo—in his paper on the achievement of Polish-American physicians, dentists and lawyers in western New York—made the following observation:

> In the case of the Buffalo Polish people, there is a strong clannishness which tended to frustrate travel from the area . . . indeed if it were not for the proximity of such an establishment (University of Buffalo Dental School), I would venture . . . that the advent of the first Polish-American dentist in Buffalo, would have likely been delayed for another decade.[48]

In 1910, there were five physicians (three dentists and six lawyers) to serve a Polish community of 70,000 in Buffalo. By 1923, there were thirty-one Polish-American physicians, fifteen dentists and twenty attorneys attending a population of 181,000 Polish-Americans in Buffalo—most of whom spoke their Polish language. In 1963, the 300,000 Polish-American population, in Erie County, New York, was represented by ninety physicians and seventy-five dentists of their own national background. By 1970, Polish-American enrollment at the University of Buffalo Dental School (the only one in Western New York) was 3.1 percent for a Polish-American population of thirty percent.[49] Because the public and Catholic Polish-American schools had classes, late entrance, and improper methods of promotion, were other contributory factors.

Currently the Polish-American clergy is aware of this neglect and deficiency. In order to assist any Polish-American student with the talent and desire to pursue a liberal arts education, Saint Mary's College has established a special student aid program entitled "Operation Talent Search," which will seek to reward any student who has an interest in Polish culture and tradition. A special fund of $25,000 has been established for full and partial scholarships for needy students. "Polish Community Lacks Youth at College Level," *Am-Pol Eagle* (February 22, 1973), p. 13.

[48] Ellen Taussig, "The Polish Community Part I: 'We've Come A Long Way . . . ,'" *Buffalo Evening News* (November 13, 1971), p. B-4.

[49] *Ibid.*, p. B-4. According to a recent study of the National Opinion Research Center, Polish-Americans are the lowest white ethnic group in the nation graduating students from college. Only the black and Spanish-speaking communities are lower. Only 5.1% of the Polish-Americans graduated from college in comparison to 76.8% of the Jewish-Americans. Similar statistics from the U.S. Bureau of Census bear this out. In graduate school attendance, the black community surpasses Polish-Americans. "Polish Community Lacks Youth at College Level, Says Educator," *Am-Pol Eagle* (February 22, 1973), p. 13.

little contact with the parents, and because nothing was done to bring the parents into the educational process—in so far as their children were concerned—one can discern the defects of the American public and parochial education systems. The schools left the parents unaffected except in those instances where the children brought home the knowledge they had learned of their new culture. Outside of the hours spent in the classroom, the children were minimally affected by the schools. Thus, while the school acted as an effective agent of cultural transmission, its penetration into the area of social assimilation was negligible. The schools did not significantly increase the generation gap, nor did they severely disrupt family relations. The immigrant community played a far more significant role in shaping family life than either the public or the parochial school. The role of formal education, in assimilating the first generation immigrants, is over emphasized. The schools had no specific programs aimed at re-socializing the children. Upon the dominant cultural pattern of the first generation family, the school appears to have had little effect. In matters of language, dress, habits of hygiene, and customs, the school did exert an influence.

Other Polish Social Organizations

Within the limits of these parishes national ideals grew.[50] Polish life emanated from the parish and then asserted itself socially and culturally. Through the years, varied activities were channeled into working groups which contributed both culturally and materially to the parish. They included social clubs for the preservation of quaint, colorful customs, singers' unions, orches-

---

[50] The salient events around which Polish history centered itself, helped much to enkindle in the masses of Polish immigrants a national idealism and a national consciousness. Polish history for the most part reads as though it were Church history; it is almost impossible to draw the line between one and the other.

Poland's entrance upon the historical scene of Europe dates with the introduction of Christianity about 960 A.D. With the conversion of Lithuania and the ensuing union of the two nations, Poland emerged as the most powerful state on the European continent in the XV and XVI centuries. Its greatest military achievements were associated with religion, e.g., the defeat of the Teutonic Knights of the Cross at Grundwald, in 1410, the routing of the Swedes from Poland, in 1655, the victory of Sobieski over the Turks at Vienna, in 1683. King Jan III merited Poland the glorious title of "The Bulwark of Christianity."

tras, art clubs, theater groups, literary guilds, historical societies, scouts and youth clubs, athletic associations, craft and sewing circles, political leagues, press associations, engineering societies and Red Cross groups. At various times, each fulfilled its respective function. The amateur Polish theater presented Polish plays and performed at national celebrations which commemorated the important events in Poland's history. Besides these activities, the organizations also donated funds to many community and parish projects. Problems which affected the immigrants' own interest or nationality or appeals from Poland for aid in reconstruction after the world wars, or a noble effort such as the purchase of one gram of radium for Mme. Curie's Radium Institute in Warsaw were acted upon locally, regionally and nationally. Funds were raised through a variety of activities, including church bazaars, dinner dances, picnics, raffles, bingo parties, spring fiestas and friendship teas. The *oplatek* dinner was one of the outstanding club traditions.

The Polish churches also fostered the development of "citizens clubs." A typical example is that of "King Casimir the Great Polish Citizens Club."

> This club was formed about six years ago (1914). Its purposes are to naturalize the men of the church, to educate its members in political subjects, and to work for the general improvement of the district, which, in this case, is solidly Polish. The club has about three hundred members, and meets monthly, the active attendance being composed mainly of men not yet naturalized. Meetings are usually conducted in Polish, but two-thirds of the members can now speak English and practically all of them can catch the drift of addresses in English.
>
> To date, upwards of two hundred and fifty men have been naturalized and many more than that have been assisted in taking out their first

---

A celebration and commemoration of any historical event would be incomplete without solemn church services and an appropriate sermon. A specific reverence was associated with the history of Poland. Her glorious past was unfolded to the Polish immigrant, and with it, national idealism, national consciousness also rose to unprecedented heights. To the church, the parish, its clergy and the Polish parochial school were entrusted the roles not only of spiritual and moral guides, but likewise the preservation and the propagation of Poland's history and her greatness. They emerged as the creators of a national idealism among the Polish immigrants in America.

papers. For the past three years, a class in English and civics, meeting twice a week, with an attendance of twenty-five to thirty, has been conducted with a paid instructor. The club also concerns itself with such local matters as garbage collection and the upkeep of streets, and sends frequent delegations to the city hall.[51]

Members, who gained prominence or rose in the professional or political ranks, were referred to as products of a given parish.

Since the Polish immigrants overwhelmingly favored social activities, organizations gradually placed a heavy emphasis on such events. Because of jealousy, rivalry or the excessive ambition of some organizations, each group went its own way to sponsor dances, picnics, banquets and other celebrations. As a result, on the same day, there could be three or more different engagements by as many different Polish organizations. To end this confusion and duplication, and to coordinate their activities in many cities, the leading Polish organizations combined into one brotherhood under the name of the Unted Polish Societies. The venture proved to be popular and successful. In time, the United Polish Societies initiated a campaign to raise funds for the construction of a building to be used by the affiliated societies, and thus the numerous *Dom Polskis*—completely free from the influence of the Polish clergy and parishes—were constructed in various American cities.[52]

In Brooklyn, New York, the Polish Home of Greenpoint—known also as New National Hall and Polish Community Center—was established in 1919. A small group of men—interested in preserving the Polish language, customs and culture—united for the purpose of maintaining a centralized headquarters in order to stimulate and foster interest in civic, cultural, patriotic and social work in the Brooklyn Community. Throughout the years, the Polish Home (certified by New York State as "Dom Incorporated") donated its meeting rooms to many patriotic, educational,

---

[51] John Daniels, *America Via the Neighborhood* (New York: 1920), p. 116.
[52] Events which were sponsored at the parish facilities, had to have the approval of the pastor and were subject to his conditions. The *Dom Polski's* were secular and therefore free from clerical domination or influence.

cultural and religious groups.⁵³ It also sponsored bowling, baseball and soccer teams.⁵⁴

The members of the Polish clergy were especially aroused to see poor Polish immigrant girls exploited economically and drifting away from their religion; in a few cases, even becoming inmates of houses of prostitution. To rectify the situation, they decided to form a voluntary organization of Polish priests who would gather funds to establish a home for the newly arrived Polish immigrant girls. As a result, all Polish priests—residing in the United States—were invited to attend a meeting in New York City, in April 1890. At this meeting, a society was formed and named "Alliance of Polish Priests in America" (Zwiazek Polskich Ksiezy w Ameryce). The members elected a president, a general secretary, and a provincial secretary. The United States was divided into provinces which coincided with the Catholic archdioceses throughout the country. The provincial secretary was made responsible for collecting the contributions from the priests under his jurisdiction. The members of the Alliance agreed to donate a minimum of two dollars, which the provincial secretary collected and forwarded to the general secretary of the Alliance in New York City.

When the necessary funds were raised, the Alliance rented a building and named it "St. Joseph's Charity Organization, Society for Polish Immigrants of New York." On February 19th, 1891, the Society was incorporated under the title of "St. Joseph's Home for Polish Immigrants." Rev. Jacob Wojcik, Rev. John Patrzycki, Rev. Matthew Barabasz, Rev. John Gulcz, and Rev.

---

⁵³ In 1969, the following served on the Board of Directors: Edward Cichon, Janina Gajewska, Zygmunt Leoniak, Wladyslaw Mazur, Jan Mierzwa, Stanislaw Pitula, Antoni Popatowski, Regina Schwab, Wladyslaw Szablowski, and Stefan Zaczek.

⁵⁴ Presently, the following organizations, clubs and unions make Dom Incorporated their headquarters: twelve groups of the Polish National Alliance of Brooklyn; two groups of the Sons of Poland; two groups of the Polish National Alliance of Chicago; M. Konopnicka Polish Educational Society—a Polish Supplementary School; Polish Youth Association; Symfonia Choir; Sea League of America; Polonia Greenpoint Soccer Team; Polish Combatants Association; Polish Falcons Nest No. 618; Moulders and Foundry Workers, Local No. 22; and Greenpoint-Williamsburg Centrala of the Polish National Alliance of Brooklyn.

Hieronim Klimecki were the founders of the new home.[55] According to Murawski, the following were the objectives of the St. Joseph Home: (1) the establishment of a home in New York where all Polish immigrants could be received; (2) to give adequate information regarding settlement or job opportunities to those who request it; (3) to help the Polish immigrants, in every possible way, to become good American citizens.

The first home, rented in Brooklyn, was followed by several other rented homes in New York City, first on Rector Street, then on Morris Street, and next at Greenwich Street. Finally, a home was purchased at 117 Broad Street, in 1897. This was a five-story brick structure on a plot which measured one hundred by twenty-five feet. It contained twenty rooms, and could accommodate sixty immigrants at one time. This site was a good location since it was only a few blocks away from Battery Park, where the immigrants landed after they were released from Ellis Island. Consequently, they had only a short distance to walk in order to reach their new home, which was administered by the Sisters of the Felician Order, under the supervision of the Alliance of Polish Priests in America.

Frequently many of the immigrants were detained at Ellis Island by the authorities because of insufficient funds, incorrect addresses of their relatives and friends, or in the event a child arrived unaccompanied by a parent or guardian. In such instances the St. Joseph representatives were of the utmost service in preventing deportation of new arrivals. If a person arrived on our shores without sufficient funds, he was usually taken to St. Joseph's Home, where he received lodging, food, and a ticket to his ultimate destination.

St. Joseph's Home also co-operated with other immigrant ethnic groups in America. Occasionally, it provided care for Irish and German immigrants, when their own ethnic societies were unable to provide needed accommodations and other services. At the same time, St. Joseph's Home received aid from the German and Irish ethnic organizations when its home was filled

---

[55] Ladislaus Francis Murawski, *The History and Development of St. Joseph's Home for Polish Immigrants of 425 West Forty-Fourth Street, New York* (unpublished project, Fordham University, 1941), p. 13.

to capacity. "Travellers Aid" also cooperated with St. Joseph's Home by referring Polish immigrants there, as well as giving aid to immigrants recommended by the staff of St. Joseph's.

At St. Joseph's Home, the staff also acted as counselors. They cautioned the immigrants not to trust strangers, including those who spoke Polish, unless definite proof was furnished that the individual could be trusted. They made an effort to ascertain the immigrant's capabilities and preferences, in order to advise him where to settle if he had no definite destination. Later, they made inquiries in order to confirm that the immigrants had reached their destinations. They exchanged foreign currency, accepted funds for safe-keeping, and stored or transported baggage and possessions. Not only did they hold the correspondence of arriving immigrants, but also they answered inquiries about relatives and friends in transit. Securing employment for immigrants, who had no friends and who desired to remain in New York, was a very important service of the Home. Many unmarried Polish immigrant girls found themselves in this category. They were invited to stay at St. Joseph's while the representatives made contacts for them in order to secure domestic positions. If a girl was placed in a household, the family employing her was visited, the working contract scrutinized, and the environment considered in order to establish that it was satisfactory. Various employers also were contacted in order to secure employment for male immigrants.

Since St. Joseph's Home was philanthropic, its main concern was to provide service to economically solvent immigrants, while providing free lodging, meals, and aid to needy immigrants. Although some immigrants were able to make small donations, the income from this source was negligible. The main source of revenue for the administration was secured from the Alliance of the Polish Clergy—whose members pledged to contribute at least five dollars annually for its maintenance—and from contributions and bequests from generous benefactors and immigrants who had once received aid and services. The Felician Sisters, to whom the management was entrusted, received no salaries for their services, thereby, considerable saving was effected by this means.

St. Joseph's Home was well known throughout the Polish settlements in the United States. Since the majority of the Polish clergy were members of the Alliance, they frequently referred to their services and objectives in their sermons. Representatives of St. Joseph's Home also addressed various Polish organizations and acquainted the Polish communities with the services which they rendered. The number of immigrants admitted to the St. Joseph's Home fluctuated widely from month to month. In 1907, during the month of November, over 2,000 immigrants were helped. During the entire year some 20,000 immigrants received service.[56]

Eventually the Felician Sisters petitioned to be relieved of the responsibility of managing St. Joseph's Home. They were succeeded by the Sisters of the Immaculate Conception, an order founded by the Rt. Rev. Msgr. Lucian Bojnowski in New Britain, Connecticut. In 1911, when William Williams was Commissioner of Immigration, several regulations were passed concerning immigrants and the agencies interested in their welfare. As a result of the new regulations, the functions of St. Joseph's Home were curtailed. With the decline of immigration from Poland, there was a gradual change in their objectives and eventually it became an establishment for unmarried girls.

When the parish had been organized, the mutual aid societies and the political clubs ceased to be the central and only representative institutions of the community; leadership was now shared with the Polish clergy. Since the priests were more literate and capable of dealing with the American environment, they were in a position to assume the leadership of their countrymen. But the mutual aid societies and the political clubs did not surrender their social functions; they simply shared the initiative in communal matters, and represented the community, along with the clergy and other associations which began to appear in rapid succession.

Polish Newspapers

Besides the benevolent societies and the church, the Polish language press also contributed to the Polish immigrants' welfare and morale. There the immigrants found all that was indispensable for their welfare: wise advice, moral upliftment, patriotism, material assistance, and a true spirit of fraternity for achieving

---

[56] *Ibid.*, p. 22.

success and triumph in America. American papers profoundly influenced all foreign language publications with innovations such as large, bold headlines, editorials, local and national news, special features, poems, photographs, recipes and cartoons. The Polish newspapers also adopted American standards in content and appearance, and featured sensational news stories, often translated directly from American newspapers. To maintain healthy circulations, the Polish newspapers had to provide information that immigrants considered to be both desirable and necessary, and which they could not obtain elsewhere. In the early days of settlement, the Polish language press emphasized news from the various regions of Poland. At the same time that it satisfied the needs of its readers for news of the homeland, it encouraged immigrants to adjust to their American surroundings by acquiring citizenship, to attend school and enter politics. It did not encourage rapid assimilation.

The Polish newspapers also informed the immigrants about trade unions. It explained how important it was for them to be organized, to be united for a cause like higher wages, shorter hours and fair treatment by their employers. The Polish press not only printed realistic stories by well-known writers, but made an effort to bring the reality of Polish life in America into the newspaper. They encouraged the readers to write to the papers about their opinions on current problems or any unusual events in their own lives. The significance of their struggles, achievements and contributions to America were written into the daily news. Because the Polish press concerned itself with the lot of the immigrants—who were lonely in America—it quickly gained their respect and confidence.[57]

---

[57] The following made significant contributions to the Polish language press in America: Wladyslaw Dyniewicz (*Gazeta Polska*), Czeslaw Dziadulewicz (*Kurjer Polski*), Bronislawa A. Eichler (*Dziennik Chicagoski*), Pawel Fox (*Postep*), Franciszek Friedel (*Ameryka-Echo*), Waclaw Gawronski (*Wiadomosci Codzienne*), Waclaw Gasiorowski (*Gornik, Gwiazda Polarna* and *Kurier Nowojorski*), Mikolaj Gmernicki (*Dziennik Dla Wszystkich*), Franciszek Gordon (*Dziennik Chicagoski*), Rev. B. E. Goral (*Nowiny Polskie*), Ludwik Haduch (*Wielkopolanin*), Mieczyslaw Haiman (*Kurier Bostonski*), Rev. Stanislaw Iciek (*Pittsburczanin*), Josef Ilowiecki (*Swoboda*), Franciszek H. Jablonski (*Zgoda*), Jozef J. Jakicic (*Wielkopolanin*), Franciszek Januszewski (*Dziennik Polski*), Tomasz Jasiorkowski (*Nowiny Polskie*), Roman I. Jaworowski (*Echo z Polski*), Wincenty Jozwikowski (*Dziennik Chicago-*

Within the community, the benevolent societies, the Church and the Polish press, sought principally to provide guidance and leadership to the community. Members of each institution or organization believed that their contributions were the most significant and vital to the entire Polish community. The Polish Newspaper played a profound role in the existence of the community's organizations. Generally, the clubs found their budgets too small to propagate their own news. Even those groups that could furnish newsletters for their members, relied upon the Polish language journals and newspapers as a necessary means of communicating more broadly with the general Polish community. Thus, Polish newspapers reported items concerning the establishment of benefits, and news of their elections and operations, lectures, plays, picnics, banquets, balls, and various other social events.

The feeling of ethnic pride showed clearly in the work of the immigrants. History has its many echoes and symbols. Great events, creative artists and great statesmen often are remembered through memorials which keep them fresh in the memory of man. There are such memorials in America. The erection of the King Jagiello monument in Central Park, New York City, or the monuments of Generals Kosciuszko and Pulaski in the nation's capital, or the monuments of Mikolaj Kopernik in Detroit, Chicago and Philadelphia, as well as the celebrations of the anniversary of the May 3, 1791 Constitution—represent the true spirit of Polish nationalism and pride. Through such activities the immigrants gained self-respect and confidence in their glorious past, while they faced a strange and often hostile environment. Polish immigrants learned to respect their homeland's history.

---

ski), Jerzy Kalczynski (*Goniec Polski*), B. S. Kamienski (*Dziennik Dla Wszystkich*), Jozef Karasiewicz (*Dziennik Polski*), Jadwiga Karlowicz (*Glos Polek*), Melchior Kedziora (*Kurier Polski*), Dr. Alojzy Klammer (*Trybuna Polska*), Pawel Klimowicz (*Ameryka-Echo*), Stanislaw A. Klukowski (*Straz*), Franciszek Kmietowicz (*Gwiazda Polarna*), Gregorz Kociel (*Patriota*), Jan Koleski (*Nowiny Minnesockie*), Edward L. Kolakowski (*Kurier Nowojorski*), Kazimierz Kolodziejczyk (*Glos Narodu*), Jan B. Kostrubala (*Dziennik Chicagoski*), Tomasz Kozak (*Robotnik*), Stanislaw Krajewski (*Dziennik Polski*), Jan Krawiec (*Dziennik Zwiazkowy*), Michal Kruszka (*Kurier Polski*), Maria Kryszak (*Glos Polek*), L. L. Krzyzak (*Weteran*), Bronislaw Kulakowski (*Telegram and Wici*), Pawel Kurdziel (*Wiadomosci Codzienneq*, and Ernest Lilian (*Dziennik Ludowy, Gwiazda Polarna* and *Kurier Polski*).

It began to form a significant part of their personal and cultural background, and provided an opportunity to gain an equal footing with Americans and immigrants of other backgrounds who could have shown pride in the country of their origin.

CHAPTER FOUR

Rise of National Fraternal Organizations

> It takes the individual acts to thousands of individuals together to achieve a goal.
> We cannot depend on any one individual; individuals come and go. But we can depend on organizations with lasting ideals.
>
> —Joseph A. Wytrwal[1]
>
> Alien friendship can only aid us; unity shall make us independent and therefore suffices for everything. Let us not reject friendship, let us value it, but let us rely only upon ourselves.
>
> —Henryk Kalussowski

For many years the mutual aid societies, the political clubs, the parishes, the schools, the saloons and the press, were the most important links in the communication process of the Polish social structure in America. These were the basic social institutions in Polish-American communities—the instrumental internal agents reinforcing Polish solidarity. They helped to deal with sickness, loneliness and death. They provided the nuclei around which the newcomers could organize their lives in America: they provided experience in building voluntary organizations; in working for large, impersonal goals; and in writing and reading lively polemical articles. Self-reliance grew into a series of popular beliefs embracing ethnic pride, solidarity, and civic, social and economic fulfillment with advancement for the group through various means of self help.

---

[1] Dr. Joseph A. Wytrwal, "The Polish National Alliance," *Dziennik Polski* (English Edition), (October 3, 1970), p. 4.

RISE OF NATIONAL FRATERNAL ORGANIZATIONS

During periods in which change occurs—and is perceived to be unusually rapid—the tendency to organize new groups becomes particularly apparent. It was during such a time of accelerating change that the impulse emerged to gather all Polish-Americans into a common national body. The Polish-American group was more numerous than in the past, and those who comprised it were in closer contact with each other than the earlier arrivals had been during the previous periods. Their experience as participants in multiple cultures made them particularly aware of change, which afforded them the ideas and the skills to respond to these changes and in turn, aroused in them the need to establish a Polish identity beyond the local and regional community, but certainly within the American social order. The national movement offered to the Polish immigrants a socially recognized expression of their position in and between several worlds, a projection of their own situation, formalizing and legitimizing it. The national movements were channels for outward mobility, and frequently for upward mobility as well. For Polish-Americans who did not participate actively in Polish local organizations, national organizations would serve to define new dimensions of Polish-American life, and to create other ways of enriching the Polish-American community.

Before long the purely local character of the Polish-American communities no longer sufficed, and in the latter part of the nineteenth century, the impulse appeared to gather all Polish-Americans into a common body. As the Polish-American parishes were the center of social and charitable societies, it was not long before a Polish pastor advanced the idea of uniting all of the various Polish-American social and charitable societies into one national organization. This was accomplished by Father Theodore Gieryk of Saint Albertus Parish in Detroit, Michigan. In June 1873, Father Gieryk published his concept in an open letter among various, then existent, Polish weeklies.[2] Father Gieryk was dissatisfied with the existing mutual aid societies, since they were not restricted to Catholics exclusively, and did not stress religion.

---

[2] Karol Wachtel, *Dzieje Zjednoczenia Polskiego Rzym.-Kat. w Ameryce* (Chicago: 1913), pp. 6-63.

Conditions were opportune for such a scheme to succeed since it, first, bolstered up the peasants' morale (*Lud Zbawi Polske*) by awakening an interest in their own national culture, and secondly, it appealed to the priests and leaders of the community, who could convince the immigrants that the national organizations would cater to their individual needs.

Seeing the wisdom in Father Gieryk's idea, John Barzynski, editor of the Polish weekly newspaper, *The Pilgrim,* his brother, Father Vincent Barzynski, Peter Kiolbassa and Joseph Gloskowski, together, took up Father Gieryk's idea to form one large national organization which would promote religious unity among the Poles. They arranged for a meeting to be held in Detroit, on October 3, 1873, for the purpose of discussing how Father Gieryk's idea could be best executed. Interested individuals in forming such an organization were invited.

At this meeting, Father Gieryk was nominated chairman, and John Barzynski was appointed secretary of the new organization, named *Zjednoczenie Polskie Rzymsko-Katolickie w Ameryce* (The Polish Roman Catholic Union in America). Every member of the organization would pay $1.00 in dues. This revenue would be utilized to attain the objectives of the organization. It was also proposed that a National Congress of Polish-Americans should be held in Chicago on October 14, 15, and 16, 1874. John Barzynski, Peter Kiolbassa, Joseph Gloskowski and Father Gieryk were appointed to act as the Pre-Convention Committee.

It was at the 1874 Congress that the foundations of the Polish-Roman Catholic Union were laid. Representatives from thirty-nine social and benevolent societies had participated and elected the following officers: Reverend Theodore Gieryk—President, Peter Kiolbassa—Vice President, John Barzynski—Secretary, August Rudzinski—Treasurer, and Reverend Joseph Barzynski—Chaplain. A Board of Directors, composed of six priests and five laymen, were also elected as part of the Executive Board. One of the clergy to be elected was Reverend Joseph Dabrowski, Founder of the SS. Cyril and Methodius Seminary in America. The objectives of the new organization—as defined, in 1874, at the National Congress, in Chicago—were: (1) to uphold the national spirit of Polish-Americans; (2) to help them preserve the

Faith of their forefathers; (3) to maintain in the youth a lively interest in matters Polish; and (4) to aid in building and improving parochial schools in the United States.³ The insurance program was not introduced until twelve years later. The 1886 Convention decided to issue insurance policies. However, it took a full year to establish a definite insurance program.

Since the original mutual aid societies offered a number of insurance policies, the Polish Roman Catholic Union decided, during these early stages of organization, to leave insurance alone, and instead to concentrate on the ideals of the organization. The following means were to be taken to attain the objectives of their organization: (1) the establishment of educational institutions for higher learning; (2) the establishment of a Polish bank for the Polish population in America; (3) the establishment of a convent for women; (4) the establishment of a teachers' seminary; (5) the establishment of libraries; and (6) the establishment of a Polish hospital. The convention also considered the establishment of an orphanage, as well as to offer help and care for newly arrived immigrants.⁴

The newly formed national organizations associated with the Polish Roman Catholic Union, supported the Polish clergy, who desired to preserve the integrity of the Polish parishes. As the number of Polish immigrants increased after the Civil War, the Poles, especially the priests, complained of the Irish control of the Catholic Church in America. The Irish dominated Catholic hierarchy, in America, opposed the establishment of separate Polish parishes; they also regarded the study of Poland's past and the cultivation of the Polish language as a bulwark against the tides of assimilation which preserved the identity of the Polish people. To prevent absorption by the Irish, the Polish priests encouraged the study of Polish history and language. Knowledge of their cultural heritage not only strengthened national Polish consciousness, but also raised the prestige of its immigrants.

Even though the representatives of the Polish Roman Catholic Union decided to hold annual meetings, they gradually grew

---
³ Dr. Karol Wachtl, *Polonja w Ameryce* (Philadelphia: 1944), pp. 164-165.
⁴ Mieczyslaw Haiman, *Zjednoczenie Polskie Rzymsko-Katolickie w Ameryce* (Chicago: 1948), pp. 32-33.

inactive and without influence. The organization represented a vague association of Polish priests and parish leaders who, in turn, represented their respective parishes. The parishes formed the foundation of the national organization and enabled the priests and lay leaders to take a far more active political role than otherwise could have been possible. But each parish was essentially a territorial institution with all of its activities concentrated upon the local Polish-American community. Besides the dissatisfaction with the Irish dominated Catholic hierarchy, there was a lack of real national issues which were common to all Polish-American parishes. Father Barzynski, with all his influence and ability, could not even induce all of the parishes in Chicago, to form one social body; their solidarity never demonstrated any cooperation other than that of a few public manifestations of a national character.

Another leader, who pointed out the need for uniting all existing Polish-American societies in the United States into one organization, was Agaton Giller, in 1879. A Polish exile and former member of the National Polish government, during the January 1863 Uprising, he lived in Switzerland. Out of his deep concern for the future of the Poles in partitioned Poland came his article, "The Organization of Poles in America" (*O Organijacji Polakow w Ameryce*) which appeared in Polish newspapers in Poland and in Chicago's *Gazeta Polska*.[5] In this article— addressed to Poles living in the United States, numbering 500,000 at the time, according to the Polish press—Giller strongly urged the Polish immigrants to unite into one powerful organization in order to promote the cause of Poland, and foremost was the restoration of her independence. Among the additional aims of the proposed organization, he mentioned: the revitalization of the masses of Polish immigrants with the Polish national spirit; the checking of the losses among the Polish immigrants who no longer felt an attachment either to their Fatherland or to their native language; the possibility of exerting greater influence on American political life through the medium of a nation-wide union of

---

[5] Stanislaw Osada, *Historia Zwiazku Narodowego Polskiego* (Chicago: 1957), I, pp. 97-108.

Poles; gaining a greater opportunity for their economic improvement through concerted action; and the possibility of serving as spokesman between the Polish and American cultures.

With his acute vision, Giller gave the immigrants not only a concrete purpose, but also a means to fulfill itself through a consciousness that the Polish immigrants—in spite of their dispersal throughout the United States—could become a political force, if they only would use their strength for the redemption of Poland. Like all great political thinkers, Giller grasped the profound, yet simple, secret: that the dormant Polish national spirit submerged among the Polish immigrants could be converted into a source of strength with fortitude, of initiative and heroism, if it was to be linked to the idea of redeeming and liberating partitioned Poland. No people could be saved except through their own initiative, and the Polish problem could be resolved only by the Poles. So Giller pleaded.

In response to Giller's plea, on February 14, 1880, Julius Andrzejkowicz invited Julius Szajnert, Julius Lipinski, Vincent Domanski, John Biadynski, Antoni Wojczynski, John Nepomucyn Papielinski, John Biachowski, Theophil Kucielski, and Peter Beczkiewicz, to attend a meeting in Philadelphia.[6] There they discussed, not only the famine that existed at the time in the Polish province of Silesia, but they also discussed and studied the political patterns of European countries so that they too, in an opportune time, might organize a "Young Poland Movement" which would liberate partitioned Poland from Russia, Prussia and Austria. They believed that the Polish immigrants would eventually become a force strong enough to exert a decisive influence in world politics, if it could be united to a common cause. Andrzejkowicz's letter, dated February 18, 1880, contained the following observation:

> "What influence may be elicited upon a nation was shown by Mazzini's genius in his idea of creating a unified and independent Italy;

---

[6] At that time there was a famine in the Silesian province, in Poland, and some of the Poles who were living in Philadelphia were raising a relief fund to aid their countrymen in Europe. While canvassing for this effort, some of the members became acquainted with Julius Andrzejkowicz, a prosperous business man, who was a partner in a paint and dye business.

to him more than to Garibaldi does Italy owe its independence. He awakened the desire of unity and independence, the accomplishment of which Cavour, the statesman, and Garibaldi, a man of action and hero, had realized."[7]

In a series of questions, Andrzejkowicz urged his fellow citizens, the Polish immigrants in the United States, to form national organizations.[8]

"What is the status of the Polish immigrant in America? Isn't America far safer than England? Aren't we strong and independent? Do we not have freedom of speech, press and assembly? Why, then couldn't we form national organizations with a strong central government endowed with unlimited confidence and power?"[9]

At the Philadelphia meeting, Julius Andrzejkowicz stressed the necessity for all Polish organizations in America to unite into an alliance or federation under the name of the "Polish National Alliance" (*Zwiazek Narodowy Polski*). It was understood that each society that joined this alliance would retain its individual character. The plan of the proposed organization was patterned somewhat on the existing federal system of government; like each state, each society was to be recognized as a distinct and separate entity with a voice and a right of representation in the central organization, in order to render possible a united effort in any particular emergency, an appeal was directed to all existing organizations to express their opinions of the proposed plan, and to indicate whether they would participate. This appeal read in part.

Compatriots, here we have found a haven of refuge; here we have freedom of association, of the press and of speech. Though we have numbers, we lack strength, for like the grains of dust, we are scattered and isolated, we are nothing, powerless to assist ourselves or to render a service to the country. Gathered together and organized in a

---

[7] Stanislaw Osada, *Historja Zwiazku Narodowego Polskiego* (Chicago: 1905), p. 111.

[8] Wladyslaw Dyniewicz also encouraged the formation of a national organization. In his article which appeared in *Gazeta Polska* in Chicago, on May 13, 1875, he urged the Polish organizations in Chicago, New York, Washington, D. C., Philadelphia, San Francisco and Milwaukee, to establish a national organization.

[9] Osada, *Historja Zwiazku Narodowego Polskiego*, p. 111.

powerful alliance, not only shall we uplift ourselves morally and materially, but we shall create a mighty power which we shall be able to use for the good of our native land. What is more important, we shall create the power of public opinion, which today is mightier than armament or the bayonet, an opinion predicated on the precepts of liberty, equality, and fraternity.[10]

Immediately thereafter an open invitation was published in the Polish press asking all Polish-American societies to join the proposed association. Societies from Illinois, California, Pennsylvania, Michigan, New York and Wisconsin responded immediately. After the completion of the first draft of the Constitution, Juliusz Andrzejkowicz designated September 20, 1880, as the date for the first National Convention of the Polish National Alliance. The place chosen was Chicago. The date of this appeal, which was the first official act of the organization, has established it as the date of the founding of the Polish National Alliance. The platform—hammered out through the interplay of vigorous minds—was incorporated into the constitution of the new organization. It is interesting and enlightening to read the purpose of the Polish National Alliance:

1. To lay the foundation of institutions for the material and moral development of the Polish element in the United States through the medium of an iron fund, which shall be permanent and undivided property of the Alliance, is hereby acknowledged as essential, to the category of institutions of this character shall belong immigration homes, schools and all institutions of general learning, libraries, homes of shelter, and commercial institutions located in acceptable places.
2. To protect the interests of Polish immigrants.
3. To promote the political establishment of Polish immigrants as citizens of the United States through the medium of the official publication of the Alliance, and through entry into relations with the American press for the purpose of protecting our interests. Every person becoming a member of the Alliance shall seek to become a citizen of the United States.
4. To provide fraternal assistance to the members of the societies

---

[10] Casimir E. Midowicz, "The Polish National Alliance," *Poland Journal of Commerce and Industry*, VII (August, 1927), p. 489.

comprising the Alliance, based on insurance, and obtained by means of compulsory assessment determined by the convention.
5. To sponsor the arrangement of patriotic affairs commemorating national memorial days, and to urge the discharge of duties dictated by national honor.
6. To advocate moderation and temperance in the use of alcoholic stimulants.
7. To guarantee the freedom of religious convictions, the P.N.A. adherring to the position that religious matters constitute the concern of the Holy Apostolic See, does not regard it proper to interfere with or constitute the same as a pre-requisite to membership to its ranks.[11]

In this way the organization was founded, and its course of action drawn. According to its charter, the Polish National Alliance was created for cultural, educational and humanitarian purposes, specifically in relation to the Polish immigrants in the United States. The comparatively rapid expansion of the organization was made possible by an efficient propaganda machine, and by editors and organizers who knew how to play on the sentiments of the Polish immigrants.[12]

From the objectives adopted by the convention it was clear in the minds of the perceptive founders of the Polish National Alliance that one of their aims must be an unqualified support of education and the realm of scholarship. They fully realized that intellectual poverty would impede their efforts at advancement on all fronts. The desire for a propitious climate in which the children of new immigrants could be reared found voice in the first issue of *Zgoda,* the official publication of the Polish National Alliance. It posed the question: "Shall the Poles wear the crown

---

[11] The Convention adopted the policy of non-Denominationalism. This it did in order to be consistent with the Articles of the Polish Constitution of May 3, 1791, and the American Constitution, both of which respect their citizens' choice of religion. Midowicz, *op. cit.,* pp. 489-490.

[12] Cultural and political leaders, various cultural organizations, and the foreign language press—although trying to keep immigrants loyal to the old values—have not been conspicuously successful in their efforts to impart its enthusiasm to the masses. We have only to read the accounts which the leaders gave in their own press, of the difficulties they have maintaining in America the language and the Polish traditions in order to realize how glacial and wholly irresistible was the trend toward a common language, a common life, and a common tradition for all the peoples in the United States.

of American citizenship with dignity? Shall they stand on equal footing with the Germans, the French, the English, in the professions, in literature, in commerce, in politics, in the crafts?" And it replied: "The field is open to all. The most able will be victorious. . . . The emigration then will rise and be an equal in the family of the Christian and enlightened nations. It will be a credit to itself and to the nation."

The Polish National Alliance in its first constitution professed "obedience to the Roman Catholic Faith, since that is the faith of the vast majority of the Polish nation," but further committed itself to a program of "toleration toward all creeds in the spirit of Poland's ancient constitution." Since its intention was to unify the Polish-Americans outside of the church—independent of religious interests—the Polish National Alliance needed a general concept or central purpose in contradistinction to the theocratic purpose of the clergy. Polish patriotism fulfilled this function. The Polish National Alliance could counterbalance the power of religion only if it found response from the masses. This it accomplished by changing the mere racial solidarity of the Polish-Americans to political idealism.[13] It initiated national celebrations of several significant historic Polish anniversaries: centennial of the May 3, 1791 Constitution, the Bicentennial of Sobieski's victory at Vienna in 1683, and the Kosciuszko Year which stirred a chord in every exiled Pole's heart.[14]

The overwhelming majority of the Polish National Alliance was Catholic; however, many clerical leaders were dissatisfied with the new national organization which, by its very existence as a secular organization, constituted a threat to the exclusive supremacy of the clergy who wished to maintain their exclusive representation in positions of leadership.[15] In addition, the Polish National Alliance also became the refuge of rebellious and dis-

---

[13] Socialists, however, were barred. All official religious services were to be conducted according to Catholic rites. Successive conventions gradually eliminated all reference to religion; thus, the bar to the admission of Socialists was removed. Anarchists and criminals are still excluded. See also Felix Thomas Seroczynski, "Poles in the United States," *The Catholic Encyclopedia*, XII (New York: 1914), p. 208.

[14] Joseph A. Wytrwal, *America's Polish Heritage. A Social History of the Poles in America*, pp. 191-211.

senting local groups. Seeing this danger, not only the Order of the Resurrectionists, but the majority of the secular priests and lay leaders—whose interests were connected with those of the clergy—took a definite stand against the Polish National Alliance. A pretext for the opposition was easily found, for the organizers and founders of the Polish National Alliance—though not in any way anti-religious—showed liberal and democratic tendencies which were interpreted as a threat to the Church. The Alliance was intended to include Poles without distinction of religious denomination. Even before the national organization was actually formed, it was denounced as masonic, heretical and socialistic. Even an American bishop was induced to excommunicate the organization and its adherents. The strong resentment against giving secular representatives equitable representation in positions of leadership led to the establishment of a rival organization. A few months after the Polish National Alliance was established, Father Vincent Barzynski, with several other priests, revived the Polish Roman Catholic Union.[16]

Father Barzynski, a member of the Order of the Resurrection Fathers, desired to create a formal national organization of all the pastors and lay leaders of the Polish-American parishes. The placement of Resurrection Fathers, as pastors in the Polish-American parishes, would assure the control of the Polish-American parishes by one Polish influential institution, which could create a unified body of Polish-American clergy outside the administrative Catholic hierarchy of America. But the number of Polish-American parishes grew so rapidly that the Resurrection Order could furnish only a minority of the priests who were required. Furthermore, the American Catholic clergy opposed the

---

[15] The misgivings which the Polish clergy had concerning the Polish National Alliance were not totally unfounded. Among the first members of the Polish National Alliance were political refugees from Poland, after the abortive insurrections, with a sprinkling of cultured Poles, referred to as the "intelligentsia." These were known for their indifference to Catholicism. Many of their children have lost their Polish nationalism along with their faith.

[16] Father Barzynski also founded St. Stanislaus College, in Chicago, in 1891. At one time it numbered fifteen professors and 210 students. He also gave the Poles their first Catholic newspaper, *Gazeta Katolicka*, their first daily paper, *Dziennik Chicagoski*. Likewise, he is responsible for forming the first teaching corps of Polish nuns.

RISE OF NATIONAL FRATERNAL ORGANIZATIONS

growth of the Resurrection Order as a foreign organization, primarily dependent on its superiors in Rome, and only, secondly, on the local bishops. The secular Polish clergy also resented the manifest theocratic tendencies of the Resurrection Fathers. The failure of the projected theocratic government forced the Polish-American clergy to realize the necessity for supplementing the parish system by a semi-democratic national organization whose special function would be to uphold and propagate—in all communities—the principle of Polish self preservation as the supreme standard of social activity, while idealizing the parish system as the only instrument worthy of preservation. In this venture, the secular clergy was willing to aid Father Barzynski and his Order.

The parish system was perfectly satisfactory to the Polish clergy as long as they were left in complete control of their parishes. They saw a need of communicating with one another, and even of forming (if possible) a regular theocratic government of the Polish-American communities in order to control better all of the unruly elements within, while defending the autonomy of the incipient Polish-American parishes against interference from without, especially from the American clergy. But, at first, they did not see any need of a direct unification of the Polish-American communities into a national unit. The patriotic motives, which influenced the initiators of the Polish National Alliance, did not appeal to the Polish clergy or the Roman Catholic Church in America and Poland. The Polish clergy was willing to work for the preservation of the cultural integrity of the Polish-American communities; language, religion, mores, but would not participate at all in the political life of Poland or any political direction whatever. This myopic and selfish view was their undoing, but also of the Poles as well.

Rather than allow the Polish-American community to lose its identity in the American milieu, the Polish Roman Catholic Union leaders instinctively threw up protective barriers. They preferred the preservation of the cultural identity of the Polish-American community for their own ends, not for the benefit of Poland. And unfortunately, Polish culture was given in limited doses. Thus they discouraged and banned activities that could serve as vehicles for American encroachment. In the struggle for national identity, the leaders were also unconsciously inclined not to encourage the participation of Poles in American institutions. But to defend the autonomy of the Polish-American parishes against interference from the Catholic American hierarchy—particularly from the Irish clergy—and to preserve the integrity of the Polish parishes from absorption by the Irish dominated Catholic Church hierarchy in America, political motives and goals were gradually added as objectives of the Polish Roman Catholic Union in America.[17]

The Polish-American clergy saw clearly that in order to hold a strong position in its relation with the Irish-dominated Catholic Church—of which they were formally a part—they would have to reveal social power based upon the will of the immigrant masses. They would have to demonstrate that they had the backing of the Polish immigrant. The Polish Roman Catholic Union —nominally a lay institution, only unofficially controlled by priests—could easily be used to promote the interests of the Polish-American clergy, not only vis-a-vis the American bishops, but even in Rome. Even with these objectives, the Polish clergy should have cooperated with the Polish National Alliance. Beyond doubt, the Polish priests were first Catholic and secondly Polish.

The Polish-American clergy—many of whom were recruited from Europe—wished their people to remain complacent, loyal and dependent on them. They tolerated participation in American life, provided their members participated as Poles. They endorsed, in the form of social recognition, any activities by which their members brought parish recognition to American circles.

---

[17] During the long period of Poland's subjugation, scarcely was any institution left to unite the Polish people, save their church. In their depressed state they came to look upon the Roman Catholic Church, in Poland, as the Israelites did toward the Tabernacle in the wilderness. It was, therefore, a rude shock to the Poles on arriving in the United States, to find that their church—which they had almost identified with Poland itself—was dominated by a hierarchy and people, largely Irish in background, with a "nationalism" fully as church-centered as their own. Where Irish priests and bishops were in control of parishes whose membership was largely Polish, clashes were certain to occur. Since, in Poland, their clergy had been usually appointed through the influence of the landed gentry, they resented seeing these appointments and the control of the church property kept wholly out of Polish hands. Thus, three defections from the Roman Catholic Church occurred between 1890 and 1900.

They assumed that each Polish-American is dependent upon the recognition he receives from the Polish-American community and personally appreciates it most. Polish-Americans were to be impersonal in their relations with the American community, while purely personal in their relation with the Polish-American community. They frowned on all forms of participation which tended to incorporate the Polish-American into American primary groups which would draw individuals away from the Polish-American community: marriage, personal friendship, and all kinds of intercourse implying direct personal solidarity. Consequently, the clergy did not approve the national propaganda promulgated by the Polish National Alliance, and disapproved the participation of Polish-American parishioners in American institutions.[18]

The Polish-American, who desired to become identified with either organization, was often caught in a dilemma. If he joined the Polish Roman Catholic Union, the members of the Polish National Alliance would say he was not a true patriot; if he joined the Polish National Alliance, the members of the Polish Roman Catholic Union would accuse him of being untrue to his religion.[19] Father Kruszka described the bitter factionalism between the two groups:

> For some time neither Catholics nor Poles existed in America, but only Unionists (PRCU) or Alliancists (PNA); whoever was not a member of the Alliance, the Polish National Alliance did not regard as a Pole; while whoever was not a member of the Polish Roman Catholic Union, the PRCU did not regard as a Catholic.[20]

Father Kruszka saw certain advantages in this strife.

---

[18] Energetically and steadily the Polish Roman Catholic Union had counteracted all attempts of Americanization, regardless of the scourge. When Bishop Eis, of Marquette, Michigan, issued, in 1901, an order to the effect that religion must be taught in English in all parochial schools, the Poles, in particular, protested. The Polish Roman Catholic Union was one of the first to raise its voice in protest. Wachtl, *Dzieje Zjednoczenia Polskiego Rzym.-Kat. w Ameryce*, pp. 29-30.

[19] To be absolutely secure, many joined both organizations. It is unfortunate that no Pole appeared on the scene to resolve this dilemma. He would have been the greatest Polish-American.

[20] Ks. Waclaw Kruszka, *Historja Polska w Ameryce* (Milwaukee: 1905), IV, p. 32.

This rivalry between the PRCU and PNA has been called "fratricide." But we must concede that this very fight brought about a rebirth, a feeling of unity, love of the fatherland, a desire for education, need for the press, libraries, celebrations, . . . among the immigrant Poles in America. . . . There is nothing so bad that it does not result in some good.[21]

During the early years of strife between the two organizations, each was disposed to duplicate the other's activities, to denounce the other's way, and to claim total support for itself.[22]

These early years of contention, however, left no obviously visible scars. Most of the ephemeral writings reflected heat rather than light; it accustomed the Polish immigrants to read and write on controversial issues. Contrary to Father Kruszka's observation, it brought about wasted energy that could have been applied constructively towards achieving goals that would have improved the Poles' station in life, influence and prestige. Instead the Pole became an oddity not desired by America, except as a source of cheap labor whereby the wealthy industrialists and capitalists profited from his sweat and toil.

Among none of the other Polish-American organizations had such a battle raged so fiercely. Since 1898, as generation succeeded generation, and the basis for its antipathy grew dimmer, the feud mellowed to more or less good-natured rivalry. Nevertheless these violent decades were wasted when something good could have been achieved, and Poles could have left their imprint on American society. Today, the magnificent Catholic churches which they built are falling into ruin or being razed as the Polish population moves away to the suburbs.

Since then, also the differences between the two organizations have grown more blurred. In fact, the following decades witnessed their cooperation in many of the Polish-American projects. Patterns of mutual support were established between the two organizations, for the members of one organization felt obliged to attend a fund-raising card party or banquet of the other, since

---

[21] Edmund G. Olszyk, *The Polish Press in America* (Milwaukee: 1940), p. 10.
[22] Wytrwal, *America's Polish Heritage. A Social History of the Poles in America*, pp. 191-235.

their own organization has recently held a similar event. The exchange of services or money, between the two organizations, may have had little real value; yet, they were visible emblems of social solidarity; the act of giving evoked latent feelings of unity and independence. This cohesiveness, between the two organizations, was further cemented through interrelated memberships.

The Polish National Alliance (headquartered in Chicago) is the largest fraternal insurance society of America of Polish descent. It possesses assets of over $145 million, and over $332 million in insurance policies. The membership stands at over 330,000 in 1,405 lodges scattered throughout nearly every state of the union.[23]

Since its inception, in 1873, the Polish Roman Catholic Union has grown to be one of the largest fraternal organizations in the United States, whose members can be found in thirty-seven states. At the end of its first fifty years of existence it boasted of 1,036 lodges, with the majority in Illinois, Michigan, New York and Pennsylvania. In 1950, there were 1,095 lodges in existence, the largest amount in the history of the organization. In 1954, the number of lodges totaled 1,053 and 1,041 in 1955. Membership in the lodges, in 1954, totaled 176,850 and 175,682, in 1955.[24]

---

[23] The Polish National Alliance conducts many special activities for its members. Its juvenile department is making an active effort to build a great reserve of youth, preparing them for loyal membership, not only in the Alliance, but also as citizens of the United States.

The fraternal also maintains Alliance College in Cambridge Springs, Pennsylvania, a four-year, fully accredited co-educational college where members may obtain a college education at nominal cost. Libraries—where the latest books may be had by members without cost—have also been established. Educational loans are granted to members and their children, enabling them to obtain an education at any university of their choice.

[24] At present, the Polish Roman Catholic Union grants scholarships to needy students desirous of studying at Orchard Lake, Michigan, or other institutions of higher learning; sponsors Polish youth clubs with the intention of instilling and preserving in their members an appreciation for the language and culture of Poland; and publishes the bi-weekly, Narod Polski (Polish People).

It also maintains the Polish Museum of America, located in Chicago. The collections in the Polish Museum include more than 20,000 different titles in the library, over 2,000 periodical titles (with many complete files); more than 500 maps; 2,000 photographs; 1,000 lineal feet of primary source materials; 6,000 manuscripts and documents; 50,000 clippings and booklets and circulars; 2,000 phonograph records; 1,000 slides and films, and 12,000 pieces now on exhibit or in storage. This vast assortment of materials, almost all relating to Polish culture or Polish-American

The spread of the spirit of independence occasioned the first Polish-American Congress, which was held in Buffalo, in 1896. The second was also held here, in 1901, while the third was held in Pittsburgh, in 1904. These Congresses sought to find remedies for the sad conditions then prevailing in the Polish-American communities. However, the efforts of the promoters were largely confined to inducing the Holy See to appoint them Polish-American bishops.[25]

During these decades, Polish-American women also formed national societies. Patriotism was not a monopoly for men. Around 1890, efforts were made to organize the Polish-American women on a national scale, not through local religious circles, but through one large organization comparable in strength and membership to a Polish-American male society. The first such attempt was the *Grosz Polski*, a society of women organized to buy land in Prussian Poland for distribution among Polish families residing in those regions. The history of *Grosz Polski* was unusually brief. It lasted barely six months, and during its brief life it failed to raise enough money to obtain, for its Chicago headquarters, the necessary office supplies.

The Polish Union of the United States of North America (*Unia Polska w Stanach Zjednoczonych Polnocnej Ameryki*) was established on September 22, 1890, in St. Paul, Minnesota. The organization had its beginnings actually, in 1889, when the clergy of the Polish National Alliance frowned on the idea of

---

history were gathered from all parts of the world. The affairs of the Polish Museum of America are being administered by a Board consisting of 56 directors, 38 of whom are members of the Executive Board of the Polish Roman Catholic Union of America.

The Polish Roman Catholic Union also affords its members an extensive athletic program with emphasis on softball and bowling. In addition, it commemorates religious and national anniversaries. In 1955, it celebrated the 25th Anniversary of the Miracle of the Vistula. In addition to all of this, the organization aids its lodges to set up Catholic Scouting Programs for the youth in their respective Polish-speaking parishes.

[25] A fourth Congress—differing radically from the three preceding ones, since its spirit was purely secular—convened under the auspices of the Polish National Alliance on the occasion of the unveiling of the Pulaski and Kosciuszko monuments in Washington, D. C. on May 12, 1910. The Congress—which was ignored by the clergy and the Catholic organizations—declared itself in favor of educational institutions for American youth of Polish descent who would be utterly removed from "clerical" influence.

permitting non-Roman Catholics to qualify for administrative positions in the Polish National Alliance. Seeing that their efforts to prevent this were fruitless, they began considering the possibility of establishing a new organization which would not only unite all Polish-American societies, but would also embody the Catholicism of the Polish Roman Catholic Union and the Nationalists of the Polish National Alliance. This objective became a reality when Father Dominic Majer organized Society Number One of the Polish Union in St. Paul, Minnesota.

The objectives of the Polish Union as outlined in Article II of its Constitution was to: (1) offer its members such insurance policies as ordinary life, twenty-year payment life, twenty-year endowment, endowment at sixty-five, ten-year endowment and fifteen-year endowment; (2) maintain a fund for the promotion of patriotic and educational projects; (3) strive for the moral, religious, and material improvement of Poles living in America; (4) commemorate national anniversaries; (5) instill a deeper patriotism to the United States; (6) develop, in Polish youth, a love and respect for its forefathers; (7) strengthen in all Union members a filial obedience to the Roman Catholic Church and (8) inspire, in the training of Polish youth, to be good and useful citizens of the United States. In 1896, the Union transferred its headquarters from St. Paul to Buffalo, and, in 1906, to Wilkes-Barre, Pennsylvania.

The 27th national convention of the Polish Union of the United States of North America (held in Chicago, September 20-23, 1970) placed great emphasis on youth and its future within the framework of the organization. The 149 delegates attending the conclave, representing 17,000 members in 13 states, voted unanimously to establish a youth department and immediately adopt a program which would attract all age brackets of youth. They also agreed to appoint a coordinator "to foster and coordinate activities for the youth and young people on a natural level." In order to accelerate the growth of the fraternal, the convention approved the following projects: (1) donate books on Polish subjects in the English language to various public libraries; (2) organize youth forums, classes in the Polish language, inaugurate sports programs, dancing classes and essay contests;

(3) set up an information bureau which would publish more literature, pamphlets and booklets expanding the benefits of belonging to a fraternal insurance society; and (4) expand the scholarship program of financial loans to members.

In the middle of the 1890's, several Milwaukee societies belonging to the Polish Roman Catholic Union, became dissatisfied with the general aims of the Polish Roman Catholic Union. The first organizational meeting took place in the parish hall of St. Hyacinth's Church. A joint meeting, of all societies involved, was finally held on November 18, 1895, at St. Stanislaus' parish hall. At this meeting the Polish Association in America (*Stowarzyszenie Polakow w Ameryce*) was established. Since that time, the Polish Association in America has grown slowly, but steadily, in the states of Wisconsin, Michigan, Illinois and Ohio. Total membership, as of 1955, numbered 7,097 at 150 lodges. In 1969, the organization numbered 5,348 members.

The Alliance of Poles in America (*Zwiazek Polakow w Ameryce*) was first established in October, 1895, and bore the title of "Alliance of Poles of Ohio." The beginning of the organization was slow and difficult. Nevertheless, the Alliance was incorporated in the State of Ohio on December 22, 1895. The aims of the Alliance are to: (1) foster unity among Americans of Polish and other Slavic extraction professing the Roman Catholic faith; (2) provide members with life insurance; (3) maintain cultural ties with Poland; (4) uphold a spirit of unity and cooperation with other Polish patriotic, educational, and social organizations; (5) protect immigrants from exploitation; (6) awaken in Polish youth the desire to study and love the language and culture of Poland; (7) publish a news weekly; and (8) observe the Alliance's Anniversary of founding on September 22 of each year. Besides issuing insurance and publishing the weekly newspaper, *Alliancer* (*Zwiazkowiec*), the organization also sponsors the Ignatius Paderewski Society, the Alliance Ladies' Guild, besides annual social functions. The home office is located in Cleveland, Ohio.

The Polish Women's Alliance in America (*Zwiazek Polek w Ameryce*) was founded in Chicago, in 1898, at a time when the universal movement for emancipation of women was being widely

RISE OF NATIONAL FRATERNAL ORGANIZATIONS 157

debated and promulgated. Although other fraternal organizations admitted women to their membership, it was not until the Polish Women's Alliance was founded and organized that certain equality rights—on the same level with the male groups—were granted to the women of those organizations.

The Polish Women's Alliance had a very modest beginning. Stefania Chmielinska, Maria Rokosz and Gabriella Laudon met to organize a club which would unite the Polish-American women of Chicago for the effective pursuance of patriotic and cultural ideals, and for the provision of mutual aid in times of need. The first president was Stefania Chmielinska. The original group consisted of eleven members. Its first assets amounted to eleven dollars. As membership in the club grew, it was decided to make its scope national by forming chapters in various cities and states, with its headquarters remaining in Chicago. Following the recommendation of its first Convention (held June 12, 1900, in Pulaski Hall on Chicago's South Side), the club was reorganized and its official title became the Polish Women's Alliance in America. The first administration was as follows: Genowefa Zolkowska, president; Stefania Chmielinska, vice-president; Lucja Wolowska, secretary; Maria Rokosz, treasurer. The membership, at that time, totaled 264. This small group of women laid the foundation for one of the largest and most influential Polish-American Women's associations, not only in the United States, but in the world.

The aims and objectives of the Polish Women's Alliance are to: (1) keep the Polish-American women ever mindful of their cultural and patriotic heritage; (2) offer opportunities for higher education to Polish-American youth; (3) provide financial assistance for the aged and those hospitalized; and (4) work for the liberation of partitioned Poland.

The Constitution of the Polish Women's Alliance of America acknowledges three categories of members: (1) honorary members; (2) insured members; and (3) the uninsured. The title of honorary members is bestowed upon women who have become outstanding in scientific, literary, artistic, national or social arenas. The following were elected honorary members of the organization, and became their pride and joy: Maria Konopnicka,[26] Helena Modrzejewska, Eliza Orzeskowa, Helena Paderewska, Marie Sklodowska-Curie and Maria Rodziewicz. Many areas in the building of the Polish Women's Alliance recall these great individuals.[27]

---

[26] In 1885 Maria Konopnicka in her writings became the protagonist of the Polish peasants, whose very existence was dependent on the sun, clouds, rain and hail. Often tears sprinkled their cheeks when of necessity they were obliged to leave the small tract of land which they called their own. Konopnicka watched with apprehension their departure for North or South America. In her short stories and poetry she embraced the peasant's soul. And in her poetry she created a species of poetic pictures in which the lot and fortune of the Polish peasant was portrayed. Some of the finest poems of longing and nostalgia had come from her pen at this time.

Konopnicka also taught opposition to the germanization and russification of her people. She also preached the dignity of manual labor and stressed the value of education. She pleaded with the peasants to get out of the intellectual darkness into the light which radiates from books and knowledge.

Konopnicka's first contact with the Polish Women's Alliance was in 1902 on the occasion of the Silver Jubilee of her literary activities. In all the large cities of Poland, especially Krakow where the jubilarian lived, celebrations were held in her honor. Programs to acquaint the public at large with her beautiful poems and novels were held in various cities of the United States sponsored by the Polish Women's Alliance.

The library of the Polish Women's Alliance bears her name. It also contains Konopnicka's letters written to the organization, after having become an honorary member. On October 8, 1910 the bells of all the churches of Lwow announced the death of the Pole and writer, Maria Konopnicka. The tomb-stone, marking her grave at the Lyczakow cemetery in Lwow, was offered to her memory by the Polish Women's Alliance.

[27] The great auditorium of the Polish Women's Alliance is honored with Modrzejewska's name. The museum of the Alliance also has in its possession some personal accessories. There is a badge of Our Lady of Czestochowa which was embroidered by Modrzejewska herself and a beautiful, artistic fan, which Modrzejewska valued since it were paintings and faces of famous Polish artists. Wytrwal, *Poles in American History and Tradition*, pp. 241-245.

Eliza Orzeszkowa (1842-1910) was an eminent Polish novelist. She stressed the importance of educating the peasants. Education, according to her, should level the differences existing between the middle class and the workers. Opportunities must be the same for all, regardless of class affiiliations.

One of the meeting-halls in the Polish Women's building is dedicated to the name of Eliza Orzeszkowa. All her books are to be found in the library of the Polish Women's Alliance.

The meeting hall of the executive Board of the Polish Women's Alliance is called the Madame Sklodowska-Curie Hall. On the main wall of this room hangs a portrait of Madame Sklodowska-Curie. It was painted by Ladislaus Krawiec from Chicago. In February, 1910 this portrait was unveiled by Madame Curie's daughter, Eve.

Maria Rodziewicz (1863-1944) was a novelist whose motto was as simple and forceful as a military command: work and persevere. In her writings she honored every kind of occupation: manual, mental and artistic. In considering the aspects

Since its inception, the Polish Women's Alliance of America has actively participated in local and national affairs, and simultaneously, maintained a program of mutual aid and assistance. War Relief Work, assistance to displaced persons, refugees, and orphanages have been the major concerns of the organization. The organization currently sends regular shipments of clothing, equipment, and medication to hospitals, schools, orphanages and other worthy institutions in Poland.[28] In America, the members maintain a home for the aged and a private summer colony for children.

Recognizing Polish-American youth as a potential force, the Polish Women's Alliance called to life a junior section called *Wianki* (Garlands). A *Wianek* is a pet-child of every division of the Polish Women's Alliance. Classes in dancing, singing, literature, as well as lectures and dramatics, foster Polish ideals and promote Polish culture among the young members, enriching

---

of human pursuits she often considered economic struggle and denationalization. She speaks of these matters openly and with courage. She weaves the thread of today with the tradition of the past. For certainly such continuation is the strength of every culture, and graves are but the foundations for new edifices. Culture does not thrive on sand and it is not formed by one generation; it is the result of many previous generations, consequentially, we must not forget what we owe to those who were before us.

The museum section of the Polish Women's Alliance is called Maria Rodziewicz Hall. The library of the Polish Women's Alliance possesses all her books.

Helena Paderewska's merits were so great that Pope Benedict XV conferred upon her the golden cross—"*Pro Ecclesia Et Pontifice.*" On this occasion the official organ of the Vatican the *Osservatore Romano* printed the following comment: "Among the people who carried emergency aid to the wounded and the invalids; to displaced persons and the homeless; to the aged and the orphans—among the benefactors who deserve world gratitude—one of the foremost places is held by Helena Paderewska, whose noted participation in all such activities is well remembered in the United States, in France, in Italy and who in her own country founded the White Cross, that central institution for the victims of war, and who, with the affiliation to the Red Cross has achieved results, which in their magnitude supersede the possibilities of woman's efforts." *Dodatek to Glos Polek* (May, 1948), p. 13.

The museum of the Polish Women's Alliance is in possession of some personal objects belonging to Helena Paderewska.

[28] In acknowledgment and gratitude for the substantial contribution made to its department of biology, the Catholic University of Lublin, Poland, has named its newly constructed lecture hall "The Polish Women's Alliance of America Hall." The organization also contributed to the "Rappersville Fund," with headquarters in Switzerland; provided scholarships for Americans of Polish descent at American universities and colleges; prepared readings on current events and literary subjects; raised funds for the General Kosciuszko monument in Humboldt Park, in Chicago; and donated the "Pulaski at Savanna" painting by Stanislaw Batowski to the Polish Museum in Chicago.

their lives and those about them. From childhood the young members are raised with an understanding of the Polish spirit; and in addition to their American education, they develop their minds and hearts jointly.

The organization, also, supports recreational programs for young people and has sponsored three successful youth conferences. One of the annual youth events of the Polish Women's Alliance districts is the presentation of debutante balls. Recently the organization has sponsored several successful youth workshops on a national level.

A semi-monthly publication, *Glos Polek*, keeps the membership informed on organizational activities, obituaries, current events, and subjects of historical, cultural, religious, culinary, civic and social value. Over 10,000 volumes of poetry, non-fiction and fiction—both in English and Polish—are available to its members from the lending library, which the organization maintains in its home office building in Chicago. Also, located on the fourth floor of the building, is the museum, where cherished mementos of its founders, various historical documents, trophies, banners, works of art and handicraft, and citations presented to the Polish Women's Alliance in America, are preserved.

In 1938, the Polish Women's Alliance celebrated its fortieth anniversary. Grace Humphrey, author of many books on Polish topics, on that occasion made the following comment:

> Over and over men in Poland said to me: "It was my mother who made me a Polish patriot." It was the women of Poland who kept burning the flame of patriotism through the difficult years of partitions and oppression. I think it is equally true that today its largely the task of Polish mothers to make their American children lovers of Poland. Boys and girls learn to love the land of their forefathers, not through compulsion, but through knowing its history, its culture, its beauty. This is one of the tasks and one of the achievements of the Polish Women's Alliance of America. On this anniversary I send you all my hearty congratulations and sincere wishes for continued progress in the years that lie ahead. [29]

---

[29] Jadwiga Karlowiczowa, *Historia Związku Polek w Ameryce* (Chicago: 1938), p. 177.

Because the financial standing of the Polish Women's Alliance is firmly established, the organization is able to: (1) sponsor a Fraternal Youth Activity Program for the purpose of training future Alliance leaders; (2) grant scholarships to its needy certificate owners; (3) provide for the needs of its aged; (4) sponsor a Junior Benefit Fraternity for Polish-American youth. The organization has 1,124 lodges licensed in seventeen states with a total of over 90,000 members. The fraternal—which issues modern and up-to-date insurance certificates—has assets totalling nearly thirty million dollars, with over sixty million dollars worth of insurance in force.[30]

The Falcon gymnastic organization was founded in Poland. It had two purposes: (1) the improvement of mental and physical health; and (2) the establishment of a free Poland. Eventually, it was transplanted to America. The first Falcon Nest in America was organized, in Chicago, on June 12, 1887, by Felix Pietrowicz. By 1894, there were twelve nests in existence in the United States. Representatives from four of these—all from Chicago—met that year and decided to form a national organization and incorporate it. A charter was granted to the group on May 1, 1894 under the name, "Alliance of Polish Turners of the United States of America." Thus, the only Polish-American organization dedicated to physical culture and athletics came into being. The first president was K. Zychlinski.

In 1905, the Falcons became affiliated with the Polish National Alliance, retaining however, their autonomy and individual character. Four years later—due to the rapid increase in membership—the Falcons felt that the advantageous moment had arrived to become once again an independent association. By amendments to the charter, in 1914, the corporate name became "Polish Falcons Alliance of America," whose purpose was to "regenerate the Polish race in body and spirit and create of the immigrant a national asset, for the purpose of exerting every possible influence towards attaining political independence of the fatherland." Soon thereafter, the Falcons divided into two groups, with headquar-

---

[30] "Two Major Fraternals to Hold National Conclaves," *Polish American Journal* (July 17, 1971), p. 1.

ters in Chicago and New York. In 1918, the Falcons introduced an insurance program. This organization continued until 1924, when a new corporation was formed and permanent headquarters were established in Pittsburgh, Pennsylvania. The Polish Falcons of America—the name under which the organization is presently known—was adopted and incorporated in Pennsylvania on March 30, 1928. The purposes of the organization were redefined at that time to include insurance and to work for the following objectives: (1) fostering in its members a love for and participation in group calisthenics, thereby providing members with opportunities to learn the meaning of unity, obedience, and stamina; (2) keeping alive a love and attachment for the land, religion, and culture of their forefathers; (3) helping the Polish immigrant adjust to the American scene; (4) and encouragement to study and use the Polish language.

At the close of the Balkan wars, in 1912, the Falcons stressed military training and de-emphasized gymnastic drills. From 1911 to 1917, the Falcon Order in America broadened its program to include military training by establishing three military schools for officers, non-commissioned officers and first-class soldiers. Thus, as a military organization it provided basic training to the cadré from which later emerged the famous Polish Legion of World War I. These future Polish Lancers—who trained chiefly to be of service to Poland—were by no means devoid of American patriotism. Their patriotism was as much American as Polish, though at times it was difficult to distinguish between pure patriotism and an obvious desire for adventure and heroic exploits. When President Wilson and President Huerta of Mexico were exchanging threats in the spring of 1914, the Poles of Cleveland offered to place in the field 1,000 trained Falcons, who—according to their leaders—possessed the same training as the United States National Guard. The Falcons were expert marksmen, all having qualified in arms during the regular Sunday target practices. They also had uniforms and weapons, and were willing to leave their jobs and their families at a moment's notice in order to fight for the American cause. When President Wilson issued a call for volunteers, in 1917, over seven-thousand well trained Falcons responded. In the fall of the same year, over 5,000 Falcons—not subject to American draft—joined the Polish military force.[31]

In Bridesburg, Pennsylvania, before the turn of the century, three men: Francis Jaskowiak, Julian Wessel and Francis Chwieroch became deeply aware of the need for an organization which would provide Polish-Americans, living in Philadelphia and vicin-

---

[31] The Falcon organization draws its membership largely from Michigan, Illinois and Pennsylvania. The membership is largely from third generation Americans of Polish descent. In 1968, the membership numbered 25,048 members.

At the 90th Anniversary Banquet of the Polish Falcons in America, held in 1967, in Pittsburgh, Pennsylvania, the participants were presented with an Honor List of the sixty Falcon members who fifty years ago joined the Polish Falcon army in France, and who are still living—remnants of the thousands who served in the Falcon Battle Forces. The London Polish Government-in-Exile—by means of a special decree—issued on the occasion of the fiftieth anniversary of the formation of the Polish Army, all privates and non-commissioned officers, of fifty years ago, were made honorary Second Lieutenants. The following appeared on the honor list of Sixty Falcons, who represent a unique Polish-American National Guard: Tomasz Augustynski (Jackson, Michigan), Bernard Bochta (Auburn, New York), Feliks Bukowski (Newark, New Jersey), Stanislaw Czarnecki (Auburn, New York), Rudolf Dudzik (Calumet City, Illinois), Captain Franciszek Dziob (Chicago, Illinois), Jan Gontarek (New Haven, Connecticut), Aleksander Grabowski (Union City, Connecticut), Jozef Hardas (Ansonia, Connecticut), Jan Jacinski (Jackson, Michigan), Boleslaw Jaszynski (New Haven, Connecticut), Jozef Jarkowski (Baltimore, Maryland), Jan Kaluza (Holyoke, Massachusetts), Gustaw Kaminski (New Kensington, Pennsylvania), Ignacy Kasprowicz (Newark, New Jersey), Piotr Keczmerski (Newark, New Jersey), Stanislaw Klemba (Middletown, Connecticut), Saturnin Klimaszewski (Union City, Connecticut), Jerzy Kogut (Union City, Connecticut) Henryk Kolakowski (Meriden, Connecticut), Jan Kotkowski (New Kensington, Pennsylvania), Piotr Krol (Middleton, Connecticut), Ignacy Kucharski (Jackson, Michigan), Michal Kusowski (Saginaw, Michigan), Bronislaw Lewandowski (Ambridge, Pennsylvania), Jan Lis (Elizabeth, New Jersey), Jan Macek (Derby, Connecticut), Tomasz Malinowski (Pittsburgh, Pennsylvania), F. Malkowski (Chicago, Illinois), Jan Mazur (New Kensington, Pennsylvania), Ludwik Mikusek (Saginaw, Michigan), Stanislaw Mrozinski (Union City, Connecticut), Stanislaw Noga (Auburn, New York), Jan Olfier (Jackson, Michigan), Jozef Olszanski (Jackson, Michigan), Major Gabryel Pawlowski (Chicago, Illinois), Captain Gustaw Pieprzny (Pittsburgh, Pennsylvania), Maciej Rapala (Derby, Connecticut), Jan Rogalski (Jackson, Michigan), First Lieutenant Zygmunt Rowinski (Detroit, Michigan), Jakob Ryzowicz (Ambridge, Pennsylvania), Jan Sitko (Jackson, Michigan), Franciszek Smagowicz (Newark, New Jersey), Aleksander Staniszewski (Middleton, Connecticut), Adjutant Michal Stypula (Pittsburgh, Pennsylvania), Pawel Szczepanski (Union City, Pennsylvania), Aleksander Szegen (Wilmington, Delaware), Antoni Szulczynski (Newark, New Jersey), Jan Tarkowski (Milwaukee, Wisconsin), Josef Tyczkowski (Milwaukee, Wisconsin), J. J. Uszynski (Newark, New Jersey), Major Artur L. Waldo (Phoenix, Arizona), August Wawrzawszek (Auburn, New York), Agnieszka Wisla (Women's Corps) (Chicago, Illinois), Zygmunt Wisniewski (Newark, New Jersey), Franciszek Wojtowicz (Middletown, Connecticut), Stanislaw Wojtusik (New Britain, Connecticut), Ignacy Zapytowski (Detroit, Michigan), and Franciszek Zielinski (Elizabeth, New Jersey).

ity, with financial aid in case of misfortune. They, together wth the help of their pastor, Father Marian Kopytkiewicz, founded on December 3, 1899, the Polish Beneficial Association (*Polskie Stowarzyszenie Kasy p. o. Sw. Jana Kantego*) under the protection of St. John Cantius, whose love for the poor knew no bounds. On January 14, 1900, its constitution was completed and approved; while on April 10, of the same year, a charter was obtained from the State Legislature. Throughout the years, membership in the Polish Beneficial Association increased steadily to the extent that, in 1955, it boasted of a total of 24,547 members. Its members live in Pennsylvania, New Jersey, Delaware and Maryland. The Polish Beneficial Association has 133 lodges, with its Home Lodge located in Philadelphia. In 1969, its membership declined to 19,206.

Today, as over the past several years, the Polish Beneficial Association helps members and their families in cases of death, permanent disability or sickness; gives financial aid to member students; supports Polish culture and heritage; participates in civic and cultural affairs and observes patriotic celebrations; and aids Polish parishes, charitable and educational institutions. To date more than six million dollars have been paid out in death benefits alone.

The year 1903 saw the establishment of the Association of the Sons of Poland (*Stowarzyszenie Synow Polski*). At the first Convention, held in September 1930, the first delegates collected a few dollars as their humble contribution to the Polish National fund in Rappersville, Switzerland, where the leading Poles of the world were conducting their struggle for a Free Poland. At the time of the convention, the organization had exactly 338 members and a grand total of $409.03 in cash. There were thirty-two delegates attending the convention, all of whom donated their time freely, receiving no compensation.

From 1903 to 1924, the Association of the Sons of Poland moulded its organization on a state level. There were constant mergers with small military groups. These groups often wore elaborate uniforms. They carried on many drills in preparation for the time that they might return and liberate Poland. In 1924, there were only two major societies remaining: one, the Association of the Sons of Poland, and the other, the Polish Military Alliance of the East. The same year both societies merged together. This merger marked the beginning of growth for the Association of the Sons of Poland, which had reached a membership of 18,000 and assets of $4,250,000, in 1964.

Its material rate of growth is impressive; however, the work of the Association in the field of social and civic endeavors are even more impressive. Here, the Association of the Sons of Poland has consistently earned the right to the noble title, so poignantly expressed in the name of the organization. The ties with Poland are very strong. Every convention considered Poland's progress and difficulties. At one convention, the delegates moved to donate a stipulated amount for the relief of flood victims in southern Poland. At another convention, a generous contribution was earmarked for the poor living in large Polish cities. During World War I, when the Central Powers and Russia fought on Polish soil, which, in turn, caused the complete destruction of the country, the eight consecutive conventions voted unanimously a special tax of two cents a month on each member to aid the hungry in Poland. This tax remained in effect until the 1924 Convention. The minutes of the 1917 Convention reveal that a special letter was dispatched to President Wilson with gratitude for his sympathetic consideration and understanding of Central Europe and the Polish problem. The minutes of the 1921 Convention contain copies of the letters sent to President Harding and Premier Brand of France seeking intervention on behalf of Poland in its bitter struggle with the Germans for the predominantly Polish region of Slask (Silesia) which is rich in coal and iron ore. The plebiscite under the control of the Western powers returned part of Slask to Poland.

There were many glorious and joyous days for the organization and its members in the late twenties and thirties, when special excursions to Poland were organized and headed by the leaders of the Sons of Poland. Many paid for the excursions themselves to visit the land of their fathers. Others went as prize winners after membership drives. A six-week tour throughout Poland was very beneficial to them. Poland gained materially by building up badly needed dollar reserves; while the Americans gained through insight and broader perspective after exposure to a richer cultural background. It enabled them to make a comparison of each country's standards of living as well as its different working democracies, which induced the travelers to appreciate more the American way of life. When the annual General Pulaski parade was organized in New York, the Association supported this venture financially, and many of its members took an active part in the event. In appreciation for the services rendered, the Central Committee bestowed upon the leaders of the Association the honor of serving as grand marshals in the parade on several occasions.

The relations with Poland were of paramount significance to the new Polish state which needed unofficial ambassadors to many countries; the Sons of Poland performed this function admirably. The Polish government was deeply grateful for this assistance and rewarded the Association of the Sons of Poland with the highest decoration at its disposal: the Order of Polonia Restituta (Order of Restored Poland). The Representative of the Polish Government, Mr. Roman, decorated the banner of the Association of the Sons of Poland, in May 1939, at a ceremony in Jersey City, New Jersey.

Working for benevolent causes in Poland did not interfere in any way with discharging civic duties and responsibilities in America. On the contrary, the strong sense of identity and continuity with a country, that was tragically enslaved for nearly a century-and-a-half, made them appreciate American freedom. The Association of the Sons of Poland had lost over forty of its members during World War II. A lasting tribute was paid to these members by offering masses for the repose of their souls at the parishes where they were parishioners. The Board of Directors and many of its members attended these masses for their departed brethren. There are many "Gold Star Mothers" among the members of the Association. The Association also accepted its responsibilities during World War II by investing in war bonds; it also urged its members to save regularly by purchasing U.S. government bonds, and also sold bonds at the main office, in Jersey City, to the public at large. Since the termination of World War II, the Americans of Polish descent and the Sons of Poland are very unhappy over the fifth partition of Poland which severed Wilno and Lwow—two ancient Polish cities—from Poland.

The members of the Association of the Sons of Poland—believing in education as a means of keeping America strong—foster higher education. It gives to its young members scholarship aid—based on merit—to attend colleges and universities. Attendance at schools for graduate and advanced studies is also encouraged. In the past few years the Association of the Sons of Poland has expanded its activities in the social area. It has organized and formed the Women's Auxiliary, which has been quite active in sponsoring many social functions as well as participating in religious, social, fraternal and charitable affairs. One significant event is the Annual Debutante Ball, which is always well attended.

The Association of the Sons of Poland has also formed the Leaders Club, an exclusive organization which consists of members from the organization who have been consistently active in its undertakings, and have introduced many new members to the Association. Every year the members of the Leaders Club are feted with a gala dinner as an expression of appreciation for their unlimited services to the Association. The Leaders Club was influential and greatly responsible for the progress of the Association..

Sports and recreation are also included in the activities of the Association of the Sons of Poland. It also maintains the Sons of Poland camp, which is a modern recreational facility. Some of the activities at the camp include swimming, picnicking, dancing, softball and baseball, and singing around a bonfire. Bowling teams, in league competition, are also sponsored.

All activities are available to each member of the Association. In addition, it issues insurance certificates from $300 to $5,000. On January 1, 1953, adult benefit certificates numbered 15,260; junior benefit certificates numbered 1,961. The largest amount of these certificates (15,744) was issued in New Jersey. New York claims 1,214 certificates, and Connecticut 201. In 1969, the Association's adult benefit certificates numbered 13,947. As of January 1, 1953, the Association numbered 122 lodges, 124 in 1954, and 123 in 1955.

The Polish National Alliance of Brooklyn (*Zjednoczenie Polskie Narodowe*) was founded on February 10, 1903. The specific aims of the Polish National Alliance of Brooklyn are to: (1) unite Polish-Americans and others of Slavic descent for the purpose of affording them an opportunity to profit by the benefits that accrue from such a union; (2) instill in them a greater love for their adopted country; (3) encourage its members to practice the corporal works of mercy; (4) preserve the faith of their forefathers; (5) make a positive Polish contribution to American culture, history and literature; and (6) encourage its youth to study and use the Polish language.

In 1969, the Polish National Alliance of Brooklyn possessed a membership of 17,983 among 152 lodges. The activities of the Polish National Alliance are varied and numerous. The Alliance purchased Polish Government Bonds during World War I, and United States Defense Bonds during the past two World Wars; it organized a committee to fight Communism; it established a scholarship program for needy students; and also constructed a summer camp for boys and girls at Oak Ridge, New Jersey. When Stephen Mizwa announced the plan to honor the 40th anniversary of the Kosciuszko Foundation with a Million Dollar Scholarship Fund, the Polish National Alliance of Brooklyn donated $25,000 to the Million Dollar Scholarship Fund. The underprivileged at the Institute for the Blind, in Laski, Poland, have benefited also from the efforts of the Polish National Alliance of Brooklyn. The official publication of the organization is the Polish Weekly, *Czas*.

The Polish National Union of America (*Polsko Narodowa Spojnia w Ameryce*) was organized in 1908; however, preliminary efforts were made prior to this time.[32] Prime Bishop Francis Hodur had for a long time desired to organize a fraternal benefit

---

[32] The organizers and charter members of the Polish National Catholic Church held insurance policies issued by the Polish Roman Catholic Union and other organizations of the Roman Catholic Church. Their membership in these insurance societies created friction and misunderstanding. Consequently, the majority of them transferred to the Polish National Alliance, a progressive secular organization. In time, individuals who were currying favor with the Polish priests made themselves heard in the Polish National Alliance. They persecuted members of the Polish National Catholic Church. It was during this time that Bishop Hodur—one of the most resourceful individuals in the Polish National Catholic Church—began to entertain the idea of initiating an insurance organization of his own.

RISE OF NATIONAL FRATERNAL ORGANIZATIONS

society within the Polish National Catholic Church; however, it was not until 1908 that conditions permitted it. In February and March of 1908, the first two organizational meetings were held, and certificates of insurance began to be issued on September 8, 1908. Prime Bishop Francis Hodur was its first member, while John Drwal became the first insured.

The ideals of the organization are aptly expressed in its preamble:

> "The Polish National Union of America shall be not only a life insurance and financial institution paying benefits in case of death, etc., but also an idealistic organization. If even we were the wealthiest materially, but if we lack the strength of character, determination and responsibility for our deeds before God, our conscience and the community, then we will have lost faith in justice, self-respect and respect for our nationality; we will perish, as other organizations and nations have perished that have given up higher ideals."[33]

We read further that the Polish National Union shall cooperate with the Polish National Catholic Church, and together they will strive to uplift the Polish people and to bring about their happiness, enlightenment and betterment. However, the Polish National Union will remain a free, independent and civic organization, aiming for the same goal, although through other means.

In a resolution adopted at the First Convention of the Polish National Union in America, in 1909, at Scranton, Pennsylvania, the following goals were strongly emphasized: (1) their efforts would be directed to free the Polish Nation from political and religious bondage; (2) to cooperate with the Polish National Catholic Church, whose aim is the salvation of the Polish people; and (3) an allegiance to the United States which is the guiding star of freedom-loving people everywhere.[34]

As the Polish-American Union in America had grown in numbers and branches, it was necessary to divide the Union territory into districts. At the 1931 Convention, six districts were established. In 1935, twelve districts were established. *Straz*

---

[33] Joseph Mastalski, "Bishop Francis Hodur," *Pamietnik Zlotego Jubileuszu Polske Narodowej Spojni, 1908-1958* (Scranton: 1958), p, 13.

[34] Stanley Kotula "On the Fiftieth Anniversary of the Polish National Union of America," *Pamietnik Zlotego Jubileuszu Polsko Narodowej Spojni, 1908-1958* (Scranton: 1958), p. 9.

was made the official organ of the organization. Its printing establishment was purchased in 1923. The creation of a National Fund enabled the Union to aid Poland in 1916. Likewise, the creation of a special "Fund for the Aged" enabled the Union to purchase a farm at Waymart, Pennsylvania, in 1929, where the Home for the Aged and Disabled was established.[35] In 1951, the organization again proved to be a pioneer among Polish fraternal organizations by offering hospitalization insurance.

In 1958, the Polish National Union had 31,000 members. It is the fourth largest Polish Fraternal Society in America. It has provided low cost insurance protection within the reach of countless families. A total of a million loans have made it possible for many people to own their homes. Mostly members of the Polish National Church have profited from the Union. But the Union was not organized solely for material purposes—like insurance and finances—but primarily for social and humanitarian work. Although originally founded as a fraternal organization for members of the Polish National Catholic Church, it also accepts, as members, Americans of Polish descent from other religious denominations. Present membership has reached 32,585 insurees for a total of $28,000,000; its assets approach $13,000,000.

The Polish Alma Mater of America (*Macierz Polska*) was organized by Father Francis Gordon, C.R., who was concerned with the lack of adequate guidance and protection for youth under eighteen years of age. Being a moderator of a Polish Falcon Group, at St. Stanislaus Parish, in Chicago, Father Gordon, in due time, transformed it into the first group of the Polish Alma Mater.[36] The ideology of the new association was patterned after the Alma Mater in Poland. Although the American Alma Mater was to be a social and cultural organization, it also introduced an insurance program on May 4, 1910, at which time the Alma

---

[35] Since its establishment until 1958, 228 individuals have benefited from the Home of the Aged. The home is located on a 500 acre farm. "Dom Starcow i Kalek na farmie Spojni w Waymart, Pa.," *Pamietnik Zlotego Jubileszu Polsko Narodowej Spojni 1908-1958* (Scranton: 1958), p. 30.

[36] It was Father Vincent Barzynski, C. R., who first struck upon the idea to form the Alma Mater, which would serve as a medium to keep alive—among the Polish American youth—an interest in Polish matters. Father Gordon took Father Barzynski's idea, and brought it to fruition.

Mater commenced business as a fraternal insurance society.[37] Today, the aim of the Polish Alma Mater is to unite Polish-American people professing the Roman Catholic religion in the United States for the purposes of: (1) upholding Christian morals while cultivating civic virtues; (2) providing opportunities for higher learning while fostering patriotism; (3) giving fraternal aid in times of need; and (4) offering insurance policies to its members.

The Union of Polish Women in America (*Unia Polek w Ameryce*) was established in Philadelphia on October 17, 1920 by Frances Szwedowa, Agnes Karlewska and Helene Janoski. The Polish White Cross Circles—which existed after World War I, and which were founded by Madame Helena Paderewska—formed the nucleus for the establishment of the Union of Polish Women in America. The founders felt that the laudable work performed by the White Cross should continue, though in a somewhat modified form due to postwar conditions.

The Constitution of the Union of Polish Women in America stipulates that the scope of this organization is to: (1) preserve among the Polish women in America their moral and religious consciousness in accordance with the teachings of the Roman Catholic Church; (2) imbue them with a spirit of American patriotism and loyalty; (3) inculcate in them—particularly the younger members—worthy Polish ideals as reflected in the literature and history of Poland; (4) encourage a more active participation in community and civic projects; and (5) provide them with benefits permitted under the Act of Assembly of the Commonwealth of Pennsylvania—approved July 17, 1935, P. L. 1092.

As of January 1, 1955, the Union's number of lodges totaled

---

[37] A fraternal life insurance society was organized welcoming to its ranks American citizens of Polish descent who profess the Roman Catholic Faith—not only for the purpose of writing life insurance, but also to associate under the guidance of the Blessed Virgin Mary, Queen of Poland—for the following purposes: to transmit to America the cultural advantages of ancient Poland; to keep the Polish language for more rapid transmission of the old to the new; to indoctrinate the Poles in the United States with the American spirit; to teach thrift and self-reliance through fraternalism; to foster the tenets of the Roman Catholic Church; to encourage civic pride and patriotism, so as to build a better United States of America. Casimir J. B. Wronski, "The Polish Alma Mater of America," *Poles of Chicago*, Leon Zglenicki, Editor (Chicago: 1937), p. 161.

74; the majority are located in Philadelphia. These lodges hold monthly meetings, and their agenda not only calls for the payment of monthly assessments, but also holds a discussion of the Union's welfare along with social and community affairs. One of the subjects which received major consideration was that of juvenile delinquency: its causes and cures. As a concrete preventive measure, several lodges have established Juvenile Circles for girls under sixteen years of age. Adult members provide these circles with appropriate entertainment and instruction which will inspire girls to strive for the ideals worthy of womanhood. Social activities— which have as their objective the development of social graces— are also sponsored by the Circles. All this is performed voluntarily and without remuneration: the mainspring is the Christian desire to serve God and country.

The United Polish Women of America is the youngest of all Polish fraternal organizations. It was founded in 1932. Fully cognizant of the fact that the works of charity must occupy a focal, and not a marginal place, in the life of every true Christian, they have outlined a model program of charity. One outstanding facet of its program is a Welfare Fund which is replenished—not by assessing its members—but rather by a voluntary periodic donation. Financial assistance is extended to any needy member whenever misfortune or disaster strikes. Its insurance activities commenced on December 1, 1932. In 1969, its membership numbered 9,356 members.

The Polish-American fraternal organizations exert a decisive influence on all phases of Polish organized life in America. Polish-American organizations formed wheels within a wheel. Theirs was the little wheel turning in the orbit of the larger wheel representing the larger society. As a satellite, the little wheel was often unsteady and uncertain, but it persisted in defying practically every physical law known to man. The fraternal Polish American organizations had a marked effect on America: its history and institutions, primarily because of their independent efforts, whether in triumph or defeat. The fraternal organizations contain more members than any other Polish-American organizations. Also, their combined financial assets outdistance those of any other organization in the Polish-American community. The fraternal organizations sponsor and support many Polish social undertakings that are not directly inspired or maintained by ecclesiastical or cultural agencies.

The Polish-American fraternal organizations offer a superb illustration of the highest ideals of inter-cultural cooperation and free enterprise. By successfully blending business acumen with humanitarian sympathy, they make insurance not only a means of creating wealth, but also an opportunity for putting the finer aims in life within the grasp of many. Above all, these organizations have led the Polish-Americans to a greater understanding of their twin inheritance: American freedom and Polish culture. By transforming cultural barriers into bridges, they help to enrich America (as well as the immigrants) to the mutual benefit of both.

CHAPTER FIVE

The Polish-Irish Encounter

> We are American bishops; an effort is made to dethrone us, and to foreignize our country in the name of religion.
> —Archbishop Ireland[1]

> People, let us pray that God might have pity on us, and might deliver us from the domination of foreign bishops, restore our churches to us, and give us bishops after our own hearts.
> —Rev. Paul Fox[2]

During the 1880's, Polish immigrants accounted for the 604,000 membership increase among Catholics in America. During the decade of the 1890's the Catholic population increased by 1,250,000 immigrants. With the arrival of the Poles, the Catholic Church had rapidly developed into the largest denomination in the United States; and by World War I, it accounted for about one-third of the nation's church members.

While all of these foreign-born prospective citizens shared a common religion, other traits of similarity ended there. Unlike other institutions such as societies or newspapers, the Catholic Church in Europe existed as a source of counsel in time of need or when bridging the strangeness through a warm welcome to the recent arrivals in a village or new community. The parish priest was their personal friend, who had baptized them at their birth, taught them their catechism, and watched over them like a father or elder brother. For the Polish immigrants, the Church

---

[1] John Tracey Ellis, *The Life of James Cardinal Gibbons, Archbishop of Baltimore, 1834-1921* (Milwaukee: 1951), I, p. 369.
[2] Paul Fox, *The Polish National Catholic Church* (Scranton: n.d.), p. 29.

in their native land fulfilled their beings with the awesome majesty of celebrated ritual and sacred music, stirred by an accompanied choir and organist which sang the Polish hymns, and the responses of the Mass in their expressive Polish language along with the memory of each distinctive holyday. It was so unlike the American Catholic Church, which they found to be cold and puritanical and primarily administrative, controlled by the Irish, who rarely spoke a foreign language or showed concern to understand the needs of the immigrants.

From the very beginning, the Catholic Poles held tenaciously to their mother tongue, whether it was in the rural areas of Massachusetts, where they formed solid Catholic communities that were models of thrift and exemplary living, or in the crowded neighborhoods of cities on the eastern seaboard, or the great Polish centers of the mid-west such as Chicago, Milwaukee, and Detroit.[3] Confronted as they often were by hostile forces which resented their "foreignism" (along with their religion), the Polish Catholics quite naturally depended on the Polish priests, schools, and press as the best sources for preserving their faith and identity. As soon as the growth of numbers supplied the means, the Polish immigrants—with their fierce national pride, their consciousness of past glories and noble deeds of heroic stature, or the bitter recollection and suffering of past partitions—attempted to reconstitute, in America, the precise form of their old religious life with its own liturgical language, music, ritual, discipline and colorful customs.

The Polish priests—who followed the Polish immigrants everywhere—made a magnificent contribution to the development of the Catholic Church in the United States. Although they were poor, they were adept at turning sweat into gold. They converted the immigrant pennies into temples of grandeur, beauty, and peace which became the pride of the Polish people. They were built amidst the gravest and gloomiest wastes of the cities. Here, the priests said Mass, served the Holy Sacraments, and preached long sermons which influenced their congregations. They suc-

---

[3] Wytrwal, *Poles in American History and Tradition*, pp. 225-239.

ceeded in preserving the Polish language, and customs through all aspects of their parochial life, especially the parochial school.

Their efforts to create autonomous religious institutions, where—regardless of economic station—an individual would receive a cordial welcome supported by morale, that unifying spirit which was seldom found in Irish or German Catholic parishes. The Polish priests were limited by the American Catholic hierarchy—many of whom were of Irish origin—and did not always understand the new leaven which had been added to American Catholicism. The Irish won control of the American Catholic Church since they arrived earlier and were strategically located. They also had the advantage of knowing the English language. By the time the Poles, Czechs, Italians and other Catholics emigrated to the United States, the Irish had won a commanding position in the Church which they would hold for many years. The steady flow of Irish priests into various urban parishes enlarged their numbers at all levels of the Church hierarchy, especially capturing the most powerful positions in the American Catholic Church. Once they had established their control of the Church, it was very easy—especially in view of the numerical superiority—to bring other Irish priests to positions of influence.

Since Catholicism was the only remaining component of Irish identity, the Irish clergy viewed other Catholics as having divided loyalties. For the Irish, Catholicism was their culture. Irish Catholicism was identical with a staunch, Church-oriented outlook and commitment. Therefore, the prelates took a deprecating view of the nature of other ethnic groups' commitment to the church:

> ". . . the Polish Catholic has greater loyalty to being a Pole than the Irish to being Irish. The Irish are more Irish Catholics, and the Pole is more a Pole. . . . If the Church gave out a ruling that every Irishman should take a bath every hour, the Irish would. The Italian wouldn't.[4]

The Irish were further differentiated from other ethnic Catholics in their attitudes toward priests. The significance of this preference for the Irish over other Catholics is revealed in an

---

[4] Edward M. Levine, *The Irish and Irish Politicians* (Notre Dame: 1966), p. 194.

anecdote about an Irishman, an Italian, and a Pole, which was told to Edward Levine by an Irish priest:

> A priest is working in the garden in front of the rectory and three men walk by. The first one says, "Let me do that for you Father." The second says, "This is how you do it, Father." The third man walks by and pretends not to see the priest. What is the national ancestry of each of the men?[5]

The Irish Catholic hierarchy thoroughly inculcated in their parishioners the Catholic dogma: the salvation of the soul was the ultimate end of man over which the Church—through its prelates and priests—had absolute stewardship on earth. The flow of religious authority begins in the parish church and continues in an uninterrupted ascent to the Vatican, where undeviating respect and obedience from its faithful is required for its success.

The adherence to the Polish language for church services, school instruction, and the press, appeared to the Irish-American clergy as an inordinate fondness for old world customs, while assuming a lack of appreciation for the language and customs of the country that had given Poles a haven for a better life. They regarded it as not only un-American, but also un-Catholic. Even though they themselves were either born, or only a generation removed from Ireland, the dominant Irish Catholic hierarchy—who monopolized the right to define the Church—was vehemently opposed to any attempt to organize national parishes.[6] While the Roman Catholic Church transcends national lines in terms of its range, within each country the Church is a sub-system of the national social system. Within the national sub-systems of the Roman Catholic Church, national differences are frequently and explicitly recognized to: (1) the respective national saints within the Church's hierarchy of saints; (2) the religious traditions in each country; and (3) the national characteristics in each nation's priesthood.

---

[5] The answer is, Irish, Polish and Italian. Levine, *The Irish and Irish Politicians*, p. 196.

[6] In 1886, of the sixty-nine bishops, thirty-five were Irish-born or of Irish ancestry, in contrast to fifteen bishops among the Germans—including Austrian and Swiss. The French had eleven; the English five; and the Dutch, Scotch and Spanish one each. William V. Shannon, *The American Irish* (New York: 1963), p. 163.

The Irish resented and regarded all variations from the American pattern as out of harmony with the national trend.[7] They believed that the exclusive use of the English language would give the Poles, at least, the appearance of belonging, and free them from the charge of "foreignism." They were willing to sacrific ethnic cohesion for the interests of religious expansion.

Cardinal Gibbons made this view explicit on August 20, 1891 at the conferral of the pallium on Archbishop Frederick Katzer of Milwaukee. He said in his sermon: "Brothers we are, whatever be our nationality, and brothers we shall remain. We will prove to our countrymen that the ties formed by grace and faith are stronger than flesh and blood. God and our country!—this our watchword. Loyalty to God's church and to our country —this is our religious and political faith." Cardinal Gibbons in his provincial view was determined that the Church in America must become like the rest of the nation, homogeneous. But the nation was not homogeneous.

> The differences in languages, customs, and social styles, among these ethnic groups, added to the divisiveness of their differing religious outlooks and relationship to the Church. Each group strongly desired to continue the use of its native language in the non-liturgical parts of the religious services; this generated severely strained feelings in polyglot parishes, especially in those that had Irish priests. And the subordination of the European priests to the Irish hierarchy could hardly have improved the angry feelings that had arisen between the groups.[8]

In 1891, Archbishop Ireland, in a letter to Cardinal Gibbons, made the following comment: "We are American bishops, an effort is made to detrone us, and to foreignize our country in the

---

[7] During the nineteenth century, the Poles were deprived of a country which had formal national and political status. In partitioned Poland, the Poles were still subordinate "minorities" within an empire. Their one semblance of national organization appeared in the only organized sub-system of the group—the Church. Given these facts, the intense attachment of the Poles to their church can be more easily understood. Moreover, the Catholic Church was, in all instances, the instrument for preserving the national group image. The Church remained the first line of defense behind which the Polish immigrants could organize themselves, and with which they could preserve their group identity.

name of religion."⁹ In a lecture delivered in Cincinnati, on May 2, 1895, Archbishop Ireland made this biased opinion explicit.

> Immigration must be restricted so as to exclude criminals, paupers. Nor should immigrants in any state of the Union be prematurely authorized to vote. A due respect for American citizenship guards against a reckless extension of it to men coming from other lands. No encouragement must be given to social or political organizations or methods which perpetuate in this country foreign ideas or customs.¹⁰

Foreign priests and nuns were not welcomed by the American Catholic hierarchy, who believed that the spiritual needs of the immigrants would be better served by American clerics. Thus, they adopted either a paternalistic stance or had followed a program of segregation. The reverend John T. McNichols, the Bishop of Duluth, argued that American priests were better equipped than foreign-born clergymen to Americanize the immigrants.

> One Italian priest still bristled with anger when he recalled for the authors that he was allowed to say Mass, but not permitted to preach to Irish parishioners for fear he would somehow subvert their "Irish-American Catholicism."¹¹

The Irish-American teaching orders also opposed the introduction of foreign nuns for much the same reason.¹² Unwilling or unable to understand the folk religion of the new immigrants, Irish-American Catholic priests, nuns and laymen equated the religious observances of the new immigrants with paganism, superstition and religious indifference.

> Masking their deep-rooted animosity toward the Italian male, in particular, some Irish-American prelates would humorously describe him as one who attended church on three occasions only: when he was hatched, matched, and dispatched.¹³

---

⁸ Levine, *The Irish and Irish Politicians*, p. 98.
⁹ Ellis, *The Life of James Cardinal Gibbons, Archbishop of Baltimore 1834-1921*, I, p. 369.
¹⁰ *Cincinnati Ohio Enquirer* (May 2, 1895).
¹¹ Luciana J. Iorizzo and Salvatore Mondello, *The Italian-Americans* (New York: 1971), p. 182.
¹² *Ibid.*, p. 182.
¹³ *Ibid.*, p. 190.

The Irish-American attitude, at the turn of the century—toward the newcomers whom they viewed as inferior Catholics—had been strikingly similar to the wider society's attitude toward Afro-Americans and Indian-Americans.

> The Irish-Americans are the most conveniently inconsistent people in the world. They are always yelling about the bigotry of the Yankee Protestants. What do you suppose would happen to the Protestants if the Irish Catholics came into power, as they soon will be in Massachusetts? Look how the Catholic Poles and the Catholic Italians, their own co-religionists, are treated in the Church. They never get their rights; they are always discriminated against. Look at the fight the French Canadians have had to put up to be given even halfway justice.[14]

The following is another instance of Italian dissatisfaction with the Irish dominated Catholic Church in America:[15]

> Italians found the Church in America to be a cold and puritanical organization, controlled and often operated by the hated Irish, even in Italian neighborhoods. Devout Catholics and critics of religion alike resented Irish domination of the Church. They demanded Italian priests and control of churches in their neighborhoods. *La Tribuna Italiana Transatlantica* charged that "Irish priests work among the Italians not to save them from sin but through fear of losing fruitful clients."[16]

Toward the end of the century, there had been a slackening in the number of Irish immigrants coming to the United States. This disturbed Cardinal Gibbons. For there was danger that the continuous stream of Catholic immigrants from southern and eastern Europe would out-weigh, in the long run, the numerical superiority of Irish-Americans, at least in the largest American cities. Also, it would be more difficult for the Irish-American

---

[14] W. Lloyd Warner and Leo Srole, *The Social Systems of American Ethnic Groups* (New Haven: 1947), p. 25.

[15] While for the Irish and Polish Catholics religion made up a central aspect of national loyalty, however for the Italians Catholicism and nationalism were opposing forces. Thus, bourgeois and proletarian papers alike condemned the Pope's temporal claims in Italy.

[16] Humbert S. Nelli, *Italians in Chicago 1880-1930. A Study in Ethnic Mobility* (New York: 1970), pp. 181-182.

prelates to defend the Catholic institutions against the onslaught of the Catholics from southern and eastern Europe.

To stimulate Irish emigration to the United States, Gibbons published an article, in Ireland, on Irish immigrants in the United States. After he reviewed the history of the movement from colonial times, and assessed, in a general way, the contributions which the Irish had made to American life, he paid tribute to the "extraordinary" contributions of the Irish in spreading the Christian religion, and in conclusion said:

> I would not, therefore, discourage Irish immigration because there are at stake more than economic considerations. There are at stake the interests of the Catholic religion, which in this land and this age are largely bound up with the interests of the Irish people.[17]

The *New York Times*, dated August 24, 1901, quoted Gibbons as having said: "The country, it seems to me, is overrun with immigrants, and a word of caution should be spoken to them."[18]

Immigrants who were not ready to reject their Catholic national cultures were treated with paternal condescension like that shown to an immature child. Implied in this attitude was the thought that the best solution to the problem was to "Americanize the immigrants in order to Catholicize America." So the Catholic Poles in America found themselves in a dire predicament: to become accepted Americans, they would have to reject their Polish heritage; to become accepted Catholics in America, they would have to reject their own Catholic Polish heritage and adopt an American version of English culture together with the equally unfamiliar form of English Catholicism. The educational requirements in the United States also presented the Poles with a double threat. In the existing parochial schools, their children would forget their ancestral language; in the public schools, they would not receive training in either language or religion.

Confronted with such difficult choices, the Poles pursued one of four different courses of action. One group chose the easiest

---

[17] Ellis, *The Life of James Cardinal Gibbons, Archbishop of Baltimore 1834-1921*, I, p. 383.
[18] *Ibid.*, p. 383.

path of Catholic "Americanization," or total assimilation. They severed relations with their Polish traditions, trying to think and act as if they were Catholics of English ancestry. Some even changed their name to disguise their Polish ancestry and to conceal their inherent, undeniable relations with the past. They became rootless and anonymous Americans.

The second group simply fell away from the church, because it represented to them a medieval anachronism impeding social and moral progress in the United States. They firmly believed that if the Church truly desired to cushion the difficulties of social adjustment for the Poles in America, it would have ameliorated their hardships and directed social actions along with a religious faith to become a significant force in their lives. The Irish-dominated Catholic Church discouraged many Polish immigrants through their aggression to control and monopolize the Church; thereby they implemented values which they considered useful and meaningful in the American environment, but undesirable to the various immigrants. The Irish would never allow the Church to serve as a link between America and the customs and old-treasured religion as experienced in Poland.

The third group openly denounced the prelates of Irish blood, who dominated the American Catholic Church, because they failed to display tolerance or understanding of the ethnic minorities in America. They took to task prelates like John Ireland, James Gibbons, John Spalding, and others of Irish stock who insisted that all national differences among the Catholic membership should be resolved through Americanization with an abandonment of foreign customs.

Consequently, many local controversies developed over the nationality of the priest, the language of worship, the nature of religious festivals, or the question of whether Church property should be owned by the Vatican Church hierarchy, or by its parishioners. Likewise, the demand for greater ecclesiastical autonomy in the American Church for foreign-language groups—further compounded the problem. These disputes evoked widespread discontent, thrusting the community churches into the fiercest ecclesiastical upheaval of its history. It precipitated another schism and the formation of the Polish National Catholic Church. On several occasions, appeals were carried to Rome to redress their grievances. The fickle and unstable Irish bishops were noted for their ambition, truculence, quickness to take offense, and revengefulness. The prejudice and ruthlessness of the Irish-American clergy—while indifferent to Polish interests—were insurmountable obstacles to overcome.

The Irish-American bishops showed little disposition to yield to the demands of the Polish-American Catholics who were exasperated at their failure to win a representative proportion of posts as bishops or cardinals, thereby gaining full parochial rights over their parishes. The Irish-American bishops were determined to deprive the Polish-Americans of their language and culture. In addition, they were intent upon compelling the Polish-Americans to adhere strictly to the role of Americanization. To accomplish these ends, they did not hesitate to resort to violent and abusive language which left wounds that were long in healing.

The Irish-American clergy was extremely tactless in administering the religious care of the immigrants. They did not realize how grave a responsibility they placed on the American Catholic hierarchy: to have all nationalities treated justly, and to have their concerns satisfied. Wisdom, diplomacy, tolerance and judicious experience were grievously lacking. When Father Ignatius Barszcz appealed to the Holy See for a separate diocese to be erected for the Catholics of Slavic origin in the United States, Cardinal Gibbons labeled him a "crank."

> In the fall of 1887 Father Ignatius Barszcz, pastor of St. Anthony of Padua Church in Jersey City, appealed to the Holy See for a separate diocese to be erected for Catholics of Slavic origin in the United States. When the priest called on Gibbons in early January, 1888, with his request the cardinal told him that he was not in favor of the plan. The Polish pastor then carried his case to President Cleveland who was obviously puzzled by it. Cleveland decided to forward Barszcz's request to Gibbons for his advice, characterizing it "as a specimen of the queer letters" he received. The cardinal composed an answer for the President to Barszcz in which he stated that the Church was opposed to placing bishops over people of different nationalities, although it provided ample services for them by supplying priests of their native country, or at least who spoke their language. Gibbons sympathized with Cleveland for the annoyance he had experienced and

told the president that the priest was something of a crank and no further attention should be paid to him.¹⁹

Gibbons—who reigned in Baltimore like a Czar—was annoyed with any nationality or individual if it differed from his Irish view. Thus, he had many difficulties with the Polish-Americans in Baltimore, who did not share his views. In a letter to Bishop Keane, dated March 28, 1890, Gibbons made the following comment: "I have many things to annoy me just now, especially are the Poles giving me trouble."²⁰ When the executive committee of the Polish Catholic Congress, in April 1902, circulated Gibbons and other American prelates with a respectful request that there be named an auxiliary bishop in Cleveland of Polish descent, he was especially annoyed. In the settling of this just request, which the strength in numbers of the Polish American faithful warranted, Gibbons revealed all of his Irish prejudices and liabilities.

> Three years later Archbishop Sebastian G. Messmer of Milwaukee informed Gibbons of the newspaper stories concerning the Polish effort to secure a bishop in his province, a move which Messmer felt would prove "a dangerous experiment" due to the fact that the Poles were not sufficiently Americanized. When a group of Poles, in Rochester, defied Bishop McQuaid and the name of Gibbons was used ambiguously in the newspapers in connection with this episode, the cardinal hastily wrote to McQuaid to tell him that two months before a delegation of Poles from Rochester had waited on him at Southampton, Long Island, but he had sent them word that under no circumstances would he even see them.²¹

When Gibbons learned that Joseph Wierusz Kowalski—the Polish minister to the Holy See—had intervened at the Vatican on behalf of the American bishops of Polish descent, his wrath had no limits. However, in his letter to Archbishop Bonzano—the apostolic delegate to the United States—Gibbons changed his tone to one of effusive piety. He claimed to have consulted his conscience, raising his eyes to Heaven, and imploring Divine As-

---

¹⁹ *Ibid.*, I, pp. 362-363.
²⁰ *Ibid.*, I, p. 384.
²¹ *Ibid.*, I, pp. 384-385.

sistance. In this manner he concluded that he *always* followed the practice of recommending vacant sees to the most suitable candidates without considering the candidates' nationality, through this procedure.

In a letter to Pietro Cardinal Gasparri, Secretary of State, he strongly protested the action of the Polish Legation at the Holy See, and also condemned the interference of any foreign government in the affairs of the Church in the United States. He also disapproved such conduct where a priest would dare appeal to laymen or a foreign government in order to coerce or unduly influence the episcopate in the selection of candidates for vacant sees. Speaking in the name of the entire hierarchy, Gibbons disavowed the charges of neglecting the Catholic Polish-Americans, and reaffirmed that there was no intention on the part of bishops, to "Americanize" any existing Polish parish. Yet he would brand any attempt to preserve a distinct and separate Polish nationality in the United States as something that would be "absolutely injurious both to the Church and to the Country."[22] He also censured their attempts to gain their share of bishops, interpreting it as a step toward isolating the Polish-American Catholics from the rest of their co-religionists.

At a meeting of the American hierarchy, Gibbons expressed, in no uncertain terms, where his sympathies lay. He delivered a strong speech against recognition of any national group within the American Church. "Ours is the American Church and not Irish, German, Italian or Polish—and we will keep it American."[23] The Irish-American bishops—who were opportunists and fawners, taking their cue from Gibbons—enthusiastically applauded agreement with him.

> The deep resentment which the hierarchy felt toward this renewed attempt at what was termed "foreign intermeddling" in the affairs of the Church of the United States was shown when a committee consisting of Archbishops George W. Mundelein of Chicago and Dennis J. Dougherty of Philadelphia was appointed to draft a protest to the Holy See against the interference of the Polish minister to the Vatican. The two archbishops communicated their ideas to Gibbons along with

---

[22] *Ibid.*, I, p. 387.
[23] *Ibid.*, I, p. 386.

the texts of the protest, and the cardinal incorporated their statements along with his own and affixed his signature to the document in the name of the entire hierarchy.[24]

A succession of dire events resulted in several unexpected and dramatic separations from the mother Church. Between 1873 and 1878 the Polish-American settlement Polonia, Wisconsin, witnessed the foundation of the first independent Polish-American parish in America. Reverend Frydrychowicz instigated the separation from the Irish-dominated Catholic Church. In 1886, Reverend Dominic Kolasinski precipitated a second separation from Rome, in Detroit, Michigan.[25] A new Apostle of independence appeared in 1894 in the person of Reverend Francis Kolaszewski from Cleveland, Ohio. When Father Kolaszewski established his church in Cleveland, the Independent Polish-Americans had established churches in Freeland, Pennsylvania, Chicago, and Omaha. In 1894, Father Borszcz attempted to create an independent church movement in Baltimore. By the following year, Buffalo and Chicago had become centers of independent agitation. In 1895, Father Klawiter, of Buffalo, rebelled against Irish episcopal authority, and formed his supporters into an independent congregation. In 1895, Father Anthony Kozlowski gathered his followers, in Chicago, into a separate independent Polish-American congregation.

Scranton, Pennsylvania attracted attention, in 1897, with the Polish Independent Movement.

> In the Polish Roman Catholic parish church in Scranton, Pennsylvania, as in many others in those early years of Polish immigration, there was friction in the relations of parishioners and priest. The people shared their grievances with the diocesan bishop, but without any episcopal response. In the course of time they decided to take things into their own hands. On a certain Sunday morning they attempted to block the priest's way and to prevent him from entering the Church. The church was their own, they reasoned. They built it

---

[24] Ibid., I, p. 386.
[25] Peter A. Ostafin, *The Polish Peasant in Transition: A Study of Group Integration as a Function of Symbiosis and Common Definitions* (unpublished Ph.D. dissertation, University of Michigan, 1948). See also George Pare, *The Catholic Church in Detroit 1701-1888* (Detroit: 1951), pp. 556-558.

with their own hard-earned money; they were taking care of it; they had their right to it. Their reasoning, however, was faulty, as they found out later to their chagrin. In the struggle between people and priest, ecclesiastical authority asserted itself, and resorted to force summoning the police—a most unfortunate blunder for ecclesiastics to commit to summon the police against their people, the "sheep of their pasture." A clash naturally resulted between the people and the police. Some of the people were clubbed and some were even jailed. To their disappointment and sorrow they found out that the Church property was not theirs, but the bishop's; that the title to it had been signed over by the Church to the bishop.[26]

Deeply conscious of the injustice they had suffered, representatives of the Polish-American community visited Father Francis Hodur in Nanticoke, a neighboring town, for advice. Having listened to their tale of grievances, Father Hodur told them that the only thing for them to do was to submit to the bishop's ruling or else to build a new church, but to make certain that they retain the title of it. Instead of submission to the bishop, the community decided to build a new church. In 1897, the new structure was ready for use. The diocesan Roman Catholic bishop refused to consecrate it or to appoint a priest. On March 10, 1897, the Polish-American community offered the pastorate to Father Francis Hodur. More than 200 people signed the petition requesting him to accept the pastorate. After a great deal of reflection and mediation he accepted the pastorate of St. Stanislas Church. On Sunday, March 20, 1897, Father Hodur celebrated his first High Mass in the new St. Stanislas Church. Father Hodur did not desire, nor intend, to sever his official connection with the Roman Catholic Church. He felt that whatever concessions he and his people might contend for, they could be granted within the framework of the Roman Catholic organization. Since he could not secure any satisfaction from the local diocesan bishop, he resolved to make his appeal to Rome. During January and February of 1898, Father Hodur travelled to Rome for a private papal audience.

Among personages of distinction and influence whom Father Hodur met in Rome were Cardinal M. Ledochowski, the Car-

---

[26] Fox, *The Polish National Catholic Church*, pp. 22-23.

dinal brothers Vanutelli and Father Gormier, papal confessor and dispenser of papal charities. In the petition laid before these distinguished churchmen—drawn up and signed by the Parish Committee of his church and co-signed by the neighboring churches of Nanticoke, Wilkes-Barre, Plymouth, Duryea and Dickson City—these churches begged the Holy See for the following three concessions: (1) That the title to church property be vested in the local parish church; (2) That parishes be free to choose their own committees, both managerial and administrative, without any interference from a priest or bishop; and (3) That they have a voice in the assignment of parish priests.

Cardinal Ledochowski read the petition over, listened to the added explanations and comments of Father Hodur, and then replied sharply and categorically: "In America all Roman Catholics are bound by the enactments of the Synod of Baltimore, of 1884, and approved by Pope Leo XIII. He who conforms to these regulations is within the pale of the Church; he who dissents from them excludes himself from the Church."[27]

In spite of Cardinal Ledochowski's sharpness and finality, Father Hodur tried to resolve the matter by trying to see the Pope personally. Father Gormier received Father Hodur very cordially. But learning of the nature of his petition Father Gormier replied: "My dear Father Hodur, your efforts here are bound to be fruitless. The entire set-up of the Church here, administered by the Holy Father, is largely financed with the money supplied by the American bishops. Their administration of the Church in their respective dioceses and their wishes must, therefore, be respected. The only way left open for you, then, is humbly to submit to the diocesan bishops."[28]

During his sojourn in Rome, Father Hodur clearly realized that he would not accomplish anything. He, therefore, cancelled his scheduled audience with the Holy Father, and promptly returned to Scranton, Pennsylvania, where he called a meeting of the St. Stanislas congregation and rendered a report which stated

---

[27] *Ibid.*, p. 25.
[28] *Ibid.*, p. 25.

the results of his mission to Rome. After the report, Michael Szczyglinski made a historical motion:

> "We Poles, members of St. Stanislaus parish in Scranton, having heard the report of our pastor, the Rev. Father Francis Hodur, regarding his efforts in Rome on our behalf, feel thoroughly convinced that it is useless for us further to appeal either to the diocesan bishop or to Rome for any redress of our grievances and that the only thing left to us is to place our reliance on the will of God, and to work together with our pastor for the good of our people and for their spiritual freedom in free America." The resolution was promptly seconded and passed unanimously.[29]

About two weeks later, after the meeting at St. Stanislas and the submission of a report to both bishops, O'Hara and Hoban, Father Hodur and his congregation were excommunicated from the Roman Catholic Church.[30] The tactless action of Pope Leo XIII unwittingly resulted in another schism which disengaged many other disgruntled Catholics from the folds of mother church. To acquaint his congregation with this inhuman and unchristian document, Father Hodur read the excommunication decree from the pulpit of his church. Following that, in the manner of Martin Luther, he burnt the papal bull and ordered the ashes to be cast into the stream which flowed at the foot of the hill where the church stands.

> As a result of this daring and dramatic act another wave of unrestrained enthusiasm swept over the congregation, and set it on fire. The people rose to their feet, sang hymns, repeated their prayers, thanked God, shook hands, embraced one another for joy, some rang church bells, others rushed forward to embrace the pastor as he descended from the pulpit, and to assure him that God was with them and would not forsake them.[31]

---

[29] *Ibid.,* p. 26.

[30] The excommunication was read from the pulpits of all the Roman Catholic churches in the Scranton Diocese, with the exception of one Polish church in Mill Creek—ministered to by Father Francis Chalcarz, who refused to read it. When he was removed from his charge by the bishop for his obstinacy and insubordination, he told his congregation to respect and honor Father Hodur, for he was an upright and honest man and a friend of the Polish people. Fox, *The Polish National Catholic Church,* p. 26.

[31] Fox, *The Polish National Catholic Church,* p. 27.

It was a veritable pentecostal scene. The people appeared wholly transformed. The spirit of faith and courage, seemed to have blessed them with Divine Love as they were entering upon a new and free life. Father Hodur organized an independent congregation, which still followed the Roman rite, but adopted Polish as the language of worship. The church also adopted a charter that provided for the clergy to share its management with the laity.

Soon other congregations followed the example initiated by Father Hodur. In September 1904, twenty-four parishes—claiming 20,000 adherents in five states—formally united to form a new denomination. Reverend Hodur—whose name became known in virtually every Polish-American household in America—possessed financial acumen combined with superb organizational ability. Through the diligent and persistent application of these qualities the new Polish National Catholic Church grew and prospered.[32] So Father Hodur's stature grew accordingly. At the first synod, Father Hodur was elected Bishop. Thus, a brilliant star, called Bishop Hodur, began to shine brightly in the heavens of America for Polish-Americans.[33]

Having reached a membership of at least 20,000 in its first seven years of existence, the movement was already well established as the one large schism to affect immigrant Catholics in

---

[32] Since its inception the Polish National Church organized 140 churches in the United States: fifty in the first two-and-a-half decades, from 1895 to 1919; another fifty in the decade of the twenties—the most active and productive decade in the history of the church; and forty churches in the last two-and-a-half decades, from 1930 to 1955. The membership, according to the *National Catholic Almanac,* for 1955, and the *World Almanac,* for the same year, numbered then 267,876 souls. To this figure can be added 2,600 which comprised the Canadian membership. The total reached 270,476. The accumulated property value of the church was estimated, in 1955, at $14,749,654 and a reserve fund of $200,000. Its indebtedness was only $1,567,956. Likewise in Poland, the National Catholic Church numbered about 100 parishes, in 1939, with a membership of approximately 400,000.

[33] Fox, in his history of the Polish National Catholic Church, gives the following reasons for its rise: (1) the overbearing way of priests and bishops in dealing with Polish-Americans; (2) the matter of ownership of church property and of the administration of church finances; (3) the refusal on the part of the Roman hierarchy to let congregations have any voice in the appointment or changes of parish priests; (4) a deep Polish nationalism; (5) bishops were not always friendly toward national sentiments; (6) although ritual was important and has its place—it was insufficient; and (7) the people's sacrifices were completely ignored by the Roman hierarchy.

America. Eventually Father Hodur received episcopal consecration from bishops of the Old Catholic Church in the Netherlands. Even the leaders of the overwhelming majority of Polish Americans who remained loyal to Rome admitted the attractiveness of the Polish National Catholic Church. Members of the Polish Catholic Congress meeting in Buffalo in 1901 warned in a memorial the American hierarchy: "They have so-called Polish bishops, whereas they accuse the Polish Roman Catholic clergy of treason to their nation when holding allegiance to Irish and German bishops."[34]

The Polish National Catholic Church, which had been maturing in silence, sprang into existence without the slow process of growth. The disillusioned Irish-American and German-American bishops had brought everlasting censure upon themselves for being responsible for the first and greatest Catholic defeat in the United States. If the American Protestants had spoken Polish and had more contact with the Polish-American immigrants, the results would have been disastrous. It was fortunate for the Roman Catholic Church that the Protestant churches were not located in the Polish-American communities. The ban of excommunication—with its antecedent horrors—had no effect on Bishop Hodur who dared to stand up and denounce the gross discrimination of the American Catholic Church. Bishop Hodur stood his ground, for he had ample support from his people.

Until the defection of Bishop Hodur, Rome was completely indifferent to the griefs, longings and aspirations of the Polish immigrants in America. The success of the Polish National Catholic Church, under Bishop Hodur, had a deeply disquieting effect on Rome which forced the Pope to realize that the Irish-Americans and German-Americans were not the only ethnic groups represented in the United States. Also, the loss of 20,000 Catholics finally made Rome aware of the numbers, strength, and contribution of the Polish Catholics in the United States. As the clouds waxed larger and darker, Rome no longer sat and watched complacently.

---

[34] Anthony J. Kuzniewski, S. J., "Polish Catholics in America," *The Catholic Weekly* (April 9, 1976), p. 10.

The complaints and abuses were of such severity that, in 1902, Pope Leo XIII sent his personal representative, Archbishop A. Symons, to examine the situation. During his sojourn in America, the Archbishop visited 160 Polish-American parishes and delivered 350 speeches in order to remove the abuses of the Irish-American Catholic bishops towards the Polish Catholics in America. That more Polish-American Catholics did not defect from the Church—which exploited, humiliated, and discriminated against them—is amazing and an expressed proof of their devoutness during the late nineteenth century. Despite manifold obstacles, the Polish immigrants continued to profess their Catholic Faith in an exemplary manner. Blessed by a strong living faith and a vigorous Polish culture, they made an impressive contribution to the life of the American Catholic Church. Monsignor H. Maino—on the occasion of Poland's 1,000 Years of Christianity—made this quite clear when he stated: "The American Catholic Church would never have attained its present size and vigor had the history of Poland taken a different course."

Orestes A. Brownson, Father Isaac Hecker, and Father Waclaw Kruszka each looked with grave concern and critically interpreted the Irish-American control of the Church; they stated frankly that the Roman Catholic Church could not become properly American until it ceased to be dominated by the Irish-Americans. In a letter of 1849, Brownson—a New England intellectual who became converted to Catholicism—had the pluck to write: "Nobody can deny that in external decorum and the ordinary moral and social virtues the Irish Catholics are the most deficient class of our community."[35] Brownson also warned against the danger to the Church if Catholicity should become identified with "Irish hoodlumism, drunkenness and poverty."[36]

Father Isaac Hecker—who labored to convince Americans that the Catholic Church was not undemocratic—pleaded for a more liberal spirit within the Church.

Father Waclaw Kruszka—another Joshua fighting in the valley—also denounced the Irish influence:

---

[35] Quoted in Carl Wittke, *The Irish in America*, p. 92. See also Arthur M. Schlesinger, Jr., *Orestes A. Brownson*, and Isaac Hecker, *The Church and the Age*
[36] Quoted in Wittke, *The Irish in America*, p. 92.

It is an undeniable fact that although the Irish form only about a third of the Catholic population, of the hundred Catholic bishops in the United States, almost all are of Irish nationality; the few German bishops being only a drop in the sea. This is a fact, and against a fact there is no argument. From this fact one can easily deduct the conclusion that the Irish want a certain priest for a bishop, just because he is Irish. . . . What the Poles in their movement for a Polish bishop want, is the following: to have bishops from any nationality—not from one exclusively—as it was practiced to this time. The Irish—as facts prove—presented always and still present candidates of Irish extraction, to the exclusion of other nationalities, as if they alone had the monopoly of wisdom and sanctity and episcopal dignity. But why do the Irish mostly succeed in Rome? Simply by persuading the Roman authorities that the Irish nationality is the only American nationality; all others are "foreign" nationalities.

Since 1854, the Poles built, every year, churches, schools, asylums, colleges . . . paid always faithfully their church taxes, cathedraticum, seminaristicum . . . and during this long period, never enjoyed any rights and privileges in the Church, never enjoyed any representation in the hierarchy. This is clearly unjust and un-American! And now, when we make a just complaint, they say to us, that there was not as yet any Polish priest worthy to become a bishop, but as soon as they will find one, they will make one. I need not say that this is a poor excuse, and an uncharitable one, not worthy of a true Christian. It is an open insult to the whole Polish clergy. For so long, were the Irish and the few Germans, the only worthy ones upon whom the Holy Ghost reigned to descend? One must be arrogant, to assert this! Indeed, to this favoritism of one and the disregard of other nationalities, we may safely ascribe the fact, that there was in the United States no gain, but a loss of millions of Catholics! The Independent Polish sect says: "If the Pope allows the organization in the United States of an Irish national hierarchy, why does he not allow the formation of a Polish national hierarchy?" And even pure Americans, I mean those of no denomination either religious or national, I have heard asking: "Where is the expression of catholicity in your church? Is it not predominantly Irish Catholic?"[37]

President Theodore Roosevelt remarked to Father Kruszka, on a certain occasion, when he found his deductions logical that

---

[37] Ks. Waclaw Kruszka, *Siedm Siedmioleci Czyli Pol Wieku Zycia* (Poznan: 1924), pp. 152-153.

he believed the Polish-Americans should have their own bishops.³⁸ Father Kruszka tried to achieve without schism and revolt what Bishop Hodur had achieved by revolt.

The fourth group chose to retain the Catholic heritage and to foster its Polish culture as much as possible by creating a new pattern of education to which instruction in Polish was central. They realized that the genuine American, the typical American, is himself a hyphenated individual. This does not mean that he is part American with some foreign ingredient added. It means that the American is international and interracial in his make-up. He is not merely an American, plus Pole, or English. But the American is the common denominator whether Polish, German, English, French, Spanish, Italian, Greek, Irish, Negro, Jew or Arabic. The hyphen connects instead of separates.

The Polish Catholic order of nuns, in the Polish-American Catholic schools, made every effort to teach the children to respect other nationalities, and took pains to enlighten them as to the great contributions of every ethnic strain in America. In the teaching of American history, they took into account the great waves of migrations to the United States, which helped form the country. They made every effort to make the students conscious

---

[38] The apparent apathy in respect to the promotion of Polish-American priests to the rank of bishops was a substantial cause for complaint in the Polish settlements. Despite their size and weight of responsibility connected with their management, these Polish ships of faith were still captained by officers of junior rank who seemed to go unnoticed in the ranks of the Catholic hierarchy in the United States. It was fifty-four years after the founding of the first parish in America that the Polish-Americans were to give the Catholic Church its first Polish bishop. Bishop Paul Rhode was consecrated bishop, in 1908, in Chicago—an example of obvious tokenism. Bishop Edward Kozlowski followed him in the same rank, in 1914. This blatant discrimination and tokenism on the part of Irish and German Catholics produced much discontent in Polish-American circles. As a matter of fact, it almost disrupted the unity of the Catholic church among the Polish-Americans.

Until 1908, not a single bishop was selected from the ranks of the Polish-American clergy. On the basis of an estimated twelve per cent of the Catholic population, which they comprised in the United States at the turn of the century, the Polish-Americans reasoned that they should have at least two archbishops and eleven bishops selected from their number; yet, the fifteen archbishops and ninety-four bishops in the United States, as of 1900, were all non-Polish. With fortified indignation they further compared their 900 parishes to the 456 German speaking parishes and discovered that for that number of parishes the Germans gave the Catholic Church in the United States, they were represented by fourteen bishops and three archbishops. The Poles were given none. To the German-hating Poles, this was like being led to Heaven by the Sultan of Turkey.

of the rich breadth of this national composition. They believed that until each pupil recognizes the factors which created America, will the individual student comprehend and continue to prize and reverence his own past. They insisted that he should claim his identity and enjoy the experience of living in two worlds simultaneously.

The fourth group—through diligent application of work and funds—was instrumental in establishing, in the United States, the large number of Polish-American Catholic parishes, schools, theological seminaries, religious congregations, hospitals, homes for the aged, charitable and social agencies as well as the various publications, and other church and civic organizations. The parishes, schools and seminaries were staffed by Polish-American priests, theologians, teaching sisters and scholars who staunchly defended Polish Catholic culture, and contributed to keeping alive the Polish language and traditions by their insistence. In 1874, the Felician Sisters came to America at the invitation of Rev. Joseph Dabrowski. In 1885, the Sisters of the Holy Family of Nazareth laid their foundation in Chicago.

The work of this last and largest group was facilitated by the Pope, who sided with the more conservative majority in his *Testem Benevolentiae*. Only Cardinal Gibbons' unusual diplomacy spared him from papal criticism which would have damned his type of "Americanism" as heresy. And indeed it was!

The work of Mieczyslaw Cardinal Ledochowski, Prefect of Propaganda and an international figure of great influence, was not particularly effective.[39] He lacked the courage to be really outstanding. From 1892 to 1902, he stood at the head of the Sacred Congregation of the Propagation of the Faith, which then guided the affairs of the Church in the United States. Under Cardinal Ledochowski, many far-reaching decisions were made

---

[39] Cardinal Ledochowski became the Archbishop of Poznan in 1866. During his tenure he roused a storm of protest by forbidding the national hymn, itself a prayer, *Boze Cos Polske*, to be sung in the churches. He was resolved to keep his office above national controversies—*civis Romanus, subditus Borussiae*. For over two years his relations with the Polish clergy was strained. When he opposed the introduction of the German language in religious instruction during the Kulturkampf, waged by Bismarck, he was thrown into prison in 1874. In 1876, he was deposed and allowed to retire to Rome. For twelve years, the position of Archbishop of Poznan, which he occupied, remained vacant.

of concern to American Catholics: as, for example, those affecting the school question, the national parishes, or the policies of Cardinal Gibbons and Archbishop Ireland. It is unfortunate that in his concern for the spiritual welfare of the immigrants in the United States he did not remove the arrant discrimination practiced by the Irish-American clergy. Instead he condemned the intrigues and agitation in the United States over priests of other nationalities to episcopal sees. In a letter, addressed to the American hierarchy, the Cardinal stated:

> Whenever an episcopal see is vacant in America, clergy and people become excited, different factions discuss possible candidates in meetings, and, through the public press, seek all means to advance their favorites. The chief cause of these divisions is that Catholics, dividing on national lines, demand bishops from the ranks of their several nationalities, instead of keeping sorely in view the welfare of the Church. This welfare is the sole guide of the Holy See in naming Bishops for all countries, and especially must be followed in the case of the United States, whither populations go from various European countries, to the end that they build up there for themselves a new "patria," where they must coalesce into one people and form together one nation. This principle shall be kept steadily in view by the Holy See, which, in consequence, will in the naming of bishops, adhere strictly to the rules of the Baltimore Council.[40]

This letter, which was known to express the personal views of the Pope, was issued in May 1892. In order to provide a wide circulation for Cardinal Ledochowski's letter, Gibbons gave it to the Associated Press.[41]

Two years after Gibbons' death, the Central-Verein met in St. Paul where Archbishop Messmer was present. Messmer was quoted as having said, in reference to the controversy of years before: "I know that Cardinal Gibbons and Archbishop Ireland positively understood that they made a mistake."[42] Nothing could be further from the truth; neither Cardinal Gibbons nor Archbishop Ireland had the charisma, the distinction, or the ability to lead the American Catholic Church through a new era.

---

[40] James H. Moynihan, *The Life of Archbishop John Ireland* (New York: 1953), pp. 69-70.
[41] Ellis, *op. cit.*, I, p. 380.
[42] Ellis, *op. cit.*, I, p. 382.

CHAPTER SIX
World War I

> Poland fell through a vicious diplomatic system. She has been restored in an age of idealism and hope. Her existence will be a tribute to the revival of international justice. But the Polish Republic will also be an eternal monument to the courage and tenacity of the Polish race, the triumph of faith and hope over suffering and despair, the victory, over the powers of evil, of all the great and beautiful ideals that inspire mankind to live and create.
>
> —A. Bruce Boswell[1]

> Walczyc o Ojczyzne z bronia w reku, to najswietszy obowiazek i najwiekszy dla Polaka zaszczyt.
>
> —Ignacy Jan Paderewski[1a]

> All the future of a nation is wrapped up in the folds of your flags. The White Eagle can once more unfold its wings. It will soon float in the light of a sky once more serene, and in the rays of victory.
>
> —President Poincare of France

On June 28, 1914, a tubercular nineteen-year-old student of Serbian extraction, fired two shots which killed the Archduke Ferdinand of Austria-Hungary and his wife, Sophia, Duchess of Hohenberg. The shots signaled the final sunset of the age of confidence and security.[2] A general era of building empires had ended. The two shots terminated all reason and jolted the contrived balance of power into a terrible holocaust. Within hours— through a tangled web of secret treaties and overpowering national

---

[1] Bruce Boswell, *Poland and the Poles* (London: 1919), pp. 301-302.
[1a] To defend one's country with arms in hand is the holiest responsibility and the greatest honor for a Pole.
[2] Joseph A. Wytrwal, *Poles in American History and Tradition*, pp. 282-318.

fears and ambitions—the assassination had started Europe on its collision course. Like a bolt of lightning from the cloudless sky, during the halcyon days of July 1914, war broke out which split the taut fabrics of Europe's alliances and dragged people from all over the world into a holocaust: from the muddy Polish plains to the steamy jungles of Africa, from the frozen Alps to the deserts of Arabia. It also, in the next four years, sent over 8,000,000 men to their deaths, and altered the map of the world.

From the moment the guns boomed in Europe, Americans of Polish stock began mobilizing their resources with a view toward directing them into two channels: aid for the cause of Polish independence, and to support the United States. Although Poland had no part in precipitating the world conflict, yet by reason of its geographic position, it became one of the greatest theaters of the war. Poland suffered mutilation from both the Central Powers and the Allies. The German artillery bombarded terrain held by the Allies. The Allies blasted away at positions possessed by the Central Powers. The Poles suffered regardless who was attacking or who was defending. In Poland, whole nations met in a death grapple. Three gigantic armies—those of Germany, Austria and Russia, numbering millions of men—were marching and counter-marching over the full length and breadth of once Polish territory, leaving in their wake death and desolation.

> Their geographical location made the ancient Polish lands once again a great battlefield; about 85 per cent of Poland today became the scene of battle and the victim of the destruction wrought by huge contending armies. Cities, towns and villages were bombarded; rural areas devastated; roads, bridges, railroad tracks, stations, water towers, shops, telegraph lines, all were destroyed during the various advances and retreats, bombardments and defenses. Several million people were driven eastward into Russia proper before the retreating Russian army. Machinery and industrial supplies were confiscated by the advancing Germans and sent to Germany; all brass and bronze was seized by them to be made up into war supplies.
> A Scotch author, A. E. Tennant, who came to Poland to study the situation wrote: "The disasters of Poland were greater than those of Belgium in proportion as the country was larger and more completely ravaged. Nay, more: Belgium, or the greater part of it, was

occupied, lived in and kept habitable by the Germans, however galling or severe their yoke might be. Poland was turned into a vast battlefield and many times fought over."[3]

Another ghastly tragedy of the Great War was the way in which compulsory military services had forced Poles to fight against Poles. Their country, conquered and partitioned, was not one of the belligerent nations, and yet a million-and-a-half of her sons were fighting fratricidal battles in the armies of three different warring nations.

Just before the war, the Polish-speaking element of Austria—dwelling in the crownlands of Galicia and Silesia, where they intermingled with Czechs and Austro-Germans—numbered nearly 5,000,000, compared with about 12,000,000 in Russia, 3,000,000 in Prussia, and perhaps as many as 3,000,000 overseas. It was a cruel fate that obliged young Poles fighting under three alien flags to make war upon their national brothers. "Look at my family," cried Count Joseph Potocki, "I am a Russian subject; my brother Roman is an Austrian subject; one of my brothers-in-law is a German subject; all of my cousins and nephews, because of circumstances of inheritance, are likewise divided among the three nations. In the bosom of the same race we are condemned to kill each other." All told, better than fifteen per cent of the soldiers in the Hapsburg armies were drawn from Polish homes, approximately 200,000 died in the war and over 300,000 sustained serious injuries.[4]

The tragedy was vividly portrayed by Henryk Sienkiewicz.

When the order for a cavalry or a bayonet charge is given, hordes of soldiers rush on each other, and when they get to striking distance and commence cutting one another down, they find that the language in which they are uttering their imprecations is the common national tongue—Polish! It frequently happens when the Red Cross go out to collect the wounded from a battlefield, they lift from a heap one man in German uniform, another in Austrian and a third in Russian, and discover that they are all—Poles.[5]

---

[3] Paul Super, *Events and Personalities in Polish History* (Bombay: 1944), pp. 99-100.
[4] Arthur J. May, *The Passing of the Hapsburg Monarchy 1914-1918* (Philadelphia: 1966), I, p. 366.
[5] Sister Mary Georgina Mielcarek, F.O.S.F., *The Re-Creation of Poland 1914-1920* (unpublished Master's thesis, University of Detroit, 1937), p. 38.

The tragedy lay in the fact that no matter which army a Pole served, he fought against a nation rather than for the country whose uniform he wore. The war created many other problems.

> The Polish territory, the cockpit of the battles of Europe was devastated from end to end. An area seven times as vast as that of Belgium had been crushed and ruined by the iron heel of war. Poland had her Louvain, Kalisz, a thriving city of forty thousand people, was leveled to the ground at the beginning of the German invasion. Although the city was neither fortified nor occupied by the enemy, it was bombarded by the German artillery and hundreds of peaceful inhabitants killed, because nine German soldiers accidentally were shot.
>
> In the midst of the desolation and ruin, thousands were without a roof over their heads. The spectre of famine and pestilence crushed whole families. Fugitives wandered through the forests or hid themselves in disused trenches or in the cellars of the numerous partially burned houses. Many subsisted on wild roots or even carrion flesh of barks of trees.[6]

The Poles, as a whole, did not believe in aggression from Germany, and they certainly never had any inkling of the possibility of aggression from Russia; therefore, the state of individual and private preparedness for the war was wholly inadequate. Before July, life went on much as usual. No one was storing stocks of basic foodstuffs; no one was amassing sufficient supplies of coal, since it was still mid-summer.

Owing to the three partitions of Poland, a successful solution to the Polish question would require sacrifices on the part of Germany, Austria-Hungary, and Russia—an Entente power. Moreover, since Poles were on opposing sides during the war, both belligerents (Germany with Austria-Hungary against Russia) appealed for Polish support, holding out to them the prospect of independence.[7] The Russian commander-in-chief, Grand Duke Nicholas, made the following appeal on August 14, 1914.

---

[6] Mielcarek, *The Re-Creation of Poland, 1914-1920*, pp. 38-39. See also J. Bukowinski, "The Destruction of Kalisz," *Free Poland* (April 16, 1915), and Julie Ledochowska, *Poland Ravaged and Bereaved*.

[7] Austria was the first to recognize the independent Polish Riflemen's Societies, and immediately after the outbreak of war incorporated them into the Austrian forces as the Polish Legion under the leadership of Jozef Pilsudski.

Poles! The hour has come when the dreams of your fathers and forefathers can at length be realized. A century and a half ago the living body of Poland was torn to pieces, but her soul has not perished. She lived in the hope that the time would come for the resurrection of the Polish nation and its fraternal reconciliation with Great Russia. The Russian armies bring you the glad tidings of this reconciliation. May the boundaries vanish which have cut asunder the Polish people! May it once more be united under the scepter of the Russian Emperor! Under this scepter Poland will arise again free in faith, language and self-government.[8]

Added to the pressures of checks and reverses suffered on various fronts, along with growing need for new reserves, Germany and Austria-Hungary resolved, late in 1916, to bid for support in former Russian Poland, by means of a proclamation which proposed the creation of an independent Poland.[9]

On the fifth of November, 1916, a group of sixty or seventy Polish officials and important civilians were invited to the Zamek (the medieval castle that had been the Warsaw residence of the Polish kings, then of the Russian governor, and in turn of the German military governor) at twelve o'clock. In the famous Hall of Columns the Poles were ranged on one side, the German officials and army officers on the other.

Through the center door where Polish kings used to enter came Von Besseler and read aloud the proclamation in German, in the name of the kaisers of Germany and Austria, granting independence "to meet the undying wish of the Poles." It was then read in Polish. At the same day and hour the Austrian governor-general was doing the same thing in Lublin. Independence for Russian Poland, a greater measure of autonomy for Austrian Poland. In the next room in the Zamek a band played the Polish national hymn, followed by the German hymn.[10]

---

[8] Alexander Dallin, "Future of Poland," *Russian Diplomacy and Eastern Europe 1914-1917* (New York: 1963), pp. 6-7.
[9] The proclamation did not unite the nation, but perpetuated the division into three parts. The reconstituted Poland consisted only of part of Russian Poland. Its frontiers were not strictly defined and its form of government only described as a "hereditary and constitutional Monarchy." Some form of union with Austria and Germany was anticipated; and it was under their joint control that the army of the new political unit was to be organized, administered and used.
[10] Grace Humphrey, *Pilsudski, Builder of Poland* (New York: 1936), pp. 159-160.

The proclamation was coldly received. When the guests left the Zamek, posters announcing the granting of independence to Poland were posted on the walls. But there was no enthusiasm. Among the students, there were no demonstrations for Germany.

> The next day a second poster appeared in Warsaw, with more promises. We will give an army to the new Polish state—now the Poles can fight under the Polish flag—the Poles who in the past always fought so heroically—and so on. Forty-five recruiting stations were opened in the city. Special privileges were to be given. At the end of one month thirty-five men had presented themselves for this great Polish army, and they applied for the sanitary battalion.[11]

Von Besseler was in despair. Instead of a million recruits, or eight-hundred-thousand, he had thirty-five applicants for the sanitary battalion.

> A joke went the rounds of the Poles in Warsaw. A man rushes up to an acquaintance on the street and demands, "Where is the nearest recruiting station?" The second man answers, "In Tworki!" (an insane asylum near the city).[12]

The "Two-Kaiser Manifesto" which promised to create an autonomous Polish state was the first expression of recognition, by any warring nation, of Poland's claims to political independence. Not to be outdone by Germany and Austria-Hungary, Russia on Christmas Day, 1916, announced in the Czar's Order of the Day, the creation of a *free* Poland to be formed from all three partitioned parts of the former Polish kingdom.

The leaders of the Polish nationalist movement in the United States represented the more elite members from the Polish-American community which comprised of editors, schoolteachers, clergy and officers of various fraternal organizations. Basically they wanted Poland to be free for they wanted it to govern itself under its famous and historical constitution. The tenets of their belief were based on the liberal ideals of mid-nineteenth century nationalists throughout Western Europe and the United States. They also wanted their people to enjoy a good education and to ad-

---

[11] Ibid., p. 160.
[12] Ibid., p. 161.

vance by practicing the noble virtues of self-reliance, thrift, pride and hard work.

To form potential military units, among the Polish Americans was a long established practice. After the declaration of war in Europe, in 1914, the Falcon military exercises, in the United States, had to be implemented more discreetly. The Falcons did not wish to violate President Wilson's proclamation of neutrality. Also, they did not want to prejudice their cause in the eyes of American citizens.

So the military exercises assumed the guise of picnics and weekend outings. Oftentimes, the trainees almost drew fire from infuriated farmers who saw swarms of strangers deploying about their pastures and woodlands. Upon one occasion the exercises in the vicinity of Poughkeepsie, New York, led to total annihilation when Poland's rustic heroes found themselves "prisoners of war" in a country jail. In response to the protests from local farmers, the sheriff with his deputies entered the maneuver area and imprisoned the would-be Polish lancers. The authorities in Poughkeepsie notified not the next of kin, but Polish civic leaders in New York City from whose Polish districts most of the "fallen" had come. The prisoners were ransomed with vouchers of future good behavior. A minor set-back, some embarrassment; yet the cause of Poland was being served![13]

The field maneuvers—inspired by patriotism and fortified with occasional toasts to Poland—were disjointed and of little military value; nevertheless, many such local companies were organized and maintained by Falcon lodges in the United States.

The Falcons soon came to realize that lodges might possibly train cadres and participate in military parades, but they could never raise, equip and maintain an army. It soon became apparent that the only hope for sustaining a field unit rested in the incorporation into one of the armies of the warring nations. In December 1916, secret negotiations were concluded between the Canadian War Office and top officials of the Polish Falcons of America, whereby Canada agreed to train a small cadre of Polish-Americans.

On New Year's Eve, while America rang in a new year, a

---

[13] Stanley R. Pliska, "The 'Polish-American Army' 1917-1921," *The Polish Review*, X (Summer, 1965), pp. 48-49.

small band of twenty-three intrepid Polish patriots secretly crossed the border into Canada in the midst of a raging snowstorm. These patriots took no farewell leaves; they told nobody who they were or who sent them; they themselves knew only that they were leaving to serve Poland.

Before long the only secret about these men was their whereabouts. Their communities missed them—and so did somebody else. Enraged and un-Spartan wives loaded down with family responsibilities lost all sense of patriotism and descended upon the Pittsburgh office of the Falcons demanding the return of their husbands. Despite all onslaughts of the female platoon, the secrecy of the mission was maintained. The wives were remembered, they continued to receive letters from husbands, but all letters were post-marked "Pittsburgh, Pennsylvania."[14]

By April 1917, when the training of these cadets was completed, the United States was already at war on the side of the Allies; thus, there no longer remained need for secrecy. It was now publicly announced that these Polish cadets were trained by the Canadian Officers Training Corps, on the University of Toronto campus, where seventeen of their number passed all of the requirements and became officers. The top five graduates were, in turn, sent to Alliance College, Cambridge Springs, Pennsylvania, where a new school for the training of Polish-American non-commissioned officers had been in operation since March 1917.[15]

In 1914, the Polish National Committee sprang into existence to assist partitioned Poland in regaining her independence. The

---

[14] Ibid., p. 50.

[15] The non-commissioned officers' school at Cambridge Springs, Pennsylvania, called for dedication and financial sacrifice. Each cadet paid $14.00 per month for room and board. He also purchased his own uniform, and he paid transportation costs to and from camp. The over-all outlay for a three month training course in many instances amounted to $150.00, was an enormous expense in a time when steel workers were earning the grand total of $3.00 per day. Yet the school never lacked applicants. Its promising graduates were selected for additional training as officer candidates and sent to Canada. Of the 389 graduates produced by the school during its existence, almost one-half qualified for officer training. In the summer of 1917, this NCO school was moved to Camp Quinton, Côtes du Nord, Canada, the official training site for the future Polish Army. Stanley R. Pliska, "The 'Polish-American Army' 1917-1921," The Polish Review, pp. 50-51.

Committee succeeded in uniting most Polish-Americans under its banner. Led by John Smulski of Chicago, the Committee—working through 500 local units—collected over $50,000,000 in goods and money for Polish freedom and relief.[16]

The fraternal organizations also established funds to aid the Polish cause: The Polish Roman Catholic Union established the *Skarb Narodowy* (the National Treasury); the Polish National Alliance established the *Fundusz Niepodleglosciowy* (the Independence Fund); the Polish Falcons established the Kosciuszko Fund and War Fund; and the Polish Women's Alliance established the *Fundusz Bojowy* (The Fighting Fund).

At the outbreak of World War I, Ignace Jan Paderewski lived in Riond Bosson, Switzerland. In those fateful days, as he surveyed the broad sweep of Polish history, Paderewski sensed the import of onrushing events and was deeply convinced that the moment of Poland's final liberation was near. As though by design, the courageous striving of Kosciuszko, the poetic prophecies of Slowacki, Mickiewicz, and Krasinski, and the noble dream of Sienkiewicz would be achieved. The massive campaign would unchain his historic land and his people from their plundered past.

Almost a hundred years earlier, in 1815, Talleyrand, one of the world's shrewdest diplomats, described the exact situation with which Paderewski was confronted a hundred years later.

> By remaining partitioned Poland will not be destroyed for ever. The Poles, although not forming a political entity, will always form a family. They will no longer have a common country, but they will have a common language. They will, therefore, remain united by the strongest and most lasting of all bonds. They will, under foreign domination, reach the age of manhood, and the moment when they reach it will not be far distant from the moment when, having won their freedom, they will all rally round one center.[17]

Sensing that America would play the leading part before the world tragedy was over, Paderewski, early in 1913, crossed the

---

[16] It also helped to raise a volunteer force of 26,000 Polish-Americans, the famous Blue Army, which fought under General J. Haller in France and Poland on the side of the Allies.

[17] Rom Landau, *Ignace Paderewski, Musician and Statesman* (New York: 1936), pp. 107-108.

Atlantic Ocean to become the spokesman of a wronged and beleaguered people. American people hardly knew anything about the war beyond the Western front. They had no conception of the immeasurable injury and suffering inflicted on the peoples of the Eastern front. It seemed impossible, for a long time, to get them to grasp the fact that Poland was as much a non-combatant and an invaded country as Belgium was.

When Paderewski visited the large cities of America, he told his audience—wherever they could be assembled—of the urgent needs of Poland, and that the Polish-Americans were unable to carry the burden alone. All Americans were asked to aid a country which was partitioned over a hundred years. His careful preparations—aided by expert observations in America and Europe—were bearing out.

Paderewski opened the most unique tour of his career at San Francisco with these words: "I have to speak about a country which is not yours, in a language which is not mine." His addresses—eloquent in their simplicity on behalf of Poland—created such an impression that they were discussed almost as much as his music. Paderewski championed not only the cause of Poland, but also the lot of all oppressed peoples when he voiced his defense of the Poles.

> Poland did nothing to bring on this war. She had neither neutrality nor national power to provoke the jealousy of her neighbor. Her crime was simply that she lay between the territories of the belligerents who sought one another's throats.[18]

Paderewski—whose refined instinct rebelled against force—allied himself with the Lwow School of thought which attributed chief responsibility for Poland's downfall in the eighteenth century to the rapacity of predatory neighbors. He, thus, defended Poland's position after its political dismemberment.

> Poland fell because her enemies were greedy, unscrupulous and strong. Poland fell because she was generous, humane, and weak.[19]

---

[18] I. J. Paderewski, "Helpless Poland," *Independent Magazine*, 83 (August, 1915), p. 192.

Paderewski's consciousness of the injustice to Poland was not personal, as he once remarked.

> I will accuse nobody; I will make no complaints against the belligerents. We have been treated according to the logic of war, which is in itself a cruelty, an atrocity, nowadays multiplied by science.[20]

Voicing his protest against racial oppression, he showed its evident paradoxes. Speaking against the Russian subjugation of Poles during the Partitions, he probably recalled personal experiences which prompted him to remark:

> To the oppressed, wronged, dispossessed, persecuted, imprisoned, tormented they began to expound about the brotherhood of nations, human solidarity, social justice, universal peace, new order, and wellbeing; at the price of renouncing national ideals they promised heaven on earth, untrammeled earthly happiness.[21]

Emphasizing the paradoxical situation of Poland during World War I, Paderewski said:

> Our country, in fact, is just as Belgium was called—cockpit of Europe —and it may now be called the battlefield of the world if not of civilization. . . . The whole world stands aghast and impotent before Poland, all amazed that it is at once the victim and the culprit.[22]

Paderewski not only presented the problem of the Poles in the light of general human interest and understanding, but he also treated these problems scientifically from an historical, ethnical, psychological, political, economic, and moral point of view. He re-echoed the traditions of Polish history. Because of his vehement protests against any kind of injustice, he preferred to rely on the superiority of right over might, and to that end he counselled love, not insurrection.

> There must be a victory of light over darkness, of good over evil, of justice over crime.[23]

---

[19] Theodore Joseph Buczynski, *Ignace Jan Paderewski As An Orator* (unpublished Master's thesis, De Paul University, 1949), p. 21.
[20] *Ibid.*, p. 21.
[21] *Ibid.*, p. 21.
[22] I. J. Paderewski, "Plea for Poles," *Free Poland*, I (April 16, 1915), p. 13.

The positive and constructive features of his message, he never seemed to leave in doubt.

> My errand is not of hatred but of love. I do not intend to incite passion, but to awaken compassion.[24]

To the children attending the parish school of St. Stanislaus, in New York City, he made the following comment:

> Always tell the renegades, those who have deserted the Polish nation, that their action is abhorrent and sinful, for our Fatherland was always great; it gave forth great daughters and sons; it accomplished great deeds; it defended faith, love and justice in the world; in addition, it was the vanguard of Christianity. Today, she is also great, but great in misery and misfortune, and that is the reason we should love her, serve her and work for her to hasten the day for a better destiny.[25]

Since the Polish language is uniquely expressive, Paderewski did not hesitate to use striking and unusual metaphors as a great orator would for particular effect. When he described Chopin's music he alluded to the Polish soul's rebellion against the partitioning powers.[26]

> This music, tender and tempestuous, tranquil and passionate, heart-reaching, potent, overwhelming; this music which eludes metrical discipline, rejects the fetters of rhythmic rule, and refuses submission to the metronome, as if it were the yoke of some hated government; this music bids us hear, know, and realize that our nation, our land, the whole of Poland, lives, feels, and moves in *"Tempo rubato."*[27]

In his commemorative and eulogistic speeches, Paderewski did not follow the biographical method by listing chronological details of the subject's life. He singled out and set forth what the person accomplished in life, what he stood for, what influence he exerted, and what was likely to be his place in history. In this manner, he indicated Chopin's achievement:

---

[23] "Mr. Paderewski's Speech," *Free Poland*, IV (April 1, 1918), p. 156.
[24] Buczynski, *op. cit.*, p. 22.
[25] "Mowa Paderewskiego Do Dzieci Polskich w Nowym Yorku," *Nowiny Polskie* (November 9, 1915), p. 3.
[26] Paderewski was one of the world's foremost pianists and best interpreter of Chopin's music. He edited the publication of his complete works.
[27] Buczynski, *op. cit.*, p. 31.

For he, not by flower-hidden works, but by deeds adorned by the most beautiful flowers gained the whole world for Poland.[28]

In describing how Chopin's notes were like messengers for the Polish race beyond its borderlands, he stressed the following point:

> Not even the nation (Russia) . . . had yet dared lift its usurping hand toward Chopin. . . . What an abyss lay between his yearnings, his grief . . . and the withering despair which flows toward us as a blast, frost-laden across the steppes, immeasurable, boundless, and hopeless. . . .[29]

In his eulogy on Sienkiewicz, Paderewski told his audience how the words of the novelist strengthened the hearts of all Poles and taught them not to despair in their suffering.

> He spoke in prose, and his words reached everywhere. For the weak, poor, injured, dispossessed, he showed a tender sympathy. . . . He loved people. . . . He loved the faith of our fathers.[30]

Paderewski usually concluded his discussion of Polish history with dramatic appeals to the pride and generosity of his listeners:

> If I have succeeded, pray speak about Poland to your kind, good friends. Tell them that far away—from your prosperous, opulent, happy country—there are great people in great poverty, in great need, suffering beyond the limit of human endurance. Tell them that these very people, in the days of your need, sent you Kosciuszko, offered you Pulaski, and not for the pleasure of fighting the English, but for the noble joy of contributing to the glorious conquest of human liberty.[31]

Though Paderewski's character was staunchly Polish, his pleas were not only national, but universal. On behalf of all oppressed people, he expressed these eloquent words:

---

[28] *Ibid.*, p. 40.
[29] *Ibid.*, p. 40.
[30] *Ibid.*, p. 40.
[31] *Ibid.*, p. 42.

> Faithful to Poland's traditions, true to the spirit of our ancestors, I am not seeking assistance for those of my blood only, or of my religion, but for all, without any distinction of race, of creed, or of opinion, for all who are sharing in common my country's unspeakable misfortune.[32]

An absence of any political or personal ambition was also characteristic of Paderewski's persuasive qualities:

> I am a Pole, faithful son of the fatherland. Thought of a strong and great Poland, free and independent, was and is the theme of my existence; its realization was and is the one goal of my life.[33]

He made this point clear several times:

> My heart and hands are undefiled. Beyond relief for Poland, I did not ask and will not ask for anything from you, either here or in Poland: I expect no rewards, and I demand no payment. I do not thirst for power.[34]

When Paderewski appeared on behalf of the Polish Victims' Relief Fund in New York, he prefaced his performance with a speech on "The Martyrdom of Poland." In those dramatic times he was magnificent. A reporter from *Musical America* made the following comment:

> Neither Mr. Paderewski's speech nor his delivery of it will soon pass from the memories of those who heard it. It lasted about an hour and touched upon the glories of Poland—the loftiness of the Polish character, the idealism and humanitarian instincts of the nation's kings and law givers even in remote centuries, the prowess of its warriors, the higher glories of its poets, painters, scientists, philosophers and musicians; upon the rapacity of its partitioners in past times and upon the illimitable horrors of its present plight.[35]

Paderewski endeavored to accomplish the following tasks in America: to acquaint the American people with Poland's dis-

---

[32] *Ibid.*, p. 45.
[33] *Ibid.*, p. 46.
[34] *Ibid.*, p. 16.
[35] Richard Schnickel, *The World of Carnegie Hall* (New York: 1960), p. 171.

tressful situation in order to send food for its starving population; to make the world conscious of the historical crime of 1795; and the need for reparation. He was also keen on rousing popular American interest in Poland's political problem and her hopes for the future; on opening the way toward official government assistance and resolving Poland's freedom—forgotten for so long in the world. Once again, he wanted to proclaim Poland's name from chancelleries and editorial offices; and lastly, to unify Polish sentiment. Under his direction, a complete official thesis was prepared for the guidance of those who needed a creed to support their emotions.

After Paderewski came to America, the separate Polish-American committees combined into one organization.[36]

> Political, social and religious differences were forgotten—all became imbued with the thought that this was the opportunity of a thousand years. New bureaus and agencies appeared. The work of propaganda for the Polish cause became an actual thing, a living force.[37]

Paderewski succeeded very well in gaining sympathy and esteem for Poland. As an unofficial ambassador, he did much to familiarize Americans with the peculiarities of Poland's problems and in this way was an asset of inestimable value to the Poles. Not the least to profit from this were the Polish representatives at Washington whose duties were greatly facilitated by the undertaking they found for their problems, due largely to the preparatory work performed by Paderewski and the multitude of Polish-Americans.

Paderewski made several journeys across the American continent, delivering speeches at universities, in working men's or women's clubs, in concert-halls and theaters. Addressing crowds of ten-thousand or groups of a few hundred, he had need to be eloquent, especially on the political score. The work of more than a century of prejudiced misinformation about Poland had borne

---

[36] *Czyn Zbrojny Wychodztwa Polskiego w Ameryce. Zbior Dokumentow i Materialow Historycznych* (New York: 1957), pp. 176-222.
[37] John P. Smulski, "Poland's Role during the World War," *Poland* (April, 1927), pp. 211-215.

heavy fruit. Paderewski, however, had nothing to overcome to open the hearts of the American people when he cried:

> Is there anything more than human pain? Is there anything more sincere than the cry for help from those who suffer? Only a great wave of mankind's pity can surmount an immense wave of human misery. In the name of Christian charity, in the name of common humanity give me some bread for the Polish women and children, some seed for the Polish farmers![38]

Paderewski's appeals for suffering Poland never failed to galvanize the Americans into action. The outpouring of sympathy and financial help for the Polish sufferers was amazing.

The social contacts that his career as an artist had made in the past years became very valuable to his cause.[39] The following prominent men and women were lending their names and efforts to the Polish Victims' Relief Fund: former President Taft, Thomas A. Edison, Frank A. Vanderlip, Herbert L. Satterlee, James M. Beck, Edward Bok, Cyrus Curtis, Joseph Choate, Joseph Leiter, Melville Stone, Cardinal Gibbons, Bishop Wilson, Cardinal Farley, Cardinal O'Connell, Miss Anne Morgan, Mrs. John Wanamaker, Mrs. Richard Watson Gilder and a score of others. Francis A. Vanderbilt, president of the National City Bank of New York, volunteered to mail 24,000 appeals to 25,000 banks in the United States seeking donations for the Polish cause.[40] Archibald, the president of Standard Oil Company, also promised help.

For the majority of American citizens the name Poland became synonymous with the name Paderewski. Never before in the history of America was the name of Poland so widely known as it now became through the efforts of Paderewski whose influence steadily increased. During the winter of 1915-1916, resolutions were introduced in Congress expressing sympathy with Poland. New Year's Day, 1916, was proclaimed "Polish Day" by President Wilson, who invited popular subscriptions to Paderew-

---

[38] Charles Phillips, *Paderewski, The Story of a Modern Immortal* (New York: 1934), p. 321.
[39] Wytrwal, *Poles in American History and Tradition*, pp. 251-254.
[40] *Czyn Zbrojny Wychodztwa Polskiego w Ameryce. Zbior Dokumentow i Materialow Historycznych* (New York: 1957), p. 189.

ski's Relief Fund. Later the same year, on July 12, President Wilson addressing a group of Polish citizens at the White House, stated:

> It was not necessary that you should come. I mean I was not forgetful of Poland and was not likely to be forgetful of her. I know the terrible conditions, the tragical conditions, that exist there, and nobody could know them without feeling his heart torn with the knowledge.[41]

This knowledge was due most likely to his conference with Paderewski. The German Ambassador in Washington, Count Bernstorff, wrote in a letter to the Chancellor Bethmann-Hollweg, how well informed the American press was about all Polish matters, and that this was due to Paderewski's activities.

During this period, Paderewski was also very active among Americans to convert them to the cause of Poland. Josephus Daniels, Secretary of the Navy from 1913-1921, described his first meeting with Paderewski:

> I never saw Ignace Paderewski until he called at my office in the Navy Department during the World War to request cooperation to help his suffering countrymen in Poland. With eloquent words on his tongue and tears in his eyes, he related the story of the dismemberment of his country as if it were a fresh tragedy, and the present hopes and needs of his countrymen. With an audience of one, he was as much moved as if he were speaking to a multitude. He opened his heart to me and from that moment I was an ardent advocate of the ambition of the Poles. Again I saw him at the White House when he was entertained by the President and Mrs. Wilson. His playing moved Wilson—he played nothing but Chopin—and his presentation of his hopes for his native land converted Wilson to the cause of Poland.[42]

This personal friendship with Daniels was deepened by later meetings and communications.

Paderewski also influenced Colonel House:

> Paderewski came as a spokesman of an ancient people whose wrongs and sorrows had stirred the sympathies of an entire world. The artist,

---
[41] Phillips, *Paderewski, The Story of a Modern Immortal*, p. 349.
[42] Josephus Daniels, *The Wilson Era: Years of War After 1917-1923* (Chapel Hill: 1946), p. 399.

patriot and statesman awakened the Congress to do justice to his native land and sought its help to make a great dream come true. His perfervid eloquence brought about the renascence of Poland and added new lustre to a famous name.[43]

That Paderewski exerted a real influence on House's thought is evident. The conferences between House and Paderewski were numerous. "We poured over maps—his maps and mine—of Central Europe," writes House, "and together we traced what we thought should be a homogeneous Poland." The balance and wisdom of Paderewski's decisions expressed during these conferences deeply impressed President Wilson's advisor: "The Poland we outlined, during those fervid war days, proved to be practically the Poland created by the Versailles Conference."[44]

From the summer of 1914 to 1916, slowly but steadily, the United States became involved in the war, at first only emotionally, then economically. By the end of 1916, America's entrance into the war seemed unavoidable. Paderewski knew that if Poland was actually to be freed, her name must be coupled with America's. In his conference with Colonel House, who showed an early and abiding interest in the fate of the Poles, he urged his claim more and more emphatically.

At an address to the Kosciuszko Foundation Testimonial, in New York on May 16, 1928, Paderewski himself—with a twinkle in his eyes and a smile on his lips—told of the dramatic climax:

> One day, January 8th (1917) in the afternoon, Colonel House said to me, "Next Thursday I am going to leave for Washington, and I wish to have with me your memorandum on Poland." Terrified by the suddenness of that request, I exclaimed: "But I have my recital tomorrow, I shall not be able to hold a pen in my hand for two days, and besides, it is impossible to prepare such a document without having the necessary data."
>
> "I must have the memorandum Thursday in the morning," he answered, and it was the end of our conversation. I immediately returned to the hotel—and spent four solid hours in preparing the

---

[43] Charles Seymour, *Intimate Papers of Colonel House* (Boston: 1926), IV, p. 261.
[44] Phillips, *Paderewski, The Story of a Modern Immortal*, p. 349.

program for my recital. Only on Tuesday, after the recital, could I turn my mind to that new, very heavy task. It took me over thirty-six hours of uninterrupted work to prepare the document which was delivered, as requested, on Thursday, the 11th at eight o'clock in the morning.

Led by the purest, by the noblest idealism, Colonel House made our cause his own. . . . When a week later I called on him, he was in a cheerful mood and said: "The President was very much pleased with your memorandum. Now get ready. The first shot will be fired very soon, and it will take your breath away."[45]

Since both belligerents were on record as favoring the restoration of Poland, in one form or another, House persuaded President Wilson to endorse the movement for Polish independence. Two weeks later, having fully digested the Paderewski memorandum, in his "Peace Without Victory" address delivered on January 22, 1917, President Wilson made his first declaration of what should follow the close of the war, saying: "I take it for granted that statesmen everywhere are agreed that there should be a united, independent and autonomous Poland."[46]

Not many weeks after the declaration, Wilson, who watched the smoke and flames of burning Europe month after month, came to the conclusion that America's entrance into the war was inevitable, and on April 2, 1917, called a special session of Congress where he presented his "War Message." On April 4 the Senate adopted the war resolution. On April 6, the House of Representatives followed suit. War was declared! Every international obstacle to the proper consideration of Poland's status as a potential Allied state was now removed. Paderewski now moved to consolidate Poland's position. On April 4, the day that the United States Senate passed the war resolution, Paderewski moved the Union of Polish Falcons, in convention at Pittsburgh, to vote for the organization of "an army of Kosciuszko to fight by the side of the United States." The American declaration of war, on April 6, cleared the way to carry this vote out.

---

[45] *Ibid.*, pp. 349-350.
[46] Paderewski's influence and greatness is inestimable. That he impressed enough people to deal with the problem of Polish independence and recognize it against great odds is a stroke of great political influence.

On June 4, 1917, the quest for a military sponsor came to an end. On that date, French President Poincare signed a decree which gave birth to a Polish Legion. To tap manpower resources for the Legion, the French sent a mission to America to begin the recruiting campaign, which received official clearance from the United States War Department on October 6, 1917, with the stipulation that Polish-Americans, native born or naturalized, would not be enlisted. Not to be enlisted were also heads of families. With this understanding, the Military Mission moved into action. It worked through the major national lodges, the local Citizens' Committees and the 1,018 Polish-American priests organized as a body since 1912.

With this concerted and enthusiastic effort Polish-Americans entered the most colorful aspect of their history. Its hundreds of settlements throughout the United States stirred with new activity. The weekends were replete with pageants, dinners, speeches, parades, and upon occasion, even church processions. The rebirth of Poland was the ultimate aim; the raising of an army was the immediate objective. Forty-three recruiting sergeants fully employed at $5.00 per day were assigned to the larger Polish communities. It was the responsibility of these sergeants to follow up the patriotic outbursts of the weekend with personal calls upon potential recruits. Contrary to rumors, these recruiters received no bonus or commission for enlistments; however, their tasks were greatly simplified by the intense nationalism of the moment. In many localities the names of eligible "volunteers" were publicly displayed in church vestibules and hall entrances. It appears that no holds were barred, no devices untried. Contrary to regulations and promises, men subject to the American draft were recruited for the Polish Army and so were fathers and men with dependents.[47]

In the beginning, the recruiting campaign produced unexpected results. In October, some 3,000 recruits were sent to Niagara-on-the-Lake, Ontario, the new training site for the Polish Army.[48] An account of this camp appeared in MacLean's Magazine.

---

[47] Pliska, "The 'Polish-American Army' 1917-1921," *The Polish Review*, X (Summer, 1965), p. 52.
[48] On one occasion, four Irishmen in Chicago were recruited into the Polish Army, sent off to camp, and immediately returned with the stern warning that in

It was, however, in unorganized music that the spirit of the Pole, that variable mingling of light-heartedness and melancholy, had its most compelling expression. Whenever and wherever Poles congregate, music in some form or other spontaneously broke forth. It was most effective in their unrehearsed mass singing. That which might well have brought "idle tears" to the eyes floated across the Niagara plain on many a soft summer night. Those who heard it will never forget the haunting charm of that song of happy youth shadowed by forebodings of sorrow to come, "Jak Szybko Mijaja Chwile" (How Swiftly the Moments Pass). Then there was the trippling care-free march of the victorious legions of Dombrowski: "Jeszcze Polska Nie Zginela" (All is not over with Poland) welling up in their merriest moments, as when in great cheering train-loads they began their long journey to France—and to Poland. But from the suffering of their beloved land came the solemn, stately "Boze Cos Polske" (O God, Protector of Poland), by common consent regarded in Niagara Camp as the National Hymn of Poland. Men and women who have heard all that is most impressive in music have often stood with tear-filled eyes as thousands of Poles poured forth in this sublime hymn the pent-up emotions of a hundred and fifty years of persecution.[49]

In November, an additional 1,300 recruits made their way to this training and staging area which could accommodate no more than 1,200 men at one time. Consequently, by December of that year, 4,300 recruits had to be housed in an abandoned, nearby cannery, in neighborhood hotels, and in private residences across the river in Polish-American Buffalo. In January 1918, the United States Government assigned its Fort Niagara to the Poles. This additional billeting site, coupled with the first overseas shipment of 1,700 soldiers, greatly reduced the congestion in the training area.

In the spring of 1918, additional efforts were made to stimulate interest in the Polish Army.

Polish papers carried testimonials of volunteers who supposedly gave up good paying jobs just to serve Poland. More forceful means were

---

future such wanton liberality would cost the guilty recruiting sergeant full price of transportation to and from camp. Upon another occasion, the recruiting of seventeen non-Poles produced no upheaval. The seventeen were Czechs, and they were regarded as "foreigners." They continued to train with the Polish Army until a Czech Legion was formed in Connecticut, in 1918, at which time they were reassigned to their own army. Pliska, "The 'Polish-American Army' 1917-1921," *The Polish Review*, X (Summer, 1965), p. 54.

[49] John Murray Gibbon, *Canadian Mosaic* (New York: 1939), p. 272.

also employed. When it became apparent that eligible young men were purposely shunning patriotic gatherings to avoid pressures of public recruitment, their very places of employment were visited, and often on-the-job recruiting was sought. It might be added that one Polish newspaper in Chicago featured a daily column entitled "*Tchorze*" ("Cowards") in which were listed the names of "slackers." Whenever such "slackers" decided to move out of their neighborhood or community, "Wanted" notices appeared in future editions of the paper describing the "escapees" and alerting the populace to look out for them and remind them of their duty.[50]

It requires great patriotism in order to join the Polish Army in wartime. Privates received their uniform, three meals a day, a canvas cot, and five cents per day, or twenty-five cents at the front. To this was added a French Government overseas bonus of $150 annually. There were no servicemen's insurance policies, since no Polish-American organization was financially capable of cooperating with the American Red Cross in defraying the premiums for such insurance. Certainly the men could not afford it. As a result, some 100 widows and orphans were thrown on local charity after the war.

About twenty-two thousand men of over-draft age volunteered; and these in due time had added to their numbers some 55,000 Poles, who had been interned in France and Italy when taken as prisoners of war from the armies of the Central Powers. With additional forces added in Europe, Paderewski's army—eventually placed under the leadership of General Jozef Haller—totalled nearly 100,000 men. When the first troops of Paderewski's army were finally dispatched to Europe, Newton D. Baker, Secretary of War, expressed his satisfaction in their ideals and virtues as soldiers.

> This American contingent of the Polish army is made up of men moved by the inspiration of the principles involved on the Allied side in this conflict, and their presence on the Western front representing both their adherence to America and the country of their adoption, and to Poland, free and self-governing, as the country of their extraction, will be a stimulating and inspiring sight.[51]

---

[50] Pliska, "The 'Polish-American Army' 1917-1921," *The Polish Review*, X (Summer, 1965), p. 54.
[51] Phillips, *Paderewski, The Story of a Modern Immortal*, p. 354.

In General Haller's Blue Army a singular tribute was paid to Paderewski, an honor never before given to a civilian in the history of the war, and to only one soldier. Napoleon. Paderewski's name was written on the roll of every company.

> Daily at roll call the name Ignace Jan Paderewski was responded to not by one man but by the thunderous chorus of every regiment. There were a hundred-thousand Ignace Jan Paderewski's in that army, as there were a hundred-thousand who had taken its oath, which in itself was a memorable declaration of the aims for which Paderewski had striven: "I swear before Almighty God, One in Three, to be faithful to my country Poland, one and indivisible, and to be ready to give my life for the holy cause of its unification and liberation. I swear to defend my flag to the last drop of my blood, to observe military discipline, to obey my leaders, and by my conduct to maintain the honor of the Polish soldier.[52]

President Poincare of France made the following comment when the Polish army left for the front:

> All the future of a nation is wrapped up in the folds of your flags. The White Eagle can once more unfold its wings. It will soon float in the light of a sky once more serene, and in the rays of victory.[53]

Arthur Rubinstein attempted to join the famous Polish Blue Army.[54] However, his knowledge of eight languages made him

---

[52] Ibid., p. 355.
[53] Ibid., p. 355.
[54] Artur Rubinstein was born in Lodz, Poland on January 28, 1886. The youngest of seven children of Ignace and Felicia Rubinstein, he gave his first solo performance before he was six. When he was eight years old he began his studies in Warsaw, and eight months later accompanied an older sister to Berlin to perform for Joseph Joachim, the celebrated violinist. He remained with Joachim for eight years, eventually meeting Paderewski, who was so impressed with the young Rubinstein that he took him under his tutelage. At eleven years of age, Rubinstein made his formal debut in Berlin, where he performed the Mozart "A Major Concerto" with Joachim conducting the Berlin Symphony Orchestra, under the direction of Emil Mlynarski, whose daughter Aniela he was destined one day to marry. Shortly thereafter he toured Russia with Serge Koussevitsky, winning universal acclaim as an interpreter of Beethoven, Liszt, Brahms, and Chopin. He aslo received plaudits from modern composers for his rendition of their works. Stravinsky's Sonata from the ballet score Petrouchka and Villa-Lobos' Rudepoema are dedicated to him. Like Paderewski, he received many awards from the governments of the world, including the "Legion of Honor" from France, the "Cross of Alfonso XII" from Spain, the "Commander of the Crown" from Belgium, and the "Polonia Restituta" from Poland. Rubinstein made his first American appearance in Philadelphia, in 1906.

more valuable at Allied Headquarters, which sent him on tour on behalf of the Allied cause. In 1916, Rubinstein was scheduled to give four concerts in Spain. His interpretation of Spanish compositions was so well received that he was forced to extend his Spanish tour to 120 concerts. His South American tour met with similar successes.

While Paderewski prosecuted the affair of the Polish army, he was active as ever in his capacity of diplomatic plenipotentiary, in America, of the Polish National Committee in Paris. On November 10, 1917, the United States Government had formally recognized the committee in Paris. In due time official recognition of the Polish army was also given. Step by step, Paderewski's work in America succeeded. On the eighth of January, 1918, President Wilson in his famous Fourteen Points, emphatically proclaimed before Congress which quickly reached the remote corners of the earth, his program for world peace. The Thirteenth Point referred to Poland: "An independent Polish state should be erected which should include the territories inhabited by indisputably Polish populations, which should be assured a free and secure access to the sea, and whose political and economic independence and territorial integrity should be guaranteed by international covenant."

Simultaneously, Paderewski was spending his vast fortune on numberless charities. They were generally connected with Polish suffering and with the political preparation for Poland's independence; but he gave large sums also to a number of foreign charities, principally affiliated with the sufferings inflicted by the war upon the citizens of the Allied nations. In his solicitations, Paderewski showed a special concern for people made helpless and destitute by the war. On so many occasions he pleaded and begged so insistently and persuasively for the relief of suffering Poland that he earned the title of the "international beggar." As an official ambassador of Poland, he did not hesitate to ask for seed for dispossessed farmers and bread for Polish workers. His appeal to Wilson caused the President to send Hoover with food for the Poles. When Wilson once lunched with Josephus Daniels, he made the following remarks:

I wish you could have heard Paderewski's speeches for his country. They compared with Patrick Henry's famous "Give me liberty or give me death," and I could understand how the self-contained Jefferson was so moved as to light the fire of liberty in his heart that was never extinguished. I knew Paderewski as a master of harmony, but as we heard his eloquent appeals for his country, I felt that it was in victory that he had touched chords more sublime than when he moved thousands as he commanded harmony from the piano.[55]

In November and December, the situation in Poland became so dire that the representatives of the American Red Cross Society of the Rockefeller Foundation, and the Commission for the Relief of Belgium took notice and endeavored to start relief work. As a result of a separate investigation, which confirmed the need of immediate relief, negotiations were begun with the German, the Austrian and the American ambassadors to formulate plans for an international commission on the relief of Poland.

When the war came to an end, Paderewski decided that his mission in America was completed, and that his place was no longer abroad, but in Poland. At the beginning of December 1918, he left New York and went to Paris, where he arrived December 15. In his book, Josephus Daniels describes his first meeting with Paderewski in Paris.

"The long-haired man who embraced you must have been your long lost brother," said my Aide, who had never seen such an affectionate meeting between men as when Paderewski and I met for the first time in Paris. Our hearts and hopes are united in hope for an independent Poland, I replied, and we have had a common dream since 1916. He loves music but he loves his country more than his mastery of melody.[56]

Colonel House also summed up Paderewski's war success in America in a clear and simple statement:

"He gave to the American Poles a single purpose." He was able to do this because he lived himself for a single purpose. *"La patrie avant tout, l'art ensuite."* But he still remained the musician. All that he did was done, it might be said, to the strains of music. It was his art that

---

[55] Daniels, *op. cit.*, p. 400.
[56] *Ibid.*, pp. 399-400.

first of all magnetized the people, gave him free address to multitudes. He dedicated that art to his cause.⁵⁷

When the United States entered the First World War, on April 6, 1917, a wave of patriotic feeling swept the numerous American Polish communities. Poles immediately assured President Wilson of their support and loyalty. In New York City a special rally was held in Union Square.

> That Poland's liberty and autonomy all depend upon the success of the United States and the Allies in destroying the German autocracy was the sentiment of the speakers in Union Square, last night, at a meeting of 5,000 Poles, called to assure President Wilson, upon the anniversary of the liberation of Poland, that those of Polish birth in the United States were united in their support of the Administration. In proportion to population, it was declared, the military establishment of the country had in it more Poles than Germans, French, or other nationality. They told of one station in Chicago where 700 Poles had enlisted in the regular army in a few months.
> Following a series of patriotic speeches by members of the United Polish Societies, Civic and Military; the girls societies laid a wreath at the foot of the Washington statue.⁵⁸

At a meeting in New York's Beethoven Hall, resolutions were also adopted and sent to the President assuring him of the loyalty of the Poles.⁵⁹

In recognition of President Wilsons' declaration for a united and independent Poland, the Polish national organizations and the Polish language newspapers in the United States have united to make registration day, June 5, a patriotic holiday for young men of Polish birth and descent; they were urged to register for the selective draft so as to be ready to serve the nation "in its struggle for the preservation of democracy throughout the world."⁶⁰

> The Polish newspapers say that thousands of young Poles have already enlisted in the army and navy. From one recruiting station in Chicago

---

⁵⁷ Phillips, *op. cit.*, p. 357.
⁵⁸ "Poles Declare Loyalty," *New York Times* (May 17, 1917), p. 4.
⁵⁹ *Ibid.*, p. 4.
⁶⁰ "Polish Newspapers Help the Draft: Mr. Wilson's Recognition of a Free Poland Brings a Hearty Response," *New York Times* (June 2, 1917), p. 9.

637 Poles have been sent to commands in the regular army. Several hundred Poles have enlisted in two weeks in Milwaukee, and in addition a Wisconsin infantry regiment has enlisted an entire Polish battalion.[61]

All of the Polish newspapers in the United States published a message to their people calling on the young to register. The message was, in part, as follows:

> We are anxious that the Poles of America on registration day should give new evidence of their spirit of loyalty in their wholehearted observance of the proclamation. At a time when unfortunately groups of men throughout the country are advising that the work of registration be delayed, or if possible, made ineffective, we are desirous to set a high standard of enthusiasm.[62]

On Sunday, the clergy of the Polish-American churches also called for full registration.[63]

Of the first 100,000 volunteers, who responded immediately to President Wilson's initial call for volunteers, no fewer than 40,000 were Poles.[64] In cities containing about a tenth of the Polish population, the Polish-American volunteers would approximate a third of the whole.[65]

The Polish Falcons proposed the organization of a Kosciuszko Army of 100,000 men to fight as a special unit in the American armed forces. Within the first three months after the declaration of war, 38,000 trained Falcons joined the United States Army.[66] In the city of South Bend, Indiana, on the first day of recruiting, ninety-four of the first hundred volunteers were of Polish origin. I. Werwinski, the leader of the Polish-Americans in South Bend, was gratefully recognized by President Wilson for his efforts.[67] The actual number of Polish Americans who served in the United States Army is not definitely known. An estimate of 300,000 is usually given.

---

[61] *Ibid.*, p. 9.
[62] *Ibid.*, p. 9.
[63] *Ibid.*, p. 9.
[64] Roman Dyboski, *Poland in World Civilization* (New York: 1950), p. 115. Albert Q. Maisel, "The Poles Among Us," *Zgoda* (June 15, 1958), p. 11. Nevin O. Winter, *The New Poland* (Boston: 1923), p. 302. *Free Poland* (June 1, 1917).
[65] Winter, *The New Poland*, p. 302.
[66] Joseph Sierocinski, *Armia Polska we Francji* (Warsaw: 1929), p. 81.
[67] *Ibid.*, p. 81.

While the loyalty of some aliens was suspected, and others selfishly declined to enlist when compulsory service was impossible, Polish loyalty was never doubted and calls for assistance were never unheeded.[68]

In Milwaukee, Wisconsin, Lieutenant Colonel Peter F. Piasecki was placed in charge of recruiting men of Polish descent for the Fifth Wisconsin Infantry. In addition to Company K, he raised four other companies of men of Polish descent to form a battalion of the regiment. When the regiment was formed, Lieutenant Colonel Piasecki was promoted to colonel and given command. The five companies reported in answer to the call of the President on July 15, 1917; and on July 31, 1917, Company K was mustered into federal service. The other companies were mustered by federal officers later at Camp Douglas. The hope of keeping the four new companies in a Polish battalion was lost when the Wisconsin regiments were reorganized at Camp McArthur, Texas. Under a reorganization plan of the 32nd Division, Company K, First Wisconsin Infantry, became Company K Infantry, which designation it retained throughout the war.[69]

When Company K—as part of the 32nd Division—landed in France on March 4, 1918, general headquarters had ordered the 32nd Division to be used as a replacement unit. This meant that the men of the company would be separated and scattered, three or four at a time, among all of the divisions at the front replacing casualties as required. To members of Company K this prospect was distasteful.

---

[68] Winter, *The New Poland*, p. 302.

[69] It was these daring and heroic men of Polish descent who were assigned to the ammunition trains while fighting in France and who had formed a separate battalion at the beginning of the war, exemplified their record during the entire conflict of the war to such an extent that they were praised from every source. Not only did they serve on every front with the Red Arrow Division, but the demand for ammunition at the front kept them continually in service supplying the other combat divisions during the heaviest fighting. Their service was dangerous, for night after night they were under intense shell fire: the Germans invariably shelled the roads in the rear to prevent, if possible, the very work these men were assignd to perform. It is the proud record of these companies that in every instance every unit of the division, and of other divisions they were assigned to serve, were invariably well supplied with ammunition. Not once during the entire fighting was there a lack of ammunition at the front, no matter what difficulty faced them in the way of supplying it.

But good news came. General Pershing—when shown the record made by the division during the training period at Waco, and the generally high standing of the National Guard in both Michigan and Wisconsin, as compared to some other states—countermanded the order and decided to use it as a combat division. When this was done the division was assembled in the Tenth training area in the Haute-Marne department and on April 5, Company K detrained at Vaux-Sous Aubigny and marched to Chaunlancey, where it remained during five weeks of intensive training under the direction of French officers.[70]

On May 14, the intensive training period came to an end and the company began to march to Langres, arriving there the following day. Here, at the Alsace front, it entrained for the scene of action, where the contending armies had settled down into opposing trenches along a 350-mile line running from Switzerland to the North Sea. On May 25, the company proceeded into the front line where they were filtered into the trenches near Hagenbach. An attempt by the Germans to raid the trenches held by Company K was successfully repulsed on May 28.

On May 29, the company went into support, at Hagenbach, and on June 2, left the trenches to retire, in reserve, to Retzweiler. During the stay there the men were kept busy with two problems: trench digging and building wire entanglements. Part of the duty of trench warfare was to keep the wire in front of the trenches properly arranged so that they could not be breached. Company K did much of this work during the time it remained in Alsace. On June 19, under the command of Lieutenant Leon M. Gurda, Company K again entered the trenches, taking a position at Stockette, near Badricourt. On this occasion the company had their first severe clash with the enemy. They remained in the front lines for twenty days. This experience was invaluable for it later, when they had to face the enemy on other fronts. Here, the men and officers engaged in raids on the German trenches, repulsed similar attempts by the enemy to enter their lines, and made scouting expeditions into No Man's Land. In every way, they became accustomed to real trench warfare.

---

[70] Claude C. Manly, *History of Company K, 127th Infantry, 32nd Division, Wisconsin National Guard 1874-1924* (Milwaukee: 1924), p. 51.

> The first capture of German soldiers by Company K was made by Corporal John Slaski on July 4. Corporal Slaski, on outpost duty had stationed himself in a tree for observation at daybreak. Through field glasses he noticed two men some distance away, stealing away from the American lines across the field. His orders were to shoot any men seen in that locality. He descended from the tree and followed, finally coming near the men who had hidden in a shell hole. When Corporal Slaski neared this place he fired a shot at them. The men saw that he was too close for them to escape and they attempted to call "comrade," but the corporal kept them under cover and ordered them to come out of the hole. His surprise, when two men dressed in American uniforms, emerged, may be imagined. He was further surprised when two "American soldiers" could not understand enough English to reply to his questions concerning their identity. His suspicions being aroused he marched both men back, at the point of a bayonet, to company headquarters, where they were searched by Lieutenant Gurda. They were dressed in American uniforms, even to underwear, but in their pockets German caps were found. The men, through an interpreter admitted that they were German soldiers and were sent back to the French division headquarters. Company K never learned what became of these men, but in war the penalty that spies must pay is death.[71]

On July 10, Company K was relieved and sent back to Retzweiler. On July 19, the Company was sent to Chateau-Thierry and the Aisne-Marne front.

On July 30, the Company occupied three separate forward positions near Roncheres. On August 1, the Company moved into another position, just south of Cierges. On August 3, the Company took up the chase of the retreating enemy who sought to form a new line of resistance along the Vesle River. On August 24, the Company was transported to the Oise-Aisne front where they took part in the Battle of Juvigny.

> It was about this time that a German prisoner was captured. He said he was a Pole and that he had a brother in the American army. His name was Kazmierczak. His brother was a member of Company K, but lately assigned, had been wounded the day before and was then in the hospital.[72]

---

[71] *Ibid.*, pp. 59-60.
[72] *Ibid.*, p. 72.

At the head of the Battle of Juvigny, Company K fought it alone victoriously unaided against superior odds. Their success here was extremely important to the battalion in the rear, perhaps even to the entire division. Had the men of Company K been defeated, killed or captured, the Germans certainly would have been able to surprise the other companies of the battalion and deliver a serious defeat. No soldiers of any war have more reason to be proud of their work than the men of Company K for their deeds at the Battle of Juvigny. The cost in dead and wounded was heavy; but terrible losses were also inflicted upon the Germans, taking 2,000 prisoners and gaining much territory.

The Battle of the Argonne is recognized as the greatest battle in which American troops participated as a separate army. No division played a greater part in this battle than did the famous Thirty-second. During the first stages of the Battle of Argonne the Thirty-second was held in reserve. The high command decided to permit the newer and less experienced divisions to make the initial attack, with the veteran divisions like the Thirty-second, the First, Second and Third in support. The new divisions made an excellent showing and fought bravely, although some critics later claimed that had the old divisions made the first "jump off," the advance of the first day would have been greater, and a far larger number of prisoners would have been taken.

"Allied officers of the high command," wrote Colonel Frederick Palmer, a famous war correspondent, discussing the Argonne battle after the war, "believe that had the Thirty-second, First and Second Divisions been placed in the center of the line, at the beginning of the battle, Romagne would have been reached on the first day, a far greater number of prisoners would have been captured and fewer lives would have been lost in the American army." This was no reflection on the other American troops, but the three divisions mentioned were veterans with the experience necessary to take advantage of every opportunity offered in the advance.

The first attack made by Company K, in the Argonne, was on October 5, in the heavily wooded valley near the town of Gesnes. From October 8 until October 14, the Company participated in the attack on the Hindenburg line, which was protected by barbed wire with entanglements, dozens of machine gun nests, trench mortars, and heavy artillery. On October 15, the Hindenburg line crumbled before the relentless drive of the Allied and associated forces and the Germans began to retreat. Company K followed the enemy in their final retreat until November 9, when it crossed the Meuse River and went into the front line. Here it remained until the morning of November 11, when the armistice went into effect, and the roll of guns that had thundered along the front for four agonizing years became silent.

Germany was entered by American troops on Sunday, December 1. Because of the splendid record of the Thirty-second, the Forty-second, the First, and Second Divisions, General Pershing had accorded these four units the honor of being the first American troops to cross the Saar River. They were also the first divisions to cross the Rhine River, and in the beginning, they were the only division stationed beyond the Rhine on outpost duty.

Even though glory consisted of getting maimed or killed (and having your name misspelled in the newspapers) more than 300,000 Polish immigrants and Americans of Polish descent served before the conflict terminated. The first American soldier who died in France was Joseph Czajka of Milwaukee. The first Chicago boy killed, was a Pole, Peter Wojtalewicz of Company G, Eighteenth Infantry. His memory was honored by a special resolution of the city council. Although the Polish population in the United States did not exceed four percent, on the casualty lists of World War I, Americans of Polish descent accounted for twelve percent of the Honor Roll!

> The Polish boys were the first and most numerous to respond when the call to arms was sounded. Their willingness to enlist and fight under the American flag won repeated praise from the highest military authorities in this country. There is not one casualty list that does not contain some names of American soldiers of Polish birth who paid the supreme sacrifice on the battlefields of France. The average number killed exceeded twelve per cent. And as there are not quite four per cent of the Polish people among the population of the United States, this fact indicates that the Poles in that war were doing

more than three times their share, that they were not one-hundred, but three-hundred per cent American.[73]

Admiral William S. Maxwell enlisted in the United States Navy, in 1916, as a fireman and retired with the rank of Rear Admiral. Maxwell was Chief Motor Machinist Mate as an enlisted man in the United States Navy. In 1923, he was appointed Warrant Machinist and served as Chief Engineer on the USS *Luka,* USS *Brant* and USS *New Mexico.* Admiral Maxwell was one of the few men to be commissioned as an Ensign in the line during peacetime and has held every rank from Ensign up and including the rank of Rear Admiral.[74]

On the home front, Polish energy in America was also enlisted in Liberty Loan drives, Red Cross campaigns, and labor activities calculated to promote the war effort. Personal and family ties accentuated the urgency of collecting funds for Polish war relief. The publication *Free Poland,* which first appeared on September 1, 1914, ran the following front page announcement: "Do your bit! Now! (1) Join the Army or Navy. (2) Join the Red Cross. (3) Buy a Liberty Bond."

When a movement was started to enlist support for the first "Liberty Loan," Paderewski made a personal appeal to Polish-Americans to support the loan. With eloquence he spoke of the duties of the citizen towards his country, ending fervently with the following words:

---

[73] Miecislaus Haiman, "The Poles in Chicago," *Poles of Chicago 1837-1937* (Chicago: 1937), p. 7.

[74] Maxwell attended Post Graduate School at the United States Naval Academy, majoring in Mechanical Engineering; the U.S. Naval Submarine School, majoring in Diesel Engineering; Naval War College, majoring in International Law, Strategy and Tactics; Industrial War College, majoring in Combustion Engineering; University of the State of New York where he received a license as a Professional Engineer, and he also registered as a Stationery Engineer for the State of Colorado. During his stay in the Navy he also served in Saudi Arabia, Kuwait, Iraq, Iran, and Egypt as United States Naval Technical Officer and Naval Attache for petroleum in the Middle East. Admiral Maxwell had written numerous articles which have appeared in the *American City, National Engineer, Universal Engineer* and *Air Repair.*

From 1944 to 1946, he was head of the battleship, "Maintenance," Bureau of Ships, in the Navy, and was first Chief Engineer of the battleship, "Missouri" when it was commissioned. Maxwell was born in Poland on May 13, 1900. His surname was *Dzwoniecki.* Following the death of his parents, he was adopted by the Maxwell family of New York.

> If you really desire to be respected and honored by the people of this country, to be recognized as truly first-class citizens, and given the place you are entitled to, do your duty.[75]

All the American Polish newspapers and publications implored their readers to "buy until it hurts." The response was unmistakable. Community and church leaders, professional groups, laborers, and housewives rallied to the call. Secretary of War, Newton D. Baker, expressed his appreciation for the war effort of the Polish-Americans in a letter written by J. White, director of the Associated Press, Washington, D. C., dated June 8, 1917:

> I am especially interested in the attitude taken by the Poles in America toward our military problem. I have had many evidences recently of an especial interest on their part in the war and America's part in it, because of the obviously direct bearing of the subject of an independent Poland, which, of course is very dear even to those Poles who have become thoroughly American in their loyalty and affiliations.[76]

The same impelling forces which led Polish-American youth to the recruiting centers, also led Polish-American workers to the Red Cross campaign centers and toward the Third Liberty Loan headquarters. Proportionately the Polish-Americans subscribed more than any other ethnic group, including the Americans of several generations. At the Polish General Convention, Paderewski made the following report:

> No other nationality, here in the United States, has taken so active a part in the Red Cross campaigns as the Poles. In proportion to their number they have been the largest contributors to this worthy cause. In some American city of 300,000 population, $3,750,000 has been collected for American Red Cross, which represents $12.50 per capita, which included a number of American millionaires. The Polish population of the same city, 7,000 people, almost exclusively belonging to the laboring class, contributed to the fund $160,000, which makes $23.00 per head.
> From reliable sources it appears that in one mining district in Pennsylvania alone the poor Polish miners subscribed $11,000,000 to

---

[75] "Urge foreign born to help the loan," *New York Times* (June 9, 1917), p. 3.
[76] *Free Poland* (June 15, 1917).

the Third Liberty Loan. One single Polish bank in Chicago received over 15,000 Polish subscriptions exceeding $1,500,000. In every large city in America with a Polish population, the number of Polish subscribers working with large American concerns could not be taken into account.[77]

The words of appreciation which the Poles, and especially the Polish press, received from the Secretary of the Treasury, McAdoo, reflects the sympathy of the American government towards the Poles.

> The Polish language newspapers published in this country assisted us most laudably in publishing not only editorials but personal appeals as well as news matter pertaining to this loan. Quite a number of them even went so far as to place most patriotically, space for display at the disposal of the Treasury Department absolutely free of charge. We feel sure that Americans, of either Polish birth or descent, have done their share most willingly in participating in this loan.[78]

The Polish-Americans also launched a campaign to check the influence of pro-German propaganda.

> A meeting of the American Loyalty League of Polish Descendants was held in the headquarters, 83 Seventh Street, yesterday to check the influence of pro-German propaganda. About 250 members cheered lustily when Edward C. Rybicki called for recruits for the army of American Poles soon to be sent to France.
>
> The meeting added 100 more names to the list of those who will go to the training camp at Niagara Falls, and $25,000 was subscribed to the Liberty Loans.
>
> Speaking of the willingness of the Poles to follow the American flag into battle on the other side, Mr. Rybicki said that through the work of the organization more than 3,000 young men of Polish descent have enlisted in the Polish contingent training at Niagara Falls.[79]

The enthusiasm in Chicago was also great.

> Over eight thousand of the twelve thousand or more men who registered with the draft board at Chicago Commons were Poles from

---

[77] Stanley Bruno Stefan, *The Preparation of the American Poles for Independence 1880-1918* (unpublished Master's thesis, University of Detroit, 1939), p. 128.
[78] *Free Poland* (July 1, 1917).
[79] "Poles Flock to Colors. Meeting Also Subscribes $25,000 to New Liberty Loan," *New York Times* (October 22, 1917), p. 22.

Austria, and over two thousand more of them came from Russia. When asked where they were born, they replied "Poland." When required to state whether it was in Russian or Austrian Poland, some of them proudly answered, "Not Austria, but Poland under the domination of Austria." Most of them said that they did not want to be soldiers, as they left Poland partly to escape Austrian military service. But many who were exempt, because they were aliens, quickly added, "I go if you need me." Scores of them proceeded at once to file their declarations of intention to become American citizens. Returning from the City Hall with their first papers to be registered as subjects of the draft, not a few of them exclaimed, "I may meet my father or brother in the Austrian trench." All of them might have added that, if captured, they would have been shot as traitors. Of no American lad's patriotism was such an acid test extracted as these young Polish men so bravely stood.[80]

The Polish-Americans greeted the announcement of the Armistice with patriotic public demonstrations. With the termination of the war, dreams of the past gave way to the realities of the present. Building their hopes into the future of the United States, the Polish-Americans peered confidently into the future, little dreaming that another World War would follow in two decades.

---

[80] Graham Taylor, *Pioneering on Social Frontiers* (Chicago: 1930), p. 213.

CHAPTER SEVEN

Dissolution and Asseveration

One part Declaration of Independence; one part the Constitution; one part love for apple pie; one part desire and willingness to wear American shoes and another part pride in American plumbing will make an American out of anyone.

—FRANKLIN LANE[1]

*No war, or battle's sound
Was heard the world around
The idle spear and shield
Was high up hung.*

—MILTON

It is to Ellis Island rather than to Plymouth Rock that a great part of the American people trace their history in America.

—LOUIS ADAMIC[2]

The period from 1919 to 1929, for the Polish immigrants in the United States, was one of hesitancy, changing moods, and mixed patriotic emotions. The establishment of an independent Polish Republic, and the consequent distinction between Polish and American citizenship, forced all Polish immigrants into a painful evaluation of their personal and emotional allegiance to the land of their birth. Out of a drawn-out process of self-examination emerged a sharper awareness of their basic commitments

---
[1] William Carlson Smith, *Americans in the Making* (New York: 1939), p. 116.
[2] Joseph S. Roucek, "Future Steps Toward Cultural Democracy," *One America* (New York: 1946), p. 627.

233

as well as responsibilities to the United States. The attachment to the ideal Poland had made it easier to reconcile one's loyalty to America. Confronted, however, with two political realities: America, the land of freedom and opportunity, and independent Poland—the process became complicated and demanded a choice. It wasn't so much their personal experiences that mattered: an attachment to the country, raising a family, starting a business, or making various commitments that determined for many Polish immigrants to remain in America. Above all, America was a land of opportunity where wealth could bring opportunities and luxuries which would not be obtainable in free Poland, just emerging from over a century of economic stagnation and backwardness—forced upon by the partitioning powers. Time and experience also changed them. Distances loosened the binding ties from the village, weakened the inherited values of peasant life, and dimmed the memory of the past. With marriage and children, the immigrants put down roots in America. Their situation and interest in America were no longer a temporary matter. Although feelings of profound ambivalence were probably never permanently settled, at least most of the fundamental uncertainties had been resolved.

In adapting to American society, the Polish immigrants have had to face the persistent and perplexing problems of how to look upon their dual heritage. The difficulty of reconciling these twin aspects of their lives is often revealed in that moment of hesitation many experienced when asked, "What are you?" Depending upon the mood and the circumstances, the answers have vacillated between "American," "Polish," and "Polish-American."[3]

This profound change, which affected the Polish-Americans, became apparent even before the first Armistice whistles blew. The change, precipitated by the war, affected differently the divided segments of the Polish-American community Many Polish-Americans returned to Poland with enthusiasm and determination to make the new State of Poland strong. They were even willing to enter the Polish armed forces and work energetically towards Poland's future greatness.[4]

---

[3] Whatever the response, it usually felt somehow unnatural. Perhaps this question would not pose such problems if an atmosphere of greater tolerance existed in the

But the majority elected to remain in America, to accept American citizenship, and to remain ardently loyal to their adopted country. To indicate that they intended to bind their future and that of their children with the United States, large numbers initiated naturalization procedures. When comparing the United States to the realistic situation (not the idealistic) in Poland, many decided in favor of the United States; Poland was a poor agricultural country which was deprived of industrialization by the partitioning powers. To establish this economic need would become one of Poland's miracles during the early twentieth century: opening a new port of Gdynia, new minerals uncovered and mined, and many factories were built and a new railroad built from Silesia to the Baltic sea.

Here were about 28,000,000 people who had for four years been ravished by four separate invasions during this one war, where battles and retreating armies had destroyed and destroyed again. In parts there had been seven invasions and seven destructive retreats. Many hundreds of thousands had died of starvation. The homes of millions had been destroyed and the people in those areas were living in hovels. Their agricultural implements were depleted, their animals had been

---

United States. Certainly if the United States was a harmonious melting pot, all races would have been accepted equally—as myths would have one believe—there would never have been any need to feel hesitant about identifying with a minority.

[4] Considering the number of Polish immigrants residing in the United States, at the time, the number of Polish re-emigrants can be considered small. According to Dr. Szawlewski, 96,237 returned to Poland during the period from 1919 to 1923. Of this number, 32,561 were born in the United States. All the individuals returning to Poland were not Poles by national origin.

The repatriates who returned from the United States could not help but bring to Poland some of the material and the intangible qualities of American life. In going from an advanced to a retarded social economy, they took with them money, higher standards of living, a spirit of optimism, reformist attitudes, and pronounced pro-American sentiments. They had come into contact with a different language, with different customs and attitudes. They could hardly have failed to acquire new skills and techniques; their tempo of life had quickened; they had seen people worship in different churches; for better or for worse, they were exposed to the American press, periodicals and literature; and they had sensed the pulsating effects of living in a strong and wealthy country. What they brought back often filtered down into the poverty-stricken areas of the country, and many of the services they rendered were of a character normally furnished by local governments in America. Even though their names failed to appear on the facades of the libraries, museums and schools of Poland, in all, their contributions were genuine. Their devotion to Poland was sometimes more altruistic than that of the upper classes that remained in Poland.

taken by armies, their crops had been only partly planted and even then only partly harvested. Industry in the cities was dead from lack of raw materials. The people were unemployed and millions were destitute. They had been flooded with rubles and kronen, all of which were now valueless. The railroads were barely functioning. The cities were almost without food; typhus and diseases raged over the whole provinces. Rats, lice, famine, pestilence—yet they were determined to build a nation.[5]

In pointing out the advantages of American citizenship, the Polish-American press was almost lyrical. The press had made it clear to its readers that the United States was their permanent home, but only as residents possessing full rights and citizenship could they participate fully in community affairs. The editors also reminded them that they should consider themselves fortunate to be in a country which encouraged its immigrants to become citizens. For this reason they should cooperate and not be obdurate.

To facilitate naturalization procedures for the Polish immigrants the Polish fraternals, especially the Polish National Alliance, provided teachers as well as classrooms.[6] Naturalization papers came to have a meaning and purpose, for the Polish-American leaders were convinced that in any demonstration of strength, the Polish-Americans would have to demonstrate their voting power. Immigrants who held first citizenship papers—or even better, naturalization papers—won recognition and esteem from Polish-American leaders. Immigrants—who did not show their intention in applying for citizenship papers—were declared failures; immigrants—who possessed them, but failed to apply for naturalization papers, within a reasonable time—were labeled dullards (*cymbaly*).[7]

---

[5] Herbert Hoover, *The Memoirs of Herbert Hoover* (New York: 1951), p. 356.

[6] To be objective about the situation, it can be stated that naturalization never was discouraged; but before the Armistice many immigrants planned to return to Poland, and then, citizenship papers were not worth the effort. Prior to 1920, Polish housekeepers asked what good would citizenship papers do them around the kitchen stove or the washtub; and during World War I, Polish editors were busy recruiting an army, made up primarily of non-citizen Poles. Encouraging naturalization at that time might have reduced the size of the army which was being drawn. However, after the war the situation changed. Polish women, after 1920, could become not only citizens, but also voters. They also had more opportunities to enter the business world.

The constitutional provisions and utterances of many prominent intellectuals in the Polish-American organizations, indicated that the Polish immigrants' first attraction was the United States. In that climate of opinion, not one member protested when, in 1924, the Polish National Alliance refused full rights to members who were Polish citizens, or when the Polish National Alliance introduced motions that only American citizens could hold superior administrative positions in the organization.[8] In 1931, an effort was made to amend the Polish National Alliance constitution whereby only American citizens would be qualified to serve as officers in the Polish National Alliance or act as delegates to the Polish National Alliance conventions.[9]

After World War I, a willingness to accept the immigrant appeared. It was accompanied by a determined effort to divest the immigrant of his traditional culture, and to persuade him to accept the American culture and way of life as quickly as possible —a process called assimilation. This has become known in sociology as the "Americanization" movement, and is commonly recognized as having been a grievous error. The theories of assimilation, during this period, tended to glorify the way of life in the United States, and to disdain the way of life among the newcomers. Many nineteenth century writings glorified the white Anglo-Saxons, and considered other races and ethnic groups as inferior. These writings attributed the democratic achievement in the United States to Anglo-Saxons and explained that the phenomenal development in trade and industry resulted from their initiative, vigor, discipline and character. This created an unfavorable attitude towards the immigrant as one who would threaten the great achievements of the Anglo-Saxons, and therefore should be forbidden entry to the United States, or compelled—when he came here—to adopt the ways of the traditional Americans (that is, the Anglo-Saxons) as early as possible. Even today, this

---

[7] Stanley R. Pliska, *Polish Independence and the Polish-Americans* (unpublished Ph.D. dissertation, Columbia University, 1955), p. 474.

[8] If these amendments failed adoption at the convention, it was only because the proponents were accused of using this scheme to perpetuate their hold on the organization. Exclusion of non-citizens would facilitate such control by the few chosen naturalized ones.

[9] ZNP *Konstytucja, Prawa, Reguly i Przepisy* (Chicago: 1931), pp. 22, 73.

particular American snobbery prevails despite the emphasis on ethnicity and its divergent assets.

During this period, many Americans raised the old claim that by heritage, institutions, and language the United States was basically an Anglo-Saxon nation, with its character already fixed and established. Immigrants—who could not readily conform to those standards—were declared "unfit" to become Americans; and instead of trying to "melt" or blend them, the United States should shut the gates of Ellis Island in order to keep them out. On May 26, 1924, the Quota Law was passed.[10] It reduced the number of Polish immigrants to 5,982 annually.

In time, the nostalgic and sentimental attachment to Poland—after the enthusiastic conclusion of World War I—faded gradually into the background. The 1920's witnessed the arrival of a comparatively small number of immigrants. During this period the Polish-American communities had been diluted through the deaths of older members from the scene, the dispersal of former residents, and the influx of other nationality groups. Reconciliation to the idea of permanent residence in the United States had weakened ties with the old country to the point where fewer Polish immigrants corresponded, even with their closest relatives in Poland. The major concern was with American issues and American programs.

Even though integration into the American community was having its effects, one must not assume that all bonds with Poland had been severed. Polish-Americans continued to make their annual excursions to Poland, where they visited relatives, acquired wives, and preached the gospel of American progress. The Polish National Alliance, the Falcons and the Sons of Poland sponsored trips for children to Poland.[11] The Kosciuszko Foundation initiated the scholarship program.[12] Furthermore, the Polish-oriented

---

[10] The racial theories were raised again at the time of the revision of the U.S. Immigration Law, in 1952. Their influence was finally and fortunately ended with the Immigration Act of 1965, which did away with the use of immigrant quotas based on nationality origins. But we have other forms of discrimination today which are more stringent than in the past. Poles cannot immigrate to the United States unless they are immediately related: brothers, sisters, parents, children or else as a political exile, who must permanently cut his ties with Poland.

[11] Karol Burke, *Jedziemy do Polski* (Chicago: 1936).

[12] Anne J. Pawelek, *An American in Poland* (Detroit: 1967).

clergy were a constant reminder of Poland. Even if the majority of the Polish immigrants wanted to confine themselves to the American scene, there were too many forces at work in Poland that pulled at the heart and mind of many Polish-Americans.

During this decade a generation matured which had never seen Poland, or who was unable to think or identify with the Polish terms of their parents. Now even parents gave more thought to the land of their children than to the land of their birth. The passing years only strengthened their fiber and their love for America, while the ties of memory and affection—that bound them to the Old World—faded into oblivion. A study, conducted among the Polish-Americans in Buffalo, revealed that only seven percent of the second generation considered themselves as Polish-Americans.[13]

The era of the hyphenated Polish-American had passed. Dreams of the past gave way to realities of the present. Polish-American community leaders were now involved in problems affecting the social, cultural, economic, and political progress of the Polish-American community and their children in America. The local problems and projects which absorbed their time, efforts and interests, and the general trend of Americanization decreased their involvement in the affairs of Poland. Furthermore, during this period no event of international importance, that took place in Poland, could compel the Polish-American leaders to ignore their own problems and focus their attention there.

The implementation of the Polish language and customs had not disappeared; but their ideals had changed. The activities—on Poland's behalf from 1919 to 1925—were confined largely to social relief and monetary loans to help stabilize the Polish economy. The reports of the Polish Roman Catholic Union and the Polish National Alliance conventions, held between 1925 and 1935, contain little material bearing directly on Poland. Each "convention" or "sejm" attested to the fact that the strong links that bound the Polish-American community to Poland really no longer existed. At most, since they were preoccupied with their

---

[13] Niles Carpenter and Daniel Katz, "The Cultural Adjustment of the Polish Group in the City of Buffalo; and experiment in the technique of Social Investigation," *Social Forces* (September, 1927), p. 80.

own local school problems and projects in the United States, these organizations mention only their devotion to Poland. For some time the Polish National Alliance was avowedly Polish; but since Polish patriotism was not a vital matter to the majority of Polish immigrants and their descendants, the Polish National Alliance gradually became a Polish-American organization which endeavored to enhance the status of the Polish-American community and its members by stressing the contribution of the Polish immigrants to the progress and prosperity of the United States.

Even in the parishes, despite the once patriotic and active priests—now engaged in expensive renovations and building programs—became indifferent and conspicuously inactive.[14] Many Polish-American pastors believed that the Polish-American community had contributed more than its share to the new Polish State. Many pastors felt the time had come when Poland should terminate its dependence on the Polish-American community. Perhaps Father A. Ignasiak, pastor of a parish in Erie, Pennsylvania, expressed himself typically when he made the following observation:

> It will be difficult to gather funds for Poland, and furthermore the Poles in Europe should begin doing something for their country. They should bring up the youth in such a way that they will appreciate their freedom and independence. There is absolutely no reason why we scattered here over the United States should help save Poland for those who never showed us any consideration and even made fun of us.[15]

Instances when the Polish-American community expressed the change in its orientation towards Poland were the Emigration

---

[14] Several other reasons could be advanced which cast light on the gradual disappearance of the patriotic and active priests. Exhaustion and age had overtaken the older Polish priests, and the younger generation of American priests of Polish descent did not seem to share the enthusiasm of the older priests in matters of national importance. They also did not show the same interest in the national patriotic ideals which stirred the older Polish-American clergy. Also since the American Catholic Hierarchy frowns upon this type of activity, many of the younger American priests of Polish descent are further discouraged from participating in this type of activity.

[15] Pliska, *op. cit.*, p. 468.

Congresses summoned by the National Division (Wydzial Narodowy).[16] Over 1,000 delegates had attended the first Congress, held in Detroit, in 1918.[17] In the presence of the Polish representatives, Dmowski and Paderewski, the Congress issued a statement of loyalty to the United States; expressed appreciation to France and England for their support of the Polish cause; and concluded with a promise to raise ten million dollars for Polish relief. Further withdrawal from Polish political life was indicated by the following objectives adopted by the National Division of the Emigration Congress:

1. In reaffirming the need for a central organization to educate the youth, it gives stipends only to Polish-American students as loans, not to Poles living in Poland or wanting to study here.
2. The National Division should defend Polish interests in America; a very pressing matter is the equality of Polish clergy; the commission recommends the matter be presented to the Vatican delegates in Washington; it feels the schism among Polish-Americans is due to lack of proper clerical representatives.
3. Poles should defend their constitutional rights in this country.
4. The National Division should concern itself with the matter of Americanizing Poles who intend to live permanently in America, but not Americanizing which forgets faith and language, and with no forcing of citizenship.
5. The National Division, to the extent of need, should concern itself with actions of assistance and material help to the needy in Poland.
6. The National Division is apolitical concerning the internal political life of Poland and will not support any party, but it will consider its duty, in case of danger to the nation and its unity, to give active support to those parties in the fatherland who stand at the defense of national interests and democratic government.

The withdrawal from Polish political affairs was accompanied by an increasing awareness of American society. Previously, Polish immigrants had been oriented towards Poland, and had ignored American local problems and needs. The conclusion of the na-

---

[16] These Congresses were meetings of delegates of all the existing associations with the exception of those who remained with the Komitet Obrony Narodowy (National Defense Committee).

[17] Mieczyslaw Haiman, *Zjednoczenie Polskie Rzymsko-Katolickie w Ameryce* (Chicago: 1948), p. 356.

tionalistic Polish-American leaders was that no Polish immigrant could possibly be interested in anything other than Poland. Family, employment and the entire life of the individual, were secondary to the country of birth. Only work for Poland gave meaning to life. This philosophy—preached in the years prior to World War I to the Polish immigrants and their descendants—finally led to a revolt. At the third Emigration Congress, the Polish-American community, made an about-face when it decidedly expressed itself in the motto: "The Emigrant Group for the Emigrant Group" (Wychodztwo dla Wychodztwa).[18] All who lived

[18] Ibid., pp. 356-357.

in America (alien born and native born) were resolved to become Americans. Strongly and openly the third Congress proclaimed that the Polish-American community cannot be satisfied with what they have done so far. The goal they sought was to create a new dimension of Polish-American living whereby they could build lives of quality with meaning, depth, promise and beauty. They would adopt new patterns and put them into operation, now at this time of growth, movement and excitement in the United States. "We for ourselves," was a rather unusual and frank expression of self-interest. It was also in extreme contrast to the previous motto of "Everything for Poland."

The break with the past orientation of the Polish immigrants in America was made public, in Warsaw, in 1934, at the second convention of the International Alliance of Poles from abroad. The Polish National Alliance and Polish Roman Catholic Union delegates made the following declaration:

> We came to this convention not as Poles from abroad, but as Americans of Polish descent. We are loyal citizens of the United States, but as citizens of the United States we would like to cooperate with you only in the cultural field.[19]

The Polish immigrants love the land of their birth, but they love the land of their adoption more. Their first and last allegiance is to the country in which they have settled and raised their

[19] Haiman, op. cit., p. 427. Dr. Coleman, former president of Alliance College, was also among the participants at this convention.

families, and where is centered every interest they and their children have.

> Our first and most important duty is to be good Americans, take an active part in all phases of life here, and take advantage in full of all opportunities and privileges, as are rightfully ours, not as a numerous minority, but as mutual originators and participants in the common good of the American Republic.[20]

However, they did not intend to forsake the heritage of their fathers. Bishop Rhode in his address at the 41st Polish Roman Catholic Union convention made the following observation:

> If we forget our Polish heritage we become nothing but ships in the wind without anchors.[21]

The 1938 Convention of the Alliance of Polish Women in America (Zwiazek Polek w Ameryce) contained the following observation:

> Our working together with Poland results from the realization that, wanting to be worthwhile citizens of the United States and to understand this new world, this new swing to life, to live in this great family of nations, we can not be among them like leaves blown around by the wind, but we must point out our worth of descent and history; we must respect our past, if we want others to respect us."[22]

Perhaps the most clearly formulated view on the value of preserving one's heritage is that of Dr. Watson Kirkconnel:

> There is nothing so shallow and sterile as the man who denies his own ancestry. The "100 percent American or Canadian" is commonly one who has deliberately suppressed an alien origin in order to reap the material benefits of a well-advertised loyalty. There can be little hope of noble, spiritual issues from such a prostituted patriotism. Unfortunately, it is abetted by the ignorant assumption of many an

---

[20] F. Starzynski, "Polish Americans," *Polish Medical and Dental Bulletin* (November, 1938), p. 18.
[21] Haiman, *op. cit.*, p. 433.
[22] Jadwiga Karlowiczowa, *Historia Zwiazku Polek w Ameryce* (Chicago: 1938), p. 189.

English-speaking citizen that an alien origin is a natural mark of inferiority. He who thinks thus is a mental hooligan—whether he be a lawyer, militia colonel, or bishop of the church. What we sorely need, on the contrary, is enough common intelligence to recognize both the rich diversity or racial gifts on this earth and the strength which racial roots can contribute to the individual.[23]

This view was dependent on a new and specific interpretation of American society and culture.[24]

Laur Society, a cultural group in Detroit, stated explicitly in its published program the ideal of this new idealogy:

> The enrichment of American culture through preservation, cultivation, and propagation of Polish heritage in language, song, dance, music, drama and literature, is the ideal of the Laur Society. This ideal is possible because it is based upon the conviction that there are enormous possibilities in ordinary people.[25]

In this third state of orientation, the Americans of Polish descent emphasize the point that they had become an integral part of the United States. However, they did not intend to disappear without a trace as had the Polish immigrants before 1870. On the contrary, grouped around their parishes, schools, local and national organizations, they wanted to make their contributions to the creation of a common American culture; believing that out of the best elements of the diverse cultures in the United States, a superior civilization would be fashioned.

Historically there have been three general attitudes among native Americans who belong to the majority group regarding the manner in which immigrant people or minorities were assimilated and acculturated into the mainstream of American society. The first period, from 1776 until 1876, could be called the period

---

[23] Watson Kirkconnell, *Canadian Overtones* (Winnipeg: 1935), preface.

[24] According to this new ideology, America is a country composed entirely of sub-cultures and sub-societies. All of these societies help form the composite which is America. Each culture contributed something to the composite. The function of the Polish-American organizations is twofold: to find the best elements of Polish culture and "national characteristics" and impart these to the younger generation; and also make the general American society conscious of the Polish contribution to the American composite.

[25] Joseph A. Wytrwal, "Avenue of Pageant Pathway," *Laur Souvenir Program* (Detroit: 1951), p. 6.

of Anglo-Saxon conformity. During this period the majority group in America assumed and enforced the preference to maintaining the English language, English institutions (as modified by the American Revolution), and English oriented cultural patterns as a model or standard for American life.[26] Anglo-Saxon conformity was essentially a consciously articulated movement to strip the immigrant of his native culture and attachments and convert him into an American with Anglo-Saxon characteristics.

During the second period, from 1876 to the 1950's (when the ethnic vote became a matter of concern) there was a strong emphasis in implementing the "Melting Pot" theory, which was based on the contrasting view that the American nationality was a composite of many ethnic strains—not just English. Something new and distinctly American would result from the amalgam.

The "Melting Pot" meant dissolving all distinguishing characteristics of speech, dress and habits. America is a crucible into which all newcomers of non-English background must be prepared to hurl their entire heritage of the past, their pride, and their prejudice, their dreams and their sacrifices, their traditions and superstitions. Out of this "Melting Pot" would emerge a new citizen: the new American with a new culture which would be better than that of his ancestors. The "Melting Pot" concept became popular because it tolerated for a considerable period, during adjustment, multi-uniformity; but it still accepted the Anglo-Saxon trunk for the foundation unto which the other ethnic cultures were grafted.

The "Melting Pot" hypothesis also gave comfort to Americans who feared the enormous infiltration of people from eastern and southern Europe. It gave assurance that with time, the ability to find employment, and the beneficent forces of America would slowly bring about the adoption of standardized American conduct and conversion to American ways, within and without.

> What is really meant by assimilation is only the acceptance and imitation of Anglo-American civilization, of Anglo-Saxon modes of life, of Anglo-Saxon business methods, of Anglo-Saxon dress and the

---

[26] Joseph A. Wytrwal, "Why Ethnic Studies?" *Teacher's Guide for Senior High School Ethnic Studies Course* (Detroit: 1972), pp. 12-21.

Anglo-Saxon language. People are considered assimilated or assimilable to that degree with which they are capable of imitating the existing order of things. Such appraisal of assimilatory abilities is false. Only those people assimilate rapidly whose own culture is not very steep, whose culture is not very valuable. It is comparatively easy for an uncultured individual or group of individuals, whose range of emotion is expressed in their own language in three or four hundred words, to learn these three or four hundred words in any language for the purpose of daily transactions and expression of emotions. But it is difficult for a spiritually higher-minded individual or group of individuals, whose culture is far deeper, needing thousands of words to express more vivid emotions, to learn these thousands of words in another language. The emotionally and culturally low individual does not leave as much behind him, over which to ruminate and think as the emotionally highly developed individual who is continually wondering whether the new is worth as much as what he has left behind him. The baser metals melt first. They melt at straw heat.[27]

Thus, no large investments were made for education or for social aid. The few haphazard attempts that were made to assimilate the immigrant groups, were based on the following assumptions.

We could crystallize millions of aliens of all nations, habits, and languages, flocking to us from every quarter of the globe into a new homogeneous race, better and finer than the world had ever known.[28]

Franklin Lane presented a good summary of this Americanization theory:

One part Declaration of Independence; one part the Constitution; one part love of apple pie; one part desire and willingness to wear American shoes and another part pride in American plumbing will make an American out of anyone.[29]

Immigrants frequently criticized the naive assumption that American clothes, practices, and customs were superior to all

---

[27] Konrad Bercovici, *On New Shores* (New York: 1925), p. 16.
[28] Robert Ezra Park and Herbert A. Hiller, *Old World Traits Transplanted* (New York: 1921), p. 114.
[29] William Carlson Smith, *Americans in the Making* (New York: 1939), p. 116.

others, and this American spirit of condescension and coercion aroused a feeling of resentment.[30]

> If he gets on, if he is able to realize here in America some of the fundamental wishes that were denied him in his mother country, he will eventually become an American in every sense that we desire to give to that title.[31]

The "Melting Pot" concept appeared early in American history. St. John de Crevecoeur, the perceptive and enthusiastic observer of the American scene, wrote in 1782: "Here individuals of all nations are melted down into a new race of men." Crevecoeur saw them as a mixture of English, Scotch, Irish, Dutch, German and Swedes—a promiscuous breed which produced "that race now called American." Emerson elaborated and sustained this vision. By the middle of the nineteenth century the poet, Walt Whitman—who regarded himself as a kind of high priest of American democracy—was writing paeans to his country, "center of equal daughters, equal sons." America, he said, was not merely a nation, but a teeming nation of nations.

In 1908, at the height of the last surge of Immigration, Israel Zangwill's *The Melting Pot,* a play about American immigrants, captured the imagination of American theatergoers. The title has been immortalized as the classic description of the immigrant's reception and future in America. The great pot pictured in the play's last act was a roaring, bubbling cauldron, in which human material from the "ends of the world" was melted and fused with a "purging flame" by God the Great Alchemist, to produce the "glory of America." "There she lies, the great Melting Pot," exclaimed the hero David Zuexano. "East and West, the North and the South, the palm and the pine, the pole and equator, the crescent and the cross—how the great Alchemist melts and fuses them with his purging flames!" Carried completely away by the "Melting Pot" concept, Zangwill continued: "America is God's

---

[30] Everett Hale, in 1852, advised that the Irishmen must be surrounded by Americans. He believed the proper ratio would be eight Irish for every hundred native-born. This would speed Americanization. Carl Wittke, *The Irish in America* (Baton Rouge: 1956), p. 115.
[31] Smith, *op. cit.,* p. 168.

Crucible, the great Melting Pot where all races of Europe are merging and reforming . . . Germans and Frenchmen, Irishmen and Englishmen, Jews and Russians—into the Crucible with you all! God is making the American."

According to the "Melting Pot" hypothesis, America was the great melting pot into which immigrants of all origins, classes, experiences and education were dumped unceremoniously. Then, as if by magic, they were confidently expected to emerge, after a very brief intensive purification, with the dross of foreignism purged away to become one hundred per cent pure and unadulterated Americans.[32] The play was well received because it voiced the wish that was lodged deep in the hearts of thousands of Americans.

It was one thing to ask an immigrant to become an American; millions of Americans boasted that they wanted to be American. It was quite another thing to tell the immigrant that he had to discard the deepest values of his life, set aside all the traits that gave life its meaning, and adopt a pattern of ideas, attitudes, and customs which seemed to have no relationship to the lives of his ancestors. In many cases, the immigrants had become Americans, precisely because they had conceived of America as the land where they would be free to live according to the values which they cherished.

A vast number of Americans refused to give up their heritage, where everyone is expected to come out the same. They realized that Anglo-American culture had beed modified by the continued impacts of many foreign cultures, by the geographical and social factors in America and further affected by the distance of this country from the original habitat of its immigrants.

This resulted in the concept of Cultural Pluralism which found vigorous expression and wide support—not among native

---

[32] Dr. Max Kapustin, an orthodox rabbi and a native of Germany, rejected the "Melting Pot" hypothesis which maintains that the United States has a plurality of cultures woven into a pattern one and indivisible. The concept of Zangwill, according to Dr. Kapustin, did not comprehend the principles embodied in the American documents for two centuries: respect for personality, group personality, faith in progress and improvement of society. "Melting Pot Theory Criticized," *Polish American Historical Association Bulletin,* Dr. Joseph A. Wytrwal, Editor (February, 1960), p. 2.

Americans, but among the immigrant population who considered the "Melting Pot" hypothesis a harmful and unrealistic concept. They discovered that the immigrants were not "melting" and were not being fused into Americans. They also realized that certain groups such as Blacks and Orientals cannot be altered by the "Melting Pot" theory; a Black remains always visible as a Black, just as Orientals, Latinos, Hindus, respectively. They also discovered that ethnic traditions need to be honored and enhanced if a community is to be viable. Individual values must be encouraged if family, neighborhood, and parish are to be meaningful. Also, minority views must be allowed to be expressed on any question if democracy is to be relevant. Furthermore, they discovered that it was not possible or desirable to fuse all immigrants into one common base, since no two humans, no two families, no two groups are alike.

The basic tenet of the Cultural Pluralists is that the immigrants have as much to contribute to American culture as to receive from it—perhaps even more. This hypothesis can be considered a "mulligan stew" approach: where the meat is always the meat and the potatoes always remain the potatoes. Everything combines to create a new whole without losing individual identity. Each gains from the other, but if one element is missing, the stew is incomplete. Thus, immigrants are encouraged to believe that they bear an ancient national culture, hoary in tradition, distinguished in achievement, and still creative in purpose and action.

The Cultural Pluralists held that America should be a federation of various cultures, a democracy of nationalities, each developing within itself in harmony with others so as to preserve the valuable cultural differences each nationality has brought to the United States. Each group is an integral part of the whole that is America; that while individuals are of Irish, or Polish, or Italian, or Greek birth, or descent, they have contributed to American life—not as Irishmen, Poles, Italians, or Greeks—but as Americans; not as people of separate groups, but as peoples of different groups united in spirit as American citizens. Each group will recognize and understand its own culture, but not for itself, per se. Rather it will seek to understand the ways it has blended with, and thereby contributed to, the total and kaleidoscopic pattern of American culture. A healthy society depends upon diversity, not conformity and uniformity. Unlike diversity, conformity occurs only in cemeteries where individuals are all exactly equal. Diversity is richness, a richness which makes learning and understanding possible.

Cultural Pluralism helped scholars to recognize the importance of the culture of the immigrant, and to acknowledge that his loyalties, values and customs should exist in America; together the other cultures came to be known as American—a multi-hybrid.

Cultural Pluralism provided an honest appraisal of the immigrant's heritage and the means for a positive contribution to American life. Cultural Pluralism demands acceptance of one's own birth, parentage, heritage, customs, mores, traditions and history. It also requires a willingness to sympathize with and accept those who are different, provided the cultures do not clash or abrogate others' rights or sensitivities. The pluralistic person sees in others, not common principles or some universal Reason, but an analogous human story; not the same story for all, but comparable stories which describe too often mankind's universal tragedy: ignorance, immaturity, disease, conflict and inevitable death. A pluralistic American is a realist; in his maturity he is ready to accept the dimensions and complexity of the American experience.

The Cultural Pluralist hypothesis ushered in a new spirit and a new attitude on the part of many immigrants toward American culture and the Americanization process. Above all, a deep rooted conviction developed that the immigrants owe it to themselves, to their children, to their native lands, and also to the United States to maintain their old native cultures zealously and aggressively. They must also resist the influence and encroachments of the American environment.

In accordance with this hypothesis, some Polish-American leaders imagine the United States as a multiplicity in a unity, an orchestration of mankind. The ideal symphony is composed of a variety of instruments which play different notes, but they all blend to give the listener a masterpiece of harmonies and inspiring music if dissonance isn't interjected by crime, riots and a host of injustices.

> As in an orchestra, every type of instrument has its specific timbre and tonality, founded in its substance and form; as every type has its appropriate theme and melody in the whole symphony, so in society each ethnic group is the natural instrument, its spirit and culture are its theme and melody, and the harmony and dissonances and discords of them all make the symphony of civilization, with its diffierence: a musical symphony is written before it is played; in the symphony of civilization the playing is the writing, so that there is nothing so fixed and inevitable about its progressions as in music, so that within the limits set by nature they may vary at will, and the range and variety of the harmonies may become wider and richer and more beautiful.[33]

Other Polish-American leaders have compared the American culture to a garden filled with beautiful flowers of many varieties, colors and scents. Among these, the Polish flower has its opportunity to blossom forth in rich and exciting beauty.[34]

Whether consciously or not, Polish-American leaders were the most persistent exponents of the Cultural Pluralist hypothesis. According to this hypothesis the ethnic groups cherish their own traditions, and at the same time refuse to isolate themselves from the larger culture.[35] Jozefa Kudlicka expressed it in the following manner:

> I am not speaking as a Pole. I am speaking as an American. I feel I am 200 per cent American because I am 100 per cent Pole.[36]

The stress on the Polish heritage, however, does not necessarily mean identification with the Polish culture, but rather with the Polish culture as interpreted by Americans of Polish descent.[37]

> The culture of any nation cannot be simply a blend of cultures of other nations. The grafting of the fruit or products of strictly Polish

---

[33] Horace M. Kallen, "Democracy Versus the Melting Pot," *The New Immigration*. Edited by John J. Appel (New York: 1971), p. 122.

[34] Jozef A. Wytrwal, "Towarzystwo Laur Zespol Tancow i Spiewu w Detroit," *Bialy Orzel* (July, 1951), pp. 12-14.

[35] The Cultural Pluralist hypothesis had been set in motion by Randolph Bourne and Horace Kallen.

[36] Lola Kinel, "Jozefa Kudlicka," *Common Ground*, I (Winter, 1940), p. 35.

culture on the foreign soil of America may enrich American culture quantitatively for a certain time but not qualitatively. Rather the emerging culture of the United States will be enriched qualitatively by the values of the Polish spirit and character in those Americans of Polish extraction who, as intelligent and educated individuals, will take an active and creative part in American life, contributing to the art, science and literature of this country in the way that Joseph Conrad enriched England and Marie Sklodowska-Curie enriched France.[38]

The Cultural Pluralist movement made the Americans more conscious of their ethnic heritage, prouder of their characteristic diversities, and more aware of the material their heritage offers for literature, art, folklore, and folkways. Wisconsin, for example, was left with a distinctive state culture rather than with a microcosm of the national culture. All official publications of the state legislature were uniquely published in three languages: English, Polish and German. The various Old-World cultures were never completely submerged in Wisconsin as they were elsewhere in the nation.

Even today, scattered here and there throughout the state, there are little nuggets of Old-World culture; the Swiss in New Glarus, the Norwegians near Mount Horeb, the Poles in Pulaski, the Icelanders of Washington Island, the Amish, the Germans, the French, the Danes, and the Dutch. "We are not a melting pot but a beef stew," stated John Rector Barton, rural sociologist of the University of Wisconsin. "We were all thrown together in the same pot, but the beef remained the same and the carrots remained the same and the peas remained the same."[39] Only each ingredient added flavor to the total recipe. The general characteristics of the dish are made up of the dominant characteristics of its elements: the Poles, the Germans, and the Russians.

The "Melting Pot" hypothesis would indicate that a success-

---

[37] There is a marked tendency to make more extensive use of the means and opportunities which the American community itself offers, and not to rely exclusively on the Polish-American community.

[38] Thaddeus Slesinski, "Past, Present, Future Report Given to Polish Cultural Clubs," *Dziennik Polski* (August 7, 1959), p. 2.

[39] William Barry Furlong, "Wisconsin: State of Insurgents," *The New York Times Magazine* (April 3, 1960), p. 119.

ful American life would require complete, passive, assimilation or cultural stagnation, regression or repression. The Cultural Pluralist hypothesis emphasized cultural particularism, an awareness and appreciation of one's heritage as well as tolerance of others, with a willingness to co-exist and not dominate other ethnic groups.

The first is more extreme than the other. The "Melting Pot" hypothesis—with its denigration of foreignism and lack of respect for everything that is not Anglo-Saxon—would destroy for America all that the immigrant could give to it. The Cultural Pluralist hypothesis would destroy for the immigrant all that America has to give him by not urging conformity, experimentation and submitting to a role of exclusiveness. Neither the "Melting Pot" hypothesis nor the Cultural Pluralist hypothesis is in any way compatible with the principles of Americanism and the true spirit and aims of American life for a healthy national existence.

There is a distinctive American people and a unique evolving American culture. Therefore, the underlying premise of the Cultural Pluralist hypothesis is not necessarily true. Contiguous racial groups can fuse, both physically and spiritually, to form a new and distinct national and racial group, with its own particular spirit and culture. Historians had established this truth. This culture is slowly, steadily evolving and expanding in a rich variegated pattern. In addition to this evolving American culture, the immigrants of the last half-century have contributed very much, and have even more to contribute.

The correct attitude to assume and the constructive principle to follow is neither total assimilation nor total isolation. Rather, it is the historic middle course: it is the process of active versus passive assimilation, the process of being changed without losing one's dentity, the process of cultural giving in the same proportion to cultural receiving. It means the need to consciously preserve—in the midst of the American environment—the ancestral, historic and familiar values of the old culture. One does not have to maintain an active loyalty or a direct political affiliation with the native land; nor does one have to be separated from all other Americans. These values must be preserved to the end that the maximum of what is true and of eternal value in the old cultures may be conserved and contributed with a minimum of loss to the expanding content of the evolving American culture. The middle course must be a natural, gradual and creative process of adopting new ways, customs, and ideas that aid in spiritual growth, economic and professional advancement while living in an atmosphere of freedom, good will and justice.[40]

The "Melting Pot" and Cultural Pluralism hypotheses, along with Poland's independence, the "Quota Law of 1924," and the changing leisure-time activity pattern of the immigrants and their descendants—were bound to create a serious and precarious situation for all of the Polish-American fraternals. Their membership could no longer be increased by new immigration. The amusement and recreation afforded by the lodge had been supplanted by the automobile, the movie, radio and eventually television. The three basic needs supplied by the lodge: insurance, service and fellowship had gradually become commercialized with the decline in

---

[40] Cultural Pluralism is more acceptable to the ethnic pallete in making them feel less or not so inferior. There is a tolerance for not only who they are, but what they are. After the invasion of millions of immigrants from all corners of the earth, the expected assimilation into an Anglo-Saxon mold became impossible.

There is also the factor that certain nationalities are more assimilable than others; e.g., Germans, Scandinavians, Canadians and Australians. But at the other extreme, there are Gypsies (a curious nomadic people with a dominant culture and no nation to call their own), various orientals, Italians, Orthodox Jews (another nomadic group that has regained nationhood), various Arab speaking peoples, Greeks, Southern Slavs (Albanians, Serbians, Ukrainians), Spaniards, Portuguese, various African and Negro tribes, Latinos. A curious fact appears that the peoples emigrating from warmer climates nearer the equator have characteristically more dominant culture patterns than do those from northern climates.

The Poles, the French, Belgians are moderately assimilable. They do not differ so extravagantly from the European norm to appear strange.

There is another factor which permits people to relax their cultural standards and be more assimilable, that is if the immigrants come from a nation of their own. When immigrants arrive from subjugated lands where their nations no longer exist, they remain more conscious of their culture, language, history, folkways: e.g., Lithuanians, Armenians, Ukrainians—even taking a more militant nationalistic posture. Since Poland has been restored and the Jews have re-found their land called Israel, they are less reluctant to change and even become modern. The phobia about orthodoxy among the Jews has quickly disappeared for genetic reasons as well as the comforts which could no longer be tolerated.

Other ethnic groups like the Amish remain unchanged for religious reasons—an additional consideration.

Furthermore as one grows in wealth, and acquires the luxuries and the trappings of an elite society, people become more assimilable. For each acquisition there must be a sacrifice. These are the premises which truly determine the outcome of one's future in America.

DISSOLUTION AND ASSEVERATION

service and fellowship. Also with the decline and disappearance of nationalism, among the Polish immigrants in America, the *raison d'etre* of the Polish fraternals would become seriously undermined if a new program and new objectives were not substituted in order to rally the Polish immigrants and their descendants around their banners. Not only were new objectives necessary, but also intensive action to hold the ranks and numbers of those enrolled. The growth, increase, and continued existence of these organizations dictated only one program to which all the Polish-American national organizations had to subscribe if they wished to survive, namely to help the Polish immigrants and their descendants, socially, culturally, and civically in the American environment.

The objectives of the Polish-American fraternals were reduced to three outstanding projects: (1) In education, to support the Polish language and Polish schools, and promote higher learning; (2) To protect the rights of Poles in the United States, with a special emphasis on equal representation of the Polish-American clergy in the ranks of the Catholic Hierarchy in America; (3) Americanization, the question of Polish-American youth, to keep alive in them the consciousness of their Polish legacy.[41]

If the trend of events, shortly before the war, had won over the Polish clergy and the Polish Roman Catholic Union to the orientation of the Polish National Alliance for an all-out effort for Poland, so now, after the war, the Polish clergy and the Polish Roman Catholic Union could equally claim the distinction of winning over—also by force of circumstances and events—the Polish National Alliance to their own pre-war orientation, namely to give primary attention to the progress of Americans of Polish descent in America. In their activities and efforts, the Polish-American fraternals have not lost or cast off all their ideals; but with the change of historical events and political conditions, their ideals were merely modified.

This change and modification of purpose affected the Polish National Alliance and the Polish Roman Catholic Union in different ways: for the Polish Roman Catholic Union, it was simply

---

[41] Stanislaw Osada, *Jak Sie Kszaltowala Polska Dusza Wychodztwa w Ameryce* (Pittsburgh: 1930), p. 43.

a matter of reconversion, a return to its pre-war objectives and activities which had been suspended for the duration; for the Polish National Alliance, it necessitated a complete change in orientation, which was accomplished in an adroit manner.

> We have fulfilled our duties toward Poland with dignity. All future efforts in that direction have to a certain degree come to an end. And now it is high time that we think of ourselves. We have much to accomplish.[42]

Acknowledging that the main purpose of the Polish National Alliance—namely the restoration of Poland's sovereignty, had been achieved—the Polish National Alliance considered itself released from its obligation to give organized aid to Poland, so that it could give primary attention to the economic, cultural, political, and social advancement of Americans of Polish descent.

Before 1939, the preponderant majority of Americans of Polish descent had almost forgotten their tribal origin and heritage; their very sentimentality about Polish institutions and customs were often no more than skin-deep. Most had never seen Poland and never expected to see it; born in America, they thought of Poland as a foreign country. Nevertheless, the Polish-American fraternals made every effort to make them conscious of their Polish descent and heritage. Every "convention" or "sejm" emphasized the importance of sustaining the best of Polish culture in America, especially the rapidly vanishing language.[43] To preserve this language, it was decided to organize evening schools in

---

[42] Pliska, op. cit., p. 469. Zwiazek Narodowy Polski, Kalendarz Zwiazkowy, 1936 (Chicago: 1936), p. 46.

[43] No one will deny that a common language adds to solidarity, but in the United States English was rapidly becoming the language of the second generation Poles, and they were the growing and dominant group. However, the older Polish-American leaders feared the ties with Poland would be severed completely when the second generation and third generation were unable to express themselves in Polish. Yet of all the cultural influences, the language undoubtedly was the most difficult to maintain. For this reason other aspects of the culture had to be maintained. As demonstrated by Irish and Jewish organizations, unity can be retained without a common foreign language.

These stalwart Polish-American leaders would not hear of any substitutes. In their "Keep the Polish Language" campaign, the directors sent letters not to the national lodge, but to the local pastors. The priests supported the move as best they could, but the apathy of the younger generations and the inadequate funds from the older generation soon ended all endeavors.

all Polish-American communities. According to Karol Rozmarek, who was president of the Polish National Alliance, no other orientation was conceivable in the turn of events that the war brought with the restoration of Poland's freedom.[44]

> The existence and the future of the Polish National Alliance, as the name indicates, rests principally on the longest maintenance of Polish consciousness in America.[45]

The new orientation of the Polish-American fraternals also included efforts to make secure and build its membership, not from without, but from within, by probing as yet untapped sources.[46] By means of intensive campaigns, new members were drawn into the organizations, and the organizations gradually regained their buoyancy.[47] In these campaigns the numerical strength, financial resources, and security of the insurance policies were especially emphasized.

But to increase the adult membership in the organization did not necessarily imply that the future of these organizations was made secure. The Polish National Alliance and the Polish Roman Catholic Union placed a special emphasis on attracting the youth to their respective organizations, and on developing in them a consciousness of their Polish descent. To prepare the youth for administrative positions in the Polish Roman Catholic Union, John Olejniczak, the Polish Roman Catholic Union president, struck a significant note in his summons for the fortieth convention, when he appealed to the various groups in the organization to select young men and women as delegates who could learn to work for

---

The Polish fraternals could have become viable institutions if they had made a concentrated effort towards establishing a Polish cultural center, not a Dom Polski, but an attractive library-museum with an auditorium and reception hall for daily activities where various other organizations could congregate and benefit from these resources.

[44] The Americanization of the second generation, the barring of immigrant re-enforcements by legislation, decentralization among Polish-American national organizations, and the growing non-intercourse between Poland and Polish-Americans were rapidly breaking down what solidarity there had been among the Polish immigrants in the United States.

[45] *Zwiazek Narodowy Polski, Kalendarz Zwiazkowy,* 1943 (Chicago: 1943), p. 79.

[46] *Zwiazek Narodowy Polski, Kalendarz Zwiazkowy,* 1936 (Chicago: 1936), p. 46.

[47] Zwiazek Narodowy Polski, *Urzedowy Protokol Sejmu XXVI, 1931, Scranton, Pennsylvania* (Chicago: 1931), p. 119.

the welfare of the organizations as their fathers had done in the past.[48]

The Polish National Alliance and the Polish Roman Catholic Union carried insurance for children, who became additional members of the organization; later, on reaching maturity, they were transferred to the adult group membership. However, both fraternals realized the disturbing loss and decline of membership among children and teen-agers. The extent of the decline is indicated by the fact that between the years 1931 and 1932, the Polish National Alliance had lost 13,054 of its youth; while the Polish Roman Catholic Union, after reaching its peak in 1930 with 44,182 young people in its organization, saw its numbers dwindle to 27,366 by 1935.[49] By December 1955, the number in the Polish Roman Catholic Union dropped to 20,865;[50] in 1956, there was a slight gain in membership to 21,522.[51] To hold members in the organization, the Polish National Alliance, in 1931, and the Polish Roman Catholic Union, started to form large scale Scout Troops.[52] This last undertaking checked the falling away of the teenagers from the Polish National Alliance ranks.[53] The Scout movement in the Polish National Alliance was modeled on the Polish system; the Polish Roman Catholic Union followed the American system.[54] In 1933, the Polish National Alliance numbered 52,106 members; the Polish Roman Catholic Union listed 7,440 members, in 1937.[55]

In 1928, the Polish Roman Catholic Union and, in 1931, the

---

[48] J. Olejniczak, "Oredzie na Sejm Zjednoczenia Polskiego," *Polacy Zagranica* (February, 1931), p. 327.

[49] Zwiazek Narodowy Polski, *Sprawozdanie na Sejm XXVII, Baltimore, Maryland 1935* (Chicago: 1935), p. 282. Franciszek Barc, *65 Lat Zjednoczenia Polskiego Rzymsko-Katolickiego w Ameryce* (Chicago: 1938), p. 85.

[50] "Annual Statement for the year ended December 31, 1955 of the PRCU of America," *Narod Polski* (April 19, 1956), p. 2.

[51] "Annual Statement for the year ended December 31, 1956 of the PRCU of America," *Narod Polski* (April 2, 1957), p. 3.

[52] Zwiazek Narodowy Polski, *Urzedowy Protokol Sejmu XXVI, 1931, Scranton, Pennsylvania* (Chicago: 1931), p. 229. Barc, *op. cit.*, p. 90.

[53] Zwiazek Narodowy Polski, *Sprawozdania na Sejm XXVII, Baltimore, Maryland, 1935* (Chicago: 1935), p. 282.

[54] Zwiazek Narodowy Polski, *Kalendarz Zwiarzkowy, 1935* (Chicago: 1935), pp. 62-64.

[55] Zwiazek Narodowy Polski, *Sprawozdania na Sejm XXVII, Baltimore, Maryland, 1935* (Chicago: 1935), p. 267. Barc, *op. cit.*, p. 95.

Polish National Alliance established in their fraternals special Youth Departments which were as important as the Education Departments or the Welfare Departments.[56] By holding membership cards in the Polish National Alliance, or the Polish Roman Catholic Union, and by participation in their recreational activities, youth could not help but preserve their consciousness of its Polish origin. The Polish National Alliance scout movement, which retained the Polish scout uniform, and required a knowledge of Polish and of the culture and history of Poland, was regarded as the most influential means of instilling in the youth of Polish descent the Polish national spirit.[57]

The task of instilling Polish consciousness in both young and old members was difficult to promote; in both organizations, the insurance element asserted itself and claimed attention more and more. The national objectives were, at times, deliberately relegated to the background by the suspension of societies and members for non-payment of dues and insurance rates. Thousands were lost to the organization during the depression years.[58] The introduction and substitution of new insurance tables with rates to meet the requirements of State laws, caused an additional loss of members. During these changes the ideological element was not even considered.[59] Fraternal insurance organizations were given charters in different States, not because of the services rendered to the members, but because they met the standards set by the States for insurance companies.[60] Some States did not permit, or else restricted fraternal insurance organizations in their social activities. Thus, the national work of the fraternals was curtailed.[61] Notwithstanding these limitations and difficulties, the

---

[56] Zwiazek Narodowy Polski, *Sprawozdania Na Sejm XXVII, Baltimore, Maryland, 1935* (Chicago: 1935), p. 258. Barc, *op. cit.*, pp. 100-103.

[57] Zwiazek Narodowy Polski, *Kalendarz Zwiazkowy, 1935* (Chicago: 1935), p. 64.

[58] Zwiazek Narodowy Polski, *Sprawozdania na Sejm XXVII, Baltimore, Maryland 1935* (Chicago: 1935), p. 228.

[59] Barc, *op. cit.*, p. 84.

[60] Zwiazek Narodowy Polski, *Sprawozdania na Sejm XXVII, Baltimore, Maryland, 1935* (Chicago: 1935), p. 59.

[61] Compare Massachusetts State Law regulating fraternal insurance organizations in Zjednoczenie Polskie-Rzymsko Katolickie, *Protokol Urzedowy Sejmu XL, Detroit, Michigan, 1931* (No imprint), p. 66.

Polish National Alliance and the Polish Roman Catholic Union, during the period under consideration, had shown feverish activities centered mostly on increasing their membership capital. In 1935, the Polish National Alliance numbered 280,385 members; the Polish Roman Catholic Union 151,515.[62] The wealth of the Polish National Alliance, for the same year, totalled $28,376,426.69; that of the Polish Roman Catholic Union, $15,439,690.73.[63] It is to be noted in the history of the two fraternals that whenever the membership in these organizations decreased, their wealth increased.

After World War I, much of the organizing vitality in the Polish-American communities was provided by the young war veterans from the American army and from the Polish Blue Army. They either formed organizations of their own or joined with a new found pride other groups which were seeking more effective and satisfying roles for Polish-Americans. Most prominent in this activity, in the early 20's, was the Alliance of American Veterans of Polish extraction, with national headquarters in Chicago, Illinois, representing Illinois, Wisconsin and Ohio. A similar organization with the same name was organized with headquarters in Detroit, Michigan. Another organization was prospering in the East comprising the states of New York and New Jersey under the name of the Polish Legion of the American Army with national headquarters in New York City.

In the year 1930, the Alliance of American Veterans of Polish Extraction, with headquarters in Chicago, Illinois, delegated their national commander, Stanley A. Halick, to the national convention of the Polish Legion of the American Army, for the purpose of consolidating both organizations into one strong organization of veterans of Polish extraction. Through correspondence the same procedure was initiated with the Michigan organization which proved very favorable and all three organizations met in Cleveland, Ohio, on September 5, 1931, at a consolidating convention forming the Polish Legion of American

---

[62] Zwiazek Narodowy Polski, *Sprawozdania na Sejm XXVII*, Baltimore, Maryland, 1935, p. 228. Barc, *op. cit.*, pp. 84-85.

[63] Zwiazek Narodowy Polski, *Sprawozdania na Sejm XXVII*, Baltimore, Maryland, 1935, p. 109. Barc, *op. cit.*, pp. 84-85.

DISSOLUTION AND ASSEVERATION

Veterans. At this convention all three organizations were equally represented by their fully entitled delegations.

At this convention, Stanley A. Halick was elected national commander, and also a ladies auxiliary was organized which was known as the Ladies Legion.[64] Following this convention, the Polish Legion of American Veterans prospered in its membership, posts and finances.[65] As a living monument to over 1,000,000 Americans of Polish extraction, who served in the World Wars I and II in the armed forces of the United States of America—of whom thousands made the supreme sacrifice—the members of the Polish Legion of America formed the organization for the following purpose:

> To uphold and defend the Constitution of the United States of America and all the principles for which it stands; To encourage active interest in all manifestations and demonstrations of patriotic nature, that the glory and sanctity of American ideals may be forever preserved; To combat the destructive propaganda of communism and other alien influences endeavoring to weaken or destroy our American institutions and democratic form of government; And to maintain and preserve the true spirit of fraternity and patriotism arising from the sacrifices in the World Wars, and to perpetuate friendships and associations arising herefrom by mutual aid and cooperation in patriotic charitable, educational and civic activities.[66]

The Polish Army Veterans Association is an organization, unique in the sense that it was originally composed of veterans of World War I who had enlisted voluntarily from the United States for service with the Polish Army in France, in 1917-1918. They experienced active service on the Western Front, fighting

---

[64] The second national convention was held in Hamtramck, Michigan, in 1932, electing Mieczyslaw Glod as national commander. The third national convention took place in Cicero, Illinois in September 1933, William F. Kalisz was elected national commander. John A. Ciaglo was elected commander at the fourth national convention held in Milwaukee, Wisconsin, in 1935. John M. Lewandowski was elected national commander at the fifth national convention held in Cleveland, Ohio, in September 1937. He was re-elected at the sixth national convention held in Maspeth, New York, in September 1939.

[65] The organizers of the new organization were: Stanley A. Halick from Chicago, Illinois; W. Goda from New York City; and Frank Wojtal from Detroit, Michigan.

[66] Helen Kwiecien Kmiec, "The Polish Legion of American Veterans, Chicago, Illinois," *Polish American Encyclopedia* (Buffalo: 1954), I, p. 174.

side by side with the armies of the United States, France, Great Britain, Belgium and Italy. In 1919, this army crossed Germany and arrived in Poland where—united with the Polish army—they fought jointly against Bolshevik aggression, in 1919 and 1920, for the frontiers of reborn Poland.

In the middle of 1920, their mission completed, most of these volunteers were repatriated to the United States where they resumed their normal activities. In May 1921, a group of the Polish Army veterans met in Cleveland, Ohio where they laid the foundation of the first foreign army veterans organization in the United States. The primary purpose was to organize the loosely scattered posts, create new ones, and bring together into one fold all the comrades who served under the Polish eagle in France and Poland.

The organization did not limit membership to those who volunteered for service in the Polish armed forces, but called the new organization the Polish Army Veterans Association of America. The PAVAA permitted any person who served in any branch of the many and varied Polish armed forces—at any time during the period from August 15, 1914 to November 11, 1920—to become a member of this newly formed body.

Within a space of twenty years—just before the United States was drawn into the conflict of World War II—the organization had 141 posts and a membership of 4,450 in twenty states, Canada and Poland.[67] The Ladies Auxiliary, which was organized in 1925, numbered approximately 4,530 members in 104 posts.

Soon after the association's inception, it became evident that the financial status of the returned American and Polish veterans required assistance. Neither government felt responsible toward the disabled or the sick. This unfortunate situation motivated and inspired the Polish Army Veterans Association to find ways and means to aid and succor their disabled and incapacitated comrades. A special fund for this purpose was established. The first person to consider the urgency for helping the disabled Polish Veterans was Ignacy Jan Paderewski. He contributed the sum of

---

[67] Post No. 130 existed in Poland until World War II.

$10,000. In appreciation for this noble and generous gesture, the special fund was named "The Ignace Jan Paderewski Invalid Fund." Paderewski's contribution inspired the individual posts to raise funds through various drives. When the depression of the 1930's depleted this fund, the organization invited General Haller, the commander-in-chief of the Polish army in France, in 1918, to visit the United States. He toured the main Polish-American communities for six months and solicited donations to help maintain the humanitarian work. This fund has been supplemented and enlarged through special drives, contributions, donations, and since 1935, through the proceeds from the annual sale of the *Blawatek* (Cornflower), the Polish poppy by the posts of the various veteran organizations. Another source of revenue is the Polish National Alliance, which since 1935, has donated part of its membership assessment each year to the amount of approximately $3,800 annually.[68]

The annual outlay for veterans of the Polish army is approximately $28,000. A few districts maintain their own Soldiers Home where the disabled and elderly veterans receive year-round care.[69]

The Polish language periodicals were generally limited to first generation members who remembered partitioned Poland. As a rule, they were among the least articulate in their respective communities, among those found on the outer social and economic fringes of American society. Many of these people had a very poor command of the English language; to them, the Polish press was a means of keeping abreast with the outside world. The Polish press continued to represent the sentiments of the older generation—those whose formative years had been spent in Poland. It had a distinctly immigrant bias and made no serious

---

[68] Jan Dec, "The Polish Army Veterans Association of America," *The Polish American Journal* (April 29, 1967), p. 3.

[69] When World War II concluded, many Poles, who fought in the Battle of Britain, at Tobruk, Narvick and Monte Cassino, found themselves stranded in many allied countries and in the displaced persons camps in Germany. With the passage of several bills, by the United States Congress, many found refuge in America. Foreseeing the possibility that many former members of the Polish armed forces would establish their future in America, the national convention, in 1946, amended its constitution and by-laws whereby those who served actively during the Second World War, in any branch of these forces, could be accepted as full members of the Polish Army Veterans Association of America.

attempt to understand the problems of the second generation. It implored the youth to follow in the footsteps of the older generation, and to preserve the customs and traditions of their parents. However, it did not have any serious influence on the thinking of the second generation. What is more, relatively few of the young were able to read a Polish newspaper, for their command of the language was limited.

Since the Polish immigrants lived in a dual culture, they wished their children to follow the same pattern. Thus, Polish-American parochial schools flourished during the 1920's; and at home, the Polish language was utilized, and some semblance of control was exercised over the young Americans of Polish descent.

Late adolescence reversed this Polish indoctrination, and the American environment prevailed. When the second generation reached adulthood, the Polish-American community became less Polish. Chicago's Polish theater passed from the scene during the 1920's. The Polish-American papers were compelled, by circumstances, to print more English articles. Under the pressure of the changing times, even the Polish-American pastors had to deliver sermons in English, if they wished to reach the hearts of the young.

The Polish-Americans had completed another chapter in their history, by 1925. Having built a miniature kingdom in a friendly territory, they were now to behold their institutions blending together with the wider society around them. Occupational mobility also had affected the mooring of Polish-American isolationism. In a land where it is possible to mount the ladder of opportunity, second generation Americans, with a better command of English and a better education, were able to rise economically and socially above their immigrant parents. The change was not sudden, since the first generation immigrants still numbered over one million in the 1920's; together with a small segment of the second and third generations, they managed to maintain the dual pattern.

CHAPTER EIGHT

The Second Generation

> We were here and endured:
> Groups of lumberjacks, carters,
> Miners of coal and gold,
> Ploughmen of fallow fields
> To gather at the cross with nostalgia:
> The humble, the dreary, the speechless,
> Living in foreign shacks, our thresholds,
> Sincere beggars of God
> To bring us nearer to death or Poland.
>
> But today—so gradually we have become
> People, whom nothing hurts us,
> Daily we leave
> Beyond the gate,
> Beyond that Gate!
> Leaving behind ourselves
> A card: "For rent" at our doorstep,
> And in the Polish papers—a few obituaries.
>
> —Jozef Makowiecki[1]

The members of the second generation of Poles in America did not find themselves in any easy position. Descendants of an agrarian folk culture, they were born into families with a rich cultural past and a deeply rooted style of life. They had developed in a different world from their parents, but through the memories of their parents—edited by the passage of time—they shared in the misty nostalgia of a special heritage. Their early years were hardly joyous, for they were exposed to the hardships of life.

---

[1] Jozef Makowiecki, "Przypomnienie," *Wiadomosci Codzienne* (July 28, 1939). Translated by Benedict Markowski.

They heard parents and their friends recall and discuss their burdens in Poland, and the unemployment, discrimination and difficulties with the English language during their early years in the United States.

The will to succeed had been deeply ingrained in their children from the beginning. They were told in clear—and often blunt language—that work in America was something sought after. The principal purpose in life was not to have fun, but to work. Few parents permitted their children to forget that one of the requisites of life was to learn how to assume responsibility soon. The admonition to "be someone better than I am" also was heard repeatedly. The children were admonished to take advantage of the opportunities denied their parents, assume responsibilities, to make a success of themselves, and to provide for their parents in old age. An unoccupied and unemployed son, in his early teens, could be made to feel he was committing an offense against his family, God and society by not having something gainful or constructive to do.

In the atmosphere of their homes, members of the second generation shared the ethnic life of their parents who continued to speak and read Polish periodicals. They attended churches where customs and religious practices imitated the customs of Poland, and raised their children in a culture isolated from that of the United States.

The parents had a reluctance to change. They had limited experience in civic affairs or gaining wealth—although thrifty by nature. They cared little for organizations, perhaps because of an attitude that encouraged strong individualism. Most of the parents struggled to learn the new language. Before they gave up the project, they mastered enough words which resulted in a language interjected with Polish and American expressions, or a macaronic English which was no better, albeit colorful. Any one of their remarks might contain a sprinkling of terms such as "store," "haircut," "grocery," "corner," "paycheck," "doctor." To their children they always spoke in Polish, who in turn, answered in English. Before they learned English, the children of the immigrants learned to speak Polish fluently. Through ridicule by others, children were made to suffer many embarrassments;

they were made to feel inferior and self-conscious that they were less American than any English-speaking person. They were compelled to forget and not use the beautiful lyrical language of their forefathers that produced the great Romantic poetry of the nineteenth century.

Sandra Severo—the fiery lady whose push shoved Detroit onto the world ballet scene—was born in Detroit, on Rivard Street between Forest and Canfield. Her accent is Middle European and authentic. But she didn't get it in Europe; she acquired it, at home, in Detroit.

> "My mother was determined that her children would not forget their heritage, so all we spoke at home was Polish. The neighborhood was very Polish, so outside the home you got Polish, too. Same at school, St. Josaphat.
>
> I have this accent because I did not speak English until I was about fifteen."[2]

The first contacts of the second generation were usually with peers of identical background, as were the associations of their parents and friends. This is understandable, for they spoke a common language, understood each other's problems, and could be counted upon for sympathy and advice. Some parents made a point of seeing to it that their children associated only with children of Polish extraction. This was part of the family and cultural discipline, as well as a matter of convenience.

In the parochial schools, the Polish language was given considerable prominence. Thus, in addition to hearing Polish spoken at home, the children learned it in school and came to use it even on the playground. Yet it was impossible for children to share their parents' ethnic life completely. They came under influences that had not touched their parents. They gained a knowledge of American traditions and institutions. They learned to speak English, and conformed to the dominant society in America. They mingled with youngsters of non-Polish origin and eventually acquired the social, personal, and economic values that motivate average youngsters in America.

---

[2] Al Stark, "Sandra Severo—The fiery lady who makes Detroit Dance," *The Sunday News Magazine* (December 3, 1972), p. 32.

If they attended parochial or public schools—which were not established by Polish-American institutions—they encountered discriminatory treatment frequently:

> Another side of the coin is that Polish youngsters have often been subject to a subtle (and often thoughtless) discrimination, even in parochial schools. A paper written for a graduate degree at Pitt said in some school situations Polish young people constituted an "underclass," with teachers being heard to remark, "What can you expect from Polish youngsters!" (The most telling account in this paper was of a Polish girl who moved to another school system, changed her name to one which sounded Scandinavian, and found the attitude and expectations of her teachers much better!)[3]

When the children attended the public school, rather than the parochial school, they were forced to bridge a cultural barrier. To be culturally integrated they must be, sociologically speaking, upwardly mobile. Cultural integration required that their academic skills and knowledge be improved to match those of the dominant American society. The task was made more difficult by many teachers who faced the dilemma of countervailing values. The teacher had a choice between two honored values: maintenance of academic standards and concern for individual differences. Most teachers chose to maintain the academic standards, which led to lower grades for the majority of minority students. Thus, the second generation children encountered additional difficulties and discouragements when they tried to climb the social ladder.

Pride is the child of prideful behavior. It is the business of standing tall in one's eyes. It is the process of finding usefulness and purpose—not in the world one dreams of—but in the world that is. Although the educators in the public schools claimed there were no distinctions, minority children frequently heard such expressions as "foreigners" and "gringos" used in a disdainful manner. Nor was this all. In school the youth might have heard a teacher refer to the immigrants from eastern and southern Europe as being of a less desirable mold than those from western and

---

[3] Clarke M. Thomas, "Pittsburgh's Polonia. Living with Discrimination." *Pittsburgh Post-Gazette Daily Magazine* (April 26, 1973), p. 31.

northern Europe. This, of course, included their parents. Often teachers discouraged the use of foreign languages. Frequently they ridiculed, or scorned, or questioned the children's traditions and belittled their nationality. Not infrequently they were exposed to teachers of Jewish descent whose parents migrated from Poland. Their presentation of Polish history—in the context of world history—was far from objective. In addition, they were ridiculed for their accent. Many times they were piqued by teachers as they garbled their surnames. And of course, there was always the teasing and name calling by classmates.

To fit into the school's social system, the children understood the role they were expected to play as students. They also learned what behavior is rewarded with A's, or praise and what behavior is punished with F's and frowns. To flaunt one's Polishness was to invite persecution, and put needless barriers to success, for it would attach the stigma of being a foreigner in an era when one boasted of his Americanism. Polish identity was important, but it would have to be subdued; it would have to be muted. If they demanded to be treated as all other Americans, they could not, at the same time, emphasize too strongly their Polish differences.

After a few months in school, the children knew far more than their parents about the new country, but were taught almost nothing about their own cultural past, or the achievements of the country of their parents. In fact, they were constantly urged to disregard old values, and often were made to feel ashamed of their parents for their foreign ways. The teachers certainly made no effort to help the children preserve a genuine respect for their own culture as they acquired a knowledge and respect for the new culture.[4]

Many left the public school with the knowledge that they could climb the ladder of success in America, if they scorn much of their Polish past and consign it to the trash can of historical obscurantism. This was not true in most situations. Instead of assisting students to become better adjusted to American life, the school personnel often drove them closer to others of their own

---

[4] If they attended Catholic schools staffed by teachers or nuns of Irish descent, they were exposed to ridicule because of their accent or Polish surnames.

nationality, which increased their sense of isolation and delayed their adjustment.

Related to the problem of discrimination was the question of education. Practically all of the children came from homes where there were large families with little or no leisure. Thus, quite often children were compelled to leave school at an early age because of the economic conditions at home. Also, many left the school without pride in their nationality, *sans* pride in their family, *sans* pride and confidence in themselves. Encouraging or striving for a higher education did not have as high a priority in all Polish families as it did in other nationality groups. Therefore, Polish families pushed their young people to get out into the world, and obtain a livelihood as soon as possible. Wherever there were large families, this became a necessity, since scholarships were not plentiful for students.

In many cities where one-quarter to one-third of the children in the schools were of foreign parentage, only a small percentage enrolled in high schools, and less than two per cent entered college.[5] Even though they had to work, and often they lacked leisure, nevertheless a few of them were well acquainted with the music, art and literature of Poland. At the same time, they had only a superficial exposure to the best in American culture.

When the second generation children terminated their education, they did not always, or even frequently, engage in common work occupations with their parents as was the custom in Poland. Diversity of occupation brought with it diversity of interest, and a division in the Polish-American home. The girl who was forced to turn over her earnings in Poland, understood the reason why: it would eventually be returned to her with her dowry, which was the custom of life in the cooperative large family. In America, the concept of an extended family had disappeared; the tradition of cooperative family efforts toward a common goal were shattered, and the assurance of a dowry, at the time of marriage, became problematical.

Living in two worlds, and attempting to master both, could

---

[5] Thaddeus Slesinski, "The Second Generation of Immigrants in the Assimilative Process," *The Annals of the American Academy of Political and Social Science*, XCIII (January, 1921) pp. 156-161.

be taxing. Many times the children of immigrants had to mediate between the traditional values of the attitudes of their parents, and that of the community. Thrust into a society that had as one of its objectives the obliteration of those vestiges of foreignism that proud parents wished to perpetuate, many children questioned not only their identity, but also their adequacy. Many experienced alienation and despair. Sometimes the increased stimulation of the city life made home and "foreign" culture seem drab.

Evidences of the increased incorporation of American elements into the cultural experience of the second generation were accumulated from a sample of Polish-American young people, eighteen years or over, in 1929. In this study Carpenter and Katz showed that their sample group obtained about half their schooling in the parochial, and half in the public school. About seventy per cent of the youth approved the complete authority of parents over adult children, and yet ninety per cent asserted that the child should be independent in choosing a vocation. As the investigators assert, "Culture behavior changes more rapidly than rationalized culture attitudes."

Probably the same influence was at work in another response of the younger group, since three-fourths declared themselves in favor of a separate Polish community, while only one-fourth maintained that the Polish-Americans should spread out and lose their identity in the larger American scene. Fifty-six per cent of the group agreed to this statement: "Poles should speak Polish in their homes, subscribe to both Polish and American books, and speak English in their business and daily contacts." On the other hand, thirty-seven per cent subscribed to the following: "The Poles should speak mostly English, subscribe mostly to American newspapers, read American books, but should retain some Polish for the value it has in maintaining Polish culture and traditions."[6]

The remarkable studies about the tendency to use the native language were made in 1927 and 1945. Data reflecting the percentage of homes, in which Polish was spoken, was gathered. In

---

[6] R. A. Schermerhorn, *These Our People* (Boston: 1949), pp. 286-287.

1927, in families where the fathers were born in Poland, forty-eight per cent spoke only Polish in the home, and fifty-two per cent spoke English and Polish. The follow-up study, in 1945, in which 8,000 homes were surveyed, forty-nine percent spoke only Polish, and fifty-one per cent spoke English and Polish.[7] In both studies the results were comparable.

Members of the second generation lived amid two societies. From the differences in the two societies emerged a dilemma of opposing values. The first society was composed of perplexed and admonishing parents, the Polish-American clergy, various fraternal and community leaders and veterans of the Polish Blue Army. All were committed to the Polish identity in all of its various forms. All were alarmed at what they regarded as the casual abandonment of Polish culture that appeared to them to be both rich and inspirational. All strongly resisted acculturation, and bemoaned the eventual extinction of a Polish identity in America.[8] All supported the State of Poland financially, politi-

---

[7] George P. Graff, "Michigan's Polish and Lithuanian Immigrants—Settlers of City and Countryside," *The People of Michigan* (Lansing: 1974), p. 86.

[8] Not having known political oppression, the second generation could not be moved by Polish nationalism. Frequently, leaders of the Polish communities in America complained that their mission was fading with the younger generation. The reason was that the second generation had not so much lost the sense of a mission as transformed it. Never having known Poland, they were not pressed by the necessity of making comparisons with that which had been left across the ocean. If they did remember anything about Poland, from their studies, they remembered only what they wanted to remember; they remembered even things that never happened, but should have happened. For them Poland was not a source of security, but of inherited bonds, often irrelevant to the needs of the time and place. Beyond the influence of the value and standards of the Old World, they developed their own. Not having known Warsaw, they could consider Chicago a great city; not having seen Wawel Castle or the Lazienki Palace, they could take pride in their local parish church. They did not fear a loss of contact with Poland which they never knew. Their experience which was limited when it came to what lay beyond the ocean, but not when it came to what was near at hand—generated confidence in their own capacity for achievement. And their experience was not one of loss or deprivation, but of continuous gain, as industry prospered, as the population grew, or as cities expanded. They were rootless and mobile, but they never lived under any other conditions; and they were, therefore, not subject to the same strains of making decisions that had burdened their parents. Even with feelings of inferiority, they were likely to accept, as a way of life, and adjust to the disorder and precariousness which troubled their parents.

This failure to appreciate Poland was primarily due to the parents' lack of awareness or information which they should have imparted to their children. At best, they had a vague awareness of the spirit of being Polish: heroic, romantic, idealistic, patriotic, or Catholic. But they could not convey Poland's greatness through facts or detail.

cally and emotionally, even when such support raised the specter of dual national loyalty. All believed that American and Polish interests are compatible, for otherwise they would be forced to make a choice between the values, each of which they desired.

The second generation was confronted with public schools, non-Polish friends, and institutions, with which they came into daily contact. In addition, there were vocal and ubiquitous individuals and groups that wished to mold all foreigners in their image of Americanism.[9]

How to inhabit two worlds simultaneously was the problem which this generation had to resolve. In the schoolroom, they were too foreign; at home, they were too American. They had to be resolute in order to absorb the criticism of their parents for being too American, and by Americans who disdained them for being too Polish. As a result there was an inevitable reaction, on their part, to the standards, interests and attitudes found in the Polish-American community and the non-Polish values and attitudes in the surrounding society.

As long as the children were young and manageable, the stern parental will prevailed. However, this cultural isolation broke down as the children advanced in the elementary and secondary school grades. This is when they began to draw comparisons, and sometimes complain about having to attend the Polish-American parish school or the Polish Roman Catholic Church.

Parents were of two kinds: Some realized that they were living in the United States, and that their children would have to grow up as Americans; they would satisfy themselves with what few vestiges of Polishness they could retain. Others insisted on attempting to rear their American-born children as though they were native Poles. Parents who chose the former course—and they were in the majority—had much the easier time. They wanted their children to retain membership in the Polish Roman Catholic Church and maintain a Polish surname and some knowledge of the Polish language; however, in all other respects they were willing that their children be American.

The average Polish-American priest made every effort in stress-

---

[9] Cardinal Gibbons and Archbishop Ireland are two appropriate examples.

ing the advantages of marrying within their own ethnic and religious background. He emphasized the advantages of having a spouse of the same faith, capable of conversing in the native language of the parents, and discharging her true duties to the family. He warned of the dangers of mixed marriages, the loss of Polish identity, and the Catholic faith. The priest also kept haranguing the parish with the admonition that the only way of preserving Polishness, in America, was by supporting the Polish Roman Catholic parishes.

To the members of the second generation the church represented Latin Masses with Polish sermons, novenas, and benedictions. It also supplied Polish schools. It was also a place where their parents and others congregated on Sundays to extend their greetings and exchange gossip. The parish hall was the scene of bazaars, bingo parties and meetings of women's church auxiliaries. To the second generation, religion appeared as an external matter, not the product of a deep conviction. The priests in the parish offered no cultural guidance, no spiritual warmth and no inspirational leadership. At the same time, the nuns failed in their mission to their Polish charges to teach them about Polish history and culture; the limits of their resonsibility were to teach the and culture; the limits of their responsibility were to teach the Polish language, the prayers, the confession of sins, and the catechism in English as well as in Polish.

This was, also, a period when the second generation began to assert its independence, desire the company of other backgrounds, attend social functions with members of the opposite sex, and disapprove the cultural milieu of their parents. The main problem was to decide which group to affiliate with, and which set of cultural values to pursue: the Polish or the American? Three psychological reaction-types were possible: the "rebel" identified with the American system; the "in-group" gravitated towards the Polish group and its values; or the "apathetic" which was a retirement from the conflict by minimizing the significance of nationality groupings.

Caught between two cultural worlds, the members of the second generation responded to the conflict in many ways. These may be classified into five categories.

The first category, uncertain of who they were or their direction in life, uncertain of their grip on the present, weak in their hope of the future—placed their trust in the "Melting Pot." It was that great and wondrous myth that Zangwill elevated to an article of faith. A society that melted meant a society where the Poles would not be different or singled out for persecution. Weary of discrimination, this category yearned to melt, because melting meant the blurring of distinctions. In the "Melting Pot" there is indivisibility that forever hid the Polish-American as a distinct entity to be attacked. This was the way to abolish contempt for Poles.

Because they believed that the "Melting Pot" was the great equalitarian credo, they rejected anything that had to do with Polish-American life: language, history, tradition, customs. Living almost perpetually in a state of conflict and tension, they were resentful of the disabilities imposed on them by their ethnic inheritance. In their frantic repression of their ethnic inheritance, the past is only allowed to return in the form of self-hate, shame of one's parents, and caricaturing Polish traits. In their refusal to accept the tension of being in a minority, and the need to balance the insistent demands of the past with the needs of the present, they went to great lengths in order to transcend their parochial origins and divest themselves as thoroughly as possible of all immigrant symbols. Uncomfortable with their Polishness, they went beyond all else in order to be inconspicuous. Many changed or altered their Polish surnames. Many distinguished themselves from the Polish-American community by leaving the Roman Catholic Church for the Episcopal, Congregational, Evangelical or other faiths. Many rejected all contact with the Polish-American community, because it was nothing but a burden to them. In some instances they even denied their Polish origin. They rationalized their abandonment of Polish loyalties by seeing it, not as desertion, but as moral growth. By professing a vague humanism or universalism, they tried to justify (at least to themselves) their reasons for casting off the particular.

Coming to terms with this kind of repression often led to alienation from the Polish-American community, including a feeling of insufficiency, even when they had some knowledge of its traditions. The word "Polish" touched a live nerve, triggered a reflex and altered them so much that they disliked everything Polish, for they saw in it that element which kept them away from the majority to whom they wished to belong.

The present was their only reality. Lacking a past, they could have no notion of a continuity, or any image of the future. For them, there could be no fulfillment. To free themselves from their ethnic origin, they loudly proclaimed that whereas trees do have roots, human beings have legs with which to move freely amongst each other. The real issue was never, to be or not to be Polish, any more than it was, to be or not to be the children of their parents. Whether under the name of Shell or Skorupski, Cherry or Wisniewski, whether within the society, among Americans or other peoples—they were still compelled to confront the forces which the majority erected against the crossing of an individual from the minority to the majority group. It is still not so open that individuals who are different from the majority can serenely and happily accept their differences.

The second category consisted of individuals who did not feel the least attachment to Polish life, but were not necessarily hostile to Polishness. Sensitive to the counterpulls of the two cultures, these individuals sought to evade the problem by avoiding all situations where ethnic origins might be considered. When they had acknowledged freely their Polish descent, they had made personal choices whether to abandon their Polish ties for one reason or another. At the same time, however, they lacked the confidence to participate in native American institutional life for fear their ethnic background would be a source of embarrassment.

The third category consisted of individuals who considered themselves part of the Polish-American community in some sense. Because of unusual opportunities or abilities, they have succeeded in winning a place in the larger community as well as in the immigrant colony. They usually acquired a good education, and through self-application and persistent effort they gained positions of leadership among both the Polish-American community and the American establishment. Often they did not live in the Polish-American community, but, at the same time, they kept in contact by membership in the Polish-American fraternal organizations, or by appearing as speakers at the annual General Pulaski Day dinners. Sometimes, they even attended the Polish Roman Catholic churches. They spoke the Polish language fluently and were more or less acquainted with the culture and traditions of their own nationality. At the same time they knew the best in American life. They served not only the members of their own racial group, but the larger community as well. Many of them were public-spirited citizens who were entrusted with high public offices by the larger community. In this capacity they rendered valuable service and gained respect and recognition from all.

Among them are bankers, business men, educators, lawyers, and doctors. This group also included the artists, writers, and musicians. It is to this group that members of the Polish-American community pointed with pride as being of the same national identity. This group had no special or economic interest in the Polish-American community. They belonged entirely to the larger community. Nevertheless, they did not deny their nationality. They did not alter their surnames, but were proud of their heritage. As American citizens—with interests and experience reaching far beyond the limits of the Polish-American community—they did not approve of the standards set by the Polish-American community leaders. There is no doubt that they exercise an Americanizing influence, but they are prone to feel out the sentiment of the majority before taking a stand on any issue involving the Polish-American community.

The fourth category, small but growing in number, encompasses individuals who were in some way stirred by the Polish heritage and were sincerely committed to their Polish-American attachments. Some of them discovered their Polish heritage a little late in life. There was something zestful and exciting in that background, which was forever passing from their lives; it had given them a smattering of Polish, a cultural distinctiveness, and a special brand of individualism. Proud of their heritage, they interpreted for the rest of the world the music, art and philosophy of their own people. They were not only keeping alive the best of their own traditions, but they were also making a great contribution to America. Wiktor L. Alski, publisher and editor of *Pittsburczanin,* made this explicit:

"There are decisive moments of our becoming conscious of being Polish. We become aware of a relationship springing from the glory and suffering of Poland. Often we realize with a sudden flash of understanding that we have within us a thousand years of Poland. We then recognize ourselves anew in pride and sympathy. Something strikes a hidden vein that bursts up like a geyser from the subconscious world within us. We grew slowly, but firmly into the soil of a new country.

Many of us found ourselves under biological, psychological or sociological pressures to assimilate properly and naturally; to become good Americans by destroying any connection with Poland, as if to assimilate happily and naturally, required such sacrifice. This idea is basically wrong! That this notion is false, is the one truth it is our mission to spread. Ours is a basic contribution in our war against the inferiority complex, the rust corroding so many Polish lives.

It is our task to teach our young fellow Poles that to belong to the Polish cultural group is no stigma of inferiority, that, on the contrary we are better Americans by contributing our rich dowry to the greatness of this country, as a valuable component of the young American nation."[10]

This category, intellectually and culturally mature, rejected the Cultural Pluralism hypothesis and the "Melting Pot" hypothesis. Neither hypothesis is in any way compatible with the principles of Americanism and the true spirit and aims of American life and national existence. Accepting neither total assimilation nor total isolation, they adopted the historic middle course. It is a process of active versus passive assimilation, of assimilating without being eradicated ethnically, or cultural giving to the same proportion as cultural receiving. It means the conscious preservation —in the midst of the American environment—of the basic and permanent values of the old cultures which must be preserved, neither to maintain eternally active loyalty and affiliation with the native land, nor for the perpetuation of hyphenated Americans eternally separated from all other Americans. These values must be preserved so that the maximum of whatever is true and of eternal value in the old culture can be preserved and contributed with a minimum of loss to the expanding content of the evolving

---

[10] "Przed 15 Laty Zmarl Red. Wiktor L. Alski," *Pittsburczanin* (November 3, 1972), pp. 1-2.

American culture. The middle course must be a slow, natural, spontaneous and creative process of active assimilation with the spiritual growth, and must express the true American spirit of freedom, justice, good will and progress.

The fifth category, small but diverse, is composed of those who have grown up with Polish attachments. They have tended to identify strongly with the parental group, and they have urged retention of Polish identity in order to affirm Polish spiritual and cultural values. Certain that their Polish heritage is as mutually enriching as that of America's, they believe that those who deliberately jettison their patrimony in search of security are poorer than they need be; and America is weaker for forsaking their ethnic heritage. Since this response was not well received by the Anglo-Saxon populations, the members of this group sometimes compensated for their consequent feelings of insecurity with a militantly defensive posture. Their concern about the Polish-American community was a natural development and reaction to an unfavorable situation. They appreciated the problems of the Polish-American community and would like to see some of its values preserved, while making a conscious effort to remove the barriers that separated the Polish-American community from the larger community. They also tried to instill and stimulate, in the third generation, love and admiration for Polish culture, traditions and ideals.

Though their love and loyalty for their parents was genuine, yet it was impossible for them to forget that their experiences were also American. This was especially true for the majority of the second generation who reached maturity between the First and Second World Wars. They were torn between two forces: the desire for acceptance by the American society, and the attraction of non-Polish values and attitudes, and the desire for group identity and survival as a distinct community. While Irish immigrants seemed to take pride in their loss of identity, members of the second generaton of Polish descent seemed anxious to find an ideological position which denies the existence of any tension between survival and integration.

For the most part, the members of the second generation wanted to be part of the society into which they were born, rather than become torchbearers in preserving the national identity of their parents. They were content with the pleasures of popular culture and sought some meaningful forms of identification and expression. They could not simply revert to the organizations and traditions of their parents for those bore the stigma of foreignness. Their problems, they felt, were not the problems parents conceived them to be; maintaining the Polish language, the Polish church, and the spirit of Polishness. When prejudice and discrimination reminded them that they were not fully equal, when they reached for higher occupational positions, they claimed their rights as native Americans.

For a time it appeared as though an unbridgeable chasm separated the older generation from the younger. However, strong family ties, the Polish language, the Polish school, and the Polish churches shaped the attitude and behavior of the child born of immigrant parents and bridged the chasm between the two generations.

The average member of the second generation rarely concerned himself with issues relating to Poland, except in periods of extreme crisis. If the Polish issue was linked to something preponderantly American, the interest would be keener and perhaps justified. Seldom would he read a Polish newspaper or take seriously Polish issues that filled the column of the American press. In fact, he might resent the efforts of a Polish patriot or immigrant to inject such issues into community affairs. Interest in modern Polish culture was also at a minimum, despite the efforts of the Polish press, church leaders, and influential laymen, who organized fraternals, libraries, theatrical and musical groups to keep alive an interest and be informed about their Polish heritage. The majority of youth were too concerned with the American way of life: the pursuit of pleasure and modern material conveniences—rather than be concerned about their own personal problems or give any thought to Polish art, literature and higher learning. What the Polish church, the Polish language press, and Polish travel agencies wished to encourage (for perfectly obvious reasons) the rank-and-file members of the second generation chose to avoid. They were in America, and it was their country. They just did not care about preserving or acquainting themselves about Polish culture.

The rise of the second generation to professional, commercial, and intellectual prominence, in the United States, is part of the American success story. Virtually all were of humble origin, without wealth or influential friends; but succeeded to influential positions through determination and dedication.

The professions, which mostly appealed to the young, were those of law, holy orders, and medicine, and to a lesser degree, dentistry. Teaching, engineering and other professions gradually acquired more appeal. The inclusion of so many professionals and intellectuals, at this period in Polish-American history, is due to two factors: (1) the skimping and saving of parents to provide their children with a higher education that led to a profession. This was regarded as the safest and most profitable investment, since they expected that the children would provide them with care and comfort during their declining years; (2) the scholarships granted by the large national organizations, or loans without interest to students—sons and daughters of their members. However, except for the politicians and the clergy, most of the professionals and intellectuals proved to be a failure from the Polish-American point of view. Only three per cent of this segment had shown a real interest, or had taken an active part in the national life of the Polish-American community.[11]

Reports on the doctors and lawyers—members of the professional and intellectual class, who grew out of the Polish-American communities—showed that having climbed the social ladder by means of their education and profession, they showed the greatest inclination to abandon the organizations which had provided them with opportunity and a means to better themselves socially, economically, and culturally. Only the Polish-American clergy and the politician, who benefited directly from the constituents they represented (especially members who were born in Poland) held firm to their Polish individuality; and it was due to their leadership that Polish-American communities were established with their unique social forms and institutions; and it was

---

[11] Rev. D. Szopinski, "Od Redakcji," *Przeglad Katolicki* (January, 1926), p. 229.

the small Polish-American businessmen who supplied financial support to these communities.

The Polish-American clergy had ascertained that many professionals of Polish descent frequently settled in non-Polish Catholic communities, enrolled their children in non-Polish Catholic schools, where they joined non-Polish parishes, either because they did not desire to associate with Polish immigrants, or for business reasons, in order to attract clients from other nationalities.[12] In most instances, they had unlearned many of the habits acquired in childhood from their lowly-placed parents, and had learned most of the values of the upper economic classes where they had settled. Engrossed entirely to the pursuit of the dollar—with no thought of cooperating with Polish-American communities—not only did these professionals refuse to be included as members of the Polish-American community, but they remained indifferent to it—abandoning it to its fate. A large number no longer considered themselves Poles; they considered themselves merely Americans.[13] Even prominent old family names were affected. Many changed their names, either for simplicity or to accommodate their public, in order to identify themselves with native-born Americans.[14] Father Bolek did not hesitate to call the majority of the Polish-American professional intellectuals simply businessmen eager for the greatest possible financial gains from their professions.[15]

---

[12] "Pogadanka o Ameryce," *Przeglad Katolicki* (March, 1928), p. 219.

[13] Dr. F. Lenart, "Potrzeba Zorganizowania Inteligencji Zawodowej Na Wychodztwie," *Kongres Wychodztwa Polskiego w Ameryce, Odezwy, Referaty, Rezolucje, Uchwaly oraz Urzedowy Protokol* (Detroit: 1935), p. 46.

[14] A Detroit attorney, Stanley A. Hoyle, who legally changed his name ten years back, died before he could realize his wish to have it changed back. His petition to have his oroginal name, Stanley A. Hojnacki, restored to him was dismissed by Probate Judge James H. Sexton after the judge was notified that Hoyle died. In his request to the court, the lawyer said his decision a decade ago to take the name of Hoyle had "weighed on his peace of mind." "Death Prevents Name Restoration," *Detroit News* (March 6, 1956), p. 27. The University of Toledo, in Toledo, Ohio, accepted a bequest to the university of $9,000 from the estate of Irene J. Paryski, the late publisher and editor of the Polish-American weekly, *Ameryka-Echo*. The stipulation on the use of the bequest is that it be used to assist American students of Polish descent who have not changed their Polish surnames and who speak the Polish language. *Polish American Journal* (December 6, 1958), p. 2.

[15] Rev. F. Bolek, "Zycie Kulturalne Polakow w Ameryce," *Przeglad Katolicki* (March, 1928), pp. 44-51.

F. Lenart—in his address at the Polish National Congress, in Detroit, in 1925—listed that, at that time, there were, in Chicago: 150 Polish-American doctors, 150 dentists, 300 lawyers, 70 druggists, 30 engineers and architects. Immediately, he raised the question: How many of these professionals contributed their share and took active part in the social work of the Polish-American community? The number was so negligible that he preferred to leave the answer to the professionals and intellectuals.[16]

No one will deny them the privilege or right to accumulate wealth through their profession. However, some might criticize them because they preferred to be considered only Americans. It is obvious that wider possibilities were open to the professionals through speedy acclimatization. Therefore, they lost their profound Polish-American characteristics, and made more rapid progress in their American surroundings. But these professionals did not pursue their career in a typically American community where ethnic differences or characteristics were unknown or reduced to a minimum. They maintained their offices, plied their trade, and numbered their clientele among Poles in Polish-American communities.

The nationalistic Polish immigrants regarded this elite class with criticism and disappointment for the following reasons: (1) The professonals and intellectuals had their origin in the Polish-American community which they now openly snubbed; (2) Only through the efforts and contribution of the Polish communities could these individuals have risen to a higher professional and intellectual level; (3) Only in the Polish-American communities did they, at first, exercise successfully their trade or profession. The Polish-American community was responsible for their success; while at the same time, these professionals did not reciprocate.[17] In most cases this meant sacrifice: members of the Polish National Alliance and the Polish Roman Catholic Union had contributed hard-earned money to their success. It is understandable

---

[16] Dr. F. Lenart, op. cit., pp. 49-51.
[17] "Co Czyni i Jak Intelligencja Polska?" *Przeglad Katolicki* (January, 1926), pp 111-112.

why members of the Polish-American community do feel bitter toward their successful professionals and consider them ungrateful.

The last reproach was justified in the reports on scholarships furnished by the Polish National Alliance and the Polish Roman Catholic Union. From the very beginning, they had charged their members a small fee each month (only a few cents), which, in time, as the membership had increased, produced a large sum of money for scholarships. The Polish National Alliance, during the years 1932-1935, had expended $72,981.99 among 673 students attending higher institutions of learning.[18] The Polish Roman Catholic Union spent $300,000 from 1908 to 1938, for the same purpose.[19] These monetary sums were loaned out without interest to students. The scholarships were not in the form of foundation grants whereby money was invested which brought dividends and the organizations then drew their funds from the principal. They were contributions of Polish Roman Catholic Union members and the Polish National Alliance members, who voluntarily stimulated a set fee which was voted on at the national conventions for the purpose of sending promising students to higher institutions of learning. It is self-evident that with more members in the organization—which would increase the revenues of each organization—and a requirement that all grantees, in turn, remain faithful members of the organization with the added stipulation, that once successful, they would contribute generously to a special fund earmarked for scholarships.[20]

Thousands of American students of Polish descent benefited from these contributions, and both organizations were proud of their achievements and the type of educational work they had undertaken. But they could not help feeling resentful at the time. According to the Polish Roman Catholic Union official

---

[18] Zwiazek Narodowy Polski, *Sprawozdania na Sejm XXVII, Baltimore, Maryland, 1935*, p. 215.

[19] Barc, *op. cit.*, p. 88.

[20] The Kosciuszko Foundation also grants scholarships. Many Polish born students received them. It would be interesting to note how many showed their appreciation after they received university placement. Very few. They made little impact on the Polish-American communities.

reports, out of $300,000 expended for loans and scholarships, only $21,200 had been refunded. Many who have benefited from these loans, evidently did not feel obligated to return the loans they received, without interest, although they attained prominence and wealth in their profession.[21]

The Polish National Alliance fared better, even though its Educational Department also had some money loaned out and not returned.[22] Thus, it was not surprising when the Polish National Alliance and the Polish Roman Catholic Union members charged these professionals—whose higher education was gained through their faith in them—with dishonesty, disloyalty, ingratitude, injustice and parsimony: for had the loaned sums been refunded on time, many other students would have benefited from these loans. The Polish Roman Catholic Union would have at its disposal $275,000 for new scholarships. These professionals deprived many deserving and talented students from the opportunities of acquiring a college education.

These revelations caused considerable stir among Polish-American fraternal organizations and intellectual groups. Why was there such a lack of cooperation between the organizations and the professionals? This had been a topic for discussion for many years. The Polish-American fraternals eliminated prejudice, even though many Polish immigrants harbored a suspicion against higher education. The fraternals had preached and stressed the necessity of a professional and educated class to insure progress and advancement for Poles in America, for they financed the education of promising students. The Polish National Alliance, and especially the Polish Roman Catholic Union, placed the blame on the professionals for having isolated themselves from the Polish-American community and for failing to take over social and cultural work among the Americans of Polish descent. In the opinion of the Polish National Alliance and the Polish Roman Catholic Union, the professional group had refused to share the

---

[21] Zjednoczenie Polskie Rzymsko-Katolickie w Ameryce, *Sprawozdania Zarzadu Glownego na Sejm XL, Detroit, Michigan 1931* (no imprint), pp. 418-420. Barc, *op. cit.*, p. 88.

[22] Lenart, *op. cit.*, p. 43.

leadership which both of these Polish organizations held successfully for the past eighty years.²³

The professional and intellectual class refused to accept these accusations. They advanced reasons for leaving the compact and economically inferior Polish-American communities. Dr. Ostafin stated these reasons succinctly in his study:

> It is typical of urban Polonia leaders to forsake narrow Polonia loyalties as they advance either in the Catholic hierarchy or the American political system. A judge or a district attorney of Polish extraction must serve the whole community, not just the Polish segment. A Roman Catholic bishop of Polish origin must emphasize his loyalty to Rome and to all the Catholics of his diocese—even though his fame and appointment may be due to the presence of organized Polonia groups. There is a tragedy in the disappointments which the exceptional sons of Poland bring to her at the moment of her victory. Polonia develops and supports her leaders, but as they go up the ladder of American opportunity, she loses them.²⁴

The controversy, over the American professional and intellectual group of Polish descent, had elicited many suggestions and comments; and it had some practical results. The Association of Polish Doctors and Dentists—at their November 1928 Convention, held in Cleveland—set forth the following program of action:

---

²³ This feeling seems to persist, for even as late as June 1, 1958, Brother E. Stanislaw, President of La Salle College, made the following observation at the sixty-ninth commencement address at the Orchard Lake schools, in Michigan. "Szdoka wielka ze dorobek nasz w Ameryce, zapoczatkowany zreszta wspaniale, skierowal sie na ksztalcenie lekarzy i adwokatow, a zupelnie pominal intelektualistow i naukowcow. . . . Nie many dosc polskich intelektualistow i dlatego dzis odczuwamy wielki brak czegos. Tym czyms jest wlasnie brak zainteresowania naszym wlasnym pochodzeniem, nasza tysiacletnia kultura. A przeciez to jest obowiazkiem Polonii . . ." Stanislaw Krajewski, "W Ameryce Brak Polskich Intelektualistow—Mowil Brat E. Stanislaw, w Orchard Lake," *Dziennik Polski* (June 3, 1958), p. 3.

Alexander Janta, in his observations on Polish culture in America stated: "No conclusions were yet drawn from the striking fact that some Americans of Polish origin, who had achieved prominence in their professions here, often betrayed an embarrassing ignorance and their appalling lack of basic information on Polish matters. In other words, and this is still a valid statement, though they may have a university education, the level of their understanding of things Polish is at best that of a parochial school." Alexander Janta, "Barriers into bridges: Polish Culture in America," *The Polish Review*, II (Spring-Summer, 1957), p. 83.

²⁴ Peter A. Ostafin, *The Polish Peasant in Transition. A Study of Group Interaction as a Function of Symbiosis and Common Definitions* (unpublished Ph.D. dissertation, University of Michigan, 1948), p. 280.

To take active part in social-national life. To contribute professional service, especially to charitable organizations.[25]

A point could be raised in defense of some of the professionals who learned from experience that belonging to the large Polish national organizations was to no avail for their leadership lacked distinction and the organization proved to have no clout in critical matters that affected the Polish-American community. Many intellectuals and professionals can cite experiences where they defended Polish, Slavic and ethnic concerns with no support from these organizations. Often their stand for justice for the Polish-American community proved detrimental to their own careers.[26] The Polish-American organizations do not have the influence or ability to exert pressure that the NAACP does.

The goals of the Polish American fraternals must be examined introspectively and critically. Success is not determined by the financial statement which reads a large net balance in the black, but how much the money is turned over, how much new money is pouring into the coffers of the organization, how many younger members are involved in the destiny of the organization.

During the same period attention was focused by the *Pittsburczanin* on a strange phenomenon which became noticeable in the leadership of the large Polish organizations. During their tenure of office (frequently acknowledged and honored as leaders of Polish-Americans), they were heralded as wholeheartedly devoted to their organizations, sacrificing their time, strength, and health for their brother-members; suddenly, after removal from office, with the election of new officers, they disappeared from the public arena and no longer took an active interest in the Polish-American affairs—not even in their Polish National Alliance or the Polish Roman Catholic Union.[27]

---

[25] "Ad Notam," *Przeglad Katolicki* (March, 1928), pp. 198-199.

[26] A good example is Benedict Markowski. Dr. Joseph A. Wytrwal, "Dred Scott . . . Alfred Dreyfus . . now Benedict Markowski," *Dziennik Polski*, English Edition (January 4, 1975), p. 4.

[27] Rozmarek, former president of the Polish National Alliance and the Polish American Congress, and Pranica, former president of the Polish Roman Catholic Union—are the best examples. Their names which were very conspicuous in *Zgoda* and *Narod Polski* are conspicuously absent. Nothing was recorded of their activities on behalf of the Polish-American community after leaving office.

CHAPTER NINE

Polish Cultural Heritage in America

Jakose po niebie
Sloneczko poluje
Tak se moj kochanek
Po swiecie sportuje.

Sedlbym do dziewecki
Widzi sie mi precki,
Przez jeden wiersycek.
Przez dwie dolinecki.

Cozbyscie wy chlopcy
Gorale robili,
Kiedy sie wom jesce
Kochac zabronili?

Co mi z tego kwiatka
Co patrze na niego,
Kiedy on ma zapach
Do kogo innego.

America is basically a country without common traditions. It is limited to regional customs which are indigenous to the area by geography, ethnic domination, or physical terrain. This is not to say that America is a country without a culture of its own, but rather that American culture is one of achievement and not tradition. America's lack of tradition can be traced to two factors: first, America's brief history has provided the country little time for traditions to develop; secondly, American society is a mosaic composed of different ethnic groups and races whose origins can be traced to all of the varied and distant continents of this wide world. As a result, Americans tend to draw on the traditions of their forefathers.

The pattern of living and thinking—which prevailed among the people of Poland—was, for centuries, characterized by a resistance to change and by a tenacity for inherited customs and beliefs. During the 19th century, the Poles were in subjection to alien powers and were on the defensive against vigorous and organized efforts to wean them from all they held dear, and to form them into something quite different. Because of this aggression, the Poles made it a point of honor to cherish not only the "faith of their fathers," but also their culture, their traditions and their customs in order to preserve their identity as a people.

Polish-Americans cling tenaciously to their customs, which are, in nearly every instance, quite as much religious as national in character. The most beautiful custom—and the one that bids to outlive all others among the Polish-Americans—is that of sharing the *opłatek* (Christmas wafer). The *opłatek* is a thin unleavened wafer, much like the altar bread or communion wafer, used in church service. It is stamped with the figures of the God child and Our Lady of Częstochowa. It is known as the "bread of love." Shortly before Christmas, the parish organist distributes the wafers; and at this distribution, each parishioner makes a slight offering to the organist who delivers the *opłatek*. These are sent to friends and relatives in Europe, and the latter do not forget those in America.

Unlike Americans of other ethnic origins, who have Christmas dinner on the 25th of December, the Poles have their solemn dinner on Christmas eve. The special meal, known as *Wigilia*, is the most prominent event during the holiday season. Although it is meatless, its gustatory delights leave a profound impression on the mind, and sometimes on the waistline.

The dinner is arranged according to prescribed traditions. To commemorate the Savior's birth in a manger, a bit of hay is placed beneath a white tablecloth. Cut into narrow strips, the *opłatki* are placed on a plate which occupies the center of the table. Prior to sitting down at the table, the father offers each member of the family an *opłatek*. If guests are present, they too partake of the Christmas bread, since it is an explicit sign of brotherhood and

Catholic friendliness. First, the mother and father break off a bit of each other's bread while exchanging wishes and embraces. Then the rounds are made until each person has broken bread with everyone else. Everyone present repeats the ceremony, eating a small piece of wafer, and breaking it with each other as a sign of brotherly love. Custom dictates that before the *oplatek* (tokens of continued love, mended friendships and goodwill to men) may be eaten, all dissensions, quarrels and misunderstandings that may exist must be dissolved. The absent members are not forgotten; a wafer with appropriate greetings is exchanged with them by mail, even abroad to Poland.

After the breaking of the *oplatek* by the family, the *Wigilia* (Vigil Supper) follows as set forth by ancient tradition and belief. The course to be served are fixed at either seven, nine, eleven or thirteen. An odd number of people should be seated at the table; a vacant 12th chair and place setting is provided symbolically for Christ or the unexpected visitor. Polish tradition also dictates that no one but the wife rises from the table during the Christmas meal, or bad luck will result during the ensuing year. Also during the feast a lighted candle is placed in the window. The plate and chair symbolize the hope that the God Child, in the form of a stranger, may come to share the *Wigilia* supper with them. From this ancient belief, comes the Polish custom of honoring and protecting any guest or stranger who comes into their home. In all Polish traditions the odd number is always preserved in offerings: e.g., gifts of roses or carnations, when visiting a home should be always an odd number—the greater the number, the greater the esteem for the person.

The *Wigilia* supper will be a meatless supper in honor of the holy birth. The menu consists of fish prepared in a variety of ways. Also *barszcz* served with mashed stuffed dumplings and mushrooms, sweet herring, shredded noodles dipped in honey and poppy seeds, *Kasha* (grits, groats, and pearl barley), peas, *pierogi* (a dough-filled cheese appetizer dipped in sour cream) filled with mushrooms and sauerkraut. The toasting beverage is *miod,* a Polish honey liquor, and followed by delicious poppy seed cakes, gingerbread, fanciful pastries, the familiar *babka* and *sernik* (cheesecake), as well as all kinds of fruit, hot tea or coffee.

After the meal, gifts are exchanged and opened under the illuminated Christmas tree. Then, *kolendy* (carols) are sung. Unlike many of the Christmas carols of other nations, the *Kolenda* is not only a prayer, but it also narrates a short story or musical drama depicting that wondrous tale of the Nativity. In "*Lulajze Jezuniu*" the Infant is called "my little pearl." In contrast, Poles have "*Tryumfy Krola Niebieskiego*" (Triumphs of the Heavenly King) a hymn filled with exulting tones.

The *Kolendy* musically express the profound religious convictions which inspired the Poles through Christ's birth at Bethlehem. Also, at this time, the neighbors would call with the *oplatek* in hand, and exchange wishes of good cheer. Sometimes the carolers go from house to house. This merriment continues until it is time to attend the "*Pasterka*"—the Christmas Midnight Mass.

During the Octave of the Epiphany, doors are marked with the initials of the name of the Wise Men, with chalk blessed on the feast of the Epiphany. The Christmas season closes on February 2, Candlemass Day. On that day, people carry candles to church and have them blessed for use in their homes during storms, sickness and death.

The practice of decorating eggs for Easter is known throughout the entire Christian world, but has been developed into an elaborate and complex art in Poland, called *pisanki*, which custom began as early as the XI century.[1] Poland has two main techniques for decorating Easter eggs: Eggs dyed a solid color through boiling and soaking them in various vegetable materials, after being cooked, are called *skrobanki*. The outline of birds, flowers and animals are delicately scratched with sharp instruments. Eggs covered with wax, etched in artistic design and then dipped in colorful fluids, are *pisanki*. The latter are found in all parts of Poland and in the United States. This art form has been adopted by other Slavic groups with their own distinct designs: Ukranians, Russians, etc. A third form of easter eggs are decorated with colored paper strips (*wycinanki*) in shapes of flowers, birds and other fanciful designs after its contents have been emptied.

---

[1] Polish legend has it that on the first Good Friday a religious man was taking a basket of eggs to market to sell. On the way he set his basket down and ran to help Christ carry his cross. When he returned for his eggs, they were all decorated.

Many Polish-Americans fashion eggs with brilliant designs for Easter gift-giving. People exchange them after Easter services as gestures of friendship. Girls offer their best handiwork to their favorite young men, and friendship takes on a new dimension. Displayed at home, they are interesting conversational pieces. Blessed by the priest, *pisanki* are believed to contain talismanic powers. Sometimes an egg, featuring a hen or rooster motif, is given to childless married women.

Polish egg designs use traditional Christian religious symbols such as the cross and lamb, which represent Christ, or the flower, signifying nature's reawakening in the spring, or the risen Christ.

Swieconka is the blessing of Easter food on Holy Saturday. This may be done either by inviting a priest to the house, or by taking the food to the church. If the food is to be blessed at the church, the food is placed in a small decorated basket and carried there. The priest recites several prayers when blessing the food: eggs, bread, butter and cakes shaped as lambs, etc.

When the priest is expected to visit the house, the dining room table is covered with the best tablecloth, and the food arranged with taste and festive trimmings. The lamb (*baranek*), usually made of butter, stands in a prominent place; a small banner is pressed into it. Different meats: boiled *kielbasa* (fresh and smoked) in coils or rings are placed on warm platters. Then the bread, *babka, mazurki, pierniki,* and other pastries; fruit, wine and vegetables are arranged artistically on the table. Hard boiled eggs, some shelled, some dyed and others decorated, are also included. Flowers and fresh greens add a pleasant spring touch to the ceremony.

Some of the above mentioned foods are symbolic. The lamb symbolizes Christ, slain for the remission of our sins. Meat is present because Jesus destroyed the old order that forbade certain meats; horseradish recalls the bitterness of Christ's passion. Eggs, of course, are symbols of resurrection and a new life.

The Easter blessing of food owes its origin to the fact that these particular foods, viz., fresh meat and dairy products, including eggs, were forbidden in the Middle Ages during the Lenten fast. When the feast of Easter brought the religious fast to an end, and these foods were again allowed at the table, the people showed their joy and gratitude by first taking the food to the church for a blessing. Moreover, they hoped that the church's blessing on such edibles would prove a remedy for whatever harmful effects the body might have suffered from a long period of self-denial.

The blessed food is eaten for breakfast on Easter Day. First, the egg, symbol of life, is cut into pieces and shared with the family and friends in a similar way as the *oplatek* is shared at Christmas. Each person takes a piece of the blessed egg exchanging the greeting, *Wesolego Alleluja*. Unlike Christmas, which is a day of family gatherings, Easter is an appropriate occasion for traditional Polish-American hospitality when everybody is invited to share their table in a season of plenty with blessings to the family all year long. The doors are open to the extended family of relatives who congregate to enjoy the Easter meal. It is informal with no special menu of courses.

An integral part of the Holy Week observance is the practice of visiting elaborate grave scenes usually set up at one of the side altars. Life-size figures of Christ in his sepulchre guarded by angels, flickering candles and votive lamps, flowers and potted palms set against a backdrop of painted Crucifixion scenes, with honor guards of parish activists and boy scouts keeping watch—all lend to set an eerie, medieval mood that is truly unforgettable.

Americans of Polish descent continue the Polish Easter customs. On Holy Thursday, the church bells are traditionally silenced; their function is performed by the *klekotki,* rattles constructed of wood. On Good Friday, the people would spend the Holy Hours, in Church, keeping their Savior company, while he hung on the cross, often before a scene of the entombment, sometimes reproduced in life-sized images in the churches. As a sign of mourning, the altar and church statuary would be draped in black or deep purple covering. On Easter Saturday, they hurry to church to have the food blessed for Easter. In the same manner they share the blessed egg and exchange good wishes at the Easter table. The custom of *Swieconka*—once typical of Polish parishes in America—has now spread to other parishes where the Americans of Polish descent form a minority and is becoming popular with many non-Polish-American Catholics. Very early on Easter morning, Holy Mass is celebrated, and after the Mass, the priest and the laity go in solemn procession three times around the church, inside or outside, depending on what weather permits. This is called the *Resurekcja*.

"*Dingus* Day," or "Switching Day," is Monday after Easter; and for centuries it has been a Polish holiday.[2] The custom permits male Poles to make the round of the neighborhood knocking on doors. If a female opens it she can expect a sprinkling with water (or perfume in the more affluent areas) and then receive a flogging on the arms, shoulders or back with a light-weight switch, or rod. In reciprocation, the female is obliged to invite the flogger in and give him a swig of spirits.

One of the loveliest and most beautiful Polish customs is celebrated on St. John's Eve (June 24th) where marriageable young ladies placed a candle in the center of a wreath and floated it down a river. If the candle burned down without going out, it meant the girl would marry within a year. What an awesome spectacle this must be near larger cities, like Krakow, which has been described memorably in the memoirs of various Polish women.

In Poland, weddings are celebrated with great zest. Partly because daily life was so hard, and partly because marriage is naturally an happy event. Weddings in Poland become occasions for a great deal of feasting, dancing and merrymaking, often extending two or three days in the country. This tradition was brought to America by the immigrants.

A Polish-American wedding is communal in nature: two families are really joined—brothers and sisters, aunts and uncles, nieces and nephews, and cousins to the last degree. Almost all of the invited guests will attend the marriage ceremony. In many Polish-American families, it usually is the custom for parents of both the bride and the groom to give the couple their blessing before they depart for the church ceremony. The couple kneeling before the bride's parents and holding hands while each parent

---

[2] *Dingus* Day grew up in Poland 800 years ago when peasant boys celebrated the end of Lent—and a lull in their farm work—by swatting their sweethearts with red willow switches, dousing them with water, or playing other tricks. Rich city boys threw perfume instead of water. Easter Tuesday was the girls' turn to get even.

takes turn in gently sprinkling and blessing the couple with a small amount of holy water. The purpose of this tradition is to signify before all, the serious responsibility of marriage and the difficulties that may be fraught, but that the best wishes of the bride's parents are bestowed on them for a happy, as well as, holy married life. This tradition is of distant origin in Poland, stemming from the perilous times when safety and long life of the couple was especially beseeched of God.

After the wedding ceremony, all proceeded to the place of the reception: either the home of the bride, or a reception hall. By tradition, the food and the locale will be furnished by the bride's parents, while the liquor, band and flowers are furnished by the bridegroom.

At the reception home, or hall, family and friends await the arrival of the bride and groom; and usually the cook for the reception greets the couple with bread and salt, symbols of the wish that food ever will be plentiful in their home. The banquet includes a great variety of food served "family style," including fresh and smoked *kielbasa* (Polish sausage), *golabki* (stuffed cabbage), *pierogi* (dumplings) and *chrusciki* (angel wings).

During the banquet, the affair will sparkle with gaiety and laughter. Dancing after the banquet is lively and spirited. Drinks are poured at the bar with the familiar expression *Na Zdrowie* (To your health!) This is an occasion when everyone dances who can or enjoys it: children dance with each other among the adults, and women dance with male partners or with other women for the sheer joy of dancing. Mrs. Josephine Kopczynski, of Pittsburgh, recalls when in some home all the furniture had to be moved out into the yard, in order to make room for the dancing.

> "They'd dance and drink all night and never take a day off from work the next day . . . not like the young kids these days. And let me tell you, Polish weddings have always had a name for fun. People from any nationality group were quick to take up an invitation to a Polish wedding."[3]

---

[3] Clarke M. Thomas, "Pittsburgh's Polonia—Weddings, Yes and Much More," *Pittsburgh Post Gazette* (April 25, 1973), p. 49.

The featured event was the bridal dance, a custom brought over from Poland. Usually reserved for the evening, it began when the father of the bride announced *"jeszcze nasza"* meaning "she's still ours!" The musicians and guests were expected to echo the same phrase, whereupon the men formed a circle around the bride, then taking turns dancing with her. The father stood among the guests, and everyone who wished to dance with the bride was expected to throw a dollar into a cigar box. As its often done, throw a silver dollar against a dinner plate so that it will ring, or even break the plate. Each partner was expected to dance only once or twice around the floor; in this manner the young bride was whirled round and round with great delight. The money collected from the bridal dance was given to the bride. This custom was probably deliberately pursued to make up for the lack of a dowry, which was part of the wedding preparations in the Old Country, but withdrawn in the New World.[4]

Marriage is the most important family celebration, and each of the steps in a ceremonial Polish wedding had its own song to accompany the conventionalized drama. There are songs for replacing the bride's veil with a cap; for the bride's departure from her parents; for the procession of the bride and bridesmaids to the marriage chamber; for the couple's departure to the groom's home. In America, the "Song of the Twelve Angels" is sung for the culminating point of the wedding: *odczepiny*—the removal of the bride's veil just before the newlyweds leave for the honeymoon. The bride sits on the groom's lap, her mother—assisted by attendants—removes the bridal veil to signify that she is no longer a bride, but a married woman, as guests join in singing "Twelve petals on a red rose, twelve angels waiting on the young bride." Lyrics tell of the various gifts the bride can expect to receive.

While many of the specifically Polish customs have died out, and most of them replaced with American customs, it is still common for Polish-Americans to invite many guests to their

---

[4] After World War I, the American custom of a "shower" grew more common among Polish-American brides-to-be; and since World War II, it has become almost as common among the girls of Polish descent as among other ethnic groups—again indicating the nearly complete absorption of Polish culture into the American tradition.

weddings, where plenty of good food, wine and liquor is provided and lively dance music is heard until the early hours of the next morning.

Polish custom requires naming a child after a saint, not necessarily the one whose feast day falls on the child's birthday. The next preference is to name a child after a hero. Children are sometimes named after grandparents, but it is not common for them to be given the Christian name of their parents. Polish-Americans celebrate festively their name's days, the feast day of their patron saint. The family gathering, the dinner, the cake and candles, assorted gifts—all are essential to the celebration. The "candle blowing" routine includes the traditional "Happy Birthday" with the traditional *"Sto Lat,"* which wishes the celebrant a long life of a "hundred years."

Because "new life" is always a cause of joy, the christening parties for infants are great opportunities for family reunions. These receptions include not only the god-parents, but all relatives of both parents, together with friends and neighbors. Sponsors at Baptism are regarded as relatives by the interested families.

Anniversaries are also ready occasions for parties, especially wedding anniversaries, with the 25th and 50th anniversaries receiving very special attention, including a renewal of their marriage vows, in church, at a special Mass offered in thanksgiving for God's many blessings.

Another prominent community celebration occurs when one of the young men of the parish is ordained a priest. The offering of his First Solemn Mass (*Prymicja*) is a source of pride and joy for every member of the parish. The festivity that follows is much like the reception at a wedding. For the Mass, the Church is elaborately decorated in Christmas-like fashion. The procession is long and includes representatives of every parish organization; the choir sings in its finest form. The offertory procession finds the parents presenting the gifts which include the chalice they have given their son. A small girl and boy present the newly-ordained priest with a pillow with the Mass pall and a spray of wheat and grapes, symbolizing the bread and wine to be used in the Sacrifice of the Mass. A close priest-friend preaches the homily, and after the Mass, the entire family and friends present themselves for the first priestly-blessing. The blessing concludes with a touching gesture: each recipient, including the mother and father, kiss the palms of the newly ordained priest on the spot where they were anointed during the ceremony as a gesture of love and respect for his new station in life. A similar ceremony takes place when the priest is assigned his first parish, or the event of a 25th anniversary, on his elevation to a higher rank in the church hierarchy.

Corpus Christi is another important religious observance which is performed with an elaborate procession visiting three decorated altars outside of the church walls.

Poles are lovers of parades, processions, flags, banners and uniforms. A Polish church on festival days resembles a national temple where the battle-flags of nations are displayed. The Polish-Americans, also, are not utilitarian; and all of this, to them, is more than useful, for it serves to bind them more closely to the church, whose feasts provide additional solemnity.

The observance of national festivals is religiously kept. May recalls the adoption of Poland's notable document of freedom, the May 3, 1791 Constitution, the Magna Carta of national renaissance; November recalls the futile heroic Revolution of 1830, the first revolt attempting to restore Poland's independence; January, Poland's insurrection of 1863, the third attempt to regain independence. In October, the Polish-Americans honor the memory of General Casimir Pulaski who was killed at Savannah, Georgia, in 1779. Parades in his honor are held in many American cities. The Pulaski Parade, in New York City, is the largest nationality parade. More than 100,000 participate. The various organizations vie with one another in preparing these celebrations, which serve to recall to the younger generations and to the immigrant Americans, Poland's contribution to America's independence.

On the death of a parishioner, the church bell is tolled each day, immediately after the Angelus, until after the funeral, when the Office of the Dead is chanted. Early Polish funerals in America were very impressive. Others were not buried with the same solemnity and pomp characteristic of Polish funerals. Harry Golden had seen a Polish funeral on the lower east side, in New

York. The parade to the cemetery was the most impressive ever staged:

> The hearse was drawn by a brace of black horses, their manes decked in crowns of ostrich feathers. Over their backs were draped a chenille net from which black tassels dangled. The horses' tails were plumed and carded and a big fan of peacock feathers waved as they pulled the hearse.
> All the hearses were a shiny black with silver fittings and many had a silver-domed roof. The sides were glass and you could see the flowers banked around the coffin. Often there were several victorias, each laden with wreaths and flowers, following the hearse. And behind them was a rented limousine for the family.
> But the reason the kids would follow the hearse along was the band which led it up the streets. There was always an enormous brass band complete with cymbals playing Chopin's "Funeral March." They played a step at a time because the funeral proceeded slowly. The horses were trained to pace and pause with each note, and with infinite precision they put one hoof ahead of the other in absolute rhythm.[5]

The fame of Polish folk music was indeed so great that one of Bach's German contemporaries, George Philip Telemann, could declare in the eighteenth century, that "a Polish song makes the whole world dance." It used to be said of the aged folk singers who travelled from village to village chanting their ballads and lyrics: "They are men who remember old songs and better times." There exist a few historical and legendary ballads that make allusion to those early days when Polish heroes, living on the border lands, were occupied with fighting the Turks, or Cossacks, on the south-eastern frontier.

There are special songs for Christmas, called *Kolendy* and *Pastoralki,* songs for Easter, at the beginning of Spring, the summer solstice, the harvest, and so on through the peasant's year. In addition to songs for special occasions, there are the usual ballads: songs of boatmen, shepherds, beggars, soldiers, romances —and pieces about domestic life. There were also humorous and satiric songs. These usually take the form of "razing" people from

---

[5] Harry Golden, "Poles and Italians Had Classy Funerals," *Detroit Free Press* (September 13, 1969), p. 15-A.

some other districts and foreigners—the Ruthenians, the Germans, and the Jews were especially subjected to good-natured ridicule. Fully half of the prodigious number of extant Polish folk songs concern love. Dancing songs were also very popular.

The Polish-Americans retained their inheritance of Polish songs, and singing them gave America an incomparably rich folk literature. Like many other children of immigrant parents, Polish-Americans absorbed these folksongs naturally, and sang them as a matter of course. Many Polish-Americans made a real contribution in their humorous and satiric songs.

The Poles express themselves uniquely in their folk dances. In this respect, Poland is the only country that has produced most of its folk dances in the sophisticated and graceful 3/4 tempo: the *Mazur, Polonaise, Mazurka* and the *Kujawiak* unlike the most common 2/4 or 4/4 rhythm of most folk dances. Polish influence, in dancing, has affected other countries as well, e.g., Sweden's national dance, the *Polska,* was imported when Zygmunt III Vasa became joint king of Sweden and Poland. The *Polka* was adopted by the Czechs and Germans, perhaps modeled or based on some of the rapid figures in Polish dances. Its origin is apparent in its name.

The accepted methods of executing the dances left enough liberty for improvisation. The *Polonaise* began as a court dance before it was adopted by the different peasant regions of Poland. It is characterized by a noble grace, a grand gesture reminiscent of the Spanish Pavanne, but a more spirited processional with courtly bows and curtseys. Traditionally, each Polish ball opens with a stately *Polonaise.*

The *Mazur* is a popular folk dance whose peculiar characteristic is to accent the 2nd or 3rd note of each bar of music. The "White *Mazur*" should close a Polish ball. The *Mazurka* is a livelier form of the *Mazur,* more stylized and mastered by Frederic Chopin. This tempo appears in the faster passages of the *Kujawiak* and *Oberek*—the latter marked in 3/8 time. By the middle of the nineteenth century, a somewhat chastened form of the *Mazurka* had swept westward as far as England, captivating Berlin, Paris and London wherever it was introduced.

The *Kujawiak* has a chivalrous characteristic where the male dancer regularly swoops down on his knee before his partner.

The *Krakowiak* originated in Krakow and is a dance of double time, a kind of gallop with much syncopation with regional variations. Like the *Mazurka,* these dances were accompanied by intermittent singing. The *Krakowiak* is usually punctuated by an improvised couplet or quatrain.

These are but a few of the large number of national dances; many more are regional in extent, such as those from southern Poland, the Tatra region. Several notable dance companies from Poland have performed these beautiful spirited dances in their handsome costumes. Throughout the United States many local amateur folk dance and song ensembles have also performed them, delivering a great theatrical impact on the viewers. The melodies are so infectious that they invite public participation, even though in all of their steps they are quite intricate.

CHAPTER 10

Polish-American Cultural Organizations

Dla Ciebie, Ameryko, Ojczyzno przybrana!
Dla Ciebie, Polsko, i dla Twojej chwaly!
W dowod umilowania kultury
I pieknych tradycyj obydwu Narodow.

—My, Potomkowie Piasta.

For You, America, chosen Fatherland!
For You, Poland, and for Your Glory!
As Testimony of loving culture
And the beautiful traditions of both Nations.

—We, Descendants of Piast

When William Thomas and Florian Znaniecki studied the Polish immigrants in the United States, from 1914 to 1919, they were convinced that the first-generation immigrants alone had been capable of preserving Polish cultural patterns; the second generation would drift away from the heritage of their fathers, the third would abandon the Polish way of life, while the fourth would be completely assimilated.[1] However, when Znaniecki returned to the United States, in 1939, he was amazed to discover that there had been an alteration, almost cyclical in nature, between the urge toward assimilation with the larger culture and the urge toward a militant assertion to identify with the subculture. What the son of an immigrant wishes to forget, the

---

[1] Florian Znaniecki, "The Significance of Cultural Associations in the Modern World," *American Council of Polish Cultural Clubs Convention Bulletin* (August, 1955), p. 20.

grandson wishes to remember. What is truly noteworthy today, is to find many Polish-Americans from the third, fourth and fifth generation who are re-discovering their Polish heritage long after their parents have become wholly assimilated. With pride, they are discovering Poland's rich culture and the achievements her great men and women have contributed to the world—each a noteworthy milestone which distinguishes them amongst the most civilized of nations.

What is even more remarkable is the great interest in genealogy, to trace one's ancestors as far back as possible—even by Americans who have lived here for several generations and should be totally assimilated. Those with French names are keenly interested in French forebears in the Detroit and New Orleans regions, as are the Dutch, German and English descendants in the New England states, the Scandinavians and Poles and other Slavs in the mid-western states, or the Spanish-speaking residents among the southern states. Minority groups have taken on a defensive posture, partially for self-preservation which implies a healthy and positive opinion of oneself; they are also concerned with retaining their customs and traditions, artistic pursuits, language, religion and favorite ethnic dishes.

From the turn of the century—but especially during the decades of the '20's, '30's and '40's—the Polish-Americans experienced their "Golden Age" of cultural life, when it was most unpopular to be ethnically oriented. This was the period of concentration and the establishment of many Polish parishes with the accompanying schools where the Felician Order of nuns adopted as their sacred duty to teach the Polish language in their schools, but failed to teach their charges about their Polish heritage.

The '30's and '40's may rightly be termed the first harvest of the Polish-language parishes. Vocations to the priesthood and religious life multiplied among the second generation Polish-Americans. The priests and sisters were facile with the ancestral Polish, which was still spoken at home. And they knew English, which had been taught in the schools of their formation. Thus, they were able to render yeoman service to the Polish-American parishes, both in their concern for the older parishioners and in their desire to imbue the younger generation with an appreciation of their Catholic faith and Polish heritage.

There were definite signs of the vibrant vitality of these Polish-language parishes in the joint efforts they sponsored. State-wide basketball leagues for these parishes brought together young men and women in healthy recreational and social contacts. Proud of their Polish associations, these men and women participated with zest, displaying their basic American enthusiasm. But in addition, this period was also active in producing numerous theatrical and musical groups which produced many original plays and composed original serious music for concerts and recitals. There were also dance companies that toured and performed original ballets as well as the beautiful folk dances of Poland. Many charitable and social organizations also arose to fulfill their respective needs, filling an apparent void that local municipal authorities neglected.

When the Polish-Americans first came to America, they did not affiliate themselves with any political party. In 1918, Republican John Kleczka of Milwaukee, was elected a United States Representative, the first Congressman in Polish-American history. The second U.S. Representative was Henry Kunz, Democrat from Illinois. The third was John Bartholomew Sosnowski, Republican, from Michigan. During this period many Polish-Americans were elected to State Legislatures: Theodore Brysk in Connecticut; John Pelka in Illinois; Eugene Heike in New Jersey; Stefan Wojtkowiak and Joseph Topolski in New York; Martin Baginski, Michael Grajewski, Stanislaw Nowak, Albert Bielawski in Michigan; B. G. Nowak in Minnesota; Edward Lusienski in Nebraska; Feliks Irzyk and Chester Skibinski in Massachusetts; Peter Pyszczynski and Clement Stachowiak in Wisconsin.

Paradoxically, the amazingly rapid advance of assimilation in the 1940's and 1950's made Cultural Pluralism seem more and more desirable. As the worst injustices of the early 20th century were redressed, people of every ethnic background were swept up in the pursuit of affluence. In obliterating differences, perhaps even becoming color-blind, Americans were moving into a world of grey uniformity in which everyone would feel rootless and powerless. Every forward step toward fuller integration enlarged centralized power and bureaucratic impersonality. Every victory for assimilation aroused new yearnings for a return to ethnicity.

Many assumed that cultural differences can be preserved without perpetuating inequalities. We now know that ethnic groups are unequal in their cultural resources as well as the social and economic standing of their members. Accentuating their differences can serve to reinforce the disadvantages of some ethnic groups. Moreover, such ethnic differences necessarily generate conflict. In itself that is not always bad. But the Cultural Pluralist point of view offers no universal standard—no overall conception of the good—which can keep ethnic strife within tolerable bounds. A democratic society requires a common culture that transcends its ethnic segments and commands their ascent. The dilemmas posed for the United States, by opposing demands for assimilation and pluralism, have become painfully acute. Both the unifying thrust of integration and the self-respect of separate group identities seem essential to the common good. Polish-Americans have presented many excellent examples (with their cultural clubs, festivals, etc.) how to combine the two.

The current "ethnic" wave of popularity, with its exhibits and folk festivals appears like an after-thought when so many other nationalities finally realized the positive needs of knowing one's ancestral roots and culture. Another factor is the enormous number of new immigrants who are arriving from many exotic countries who cannot obviously hide their identity, but who, in many instances, also have a proud and militant posture about their own culture.

In the midst of these more dominant groups, Polish-Americans are indeed struggling to survive. In the past, when ethnic neighborhoods were popular and Polish towns, like Hamtramck, could be pointed to with pride, forced integration with other races and nationalities in order to deliberately destroy their eithnic purity—besides other exterior pressures—has wreaked its havoc on all of the Polish-American communities with their Polish institutions, parishes, theaters, club houses (Dom Polskis') resulting in an exodus of the Polish population where it once was so well established and comfortable for them.

Today, there is a marked tendency to explore and study the culture of ethnic descent, and to sample the everyday pleasures of being Polish.[2] As a result, many new varieties of Polish-American cultural associations have evolved. Many members of these associations are also active participants in American culture and politics. The factors responsible for this greater awareness are: the development of an ideology which emphasized the importance of knowledge, the appreciation of Polish cultural elements, and the increasingly higher educational level of Americans of Polish descent. Thus, the organizations seek to make the Polish cultural contribution to world civilization known where it is ignored, appreciated where it is scorned, cherished where it is neglected, and respected where it yet fails to command its deserved attention.

The Adam Mickiewicz Library and Dramatic Circle, in Buffalo, was among the first Polish-American societies which concerned itself with the cultural welfare of Polish-American youth by offering theatrical productions in the Polish language, simultaneously maintaining a library and other reading rooms with a vast assortment of books and periodicals in Polish and other languages. The society, which honored Adam Mickiewicz, was organized, in 1895, in the home of Joseph Slisz, a bookseller.[3]

---

[2] "WSU and U-M to teach Polish Pride," *Detroit Free Press* (July 4, 1976), p. 4-A.

[3] Poles, in America, were not the only nationality to honor Mickiewicz. Mazzini, the well-known Italian patriot and writer, dedicated one of his articles in a London Monthly to Mickiewicz. Another enthusiast of the Polish poet was George Sand, who in the Paris *Revue Des Deux Mondes*, included Mickiewicz as one of the four great poets of the world: Dante, Goethe, Byron and Mickiewicz. In Italy, Mickiewicz was called the Polish Dante. A united and free Italy paid tribute to Mickiewicz by erecting a bust of Mickiewicz in Rome. The French decorated Paris with a beautiful memorial of him by the famous sculptor, Bourdelle, on one of the most beautiful streets of Paris. The memorial represents Mickiewicz in the figure of a pilgrim illustrating his writings on the pilgrimage of the Polish Nation. The remains of the poet were transferred from Paris and placed among the tombs of the Polish kings, in the Cathedral on Wawel Hill, in Krakow.

Mickiewicz was the first to acquaint the French with the American writer and philosopher, Ralph Waldo Emerson, and introduced his work to his colleague-professors, Quinet and Michelet at the College de France. The American writer, Margaret Fuller-Ossoli, also knew Mickiewicz.

The society began its activity by staging amateur productions: at first one-act, later two-act, and finally three-act plays. Rev. John Pitass was generous to the newly formed society, and helped it tremendously by paying the first year's rent for the use of the clubrooms.[4]

When the rented quarters became inadequate, the society purchased land on Fillmore Avenue and erected its own building to serve the expanded activities. Money for the building was raised with the income from various musical and vocal evenings, lectures, dances and plays which the members presented. The present building, enlarged in 1917, is a two-story frame dwelling with facilities for the library, meeting rooms, casino, board of officers and secretary rooms, billiard rooms, kitchen and hall. Besides the collection of books, the library provided Polish, American, French and German magazines, and Polish newspapers printed in America. The library is often visited by non-members, since anyone who is interested in Polish-American history, culture or civilization may utilize these resources. According to the librarian, K. J. Wloch, the library contains 1937 books in Polish, 95 in English, 180 plays, and many pamphlets.[5]

Instead of having its own theatrical group, the organization sponsored existing Polish-American theatrical ensembles. It also sponsored groups of artists from England and Poland. One of the theatrical groups which it sponsored was the internationally famous Polish dance ensemble, *Mazowsze*.[6]

To acquaint the Americans with the Polish heritage and Polish cultural accomplishments, the society initiated the observance of Polish anniversaries and national holidays. In 1964, the

---

[4] Among the benefactors of the society were also the following: Rt. Rev. Msgr. Peter Wawrzyniak, from Mogilno, Poland; Rev. Dr. Stanislaw Sobieniowski; Polish poet, Stanislaw Belza; Nobel Prize laureate, Wladyslaw Reymont; Rev. Dr. Alexander Pitass; Colonel Dr. Francis E. Fronczak; Anthony Schreiber; A. J. Walkowiak; Casimer Bilski; Joseph Slisz; S. S. Nowicki; S. Napieralski; Waclaw Horst; Pankracy Maciejewski; and Zygmunt Racki.

[5] The first sixty-three books donated to the library, in 1895, by Stanislaw Murawski, Jozefa Ruczaja and Jozefa Slisza, are still in the collection. They were not lost or stolen. All of the books were published in Poland and fifty per cent were religious. After World War II, the families Jenorog, Dabrowski, Strzelczyk and Wloch donated over 400 books which were published in Poland.

[6] Jay Carr, "Polish dancers dazzle audience," *The Detroit News* (March 6, 1971), p. 7-A.

600th anniversary of the formation of the Jagiellonian University, of Krakow, was observed with a special program in English and Polish. In 1967, the 100th anniversary of the birth of Madame Marie Sklodowska-Curie was observed with a program in the English language.[7] The anniversary of the first strike on American soil by Poles was also celebrated.[8] During the past few years many other anniversaries were observed: the 50th anniversary of the death of Henryk Sienkiewicz, Nobel Prize Winner; the 100th anniversary of the birth of Marshal Jozef Pilsudski; the 100th anniversary of the birth of Stanislaw Wyspianski, painter, dramatist and poet; and the 25th anniversary of the tragic death of General Wladyslaw Sikorski.

In 1965, a lecture series was inaugurated to commemorate the Polish Millennium by the Polish-American Council on Cultural Affairs, Inc., and supported by the diocesan Millennium Committee. The Polish lectures were given in Mickiewicz Hall. Seven of the lecturers were members of the organization. The organization also presented many literary evenings, where the following were presented: Aleksander Janta, Marian Hemar, Jan Roztworowski, Bohdan Pawlowicz, Rudnicki, Jozef Siwiak, Krzysztof Wloch, Stanislaw Czerwiec, Dr. Tatarkiewicz, Dr. Mianowska from Warsaw, Dr. B. Richard Bugelski, Dr. Drzewieniecki, Dr. Kozak and Dr. Mrozowski from Buffalo.

To acquaint the Americans with original Polish folk art, the

---

[7] Madame Sklodowska-Curie has been honored, as no one before her, by the scientific world with two Nobel prizes for physics and chemistry. In her letter to the Nobel Committee she insisted that they should refer to her as Marie Sklodowska-Curie and not simply as Marie Curie. She gave the results of her work freely to the world; took out no patents for discovering two heavy elements radium and polonium or the difficult technical process for extracting these elements; and also pioneered in hospital work during World War I with the life saving X-rays. Her discovery of *Polonium* placed her homeland in the Table of Chemical Elements, while her husband's name was immortalized by the term, *curie,* a unit for measuring chemical energy.

[8] In 1619 during the second term of office of Governor Yeardley, the London Company granted the right to vote to 1000 men of English descent, who lived in Virginia. The Poles, who worked in Jamestown as specialists in the production of glass, tar, pitch and soap were refused the right to vote. On July 30th, 1619, the Poles went on strike, not for material benefits, but for democratic rights. The strike was successful, and they received the right to vote. *An Introduction to Records of the Virginia Company of London* (Washington, D. C.: 1950), I, p. 251. Wytrwal, *Poles in American History and Tradition,* pp. 13-14.

organization organized a display of Polish folk art in September 1967. The exhibit was made up of many tapestries, wall hangings, hand made rugs, vases, embroideries, dolls in folk costumes and wood and iron sculptures. This exhibition was opened by the acting Mayor, Chester Gorski. It was well received by the radio and press. Another exhibit "Beautiful Poland and Achievements of the Polish Nation" was prepared in May 1969. This display traced the history of Poland from its early beginnings to the present. Special attention was focused on the contributions of the Poles to American history. The exhibit was opened by Mayor Frank A. Sedita. It was also well received by the press, radio and television.

To help other organizations in their cultural endeavors, the Mickiewicz Society gave the use of their clubrooms, free of charge, to such groups as Szaniec, Polish Students Group, Boy Scouts, Friends of Scouts, Polish schools, Polish-American Council on Cultural Affairs, Inc., stamp collectors and various coordinating committees. It also gave instruction in the Polish national dances without cost.

Throughout the 75-year history—according to Marian Strzelczyk, president—the Mickiewicz Society has worked to acquaint Polish-Americans and others in the community with Polish culture, thus instilling a deeper love for all that is Polish among the Americans of Polish ancestry and familiarizing others with the richness of Polish customs, traditions and her contribution to world civilization.[9]

Just after the World War I, Polish musical organizations made a strong bid for the same activity and interest which German societies had displayed earlier. The Polish Opera Club— formed in 1919, in Milwaukee—was the only one of its kind in America. It performed numerous Polish and other operas, in Milwaukee, Chicago and Detroit. In 1925, the club imported a Hollywood star, and produced a motion picture version of the Polish opera, *Halka*. The scenes were filmed on a farm southwest of Milwaukee. The group became dormant in 1927.[10]

---

[9] Marian Strzelczyk, "Contributions to Polish Culture," *Ksiega Pamiatkowa Diamentowego Jubileuszu Kola Dramatycznego i Czytelni Im. Adama Mickiewicza* (Buffalo: 1970), pp. 13-15.

The most prominent of all Polish-American cultural organizations, involving cultural exchange between Poland and the the United States, is the Kosciuszko Foundation, founded in 1926. Its origin was the Polish Scholarship Committee, which was formed in 1923. The Committee was dissolved in 1926, and in its place the Kosciuszko Foundation was established as a living memorial to General Tadeusz Kosciuszko, on the eve of the one hundred and fiftieth anniversary of his enrollment in the American Revolutionary Army.[11] The primary objective of the Foundation was to improve cultural relations between the United States and Poland. The following are the objectives which the Foundation aims to realize:[12]

1. To grant voluntary financial aid to deserving Polish students desiring to study at institutions of higher learning in the United States of America; and to deserving American students desiring to study in Poland.

2. To encourage and aid the exchange of professors, scholars, and lecturers between Poland and the United States of America.

3. To cultivate closer intellectual and cultural relations between Poland and the United States in such ways and by such means as may from time to time seem wise, in the judgement of the Board of Directors of the Corporation.

From its inception, until World War II, the Kosciuszko Foundation had exchanged between Poland and the United States 170 students, research scholars, industrial apprentices, and professors; 101 Americans studied in Poland, and 69 Poles studied in the United States. The scholarship grants totalled $125,000. Approximately ten per cent of the total number of Polish professors and younger instructors, of pre-war England, had received aid from the foundation.[13] The late professor Eric P. Kelly, who had received a scholarship and spent some time in Krakow, became a

---

[10] H. Russel Austin, *The Milwaukee Story. The Making of an American City*, p. 152.

[11] Dr. Henry Noble MacCraken, President of Vassar College; Samuel M. Vauclain, President of Baldwin Locomotive Works; and Stephen Mizwa, former president of Alliance College, were among its founders.

[12] Kosciuszko Foundation, *Annual Reports of the Executive Director* (New York: 1926), First Report, p. 33.

prolific writer about Poland. His story of medieval Krakow, *The Trumpeter of Krakow,* now in its twentieth printing, won the Newberry Medal as the most distinguished contribution to American literature for school children, in 1928. Eight Chopin scholarships of $1,000 each were granted from 1952 to 1957 on the basis of national competitions. The expense of auditions came to $2,020.35 and the total for Chopin Scholarships amounted to $10,020.35. Van Cliburn, pianist at the Juilliard School of Music, was awarded the Chopin Scholarship in 1952-1953. During the same period scholarships were awarded to 150 students and scholars in the amount of $48,122.

The Kosciuszko Foundation also engaged in a variety of other activities. It was able to grant many Polish-American students study in Poland by offering them not only free tuition, but also greatly reduced fares on the Polish-American steamship lines. In 1927, it distributed leaflets about General Kosciuszko to schools in large American cities. It also formed a "Peter Yolles Dissertation Fund" to purchase dissertations of students of Polish descent on Polish topics.

Since its founding, the Kosciuszko Foundation has sponsored seven major programs in the form of "celebrations" of national and international interest designed to draw public attention to Poland and the achievements of her people. The first project was the nation-wide essay contest on the topic "Kosciuszko's contribution to America." The second was "Kosciuszko's Recognition Day" in which the President of the United States and the governors of the thirteen original states participated in the day's program by issuing special proclamations. The third project was the celebration of the sesquicentennial of the Revolutionary War Victory at Saratoga, where Kosciuszko had selected and fortified strategic American positions. The fourth project was the celebration of the 250th anniversary of Sobieski's spectacular victory at Vienna, commemorating the defeat of the Turks at Vienna, in 1683, by Jan Sobieski, King of Poland.

The fifth celebration was held in 1928, on the occasion of Poland's 10th anniversary of regaining her independence. The

---

[13] Stephen P. Mizwa, "Polish-American Cultural Relationships," *Poland*, Bernadotte E. Schmitt, Editor (Los Angeles: 1945), p. 363.

Kosciuszko Foundation sponsored a testimonial dinner for Ignacy Jan Paderewski under the auspices of a national committee headed by Herbert Hoover. On that occasion the Foundation published a handsomely illustrated booklet entitled "Paderewski, His Country and Its Recent Progress," which was distributed throughout the nation.

The sixth celebration was perhaps the most significant celebration in the history of the Kosciuszko Foundation. It was a commemoration of the 400th anniversary of the death of the renowned Polish astronomer, Mikolaj Kopernik, and the publication of his brilliant and radical thesis, *De Revolutionibus Orbium Coelestium*, which altered man's perception of the universe.[14] Under the auspices of a national committee—organized by the Foundation, composed of leading scientists and educators, including many Nobel Prize winners—America paid tribute to Kopernik at a special Kopernik Quadricentennial, held at Carnegie Hall, in New York, on May 24, 1943, under the direction of Dr. Harlow Shapley of Harvard University. Also, in attendance was Albert Einstein and other eminent scholars, and numerous representatives from educational institutions. The Foundation published two specially prepared books on this subject which were in great demand by individuals and educational institutions throughout the land.

Also at this time, the Kosciuszko Foundation awarded "Citations" to ten modern pioneers of human progress, among them were the following: John Dewey, Walter E. Disney, Albert Einstein, Henry Ford and Orville Wright.

The seventh celebration was the 100th anniversary of the death of Frederick Chopin. A national committee headed by Dr. Howard Hanson, the distinguished Dean of American composers and Director of the Eastman School of Music, was established by the Foundation to commemorate the event. Many all-Chopin recitals took place in all parts of the country, culminating in an all-Chopin concert in the Metropolitan Opera House with Artur Rubinstein as soloist. On the occasion of the Chopin Cen-

---

[14] Benedict Markowski, *Kopernik the Great Humanist* (Detroit: 1973).

tennial, the Foundation sponsored the publication of a handsome volume on Chopin and established two Chopin scholarships.

The Kosciuszko Foundation also sponsored annual balls at the Waldorf-Astoria Hotel, in New York City. For many years, the annual ball has been recognized as the important event of the season in New York's schedule of activities. Most significantly, it provides ever-increasing opportunities for stimulating a broader interest in the great events that make up Poland's history, and for a deeper appreciation of its rich culture.

Starting from its earliest days the Kosciuszko Foundation has taken special steps to recognize and honor outstanding contributions by individuals of all national backgrounds, who through a variety of endeavors have contributed to a fuller understanding of Poland and its culture. Among the many, so honored in the past for contributing to American and Polish culture, are the following: Dr. Henry Noble MacCracken, former president of Vassar College; Professor Eric P. Kelly, the first Foundation Exchange Scholar to Poland; Arthur Rubinstein, the greatest living interpreter of Chopin.

Through their direct and indirect influence the Kosciuszko Foundation is responsible for having published about twenty books, in English, on Polish topics. In addition to *Nicholas Copernicus: A Tribute of Nations*, the Foundation had published the collected biographies of *Great Men and Women of Poland*, as well as a biography of *Paderewski*, which it distributed the first five-hundred deluxe editions *gratis*—sending the first autographed copy to President Roosevelt. Over one hundred monographs and pamphlets, treating some aspect of Poland and the United States, have been published in American periodicals, and vice versa. To mark Poland's millennium, the Kosciuszko Foundation decided that whatever books it would publish or sponsor, it would designate them as part of "The Poland Millennium Series of the Kosciuszko Foundation." The first book in this series—published in April 1955, by Princeton University Press, in cooperation with the Kosciuszko Foundation—was *Czartoryski and European Unity, 1770-1861* by Marian Kukiel. Another book in the series is the earliest comprehensive two-volume *English-Polish and Polish-English Dictionary*, compiled by Kazimierz Bulas of the Rice Institute, in Houston, and Francis Whitfield of the University of California at Berkeley. Close to 56,000 copies of both volumes have been sold.

The Kosciuszko Foundation also serves as an information center pertaining to all phases of Polish-American cultural relations. Since 1925, thousands of inquiries have been answered on Polish culture, art, history, music, folklore, literature, biography, festivals, commemorations, international exchange or progress in science. The most frequent requests are for information on educational opportunities in Poland or for Polish students in the United States. Publishers of books and periodicals frequently request illustrations; American students writing their theses or dissertations write or visit the Foundation for suggestions and information. To render service in this field, the Kosciuszko Foundation has gradually collected an extensive reference library.

The Kosciuszko Foundation has established an art gallery which contains the most representative collection of Polish masters in America: Jan Matejko, Jozef Chelmonski, Jozef Brandt, Alfred Wierusz-Kowalski, Leon Wyczolkowski, Jacek Malczewski, Juljusz and Wojciech Kossak, Jan Styka, Wlodzimierz Tetmajer, Julian Falat and others. The Kosciuszko Foundation Museum is in its beginning stage: nevertheless, the following items are in the collection: the first and second editions of Copernicus' *De Revolutionibus Orbium Coelestium*, one of Kosciuszko's letters, and steel engravings and prints of Kosciuszko.

During World War II, the Foundation rendered aid to Polish refugee scholars. Twelve professors were brought to America, and two hundred professors, younger scholars or Polish intellectuals of non-academic standing, from the entire world, have received aid. In addition, the Foundation supplied the necessary funds to enable eight hundred Polish students in Swiss interment camps to continue their studies in special university camp centers. For this aid to Polish professors and students, the Foundation appropriated and spent $75,000.

Since the termination of World War II, the Foundation has participated in the educational reconstruction of Poland by sending books and periodicals in various fields which were published in the United States since 1939. Through the influence of Stephen

Mizwa, the late director of the Kosciuszko Foundation, the American Mathematical Society—have sent seven crates of mathematical publications. By February 1947, the Kosciuszko Foundation managed to send to Poland sixty crates of books and surgical instruments. The Kosciuszko Foundation also inspired the National Books for Poland Committee, under the direction of Professor Shapley of Harvard University. Through its efforts the Copernican Observatory, at the University of Torun, received a modern telescope from the astronomical observatory of Harvard University. The Kosciuszko Foundation also supplied medical books and journals to re-establish medical and school libraries.

With the cessation of hostilities, the Foundation's main channels of activities have been scholarships, informational services, and cultural programs in the Kosciuszko Foundation House. From January 1, 1946, to June 30, 1952, there were 365 activities (meetings, conferences, lectures, concerts, art exhibits) held in the Kosciuszko House. During the following five years 494 activities were held. Since the Foundation moved to its Kosciuszko House, 859 varied programs were held at the new center.

The project for which the Kosciuszko Foundation is perhaps best known is its scholarship program, which falls into three major categories: assistance to qualified American students, regardless of national extraction, who are pursuing some aspect of Polish studies; scholarships to Americans of Polish extraction, regardless of their field of study; and student exchanges with Poland when permitted.

These include the Chopin Scholarship for piano study, the Schaefer Scholarship in any field of study; the Stan Lesny Scholarships for the study of Engineering, Mathematics and Natural Sciences; the Helena Modjeska Memorial Scholarship to a student majoring in dramatic art; the Dr. Marie E. Zakrzewski Memorial Scholarship for medical studies; exchange programs to study in Poland; and other forms of financial assistance.[15]

---

[15] The Chopin Scholarship award is given annually to a student of the piano competing on a nationwide basis. Twenty awards have been made to date. Among the many winners who have established prominent careers, perhaps the most famous recipient of this award was Van Cliburn, who won the Chopin Scholarship, in 1952, at the age of seventeen—many years before receiving recognition elsewhere in this

The Kosciuszko Foundation budget, for the 1974-75 fiscal year, was $392,579.00. Of this $171,750 was used for scholarships and grants. This does not include $60,000 in waivers of tuition and other benefits the Foundation staff was able to secure for its grantees. In addition, $60,000 was used for cultural programs of the Foundation: the publication of books, lecture programs, exhibits, etc.; $42,900 was used for administrative expenses: postage, printing, light, heat, telephones, etc.; $92,929 was used to pay salaries for the eight employees working for the Foundation.

In 1976, the Foundation announced its program of medical studies in Poland. Each year it will enable twenty-five Polish-American students to study in Poland in a program planned to enable them to complete their medical studies so as to practice in the United States. A distinguished committee of physicians, educators, and Foundation trustees selected the first group of twenty-five students who will leave for Poland for further study. In this way the Foundation hopes to overcome part of the discrimination against Polish-Americans which apparently exists in American medical schools.

In the Spring of 1927, Dr. Stefan Jarosz, a noted geographer of Poland, visited the United States as a delegate of the Polskie Towarzystwo Tatrzanskie and Zwiazek Podhalan. The purpose of his mission was to awaken interest in the Tatra folklore and culture among the Polish immigrants, and to stimulate tourist traffic to the Tatra mountain region of Poland.[16] This trade was

---

country and Russia. He, in turn, has contributed generously to the Chopin Scholarship award.

[16] Along the border with Czechoslovakia, Poland has a series of high and majestic mountains, of which the grandest are undoubtedly the Tatras. This region of Poland—centering about the resort of Zakopane—is filled with a unique history, legends and folklore. It frequently is the site of Olympic Ski Championships. Originally this region was not noted as a resort, at least not until Dr. Titus Chalubinski's explorations of the region in the 1880's, directed interest there. Prior to that time, it was primarily a grazing ground for hundreds of sheep, which still meander along the scenic mountain slopes, and a refuge for the oppressed and lawless. In many respects, it was similar to the American west, or to any frontier region where the spirit of individualism, independence and lawlessness developed to a much higher degree than in more settled and established areas. The Tatras are comparable to England's Sherwood Forest; it was the home of Janosik, Poland's Robin Hood. The Polish highlanders are the descendants of those vigorous and virile frontier men. In Poland they are called *Gorale*.

These highlanders have captured the imagination of artists throughout the world.

to provide additional income for the needy mountaineers. Dr. Jarosz lectured in the principal cities where Polish mountaineers resided. The Polish-American mountaineers were delighted to hear of a person who came from their native region. The *Gorale* who lived in Passaic, New Jersey invited Dr. Jarosz to deliver a lecture. His inspirational talk about the Tatra Mountains deeply moved those assembled. In this moment of enthusiasm, they decided to organize a Polish Highlander Club. However, this society was not destined to last very long. The hastily organized club was not founded on a solid basis. There were many who could not comprehend the true object of such an organization. Jan Gromada, who became president in later years, tried to salvage the Highlander Club, but some of the members sowed seeds of misunderstanding which hindered his attempts. Finally, in March 1936, Jan Gromada resigned along with a large number of the group who shared his views. Consequently, the Polish Highlanders' Club, in the hands of the few, shortsighted men, slowly withered away.

Jan Gromada, who came to the United States, in 1927, from Poland, and settled in Passaic, New Jersey, in 1929, could not bear to see the lofty purpose of a *Gorale* organization from disappearing. Therefore, on December 26, 1936, he called a meeting of all *Gorale* who were sincerely interested in preserving Tatra culture. Some thirty persons attended this meeting. Jan Gromada proposed to form an idealistic, cultural organization, whose object would be to acquaint the American public with the Tatra art and customs, and to preserve the Tatra tradition within their own families. The assembled agreed unanimously to this proposal.

By unanimous vote, Jan Gromada, a *Goral* musician, dancer and embroiderer of Tatra costumes, was elected president. Other elected officers were: Joseph Urbas, Maciej Siedlarczyk, Andrew Bigos, Michael Krezel and Maria Wojtanek. The newly organized society was called "The Polish Tatra Mountaineers Alliance

---

Kazimierz Prerwa-Tetmajer wrote a number of works whose settings were staged in the Tatra Mountains, one of which *The Tale of the Tatras*, is available in an English translation. Paderewski brought the music of the highlands to the attention of the world in his *Album Tatrzanski* and his opera *Manru*. Karol Szymanowski introduced the Gorale to the world in his ballet entitled *Harnasie* (the Highland Lads).

of America" and became a member of the Polish Highlanders Alliance of Chicago, a national organization. On November 10, 1941, "The Polish Tatra Mountaineers Alliance" was incorporated by the State of New Jersey.

In order to fulfill the aims of the organization, Jan Gromada had to obtain authentic Tatra costumes, form an able dance group and organize an orchestra to accompany these dances. Since he was an embroiderer and tailor, by trade, in Poland, Jan Gromada made several of the costumes himself. He imported the others from Poland at his own expense.

Since "The Polish Tatra Mountaineers Alliance" was founded, it had been true to its purpose, producing thirty-five stage plays, presenting innumerable folk dances and folk art exhibitions, and arranging for a host of cultural lectures. To facilitate communication with its many members scattered throughout the United States, it published the *Tatrzanski Orzel* (the Tatra Eagle), a quarterly newsletter containing information not merely about its members, but about the customs and traditions of the Tatra highlanders. Thaddeus V. Gromada and Jane Kedron served as editors.

In one of the issues of *Orzel Tatrzanski,* Thaddeus Gromada, the editor, noted the following:

> ". . . there is something more that makes us proud of our Tatra highlander ancestry and that is the great tradition of freedom and liberty in Podhale. Earlier we noted that the Gorale had to contend with a hostile environment which included harsh climate and poor soil, periodic floods, etc. So the economic conditions were never good. But the mountaineers were willing to put up with these inconveniences because they wanted to live as free men. Therefore, they will remind you lowlanders that they were never serfs, that Podhale was royal territory endowed with special privileges and guarantees. If for some reason a certain magnate like Komorowski endeavored to infringe upon these rights, the highlanders would rebel and fight."[17]

From its very inception the organization has aided and encouraged its members to educate their children as good and useful

---

[17] Quoted in Eugene Kusielewicz, "The Tatra Mountaineers' Alliance," *The Polish American World* (June 15, 1962), p. 2.

American citizens. At the same time, the organization has always insisted that native American citizens, amongst Polish highlanders, should not be deprived of an opportunity of studying and appreciating the rich cultural heritage of Poland and especially of the Polish Highlands. Such activities never did create any conflicts in a country where unity has been achieved through diversity and not through monolithic conformity. "I should like to consider America not only one homogeneous block, but rather a beautiful tower of jewels imported from many foreign countries," said John David, in 1924.

An important event in the annals of Polish-American relations was the establishment of "The Polish Institute of Arts and Sciences in America." The germ of the organization was planted by Polish scholars from the Kosciuszko Association, which was established on December 28, 1940. An academic association, it was composed of members from the former Polish Academy of Sciences and other Polish educational associations who had been able to escape north into Lithuania or south into Romania during the crucial weeks of the destruction of Poland, in 1939. Eventually, these scholars made their way west. When they arrived in the United States, the Polish-American organizations working with the Polish legation in Washington provided funds to allow them to continue their scientific work. To furnish a center for them and keep them from being lost in the American milieu, an American branch of the Polish Academy of Arts and Sciences was formed with Dr. Oscar Halecki as its chairman.[18] The new institution had two objectives: to work toward the development of Polish education, and to disseminate knowledge about Poland and Polish culture in the United States in order to improve cultural relations between Poland and the United States.[19]

The Kosciuszko Association, consisting of eighty members scattered throughout the United States, during its early period of existence, organized two general meetings and several lecture

---

[18] Clarence A. Manning, *A History of Slavic Studies in the United States* (Milwaukee: 1957), p. 64.

[19] Its officers were, Dr. Oscar Halecki, president; Dr. Bronislaus Malinowski, vice-president; Dr. Waclaw Lednicki and Stephen P. Mizwa, directors; and Dr. Irena Piotrowska, secretary and treasurer. Dr. Piotrowska was the only one in the administration who was American-born.

series. It also prepared articles on various branches of knowledge for the Polish-American press. Financial support for Polish emigré scholars was also provided. In 1941, members of the Association had prepared a plan for a cooperative work the "Republic of Poland, 1919-1939" which eventually formed the basis of a book, entitled *Poland,* published in 1945, by the University of California Press.

Eventually the Kosciuszko Association was reorganized and the "Institute of Polish Arts and Sciences" was formed, in 1941. It became the main association not only of Polish educators and scientists, but also of Americans interested in Poland. The Institute is divided into several sections and with specific areas of interest: (1) history and political studies, (2) cultural research, (3) legal, social, and economic studies, (4) history of literature and art, (5) theoretical and practical sciences. A special commission considers topics that do not fall under any of the listed areas. Since its establishment, the Institute has organized formal sessions, scholarly conferences, and discussion meetings. Through its director and other members, the Institute has participated in many scholarly conventions held in the United States. The Institute has also embarked on a project to catalog all Polonica in American libraries. Also, in collaboration with the Kosciuszko Foundation, the Institute has sought to encourage book collection drives for the Polish libraries and scholars in Poland. At the Institute, a library of one thousand volumes was established. In October 1942, the Institute began to publish a quarterly *Bulletin of the Polish Arts and Sciences in America*. In addition, the Institute has published nine major monographs under the title of *Polish Institute Series*. In 1956, *The Polish Review,* a quarterly in English—dedicated exclusively to Polish topics, including the analysis of events in contemporary Poland—was inaugurated.[20]

In April 1971, the Institute—in cooperation with the School

---

[20] Although many Polish scholars living in the Free Western World frequently enjoy the hospitality of American, British and French journals, the lack of a periodical devoted only to Polish affairs in the English language was needed. To fill this gap and to become a source of objective information and a rallying point for study of all aspects of Polish cultural life, past and present, has become the purpose of *The Polish Review*. It opens its columns to all Polish scholars and writers in the Free World and to scholars of all Free Nations writing on Polish subjects.

of International Affairs and the Institute of East Central Europe, divisions of Columbia University—sponsored a three-day symposium.[21] The three hundred scholars from primarily American and Canadian Universities included specialists in disciplines ranging from demography to mathematics to literature and Polish historical-political relations.[22] To the participants the communality was obvious: the papers and their authors were all reflections on Polish culture. The three-day Congress of Polish-American scholars and scientists served as a forum of exchange between men of differing disciplines who shared cultural history along with their cultural perceptions. The Congress revealed to the world those contributions of Polish thought and creativity which had made an impact and continues to offer such to the progress of the world.

The most popular seminar concentrated on Polish assets and their liabilities under the title of "Problems Related to a Psychological Explanation of Polish History." The discussion panel included psychiatrists, sociologists and historians who for three hours attempted to define the Polish national character. The significant traits that were suggested included bravery, romanticism, ultra-idealism, independence of thought, tolerance, arch-Catholicism, gentleness and the inability to achieve compromise. Generally each characteristic trait could be explained or countered through the events of each epoch. There was, however, general agreement among the panel members that a new methodological approach was needed to study national character.

One member of the audience suggested that there was one aspect of the Polish spirit that seemed pervasive and that while it may not have been mentioned by the panel, the discussion had attested to it. "Poles are not very good at dialogues," he said. "They have a tendency and flair for monologues."[23]

The history of a nation can be a well spring of inspiration from which people draw strength in their struggle for independence and national identity. To Polish patriots everywhere, the

---

[21] "300 Polish-American Scholars End a 3-Day Symposium Here," *New York Times* (April 20, 1971), p. C-43.
[22] Participants from Detroit included Benedict Markowski and Dr. Joseph A. Wytrwal.
[23] "300 Polish-American Scholars End a 3-Day Symposium Here," *New York Times* (April 20, 1971), p. C-43.

memory of Poland's many centuries of stable, national life has often provided the vision and the rallying cry so essential in that continuing quest for an improved tomorrow. In other words, a country's history is one of its most important national resources. One organization vitally concerned with this matter is the "Jozef Pilsudski Institute of America for Research in the Modern History of Poland, Inc." This association describes its basic goal, its principal reason for existence, in one all-encompassing slogan: "The propagation and defense of the historical truth about Poland."

The "Institute for Research in the Modern History of Poland," was created in Warsaw, in 1923, for the purpose of combatting those still-circulating distortions about Poland which had been spread by Russia, Prussia and Austria during the Partition era. After the death of Pilsudski, in 1935, the name of the Institute was changed to the "Jozef Pilsudski Institute for Research in the Modern History of Poland," although its activities remained unchanged. The Institute made available to historians and students its rich archives, and scientific research work was conducted with the participation of scholars.

During World War II, the archives were almost totally destroyed. In 1943, a group of Polish war emigrés, together with some Polish-American leaders, created the Institute anew—this time in New York City. Since the end of the Second World War saw Poland come under a new foreign domination, the Institute has remained in America.

With its establishment in America, the Pilsudski Institute set to work collecting books and material dealing with the following periods of Polish history: (1) From Poland's uprising against Russia, in 1863 until the beginning of World War I; (2) World War I (1914-1918); (3) The regaining of Polish independence and the Polish-Russian War of 1918-1920; (4) The period of the independence of the Republic of Poland (1918-1939); and (5) World War II (1939-1945) with emphasis on the activities of the Polish Underground Army (AK) and the Warsaw Uprising.

The Institute possesses a large library as well as an imposing collection of original documents and other historical materials which are source material for other historical studies. The collection and preservation of these significant documents and materials constitute the primary task of the Institute. The second task consists in organizing research based on documents already collected. In this endeavor the Institute has the support and collaboration of a number of Polish scholars. The third task is in the field of publications. It already has printed various works (in Polish and English) for example: *Selected Writings of Jozef Pilsudski, Poland in the British Parliament,* 1939-1945, three volumes, edited by W. Jedrzejewicz, and the *Rebirth of the Polish Republic* by Tytus Komarnicki.

Besides this basic activity, the Institute periodically organizes lectures and publishes a bulletin. Also, at great expense, the Pilsudski Institute had restored the documentary film on Pilsudski. The Institute—being an educational, non-political, non-profit institution—is supported by voluntary tax-deductible donations and membership fees.

The Polish American Historical Association was organized, in 1942, in Chicago, as a part of the Polish Institute of Arts and Sciences in America. It has the following objectives: to keep some record of the history of the Polish immigrants and their descendants; to preserve the record of their achievements; and to promote study and research on the social background of Americans of Polish descent. Consisting of Americans of Polish descent, the Association publishes the *Polish American Studies,* which is issued semi-annually, and is sent free to all of its members. The *Polish American Studies,* in addition to scholarly articles and important documents, contains bibliographical lists and reviews of books concerning Americans of Polish descent. It also contains news about the activities of the members of the Association. Members also receive a special mimeographed Polish American Historical Association *Bulletin* which is issued quarterly. The Polish American Historical Association holds regular meetings, in addition to furnishing its membership with opportunity to read and discuss scholarly papers, which enable them to exchange views and ideas. Membership—which is not limited to persons of Polish descent—is secured through election by the Executive Board, upon nomination by a member, or by direct application.

The Institute of Research on Poles in America (Instytut

Wiedzy o Polonii Amerykanskiej)—established in 1948, at the Polish Seminary in Orchard Lake, Michigan, by Dr. Stefan Wloszczewski—sponsored lecture courses concerning the Polish seminary in the State of Michigan. Several pamphlets, relating to the history of the Polish immigrants and their descendants, have also been published.

The "Chicago Arts Club," which has been in existence, since, 1926, has been established by a group of young Americans of Polish extraction. It has the following objectives:[24]

1. To broaden our knowledge, appreciation and enjoyment of serious music, art, and literature.
2. To render moral and material aid to promising writers, musicians, and artists.
3. To make Polish music, art, and literature better known in the United States.

According to Clara Grabowski, the following were also enumerated as objectives of the "Chicago Polish Arts Club."[25]

1. Let us resolve to develop heroes and heroines of our own.
2. Let us resolve to learn just as much as we possibly can about the fundamentals of literature, music and art (to be intelligent as an audience and cultural persons).
3. Let us resolve to acquire the greatest possible skill in that highest of the arts, the art of human relations.

One of the first projects sponsored by the Chicago Polish Arts Club was the lecture by Wladyslaw Benda. Other early activities of this group included: a memorial meeting honoring Reymont and Zeromski in Fullerton Hall of the Art Institute; a Sunday afternoon concert featuring Ina Bourskaya, at Ravinia Park; art exhibitions; debut recitals; and scholarships.

In 1933, the Club arranged for a special exhibit of paintings of Polish and Polish-American artists during the Polish Week of Hospitality at the Century of Progress Exhibition. Literary con-

---

[24] Thaddeus Slesinski, "The Development of Cultural Activities in Polish American Communities," *Polish American Studies*, V (July-December, 1948), p. 100.
[25] Helena Znaniecki Lopata, "The Function of Voluntary Association in an Ethnic Community: Polonia" (unpublished Ph.D. Dissertation, University of Chicago, 1954), p. 229.

tests for school children of Polish and non-Polish descent were also sponsored. By 1952, the Chicago Polish Arts Club had three sections devoted to music, plastic arts, and literature. At the regular meetings, visiting professors and musicians were presented with marked frequency. The Chicago Polish Arts Club was the first of its kind in America, but other cities soon started similarly directed clubs.[26]

The desire to encourage cooperation and to provide a modicum of unity to the various Polish cultural clubs across America in their efforts to expand America's awareness of its cultural heritage, and to improve the quality of life for as many as possible, as well as to inform all Americans of the significant contributions of Americans of Polish descent to America—led to the formation of the National Association of Polish Cultural Clubs, in Grand Rapids, Michigan, in 1940. Prominent in the movement was John C. Hajduk of Chicago, and Florence Turowska of Youngstown, Ohio. Hajduk was elected president, and Miss Turowska secretary. Unfortunately, America was in the midst of World War II, and the energies of the fledgling organization were diverted into areas of more urgent need. The national association languished, and in the next few years declined to the point of inactivity.

Dr. Zygmunt Stojowski, a renowned pianist, composer and pedagogue, heard about the plight of the National Association of Polish Cultural Clubs and decided to do something about it. He succeeded in calling a national conference of Polish cultural clubs which was held in Buffalo. Here, under his devoted leadership, the American Council of Polish Cultural Clubs was born, and a national arts bulletin, edited by Thaddeus Slesinski of Chi-

---

[26] The first link between Americans of Polish descent interested in "culture" was formed by Professor Dybowski, of the Jagiellonian University, who toured the United States lecturing under the auspices of the Kosciuszko Foundation. The first cooperative effort, in 1936, was the sale of the Chicago Polish Arts Club publication, *An Anthology of Polish-American Poetry*. When the Chicago Polish Arts Club undertook the publication of this anthology, in celebration of its tenth anniversary, news releases were mailed to all Polish language newspapers in the United States in an effort to secure material for the volume. It was due to the cooperation of these newspapers that the Chicago Polish Arts Club was successful in its undertaking. A thousand copies of this anthology, edited by Dr. Thaddeus Mitana, were sold during the next few years.

cago, was inaugurated.²⁷ The general reasons for the existence of the American Council of Polish Cultural Clubs is stated in the Preamble to the Constitution.

> To perpetuate and develop the culture created by our forefathers; to encourage higher education and scholarships among people of Polish descent; to foster in Americans of Polish descent a consciousness and pride of their own heritage; to enrich the forming pattern of America's great culture by weaving into it the best from Polish sources of inspiration, and of accomplishment, we associated ourselves together.²⁸

The following are the means by which the objectives of the Council are to be attained:²⁹

1. Maintaining a clearing house for the interchange of information and ideas which pertain to the promotion of Polish culture in America, and should be translated into initiative and action on a national scale.
2. Proposing program material and suggesting plans for cultural activities which would stimulate interest and provide member Clubs with worthwhile guidance for the fulfillment of their objectives.
3. Encouraging the formation of new cultural clubs, particularly in such communities where they do not exist.
4. Cooperating with other Polish, or Polish-American organizations, or activities of a similar purpose in order to maintain close contacts with the creative forces of contemporary Polish cultural life.

The annual conventions of the Council provide affiliated clubs and the general American public with answers as to the direction of the Council's development. The conventions also serve as channels for the exchange of ideas and experiences. They also furnish the opportunity to evaluate the progress of the Council and the associated clubs. The following projects were initiated by the Council. The Norwid Literary Contest was organized for the years 1952 and 1953. The Marcella Sembrich-Kochanski Voice contest was organized in 1954. Postcards with reproductions of photographs of Joseph Karsh of the Polish royal treasures, stored

---

[27] Bruno S. Figura, "Zygmunt Stojowski, Father of the ACPCC," *Polish American* (August 16, 1969), p. 10.
[28] "About the A.C.P.C.C.," *American Council of Polish Cultural Clubs Convention Bulletin*" (August, 1955), p. 16. Slesinski, *op. cit.*, p. 103.
[29] *Ibid.*, "About the A.C.P.C.C.," p. 16.

in Canada, were also distributed. The Mickiewicz Centennial was translated into action on a national scale. In addition, the Council inaugurated a quarterly bulletin for the benefit of individuals and affiliated clubs.[30]

The Polish Arts League of Pittsburgh was formed on February 7, 1948, at 1407 Chelton Avenue, the residence of Olga Klug-Iwanowski. The early meetings were held in the Polish Room, of the Cathedral of Learning, University of Pittsburgh. The members of the League work in close cooperation with various groups and actively support and promote Polish culture by lectures and exhibitions.[31] The League is affiliated with the American Council of Polish Cultural Clubs, and locally with the Arts and Crafts Center. The League takes particular pride in that they assist students in scholarship aid at the University of Pittsburgh, Carnegie-Mellon University, and Duquesne University. Over the years the League has—jointly with the Polish Room Classroom Committee at the University of Pittsburgh—sponsored receptions, cultural programs for visiting Polish artists in the cultural and educational fields. Among its achievements were the binding of Paderewski's manuscript to his opera, *Manru,* along with furnishing the cabinet, together with the archives, now on display in the Polish Room, in the Cathedral of Learning. To make Polish art, music and literature better known, the League had also donated volumes on Polish culture to the Central Branch of the Carnegie Library, the Hillman Library of the

---

[30] The following are members of the American Council of Polish Cultural Clubs: Krakowiak Polish Dancers, Boston, Massachusetts; Polish Arts Club, Buffalo, New York; Polish Club of Alliance College, Cambridge Springs, Pennsylvania; Polish Arts Club, Chicago, Illinois; Society of Polish Arts and Letters, Chicago, Illinois; Friends of Polish Art, Detroit, Michigan; Polish Heritage Society, Grand Rapids, Michigan; Helena Modrzejewska Polish Cultural Club, Los Angeles, California; Polanki, Milwaukee, Wisconsin; Polanie Club, Minneapolis-St. Paul, Minnesota; Polish Arts Club, Newark, New Jersey; Club Polonaise, Passaic, New Jersey; Polish Heritage Society, Philadelphia, Pennsylvania; Polish Arts League, Pittsburgh, Pennsylvania; Polish Arts Group, Rochester, New York; Paderewski University Club, Scranton, Pennsylvania; Chopin Fine Arts Club, South Bend, Indiana; Polish Arts League, Syracuse, New York; Polish American Arts Association, Washington, D. C.; Polish Arts Club, Youngstown, Ohio.

[31] Recently, a lecture on the "Polish Theatre Today and Yesterday" was presented in the Cathedral of Learning, on the campus of the University of Pittsburgh. Also, an exhibit of Polish masters, arranged by the local Polish Arts League members, was held.

University of Pittsburgh, and to the university libraries of Carnegie-Mellon and Duquesne Universities.[32]

On May 25, 1950, Francis S. Chojnacki placed a brief announcement in a local newspaper to the effect that there would be a tea social at the Edelweiss Restaurant. Chojnacki extended an invitation to Denver Americans of Polish descent and to those of Polish kinship through marriage, to attend. The framework for the Denver Polish Club was established at that first meeting, and it grew into a viable active, fellowship with its own club quarters located at 1660 Ogden Street.

Over the years, the Denver Polish Club has financed many projects for St. Joseph's Polish Church. It also sponsored a Polish-American radio program, folk dance groups, and language classes. And it participated in civic and cultural endeavors. In 1962, the Polish-American community of Denver was honored by the city administration in naming a Denver Park in honor of Brigadier General Casimir Pulaski. The request for Pulaski Park originated at the annual General Pulaski Day banquet, sponsored by the Polish Club of Denver, in 1961.

The Polish Cultural Garden, in Cleveland, has monuments of the following illustrious Poles: Paderewski, Chopin, Sienkiewicz, Kopernik, Marie Sklodowska-Curie, Maria Konopnicka, Helena Modrzejewska and Adam Mickiewicz. The Polonaise Art Club was one of the sponsors of the Mickiewicz monument.

Many Polish cultural clubs have been established at American Universities. The name of the Polud Club has an interesting origin. Since the organization is open only to students of Polish descent, its founders adopted the first three letters of Pole, and added U-D, short for the University of Detroit. The purpose of the club is to unite students of Polish extraction, nationally, socially and educationally. The club also attempts to further the practice of Polish customs; and to stimulate interest in Polish-American studies and culture. The Club also attempts to give

---

[32] The presidents of the Polish Arts League of Pittsburgh have been: Olga K. Iwanowski, John M. Budarz, Martha Kluz, Stephanie J. Matula, Martha G. Albosta, Victoria Hruska, Eugene R. Handzlik, Henry J. Zygmunt, Marie Iwanczyk, and Antoni Tabak.

members a better insight to the country of their origin by means of cultural meetings.

The idea of the club originated with Wanda Ogorek, who banded several other students, members of the Laur Dancing Society of Detroit; and in one year, the club (with students of Polish descent) grew from the smallest on the campus to the largest—boasting a membership of 200 members.[33] In 1959, the club celebrated its tenth anniversary.[34]

In addition to the regular monthly meetings, members hold the traditional *Wigilia,* or Christmas Dinner, open to members and non-members alike. A guest speaker of Polish descent is presented. Past speakers have included Father Joseph Osuch, S.J., of the Theology Department, and Judge Lewandowski. Some of the other accomplishments of Polud include the following: the establishment of the first cultural booth at the University of Detroit carnival, participation in Pulaski Day Parades, and radio broadcasts on famous men in Polish history.

The Hamtramck Philharmonic and the Lutnia Singing Society are also significant organizations in Detroit. The Hamtramck Philharmonic under the direction of Frank Grabowski for over 45 years performed concerts quite regularly. Lutnia Singing Society was distinguished by winning first place in the national competitions for Polish choruses: as a whole group, or the male and female sections separately. Lutnia has also published many recordings which were well received.

The Polish American Academic Association was formed in America, in 1951. Its objective was to gather together, in a stimulating environment, the intelligentsia of the Post World War II immigration. The Association sponsored a stimulating sequence of lectures, discussions and authors' evenings, at which famous Polish authors read their own works. These intellectuals were often brought over from various continents of the globe. Among the celebrities were such names as Kazimierz Wierzynski,

---

[33] The following were members of the Laur Dancing Society: Dr. John Toton, Dr. Joseph A. Wytrwal, Jane Gontko, Josephine Dobosz, Helen Wielbik and Isabel Gutowski.

[34] "Polud Club Celebrates Tenth Anniversary," *Polish American Historical Association Bulletin,* Dr. Joseph A. Wytrwal, Editor, Bulletin Number 177 (April, 1959), p. 1.

Maria Kuncewicz, the world-famous novelist, Czeslaw Milosz, the novelist and poet, Beata Obertynska, and many others.

Chapters of the association have been founded in Milwaukee, Detroit, Buffalo, New York and Cleveland. The bi-annual convention is hosted every two years by a different chapter. The 1965 convention was held in Buffalo, the 1967 convention was held in Detroit, and the 1969 convention was held in Chicago. The convention is traditionally held during the Labor Day weekend. During the convention—crowned by a large and sumptuous banquet—the successes and failures of the preceding two years are summed up and weighed. Also, old aims are reconsidered and new directions are given their commencement. The national convention is the sole body with power to change the Association's statutes and elect a new National Executive Committee.[35]

The Alfred Jurzykowski Foundation was established, in 1960, in New York City, by the civic-minded industrialist, Alfred Jurzykowski (1889-1966). The objective of the Foundation is the preservation and development of Polish culture. One of its tasks is to make annual awards to scientists, scholars, writers, composers and artists of Polish ethnic background, regardless of their place, residence, or citizenship. The awardees literally reside in numerous countries throughout the world. Over the years, the Jurzykowski Foundation's operation has benefited tremendously Polish cultural life, in particular, in many American cities. On February 9, 1973, the Foundation presented for the ninth consecutive time, its awards honoring men and women prominent in the arts and sciences. Many of the current recipients are from the United States or Poland.

The Polish Arts and Culture Foundation, in San Francisco, is a private foundation dedicated to sharing with Americans the

---

[35] The Chicago chapter numbers over 150 active members, and 250 members-at-large, who attend the important activities of the organization. The driving force of the Chicago chapter is Andrew Azarjew, former editor of *Dziennik Chicagoski*. He led the chapter from its beginnings, either in capacity as president, or as its mentor. He has contributed greatly to expand the association's membership and activities. One of the projects, he and his co-workers have fostered and succeeded in, is the magazine *Mercury* (*Merkuriusz*) published in England, jointly with London's Polish Students' Association. In Chicago, Azarjew initiated two publications of note: *Zew Mlodych* (*The Call of Youth*), and later, *Nowe Drogi* (*New Paths*). Both were eventually discontinued because of lack of financial support.

wealth of Polish cultural achievements, art and history. The Foundation's premise is that Poland's thousand years of culture are certainly deserving of the widest possible audience, disregarding any political persuasions. The United States has been continually enriched by the legacy of her emigrés through their ideas and achievements. The Foundation considers all of the artistic and cultural achievements of Poles everywhere from all historical periods.

The Polish Arts and Culture Foundation arranges exhibits and lectures with materials from the Foundation's collection and with items lent privately by Polish-Americans living in the San Francisco Bay area. The Foundation has available for lending: films, publications, taped lectures in English, and taped music, musical scores, as well as slides suitable for programs, conferences or the classroom. Also available for display are Polish regional costumes, examples of arts and crafts, posters and paintings. With this collection the Foundation plans eventually to establish a permanent museum and library. The Foundation is a private, non-profit organization. It is not supported by any government. It relies upon individual contributions to support its activities. Donations to the Foundation are tax deductible.[36]

At the suggestion of Rev. Anthony Matla, the Polish-American Cultural Club of Mosinee (Wisconsin) was organized in 1972. The goals of the club are the study of Polish History, Art, Music and Literature. Proceeds from the club's activities are designated for the preservation of Polish heritage and possibly scholarships for youth.[37]

The American Institute of Polish Culture, in Miami, Florida, was founded, in 1972, by a prominent group of members from the Miami community. The chairman, since its inception, is Blanka Rosenstiel. The aims and objectives of the Institute are

---

[36] Officers of the cultural unit are: Wanda Tomczykowska, president; Prof. Peter Dale Scott, vice-president and secretary; and Wanda Polena, treasurer.

[37] The following Board of Officers were elected: Advisors: Mr. and Mrs. Adam Bartosz; Associate Advisor: Mrs. Matla; Chaplain and Director: Rev. Matla; Chairman: Mrs. Mary Sitko; Vice Chairman: Mrs. Margie Geary and Mrs. Pauline Gronski; Recording-Secretary: Mrs. Arline Stark; Treasurer: Mrs. Stefanie Kaptur. Directors are: Eva Pietrzykowski, Helen Orzechowski, Raymond Wysocki, Hattie Weyer, Bernadine Kluz, Viola Cichy, Gertrude Kazmierczak, and Dorothy Kranowski.

twofold: first, to bring to the forefront and share with all Americans Poland's rich heritage, whose achievements through the centuries have played a vital role in the formation of Western civilization. Second, to develop an institution that provides a center with educational facilities and resources for aiding and exhibiting the present artistic contributions of Americans of Polish and Slavic backgrounds. The Institute is located in a modern building, in downtown Miami, at 1000 Brickwell Avenue.[38]

The Copernicus Society of America, formed in 1973, by Edward J. Piszek, president of Mrs. Paul's Kitchens, as a cultural and educational foundation to advance Polish arts and sciences, and to pay tribute to the Polish astronomer, Mikolaj Kopernik, who demonstrated that the Earth is not stationary, but moves around its own axis while circling the Sun.

The activities of the Copernicus Society are varied and many. In December 1973, the Society underwrote expenses of four students, selected by the Smithsonian Institution, to make a pilgrimage to Poland to retrace the life steps of Kopernik. The report of this project was published in the March 1973 and April 1973 issues of the *Smithsonian* magazine.

The Copernicus Society also arranged an exhibit of original instruments used by Kopernik during his years of research and discovery at the Jagiellonian University in Krakow.[39] The price-

---

[38] On January 30, 1973, the Institute sponsored a piano recital with the world-renowned pianist, Witold Malcuzynski. In October 1973, the Institute sponsored a lecture by Krzysztof Zanussi, the leading Polish film director. On October 29, 1973, an exhibit was organized of paintings, watercolors, photography and sculpture by four artists of Polish background. On November 29, 1973, the Institute participated with the Copernicus Committee of Miami in the Copernicus Symposium, held at the University of Miami. On January 23, 1974, the Institute, co-sponsored with the Museum of Sciences, an illustrated lecture at the Museum of Sciences by Zofia Kielan-Jaworowski on "Dinosaur Hunting in the Gobi Desert." On February 19, 1974, the Institute sponsored, for public television, the New York Harp Ensemble featuring four internationally known harpists. Two harpists were of Polish origin: Eva Jaslow and Barbara Pniewska. On March 21, 1974, an illustrated lecture on the "Art of Renaissance Poland," by Mr. Riabov, was sponsored.

[39] The instruments on loan from Poland included the largest preserved medieval astrolabe, dated 1481, an instrument for observing the positions of celestial bodies; one of two extant Torquetums, which are used in astrology to read off ecliptic coordinates, and dated 1487; and an Arabian astrolabe, dated 1054. The most precious of the instruments in the university collection is the gold Jagiellonian Globe, dated 1510. The approximately six-inch globe is encircled with an armillary sphere and

less scientific instruments were mounted by the Smithsonian Institute for display at the Smithsonian Institution and at the following cities: New York, Philadelphia, Detroit, Milwaukee, Chicago, Ottawa, Canada, London, England and at the Bibliotheque National, in Paris.

The Copernicus Society also has published a beautifully illustrated book, *Copernicus and His Epoch*. The society also provided Copernicus lapel buttons to wear during the commemorative year of Mikolaj Kopernik.

The Polonus Philatelic Society was organized February 26, 1939, in Chicago. The Society is composed of members who are interested in saving stamps. The society includes the foremost specialists on stamps of Poland. Throughout the world these members are actively engaged in promoting Polish philately by publishing its own magazine; by writing articles for the philatelic press on the stamps of Poland; by arranging a fine annual exhibition of Polish stamps; by buying, selling and exchanging stamps and covers at each meeting, or by mail; and finally, by getting together with others to promote their hobby. They are also in constant touch with philatelic sources in Poland. Another objective of the orientation is to promote an awareness of Polish culture, literature and history through philatelic means.

The Polish-American Numismatic Association, of Chicago, has issued a medal honoring the 500th anniversary of the birth of Mikolaj Kopernik. The designer of the medal was the Polish artist, Waclaw Kowalik. The Polish-American Numismatic Association is a non-profit organization.[40]

In modern times cooperation among these ethnically-oriented cultural clubs is only one indicator among many that the old cultural separation between peoples of different nationalities is nearly gone. For the most significant trend in modern times is cultural cooperation between nationalities, as Dr. Florian Znaniecki stated in his book, *Modern Nationalities*. Americans look

---

has a clock mechanism moving the indicator and the sphere. The clock tells the hours, days, months, and the position of the Sun in the sky.

[40] *Narod Polski* (April 19, 1973), p. 11. The Polish American Congress, Michigan Division, also issued a commemorative silver medal for the International Copernicus Year, in 1973.

for common interests in other people, and group with them for the preservation of those interests. For Americans now realize that every nationality can contribute something to the creative growth of other nationalities, by what we call "cross-fertilization of cultures."

The children, and especially the grandchildren of the Polish immigrants, are revealing a lively interest in the history, literature and art of the land of their forefathers. Pride in these achievements has not weakened their American patriotism; but they are resolved that in the national culture of the future, the warmth and refinement of Polish civilization shall have its place alongside the solid and historic institutions contributed by the colonists and immigrants from Western Europe. Furthermore, descendants of the Polish immigrants believe that the people of many nationalities, functioning together, can develop creatively a world culture; and that this is the only effective way of unifying all mankind. Such cooperation requires that nationals of different cultures should understand, and appreciate one another. At the first step, in this direction, every individual should participate in at least two cultures, and fully appreciate both; that is exactly what members of the Polish-American Cultural associations, in the United States, are doing. As participants in American culture, Americans of Polish descent are aware that America is no longer a closed "Melting Pot," but the main cultural center of the modern world.

CHAPTER 11

The Valiant Years (1939-1945)

> Conquer, you will not conquer.
> Suppress, you will not suppress.
> Root out, you will not root out.
> Neither guns nor bayonets, neither scaffolds nor mines.
> Neither counsel nor treachery will avail you,
> As sure as God is God, for His is the Cause.
>
> —August Cieszkowski

> The victor will not be asked afterward whether he told the truth or not. In starting and waging a war it is not right that matters but victory.
>
> —Adolph Hitler

> Poland is immortal. We will free her from the chains of slavery and rebuild her from ruins, so help us God.
> Poland will not perish, my wearied brethren, she will not perish, but will live forever in power and glory, for you, for us and all humanity.
>
> —I. J. Paderewski

The year 1939 was the year of the World's Fair. It was also the beginning of the age of nuclear fission which started that year with an announcement that scientists had succeeded in splitting uranium by means of a bombardment of neutrons. This was scarcely noted in the press and certainly not by the visitors to the 1939 World's Fair with its trylon and perisphere, its "Town of Tomorrow," its General Motors show, and a Japanese Shinto shrine enclosing a replica of the Liberty Bell made of diamonds and pearls.

Americans, in the late '30s, lived in a world emerging from the grimness of a massive depression. Although the threat of war was a continual fear, its real horror had not affected American lives, and public attention was diverted elsewhere. On the very eve of World War II, it was possible, even inevitable, for individuals in all parts of the world to be optimistic. The war-like moves of Italy and Germany contradicted the announcements of the government travel bureaus which were advertising: "Italy—Land of Traditional Hospitality," and "Bypaths of Beauty Beckon you to Germany."

It was an era of pleasurable escapism. The following songs were heard: "Imagination is Funny—It Makes a Cloudy Day Sunny," "It's a Big, Wide, Wonderful World," and "It's a Lovely Day Tomorrow."

This was the pre-television era. The silver screen never shone more brightly than in the brilliantly lit grandiose movie palaces that sprang up on Main Street. Razzle-dazzle marquees lured the movie-mad public into lush settings that made every patron feel like a sultan. Lobbies gleamed with marble and gold, fountains splashed, clouds drifted and stars twinkled. There were circus-style playrooms, and Versailles-like lounges to accommodate the vast audiences of all ages.

It was an era filled with numerous personalities: especially glamorous and idolized movie stars. The actresses were beautiful women with handsome leading men playing opposite them in a variety of colorful, exotic, spectacular, but above all, romantic films. Even the love songs had memorable music with lyrics which increased the sales of phonograph records and sheet music.

The movie of the year 1939 was "Gone With the Wind." Other motion pictures were "Charley's Aunt," "Kiss the Boys Good-bye" and "The Shadow of the Thin Man." Claudette Colbert was featured in an "unorthodox love scene," with Ray Milland in "Skylark." The description was the result of her being the aggressor in a screen kiss. "Snow White and the Seven Dwarfs," Walt Disney's first full-length cartoon, delighted young and old.

The radio transported the Americans into a magic world where it supplied the sound, while the Americans supplied their

THE VALIANT YEARS (1939-1945)

own pictures. Families gathered around to listen to Kate Smith, Gabriel Heatter and Bill Kenny of the Ink Spots, who were singing those beautiful high notes. Fibber McGee and Molly were holding forth at 79 Wistful Vista, and a little bellboy with a clarion voice advised the listeners to call for Phillip Morris. There, also, was "One Man's Family," "Dinah Shore," "Bulldog Drummond," and the late-night favorite that began with a door creaking and a slightly mad, crackling voice: "Ghost stories, weird stories, and murders, too . . ." entitled "The Hermit's Cave." Radio also gave Americans a Halloween scare they never forgot when a 23-year-old actor, Orson Welles, simulated a news broadcast of a fictional invasion by men from Mars, sending thousands of people into the streets in panic, and some to their deaths.

The Number One novel on the best seller list was John Steinbeck's *The Grapes of Wrath*. The highest Adolph Hitler got on the best-seller list, that year, with *Mein Kampf*, was number seven. Americans were also reading such books as *Pistols for Hire* in which Flick Parsons set out to capture the notorious Billy the Kid. In the comics, Li'l Abner was having his troubles with Madam Rhumboogie. There was Chief Wahoo, Flash Gordon, Mickey Finn, Napoleon, Superman and others.

The year 1939 was the year of big bands, of "jitterbugs" and names like Goodman, Dorsey and Miller. It was also the year of the holocaust; of the Nazi conquest of Czechoslovakia and the Ribbentrop-Molotov pact. Brutal militarism was on the march abroad, while Prime Minister Neville Chamberlain spoke hopefully of "peace in our time."

The Poles had expected war, but were tactically surprised. Following the advice of the Western Powers—not to incite Hitler's fury—the Polish government delayed its general mobilization so that a large part of the Polish armed forces was unable to participate in the fighting. Even though negotiations for a peaceful settlement were being considered apparently by Germany and Poland, on August 22, Hitler told his generals that he had Poland in exactly the position he desired, adding: "I am only afraid that at the last moment some swine or other will yet submit to me a plan for mediation."[1] On August 24, Roosevelt appealed directly to Hitler and President Ignacy Moscicki of Poland to solve their differences by direct negotiations, arbitration or conciliation. President Moscicki agreed to negotiations and conciliation, and Roosevelt forwarded the reply to Hitler who remained silent. On August 31, Hitler—while replying to President Roosevelt that he had "left no stone unturned" in seeking a peaceful settlement—ordered his troops into Poland at dawn, on September 1, 1939.

World War II began with the *blitzkrieg*. Although it was not a German concept, the Germans did perfect the technique and gave it a name, which literally translates into "lightning war." From the north, west and south, poised German fighting men marched and flew into Poland to win more *lebensraum* for the power-hungry *fuehrer*. The *blitzkrieg* moved with speed and ruthlessness leaving death and destruction in its wake while spreading terror ahead.[2]

The *blitzkrieg* broke over Poland at dawn, on Friday, September 1, 1939, and embroiled the world in the most destructive war in history. It lasted six years, which is not a long

---

[1] Arnold A. Offner, *The Origins of the Second World War. American Foreign Policy and World Politics, 1917-1941* (New York: 1975), p. 130.

[2] The concept of the *blitzkrieg* is based on the highly mobile, armored striking force centered around tanks, self-propelled guns, and trucks to transport the infantry, breaking front lines, wrecking command areas and cutting-off rear supply routes. Disorganized and without means of direction or resupply, the enemy is unable to offer a coordinated defense against the slower, non-motorized infantry that follow to "mop up." Coordination is provided by radio, telephone, telegraph, and the airplane—the second arm of the blitzkrieg. Bombers, rangers far behind enemy lines, destroyed bridges, railroads, communication centers, and industrial plants. The blitzkrieg deals the enemy a triple blow: his ability to mobilize, direct, and supply his forces is impaired; the industrial base for his long-range supply is crippled; the terror and destruction raining from the skies undermine civilian morale.
The three principles of blitzkreig warfare are: surprise, speed and concentration. Surprise made for speed; speed enhanced surprise; concentration bolstered both. In the Polish campaign surprise was achieved by negotiating until the last moment and then attacking without even a declaration of war. Hand in hand with concentrated *Schwerpunkte*, speed was assured first by the Luftwaffe which eliminated the Polish air forces and disrupted the Polish command and communications; second, it tore open the Polish front by tank formation which penetrated deep into Polish rear areas. The deep breakthrough paralyzed the opposition and led to annihilation when Poland, with its moral and material resources exhausted, was no longer able to wage war. Nevertheless, the Poles were superb strategists at war, and even with a cavalry they were able to devastate columns of armored vehicles and take hundreds of German prisoners.

THE VALIANT YEARS (1939-1945) 339

duration since history has recorded many much longer wars, but it did produce the largest armies, the longest battle lines, and until then the most devastating weapons of any war; it inflicted more suffering, left more destruction in its wake on two hemispheres of the globe and became the costliest war until then. In Germany, race relations had become strained and hateful, and all accepted values had disappeared. The war affected irremediably the world, and resulted in the killing of six million Jews. It placed some seventy million people in uniform, and killed as many as thirty-five million, including many millions who were never in uniform; it was a war that slaughtered indiscriminately more than any war which preceded it.

In one of the most momentous days in the history of the world, the Germans employed two Army Groups: in the North, under General Fedor von Bock; and in the South, under General Gerd von Runstedt. Their total strength was approximately 1,500,000 men.[3] With a force of more than fifty divisions (five were identified as panzer and four were motorized infantry) and approximately 2000 offensively armed aircraft at their disposal, the Luftwaffe commanded the skies, reconnoitering, bombing and terrorizing the country below. While hordes of Heinkel 111 bombers were blasting a path for the panzers from the sky, the Stukas, screaming and shooting, spread terror and havoc by supporting the panzer units, which easily broke through the Polish lines and drove deep into Polish territory. Nor were they alone on the ground. Mechanized artillery, motorized infantry kept up; even the marching infantry seemed to advance with terrifying speed. Most of the Polish planes were destroyed in the opening hours of the war; by September 3, the Polish Air Force was eliminated as a fighting unit. The Luftwaffe, now in command of the skies, turned to direct support of the ground forces by bombing and strafing Polish troops. By that time, Army Group North had cut the Polish corridor by simultaneous thrusts from East Prussia and Pomerania and had turned south toward Warsaw; at the same time Army Group South had crossed the Polish

---

[3] Hitler held in reserve, or was forming sixteen second-line divisions supported by 500 aircraft. However, they saw no fighting.

frontiers on a broad front and were pressing toward Lodz, Warsaw, and Krakow.

Poland's task in defense was formidable. Poland is a vast plain providing a path between Germany and Russia. For centuries, since Poland has no natural eastern or western boundaries to protect her territory, this plain has been trampled by armies moving between east and west. In addition, in 1939, Poland was so constituted that to protect her vital industrial and agricultural areas, she must spread her armed forces over a broad perimeter and expose her flanks. Troops in the Corridor could easily be cut off, as the Germans so ably demonstrated: units in the area around Poznan and Krakow became vulnerable by encirclement. Yet these areas contained a large part of Poland's agricultural, mineral, and industrial resources. To lose them would make continued defense almost impossible. Rather than concentrate her forces on a narrow front, Poland elected to defend her entire area. Thus, no central reserve was created from which the gaps in the defense system would be filled. If Britain and France would have attacked from the west immediately after Germany's attack of Poland, before the Polish forces had to capitulate, there still would have been a chance to succeed and World War II could have been concluded in the first month of the war.

Poland had only thirty front-line infantry divisions, one poorly equipped cavalry division, which boasted some obsolete tanks, a handful of brigades mounted on horseback, and ten reserve divisions. Of her 935 aircraft, only 400 were modern enough to face the *Luftwaffe*. Polish mobilization was still incomplete when the Germans attacked. Only well-prepared defenses, in depth, could have held back the Germans on terrain so ideally suited to the new *blitzkrieg* tactics. Except for the rivers there was virtually no natural obstacle on the vast Polish plains which stretched from the German frontier to the forests and marshes of the eastern borderlands. There was virtually no defense against the air attacks on cities, airfields, supply and communications centers. Nevertheless each village and town was an obstacle of resistance and evidence for the atrocities which took place. Today, the commemorative tablets, and shrines left their mark for the reprisals against the Germans by the valiant Poles.

British and French help did not come as was promised by treaty. Furthermore, if the Allies under the direction of Churchill had attacked Germany instead of conducting a prolonged and wasteful campaign on many fronts, World War II would have been concluded sooner. They never came to the relief of Poland, but chose Africa instead. Norway also was too close, until the German Air Force attacked England. If the entire effort of the war was directed against Germany, the other fronts would have capitulated and war would have been concluded in half the time. The waste of human carnage, both civilian and military, besides all the buildings and treasures created through the centuries which depicted man's achievement was wasted in this futile endeavor. Much blame for the war must be laid at the feet of Churchill and Roosevelt. Theirs were numerous sins of omission and commission as our idols with feet of clay.

The German *blitzkrieg* moved with startling rapidity; the conquest of Poland was achieved before Poland's allies could come to grips with the military situation confronting them. The Poles fought with valor but with little hope of success. Most of their weapons were of World War I vintage; they had almost no tanks; horse cavalry pitted against panzers resulted in cruel slaughter and often effectively hindered the German advance.

Despite the brave action of units, the numerically and technically superior German armored divisions cracked the Polish defenses—often spontaneously organized in order to delay the German advance. By September 6th, Krakow had fallen and the Polish armies were either surrounded or in retreat. German mechanized units raced ahead to cut off retreat routes and to prevent the Poles from organizing a coordinated resistance. Roughly one-third of the Polish ground forces, surrounded in the Kutno area, made a desperate attempt to break out toward Warsaw. They failed. The survivors surrendered on September 17. The same day, Brest, to the east, fell before the armored assault of General Heinz Guderian's Panzer Corps.

On September 17, 1939, the Red Army began pouring across the Polish frontiers from the east. Shortly afterwards—after minor disputes with the Germans were settled and certain modifications agreed upon—the USSR seized control of all territory east of the line running along the rivers Pisa, Narew, Bug and San—an area of more than 77,000 square miles with a population of 13,200,000. This territory the USSR received as a result of the pact signed in Moscow, on August 23, 1939, by Soviet foreign minister Molotov and the foreign minister for the Third Reich, von Ribbentrop. The Nonaggression Pact publicly proclaimed that each country would remain neutral if the other went to war and secretly provided that in the event of war they would divide Poland approximately in half.

Hitler invited Stalin to occupy his half on September 3, 1939. Not only did Hitler want to dispose of Poland in a hurry so he would be free to face Britain and France, but if Russia participated in the military destruction of Poland, the stigma of aggression would not be borne by Germany alone. Perhaps, because Russia's forces could not be mobilized quickly enough to begin earlier (a small war with Japan was being concluded in the Far East); or perhaps, because she was willing to let Germany carry the burden of Poland's defeat—Russia refrained from direct attack until September 17th.

Even though the Russians merely claimed the eastern Polish area by license in its August 23 nonaggression pact with Germany and a secret protocol partitioning the country, the Soviet Union took a number of actions in order to justify, both morally and legally, its seizure of territories belonging to the Polish Republic. Calling their advance a "liberation march," the Russians explained their action to the world as a move to extend assistance to their Ukrainian and Byelorussian brothers, a calculated maneuver of aggrandizement to expand its western frontier. Now that Poland was rendered helpless, the USSR attacked Poland, the land which she had designs on for centuries. The Russians also stated that their action was based on the right of self-determination of the Ukrainians and Byelorussians, who represented a clear majority of the population of the annexed area. Their "democratically" elected assemblies voted in favor of incorporation into the Ukrainian and Byelorussian republics of the Soviet Union. But this was only a calculated deception utilizing a cause which was festering a long time in the Soviet Union. They turned a liability into an asset.⁴ Poland was not conquered when Russia attacked.⁵

Another achievement of the Poles, during World War II, was the successful theft of the V-2 Rocket from the Germans by the Polish underground, known as the *Armia Krajowa* (the Nation's Army). The Germans were testing the V-2 Rocket in Southern Poland when the A.K. in a daring and clever raid stole one of the rockets and then smuggled it to England where scientists could examine it and develop their own new weapons. Kazimierz Szrajfer—now a Canadian pilot—participated as one of the two courageous pilots on that eventful and highly dangerous mission which resulted in shortening the duration of the war.

The Poles were the first who had the courage to defy Hitler, a ruthless dictator.

Poland paid the highest price of all the belligerent nations: of the 35 million prewar citizens of Poland, over 6 million perished; that is

---

⁴ The Byelorussians were never stirred toward independence and were most happy to be a part of Poland. They were made unhappy when the Curzon Line, designed by the British to settle the Polish-Russian boundary, only split these people in two: half in Poland and half in Russia. Only the Ukrainians behaved ignominiously toward Poland through secret excitement by the Nazis, even prior to the war's commencement. Ukrainians counted on total independence from Poland and Russia. The atrocities performed by them against innocent villagers, for no reason at all, are still remembered and shared by many Poles. In order to encourage a people to fight their own brothers, the Nazis initiated a propaganda campaign of hatred to build and generate enough effort and determination against innocent people in order to achieve a determined goal. The Germans made numerous promises to the gullible Ukrainians and Russians. To this day, there is no identifiable majority of Ukrainians in the Ukraine territory, for after the war, Stalin transferred and resettled Ukrainians, Armenians, Lithuanians and other intensely nationalistic groups to remoter parts of the U.S.S.R., where they would be in alien territory. Most Poles were resettled in Poland with its new boundaries.

⁵ In comparison with other European powers, it took the German and Russians a month to defeat the Poles, who fought alone without any help or support from Allied powers. Yet France capitulated in two weeks. Norway and the Scandinavian countries also capitulated in the same fashion. Even Great Britain could have been defeated without the benefit of the Polish ace pilots in the RAF. All of these countries already had the support of the Allied Powers, including the United States. Prior to Poland's invasion, both Austria and Czechoslovakia capitulated without defense. Hitler expected a quick annexation of Poland. Poland's valiant defense was unexpected. Yet Poland had no choice for survival, even as a beleaguered nation. Had not Poland defended her boundaries, Europe would be under the total influence of Fascism all the way to the Pacific. The U.S.S.R., Spain, Portugal, Italy and North Africa were under the control of Fascism already. Which form of evil is preferred is questionable. The issue is not settled yet, for factions of each ideology are still fighting today—more than thirty years after the conclusion of the war.

220 out of every 1,000 that were killed . . . Only about 66,000 Poles, however, were killed in active battle. The rest died in bombed cities, in prisons, and above all, in concentration camps.[6]

Hitler's timetable was abruptly halted, and the Allies gained a breathing spell. Even though Hitler and Himmler searched Poland, they could never find a Quisling.

Many Poles were willing to continue the struggle and made their way into forests where they fought as partisans and raiders, attacking communication centers, sabotaging, waging guerrilla warfare. Resistance units in the areas of Wilno, Tarnopol, Krakow, in the Ukraine and elsewhere, attest to the courage as well as to a people's martyrdom. Many Poles were willing to continue the struggle abroad. According to the figures of the International Labor Office, there were 32,000 Polish civilians and 70,000 Polish soldiers who crossed into Romania, Hungary and Latvia. Many young Poles escaped in the following years to join the Polish armed forces fighting in other parts of the world. Soviet intervention cut off important units of the Polish army, which were prevented from escaping to Romania. Their deeds reflect a capacity to defy the enemy wherever the trap had not been completely shut.

France and Britain declared War fifty-four hours after Germany's attack on Poland. Although Britain and France declared war on Germany on September 3rd, however, they did not attack Germany for two weeks while fighting raged on in Poland, and the German armies pillaged Polish villages and towns, arrested and executed Poland's defenders and elite; while simultaneously the German Air Force was hurtling bombs on Polish cities, devastating them. During this crucial time when not only days counted, but even hours and minutes were significant in defending Poland, a nation that would save Europe from German domination could have been spared the great holocaust of World War II and perhaps even concluded the war in the first months. September revealed the stupidity, hypocrisy and treachery of both Britain and France. Through their dilatoriness they did not avoid or spare themselves of involvement in the war; it definitely prolonged

---

[6] Jan Szczepanski, *Polish Society* (New York: 1970), p. 34.

the war. America's late entry also contributed unnecessarily to Poland's enormous tragedy. In this instance Hitler's conviction about France and Britain was correct in that no one would come to the defense of Poland immediately.

Instead of bombs, British airplanes roamed over Germany, dropping leaflets for propaganda purposes. One of the great absurdities of World War II! On September 5, British planes dropped three million leaflets over the Ruhr region. On September 6, 8 and 9, British planes again dropped leaflets, which was repeated again on September 24 and 25—in all, eighteen million leaflets were dropped since the war broke out. This action alone conveys a greater partiality for the welfare of the German people than for the fate of the Polish people. Even the focus of the war was improper as far as the British Government was concerned.

> Strict orders were issued to the British Air Force not to bomb any German land forces, and these orders were not modified until April, 1940; similar orders by Hitler to the *Luftwaffe* were maintained for part of this same period. When some British Members of Parliament, led by Amery, put pressure on the government to drop bombs on German munition stores in the Black Forests, the air minister, Sir H. Kingsley Wood, rejected the suggestion with asperity, declaring: "Are you aware it is private property? Why, you will be asking me to bomb Essen next!" Essen was the home of the Krupp munitions factories.[7]

Also, the British Navy went into action so slowly that the German "pocket" battleships were able to escape from their ports and from the North Sea out on the high seas where they could become commerce raiders. With the aid of such allies, it is a wonder that the war was won—but only after the United States entered into the conflict to deliver them from their mistakes. The might of Britain's great sea power—propagandized so effectively by Churchill—was after all a great myth!

Ivan Maisky, the Soviet ambassador to the United Kingdom, made the following comment in his memoirs:

---

[7] Carroll Quigley, *Tragedy and Hope. A History of the World of Our Time* (New York: 1966), p. 667.

> I remember meeting Greenwood in Parliament in the middle of September. We talked of the German-Polish war. Greenwood was in utter confusion.
> "It is terrible, terrible!" he said loudly. "Our Government gave the most solemn promises to come to the help of Poland in the event of a German attack—and what are we doing? Surely the British and French loan of eight-and-a-half million pounds to the Polish Government is not help! We haven't sent a single plane to Poland, and we are using our own planes to drop useless leaflets over Germany!"[8]

When the war was ten days old, John Gunther had an opportunity for a conversation with Winston Churchill. While Poland was at the moment being submerged and the West remained quiet, Churchill—who was already falling into senility before he was overtaken by old age—made his observations on the war to Gunther:

> He thought that the Nazis were bound to strike elsewhere soon, possibly in Hungary or Yugoslavia, possibly in Switzerland or the Low Countries.[9]

During the first two weeks of September, when the greatest speed and energy were required in affording assistance to Poland, the French army displayed little, if any action. The first French war communique, dated September 4, stated: "Operations have begun on land, at sea and in the air." The second French war communique, dated September 5, stated: "French troops have entered into contact with the enemy along the whole line between the Moselle and the Rhine." The third French communique, dated September 6, reported crossing into "no man's land," the strip of land from three to twelve miles wide, separating the Maginot Line from the Siegfried Line. From September 10 to 12, the French communiques reported the systematic advance of the French troops in the region of "no man's land." The French army did not yet seriously attack the Siegfried Line or pour bombs on the German fortifications.

On September 12, General Gamelin, alarmed at the way

---

[8] Ivan Maisky, *Memoirs of a Soviet Ambassador*, translated by Andrew Rothstein (New York: 1968), p. 9.
[9] Gunther, *Procession*, pp. 133-134.

THE VALIANT YEARS (1939-1945)   347

things were going in Poland, sent a secret order to General Pretelat, the commander of the Saar "offensive," ordering him to halt and assume a defensive posture. When Poland capitulated, the French War Cabinet directed to pull back its forces to the Maginot Line. On October 4th the withdrawal had been completed. General Gamelin was pleased that the Germans had obliged by letting the French forces go peacefully. At least France had made a gesture on behalf of the Poles; thus honor, according to General Gamelin, was satisfied.[10]

The blockade of Germany was established in such a perfunctory fashion that large quantities of French iron ore, as well as other commodities, continued to go to Germany through the neutral Low Countries in exchange for German coal coming by the same route. These exchanges continued for weeks. On his part, Hitler issued orders to his air force not to cross the Western frontier except for reconnaissance, and to his navy not to fight the French, and to his submarines not to molest passenger vessels and to treat unarmed merchant ships according to the established rules of international law.

When Strasbourg was being evacuated, at the outbreak of of the war, the Germans obligingly aided by turning on searchlights from their side of the river; for several months, power plants in the German Saar continued to supply French frontier villages with electricity.[11]

Hitler and his generals knew that the essential political and military prerequisite for the success of the Polish campaign was that Poland's western allies did not aid her by attacking the Rhineland. In the west, Germany had only eleven first-line divisions, one division of fortress troops, thirty-five second line divisions and no armored or motorized units. The French had fifty-seven front-line divisions, forty-five reserve divisions, two mechanized divisions, one very heavily armored and powerful

---

[10] Thus ended France's first and last offensive of the war. During it, the morale of the French troops has been promisingly high—"We're starting to invade them!" wrote an infantry NCO, Rene Balbaud—but frustration at the subsequent withdrawal was correspondingly great. Out of the experience gained, the Army settled down to the dubious consolation that German anti-tank shells had been observed to bounce off French tanks.

[11] Alistair Horne, *To Lose A Battle France* 1940 (Boston: 1969), p. 102.

tank division. In addition four British front-line divisions were also soon under the French commander-in-chief, General Maurice Gustav Gamelin. This immense Allied superiority on the ground was enhanced by the fact that the German troops were mostly either elderly reservists or raw recruits. Germany was inferior in the air both in bombers and fighters, except for the dive-bombers in which case French artillery superiority more than redressed the balance.

> In Germany, the Wehrmacht leaders observed France's supineness in the west with mixed amazement and relief. Aware of their own Army's unreadiness for full-scale war, they have viewed Hitler's plunge into Poland as one more lunatic gamble; when France and Britain declared war, they were terrified that, this time, Hitler's bluff had been called and that immediately they would face a powerful breakthrough offensive in the west. According to General Westphal, during the whole Polish campaign, the frontier from Aachen to Basle was held by no more than twenty-five-reserve, militia and depot divisions, with not a single tank under their command and with enough ammunition for only three days' battle. At the Nuremberg Trials, Milche declared that the Luftwaffe stock of bombs had been so small that the Polish campaign had consumed half of it; and Jodl, the Wehrmacht Chief of Operations, claimed that, because of ammunition shortages, in Poland, "we only managed solely because there was no battle in the west." The Siegfried Line, despite Hitler's boasting, was nothing like as formidable as the Maginot Line, and was far from complete; according to his Chief of Staff, when Runstedt inspected it for the first time, he laughed. If the French had seriously attacked it in September 1939, their troops would at least have gained the training which was to prove so badly lacking seven months later, while many responsible German generals believed (and indeed still do) that the French could have reached the Rhine within a fortnight, and possibly have won the war. From Berlin, Joseph Harsch reckoned that German morale "was probably no better able to withstand the shock of invasion in September 1939" than French morale the following summer.[12]

With such tremendous superiority the French could have breached the Siegfried Line, as Gamelin himself later admitted, but they were haunted by memories of the bloody offensive of 1914-18, and remained on the defensive. Gamelin had promised

---

[12] Alistaire Horne, *To Lose A Battle France* 1940 (Boston: 1969), p. 100.

the Poles a full-scale attack on the Siegfried Line by the sixteenth day after the German attack on Poland, but clearly the promise was never meant to be honored. Had it been, the Rhine could have been reached within a fortnight, with incalculable consequences for the morale and military prospects of Germany and the Allies. In this regard, the French and British were almost as guilty as the Germans for World War II, but their guilt was one of neglect rather than aggression.

Such a western offensive would have impressed the Russians also. They had doubted, with good reason—until the British and French declarations of war had been made—whether the western powers would declare war, but they were equally uncertain of Nazi fidelity to the signed treaty. They were anxious to seize their share of Poland, but they were not ready for war, even with Poland—still less with the west.

World War II—which shattered the lives of many—was the beginning of great suffering, heartbreak, misery and human savagery amidst heroism, idealism, and patriotic fervor. It spared no one—not even children. Defenseless cities, the length and breadth of Poland, were bombed over and over again. Hitler regarded Warsaw as the symbol of Polish nationalism, and therefore a prime target of his planned attack on Poland. Warsaw was to be encircled, starved, captured and destroyed. In Warsaw, that Sunday, it was a red, flaming dawn as firemen and householders tried to subdue the fires and dig the dead and injured out from under the destruction German air supremacy had wrought. Before evening, not a single Polish fighter plane was left to defend the capital. When the near misses shook the churches and the congregations streamed forth into the streets, the pilots swooped down to mow the people with their machine guns.

It wasn't a war waged on a battlefield. It was savage, sadistic and premeditated murder. The unconquerable Polish cavalry, although more mobile and effective, could not endure against German tanks which were protected by German air power. Outnumbered five to one, Poland's archaic air force was quickly wiped out.

At Westerplatte, a district of Gdansk, an heroic stand was made which was to become World War II's first legend. The garrison of five officers and 260 men—penned in on a square mile peninsula with supplies for only twelve hours—held out for seven days. From all sides and above the fortification was hammered by German weapons, including a battleship firing point-blank from 800 yards. The garrison fought for life and honor against all the might and fury of the disciplined and ruthless German race. They defied air, land and sea bombardment and killed several hundred attacking Germans. In the end dysentery, exhausted rations and lack of ammunition dictated surrender. Fifty Poles survived. Major Henryk Sucharski, from Greboszow offered his sword to a German general in token of surrender. The general did not accept it; instead, he saluted the major and told him to keep it, because he was a brave soldier. Sucharski kept it during the entire time he was a prisoner, until the Americans freed him from a POW camp.

This was such a destructive war in which monuments built for the ages, were laid waste in moments. There were few incidents of its kind in the annals of history which delivered such a shock of outrage than the German raid on Warsaw which destroyed the nation's most precious heritage. The centuries-old cathedral, the royal castle, the opera house, palaces, historic buildings, libraries, museums, and universities with their priceless treasures: these paintings, sculptures, musical instruments and rare manuscripts were lost forever. The Poles are innately and intensely patriotic people. They do not wear their patriotism on their sleeves, nor does it come easily to their lips. They feel it. As Warsaw and its historic structures were slowly burning down, from fires set by German bombs, the Poles did not merely remain idle in their grief. Through the well-organized underground resistance they moved many treasures by sealing them in destroyed buildings or transporting them secretly to hidden places for the duration of the war. How many transports of art treasures—intended for German museums—were strangely detoured and prevented from leaving the country?

But it was typical of the race that before the ashes had cooled, they made the resolve that Warsaw would rise again.[13]

---

[13] And so in central Poland, Warsaw stands again. A symbol for all of us, a message to say that glory, beauty or the achievements of centuries can be leveled to

The heroic resistance of the Poles against a ruthless dictator aroused the admiration of the world. Newspapermen, cartoonists, political leaders, poets, scholars, all helped to popularize the Polish cause. Now, it was "the glory that is Poland," not the "glory that was Poland." Even the German Field Marshal Kesselring, who directed the German Luftwaffe in the German-Polish campaign, paid tribute to the Polish armed forces who bore the brunt of the fighting against Nazi Germany. The Poles not only upset the timetable of the ruthless Germans, but they gave the Allies a breathing spell.

> The fighters of the Polish air force numerically and qualitatively claimed our respect, although their bombers lagged considerably behind.[14]

Kesselring also noted Warsaw's effective fighter planes and flak defense.

> I often visited the Stuka squadrons on their return from bombing raids over Warsaw, spoke with the crews about their impressions and inspected the damage where aircraft had been hit by flak. It was almost a miracle that some of them got home, so riddled were they with holes—halves of wings were ripped off, bottom planes torn away, and fuselages disembowelled with their control organs hanging by the thinnest threads.[15]

Kesselring also paid tribute to the Polish High Command that the Polish forces had enormous fighting spirit, and in spite of the disorganization and loss of communications, they were able to strike effectively at the German points of effort.

Peter Townsend also commented on the gallantry of the Polish airmen:

> Hopelessly inferior in numbers and equipment, the Polish airmen fought back with desperate gallantry. In a second assault on a Lublin airfield, Hajo Hermann's Heinkel III was attacked by a Polish fighter. "He was a marvelous fellow—he rolled over on his back and shot at me," said Hermann, who had to limp back on one engine.[16]

---

the ground by the hordes of barbarians, but that its culture will persist and its cities will rise like the phoenix from its ashes.

[14] Albert Kesselring, *Kesselring A Soldier's Record* (New York: 1954), p. 40.
[15] Ibid., p. 43.
[16] Peter Townsend, *Duel of Eagles* (New York: 1970), p. 193.

General Heinz Guderian, commander of the XIX Corps—containing one panzer and two motorized infantry divisions whose task was to advance from Pomerania, across the Brahe between Zempolno and Konitz, and move as far as possible to the Vistula, thus cutting off enemy forces in the Polish Corridor—also commented on the valor of the Polish forces.

> It was all too much for the Poles. They were simply overwhelmed. Courage, however, they were not short of. Guderian reported that on 3 September during the battle of the Corridor some of his panzers had been charged by a Polish Cavalry Brigade with sword and lance. Their losses were appalling. So were those of a Polish artillery regiment overrun by panzers (Hitler himself was astonished by the destruction when he visited on 5 September), of Polish infantry and of their supply columns.[17]

No food, no light, and, in addition, German air raids and constant shelling—such was the life of Warsaw where people worked for weeks constructing trenches, mine fields, tank traps and dugouts. They were machine-gunned and some of them were killed, but they carried on. Even young boys and old men took to the trenches to save Warsaw where the *blitzkrieg* was finally stopped, and the German advance terminated—by the trenches—they had dug only a few days before. Stopped at the city's outskirts, Hitler ordered his troops to dig in and the siege began. Julien Bryan, an American reporter, stranded in beleaguered Warsaw, captured much of its spirit and suffering on film. His camera lens documented for all times the bestiality of the Germans.

> Is an old wooden church in a workingmen's section a military objective? Is a Catholic hospital a military objective? Are tenement houses in the poor quarters of a city military objectives? Are the tombs of the dead military objectives? The human eye may deceive an observer. The human tongue may hide the truth. But the camera lens is as ruthless in the depiction of actuality as totalitarian rulers are in falsifying it. Bryan had not set out to hunt for atrocities. He is a reporter with a soul of an artist and is interested primarily in human beings. He wanted to record life as it was lived by the common man

---

[17] John Strawson, *Hitler's Battles for Europe* (New York: 1971), p. 91.

in a modern city under siege—and not death! The fact that most of his pictures were taken in the poorer quarters of the city or its outskirts, in fields where people were working, only emphasizes the utter lack of military justification for the deeds of *Schrecklichkeit* which his words and pictures so unforgettably reveal.[18]

The "lightning campaign" against Poland was no easy undertaking. The Poles put up a stubborn resistance, and although the campaign lasted only four weeks in all, the Luftwaffe lost during that time no less than 743 men and 285 aircraft, including 109 bombers and Stukas. Dire distress and hardships pervaded the postwar scene. Partitioned Poland now numbered thousands of orphans and widows, cripples and invalids, psychotics and persons otherwise disabled. Countless families were severely undernourished and underclad; and all this against a background of scorched fields, idle factories, and desolate towns and villages.

Reverberations of this desperate conflict in eastern Europe interrupted the course of the Polish-American communities. All America was outraged when the news of the German invasion of defenseless Poland crossed the Atlantic. A shudder of horror ran through the Polish-American communities.

> It was well-nigh impossible to describe the pain which Polish Americans endured when Hitler and Stalin invaded and conquered and partitioned Poland. Pain is the word. It was literally physical with many. They huddled around radios, unable to restrain sudden sharp, agonized cries of hurt outrage, hate. Many suffered more acutely during the bombings of Warsaw than they might have were devastation and falling debris overwhelming their own homes in Chicago, Buffalo or Detroit.[19]

Members of the Polish-American communities, as they awaited details of the invasion, remembered the great days that had been lived, the great things that had been achieved, among them the restoration of Poland, through a mysterious dedication that had enabled hundreds of thousands of young men to serve something greater than themselves during World War I. They were filled with admiration for the Polish army which desperately resisted

---
[18] Julien Bryan, *Siege* (New York: 1940), pp. 10-11.
[19] Louis Adamic, *Two-Way Passage* (New York: 1941), p. 135.

German advances in Poland. The Polish army left no doubt of its valor. It was Poland's finest hour and greatest story.

When the Polish armies were routed and Warsaw had fallen to the Germans, third and fourth generation Americans of Polish descent, or Americans living for three or more generations, who were partly Polish—were often filled with more emotion and greater pain than the children of the immigrants; for unlike the latter, they in most cases did not need to work out those immigrant feelings or struggle with their identity. One young third-generation American, who was half Polish, one-fourth German and one-fourth old stock American—scarcely slept during the first two weeks of September 1939. When he did fall asleep, he would wake up weeping.[20] Nationality had become important because the grandchildren expected it to compensate for the loss of the stable and traditional cultures of their parents. It also reflected a desire for national identification, a wish to be proud of the group to which one belonged. They wanted the entire world to know that they were of Polish descent and they did.

On October 15, 1939 more than 100,000 Americans of Polish descent—most of them in tears—marched up Fifth Avenue in the third annual General Pulaski Day parade. The great celebration was likened to a funeral procession with many non-Poles sobbing on the sidewalks. Francis Cardinal Spellman was the chief reviewing officer at St. Patrick's Cathedral. Ted Maksymowicz, dressed in a costume similar to that of the trumpeter of Krakow, sounded the traditional Polish call to arms, the Heynal, in front of St. Patrick's Cathedral. The bugle call, which was sounded hourly in Warsaw, during the Nazi invasion, brought a grim reminder to Fifth Avenue that Poles were dying at that particular moment, victims of German and Russian aggression. Later that evening some 15,000 crowded into the 163rd Regiment Armory for a General Pulaski Memorial Service. Former President Hoover told the audience: "The spirit of a great race does not die from oppression. Poland is not dead. Poland will rise again." Archbishop Spellman—at a Mass in St. Patrick's Cathedral opening "Polish Day" at the World's Fair—said from the pulpit: "As one

---

[20] Adamic, *op. cit.*, p. 138.

who mingled with Polish people, who attended seminaries with Poles, who has read the history of Poland, who knows Poland and loves her, I offer you my sympathy and I wish to encourage the people of Poland, as Pope Pius XII has said, and so do I say, Poland will never die."

The outbreak of World War II found the Polish-American community unprepared for any political activity on behalf of Poland. The tragedy of destruction and occupation of Poland by Germany, the treacherous stab in the back of September 17, the heroic battles of the Polish army—whose culminating exploits were the defense of Westerplatte and of Warsaw, the transfer of the Polish Government to Romanian territory, and its internment there, the formation of a new government in Paris—all of these historical events, following the unparalleled calamity that befell the Polish State and the Polish people—had failed to produce a political response from the Polish-American community.

Not a single Polish word was heard in the U.S. Congress during the months of Poland's struggle. No declaration had been made in the name of the Polish-American community condemning the Fourth Partition of Poland. The major Polish-American fraternals had expressed in fervent words their sympathy in the tragedy of the Polish nation and had passed corresponding resolutions. However, there is a vast distance between resolutions and political action.

When the Council for Polish Relief was founded, it was assumed that this organization would also undertake the political representation of the vast masses of Americans of Polish descent and the Polish-American communities. There was hope that the Polish Council would formulate a program of action as the representatives of six million Americans of Polish descent, and begin to act in defense of the independence of the Polish State. These hopes were futile. The Council restricted itself to only one phase of aid to Poland: relief. To obtain funds for relief they staged rallies and benefit programs. They also offered prayers in their churches.[21]

---

[21] As early as August 29, 1939, while there was still the fervent hope that the crisis would be averted, the Polish Consulate reported that more than one million dollars was sent to Warsaw in the previous month. *New York Times* (August 29, 1939).

It was the Polish-American Council, which considered itself to be the central organization of the Polish-Americans, and which was not fulfilling its role as the representative body, that caused the complete inactivity for the Polish Cause, which was reflected in the attitude of the American people and the U.S. Government. Two other factors contributed to this stagnation: the first was American neutrality, which the Polish-American Council, together with the fraternal orders had not been able to reconcile with the political problems of Poland, thereby formulating a positive appeal to demand aid in the defense of Poland's independence. The second factor was the attitude of the Polish Government in London and its representatives in the United States. General Sikorski and Mikolajczyk believed that the matter of defense of Poland's rights should be left to the competence of the Polish Government, and that any action, undertaken by Americans of Polish descent in this field, was neither necessary nor helpful.[22]

To obtain support for the Polish cause, in the early stages of World War II, the Polish government-in-exile made attempts to revive the extreme Polish nationalism of World War I in the Polish immigrants and their descendants in America. The attempt—made through the *Polish Review*, a periodical published in New York by the Polish political exiles—failed.[23]

---

[22] The five years of Polish participation in the Second World War were marked by three characteristics. The German invader, who occupied the major part of ethnically Polish territory, was unable to induce any of the representative figures of the nation to play the ignominious role of "Polish Quislings." The attitude of the Polish masses was one of determined resistance which even the terror of the SS and the Gestapo failed to break.

Secondly, a relatively large part of the Polish governmental apparatus and a sizable contingent of the army managed to find their way to the West. There, the armed forces were increased in size by conscripts and volunteers from among Polish nationals living abroad. In the middle of 1942, the army of General Wladyslaw Anders was transferred from the Soviet Union to the Middle East and later to Africa. As a result, the Polish Government in London, disposed of considerable armed forces which greatly contributed to the combined Allied war effort.

The third characteristic was the ability of the exiled government to maintain a considerable degree of consistency despite the immense pressures to which it was exposed. Equally remarkable was the capability of the Polish exiles to maintain contacts with the representatives of the non-communist underground military organization on Polish soil.

[23] Each issue of the *Polish Review* contained one or more articles either on the fighting which was carried on by the Poles dispersed over the various continents, or

THE VALIANT YEARS (1939-1945)   357

In 1941, the Polish and Canadian military authorities opened a camp at Owen Sound, Ontario for the training of Americans of Polish descent volunteering for service in the Polish Army.[24] On October 25, 1941, *Dziennik Dla Wszystkich* reported that eight Americans of Polish descent were serving in the Polish Army.[25] On October 30, 1941, it reported that Jan Kurek and Mieczyslaw Lukasik joined the Polish Air Force.[26] On November 25, 1941, it reported that the following Americans of non-Polish descent joined the Polish Army: Ralph Alobr, Edmund Bushaw, Edward Sauciunas, Scott McCrossen and George Schumaker.[27] Ryszard Wansort from Buffalo, New York and Jan Racinowski from Batavia, New York also joined the Polish Army.[28] Several days later, *Dziennik Dla Wszystkich* reported that Ludwik Pietruszka, Ryszard Wansart and Edwin Bashau joined the Polish Army.[29]

---

on the "glorious past" of the Polish nation. Additional articles dealt with the activities of the Polish exiles in London; the activities of the Germans in Poland; and the activities of the Polish underground in Poland. There was very little discussion of the existing Polish political parties. The Russian communists were ignored; and only a few remarks were included on the Polish Government-in-Exile, in London.

Each issue also contained one article, usually illustrated, concerning the artistic work of one or more Polish artists, writers or composers. Artists, writers, or composers of non-Polish background were either ignored or mentioned only in reference to a Polish situation. The *Polish Review* appeals were directed toward a rather highly educated group of Americans of Polish descent. This was a departure from the publications of the earlier years. The adjustment to the higher educational and social economic level of the Americans of Polish descent, and the various appeals did not produce the same type of nationalistic activity as had the earlier pre-World War I publications.

[24] During World War II, the United States Government permitted American citizens to volunteer for service in Allied armies on condition they do not swear allegiance to the Allied countries. General Sikorski made this arrangement with the United States government.

[25] They were: Stefan Lwowski (Plainfield, N. J.), Edward Chledowski (Chicago, Ill.), Jozef Skiba (Brooklyn, N. Y.), Tadeusz Jaskolski (Chelsea, Mass.), Edward Skupienski (Phoenix, Ill.), Eugenjusz Rybarczyk (Terryville, Conn.), Edward Pietrzak (Chicago, Ill.), and Wieslaw H. Dziulikowski (Passaic, N. J.). "Pierwsze Awanse. W Wojsku Polskim w Kanadzie Nastapily Juz Pierwsze Awanse," *Dziennik Dla Wszystkich* (October 25, 1941), p. 3.

[26] "Do Windsoru Do Armji Polskiej w Kanadzie Wyjechali Jednoczesnie Dwaj Mlodzi Przedstawiciele Buffalo," *Dziennik Dla Wszystkich* (October 30, 1941), p. 2.

[27] "Ochotnicy z Buffalo i Okolicy Zwieksztaja Szeregi Armji Polskiej," *Dziennik Dla Wszystkich* (November 25, 1941), p. 14.

[28] *Ibid.*, p. 14.

[29] *Dziennik Dla Wszystkich* (November 29, 1941), p. 5.

General Sikorski and other prominent Polish leaders made extensive tours in the United States visiting the Polish-American communities in the larger cities, often in the company of national and local fraternal leaders. In community after community, they delivered numerous speeches urging Polish-American residents to participate actively in World War II. Local prominent fraternal and church leaders were lending their names and efforts to the cause. The recruitment did not go well. General Sikorski and the Polish Goevrnment-in-Exile overestimated the probable response of the younger Americans of Polish descent. These young people were willing to fight, but only in the American army.

Even the first generation immigrants, who came to America before World War II, did not show much interest in joining the Polish Army in England that was to fight against Germany in order to free Poland. Refugees and dignitaries, recently from Poland, did not do so either; and a good many of them were not even interested sufficiently to work or speak on behalf of recruiting soldiers for the noble cause.[30]

When General Sikorski made his second trip to America, he accused the Polish-American community of not doing its part in helping Poland. His remarks antagonized Americans of Polish descent, and several voices were heard which reflected the change of attitude from that of the situation of World War I. The PNA *Alliance Daily* reported: "We have our own problems."[31] The poor response to the recruitment campaigns, the lack of a central Polish-American Association, and the concern with American war problems—all had indicated, beyond doubt, that the Polish-American community's attention was no longer concentrated on Poland. Furthermore, the presence of a legally accepted Polish Government-in-Exile, in London, prevented members of the Polish-American community from undertaking any political activity or task to speak on behalf of Poland. Not extreme nationalism, but rather an empathy for Poland and its people, was reflected in the Polish-American community. The number and size of contributions and assessments for Polish relief had been increased. In

---

[30] R. A. Schermerhorn, *These Our People* (Boston: 1949), p. 287.
[31] Dr. Karol Wachtl, *Polonja w Ameryce* (Philadelphia: 1944), p. 421.

addition, drives to raise funds for ambulances, surgical supplies, food and clothing for the Polish forces, were also organized.³²

World War II, however, did stimulate the Polish-American community's interest in international affairs and Poland. The Polish-American community was far from "Laodicean" in its support of President Roosevelt's action on behalf of the anti-Axis powers. The Lend-Lease Policy was loudly applauded. The Polish Army Veterans of America adopted, on April 3, 1921, a resolution which recommended that President Roosevelt secure the cooperation of Great Britain in developing a program which would render effective aid to Poland. The Polish-American community also approved, in November 1931, President Roosevelt's repeal of the Neutrality Act. Council Six of the Polish Roman Catholic Union voted unanimously to assure President Roosevelt that it favored the repeal.³³ When in mid-August 1941 Winston Churchill and President Roosevelt drew up the Atlantic Charter, the Polish-American community hailed the eight point statement of peaceful aims as just and equitable, and as the "supreme achievement of our international political activity."³⁴

In the autumn of 1941 and during the winter of 1941-1942, a number of Polish-American groups—headed by the Association of National Defense in New York and the Committee of National Defense in Detroit—proceeded with their work towards the creation of a Polish-American organization whose sole aim would be to fight for Poland's political rights and a vigorous support of American efforts to bring the war to a victory, which would assure peace throughout the world based on the principles of the Atlantic Charter.

These organizations—schooled in the spirit of Jozef Pilsudski's political philosophy—endeavored to draw up a program for the Polish-American community, which would give moral support to

---

³² Members of the Polish National Alliance voluntarily submitted to a five cents a month assessment, per member, for the Polish War Relief Fund which amounted to $786,307.29 according to the Polish National Alliance treasurer's report, in April 1951. M. Tomaszkiewicz, "Na Fundusz Ratunkowy," *Zgoda* (April 15, 1951), p. 2.

³³ United States Congress, *Congressional Record*, 77th Congress, 1st Session, p. A 5036.

³⁴ F. F. Wassell, *Attitudes of the Various Polish-American Organizations Toward American Foreign Policy Affecting Poland: 1939-1945* (unpublished Master's thesis, Columbia University, 1946), p. 42.

the Polish nation still carrying on the heroic struggle for its independence; it would also reveal the danger threatening Poland, not only from Germany, but also from Russia. This was particularly imperative since the conciliatory policy of Great Britain and the United States toward Russia, as well as the policy of the Polish Government-in-Exile, in London—moving in the orbit of the great Allies—was often misleading Americans because of the frequent concealment of the true facts: viz., Soviet Russia's hostile attitude towards Poland.[35]

The basic program of their political activity was expressed in their memorandum of May 12, 1941, signed by over 100 persons from various cities of the United States. This was submitted to President Roosevelt by a number of prominent representative Americans of Polish descent headed by Maximilliam F. Wegrzynek. This memorandum—the first political document issued by Americans of Polish descent on the Polish cause, during World War II—had pointed out the necessity of reconstructing Poland within its September 1, 1939 boundaries in the East and enlarged in the West—a Poland with a free Baltic coast and a free Lithuania, Latvia and Estonia, in agreement with the principles of the Atlantic Charter.

This appeal was submitted at the moment when Molotov was visiting London and Washington, endeavoring, even then, to secure the approval of England and the United States for the

---

[35] Binen Heller, a Pole of Jewish descent, wrote an anti-Nazi poem entitled "Warsaw, 1939" and sent it to a Moscow publication, early in 1940. It was rejected. Another refugee writer made the following comment: "The only thing allowed us, demanded of us, in fact, was to write about the anti-Semitism of the former Polish rulers." Yehoshua A. Gilboa, *The Black Years of Soviet Jewry 1939-1953* (Boston: 1971), p. 19.

Henryk Erlich and Victor Alter, leaders of the Jewish Socialist Bund of Poland, had escaped in September 1939 from the German occupied part of Poland to the area annexed by the Red Army. They were arrested shortly afterwards on charges of collaborating with the Polish secret police and planning to commit acts of sabotage in the Soviet Union. They were taken to Moscow for questioning. After their release from prison, on September 24, 1941, Erlich and Alter notified the Polish ambassador in Moscow, Stanislaw Kot, that they had addressed an appeal to the Polish Jews in the USSR to enlist in the Polish forces that were then being organized on Soviet soil "in order to restore Poland's right to a life of freedom, and in order to liberate the world from brown (Nazi) servitude." On October 15, 1941, Erlich and Alter were evacuated from Moscow to Kuibyshev. On December 4, 1941, Erlich and Alter were arrested again; shortly afterwards they were shot. Gilboa, *The Black Years of Soviet Jewry 1939-1953*, pp. 43-45.

Fifth Partition of Poland. The appeal to President Roosevelt revealed Russia's intention to carry through such a partition; whereas the Polish Government-in-Exile—which was the most competent body to act in this respect—was concealing the true facts.

As a result of this memorandum, a convention was held in New York City on June 20-21, 1942, in which delegates of the various organizations took part. A resolution was passed calling for the creation of a political organization of Americans of Polish descent under the name of National Committee of Americans of Polish descent. Some of the objectives of this new organization were:

> Defense and maintenance of the sovereignty and integrity of the Polish State evolving from its history, its treaties and international law.
> Cultivation among Americans of Polish descent, the realization of their duties of steady loyalty to the United States and steadily increasing activity for the benefit of the United States.
> Initiation of the American people in the historical role of the Polish State and its importance as a bastion resisting aggressive imperialistic doctrines.

The prominent leader and editor of the Polish *Nowy Swiat*, M. F. Wegrzynek, was elected president of the new National Committee of Americans of Polish descent.[36] The National Committee's political activity was manifested in a number of statements published by the Executive Board, which proclaimed a decisive and uncompromising defense of Poland's rights. This defense—conducted in a daring and outspoken manner—was resisting all attempts on the part of other elements whose intention was to submerge Poland's rights. The National Committee not only took issue with Poland's enemies, the Germans and the Soviets, but also adopted a critical attitude toward the policies of England and America, whenever these policies deviated from the principles of the Atlantic Charter and threatened the interests of America and Poland.

The course of events had forced the National Committee to

---

[36] Wegrzynek held this post until his death on November 8, 1945.

view with a good deal of criticism the policy followed by the Polish Government-in-Exile, in London, under the leadership of General Sikorski and Premier Mikolajczyk. This was due to the latter's submissive attitude in the face of increasing Soviet danger to Poland, a danger that was threatening Poland's independence and integrity. The members of the Polish Government-in-Exile continually concealed the true facts of the attempts made on the rights of Poland and those of her citizens.

The decided stand of the National Committee Executives and of its members—and in particular, the unyielding attitude of its President, M. Wegrzynek—had assured a uniform challenging course for the organization in its struggle for Poland's independence. The political line followed by the National Committee was reflected most clearly in its press organ, *The Organization Bulletin*. In a number of important articles, frequently containing ideas and conceptions well in advance of the course of events, this publication gave direction to Polish political thought and voiced the necessity of defending the principles and ideals of America as well as the duty of applying them in our foreign policy. The *Bulletin* soon extended its influence to other continents, and became one of the most important organs voicing Polish independence as well as American political thought.

An individual who devoted much work and thought to the molding of the National Committee's ideology was Ignacy Matuszewski.[37] He had brought into the organization his creative mind, his far-seeing political conceptions, his knowledge of the people involved, and all the ramifications of international relations. His voice was a guide and his unyielding attitude and devotion to the Cause were the conscience of those who united in the struggle for the defense of Poland.

Apart from the *Bulletin* the National Committee published a number of pamphlets in Polish and English. The total number distributed reached 230,000 copies. These pamphlets—written by

---

[37] Colonel Ignacy Matuszewski arrived in the United States in the fall of 1941. He started animating the Polish-American press by his journalistic talents and his super-nationalistic ideology. He became the political writer of *Nowy Swiat*, a Polish language paper published in New York City by a wealthy prewar importer of Polish hams, Maximilian Wegrzynek, who also was a publisher of a super-nationalistic Hungarian paper.

THE VALIANT YEARS (1939-1945)   363

prominent Polish and English authors—served to acquaint the American people with the Polish cause. The entire organization of the National Committee made an effort to distribute this literature as widely as possible.

After two years of the National Committee's activity (all due to President Wegrzynek's efforts) a league of Polish-American organizations was formed under the name of the "Coordinating Committee of Polish-American Associations in the East." Its purpose was to steer such organizations unto the proper path of political activity for the Polish Cause. M. F. Wegrzynek became President of this organization. In the course of further developments, the Polish American Congress came into being at a convention in Buffalo, May 28 and 30, 1944. Karol Rozmarek, President of the Polish National Alliance, was elected President of the Polish American Congress.

All the members of the National Committee welcomed with joy this organization of the Polish-American communities whose purpose was the defense of Poland's rights. The president of the National Committee was elected vice-president of the Polish American Congress, and in addition, a delegate of the National Committee was included on the Board of Directors of the Congress. The inclusion of many members of the National Committee on the Executive Board of the Polish American Congress and the State Divisions enabled both organizations to establish fruitful collaboration.

As a member of the Polish American Congress, the National Committee retained its structure as an organization, and continued to follow the course of its work for Poland that had been set forth for the last few years. The Polish American Congress is an Association of numerous social and professional organizations. The National Committee is an organization of individuals, taking part in the independent movement, in comformity with their fifty-year-old tradition. The National Committee is a fighting organization, keenly reacting to the course of events, and in many instances preparing the group for further political action.

In 1940, America passed the Selective Service Act. Also, America sent old destroyers and bundles to Britain, and protests to Tokyo and Berlin. Time and two oceans, Americans hoped, would take care of the rest.

Meanwhile, Americans earned a living, went to the movies and read *How to Win Friends and Influence People* by Dale Carnegie. However, not all Americans were so complacent. Members of the Polish-American communities immediately condemned the Germans who had committed nameless and shocking atrocities, crimes against humanity, offenses not justified in the name of war, horrors not usually incident to armed conflicts, in their drive to deprive the citizens of the Polish State of life, liberty and the pursuit of happiness. During the next six years of the Second World War, Americans of Polish descent expressed more fully their newly discovered capacities. Among the first, who flocked to the colors, was Lieutenant Bronislaw Godlewski of Chicago. Only seventeen, he was rejected by the American army, but managed to join the Polish Air Force. Patriotism and the inspiration of duty were his motives. He won three national decorations for bravery: Polish, British and American.

CHAPTER 12

In the Service of Their Country

*"Abysmy mogli byc z nich dumni"**

The Japanese sudden and deliberate attack on the U.S. Naval base, at Pearl Harbor, in the Hawaiian Islands, plunged the United States into World War II. Before the attack by carrier-borne Japanese airplanes was over, 19 U.S. warships were sunk or disabled, 150 airplanes were lost, and more than 2,000 servicemen were dead. One of the battleships sunk in the attack was the heavily gunned, 32,000-ton warship, the *Arizona*. Among the 1,102 Navy dead, locked within the rusted hull, were the following Americans of Polish descent from the State of Michigan: Clarence William Lipke, Theophil Czekajski, Joseph Baraga, Stanley Czarnecki, Edwin C. Jastrzemski, and John Stanley Malinowski. A few hours after the Japanese attack on Pearl Harbor, the War Department notified Peter Niedzwiecki of Grand Rapids, Michigan, that his son, Robert, had fallen in the attack.

During the extended conflict Polish-Americans supported the war effort with undiminished energy and devotion. Although the American soldiers of Polish descent had no fortitude for fighting or glory for their own sake, they became prominent on all fronts, and in all fighting forces. They took part in the fiercest fighting whether the infantry, cavalry or armored units; they also served in artillery and tank brigades, on warships and submarines. They excelled in airborne operations as pilots. Their service in reconnaissance and intelligence units, in front-line medical and engineerng corps, and their contributions to the development of

---
* "So that we could feel proud of them."

weapons (Stan Ulam for example) were significant and deserve mention.

After Pearl Harbor, the following immediately joined the U.S. Navy: Czeslaw P. Nabywaniec, Julius F. Ostrowski, Henryk J. Jakubowski, Leon S. Szatkowski, and Jan S. Slawisz.[1] Stanley Szczechowski, commander of General Krzyzanowski Garrison, N. 298, sent the following telegram to Franklin D. Roosevelt:

> We the members of General Krzyzanowski Garrison, No. 298 Army and Navy Union, U.S.A. assembled at our regular meeting Wednesday, December 10, pledge our full support and loyalty, and are at your disposal for any service you see fit.[2]

Many of the officers in the armed forces were civilians drafted for service. Americans of Polish descent learned quickly the art of command and often showed remarkable qualities of leadership. Many gained the headlines by their heroic exploits which established American military power in the skies during the twentieth century. Many were named for the Medal of Honor award and were added to America's roster of heroes.[3]

The first American flyer, who became a German prisoner in World War II, was Lt. Clarence Lipski of Great Neck, Long Island, New York. For a while he was regarded as the first American hero lost on a bombing mission over Northern France. He fell into German captivity when the Flying Fortress, piloted by him, was shot and downed by a Nazi barrage.

Frank Gabreski was not an aviation enthusiast as a young man in Oil City, Pennsylvania. While enrolled as a pre-medical

---

[1] *Dziennik Dla Wszystkich* (December 9, 1941), p. 12.
[2] *Dziennik Dla Wszystkich* (December 11, 1941), p. 16.
[3] It was during the Civil War, while the Medal of Honor requirements were being formulated that an unidentified Senator said: "Honor is something that no real soldier likes to talk about. Those that want to honor him should provide him with a token that he can wear without words." The Medal of Honor originated in 1861. It was enacted by law, in 1863, by President Abraham Lincoln. The Medal of Honor is the highest military award for bravery that can be presented by the United States of America. The decoration is presented to its recipients by the President or a high government official "in the name of the Congress of the United States,"—and because of this it is very often called the "Congressional Medal of Honor." Since World War I, the Medal of Honor is awarded to members of the American armed forces "for a deed of personal bravery or self-sacrifice, above and beyond the call of duty in actual combat with an enemy of the nation."

student at Notre Dame University, he developed an interest in aviation. Eventually he left Notre Dame University to enter the Army Air Force's Aviation Cadet Program. When America was plunged into World War II, Gabreski was stationed at Pearl Harbor. When he finally got into the air on that fateful day, the Japanese attackers were gone. A few weeks later he was ordered to England where he initially flew combat with one of the Polish squadrons of the Royal Air Force. His days with the Poles didn't result in any victories, but from them he did gain a determination and aggressiveness that was to make him one of the great fighter pilots of the war. From the Poles he also learned the tactics of closing with the enemy to the point that you just couldn't miss.[4]

When Gabreski joined the 56th Fighter Group of the 8th Air Force, he proved himself a good commander in the air, and when he learned the ruggedness of the P-47, he began to run up his score. Gabreski became an ace on November 26, 1943, and as he put in more escort missions with the bombers, his tally of strikes grew steadily. At the time of the Allied invasion of the Continent, on June 6, 1944, Gabreski had 21 victories to his credit. The day after D-Day two 109s and a Focke Wulf 190 fell before his guns. By the end of June his score stood at twenty-seven. On July 5th, he got number twenty-eight. This was to be his last victory in World War II, but his total would never be surpassed in the European Theater of War.

Gabreski flew his 166th mission on the 20th of July escorting bombers to Frankfurt, Germany. During his return, he led the fighters down to strafe a Luftwaffe airdrome. Making his second pass he got too low, bounced his F-47 on a knoll and bent his propeller. The resulting vibration was too much. He had to crash. For five days he managed to evade the enemy, but was finally caught and spent the remainder of the war in a German Stalag.[5]

Lieut. George A. Pucilowski, from Detroit, roamed the European skies shooting down Nazi fighters, saving comrades' lives and collecting medals. He is the holder of the Distinguished Flying Cross and Air Medal with ten Oak Leaf Clusters. He was first

---

[4] William N. Hess, *The American Aces of World War II and Korea* (New York: 1968), p. 28.

based in England, then in Africa, and participated in most of the early fortress raids on Germany. He took part in the raid over Rotterdam, which is believed to have been the first battle in air history between heavy bombers without fighter escorts and enemy fighters. He earned the DFC after saving a fellow airman's life above Bizerte after his bomber, "Kowboy" had been crippled by flak. After administering first aid to two wounded crew members, he gave his own oxygen mask to one of the men and was credited with saving the flier's life. One of Lieut. Pucilowski's Oak Leaf Clusters is for the destruction of an ME 109 (Messerschmitt) over Cagliani, Sardinia. Lieut. Pucilowski flew 1,200 hours in completing fifty missions as a flying fortress bombadier during his overseas duty in North Africa and Europe. His combat career brought him the Air Medal eleven times.[6] His further quest for medals was terminated when he was selected to teach bombadiers his techniques.[7]

Lieut. Edward P. Maliszewski from Grosse Pointe Park, Michigan was a co-pilot of a Flying Fortress which fought off thirty German planes while returning to an English base following a bombing assignment over Lille, France. Lieut. Maliszewski brought down four to eight of the German planes and got back to England with one motor dead, the controls half frozen and the wing tip "foiled up like a sardine can." The plane was virtually riddled with enemy shells. King George VI saw the Fortress on its return and remarked: "It is a marvel that it could ever come back." When the Flying Fortresses made their damaging assault on Nazi naval installations and submarine yards at Kiel and Flensburg, Lieut. Maliszewski was at the controls of one of the big bombers. Lieut. Maliszewski has been awarded two Distinguished Flying Crosses, the Purple Heart and the Air Medal with a string of Oak Leaf Clusters. One of the medals was presented personally by King George VI.

Staff Sgt. Edward A. Piotrowski, of Dearborn, Michigan, is a

---

[5] He saw duty again in the Korean War.
[6] "Wins Air Force Medal," *Detroit News* (May 2, 1947).
[7] "Detroit To Rouen Bombadier Takes His Aim at Nazis," *Detroit News* (August 19, 1942). "Hero and His 12 Decorations Back," *Detroit Free Press* (October 6, 1943).

IN THE SERVICE OF THEIR COUNTRY

veteran of fifty flights over Axis targets in the Mediterranean. He received the DFC and the Air Medal. To the cluster are appended thirteen Oak Leaf Clusters, each representing an act sufficiently meritorious to win him the Air Medal again. His peak adventure came when he had fired all his ammunition except one round at an attacking Messerschmitt. The German plane spat bullets as it plunged toward him. Piotrowski waited until it was within thirty yards and let go his final round. The German went down and the Sergeant placed another notch on his gun.[8]

Pfc. Edward J. Knieja has been commended both by the Marine Corps and the Navy for heroism in taxiing Marine and Navy planes to safety while Henderson Field, on Guadalcanal, was under heavy Japanese attack. Knieja has also been awarded the Legion of Merit with a presidential citation for the same "dauntless courage and for exceptionally meritorious conduct and outstanding services while with a Marine scout bombing squadron from October 13, 1942 to December 13, 1942." His citation read in part: "During this period of intense hostile activity, the then Pfc. Knieja served as a plane mechanic with highly commendable skill. He disregarded many air raid alarms and constantly stood by his ship at great personal risk to complete repairs and preparations for its missions. Once, when an artillery shell exploded between the aircraft and himself, Knieja disregarding his own safety, taxied his plane to a less dangerous area, where he readied it for action."[9]

Staff Sgt. Joseph Sawicki—whose parents were born in Poland—has been given the Polish Cross of Valor, the highest honor given by the Polish Government-in-Exile for his part in a bombing raid on Gdynia, Poland. The entire squadron volunteered for the assignment, and participants had to be selected by number. Sawicki offered half a month's pay to any man who would give him a winning number. Sgt. Sawicki, who joined the Polish Air Force in 1941, participated in numerous raids over Germany and enemy territory was a tail gunner of the Polish manned *Welling-*

---

[8] "Dearborn Gunner is Cited 15 Times," *Detroit News* (August 6, 1943).
[9] *Detroit News* (June 14, 1943). *Detroit News* (October 29, 1943). Knieja graduated from Chadsey High School, Detroit, in 1934. He enlisted in April 1942.

ton, before switching to a Flying Fortress. Sgt. Sawicki won the U.S. Air Medal and an Oak Leaf Cluster.[10]

Staff Sgt. Thomas F. Kusowski, at the age of seventeen, was awarded the Army Air Force Medal for exceptionally meritorious service as an aerial gunner on a foray against the German submarine base at Lorient, France. He was credited with shooting down a German plane that attacked the Flying Fortress on which he was a gunner.

For extraordinary heroism and achievement, Corporal Gerald J. Bogacki, of Detroit, was awarded the Oak Leaf Cluster in lieu of an additional Distinguished Flying Cross. Corporal Bogacki's citation is for "extraordinary achievement while participating in operational flight missions . . . dropping supplies and transporting troops at advanced positions. The flights involved flying at dangerous altitudes over mountainous terrain under adverse weather conditions, and often necessitated landings within a few miles of enemy bases."[11]

Sgt. Thomas Klimaszefski, of Alpena, Michigan—a radioman of the famous "Ten Dead Men" flying fortress—received an Air Medal for service in North Africa. Ernie Pyle told the story of Sgt. Klimaszefski in three dispatches to the *Detroit Free Press.* He wrote of them as "ten dead men who came back to their base in North Africa with their crippled Flying Fortress—two motors shot away—after flying across mountains where the lowest pass was 1,600 feet—with an altitude of 1,500 feet."

Lieut. Edward F. Koziarski, of Detroit, also received the DFC. A flying navigator, he was a member of a bomber group cited by the President for the bombings of the Muhlembau Aircraft assembly plants at Brunswick, Germany. His unit, a part of the 3rd Air Division, was also cited for the shuttle bombing of Regensburg, in August 1943.

Captain Walter J. Koraleski, of Detroit, was awarded the DFC for shooting down a German plane, almost in the shadow of the Eiffel Tower. Koraleski's plane was attacked at house top level, over Paris, by two German fighters. In the fight that fol-

---

[10] "Bombing of Polish City Wins Flier Polish Medal," *Detroit Free Press* (December 3, 1943).

[11] *Detroit News* (September 21, 1943).

lowed, Koraleski took credit for one of the enemy planes and his wingman shot the other.[12] He also received the Air Medal with three Oak Leaf Clusters and a Silver Star for driving off an attack on two straggling bombers by nine German fighter planes. His further exploits were terminated when he became a German prisoner of war, in 1944. A veteran of seventy-six missions, he was a flight leader in the Thunderbolt squadron, in England.[13]

Staff Sgt. Michael Zuk, of Detroit, was awarded the Distinguished Flying Cross and ten presentations of the Air Medal, with a Silver star and four bronze Leaf Clusters. Zuk was cited for the DFC for going to the aid of a wounded fellow-crew member—in spite of the risk of extreme cold when his heating suit was no longer attached to the plug—by using the incapacitated man's gun to drive off attacking planes.[34] On a previous occasion Zuk was part of the crew of the famous All-American, which flew back miraculously from a continental mission, almost severed by enemy fire, and actually broke in two upon landing.

T/Sgt. Henry H. Switanowski was awarded the DFC for climbing out into an exposed position without his parachute in order to free five bombs which had become jammed and endangered the safety of his plane.

Lt. Eugene A. Zielinski, from Detroit, earned the DFC and the Air Medal. Lieut. Zielinski was piloting a P-39 fighter when his fighter group fought off seven Japanese planes, downing five within a few minutes. Zielinski was credited with two Japanese planes. The Japanese raiding planes were attempting to break up an American bombing raid on Salamaua.

Lieut. Alvin Ignatowski completed thirty missions in the South Pacific. A navigator on a B-24 Liberator, he received the DFC with one Oak Leaf Cluster, the Air Medal with three clusters, and the Purple Heart.

Edward A. Jakubiak, navy aviation ordinanceman, has been posthumously awarded the Air Medal and the Gold Star for par-

---

[12] "Detroit Captain Decorated For Air Battle Over Paris," *The Detroit News* (March 2, 1944), p. 5.
[13] He was a graduate of Southeastern High, in Detroit.
[14] "11 Decorations for Detroiter," *Detroit News* (June 15, 1944).

ticipation in bombing missions against Japanese Forces in the Pacific area.[15]

Lieut. Raymond J. Jozefowicz, of Detroit, earned the DFC with three awards of the Air Medal for twenty-six strikes as pilot of a fighter bomber over the Japanese home islands.[16]

Henry Grabowski, radioman in the Air Force, of Detroit, was one of the first Navy airmen to fly over Japanese home territory on bombing missions. He received the Air Medal.[17]

Pfc. Alexander Galek, of Detroit, won the Soldier's Medal for rescuing fellow members of his crew when their plane crashed in flames.[18]

Staff Sgt. Charlie Grudnicki was awarded the DFC for "marked ability and heroic devotion to duty." He also received the Air Medal.[19]

Tech. Sgt. William S. Lukasik, from Detroit, received the DFC. He also holds the Air Medal and three Oak Leaf Clusters. As a Flying Fortress aerial gunner, he received the DFC for extraordinary achievement. He completed twenty-five bombing assaults on continental Europe.

Sgt. Stanley T. Maciejewski, who received the DFC, was a radio operator and a gunner on a Flying Fortress.

Lt. Louis J. Majewski, from Hamtramck, Michigan, received a DFC and the Air Medal and three Oak Leaf Clusters for missions over Europe, along with the Purple Heart.

Captain John Marusiak, from Hamtramck, Michigan, won the DFC, the Distinguished Unit Badge, and the Air Medal with eleven Oak Leaf Clusters.

Staff Sgt. Casimir A. Nastal, of Detroit, was a gunner in the famous "Memphis Belle" Flying Fortress. He received the DFC and the Air Medal with three clusters.

Staff Sgt. Theodore Nastal was a member of the famous "Thunderbird" flying fortress. He also won the DFC.

Lieut. Robert J. Nykiel, from Royal Oak, Michigan, a marine

---

[15] *Detroit News* (October 19, 1946).
[16] *Detroit News* (August 3, 1945).
[17] *Detroit Free Press* (June 30, 1944).
[18] *Detroit News* (November 6, 1944).
[19] A graduate of Chadsey High School, he enlisted in December 1941.

fighter bomber pilot, flew seventy missions from the Philippines. He won the DFC.

Ensign Mitchell G. Zbikowski, a veteran of eighty missions in the Pacific, is also a holder of the DFC.

Many others received the Distinguished Flying Cross and the Air Medal.[20]

The Navy Cross was awarded to Chief Machinist's Mate Walter Niemiec for his extraordinary heroism during a naval engagement with the Japanese, in the South Pacific, on August 9, 1942. Niemiec, who was seriously burned, finally collapsed while rescuing an engine crew that was trapped in the ship. The citation which he received from the Secretary of the Navy, Frank Knox and Admiral William F. Halsey, praised the veteran seaman for his courageous conduct. He fought his way through wreckage, fire and dense smoke to the compartment, previously abandoned, pried open a jammed door, and carried the men to safety. He continued to rescue the trapped men until he collapsed—the citation read. Niemiec had been in seventeen major engagements prior to this one, including Wake and Midway.[21]

Pfc. William L. Piaseczny, a graduate from Hamtramck High School, was awarded the Navy Cross for extraordinary heroism in action against an armed enemy on Guadalcanal. The citation,

---

[20] The Distinguished Flying Cross was also awarded to the following from Detroit, except where specifically indicated parenthetically elsewhere in Michigan: Staff Sgt. Frank Glenski, Staff Sgt. Barney J. Grabowski, Lt. Alfred P. Grodzicki, Lt. Stanley Holewinski, Staff Sgt. Casmer Juszczyk, Staff Sgt. Benedict Jozefowicz, Lieut. William F. Koniegska, Staff Sgt. Leonard S. Koscielny, Staff Sgt. John Kovaleski (Saginaw), Michael J. Kucyk (Wyandotte), Lieut. Louis J. Majewski (Hamtramck), Lt. Thaddeus J. Michalski, Tech. Sgt. John J. Niemiec, Tech. Sgt. Arthur D. Nowakowski, Lt. Leonard J. Olkowski (Dearborn), Tech. Sgt. Walter V. Olowniuk, Private Stephen Pelech (Hamtramck), Sgt. Alex Pesko, Captain Edwin F. Pezda (Hamtramck), Lt. Robert B. Pokorny, Staff Sgt. Theodore Poniewierski, Staff Sgt. Walter Pudlo (Hamtramck), Tech. Sgt. John C. Robak, Tech Sgt. Michael J. Siwek (Hamtramck), Staff Sgt. Henry J. Skorupski (Grand Rapids), Captain Thomas J. Sobieski, Richard J. Sulewski, Tech. Sgt. Joseph J. Stankevich, Lieut. John S. Stepanski, Staff Sgt. Norbert F. Swierz (Dowagiac), Lieut. Joseph Troyanowski, Staff Sgt. Zygmunt C. Warminski (Hamtramck), Staff Sgt. Ben J. Wdowicki, Staff Sgt. Frank E. Wilk (Romulus), Sgt. Frank J. Wilk (Dearborn), Lieut. Frank T. Wodzinski, Staff Sgt. Stanley Zaborowski, Stanley S. Zajac (St. Joseph), Staff Sgt. Steve J. Zajac and Lieut. Maryan J. Zaleski.

The Air Medal was awarded to the following officers from Detroit except where specifically indicated parenthetically elsewhere in Michigan: S/Sgt. Kajetan A. Jezalowicz, S/Sgt. Leo J. Kaminski, T/Sgt. Edward Korzeniewski, Sgt. Edward Koska, S/Sgt. Henry Kubinski (Hamtramck), Lt. Albert A. Kukurowski, S/Sgt.

by Admiral William F. Halsey reads: "During an engagement with the enemy, a member of Pfc. Piaseczny's platoon was wounded and fell in an exposed position. Two attempts to remove the wounded man failed and a hospital corpsman was killed in the third attempt. Pfc. Piaseczny demonstrated complete disregard for his own safety, moved forward under a hail of enemy fire and successfully removed his comrade to a place of safety."[22] Piaseczny also participated in the landing operations on Guadalcanal.

Walter J. Josefiak received the Silver Star for gallantry at Iwo Jima from President Truman. The citation lists the killing of three Japanese soldiers: one in hand-to-hand combat after Josefiak's rifle had jammed. He attacked the Japanese patrol of seven men single-handed, killing one and wounding another. Though seriously wounded, he fought through the engagement before accepting aid for his wounds. After graduating from DeLaSalle College, Josefiak joined the Marines in 1942.[23]

For twice charging pillboxes with his sub-machine gun and grenades—killing thirty-five Japanese soldiers—Marine Sgt. Steve Gerycz, of Detroit, was awarded the Navy Cross, the second highest citation for valor. Gerycz won his citation on Peleliu. According to the official statement, Gerycz took matters into his own hands on two occasions when his company's advance was halted by strategically placed Japanese emplacements. In both instances he rushed his position wiping out the defenders. A former machinist at the Detroit Seamless Tube Company, he enlisted in January 1942.[24]

Harry Kulchesky (Hamtramck), S/Sgt. Richard L. Lemanski, Lt. Edward J. Malinowski, Capt. John Marusiak (Hamtramck), S/Sgt. Stanley L. Motyka (Wyandotte), S/Sgt. Leo C. Naimolski, T/Sgt. William E. Nakonieczny, Sgt. Chester F. Nowakowski, Lt. Walter Nowicki, Lieut. Paul I. Paskiewicz, S/Sgt. Henry J. Pawelski, Sgt. Frank J. Pawlick (Saginaw), Sgt. Edward P. Pisarski (Hamtramck), Lieut. Frank P. Prokop, Sgt. George H. Pustelnik, Henry J. Pybik, Sgt. Edmund Rogowski, S/Sgt. Joseph J. Rzepka, Lieut. Leo A. Stopa, Sgt. Leo C. Suszek, T/Sgt. Edward Szemplewski, Lieut. Edward Szkodzinski, T/Sgt. Anthony C. Trebnik, Bernard J. Tyckoski (Flint), T/Sgt. Michael A. Urban, S/Sgt. Harry J. Waskewicz, Lt. Barney Wasowicz, Sgt. Walter C. Wawrzynek (Hamtramck) Edward A. Wesolowski (Hamtramck), S/Sgt. Carl S. Wydra, and S/Sgt. Michael Zuk.

[21] "A Detroiter Hero Wins Navy Cross," *Detroit News* (March 5, 1944).
[22] "Detroit Marine Wins Navy Cross," *Detroit News* (June 6, 1943).
[23] *Detroit Free Press* (March 29, 1943).
[24] *Detroit News* (May 24, 1945).

IN THE SERVICE OF THEIR COUNTRY 375

Marine Private Edward K. Koslowski, of Hamtramck, Michigan, was awarded the Silver Star "for conspicuous gallantry and intrepidity against the enemy," on Guadalcanal. He was credited with twice attempting to bring back wounded comrades from exposed positions. One died before rescue could be completed. The other was returned to safety. "At all times," the citation continues, "he demonstrated the highest courage and complete disregard for his own safety to aid his wounded comrades."

Steve Kubik from Imlay City, Michigan, a gunner's mate—who drifted in a lifeboat with nine others for forty-six days after their ship was torpedoed, in 1943—was awarded the Purple Heart for military merit. The ten men drifted more than 1,500 miles, their only food consisting of an occasional fish they were able to catch with a hook improvised from a bucket pail. They had blankets and a small quantity of water. One youth became insane and jumped overboard before a British warship rescued them.[25]

John Lesinski, Storekeeper Second Class, has been awarded the Navy Marine Corps Medal for bravery. He aided the wounded, although he had himself been hit, and the order to abandon ship had been given. Lesinski won his decoration at the Battle of Leyte Gulf when the destroyer escort, which he was serving, was hit by the Japanese.[26]

Pfc. Hubert D. Milanowski, a member of the Marine Corps, received the Silver Star Medal. During one of the heaviest Japanese attacks on Guadalcanal, Milanowski—assigned to a communication platoon—was separated from most of the unit. With four comrades he immediately set out for the front lines and engaged successfully in hand-to-hand combat with the enemy until wounds put him out of action.

Corporal John S. Stoklosa, from Detroit, was awarded the Silver Star Medal for conspicuous gallantry while the aircraft carrier Hornet was under heavy Japanese air attack. The citation accompanying Stoklosa's medal reads: "Jolted from the heat of his anti-aircraft gun by the concussion of an exploded bomb,

---

[25] *Detroit News* (February 20, 1944).
[26] He was the son of Congressman John Lesinski, Sr. from Detroit. He also served in Congress, replacing his father when he died.

Corporal Stoklosa, although severely wounded, immediately returned to his battle station and, without medical attention, continued his fire throughout the duration of the attack." During the battle of the Santa Cruz Islands, the Carrier Hornet was sunk. His brother, Peter Stoklosa, was killed on Guadalcanal.

Pfc. Edward J. Tarnowski, member of the Marine Corps, was decorated for braving surf and continuous enemy fire to save the life of a wounded companion. Seeing that cautious efforts were failing, Tarnowski plunged into the sea and rescued from drowning the wounded Marine in the face of fierce Japanese fire. This occurred during the island invasions in the Pacific.

Machinist Mate 2nd Class, Walter A. Wojciechowski was commended by the Navy for his part as member of the crew of a submarine which sank a light cruiser, a destroyer, and severely damaged another destroyer, in the South Pacific. Despite depth charge attacks the submarine and crew returned safely from their patrols.

Leo Zalewski was presented with the Bronze Medal by Captain H. S. Dilcher. A Navy yeoman, Zalewski was cited for heroic action in assuming command of a gun crew on his ship, off Okinawa, and helping to drive off a Japanese air attack.

Charles W. Lapinski, gunner's mate third class, was awarded a departmental citation for the oustanding performance of the Navy Armed Guard Crew, to which he was attached.

Marine Corporal Anthony E. Kujawinski from Grand Rapids, Michigan, received the Purple Heart and the Silver Star, for distinguished action in the Pacific.

Warrant Officer Leonard J. Lapinski was awarded the Bronze Star for heroism in New Guinea.

The Posthumous award of the Navy and Marine Corps Medal was made to Navy Lieut. Stephen G. Mroczkowski, who refused first aid, although mortally wounded. He aided in the removal of the crew to safety when his ship was sunk by a Japanese submarine.[27]

When the first Nazis shell hit him, Sgt. Martin W. Baginski of Detroit, didn't even duck. Things were happening too fast, and

---

[27] *Detroit News* (June 1, 1945).

he had to keep an eye on the approaching Panzer unit. The second shell hit him in the knee and Baginski had a hedgerow to hold on to. While under heavy fire, Sgt. Baginski left his fox hole to direct fire on German mortars and aid in capturing an enemy patrol. Then the third shell caught his hand and he went down. "By that time it was time for me to see what made my stomach hurt and why my right knee would not support me."[28] The doctors examined Baginski and found that shrapnel had entered his right lower abdomen and his knee cap. Baginski, who kept communication open near St. Lo—despite his injuries, directed the artillery fire which held off the Nazi thrust at the American lines —was awarded the Silver Star, the Bronze Star and the Purple Heart. For the drive from the Normandy beach to St. Lo, where he was wounded, Baginski also won a Presidential Unit Citation, awarded to the combat team composed of his unit, the 116th Infantry Regiment and the 29th Division. After three months in the hospital, Baginski was sent back to France where he interviewed battle-worn veterans and helped them calm their war-shattered nerves.

Willie Grabiarz—who was born February 23, 1923—joined the Army in 1941, when he was only eighteen, as a volunteer. He participated in five great battles in the Pacific. For his bravery he received nine distinctions—among them the Purple Heart. The nineteen-year-old soldier won the Congressional Medal of Honor posthumously. General Douglas MacArthur wrote the Buffalo lad's parents:

> His service under fire was characterized by his complete devotion to our beloved country . . . I have lost a gallant comrade-in-arms and with you mourn a splendid gentleman.[29]

When Grabiarz's commanding officer, First Lieutenant John J. Gregory, was wounded on the streets of Manila, on February 23, 1945, Grabiarz rushed to the side of Gregory, only to be wounded in the shoulder himself. Ignoring both pain and his injured useless arm and his comrades' shouts to seek cover, Grabiarz continued

---

[28] *Detroit Free Press* (August 8, 1944).
[29] Ellen Taussig, "The Polish Community Part I: 'We've Come A Long Way,'" *Buffalo Evening News* (November 13, 1973), p. B-5.

his efforts to drag Gregory out of range. Finding this impossible, he rejected the opportunity to save himself and deliberately covered Gregory with his own body to form a human shield, calling as he did so for a tank to maneuver into position between him and the hostile emplacement. Before the tank could interpose, Grabiarz was riddled with bullets—none of which struck his commander, who survived. Recently the "Scajaquada Creek Expressway," in Buffalo, was renamed "Grabiarz Expressway" in his memory. John J. Gregory, who still lives in Worcester, commended the Buffalo Council for honoring Grabiarz. He also stated: "I will never be able to express enough thanks for what he did. I remember him daily in my prayers."

T/Sgt. Walter J. Kumencki was wounded by a Nazi sniper in Italy's "No Man's Land"; he dodged more bullets for fifty hours, while hiding in foxholes, and then reached the safety of American lines. In a letter to his mother, he minimized his wound and the part he played in reaching a comrade during those fifty hours. But the Army release told the entire story. A tank in which he was riding was disabled near San Pietro. The commander was killed and the gunner wounded. Kumencki dragged the gunner out, but was shot in the hip by a sniper. He managed to drag himself and the gunner to a foxhole. Kumencki then left his foxhole to seek help, and upon his return, the gunner disappeared. Kumencki eventually got to the American lines, and then learned that American soldiers found the gunner and brought him to safety.[30]

Pvt. Edward A. Modrzejewski of Roseville, Michigan was awarded the Silver Star for leading an attack on a Japanese position at Buna, New Guinea. Lieut. General Robert L. Eichelberger, commander of Allied Forces in Papua, conferred the decoration. His citation of Modrzejewski read: "On November 30, he displayed exceptional courage while his company led a night attack. He averted a possible stalemate as members of his platoon advanced along the edge of a clearing, by leading the men forward

---

[30] "Detroit Hero's Exploit Bared by the Army," *Detroit Free Press* (March 14, 1944). He graduated from Hamtramck High School.

into enemy territory and aiding them to hold the vital position gained by the forced withdrawal of the enemy."[31]

For heroism in risking his life to save that of his platoon leader, Pfc. Bronislaus Niemiec, of Detroit, won the Silver Star. Niemiec exposed himself to heavy enemy fire, at Bougainville, to reach the wounded officer and carry him to safety. Despite the fact that Niemiec was shot on the way back, he succeeded in getting the officer to a first aid station in time to receive blood plasma to save his life.[32]

Brigadier General Wozenski was one of the Army's most decorated officers. He was cited for his heroic recovery of a savagely contested hill during the invasion of Sicily. "Upon him, for a tense while, the fate of the U.S. invasion rested," *Time* magazine reported.[33] "Wozenski jumped into a mobile tank-destroyer and, singlehanded, routed the Germans taking the hill that still bears his name." He received the Distinguished Service Cross with Oak Leaf Cluster, the Silver Star with Oak Leaf Cluster and the Bronze Star for his heroism during the Sicily invasion, as well as those of North Africa and Normandy.

Sgts. Paul and Edward Zielinski, a pair of twins from N. Detroit, Michigan, died three days apart in World War II. Paul, who was awarded a Silver Star, died in action with the 45th Infantry Division, in France, October 20, 1944. His brother, Edward, who had been wounded several times, was killed three days earlier, in Belgium, while fighting with the 39th Infantry Division. They were born June 29, 1917. Pine trees in their honor were planted in Lipke Park, in 1967.

Leon R. Dardas graduated from the University of Michigan with a law degree, in 1940. Having served as assistant city attorney for a number of years, Leon Dardas interrupted his law career to enter the U.S. Army. While enlisted, Dardas eventually became involved with the top priority Counter Intelligence branch of the U.S. Army, and later served under General George S.

---

[31] "Roseville Man Decorated for Gallantry at Buna," *Detroit News* (April 2, 1943).

[32] "Detroiter Wins Silver Star for Saving Life of Officer," *Detroit News* (August 6, 1944).

[33] "Wozenski WW II Hero is Commanding General," *Polish American Journal* (September 2, 1967), p. 5.

Patton. His dedicated service to the men he directed eventually earned him the Bronze Star and a promotion to 1st Lieutenant, at which stage he emerged from the armed forces.[34]

Sgt. Edward T. Wojewodzic, from Michigan, was cited for the Legion of Merit. The award was posthumous. During a mountain patrol in the Southwest Pacific area, he reconnoitered, under heavy rifle and sporadic machine gun fire, and thwarted a flanking movement by a Japanese patrol. He then led a daring frontal attack that routed the enemy and saved his unit many casualties. Sgt. Wojewodzic was killed in this action, in which he "showed the quality of a leader and great gallantry," according to the citation from General Douglas MacArthur. According to the dispatches, Sgt. Wojewodzic was at the rear of a patrol struggling up a muddy mountainside when a strong Japanese outpost was encountered. The Americans attempted a flanking movement, and when a gap developed in their lines, Sgt. Wojewodzic observed the vulnerable position; he led a squad to close it under heavy fire—losing his own life.

Pfc. Frank Mucha of Hamtramck, S/Sgt. Edward A. Opanowski, Stanley J. Pawlowski from Menominee, Michigan, and Lieut. John W. Wesolowski, also received the Legion of Merit Award. Wesolowski was cited for training his unit and leading it into action.

Pfc. Edward Osowski has been awarded both the Silver Star and the Bronze Star for heroism at Attu and Kawajalein. He lost his leg on Okinawa. He also took part in the Kiska and Leyte campaigns. Osowski received the Silver Star for rescuing two wounded comrades under machine gun fire during the battle for Holz Bay at Attu. The Bronze Star was for neutralizing enemy fire with a light machine gun on Kawajalein, allowing his own machine gun crew to advance and destroy the enemy positions.[35]

S/Sgt. Joseph A. Peczynski, from Detroit, won the Silver Star for rescuing a wounded tank driver which was under heavy

---

[34] In 1954, Dardas received his appointment to a seat on the Municipal Bench, in Buffalo, and was later returned that position through a public election. He was elected to the Circuit Court, in 1959, and ascended to the bench in January 1960, a post which the Judge has held since. He was born in Bay City, Michigan, in 1915. His family operated a meat packing firm during the depression years, in Buffalo.

[35] Wounded Detroiter Awarded 2 Medals," *Detroit News* (September 13, 1945).

IN THE SERVICE OF THEIR COUNTRY

fire on the Western Front. Peczynski also made four trips along a road exposed to brisk enemy fire, by taking ammunition and food into the besieged town, in his tank, and then evacuating the wounded men on his return trip. He was with the 12th Armored Division.[36]

Sgt. Joseph J. Niszczak, a Chadsey High graduate from Detroit, was awarded the Soldier's Medal. The Soldier's Medal is the fourth highest Army decoration. It is presented to any soldier, including reservists and National Guardsmen, who distinguish themselves by heroism, but does not involve actual combat with the enemy. Authorized by Congress in the late 1920's, only one medal can be awarded to any one person, but for any successive deeds of merit an Oak Leaf Cluster may be attached to the suspended ribbon.

Frank J. Belzowski, Albin J. Sadowski, Corporal Anthony Sadowski, Pvt. Francis H. Stasiewicz, Sgt. Walter A. Cetlinski, Pvt. Stephan A. Andruszkiewicz and Pfc. John Siekierski also received the Soldier's Medal.[37] Cetlinski saved an eight-year-old girl who had fallen into a pool. He did not reveal his identity, but onlookers notified his superiors, who recommended him for the Soldier's Medal for his heroism.[38] Andruszkiewicz was decorated for rescuing a man from drowning at Hamilton, Bermuda. He saw a man fall into deep water from a dock, and realizing he was unable to swim, jumped into the water and brought the man to safety.[39] Siekierski rescued a fellow soldier from drowning. He risked his own life to bring his companion to shore, and then administered artificial respiration.

During the unloading of a transport, in Algeria, a fire broke out in the hold near high explosives. Corporal Joseph A. Sidzina, of Detroit, climbed into the blazing hold with another soldier and succeeded in extinguishing the flames. Corporal Sidzina was cited for heroism beyond the normal call of duty which averted destruction of his ship and saved several lives. He was awarded the Soldier's Medal.

---

[36] *Detroit News* (March 13, 1945).
[37] All from the State of Michigan.
[38] *Detroit News* (February 14, 1945).
[39] "Two Detroiters Given Medals for Heroism," *Detroit News* (May 23, 1942).

Lieut. Leo J. Gronek, of Detroit, received five Battle Stars, the Purple Heart and the Bronze Medal. At Murielles, France a part of his nose was shot away but he was too busy to notice it. Just outside the German border, a jerry mortar shell got him in the shoulder. His Bronze Star was awarded for transporting men across a river, in Germany, all at night under heavy fire.[40]

General MacArthur awarded Pfc. Edward J. Kaminski the Distinguished Service Cross. Pfc. Kaminski was cited for destroying two enemy tanks on Luzon in a surprise night attack in the Philippines. Although every flash of his anti-tank gun revealed his position to the enemy, Kaminski continued to fire at point-blank range—even when a Japanese shell, bursting near him, left him temporarily blinded and thoroughly shaken.

Sergeant Alexander A. Drabik, from Toledo, Ohio, was the first American to cross the Ludendorff Bridge over the Rhine River at Remagen, earning for him the Distinguished Service Cross and the acclaim of a hero.[41] Ludendorff Bridge was the last span across the Rhine. A German officer, Captain Karl Friesenhahn, failed to destroy the bridge. It was a blooper of the greatest magnitude. Of Sergeant Drabik, Captain Friesenhahn said, long after the event: "He was the greatest hero of World War II." By storming the bridge on March 7, 1945, with eleven of his men—all the while under fire by Hitler's battered defenses on the opposing side—Sgt. Drabik received credit for abbreviating World War II which, in turn, reduced casualties by as many as 50,000 lives.[42]

Corporal Walter J. Holowezki was cited for campaigns on

---

[40] *Detroit News* (July 19, 1945), p. B-5.

[41] It is said that Sgt. Drabik was the first foreign soldier to cross the Rhine since the Napoleonic Wars.

[42] In 1955, President Eisenhower invited eleven survivors, including Drabik, to the White House on the occasion of the 10th anniversary of the capture of the bridge at Remagen. The president decided independently to establish the Society of the Remagen Bridgehead. He said that the eleven survivors symbolized "the dash, the ingenuity, the readiness to seize opportunity, that characterizes the American soldier." When Drabik's name was called first, President Eisenhower said: "This makes you the first member as far as I am concerned." Immediately a chorus of voices said: "He was the first one across the bridge." "Wonderful!" the President exclaimed and shook their hands warmly. *Polish American Journal* (June, 1975), p. 5.

IN THE SERVICE OF THEIR COUNTRY 383

Tarawa and Saipan. He, also, received the Bronze Star and the Purple Heart.

A posthumous award of the Silver Star was made to Pvt. Sylvester J. Ignasiak, of Detroit, who exposed himself to heavy enemy fire on the Italian front by informing a tank officer where the German positions were located.

Sgt. Wallace J. Jaresz, of Detroit, received the Silver Star. He was also cited for "gallantry in action" with the 78th Infantry Division near Schmidt, Germany.

Pvt. Larry Chwalek, from Detroit, won the Bronze Star for fighting side by side with his platoon in an attack on a German position in Italy despite wounds from a hand grenade. After the position had been captured, he submitted to treatment.

T/Sgt. Aloysius Wolak, from Detroit, received the Silver Star for taking command of his rifle platoon when it was isolated on the French front, and then led the men back, through a fierce bayonet assault, to the main body of American troops.

Captain Edward J. Zabinski, from Detroit, received the Soldier's Medal. He braved flames and exploding ammunition to rescue the trapped crew of a crashed bomber.

Pvt. Walter L. Zuzga, from Detroit, received the Purple Heart and the Silver Star for ignoring his own wounds and braving intense enemy fire to assist four comrades.

Walter Wujcicki won the Mariner's Medal, and Navy Machinist, Louis J. Walczak, from East Detroit, was given the Presidential Citation.

Many officers of Polish descent, from Brooklyn, served with distinction: including Colonel Michael Fibich, who commanded a field artillery battalion; Colonel William Anuszkiewicz, of the 6th Air Force, who served in the South Pacific; Lieutenant Colonels Henry Kucinski and Anthony Malinkowski, who commanded infantry battalions; Lieutenant Colonel Edward Nosek, who commanded a battalion of engineers in Africa and Normandy; and many others.

One of the most prominent of the Brooklyn officers was Colonel Benjamin T. Anuskiewicz, who commanded a chemical amphibious battalion. Colonel Anuskiewicz served in the D-Day operation in the North Pacific theater. He was twice wounded and received both American and French decorations. It was not his first experience as an American soldier. He also had served in the First World War, and he was a member of the expedition which followed General Pershing into Mexico in pursuit of Pancho Villa. After World War I, although still suffering from the effects of his wounds, he became an outstanding leader in Brooklyn's civic life.[43]

Sgt. Joseph J. Sadowski, of Perth Amboy, New Jersey, sacrificed his life for his comrades. This gift of valor won him the Nation's highest award, the Congressional Medal of Honor which was awarded posthumously to his parents. His was the last citation signed by President Roosevelt. The city of Perth Amboy honored Sgt. Sadowski by naming a parkway after him. A Catholic War Veterans Post No. 492 also bears his name.

Smashing a counterfeit ring, in Sicily, resulted in the confiscacation of $500,000 worth of bogus 1,000 lira notes. This feat was acknowledged to Benjamin W. Sobanski, of Detroit, agent in charge of the counterfeit squad attached to the Army's Criminal Investigation Division at Allied Force Headquarters, in Italy. Sobanski had arrested the ringleaders after weeks of undercover investigation. His efforts—far beyond the normal call of duty—led to his recognition as a leading authority on counterfeit currency during the European theater of war.[44]

Although S/Sgt. Alexander Kaczmarczyk died at sea on the twelfth day of Captain Eddie Rickenbacher's twenty-one day saga of endurance and fortitude, Sergeant John Bartek did survive this ordeal.[45]

Sergeant Tony Postula, with two companions, survived thirty-two days of hunger and thirst in the Pacific.

Leo Lapacinski had killed thirty-six Japanese soldiers in the battle of Tulagi, in the Salomons.

Marine "Skee" Wilski had killed one hundred Japanese soldiers on Guadalcanal. His exploits were published by Corporal

---

[43] Ralph Foster Ward, *Brooklyn in America* (New York: 1950), p. 214.
[44] "Detroiter Smashes Counterfeit Gang," *Detroit News* (April 27, 1945).
[45] Captain Edward V. Rickenbacher, *Seven Came Through* (Garden City: 1943), pp. 21-45.

Barney Ross, who described them to George K. Shaffer, staff writer of King Features Syndicate Incorporated.

Sergeant John J. Zygmunt—armed with a bazooka—held up eight German Tiger tanks and destroyed one of them. This was the first time an American bazookaman had eliminated a Tiger Tank!

The Polish-American soldiers were undaunted and usually led in the attack. The first American soldier to disembark on Sicily was Sgt. Joseph Parylak; the first to land at Anzio was Pvt. Walter P. Krzysztofiak of Summit, Illinois; the first American chaplain to set foot on French and German soil was Captain Vanantius Szymanski of Detroit. The first American woman to land on Munda and New Georgia was Army nurse Second Lt. Dorothy P. Shikoski from Green Lake, Wisconsin. Lt. George Klimowicz, of Stevens Point, Wisconsin, was one of three American officers who first entered German territory, in August 1944.

Many soldiers, from the State of Michigan, received the Silver Star for distinguished service to their country.[46]

Many men from the State of Michigan were decorated with the Bronze Star.[47] Also many Michigan men were decorated with the Purple Heart.[48]

---

[46] Floyd S. Adamczak (Muskegon), Sgt. Henry Chrostowski (Hamtramck), Corporal Raymond Kriniak (Alpena), Pvt. Joseph Kudella (St. Johns), Sgt. Joe F. Lesniewski (Hamtramck), Pfc. Casmer Mazur (St. Clair), Pfc. Hubert D. Milanowski (Grand Rapids), Corporal Bronislaw F. Nowicki (Hamtramck), Pfc. Floyd A. Szujkowski (Saginaw), Pvt. Charles Urbanik (Saginaw), Sgt. Francis E. Waldo (Kalamazoo).

The following hailed from Detroit: Henry J. Jurkiewicz, Robert J. Kopacz, Pfc. Walter J. Kowalski, Eugene J. Kruszewski, S/Sgt. Casimir J. Maliszewski, Lieut. Chester M. Masztakowski, Pvt. Theodore Moronczyk, Sgt. Thomas J. Muskiewicz, Pfc. Walter J. Oleszkowicz, S/Sgt. Stephen J. Piwok, Pfc. Edward T. Przyborski, Pvt. Walter A. Strzelka, S/Sgt. Joseph Twork, Pvt. Theodore I. Wiercinski, Sgt. Chester S. Wydrzynski and Corporal Joseph T. Zdanowski.

[47] Walter J. Kawa (Hamtramck), Corporal J. Kopiel (Hamtramck), Pvt. Walter Krakowski (Bay City), Major Paul H. Muske (Dearborn), Captain Walter J. Narkun (Hamtramck), Sgt. Frank Nowasad (Hamtramck), M/Sgt. William F. Pieprzak (Lenox), Lieut. Robert S. Roginski (Wyandotte), S/Sgt. Alexander H. Sanok (New Boston), Corporal Bernard V. Seneski (Ecorse), Pfc. George Truchan (Hamtramck), Pfc. Harry Zawacki (Hamtramck).

The following came from Detroit: Pfc. Alphonse Bagrowski, Pfc. Edmund Cylkowski, Marine Corporal Stanley F. Fortuna, Lt. Walter R. Grapczynski, T/Sgt. Walter Gwizdz, S/Sgt. Henry J. Hadacz, Arthur S. Hardyniec, Corporal Arthur S. Horzewski, Sgt. Chester Jendrewski, T/Sgt. Marion J. Zemsta, Pfc. Stanley Woj-

Divisions numbering large numbers of Polish-Americans also gained headlines by their heroic exploits:

> The 32nd (Red Arrow) division won fame again, but in a different hemisphere. It fought the Japanese in the South Pacific. The division was the spearhead of the Buno-Gona campaign, suffering heavy casualties. Company K, made up of men from Milwaukee's south side, mainly of Polish descent, battled the Japanese under almost incredible conditions for days until, when it was relieved, scarcely a dozen of its men were still able to walk.[49]

In every theater of War crosses mark the graves of Polish-American soldiers. Pfc. Robert Niedzwiecki, of Grand Rapids, Michigan lies buried at Pearl Harbor.

narski, Pfc. Henry A. Kendzior, Pvt. Joseph J. Klecha, S/Sgt. Walter E. Klimczak, S/Sgt. Frank C. Klimowicz, Corporal Edward A. Kotowski, Pfc. Michael Kowal, Pfc. Joseph T. Kowalewski, Lieut. Bernard S. Kowalski, M/Sgt. Chester J. Krupinski, T/Sgt. Joseph Kucharski, Lieut. Edward W. Kulakowski, M/Sgt. Joseph Kwasnik, Pfc. Harry J. Latkowski, Corporal Joseph Lazonski, Sgt. Walter U. Lesinski, M/Sgt. Stanley Lysogorski, M/Sgt. Brune Barylski, Sgt. Stanley C. Madej, Sgt. Arthur Marcinkowski, Sgt. Walter Miara, Irvin L. Nizyborski, S/Sgt. Arthur H. Novak, Corporal Casimr F. Opoka, Pfc. Edward Osowski, Sgt. Arthur A. Ostrowski, S/Sgt. Rudolph J. Papiak, S/Sgt. Melvin J. Partyka, Coxwain Joseph Pawlowski, Lieut. Edward L. Pazuchowski, Corporal Don Piasecki, M/Sgt. Leonard J. Piwinski, Pfc. George S. Plotkowski, Sgt. Raymond L. Plotkowski, Sgt. Alexander L. Polanski, Corporal John J. Potrzeba, Navy Coxwain Joseph Rawlowski, Corporal Andrew M. Rawski, Pfc. Joseph J. Rogawski, Captain John J. Rolak, Pvt. John C. Rozman, Pvt. Frank J. Sanocki, Pvt. Edward Sedrowski, S/Sgt. Adam S. Sliwinski, Pfc. Stanley J. Smalec, Lieut. Benjamin W. Sobanski, Pfc. Anthony Stec, Sgt. Cyril C. Straka, S/Sgt. Joseph F. Stryniaski, Pfc. Edward S. Surowiec, Sgt. Walter J. Szczypinski, Sgt. Casimer Szostakowski, Joseph C. Szwed, Corporal Benjamin Szwejkowski, Pvt. Raymond S. Szyczewski, S/Sgt. Walter B. Szymusiak, T/Sgt. Stanley Trombka, Sgt. Joseph A. Turek, Captain Jerome F. Tuszynski, Pfc. Edward P. Urbanek, Corporal Chester Vizicki, Sgt. William Walenczak, T/Sgt. Lawrence M. Walkowski, Pfc. Leonard G. Wahol, M/Sgt. Harry Warholak, Sgt. Richard J. Widelski, Edward T. Winiarski, Lieut. Norbert J. Wisinski, T/Sgt. Michael Wojciechowski, Pfc. William J. Wojnar, Pfc. Stanley Wojnarowski, S/Sgt. Thaddeus F. Wozniak, S/Sgt. Roman B. Wudarski, M/Sgt. Edward S. Wykowski, Pfc. Raymond J. Wyszynski, Lieut. Stephen A. Zalenka, Pvt. Boniface S. Zelenski, Captain Oleg Zaleski, T/Sgt. Marion J. Zemsta, Pvt. Edward J. Zibikowski, Corporal Henry J. Zmuda, S/Sgt. Stanley A. Zmuda, and S/Sgt. Charles F. Zukowski.

[48] Sgt. Eugene S. Burzynski (Bay City), Pvt. Stanley J. Rykulski (Flint). The following are from Detroit: Pvt. Casmire Chojnacki, Sgt. John V. Kolar, Benedict Lemanski, Pvt. Stanley A. Lewicki, Pvt. John T. Muszynski, Pvt. Chester J. Niedbala, Pfc. Chester B. Nowak, Pfc. Frank G. Ochmanski, Pvt. Alfred L. Pniewski, Pfc. Casimir R. Przybyl, Edward Rosochacki, Arnold J. Rzadkowolski, Pvt. Edward H. Stankiewicz, Pfc. Henry A. Sytkowski, Lieut. Joseph F. Szczygiel.

[49] Russell Austin, *The Milwaukee Story. The Making of an American City* (Milwaukee: 1946), p. 03.

In a German cemetery, next to General S. Patton, lies Pfc. John Przywara of Detroit.

Sgt. Alexander J. Kaczmarczyk, of Torrington, Connecticut, disappeared in the mid-Pacific on the twelfth night of Captain Rickenbacker's famous adventure.[50]

Somewhere on Guadalcanal a cross marks the grave of Corporal Stanley Narkon, a young Marine who was born in Nassau County, Long Island, New York. The son of a Polish immigrant, Stanley Narkon was one of Nassau County's first boys to die in World War II. The *Saturday Evening Post* featured him on its cover as the exemplary American Marine.

Contributions, of a different nature, to the war effort were made by several other Americans of Polish origin. Lieut. F. D. Hamerski, who teamed with Sgt. Melvin Campbell, built a device for training anti-aircraft gunners which provided all the realism of real equipment without the noise of gunfire.

Francis N. Piasecki, an engineer, associated with the PV Engineering Forum of Philadelphia, invented a new type of helicopter which was adapted by the armed forces and used in invasions.

Carl Harbut, of Baltimore, contributed new ideas which were utilized by the Glen Martin Company of Baltimore, builders of bombers.

The hydrogen bomb has now become the mutual deterrent to war. It was Dr. Edward Teller whose drive, foresight and patriotism made the H-bomb possible, but, as he himself admitted, he is not "the father of H-bomb." The bomb was the "work of many" who labored on the project. According to scientists—one of the most important among the "many"—is Dr. Stanislaw Ulam who—when the war broke out—joined John von Neuman, Hans Bethe, Edward Teller and other scientists who were working on the atomic bomb, in Los Alamos.[51] One morning at Los Alamos, in 1949, Dr. Teller was considering with his coterie of expert theoretical physicists, a possible design for the H-bomb. To de-

---

[50] Rickenbacker, *op. cit.*, pp. 21-45.
[51] Dr. Stanislaw Ulam was born in Lwow, Poland, in 1909. In 1935, Dr. Ulam, son of a Polish lawyer, left Poland and settled in the United States where he taught mathematics at Princeton, Harvard, and Wisconsin.

termine whether the design would work, many complex mathematical computations were necessary. At that time, the best high-speed computing machine available to the scientists was the ENIAC located at the Aberdeen Proving Ground, in Maryland. The necessary information, with which ENIAC was to be programmed, was sent back to Aberdeen.

Simultaneously, at Los Alamos, another group, composed of only two mathematicians, Dr. Stan Ulam and his associate Cornelius Everett, tackled the computing problem independently. It was a question of man versus machine. In this case, man won. As Teller has written:

> The big modern computing machines open up possibilities for complex calculations which seemed to be beyond our reach only a few years ago, but real mathematical ingenuity, coupled with hard work, can on some occasions overcome computational difficulties with even greater success than the best apparatus so far invented. This is precisely what happened in the case of Ulam's calculation. It proceeded with a speed that surpassed all expectations. Results were available even before the lengthy instructions to the machine had been completed. Those who like to contrast the ingenuity and endurance of the human brain with the lightning speed of standard operations on a machine will be able to conclude: In a real emergency, the mathematician still wins—if he is really good.[52]

Unfortunately for Teller, Dr. Ulam was more than good. He was perfect. On the basis of his calculations, he declared the H-bomb as previously and hopefully conceived to be completely impracticable. Teller refused to believe Ulam's calculations. He was so depressed by the news that he became suspicious of Dr. Ulam. Then the results came in from the ENIAC computer in Aberdeen. They proved Dr. Ulam's calculations correct in every detail. Teller then apologized to Ulam for having suspected him of being against the project and purposely "dragging his feet."

After Teller had his original H-bomb concept reduced to impracticability by Dr. Ulam's mathematics, he and his theoretical group began their experiments anew, and decided to test their preliminary measurements in an actual experiment on the remote

---

[52] Lloyd Shearer, "Who Really Invented the H-bomb? Now It Should Be Told," *Parade the Sunday Newspaper Magazine* (February 23, 1964), p. 5.

South Pacific atoll of Eniwetok. This test bore the code name "Greenhouse." Before "Greenhouse" got under way, in 1951, Dr. Ulam gave birth to a new idea, a new approach to the major problem at hand. He took his idea to Dr. Norris Bradbury, director of the Los Alamos Scientific Laboratory, then to Teller, who, in his writings, refers to it as "an imaginative suggestion."

Teller pondered Dr. Ulam's new approach, then he decided to try it. He asked Frederic de Hoffman, his assistant, to see if the suggestion was mathematically possible. Hoffman wrote the following comment concerning this incident:

> Edward told me he had a new idea. He asked me to stick some figures in my desk calculator and see if the idea was feasible. I made the calculations, then told him the suggestion would work. When I wrote up the report, I signed it with Edward's name. He wanted me to put both names on it, but I told him that his suggestion was everything, the calculation nothing. The report went with his name alone.[53]

The suggestion, originally presented to Dr. Teller, by Dr. Ulam, gave birth in turn to an ingenius idea by Dr. Teller that made possible the American H-bomb. On September 24, 1954—after we had exploded a new series of hydrogen bombs in the Marshall Islands—Dr. Norris Bradbury conducted a well-reported press conference. In the course of the conference he exhibited a report which he termed "the basic document which described the 1951 idea which led to a successful thermonuclear weapon." This document lists Dr. Teller and Dr. Ulam as joint authors.

When scientists affirm that Dr. Stan Ulam was the key scientist in helping to create the H-bomb, they have a good deal of documentary proof to confirm their belief. That is why in President Truman's memoirs, *Years of Trial and Hope,* one finds, relative to the H-bomb, the following comment: "Late in 1950 and early in 1951, Dr. Ulam and Dr. Teller, at Los Alamos, made new discoveries that changed the picture." This is why a statement to the Santa Fe *New Mexican,* September 28, 1954, the great physicist, Dr. I. I. Rabi, who also worked on the project said: "The scientific solution (of the H-bomb) was the result of a

---
[53] Ibid., p. 5.

suggestion by Stan Ulam of Los Alamos." This is also why Senator Clinton P. Anderson of New Mexico, probably the most knowledgeable senator on nuclear energy in Congress, repeatedly refers in speeches and newspaper press releases to Ulam's part in the H-bomb development.

On December 2, 1967, the U.S. Atomic Energy Commission released the names of the scientists who were associated with the atomic project at the University of Chicago. Among the many scientists, the following Poles were listed: Gerard S. Pawlicki, Leon Sefranski, Teodor R. Bolinski, Edwin Fudyja, Kazimierz Lesnieski, Leon Wojtonowski, Julian Ostopowicz, Pawel Baranowski, and Emil Konopinski.[54]

The greatest secret of World War II, after the atom bomb, was the exploitation of the information obtained from decoding German messages prepared by a cipher machine named the "Enigma." So valuable was this breakthrough in intelligence that it was given a special security classification, "Ultra." "Ultra" told the R.A.F. Fighter Command—well in advance of radar detection—how many bombers would be directed against England and when. This enabled the British to parcel out their few fighters so that some would always be available to defend England from an oncoming wave. These tactics denied the Germans superiority in the air over England, and consequently any possibility of an invasion.

During the campaigns in North Africa, "Ultra" kept General Bernard L. Montgomery informed fairly exactly of General Erwin Rommel's order of battle, and, in some cases, of his plans. It also enabled the British to know when supply ships would disembark from Italy, and then sink them; this eventually starved Rommel of vital fuel, ammunition and replacements. Another

---

[54] Dr. Konopinski, who at the age of twenty-seven became full professor, might have spent his life on the production line of an automobile factory if it was not for the financial support arranged by his high school principal, E. M. Conklin, a Rotary Club member. Through the Rotarians, $700 was raised to send the all "A" student to the University of Michigan. At the University he made straight A's for the next nine years, receiving scholarships for his outstanding work. Though a modest man, Dr. Konopinski has always had a high goal. On his application to the University of Michigan he was asked, "Have you any person in mind whose position you would like to fill?" His answer: "Yes. Eminent authority on matters physical and mathematical—Professor Einstein."

interception led to the Battle of Cape Matapan, which turned the Mediterranean from an Italian to a British lake. In 1943, "Ultra" revealed where the U-boats met their milch-cow supply submarines. Throughout the fighting in Normandy, "Ultra" delivered masses of decoded messages from Hitler and his officers, often within hours of dispatch. "Ultra" was responsible for the destruction of a large part of the German army in the west.

Everyone now agrees that "Ultra" was of supreme importance, and that without it the war would have lasted considerably longer. However, not many know that the credit for deciphering one of the great code apparatuses, the "Enigma" belongs to the Poles.[55] On July 15, 1928, the Polish cryptoanalysts noticed a decided change in the letter frequencies of German army cryptograms, which they were intercepting. The Poles quickly concluded that the Germans had begun using the "Enigma," which was invented and publicly sold early in the 1920's. Purchase of one of the commercial models showed that the Reichswehr had altered it for secrecy.

In 1932, the Polish Buiro Szyfrow (cipher bureau) obtained additional manpower in the form of three young mathematicians: Henryk Zygalski, Marian Rejewski and Jerzy Rozycki. They had achieved a partial solution in their office, hidden in the forest of Pyry, outside Warsaw, when Poland's French allies furnished some key "Enigma" documents. Major Gustave Bertrand of French cryptographic espionage had obtained them from a Reichswehr cipher unit employee, Hans-Thilo Schmidt, who wanted money. With this help the Poles completed their solution, and on July 26, 1939, presented two reconstructions of the machine to the French and two to the British. These machines enabled the British code-breaking unit at Bletchley—a small town 50 miles northwest of London—to solve the later variations of the machine and other machines used for different branches of the German armed forces.

At least one-hundred Polish-American priests served as chaplains in the armed forces: on land, sea, and in the air. Father Edwin J. Kozak, O.M.C., of Baltimore, Maryland, left his parish

---

[55] F. W. Winterbotham. *The Ultra Secret* (New York: 1974).

in Shamokin, Pennsylvania, to enter the Chaplain Corps. He became the first Catholic priest to qualify for the parachutist corps; he served with American paratroops during the invasion of North Africa and Sicily. Father Stanley C. Brach, of Newark, New Jersey, was the first Polish-American chaplain to be taken prisoner when he was captured by the Germans.

In World War II, more than 900,000 served in the Armed Forces.[56] The Marine Corps was liberally sprinkled with Andrzejewskis, Karasiewiczes and Modzelewskis. The Army and Navy had their share of "skis," "wiczs" and "wiaks." And so did the WACS, SPARS, and WAVES. According to Army and Navy records, approximately twenty per cent of the United States Armed Forces, on the eve of World War II, consisted of men of Polish extraction.[57] Americans of Polish descent were among the first to enlist in the United States Armed Forces. A recruiting officer of the United States Navy—in charge of the recruitment office at New Haven, Connecticut—reported that, in 1940 and 1941, at least fifty per cent of the volunteers, at his station, consisted of Americans of Polish extraction. Other recruiting stations in Polish-American areas had similar reports.[58]

During the Second World War 1,250 Americans of Polish descent, from Perth Amboy, New Jersey, served in the U.S. Armed Forces, with 49 dying for their country. In 1941-45, 18,000 Polish-Americans were inducted into the army from Kings County, New York. More than two thousand were wounded, and twelve hundred were killed in action.[59] The records of Mount Carmel Church, in Bayonne, New Jersey, show that nearly 3,000 parishioners served in World War II. Ninety-five gave their lives.

Not all Polish-American mothers could boast like Mrs. Rose Radziminska, California's Number One War Mother, or like Chicago's Mrs. Frances Dyke, of having eleven sons in the service.

---

[56] Albert Q. Maisel, "The Poles Among Us," *Zgoda* (June 15, 1958), p. 11. Sigmund H. Uminski, "Individual Polish Americans and World War II," *Polish American Studies*, III (January-June, 1946), p. 37.

[57] Sigmund H. Uminski, "Individual Polish Americans and World War II," *Polish American Studies*, III (January-June, 1946), p. 37.

[58] *Ibid.*, p. 37.

IN THE SERVICE OF THEIR COUNTRY

The Veterans Administration, in Washington, conducted a survey to establish the American families with the most sons in the United States Army during the Second World War. The honor went to Mr. and Mrs. Marcin Zygmunt of Scranton, and Mr. and Mrs. Walter Sobkowiak of Chicago. Each had seven sons fighting on the fronts during world War II.[60]

Mr. & Mrs. Anton Polewski had six sons in the service: Captain Walter Polewski, who served in Asia, was the first Milwaukee Chaplain killed in action; Louis Polewski served with the Seabees; Pfc. Florian Polewski served with the Army in France; S/Sgt. Joseph Polewski served with the air corps in the Pacific area; Corporal Sylvester Polewski served with the army in the Pacific area; and S/Sgt. Steve Polewski served with the air corps in the Pacific area.

Mrs. B. Debkowska, of Reading, Pennsylvania, also had six sons in the service.

Among other families of Polish extraction who had five sons in the armed forces simultaneously was the John Krukar family of Milwaukee. The Krukar boys, who served, were: Pfc. Raymond A. from the famed old Company K, in the South Pacific; S/Sgt. Emil J. from Company K who was later transferred to the European theater; Corporal Albin S. of the army in the Pacific area; Marian A. of the Navy; and Pfc. Clemens of the army, in the Philippines. Pfc. Raymond A. was cited for saving a nurse from drowning.

Five sons of Mrs. Magdalen Olszyk also served. They were: Lieut. Louis M. with the Marines; Yeoman 1/c Stanley R. with the Navy; Lieut. Edmund G. with the Army; Sgt. Alvin J. with the army; and Signalman Harry A. with the Navy.

Still another family which had five sons in the service is that of Bronislaus Zyszkiewicz, from Milwaukee. They were: Stanley, Henry (killed in action), Joseph, John, Leo and Ervin.

Mrs. R. Morawska, of Reading, Pennsylvania, also had five sons in the service simultaneously. So did the following mothers: Mrs. M. Kujawa of St. Cloud, Minnesota; Mrs. W. Powalski of

---

[59] Ralph Foster Weld, *Brooklyn Is America* (New York: 1950), p. 214.
[60] "Seven Sons in Service," *Polish American Journal* (November 11, 1966), p. 1.

Cannonsburg, Pennsylvania; and Mrs. Rose Redzinski of Los Angeles, California.[61]

Mrs. Mary Wiznak was one of three "five star mothers," in Michigan, during World War II, with five sons in military service: George, John, Raymond, Thomas and Michael. On behalf of her sons' participation she was honored by Edward J. Jeffries, Jr., then mayor of Detroit.[62]

Mmes. Dykta, Gardecka, Kupiszewska, Lapinska, Nabozna and Waszkiewicz, all from Reading, Pennsylvania, had four sons each in the Service. Marja Wilczynska reports similar examples in the Polish-American parishes of Baltimore, Maryland.[63]

Partly owing to the Kosciuszko-Pulaski-Krzyzanowski tradition, Americans of Polish descent have long been numerous and notable in the officer's corps of the United States Army. Scores have graduated from West Point Academy.[64] The following attained the rank of general in World War II: Joseph Barzynski, John Rataj, Maurice Rose, John Wisniewski, Matyka and Krygier. General Rose, who commanded the Third Armored Division, was killed in March 1945, when captured by the enemy during one of his famous outfit's spearheading operations in Germany.

The number of ways in which Americans of Polish ancestry have contributed to the war effort was as numerous as the battlefields on which Polish-American soldiers have fought. The attack on Pearl Harbor brought a new challenge. The nation was at war and with it came a new way of life: meatless days, the O.P.A., rationing, the swing-shift—as the nation marshalled all of its resources in a comprehensive effort for survival. Key leaders, in all communities, were urged to make special efforts to see to it that all classes and groups were represented, and to enlist the support of prominent Americans in heading War Loan Drives.

---

[61] "Slav Boys in the Service," *The American Slav* (December, 1942), p. 18.

[62] "Mrs. Mary Wiznak had five sons in WW II," *The Detroit News* (April 20, 1976), p. 7-C.

[63] Marja Wilczynska, *Unforgotten Heroes* (Baltimore, 1947).

[64] In 1939, the West Point Class of 456 cadets was headed by Stanley Dziuban of Polish extraction. Captain Thomas A. Parz was the top cadet of the 1971 graduating class at the West Point Academy. When President Nixon visited the Academy on graduation day, Parz, a cadet commander of 4,000 academy cadets, had the honor of presenting President Nixon with a cadet saber and wished the president "continuing success" in the execution of his responsibilities.

Particular stress was placed on keeping accounts, acknowledging purchases of saving bonds, and reporting them. Careful records were kept of all such purchases, including their names and addresses, and the amounts they purchased.

In the Fourth War Loan Drive, in Chicago, the Polish-Americans led all other purchasers with over $14 million. They were first, also, in the Fifth Drive with more than $20 million. Up to September 1944, the Polish National Alliance had $14 million bonds; the Polish Roman Catholic Union's purchase amounted to $9 million. Several United States bombers during World War II bore Polish names: "Polish Falcon of America," "Spirit of Warsaw," and "Paderewski." These names were given at the request of the Polish Falcons Alliance of America in recognition of the sale of U.S. War Bonds to the sum of $1,622,000.

Mrs. Francis P. Tarnapowicz of Pittsburgh, chairman of the 4th Area Nationality Group Division—was responsible for the sale of nearly $270 million in bonds among 101 national groups in Pennsylvania.

Anthony J. Slonina, mayor of Chicopee, Massachusetts, aroused the Polish-Americans so much that they purchased enough U.S. Bonds to buy five U.S. Bombers with Polish names.

Private John J. Wondolowski, set an example for civilian Americans to invest in war bonds, when early in 1942, at Fort Hancock, he purchased five-thousand-dollars worth, the amount of his life savings.

Also, Casimir A. Sienkiewicz, who was vice-president of the Federal Reserve Bank of Philadelphia, was deputy chairman of a campaign to sell four-hundred-million-dollars of war bonds in eastern Pennsylvania, southern New Jersey and Delaware.[65]

Confronted by the crisis of war, the Polish-Americans also broadened the scope of their activities. The parish became the outlet for many local activities: servicemen's clubs, package sending committees, letter writing groups, and bulletin distributions.

---

[65] In 1918, Sienkiewicz entered the U.S. Army, but was soon given a leave of absence for the World War I Third Liberty Bonds campaign. Before he returned to Ft. Meade, Maryland, he raised twenty-five million dollars among Polish and Slavic Americans for the bond campaign.

The women of the parish formed knitting circles which supplied servicemen with woolens; they prepared and rolled bandages; and served as Red Cross aides. Young women served as nurses, organized hospital relief, and furnished supplies to the wounded. The Young Ladies Sodalities sponsored parties for servicemen, or took part in special devotions and prayers for the men and women at the front. Many took off their kitchen aprons, pinned up their hair, put on slacks and machinist caps, grabbed lunchpails, and went off to assembly lines and production work. They were especially conspicuous in the factories producing great quantities of bombs, artillery shells, shell fuses, batteries, oil refining equipment, electric motors, gears, steam and Diesel engines, marine equipment, airplane parts, flying suits, shoes, field rations, excavators, power shovels, bulldozers and landing barges. They also worked as riveters for all kinds of war material.

Just out of her teens, Vina Slomka Stack, in 1943, volunteered for a Detroit-organized USO troupe which spent nearly two years singing to weary GIs. More than once she had to be cautioned about battlefield dangers. "Young lady, you're getting too close," she was warned by General George S. Patton, famed commander of the 3rd Army.[66] She counted Patton as a friend and met several other war leaders, including General Eisenhower. What she liked most was mixing with the GIs. She had a trunk full of war souvenirs they gave her, and over 1,000 pictures of her with different soldiers. Dressed in Army fatigues, Vina Slomka Stack, who used the professional name of Vina Del Mar, appeared often on the same program with Bob Hope and other Hollywood entertainers.[67]

Polish-American school children and high school youngsters were also involved in the war effort. They organized salvage campaigns to collect aluminum, rubber, copper, steel, waste paper, tin cans, waste fats, and even silk and nylon stockings. The children also bought war bonds and stamps, and at the same time

---

[66] "Mrs. Stack Singer with USO, Dies," *The Detroit News* (November 13, 1962), p. 6-C.

[67] On her return to civilian life, she sang professionally and appeared with some operetta companies. She also was active in local singing groups and Polish nationality groups. She also sang at rallies for Governor-elect George Romney.

promoted their sale in the neighborhood. They enthusiastically attended first-aid courses in order to be ready for any emergency; and they prepared their own family Victory Gardens. Many learned to battle incendiary bombs and signed up to be air raid wardens; they were issued white helmets and stirrup pumps for bomb disposal.

Besides generously supporting the Red Cross, the Catholic Bishop's Relief, the USO and CSO, Polish-Americans organized several special committees to aid war victims in Poland, and Polish refugees and exiles in Europe, Asia and Africa. Through the American Relief for Poland—founded in 1939 and directed by F. X. Swietlik—they contributed almost $10,000,000 to alleviate suffering. Through the Polish Catholic League—organized in 1942, and headed by S. T. Kusper—they provided the means for religious ministration to needy brethren. Members of the Polish National Alliance voluntarily submitted to a five cents per month assessment for each member earmarked for the Polish War Relief Fund which amounted to $786,307.29, according to the PNA treasurer's report of April 1951.[68] Finally, through the Polish American Congress—established in 1944—they financed additional relief activities in Poland.

With characteristic Teutonic thoroughness, the retreating Germans dynamited the railroads, telescoped the locomotives and rolling stock, blew up bridges, looted factories, scorched farmlands, slaughtered and confiscated livestock and provisions, burned towns and villages—leaving millions homeless. They stole whatever was worth taking even from the few remaining shops that eeked out a living, not to mention the millions of lives of citizens killed, maimed or imprisoned in the worst concentration camps ever recorded by history. These concentration camps were also notorious for the numerous hideous medical experiments which were performed on the innocent inmates of the camps.

In the succeeding months, the Polish American Congress also kept the cause of Polish freedom alive in America. They unsettled the conscience of the world with their accounts of the spread of terror and persecution throughout Poland, the imprisonment or

---

[68] M. Tomaszkiewicz, "Na Fundusz Ratunkowy," *Zgoda* (April 15, 1951), p. 2.

execution of political rivals, or the Communist decrees which was wiping out the last vestiges of democracy in Poland—a nation which faced more than its share of strife and bloodshed over the centuries.

Between 1939 and 1945, a number of highly intelligent and well-trained Poles found refuge in the United States. Though small in number, this predominantly professional and semi-professional group gave to their adopted country the elements of a new strength. For among them were scholars who brought to America a greater respect for scholarship, and musicians who brought her a deeper love of music. And there were writers and painters with international reputations among them, and some of them were great physicists, biologists, chemists. Others brought new methods to business and industry. America was not poorer but considerably richer with their arrival. Their influence was out of all proportion to their numbers.[69]

When the Japanese attacked Pearl Harbor, all of the knowledge and skill that the refugees possessed was pressed into the service of America. Now, there was work for them in the scientific laboratories which was proceeding at a faster pace; and in the large industrial plants, where war materiel was produced on assembly lines. In addition, there was need for them as teachers and doctors, for so many young American teachers and doctors had gone to war. In classrooms, in laboratories, in government bureaus, the refugees mobilized their knowledge and efforts toward national goals. Their presence made carefree Americans realize what living in a country at war was like. Most of them had taken out citizenship papers as quickly as the law permitted. Many volunteered for service in various military units.

This chapter only summarizes the total effort of the Polish-Americans during World War II. To describe all of the significant contributions by soldiers and civilians, the educated, or the professionals, as well as the stalwart laborers, mothers and children who remained at home—would require a whole book. Space barely permits the author to merely touch on some of the many significant efforts contributed by Polish-Americans during World War II.

---

[69] Joseph A. Wytrwal, *Poles in American History and Tradition*, pp. 394-401.

CHAPTER 13
Yalta

Who rules East Europe commands the Heartland;
Who rules the Heartland commands the World Island;
Who rules the World Island commands the World.
   —Sir Halford John MacKinder[1]

The gentle French dreamer, Fourier, predicted
That one day the oceans would run with lemonade.
Our leaders drank the sea water,
And they shouted: "It tastes like lemonade."
Then quietly they crept to their homes
To retch and vomit.
   —Comment on Communism by Adam Wazyk

After Poland's defeat, in 1939, many Polish political leaders had taken refuge in London, where they had been recognized as the legal Polish Government-in-Exile. Many exiled Poles had played an important part in the defense of Britain, in 1940, and Polish units fought with the British in Africa and Italy. At the end of the war, the Poles thought that they would be restored to a Poland which would enjoy sovereignty, independence and freedom. They also thought Poland's boundaries would be as large as they had been in 1939. They also hoped that they would be compensated for their sufferings by receiving German territory in the west. General Sikorski in his speeches—during his visit to the United States, in December 1942—made this clear:

> The inviolability of our frontiers—wider than before the war—a broader access to the sea—these are the aims for which Polish soldiers are fighting and for which the Polish Nation is bleeding.[1a]

---
[1] Sir Halford John MacKinder, *Democratic Ideals and Reality*, p. 150.
[1a] "General Sikorski's Speeches During His Visit to the United States in December 1942," Polish Information Center (New York: 1942), p. 9.

Poles expected these demands to be supported by the British government which had originally gone to war to defend Poland against Germany.

Diplomatic relations were restored between the Polish Government-in-Exile, residing in London, and the Russians after Germany had captured Russian-held Poland in 1941. At this time, the Poles wanted assurance that the Polish boundaries set by the German-Russian partition were not binding, but Russia refused to make any commitment.[2] Because of the frontier question, the relations between Poland and the Soviet Union had long been strained.

From the beginning, Stalin had insisted that he would retain the frontier which he had gained as a result of his non-aggression friendship pact with Hitler, in 1939. He asserted that this frontier was based upon the Curzon line, that the British had agreed to it at the end of the First World War, and that the Soviet Union had been unjustly deprived of it at the Peace Treaty of Riga. He suggested that Poland should be compensated for her losses in the east by taking German territory in the West. Eventually, he wanted Poland to take not only a slice of East Prussia but also a great swathe of German territory up to the river Neisse. First under General Sikorski, then after his death under Mikolajczyk, Poles obstinately refused to compromise.[3]

---

[2] After the annexation of Latvia, Lithuania, and Estonia and the occupation of half of prewar Poland, Stalin asked for British recognition. On October 15, 1940, the British government had offered to recognize the *de facto* sovereignty of the Soviet Union over Estonia, Latvia, Lithuania, Bessarabia, Bukovina, and "those parts of the former Polish State now under Soviet control." The price then was only that "the Soviet Union would apply to Great Britain a neutrality as benevolent as that applied to Germany." Robert Beitzell, *The Uneasy Alliance, America, Britain and Russia 1941-1943* (New York: 1972), pp. 7-8. See also Llewellyn Woodward, *British Foreign Policy in the Second World War* (London: 1962), p. 145.

[3] President Roosevelt did not participate in these discussions. He feared the consequences of trying to thwart Stalin over what he regarded as a purely Russian interest. Also, he did not want to take the risk of losing the Polish vote in the American elections.

A poll—organized in the summer of 1943, by the United States government agencies to determine the political attitudes of Polish-Americans toward the problem of Poland—brought to light some extremely interesting indications: nine out of ten Polish-Americans believed that they should do everything they could to help Poland; forty-one percent felt that the United States should guarantee a fair territorial settlement for Poland, "even if it meant fighting Russia"; only one-third declared

The severance of relations by the Soviet Union with the Polish Government-in-Exile, in London, was the only major breach in the wartime alliance. The cause of this open split, within the ranks of the United Nations, was the announcement by the German Government, during April 1943, of the discovery of mass graves of Polish officers at Katyn forest, between Minsk and Smolensk, in western Russia. With a virtuous show of horror, the Germans had alleged the Soviet Union was responsible—calling for an international investigation. The Polish Government-in-Exile had long been disturbed by the disparity between the number of enlisted men and the number of officers that it had found in the Soviet Union when the two nations (Poland and the Soviet Union) became allies in the common struggle against Germany.

Although Churchill bluntly warned against it, and asked the Poles whether they could bring the dead back to life, General Wladyslaw Sikorski, Prime Minister of the Government-in-Exile, requested the International Red Cross to conduct an inquiry into the German charges on April 17, 1943.[4] By April 21, the Germans had disinterred 14,500 corpses.[5] On April 21, Stalin said

---

that they would be satisfied with Poland's prewar boundaries. The majority were in favor of a "Bigger Poland." Joseph S. Roucek, "Polish Americans," *One America. The History, Contributions and Present Problems of Our Racial and National Minorities* (New York: 1946), pp. 140-141.

[4] Churchill did not doubt the Soviet Union was responsible for the massacre, and the British Government "in strictest confidence" informed Washington that "the Soviet Government had broken with the Poles . . . to cover up their guilt." Robert Beitzell, *The Uneasy Alliance. America, Britain, and Russia, 1941-1943* (New York: 1972), p. 157.

After the war the evidence was examined by a select committee of the U.S. Congress—the first truly impartial inquiry—which reported on July 2, 1952. This group, which included in its membership two Michigan congressmen (Thaddeus M. Machrowicz and George A. Dondero), declared that "its investigation proves conclusively and irrevocably" the guilt of the "Soviet NKVD (Peoples' Commisariat of Internal Affairs)." W. Sprague Holden, "A Crime Without Parallel," *The Sunday News* (October 24, 1971), p. 5. E. Zdzislaw Stahl, "Byly Oficer 'Smerszu'o Katyniu," *Nowy Dziennik* (July 3, 1975), p. 6.

[5] Diaries, letters, documents and other personal effects positively identified 4,143 of the victims and fixed the time of the executions at a date well before the German conquest. Names and ranks of victims fill more than 60 pages of an appendix, along with an "incomplete list" of Russian officials and secret service personnel involved in the murders. By rank, the dead included three Polish generals, 100 colonels and lieutenant colonels, 300 majors, 1,000 captains, 2,500 first and second lieuten-

that the Polish call for an investigation was incontrovertible evidence of contact and collusion between Hitler and the Sikorski Government, and therefore, he had decided to "interrupt relations with that Government."

The interrupted relations were never healed. Stalin—determined to ensure a friendly government in Poland—now turned to the formation of a more friendly Polish group in Russia.[6] On July 25, 1944 the Russians announced the formation of a Polish National Liberation Committee, a communist dominated group nurtured by Moscow (later called the Lublin Committee), to manage Polish affairs in Soviet-liberated Poland. A few weeks before Yalta, the Russians recognized the Lublin Poles in the face of Roosevelt's and Churchill's urgent pleas for delay. The Lublin Committee sponsored the Union of Polish Patriots who denounced the London Poles. Efforts by the British to settle the Polish Russian differences brought few results.

On July 29, 1944, as the Russian armies approached Warsaw's suburbs, the Russian radio broadcasted to the citizens of Warsaw a message urging them to rise against the Germans. The London Polish Government-in-Exile, with the help of its underground army in Warsaw, hoped to seize control of their capital

---

ants and more than 500 cadet-officers. The Katyn massacre of World War II deserves a place in infamy with other appalling mass slaughters.

Recently a stark, 20-foot monument of black granite—a memorial to the victims at Katyn—was unveiled. It was financed by Polish exiles all over the world. On this occasion, the *Detroit News,* in an editorial opinion, made the following remark: "There is no doubt about Soviet guilt for this atrocity. The despicable incident was discovered and reported by Nazi Germany, in 1943, and after the war it was investigated by British and American authorities. There was indisputable evidence that the Red Army killed the officers. . . . The Katyn Forest massacre occurred. The atrocity was committed by the Soviet Union. The event should be remembered." "An off 'fraternity in arms.' " *The Detroit News* (September 21, 1976), p. 6-B. See also "War Memorial to Polish Dead Rouses Storm," *Detroit Free Press* (September 20, 1976), p. 6-B. "Polish Massacre Blamed on Russians," *The Cincinnati Enquirer* (July 6, 1972), p. 3. John P. Elliot, "The Decapitation of a Nation," *Gwiazda Polarna* (January 6, 1974), p. 5.

[6] Strong anti-Soviet sentiments existed in Poland. And Stalin had to prepare to cope with hostility in the Polish populace. These difficulties had roots in Polish national tradition, in the strength of the Catholic Church, in the upper and middle class character of Polish leadership in prewar society, in deep resentment against the Soviet Union over the occupation of Eastern Poland with German approval and in the freshly proclaimed loss of Polish territory beyond the Curzon line. The Polish government in exile represented those very strong elements of Polish opinion which were nearly as anti-Soviet as they were anti-German.

before the Russians moved in and destroyed the chances of an independent Poland. If they could recapture it from the Germans with their underground army, this would compensate for past humiliations and give them a valuable bargaining counter against the Soviet Union. On August 1, the Polish underground army, led by General Bor-Komorowski, attacked the German forces in Warsaw. By August 6, the Poles were in control of most of their capital; but two days later the German SS moved in. Between August 8 and October 2, when Bor-Komorowski surrendered, the entire city of Warsaw was razed.[7]

The Warsaw episode aroused bitter controversy. The Russians contended that heavy German counterattacks, not only halted their advance, but forced a retreat, and they were powerless to go to the Poles' assistance. Stalin also claimed that his northern offensive had been concluded, and that he did not want to get involved in street fighting in a large city. The Poles interpreted the Russian halt as intentional and put another interpretation upon Stalin's inaction. In the course of the Warsaw battle, the Germans killed off most of the underground leaders loyal to London, and destroyed the Polish Government-in-Exile's last chance of influencing post-war Poland. It was also a move to destroy the vestiges of an independent Poland and establish the Lublin Committee as the new Polish Government. Warsaw was a turning point for Allied coalition.

Churchill—worried that the United States might be tempted to return Britain's crown colony of Hong Kong to China as a reward to the Chinese for their part in the struggle against Japan—wanted Stalin's support for the continuation of the British Empire. In return, as Churchill has written in his memoirs, he—

---

[7] During those weeks, when the Warsaw patriots fought with makeshift weapons against one of the most brutal operations ever conducted by the SS, the Russian armies across the Vistula made little or no attempt to cross the Vistula and enter Warsaw proper. The Western Allies were powerless to help the Poles. A few planes flew from bases in Italy to drop supplies, but their help was negligible. The Russians refused permission for British and American troops to land behind the Russian lines. Churchill repeatedly urged Stalin to extend some assistance to Warsaw, and on August 20, Roosevelt and Churchill sent a joint appeal, but no aid was forthcoming. On August 16, Moscow informed the U.S. Ambassador that "the Soviet Government does not wish to associate themselves either directly or indirectly with the adventure in Warsaw."

during private talks in Moscow, in October, 1944—agreed to recognize the Soviet Union's sphere of dominant influence in Eastern Europe.[8] He also agreed to Stalin's demand that Russia's boundaries would be moved west at the expense of Poland. As a result, the war-racked Polish nation would be picked up like a carpetbag and set down a few hundred miles to the west, satisfying Russia's appetite, penalizing Germany, and sacrificing and taming Poland in the process.

In February 1945, Roosevelt, Churchill, and Stalin—together with the Foreign Secretaries of their respective countries—gathered at Yalta in the Crimea in what was to be their last meeting. It was a conference characterized by personal and secret diplomacy to a degree incompatible with democracy.[9] The most emotional issues, considered at Yalta, involved Poland. All three leaders had a special national and political interest in the resolution of the Polish question. Stalin was most immediately concerned because Poland was the neighbor of the Soviet Union on the west. Churchill felt some obligations to the prewar government of Poland, which had fled to London in 1939, and was still recognized by Great Britain and the United States as the legitimate government of Poland. Roosevelt could not forget that six million Americans of Polish descent—who were strongly anti-communistic, and normally voted the Democratic ticket—looked especially to him to protect the interests of their ancestral country.[10]

At the Yalta conference Stalin imposed his will upon Poland. Russian national aims were achieved without subjecting the Polish question to a peace conference. More important, both Churchill and Roosevelt acceded to Stalin's demand on the cession of eastern Poland to Russia. The new boundary of Poland was to be the Curzon Line. The western frontier changes made

---

[8] "Historical Note. Joking at the Summit." *Time* (August 20, 1973), p. 33. "Churchill Secrets Bared," *Detroit Free Press* (August 2, 1973), p. 12-F.

[9] Even at Yalta Roosevelt had secret meetings with Stalin behind Churchill's back. Anthony Eden, Britain's wartime foreign secretary, holds Roosevelt responsible for Soviet control of Eastern Europe. "Roosevelt Bungled on Reds—Eden," *The Detroit News* (March 21, 1965), p. 9-B.

[10] Polish-American editors and politicians, in New York, Detroit and other cities, were threatening to turn their constituents against Roosevelt, in the fall, if he failed anti-Communist Poles in their hour of need. James MacGregor Burns, *Roosevelt the Soldier of Freedom 1940-1945* (New York: 1970), p. 483.

the new Poland wholly reliant upon the Soviet Union. Millions of Germans had to be expelled from their homes in the Oder-Niesse territory. This ensured that Poland would be permanently faced by the German demand for revenge, and only the Soviet Union could defend her against the German threat. Between the wars, Poland was supposed to defend Europe against Russia; after 1945, Poland became Russia's bulwark against Europe.

Roosevelt and Churchill had more difficulty in reaching an agreement with Stalin concerning the future government of Poland. Finally, the three men agreed that the provisional government of Poland—recently established at Lublin, by the Soviet Union—should be expanded to include representatives of the Polish Government-in-Exile and of the other "democratic" Poles in Poland and abroad. Roosevelt and Churchill accepted that arrangement, however, only on the understanding that the reconstituted provisional government would hold early and free elections to establish a permanent government representative of all the people of Poland.

When Roosevelt returned from his conference with Prime Minister Churchill and Premier Stalin in Crimea, during February 1945, he knew that there would be resentment for the Yalta solution of the Polish problem which could only be interpreted as betrayal of their cause and the preservation of the noble democratic principles. "Everybody does not agree with us, obviously," he said, of this "outstanding example of joint action by the three major Allied powers in the liberated areas."[11]

It did not take long for Roosevelt to realize that the Yalta Conference was a serious defeat to U.S. diplomacy.[12] On April 1, 1945, Roosevelt sent a telegram to Stalin expressing concern over the lack of progress in implementing the Yalta decisions on Poland. "I intend . . . in this message," he wrote, "to lay before you with complete frankness the problem as I see it." There followed a strong criticism of the apparent Russian view that the government established in Lublin, under Russian protection and later moved to Warsaw, the "Lublin-Warsaw government," should serve as the core of a new provisional government. Roosevelt

---

[11] Joseph P. Morray, *From Yalta to Disarmament. Cold War Debate* (New York: 1961), p. 10.

warned that the solution resulting "in a thinly disguised continuance of the present Warsaw regime would be unacceptable and would cause the people of the United States to regard the Yalta agreement as having failed."[13]

Churchill perceived earlier that the Yalta Conference was a failure. A month earlier, on March 13, Churchill proposed to Roosevelt that Yalta be proclaimed a failure.[14] Roosevelt, however, in a sharply worded reply, repudiated the suggestion.

> I cannot agree that we are confronted with a breakdown of the Yalta agreement until we have made the effort to overcome the obstacles incurred in the negotiations at Moscow. . . .[15]

The Yalta Conference altered the relationship between the United States and the Soviet government drastically and opened the Cold War. Roosevelt was vague, loose and ineffective in his planning for the postwar situation. Anthony Eden, Britain's wartime secretary, blamed Roosevelt for most of the Cold War troubles that had developed since 1945.[16]

On April 28, 1945, two weeks after Roosevelt's death, Churchill sent a message to Stalin. In the message, Churchill stated his case with passion and eloquence.

> Difficulties arise at the present moment because all sorts of stories are brought out of Poland which are eagerly listened to by many members of Parliament and which at any time may be violently raised in Parliament or the press in spite of my deprecating such action and on which M. Molotov will vouchsafe us no information at all in spite of repeated requests. For instance, there is talk of fifteen Poles who were said to have met the Russian authorities for discussion

---

[12] Recently a group of psychiatrists suggested in a report that President Franklin D. Roosevelt may have been suffering from "organic brain disease" at the time he took part in the Yalta conference where many decisions about the era, following World War II, were included. Roosevelt was used as an example of possibly "emotionally VIP in history" in the report which urged the creation of a panel of medical experts to examine government officials to help resolve the question of competence to serve. "Was FDR Incompetent," *The Detroit Free Press* (February 7, 1973), p. 12-D.

[13] Morray, *From Yalta to Disarmament. Cold War Debate*, p. 10.

[14] "Was FDR Incompetent?" *The Detroit Free Press* (February 7, 1973), p. 12-D.

[15] Morray, *From Yalta to Disarmament. Cold War Debate*, p. 15.

[16] "Roosevelt Bungled on Reds—Eden," *The Detroit News* (March 1, 1965), p. 9-B.

over four weeks ago, and of M. Witos about whom there has been a similar, but more recent report; and there are many other statements of deportations, etc. How can I contradict such complaints when you give me no information whatever and when neither I nor the Americans are allowed to send anyone into Poland to find out for themselves the true state of affairs? There is no part of our occupied or liberated territory into which you are not free to send delegations, and people do not see why you should have any reasons against similar visits by British delegations to foreign countries liberated by you.[17]

Churchill's method of dealing with Stalin was characterized as that of a dog (subject of a Greek fable), which wagged its tail while biting. The rabbit (Stalin) asked: "If you are my friend, why do you bite me? And if my enemy, why do you wag your tail?" Stalin, however, chose to ignore the tail wagging and answered only the bite in his reply of May 4, 1945.

I am able to inform you that the group of Poles mentioned by you comprise 16, not 15, persons. The group is headed by the well-known General Okulicki. The British information services maintain a deliberate silence, in view of his particular officiousness, about this Polish General, who, along with the 15 other Poles, has "disappeared." But we have no intention of being silent about the matter. This group of 16, led by General Okulicki, has been arrested by the military authorities of the Soviet front and is undergoing investigation in Moscow. General Okulicki's group, in the first place General Okulicki himself, is charged with preparing and carrying out subversive activities behind the lines of the Red Army, subversion which has taken a toll of over a hundred Red Army soldiers and officers; the group is also charged with keeping illegal radio-transmitters in the rear of our troops, which is prohibited by law. All or part of them—depending on the outcome of the investigation—will be tried. That is how the Red Army is forced to protect its units and its rear-line against saboteurs and those who create disorder.[18]

Beginning with the Teheran Conference, Americans of Polish descent began to realize that three heads of state were undertaking to make decisions which involved the lives of millions of people in lands which did not belong to the statesmen concerned.

---

[17] Morray, *From Yalta to Disarmament. Cold War Debate*, p. 25.
[18] *Ibid.*, p. 27.

The practice of awarding territory to the Soviet Union commenced at Teheran when eastern Poland, without consulting Poland, was ceded.[19]

This transfer was executed by the Big Three Powers without formally consulting the wishes of the Polish people, even though the second point of the Atlantic Charter clearly states that there are to be "no territorial changes that do not accord with the freely expressed wishes of the peoples concerned."

There is a wide difference between stealing territories and having them freely awarded by the lavishness of one's allies. Finally, it is most difficult, if not impossible, to reconcile these territorial transfers either with the Atlantic Charter, which the Soviet Union recognized, or with the repeated statements made by them, viz., that they sought no territorial gains but merely wished to drive the German racist beasts from their soil.

On May 29, 1944, Americans of Polish descent organized the Polish American Congress. Its twofold purpose is to give expression of their "undivided service, love, and attachment," to the United States and to "give full support and aid to the Polish nation."

A few insignificant groups disagreed with the objectives of the Polish American Congress. The Polish American Congress criticized the Polish government for what they considered to be its too unyielding attitude on the problems of Polish-Soviet boundaries. Another group of Polish-American intellectuals, mostly Socialists, headed by Socialist, Oscar Lange, favored the Curzon line.[20] Early in November 1943, another group appeared in Detroit as the Kosciuszko League. It urged agreement and collaboration with Soviet Russia. Its name emphasized its solidarity with the Polish Kosciuszko Division of the Soviet Army. The members of the Kosciuszko Division were former Polish war prisoners who were formed into new army divisions under Russian command.

Polish-Americans immediately condemned the Russian annexa-

---

[19] The Soviet Union received territory and concessions without reciprocal grants on her part.

[20] Oscar Lange was a former lecturer at the Jagiellonian University, in Krakow. During World War II, he was professor of economics, at Chicago University.

tion of eastern Poland. Through the Polish American Congress they urged the United States government not to recognize the changes brought about in the course of fighting in Europe.[21] The Polish American Congress also asserted Poland's claim to the eastern pre-war Polish provinces which was based on the objectives enumerated in the Atlantic Charter solemnly proclaimed and adopted by both Winston Churchill and Franklin Roosevelt. As to the ceding of any territory of eastern pre-war Poland, the Polish American Congress proclaimed:

> Poland . . . our faithful fighting ally . . . must not be shorn of one-half of her territory . . . Any compromise on the fundamental principles of the Atlantic Charter would be a repudiation of the very reasons for which our boys think they are fighting and dying . . . America must have the moral courage to face certain unpleasant realities. Russia's unpredictable change of policy, opposition to legal governments, defiance of the Atlantic Charter, are grave danger signals . . . They all confirm the mounting evidence that Stalin wants to supplant Hitler as Master of Europe.[22]

The Polish American Congress asserted explicitly, in its publications that the decisions reached at the Yalta Conferences were contrary to the objectives stated in the Atlantic Charter, contrary to international law, and in violation of the fundamental principles of democracy. Furthermore, the Yalta decisions deprived Poland of equal rights and destroyed her independence. The basic principle which had guided the opinion of the Polish American Congress was strict interpretation of the Atlantic Charter and support of the Polish Government-in-Exile, in London.

Karol Rozmarek, president of the Polish American Congress, made an attempt to enlist the support of President Roosevelt for

---

[21] Under the leadership of the Polish National Alliance, a "Congress" was held in Buffalo, New York, in May 1944. Representatives of the Polish American fraternals, professional associations, cultural, educational, religious and ideological societies had attended and established the Polish American Congress. The Polish American Congress was intended to integrate American Polonia into one super federation of fraternal, parish, and community groups to assert the coincidence of American, Polish, and Polonia interests.

[22] C. Rozmarek, "Poland and the Atlantic Charter," *Polish American Congress Bulletin* (February, 1944), p. 9.

the Polish cause. His requests to see the President were turned down on the basis of heavy schedules and the poor health of Roosevelt. Only when Rozmarek requested Mayor Kelly of Chicago to assist him in this endeavor, did Roosevelt receive Rozmarek. Rozmarek urged Roosevelt to take a more definite stand on the Polish issue. Roosevelt replied that he could not do so because this might lead to World War III with Russia. Rozmarek did not share this view, and pointed out that the President had a powerful weapon in his hand in the form of Lend-Lease. If the President informed Stalin firmly that unless Stalin adopted a reasonable attitude towards the Polish Government, Lend Lease would be terminated, this, in Rozmarek's opinion, would be sufficient to convince Stalin that America would not permit a new partition of Poland. Roosevelt—fearing the loss of Polish-American votes for his role at the Yalta conference—assured Rozmarek of his friendship for Poland, but would not make any specific promise, since he had already participated in the partition of Poland.[23]

Americans of Polish and non-Polish descent also disapproved of the Yalta agreements. Representative Alvin E. O'Konski, Republican of Wisconsin, called the Polish settlement "a success for Propaganda Minister Joseph Goebbels, second only to that of Munich." O'Konski also stated:

> The selling out of Poland is a stab in the back to freedom and a stab in the back to the freedom-loving country that has done much to crush Nazism.[24]

---

[23] According to information given to Dr. Edward J. Rozek, by Professor W. W. Kulski of Syracuse University—who has done some research on the 1944 pre-election campaign—it appears that several weeks before the election, Rozmarek had promised Thomas E. Dewey that the Polish-Americans would support him in his candidacy for the United States presidency. Roosevelt had not planned any tour of the country, but, immediately before the election, was persuaded by Democratic leaders to make an appearance in the major cities. When he arrived in Chicago, various delegations were assembled on the railroad platform. Among them, somewhere in the middle, was Rozmarek and his group. When the doors of the Presidential section of the train were opened, Franklin Roosevelt asked to be wheeled to Rozmarek first. Upon approaching him, the President stretched for both hands and said, "I am delighted to see you again, and I hope you will support me so that I can see that justice is done to Poland." Rozmarek was touched by the Roosevelt gesture and replied, "Yes, Mr. President, we shall stick with you to the end."

Jan Ciechanowski, Polish ambassador to the United States, during the war, also denounced the Yalta Treaty:

> As I left the House of Representatives I knew that Poland had been "sold down the river," that an illegal act had been committed, by virtue of which, contrary to international law and justice, the sovereignty of the Polish nation, vested in its legal government, had been appropriated by the Big Three powers without giving the people, or their legal representatives, the chance of having any say in the matter, without consulting the wishes of the Polish nation, in violation of the principles of self-determination and of all the traditions for which the United States had always stood in the past.[25]

In the confidential message to his Government, Ambassador Ciechanowski reported that on October 8, 1944, during the Pulaski Parade in New York City, he spent three hours with Governor Dewey on the reviewing stand, during which Dewey told him that Roosevelt's passive policy towards Poland revolted him and that he, if elected, intended to take a firmer stand against the Soviet appetites. On October 6 and October 20, Ambassador Ciechanowski visited former President Herbert Hoover, whom he had known for eighteen years. Hoover expressed a belief that at Teheran President Roosevelt undertook an obligation towards Stalin to preserve a passive policy towards the Polish question and that he had agreed to the Curzon Line with compensation for Poland in the west. According to Hoover, "Poland was doublecrossed" by Stalin and Roosevelt. "To my question," wrote Ciechanowski, "what Poland should do," Hoover replied:

> The only thing left for you is to appeal to public opinion. The President, the same way as Churchill—for their own political reasons and under the pretext not to spoil the relations between the Allies— demands from you silence and secrecy. You should, on the contrary bring the whole thing before the American and British public opinion. American public opinion will not fight for the Polish frontier if it will be said that an agreement was reached between you, even if under some pressure. But if it came out into the open that Russia is striving

---

Dewey was furious that Rozmarek had broken his word. Edward J. Rozek, *Allied Wartime Diplomacy a Pattern in Poland* (New York: 1958), p. 324.

[24] *New York Times* (February 14, 1945), p. 11.
[25] Jan Ciechanowski, *Defeat in Victory* (New York: 1947), p. 360.

to control Poland, which she is undoubtedly doing, then you will get such indignation and protest from American public opinion between the Atlantic and the Pacific Oceans that no American Government could conduct an appeasing policy toward the Soviet Union.[26]

Hoover then added that in view of the danger to the United States—rising out of the pro-Soviet policy of the New Deal—such a sobering of public opinion would be a great kindness to the American nation.[27]

Paul Super made the following comment on the Yalta Agreement in a letter sent to a large list of selected friends.

> Some of those who know my long connection with Poland very likely expect something from me regarding the Yalta decisions so far as they affect Poland, and regarding Poland itself, where I lived for 18 years, and to which land and people I have devoted 23 years of hard work. I say nothing about politics in my *Bulletin,* as that publication is strictly non-political.
> 1. As to the Polish section of the Yalta decision, never in a hundred years have the American people had an act committed in their name of which they have so much reason to be ashamed. As an American of long American ancestry, and proud of his country, I protest against the acceptance of this arrangement by our Senate.
> 2. For those who know just what is happening in Poland, and who love truth and justice and righteousness and humanity, these are very sad and heavy days indeed, days of pain and sorrow, of tragedy and alarm.
> 3. I have spent nearly half a century trying to serve the cause of Christ in the world. To me, the fate of Poland today marks the twilight of Christianity in eastern Europe. In all those lands its sun is setting; the night will be very dark; and who knows how far the darkness will extend.
> 4. An Old Testament prophet stated the situation accurately in Amos 5:15, as though a man escaped from a lion, and a bear met him. This is my comment as one who has spent many years in Christian work and who knows Europe from Liverpool to Stalingrad.[28]

The National Committee of Americans of Polish Descent sent telegrams to all the United States Senators protesting the Yalta

---

[26] Rozek, *op. cit.,* p. 300.
[27] Ibid.
[28] Paul Super, *Twenty-Five Years With the Poles* (Trenton: 1947), p. 343.

decisions affecting Poland. The telegrams urged the upper house to oppose American participation in another partition of Poland. The telegrams called the Polish Provisional Government of National Unity "a set of Soviet puppets."[29] Publishers of 41 Polish language newspapers—representing approximately 6,000,000 Americans of Polish descent—also petitioned the United States Senate not to ratify the Yalta plan regarding Poland.[30]

The *Catholic World* condemned the Polish settlement. It cited Russia's refusal to permit a Red Cross investigation of the story that the Red Army had murdered 14,500 Polish officers in Katyn Forest, and stated that if America allied herself with Stalin, she would have the crimes of Russia on her soul. The publication further stated: "to any good American or Englishman, Yalta may well seem the most galling incident in History."[31] The *American Journal of International Law* commented on the Polish decision editorially. It also considered the legality of the transaction. L. H. Woolsey stated that the Polish decision was in some respects exactly contrary to the principles of the Atlantic Charter. He called the partition of Poland an act under "untoward circumstances of military occupation, foreign administration, movement of population, repression of sentiment, redistribution of lands and the like."[32] Herbert Wright reviewed the historic background of the boundary settlement and concluded that there was no basis for the Curzon Line.[33] He stated that the 1939 frontier had been accepted by the Soviet Union in the Treaty of Riga, in 1921, and confirmed by the Treaty of Non-Aggression, in 1923, and he saw no reason for changing it.

In 1947, a "Justice for Poland" group adopted a resolution calling upon President Truman to denounce the Yalta agreements and demanded the withdrawal of Russian occupation troops from Eastern and Central Europe.[34] Again, in 1948, representatives of

---

[29] *New York Times* (February 15, 1945), p. 6.
[30] *New York Times* (February 19, 1945), p. 10.
[31] *Catholic World* (April, 1945), p. 5.
[32] L. H. Woolsey, "Poland at Yalta and Dumbarton Oaks," *The American Journal of International Law*, Volume XXXIV, 1945, p. 298.
[33] Herbert Wright, "Poland and the Crimea Conference," *The American Journal of International Law*, Volume XXXIV, 1945, pp. 305-310.
[34] *New York Times* (June 9, 1947), p. 6.

21 Polish-American groups—meeting under the auspices of the Coordinating Committee of American Polish Associations—demanded the abrogation of the Yalta Agreement with Russia.[36] In May 1950, the *Saturday Evening Post* carried an editorial by Ann Su Cardwell calling for the repudiation of the Yalta agreement.

In August 1951, the *New York Times* in editorial opinion declared:

> History will record that at Yalta the United States repudiated some of its solemn obligations, yielded to Russian imperialism and gave way to appeasement which will be regretted for decades and all for mythical reasons. The true reason for Yalta remains an inscrutable mystery. The result of Yalta remains a triumph for Communist diplomacy.[36]

General Eisenhower also attacked the Yalta agreement in his preconvention speeches. He asserted that he had no part in the conferences himself as a military leader. Eisenhower further stated that he knew nothing about the decisions until he read them in the newspaper.[37]

A denunciation of the Yalta agreement was also written into the Republican platform.

> Teheran, Yalta, and Potsdam were the scenes of those tragic blunders with others to follow.... The leaders of the Administration in power acted without the knowldege or consent of Congress or of the American people. They traded our overwhelming victory for a new enemy and for new oppressions and new wars which were quick to come. The government of the United States under Republican leadership will repudiate all commitments contained in secret understandings such as those of Yalta which aid Communist enslavement.[38]

Wassel in his study summarized the significance of the Yalta experience as follows:

> Yalta has become a symbol of those who are apprehensive about world affairs today. To say that most of the talk was mere verbiage

---

[35] *New York Times* (April 12, 1948), p. 7.
[36] *New York Times* (August 20, 1951), p. 11.
[37] *New York Times* (June 15, 1952), p. 50.
[38] *New York Times* (July 11, 1952), p. 8.

only misses the real significance of Yalta. The significance lies in the fact that Yalta was a lesson in international politics to the American people. And it is a lesson they will not soon forget.[39]

Delegates from the Polish American Congress had met with Presidents Roosevelt, Truman and Eisenhower to plead the cause of a free and democratic Poland, and to oppose the terms of the Yalta agreement. They also had presented the cause for an independent and integral Poland to the United Nations Conference, in San Francisco, in the fall of 1945. Rozmarek and three other members of the executive board of the Polish American Congress attended the Paris Conference, in 1946, and personally conferred with leaders and diplomats of Democratic countries, in Paris and London, where they presented the viewpoint of Americans of Polish descent.

In 1955, ten years after the Yalta Conference, the U.S. Department of State released the text of official documents to the ill-fated meeting of Franklin Roosevelt, Winston Churchill and Joseph Stalin, in the Crimea, where the peace was lost before the war was won. The documents were crammed with illuminating details of the mood and manner in which the Big Three sliced up the world. They reveal an almost total absence of the pursuit of justice through the hard complexities of the world as it is.

Senator William Knowland made the following comment when the documents were released:

> If the disclosures discourage two or three nations from thinking they can sit down behind closed doors—with no responsibility to their elected representatives and to the people—and proceed to parcel out nations and people without their consent, they will have served their purpose. Whether it be at Yalta, Potsdam or Geneva, a useful purpose will be served if every official who partcipates in negotiations realizes that he has an ultimate accounting to the people and that his decisions will have to stand the light of history.[40]

The U.S. State Department's Yalta record revealed that the Peace was lost by ignoring justice and the facts of life. How the

---
[39] Wassell, op. cit., p. 50.
[40] *Time, the Weekly Magazine* (March 28, 1955), p. 15.

fate of Poland was settled, at Yalta, is a story that contains all the elements of the larger story of how Roosevelt and Churchill lost the peace. As the Yalta Conference opened, it was obvious that the Red Army would conquer all of Poland within a matter of weeks. Stalin did not need a Yalta agreement to give him eastern Poland. Stalin's motive, at Yalta, was political, not geographic. Nobody knew better than the Russians that the Poles would not make docile slaves. With Germany and France out of the future great-power picture, Britain and the United States were the only countries to which Polish patriots would look for help. Stalin needed to destroy this hope—to show the Poles that the western powers would, in practice, throw the principles of the Atlantic Charter overboard. The Charter emphasized, as principle of world order, the right of self-determination for such countries as Poland.

The first objective of Stalin was to get the United States and Britain to abandon the former Polish government residing in London. Right at the start of the polemical sham battle over Poland, Roosevelt exposed the poverty of the Anglo-American effort. There were two related avenues, for a strong U.S. approach: the high principles of self-determination for even the smallest state, and the heavy pressure of such practical measures as Russia's stake in the future of West Germany. Instead, Roosevelt and Churchill couched their main plea to Stalin in terms of petty politicians asking favors. At that level, Stalin inevitably bested them.

> "There are six or seven million Poles in the U.S.," began Roosevelt. ". . . It would make it easier for me at home if the Soviet government would give something to Poland." Stalin could not have cared less how Roosevelt's popularity rating fared in Buffalo's Sixth Ward. To such arguments the Soviet dictator had a bland counter: "What will the Russians say?" Without the Polish territory he coveted, said Stalin, "I cannot return to Moscow."[41]

Roosevelt and Churchill also stooped to wheedling flattery. They urged Stalin to be magnanimous. At least, said Roosevelt, return the Polish oil province of Lwow. Churchill lifted the appeal

---

[41] *Time, the Weekly Magazine* (March 28, 1955), p. 31.

to an oratorical height: "This is what is dear to the hearts of the nation of Britain . . . that Poland should be free and sovereign . . . mistress in her own house and in her own soul . . . (our) interest is only one of honor." Stalin refused. Churchill and Roosevelt capitulated much to Stalin's surprise.

Two years later, in January 1947, the Polish provisional government—recognized by the Big Three—held its elections. They were rigged to insure Communist control. The Yalta agreement did give Stalin part of the Polish territory which his armies overran. So shocked were the Poles at the action of Roosevelt and Churchill that the Communists were able to fasten their grip on Poland without meeting dangerous resistance. The Polish lesson was not lost on the Hungarians, Slovaks, Bulgarians, Romanians, and Czechs. If the Poles—eastern Europe's stoutest fighters for freedom could not depend on the United States and Britain—what hope was there for them? And so the Communist grip upon all of Eastern Europe tightened without meeting dangerous resistance.

It is the fashion to criticize Stalin these days and minimize his achievements, but in some respects these bordered on the colossal. With a mighty concentration of will, and an utterly ruthless imposition of his will on Roosevelt and Churchill, Stalin achieved all of his aims without war. John Gunther in *Procession* made the following observation:

> The arrangements made at Yalta represented probably the greatest triumph in Stalin's life, although Roosevelt and Churchill did not mean this to be so. What Stalin got, as events turned out, was a virtually free hand in Eastern Europe which enabled him to build up the Communist regimes which now rule East Germany, Poland, Hungary, and the other European satellites.[42]

Aleksander I. Solzhenitsyn, author of *The Gulag Archipelago, 1918-1956*—an historical account of the Soviet penal system—made the following comment in his book:

> In their own countries Roosevelt and Churchill are honored as examples of statesman-like wisdom. To us, in Russian prison discussions, their systematic short-sightedness and stupidity stood out as astonishingly obvious. How could they, in their descent from 1941 to

1945, fail to secure any guarantees whatsoever of the independence of Eastern Europe?[43]

Recently Richard Burton was banned from working for British Broadcasting Corporation because of his recent harsh criticism of Churchill. Burton described Churchill as "a coward, a power-corrupted warmonger and a medieval bandit-king."[44] No truer words were spoken.[45]

In all these deliberations on Yalta no one refers to Eleanor Roosevelt and her point of view and why she supported the President's view (or was it hers?) to sell Poland into bondage. Eleanor Roosevelt is well known for her Socialistic orientation and her sympathetic understanding of Communist ideology. To this date it is not known how much influence she did have on persuading her husband to be more benevolent towards Communist ideology.

Also to this day the question is why did Roosevelt and Churchill make the concessions they did and how the wrongness of those concessions can be recognized in future situations where similar temptations, and pressures may occur. This is what we confront when we turn from recriminations over Yalta to the long task of expiating it.

---

[42] John Gunther, *Procession* (New York: 1965), pp. 53-54.
[43] Aleksander I. Solzhenitsyn, "Stalin: Weaken the Will to Strengthen the State," *The Cincinnati Enquirer* (December 30, 1973), p. 7-E.
[44] "BBC bans Burton for attacking Churchill," *The Detroit News* (November 30, 1974), p. 17-A.
[45] Churchill was petty and aggressive from childhood. A recent British historian says that Winston Churchill was stabbed in the chest close to his heart when he was a ten-year-old schoolboy, during an argument with a classmate over a penknife! "Churchill Stabbed" *Detroit Free Press* (September 20, 1973), p. 18-D.

CHAPTER 14

The Pax Americana (1945-1950)

*So, then, to every man his chance—To every man, regardless
    of his birth,
His shining, golden opportunity—To every man the right to live
To work, to be himself, and to become
Whatever thing his manhood and his vision can combine to
    make him—
This, seeker, is the promise of America.*

—Thomas Wolfe

When the surrender of Japan was announced, about 6:00 P.M., August 14, 1945, the country had been waiting for it with nerve rasping tenseness for many hours. The news broke over the country like a thunderstorm, washing away the fatigue and boredom of the long wait. Automobile horns, sirens, factory whistles and shouts of joy signaled the victory celebration and conclusion of the terrible war. Workers in the factories threw down their tools and rushed into the streets. Lawn mowers were left standing in yards, suppers on tables. Traffic snarls developed as people tried to drive to downtown areas to join the celebration. Girls gave ardent kisses to servicemen on crowded avenues; even a few civilian lads received such favors. Noisemaker stands sprang up like magic on every corner. The celebrations on the main streets lasted nearly all night long; and in the morning hours, a few weary celebrants could still be sitting, head in hand, on the curbstone, or trudging barefoot down the street, feebly tooting cardboard horns.

Then the Pax Americana era began. President Harry Truman took a firm grip on his new job. After twelve years of the worst depression in our history, followed by four years of World War

II's austerity and hysteria, the mood of the American people, in 1945, resembled in many ways the mood of their parents in 1919. They were ready to pull themselves together into something resembling a normal life. They were tired of politics; they desired the early return of their men from the armed forces; and they wished to be left alone to pursue their own interests. Unlike their parents, they recognized that the United States could not escape from world politics. The Congress in office, in 1945, and the one elected, in 1946, reflected the sentiments of the people. On issues of foreign policy, they supported the President with little thought of partisan advantage. They were indifferent or even hostile to his proposals for domestic reform.

The next five years were the crucial ones. The United States was the colossus. The war had left Europe in shambles. Russia still had its dauntless army, but no industrial power. Asia was a fragmented riddle. Only America was secure and prosperous. There was every reason to believe that from 1945-1950 would indeed be "the best years." But in a way they were among our most tragic and confused years. The outstanding event of 1945 was the signing of the United Nations Charter. But at home, as well as abroad, there were certain uneasy exceptions. The United States met the crisis in Greece with the Truman Doctrine, and the Berlin blockade with an airlift. The Iron Curtain was pierced with the Voice of America. The Marshall Plan, NATO and Point Four strengthened the allies of the United States.

The war's end brought immediate lifting of rationing on gasoline, canned goods, and fuel oil. Automobiles lined up at local filling stations, and motorists, once again, could say "Fill 'er up." With war contracts canceled, many war plants laid off workers, and some were closed entirely. The Signal Battery, in Milwaukee, closed; discharging 2,198 production workers, two days after the war ended. The state industrial commission's unemployment compensation department got 5,000 applications by the next day. Banks also reported heavy cashing of war bonds.

Soon the American system of welfare capitalism was booming. Sixty million jobs, once a dream, were now considered barely enough. Industry—changing from war production to consumer goods—began to reabsorb the workers. Notable advances in technology enabled industry to offer the public an enticing array of new products, including an eight-inch TV screen, electronic devices, plastic and synthetic products, chemicals to fight dirt and insects, and drugs to combat disease and nervous tension.

The consumer market was at an unparalleled high. There was money saved from the war rationing years when there was little to buy. There was a new, carefree desire to spend it, and an unsatiable demand for goods. In particular, consumer goods remained scarce. Orders took time to fill. Long lines of people formed wherever scarce items were placed on sale: butter, meat, nylon stockings, and even men's shirts and underwear. There was an acute housing shortage. War-time priorities did not allow construction of civilian dwellings to prepare for the post-war rush to the altar. Brides were lucky to be carried over thresholds.

The auto industry limped and staggered through 1946 with stop and go productions. There were strikes and shortages of a variety of parts to automobiles. Government controls impeded production and hampered the flow of materials. Industry could hardly afford walkouts at a time when the demand for goods was high. Labor unions struck for higher pay. The longest strike (119 days) in General Motors Corporation history ended March 12, 1946, when General Motors agreed to pay $18\frac{1}{2}$ cents hourly wage increases to the UAW-CIO. Employee wage loss, during that strike, was $130 million. Other strikes: electrical, packing house, steel, coal and rail—amounted to the biggest work stoppage since 1919, after World War I.

In 1946, the year America's servicemen returned from World War II, 2.3 million couples were married. Many of the divorces occurred almost before the honeymoon was over. A record 610,000 divorces (one-fourth of the couples married) were granted in 1946. The marriages ended as quickly as they began, because earnings at home didn't measure up to the sums needed to establish a new home. War experiences had changed young men; couples couldn't understand each other anymore. The birth rate, however, was not down in 1946. That year was just in the middle between 1942 and 1950 when 30 million babies were born.

For the soldiers who couldn't—or didn't want to—find work

there was the "52-20 Club," that is, unemployment pay of $20 for 52 weeks after discharge from the armed services. When six million veterans had drawn their benefits (the average was for two months) by August 1946, officials were worried if the boys would ever go back to work. The government rewarded its veterans with a GI Bill that helped them buy homes, obtain job training, and go to college. The colleges were overflowed with veterans of all ages studying on the GI Bill of Rights. New opportunities were made available for Blacks as the armed forces were desegregated.

Travel had not exactly broadened the viewpoint of the veteran. The polls revealed hostility on the part of veterans toward labor unions, Jews and Blacks. Half of the group covered by one War Department survey predicted racial "trouble" before the decade concluded. A major breakthrough in the racial crisis came when Jackie Robinson became the first Black to play big-league baseball. Joe Louis, heavy-weight boxer, retired for the first time, undefeated.

Rodgers and Hammerstein sparked the most successful decade in the history of Broadway musicals with "Oklahoma," "Carousel," and "South Pacific." The movie, in 1946, "The Best Years of Our Lives" showed a poignant wedding scene: a disabled veteran—hands blown off during the war—offering a wedding band —held in prosthetic hooks—to his bride. Best sellers indicated a taste for escapism: *Forever Amber, Peace of Mind, This Side of Innocence.* Ernest Hemingway bid a gentle literary farewell with *The Old Man and the Sea.*

Song hits had quaint lyrics that were also amusing and memorable: "They Say It's Wonderful," "Ole Buttermilk Sky," and "Shoo-Fly and Apple Pan Dowdy." The country smiled at the liberated antics of Edben Ahbez and his song, "Nature Boy," rendered by the velvet voice of Nat (King) Cole. A wobbly ankled singer, with sideburns, made "rock and roll" a craze.

The age of suburban living came into its own. Americans moved into massive housing developments located in the suburbs. Shopping centers consumed vast acres of land for multiple store complexes with enormous parking lots situated at intersections and converging expressways. Television produced forests of antennae

THE PAX AMERICANA (1945-1950) 423

atop the house tops. The Empire State Building added a TV tower. Neighborhood movie houses closed like banks during the Great Depression. The onset of the jet age reduced traveling time for great distances. As jet transportation broadened our horizons, rockets were shot into the atmosphere. A man scaled Mt. Everest, and looked toward landing on the moon. The filter cigaret was born and became the butt of comedian jokes. The "new look" dropped hemlines to the ankles. "Zoot suits" caught the fancy of "hepcats."

There were about eight or ten million people who were homeless when World War II was terminated. They had been driven from place to place by the invading armies until they literally had no home. These were the "displaced persons" known eventually as D.P.'s. They were herded together into detention camps, at first, and these were run by the various occupying armies with the help of UNRRA—the United Nations Relief and Rehabilitation Administration. This was intended to be a temporary measure while the United Nations studied the situation.

The political situation in Poland, after World War II, and the presence of large numbers of Polish citizens, in western Europe, who did not want to return to Poland, had influenced the United States Senate and the House of Representatives—in sympathy with the plight of the European refugees—to pass the Displaced Persons Act in 1948. The Act provided that 205,000 displaced persons—possessing good health—might be allowed to enter the United States in the two ensuing years on condition that homes and jobs awaited them in the United States. In 1950, the Act was extended for an additional year, and the number increased to 369,000, together with 29,000 orphans.

The first ship to bring "D.P.'s" to America, under the Displaced Persons Act, was the *General Black*, which sailed from Bremerhaven in mid-October 1948. On board were 813 people who had fled from place to place as the armies advanced. Some of them had not been able to settle down anywhere since Hitler invaded Poland, nine years ago. Many of the children had never known what it was to have a settled home. Scores of scientists, writers, and teachers were among the many thousands of Poles brought to the United States from the prisoner-of-war and Displaced Persons Camps, through the efforts of such organizations as the Polish Institute of Arts and Sciences, the Polish American Congress, the Polish National Alliance, and other organizations.[1]

The Polish American Congress formed, in 1948, "An American Committee for the Resettlement of Polish Displaced Persons." Judge Blair F. Gunther was elected chairman of the committee which had the following objectives:

> To assist in the selection of those Displaced Persons of political ethnic origin from European Displaced Persons Camps, who are eligible for entry into the United States; to provide them with the necessities of life, to assure them their transportation from the port of landing to their designated place of residence in the United States, to secure employment for them and a place to live in full cooperation with the Federal Displaced Persons Commissions and all related governmental, civic, and private agencies and to secure funds to successfully accomplish the above mentioned program.[2]

The program involved the cooperation of the United States Government; the Polish groups in Europe; and individual Americans of Polish descent who had signed assurances involving certain risks, as they had to be responsible for persons whom they undersigned. The whole procedure involved an effort to find employment, housing, and transportation. By the time the Displaced Persons Law had expired on December 31, 1951, the American Committee for the Resettlement of Polish Displaced Persons, had obtained 35,000 assurances.[3]

The Resettlement Committee has also been instrumental in resettling 16,000 Polish displaced persons and ex-Polish soldiers from England to the United States. The Polish Immigration Committee of New York—supported by a monthly remittance from the Polish American Congress—had been successful in bringing to America more than 12,500 Polish displaced persons.[4] The Committee—assisted by Charles Rozmarek, Polish-American con-

---

[1] Wytrwal, *Poles in American History and Tradition*, pp. 415-428.

[2] Helena Znaniecki Lopata, *The Function of Voluntary Association in an Ethnic Community: Polonia* (unpublished Ph.D. dissertation, University of Chicago, 1954), p. 112.

[3] *Ibid.*, p. 113.

[4] Report of President Charles Rozmarek at the Third Convention of the Polish American Congress, Atlantic City, May 30, 1952.

gressmen, and Rt. Rev. Msgr. Felix Burant, President of the Polish Immigration Committee—was also instrumental in influencing the passage, in Congress, of emergency immigration legislation which provided for the admission of 240,000 immigrants above the quotas to relieve the refugee problem in western Europe.[5] A major share of the 240,000 refugees, who entered the United States, were from Eastern Europe.[6] The need for the Resettlement Committee was necessary.

> The Committee is continuously receiving letters of complaints from Polish deportees by Hitler, still in Germany. and recent escapees, asking why they cannot come to America. They have a tremendous feeling that America has unjustly treated their nation and that the United States has not fulfilled its moral obligation to these people. The Committee's job is to explain the situation to them and not excite them to become Anti-American. The Committee has attempted to create a feeling that these Polish people are not forgotten in Europe, by the people in America.[7]

The Committee had received many invitations to attend different national and local conferences concerned with the refugee problem. The executive secretary of the Committee is a member of the greater New York Welfare and Health Council, Committee on Services to New Immigrants.

The Catholic League for Religious Assistance to Poland dates back to World War II days when the League was founded under the leadership of Bishop Stephen Woznicki. At that time its stated purpose was to have money available to help Poland after it would regain its freedom. It gave financial assistance in rebuilding churches destroyed during the war, in restoring liturgical vessels, such as chalices, ciboriums and tabernacles to places of worship, and even provided badly needed vestments and priestly garb.

---

[5] In 1975, the Polish American Immigration and Relief Committee celebrated the 25th anniversary of its humanitarian work. More than 54,000 Polish refugees and displaced persons have been helped. The present president of the organization is Monsignor John J. Karpinski.

[6] Rt. Rev. Msgr. Felix Burant, *Statement to the sub-committee on Immigration and Naturalization* (Polish Immigration Committee, 1953), pp. 1-4.

[7] Thaddeus Theodore Kryniewicz, *The Polish Immigration Committee in the United States—A Historical Study of the American Committee for the Relief of Polish Immigrants: 1947-1952* (unpublished Master's thesis, Fordham University, 1953), p. 53.

Currently funds are channeled mainly into three institutions, the Polish College and the Polish Institute (both in Rome), and the Polish Seminary in Paris, France. It takes $150,000 annually to support these three schools, two of which are seminaries and the other, the Institute, prepares teaching faculty for the seminaries. The League also finances the necessary travel of Cardinal Stefan Wyszynski, primate of Poland. Catechetical aids, and religious periodicals are also provided from the League funds.[8]

Increased Americanization did not prevent many Americans of Polish descent from working for Polish Relief and Polish independence during the post-World War II period. However, the "All for Poland" attitude was gone. There was more concern with local problems, and with the general and post-war problems of Americans. A majority of the Americans of Polish descent had spent their money, during the war, for American Defense and War Bonds rather than on Polish relief. After World War II, the main activity of Polish-American organizations involved cooperation with various agencies and governments to bring Polish displaced persons into the United States. It is hard to determine which factor—increased Americanization, or unwillingness to take a risk—were responsible for this situation.

The Polish American Congress had established an "Educational and Cultural Commission." Its main contribution had been the support it gave to the Polish Arts and Science Institute (Polski Instytut Naukowy) and the Paderewski Foundation. The 1953 report of this commission enumerated a series of motions which are interesting in light of the previous inter-organizational associations and their aims.[9]

1. The Commission urges that each of the thirty state divisions support, exploit, and promote the teaching of the Polish language at the public high schools and in the various colleges and universities, especially courses in the methods of teaching Polish, so as to increase the number of licensed teachers. Since 1948,

---

[8] The Catholic League's headquarters is now in Chicago. An episcopal committee of nine bishops of Polish ethnic background directs its activities with Bishop Alfred Abramowicz, auxiliary bishop of Chicago, serving as national chairman.

[9] Zygmunt Dybowski, *Protokol 3cej Krajowej Konwencji Kongresu Polonji Amerykanskiej* (Chicago: 1952), pp. 106-108.

Polish has been added to the curriculum of six colleges and two high schools.

2. That a "suitable national General Kosciuszko commemoration enterprise be sponsored. . . ." Also it reports that a second portrait has been added to the West Point Academy thanks to the New York Division of the Polish American Congress.
3. The Commission again recommends that the State Divisions watch and protest every book, film, or news story that slants, omits or defaces the true picture of Poland, or the Pole, or the Polish American. During the past four years, there were protests against five films and fourteen books.
4. That the Board compile, every six months, a list of books about any Polish subject in the English language and send the list to all state divisions and federations so that they can purchase and place them in the main public libraries; suggestions on how to publicize them were also included.
5. The central office of the Polish-American Congress have complete microfilm records made of the twelve daily newspapers and donate these microfilm records to the Library of Congress, New York, Boston and Chicago Libraries.
6. All members and organizations be asked to collect and send old records, protocols, letters, clippings and other data relating to the Polish American Congress and Polish American Organizations and doings to the libraries and museums of the PRCU and PNA in Chicago. Also that Paderewski data, files, signatures be sent to the Paderewski Foundation, and other data, including signatures to the Kosciuszko Foundation. These will serve as history records for future Americans. World War I and other early day records are no longer available—lost to the present and future generations.
7. That Polish-Americans show greater interest and enroll themselves in the five Polish-American colleges: Madonna College, Alliance College, St. John Kanty College, St. Mary's College in Orchard Lake and Don Bosco College in New Jersey. The colleges are urged to increase their advertising in the Polish language press.
8. That individuals who find slanted writings about Poland should communicate to the Polish American Congress, in Chicago for proper action.
9. That annually ten per-cent of the Polish American Congress Funds be utilized for educational and cultural purposes. We recommend financial support for the Polish Institute of Arts and Sciences and the Paderewski Foundation before the end of the year 1952. It is fitting that this ten per-cent be dedicated to the above outlined cause and we recommend it be apportioned to

similar institutions like the Polish Singers' Alliance, *Szkolki Doksztalcajace* (supplementary education emphasizing Polish culture) and the Polish American Encyclopedia Commission.

10. Recommend sending a telegram to General Eisenhower, then president of Columbia University.

The recommendations indicate a tremendous change of emphasis towards Americanization. The recommendations are written in English, and their primary concerns are directed toward a positive public opinion towards Poland and Polish-Americans. Two points are made about protecting the good name of Poland. No mention is made of parochial schools and their problems. The recommendations also contain the first mention of teacher qualifications, a subject which is very much on the minds of Americans, but which has not been of serious concern to the Polish-American leaders. No mention is made, however, of the physical maintenance of schools. Throughout the history of the Polish-American communities little discussion is made of physical facilities for parochial education or the problem of overcrowding. The Polish American Congress does not mention lack of books for Polish-American schools. The recommendations presume a higher intellectual and educational level of Americans of Polish descent, in contrast to earlier stated concerns over literacy. Most of the work—one assumes from the recommendations of the Polish American Congress and the cultural and educational commission —lies in protests and reviewing articles on Polish-American communities and topics which have appeared in the daily, monthly, and quarterly publications in the United States and abroad. The actual task—such as the collection of historical data—was performed by member associations, foundations, and libraries.

If the automobile opened up America geographically for the members of the ethnic groups, and the movies introduced them to the mansions of the American "aristocracy," then radio and television have brought America into their own homes. The last stronghold of group separation—the home—has fallen. There is no longer a walled-off ethnic island. The war had enormous psychological effects on the Polish-American community. It enhanced the Polish-American status in American society, accelerated the already well-advanced process of assimilation, and increased the confidence of the Polish-American people. Few, now, were prone to view themselves as Poles. In some quarters such designations were decidedly resented. They had become Polish-Americans or Americans of Polish descent.

The era after World War II was one of continued progress and prosperity for the Polish-Americans. The lush years had brought new wealth and affluence to members of the older generation who were solidly entrenched in business, and the various professions. Polish-American names became more and more identified with charitable, educational, and community projects. Thousands of Polish-Americans returned from the battlefields to continue their education, or resume careers in business, law, medicine, engineering, teaching, journalism, and a host of a hundred different occupations. At the same time, the Polish-American communities received cultural transfusions from many directions. Displaced persons, refugees, and university students began arriving in increasing numbers.

The fresh wave of refugees, exiles, and immigrants—despite the wide gulf separating the new from the old—gave a new lease to Polish life in the United States.[10] The wellsprings of Polish identity were replenished by the new arrivals. The circulation of Polish newspapers in the United States increased. Polish singing and dancing was revived. New matrimonial frontiers were opened up for some of the second generation girls. Also, Polish-American lawyers were attracting new clients for a variety of reasons. The business of Polish products was stimulated; more Polish records and foods were sold. Polish steamships and airlines became known.

Once conditions became stabilized, a mounting number of

---

[10] According to Danuta Mostwin, in her study, among the postwar immigrants: 27 per cent had university degrees, 20 per cent had university training, and an additional 23 per cent had completed high school. In a survey, 50 years earlier, dealing with Polish peasants who emigrated, the figures in each of these categories was much lower. Also 5 per cent landed inside the upper American social class, 13 per cent in the upper middle, and 27 percent in the middle class. Family income showed nearly 20 per cent over the $20,000 a year level, 22 per cent in the $15-20 thousand level and only about 5 per cent under the $5,000 level. Also Mostwin's study indicates that 62 per cent fled for political reasons, with 5 per cent citing economic reasons. In the survey of the peasants, a half century ago, the economic reason was the principal motivating force. "Polish Immigrants to U.S. since war socially higher," *Gwiazda Polarna* (February 27, 1971), p. 5.

Americans of Polish and non-Polish descent, found their way to Poland. By the late 1950s and early 1960s, popular motion pictures—filmed in Poland—and the appearance on the American stage of Polish actors, comedians, popular and folk singers and dancers, notably Slask and Mazowsze folk dance companies—helped present both Poles and their American kin in a more sympathetic light.

Poles, who came on student visas represented a distant element that should not be confused with any of the other immigrant arrivals. As a rule, they were educated, poised, and intelligent young men and women who took special pride in their Polish heritage. Most of them attended colleges and universities throughout the country, and seemed to be distributed widely throughout all branches of learning. Some were sponsored by relatives who informed them that they had to work their way through college; others were provided by means in one fashion or another: Kosciuszko Foundation Scholarships, or government exchange programs.[11] A number married Americans of Polish and non-Polish extraction and decided to remain in the United States.

The long sought for peace did not resolve many major problems. It seemed as if a nemesis was at work. With each attempt at a resolution, other problems would result, or different unrelated issues would develop on the local, state or international level to keep newspaper headlines in live copy, and people distracted from the vital concerns that would affect their life.

---

[11] Many Polish-American pastors sponsored students who were priests. They offered housing and other benefits. In many cases they were disappointed and financially poorer. The priests—who claimed to be scholars—were really opportunists interested in their own selfish advancement and material well being. These scholar-priests were certainly a sad reflection on the Catholic University of Lublin. This contact with Polish priests left many Polish-American pastors wiser, sadder and poorer. It also affected their interest in helping other Polish priests in Poland, which is sad, because there are deserving priest-scholars who should be helped.

CHAPTER 15

War in Korea

*And thru some mooned valhalla
  there shall pass,
Battalions and battalions, scarred
  from hell;
The unreturning army that was
  youth,
The legions who have suffered and
  are dust.*

—Siegfried Sassoon

The year, 1950, was the beginning of a new era for the proud and confident United States that thought it clearly knew right from wrong, and could enforce its idea of right as decisively as it had during World War II.

There were many good songs and music to be remembered, some of them highly individualistic. Johnny Ray, who was about 75 percent deaf, wretched out a big record with contortions and grimaces as he sang, "If your sweetheart sends a letter of good-bye. . . ." It was called "Cry," and you can still hear it on occasion. But it was Mario Lanza who became the singing sensation of the decade with an operatic voice: controlled, passionate and resonant —a phenomenon which could also render such popular songs as "Be My Love." Patti Page sang "Tennessee Waltz"; Rosemary Clooney—"C'mon a My House"; Teresa Brewer—"Music, Music, Music"; and Frankie Laine sang "Jezebel." This was the decade for Perez Prado's "Cherry Pink and Apple Blossom White," Leroy Anderson's "Blue Tango," and Vaughn Monroe's "Old Soldiers Never Die"—the latter in honor of General Mac-

Arthur after the president removed him from his overseas command.

Television changed the recreational habits of our nation. Huge audiences watched "I Love Lucy," "Your Show of Shows," and Milton Berle, the "Uncle Miltie" who walked on his ankles and pratfell his way to success in the medium overtaking radio in home entertainment. Television had just introduced to the nation young Garry Moore, with his crew cut and penny loafers, and Perry Como, with his soft barbershop baritone and alpaca cardigan sweater.

It was also the decade in which dizzy fads bubbled up: ducktail haircuts, hula hoops, 3-D movies, the Twist, and the Davy Crockett mania, which launched a $100-million market for Davy Crockett coonskin caps, clothes, guitars, records and pup tents. The Yankee dynasty which would once again win the World Series, in 1950, fielded such legends and near-legends as Dimaggio, Rizzuto, Bauer, Berra and Martin. In 1950, the big movie in America was "All About Eve." Then there were flying saucer reports which scared some, inflamed the imagination of others with a neon glow. But some of the "flying saucers" sighted turned out to be Air Force weather balloons, and for the cynics that confirmed their delight.

According to the United States Census, 861,184 Americans claimed Poland as their country of birth; 1,925,015 had one or both parents born in Poland. The decline in the number of foreign-born Poles, and the relative stability in the size of the second generation, suggested a third generation of Polish-Americans was becoming a more important segment of the population.

On Sunday, June 25, 1950, baseball was displaced by news that war had broken out in an obscure little Asian nation called Korea. Some 60,000 North Korean troops—spearheaded by 100 Russian-built tanks—had crossed the 38th Parallel into the Republic of Korea to the south, and the UN Security Council had demanded a cessation to the hostilities. When the hostilities began, President Truman sent U.S. warplanes into the battle. Our chief delegate to the United Nations, Warren R. Austin, declared that the immediate effect of this "historic action should be to stop bloodshed and aggression in Korea." He also stated that "the larger effect should be to discourage aggression everywhere. The Korean War marked the first real test of Free World solidarity in the face of the Communist force. In repulsing this attempted Communist aggression, the United Nations—led by the United States—served notice that it would not hesitate to aid those nations whose freedom and independence was under attack.

June 25, 1950, was the rude awakening into a new age, and the concept of a "limited war" was ushered in. It was also the beginning of the maddeningly paradoxical era of America's Asian involvement. When the Chinese entered the war, they swarmed across the frozen Yalu River; they stormed up Pork Chop Hill to fearsome bugle calls, and stalemated our best at the Punchbowl. The United States landed Marines at Inchon, and died beside the ROK's, the Australians, the Turks, and other United Nations allies. Harry Truman called it a "police action," it was war.

The enemy was an unrecognizable "horde," a mass of oriental humanity dressed in quilted jackets who carried banana-clip burp guns and fought valiantly. In three years there were 33,629 U.S. battle deaths and 130,000 total casualties.

In the United States, Americans learned to pronounce words like Pyongang, Seoul, Pusan, and Wonsan, and, finally, Panmunjom. Americans learned of a new national paranoia: fear of the "comies," the "reds"—a fear that would give prominence to Senator Joe McCarthy and later destroy his career. Also, Herb Philbrick, the real man and the TV character on "I Lead Three Lives," became a folk hero. When our POW's came home, the country learned about brainwashing, and about the 21 who chose to stay behind.

When the Korean War commenced, Colonel Francis Gabreski, a winner of twelve Distinguished Flying Crosses, was back on active duty with the Air Force—eager for combat once more. In May 1951, the orders arrived for him to report to the 4th Fighter Interceptor Wing in Korea. There, as the "Old Pro," he found combat much different from World War II. The flights covered an area of square miles, and the attacks had to be coldly calculated. He proved adept at the game by downing his first Mig on July 8, 1951.

He had one more victory with the 4th before he was given

command of the 51st FIW, which he led to fame and many victories with a courageous spirit and determination. With a few veteran pilots, he moulded them into a very successful unit which led the way for him to become one of the first jet aces. Gabreski scored $4\frac{1}{2}$ times with the 51st. The half victory was shared with another former ace of the ETO, Major Bill Whisner. As a matter of fact, when Whisner finished the Mig off, Gabreski ordered him to take credit for it. He refused, and after a few days' hassle, it was finally split between the two. Gabreski had done so in an attempt to make Whisner the first ace of the 51st.[1]

In an editorial on August 8, 1959, the *Detroit News* called Gabreski the nation's greatest living ace, and said: "he has been too long denied the rank that should be his according to his record, character, command quality, and devotion to the United States."[2]

A jungle infiltration course at Fort Benning, Georgia is named after Captain E. C. Krzyzowski, who lost his life in an assault, in Korea, in 1951. There also is a metal bridge, in Korea, named after Captain Krzyzowski. For his heroic action in Korea, Captain Krzyzowski was awarded the Congressional Medal of Honor posthumously.

Colonel Bernard J. Pankowski was commander of the largest battalion in the U.S. Army—the 304th Signal Battalion in Seoul, Korea. A native of La Porte, Indiana he graduated from the U.S. Military Academy, in 1946. He received his M.S. degree in electrical engineering, in 1952, from the Massachusetts Institute of Technology, and an M.S. degree in business administration from George Washington University, in 1965. He also attended the Command and General Staff College at Ft. Leavenworth, Kansas, and the Industrial College of the Armed Forces at Fort McNair, Washington. The Signal Battalion provided command and control communications for the United Nations Command and the Eight U.S. Army Headquarters. He wears the Army Commendation Medal with an Oak Leaf Cluster.

Lt. Col. Adam A. Komosa was Senior Regimental Advisor

---

[1] William N. Hess, *The American Aces of World War II and Korea* (New York: 1968), p. 29.

[2] "Col. Gabreski's Feats Recalled," *Dziennik Polski* (May 13, 1960), p. 4.

to the 29th R.O.K. Regiment, 9th R.O.K. Division. He received the Korean Wharang Distinguished Service Medal, and a personal Commendation from Sygman Rhee.

Edward F. Wozenski served as executive officer with the 169th infantry, 43rd Division. He was promoted to Colonel in 1950, the year the 169th was called into federal service for the Korean emergency.

Lt. Col. J. W. Bezusko—flying in F80 jet fighters—completed 157 combat missions in Korea before returning to the United States.

Commander Norbert F. Walczak was awarded the following medals: National Defense, Korean Campaign, and United Nations Service.

The Korean War ended in 1953. Nobody had fled to Canada or burned their draft cards. South Korea had been saved for the free world . . . or for the pending aggression of Communist invasion from North Korea.

CHAPTER 16

The War in Vietnam

> *I think continually of those*
> *who were truly great—*
> *The names of those who in their*
> *lives fought for life,*
> *Who wore at their hearts the*
> *fire's centre.*
> *Born of the sun, they traveled*
> *a short while toward the sun,*
> *And left the vivid air signed*
> *with their honour.*
>
> —STEPHEN SPENDER

The contributions of Americans of Polish descent to the building of America has been noteworthy. In many respects they have greatly enriched American culture. They yield to none in their patriotism. Many contemporary young men and women of Polish ancestry—inspired by the idealism of their age and by their illustrious Polish-American predecessors—have responded to the call to arms when it was sounded in Vietnam, just as their ancestors had, in 1951, when the call came from Korea, or in 1941 and 1917, when armies marched through Europe. They also served before that in times more distant. The lamentable involvement in Vietnam, which started with a resolution from Congress, seemed to them almost a holy cause to oppose an atheistic ideology with a long term strategy for indenturing the peoples of the world. They remembered well how the Soviet Union, immediately after World War II, ruthlessly engulfed defenseless little nations in Eastern Europe.

Because Polish-Americans accepted their obligations and responsibilities, and met the challenge of duty, honor, and country, they exchanged youth for manhood on the battlefields of Vietnam where they were killed on lonely patrols, without witness, or slain in captivity. In a war, which has given us no songs, few slogans, or articles of faith, they fought valiantly. Those heroic acts of valor did cost them their lives, but they were lessons of loyalty, bravery and patriotism so that others might live.

And Americans of Polish and non-Polish descent read of their valor in the newspapers, and watched filmed newscasts of the devastating battles which revealed the carnage and savagery unleashed upon the Vietnamese. The war, which started on January 1, 1961, was a strange interlude, a long feverish nightmare where strategic land was gained, lost, and regained several times while the populace migrated back and forth to safer zones. It lasted officially for twelve years and 26 days; it also surpassed the Revolutionary War as America's longest conflict. It was the fourth most costly conflict, in battle deaths, among the nine wars that the United States had fought. There was much advice from the administration level and the Pentagon, but a minimum of leadership or generalship. At the conclusion of the war, there was a hard core of sympathizers for the war, as well as a hard core against it; there was also a vast sea of impassivity about the whole debacle with a great relief at its termination.

American military strategy stressed two types of operation. One was intensive bombing of areas believed to be occupied by the Vietcong, of strategic points in North Vietnam, and of the roads along which men and supplies came into South Vietnam from the north. The second was "search and destroy" missions, which included air and ground attacks against any places where the enemy might be found. The American commanders believed that they must inflict intolerable casualties upon the enemy, and the success of the missions was judged by the number of Vietcong or Vietcong sympathizers killed. In this type of warfare whole villages, including civilians, were considered likely as combatants and to be numbered among its casualties. Another aspect of American tactics was the protection of as many South Vietnamese hamlets as possible against attack by the Vietcong. The part of the American program—commonly described as "pacification"—relied upon small teams of soldiers and civilians, who were stationed in hamlets in the hope that their presence would deter attacks by the enemy and reassure the residents that they could follow their normal mode of life.

Most of the Polish-American participants of the war returned vindicating the deep patriotism of their fathers and grandfathers, which had been cherished from generation to generation for the advancement of the public good and the glory of America. Many returned weighed down with military medals, some lighter from the loss of limbs. A lot of them did not win any medals. Many did not return at all from the Vietnam war, either whole or crippled. The Vietnam war consumed 50,000 American lives, and 304,000 wounded in battle.

Major Robert J. Modrzejewski was one of those who came home with a medal—the Medal of Honor to be precise, the nation's highest military award! President Lyndon Johnson, in the name of Congress, presented the medal to Major Modrzejewski in a special White House ceremony with appropriate pomp and military circumstance. The citation was for conspicuous gallantry and intrepidity at the risk of his life, above and beyond the call of duty, while serving as Commanding Officer, Company K, Third Battalion, Fourth Marines, Third Marine Division, in the Republic of Vietnam, from July 15 to July 18, 1966.

> On July 15, during operation Hastings, Company K had landed in an enemy infested jungle area to establish a blocking position at a major enemy trail network. Shortly after landing, the Company encountered a reinforced enemy platoon in a well organized, defensive position. Major (then Captain) Modrzejewski led his men in the successful seizure of the enemy redoubt, which contained large quantities of ammunition and supplies.
>
> That evening a numerically superior enemy force counterattacked in an effort to retake the vital supply area, thus setting the pattern of activity for the next two and one-half days. In the first series of attacks, the enemy assaulted repeatedly in overwhelming numbers but each time was repulsed by the gallant Marines.
>
> The second night the enemy struck in battalion strength, and Major Modrzejewski was wounded in this intensive action which was fought at close quarters. Although exposed to enemy fire, and despite his painful wounds, he crawled 200 meters to provide critically

needed ammunition to an exposed element of his command and was constantly present wherever the fighting was heaviest, despite numerous casualties, a dwindling supply of ammunition and the knowledge that they were surrounded, he skillfully directed artillery fire to within a few meters of his position and courageously inspired the efforts of his Company in repelling the aggressive enemy attack.

On July 18, Company K was attacked by a regimental size enemy force. Although his unit was vastly outnumbered and weakened by the previous fighting, Major Modrzejewski reorganized his men and calmly moved among them to encourage and direct their efforts to heroic limits as they fought to overcome the vicious enemy onslaught.

Again he called in air and artillery strikes at close range with devastating effect on the enemy, which together with the bold and determined fighting of the men of Company K, repulsed the fanatical attack of the larger North Vietnamese force.[1]

Major Modrzejewski's unparalleled personal heroism and indomitable leadership inspired his men to a significant victory over the enemy force and reflected great credit upon himself, the Marine Corps, and the United States Naval Service.

President Johnson—looking at Major Modrzejewski, after hanging the medal of honor around his neck—said he felt proud and confident because he could see in the face of the Milwaukee, Wisconsin marine "the answer to aggression."[2] In the story of Modrzejewski's triumph, said President Johnson, "the voice of a people's character and a nation's greatness is brought before us; we should all understand that is a voice with steel in it."[3]

Marine Lieutenant Colonel J. Bronars, of Chicago, received the Silver Star Medal from General Wallace M. Greene, Jr., Commandant of the Marine Corps at Camp Pendleton, California. The medal was awarded for the colonel's actions as the Senior Marine Advisor in the Rung Sat Special Zone, Viet Nam. At

---

[1] "Major Robert Modrzejewski Receives Medal of Honor in White House Ceremony," *Dziennik Polski* (March 14, 1968), p. 2.

[2] The story of Modrzejewski's life is that of a love affair with the Marine Corps. He entered it shortly after graduating from the University of Wisconsin, at Milwaukee, in June 1957. He was born on Milwaukee's south side, on July 3, 1934; attended Hayes elementary school, and was graduated from Pulaski High School, in 1953. He received a bachelor of science degree from UWM, and enlisted in the Marine Corp in 1960.

[3] "LBJ Sees Modrzejewski 'Answer to Aggression,'" *Polish American Journal* (March 30, 1968), p. 1.

that time the Rung Sat Special Zone was the largest Viet Cong infested area in Vietnam. According to the citation which Colonel Bronars received with the medal—he "unhesitatingly led one assault on a fortified insurgent; and volunteered for and participated in a daring ambush attack deep in Viet Cong territory." He also "calmly conducted a successful medical evacuation of an American Army Lieutenant and five Vietnamese soldiers while under sniper fire."[4]

Lieut. Paul S. Krzynowek, of Bedford, Massachusetts, was an electronic warfare officer aboard an EB-66 bomber. He flew thirty-three combat missions. On December 6, 1967, his bomber crashed and he failed to return. In his last letter to his wife, Claudia, he expressed himself poignantly: "But if I should die, remember that I died doing what I loved, fighting for the country I loved, the principles of life I admired so greatly, and the beliefs I hold above life itself. And I died for you," he wrote ending, "and the children we shall never have. Whatever is worthwhile has its price, and this is my price. This was my choice and my chance."[5]

The Viet Cong wanted Air Force Captain Alexander Zakrzeski dead or alive. As a forward air controller, or FAC, his job in Vietnam was to pilot a light plane over enemy positions and direct air strikes. Zakrzeski was so good at it that before he returned home the Viet Cong had offered the equivalent of $500 for his capture—dead or alive. The 25-year-old chemical engineer, from Linden, New Jersey, was awarded the Distinguished Flying Cross three times and the Air Force Medal eleven times. He has qualified for nine additional air medals. He has been nominated for the Silver Star, the Bronze Star of valor, and two more Distinguished Flying Crosses. He also earned six Vietnamese medals.[6] The medals were earned for flying his spotter plane at a low altitude, and slow in order to search out the enemy. In the Than Thiet action, his spotting warned an approaching South Vietnamese force of an ambush and brought repeated air strikes down on the guerrillas.

Joseph Stremplewski's combat duty in Vietnam was recognized

---

[4] "Silver Star Medal for Bravery," *Polish American* (December 11, 1965), p. 9.
[5] "I died for you and children we shall never have," *Polish American Journal* (March 30, 1968), p. 5.

for the 20th time when he was awarded the Distinguished Flying Cross, and an Air Medal to go with eighteen other Air Medals which he earned, making him Chicago's most decorated serviceman. In 525 combat missions, Stremplewski estimated he was the target of "hundreds of thousands of bullets." His combat duty was with the 334th Armed Helicopter Company of the 1st Aviation Brigade.[7]

Lieut. Commander John R. Winkowski—a navy jet pilot, and a native of Milwaukee, Wisconsin—has been awarded the Distinguished Flying Cross for heroism in Vietnam. As a member of fighter squadron 41, aboard the aircraft carrier Independence, he flew 113 combat missions in an F-4B Phantom 2, delivering more than 40 tons of bombs and rockets in Vietnam. In addition, Winkowski has been awarded eight Air Medals, two Navy Commendation Medals, and a personal commendation from the commander of the 7th fleet for participation in the destruction of the first surface to air missile site attacked and destroyed in Vietnam.

Major Joseph L. Lukasik, native of Dickson City, Pennsylvania, has been decorated with ten military medals at Luke AFB, Arizona. Major Lukasik was awarded the Distinguished Flying Cross, seven awards of the Air Medal, and two awards of the U.S. Air Force Commendation Medal for action in Southeast Asia. An F-104 Starfighter pilot, Lukasik received the DFC for heroism in military flight. He was cited for his outstanding skill, courage, and determination in devastating air attacks against hostile positions. He was awarded the Air Medals for his outstanding airmanship and courage on successful and important missions under hazardous conditions.

Captain Francis J. Gawell has been awarded the U.S. Air Force Medal at Langley AFB, Virginia. Captain Gawell, a navigator, won the award for his personal bravery and airmanship in Vietnam. The Captain served in the Tactical Air Command which provided combat reconnaissance, aerial firepower, and assault airlift for U.S. Army forces.[8]

---

[6] " 'Wanted' Yank Picks Up Medals by the Chestful," *The Detroit News* (March 24, 1966), p. 1.

[7] "20th Decoration for Viet Hero," *Polish American* (February 10, 1969), p. 1.

[8] "Awarded Air Force Medal for Bravery," *Polish American* (November 27, 1965), p. 1.

Major Albert J. Lenski, from Chicago, has been decorated with two Distinguished Flying Crosses for heroism as an F-105 Thunderchief pilot over North Vietnam. Major Lenski flew cover for a search and rescue operation of two downed crew members in a heavily defended enemy area. During an attack by enemy aircraft, the major's wingman was shot down. Although critically low on fuel, and with suspected battle damage to his own aircraft, he returned to the area to pinpoint his wingman's position. On another mission, Major Lenski bombed a highly important and heavily defended transformer yard. While inbound to the target, he engaged and dispersed a flight of enemy jet aircraft attacking another bomb flight. The Major then flew through intense and accurately directed flak in order to place his ordinance on target. Upon departing the target area, he was attacked by two enemy jet aircraft while experiencing a fuel system emergency. Major Lenski demonstrated outstanding airmanship in expertly evading the attacking aircraft. Major Lenski, who flew 100 combat missions during his tour in Southeast Asia, also was awarded ten Air Medals for outstanding airmanship and courage on other missions. Major Lenski also served as an F-106 Delta Dart instructor, at Tyndall, in a unit of the Air Defense Command.[9]

Captain Richard A. Slowik, of Belleville, Michigan, received the Air Medal and citation for his work as an air controller in Southeast Asia, in July 1968, when he directed tactical air power in the destruction of a large enemy bunker complex.[10]

Sgt. Raymond J. Kosierowski, from Brooklyn, New York, an ammunition specialist, received the Air Force Medal for Meritorious Service at Da Nang AB, Vietnam.[11]

Sgt. Shephen J. Matewicz, from Romulus, Michigan, who served as chief of plans and programs, received the Bronze Star Medal for his meritorious achievement while engaged in military operations against Viet Cong forces at Phu Cat AB, in Vietnam.[12]

---

[9] "Decorated for Heroism in Vietnam," *Polish American* (December 9, 1967), p. 5.

[10] "Air Medal Awarded to West Sider," *West Side Courier* (March 8, 1973), p. 8.

Sgt. Donald B. Jelonek, from Buffalo, New York, received the Distinguished Flying Cross for his aid in repulsing enemy forces in the village of Duc Duc.[13]

Marine Private John J. Falkowski, from Chicago, Illinois, served with Marine Medium Helicopter Squadron 365 at the Marine Corps Air Facility, Futema, Okinawa. He received the Air Medal for participation in aerial flights in support of the Vietnam forces.[14]

Eugene Dzikowski was awarded the Bronze Star for heroism on February 8, 1968. A member of the 35th Ranger Division, Specialist Dzikowski repeatedly endangered his own life attempting to rescue injured comrades while under Viet Cong fire. He also directed his men into enemy fire in a fierce attempt to disorganize the Viet Cong attacks.[15]

Sergeant John S. Dziengowski won an Army Commendation Medal for heroism, and a recommendation for the Bronze Star Medal for bravery during the Viet Cong Tet offensive, in Hue, in February 1968. A member of the 5th Battalion, 7th Cavalry Division, Dziengowski accepted his "medal for heroism" during ceremonies at Camp Evans, Vietnam, where he was assigned. His citation reads in part:

> Sgt. Dziengowski has distinguished himself by heroism in action during a combat mission near Hue. Upon spotting an armed enemy soldier running from a place of cover, Dziengowski, disregarding his own safety, pursued the insurgent and succeeded in halting him by firing several bursts over his head, thus gaining valuable information on the enemy movement.
>
> His display of personal bravery and devotion to duty is in keeping with the highest tradition of the military services, and reflects great credit upon himself, his unit and the United States.[16]

---

[11] "Sgt. Kosierowski Received Medal for Viet Service," *The Brooklyn Star* (October 23, 1970), p. 8.

[12] *Romulus Roman* (April 21, 1971), p. 1.

[13] *Am-Pol Eagle* (June 1, 1972), p. 16.

[14] "Awarded Medal for Heroism in Vietnam Flight," *Polish American* (July 17, 1965), p. 1.

[15] "Bronze Star Awarded Dzikowski," *Detroit American* (May 22, 1968), p. 10.

[16] "Soldier, 21, Awarded 'Medal for Heroism,'" *West Side Courier* (July 3, 1968), p. 12.

Sergeant Dziengowski received the Bronze Star for saving one of his fellow soldiers while under heavy fire in Hue. Only four out of his platoon survived that battle.

Private Dennis E. Wisniewski, of Chicago, was awarded the Bronze Star for heroism, an award for meritorious service, and the Combat Medical badge. The Bronze Star was awarded for heroism as a medic on February 3, 1969. He was serving with a rifle squad of A Company, 4th battalion of the 21st infantry. The squad discovered an enemy tunnel complex while on a combat mission. When a soldier entered one of the tunnels, he was injured by a hand-grenade blast. Wisniewski pulled the man from the tunnel and administered first aid which saved his life. Wisniewski was fatally wounded, March 1, 1969, in a mortar attack while fighting with the American combat medical division.[17]

Sgt. Raymond J. Koczan has been awarded the U.S. Army Commendation Medal for heroism with a "V" for valor. The citation describes his action.

> On Oct. 2, 1969, Koczan distinguished himself during a medical evacuation in Phouc Long Province, Republic of Vietnam. When his unit became engaged with a determined enemy force located in concealed positions, with complete disregard for his own safety, Koczan unhesitatingly exposed himself to intense hostile fire as he moved forward to the point of heaviest contact and began placing a heavy volume of suppressive fire on the enemy positions. His covering fire enabled the medical evacuation to land and extract the wounded. His actions were an inspiration to the other men and contributed immeasurably to the success of the mission. Koczan's display of personal bravery and devotion to duty reflects great credit on himself, his unit and the army.[18]

Koczan was also awarded the Bronze Star Medal.

Spec. 4/c Larry Kaluch received the Bronze Star for rescuing his commanding officer from a tunnel fire in Vietnam.

Spec. 4/c Zdzislaw E. Nowacki was awarded the Soldier's Medal for heroism. It was given in recognition of Nowacki's courage in disarming a fellow soldier who was menacing No-

---
[17] *Polish American* (August 9, 1969), p. 1.
[18] "Wins War Medal," *Glos Narodu* (April 30, 1970), p. 5.

wacki's unit area with a rifle. According to the orders authorizing the award of the medal, the man for no apparent reason, began shooting at any thing that moved and threatened to kill anyone who approached him. "With complete disregard for his own safety, Specialist Nowacki calmly and reassuringly convinced the man to put down his weapon and sit down and talk over his problem" the award read. "His valorous action was responsible for saving countless lives of his fellow soldiers."[19]

A Marine Corp Lance Corporal Louis Cherwack was spending his eighth month in Vietnam when on March 24, 1967 he volunteered to go into the forward area to look for enemy mines and booby traps. He accidentally stepped on a Viet Cong mine. The impact of the explosion severed his right leg four inches above the knee, and the left by five inches below the knee. He was awarded a Purple Heart and a Bronze Star with the "V" for valor. Cherwak views his war experience with pride: "Its freedom. I couldn't have lost my legs for a better cause."[20]

Marine Captain Nicholas H. Grosz, Jr. of River Edge, New Jersey, received the Navy Cross for valor. The nation's second highest citation for valor was given Grosz for heroism when he was commanding officer of Headquarters and Service Company, 2nd Battalion, 7th Marine Regiment. The citation read:

> When savage small arms, automatic weapons and mortar fire pinned his company down in a muddy and exposed rice paddy area, Grosz immediately informed his battalion of the seriousness of the situation and summoned help.
> Completely disregarding his own personal safety, he repeatedly ran the gauntlet of intense enemy fire to personally evacuate four wounded Marines.[21]

Corporal Robert S. Liszcz of Hempstead, L.I., was killed in a surprise mortar attack by the Viet Cong on March 16, 1967, but the spectacular deeds of the soldier were not known until after his death. It was on November 4 and 5, 1966, that Liszcz, then a

---

[19] "City Man Cited for Viet Heroism," *Wiadomosci* (September 3, 1970), p. 2.
[20] Richard Cady, "Courage Braces Legless Viet Hero," *The Detroit News* (July 3, 1967), p. 3-A.
[21] "Cpt. Grosz Given High Navy Cross," *Polish American Journal* (December 10, 1966), p. 1.

private first class in the 196th Infantry Brigade, risked his life over and over again to carry wounded soldiers out of a dense jungle. He carried the men to an open area where helicopters could land to fly the wounded to field hospitals. The Army specifically pointed out that Liszcz volunteered to aid the trapped soldiers. "He was the kind of guy who would do anything for anyone," wrote one of Liszcz's buddies in a letter to Liszcz's parents. "He was an exemplary soldier," added Liszcz's platoon leader. "Robert had the respect of all the non-commissioned and commissioned officers."[22] The true story of Robert's heroism unfolded after his death when his family received the official citation from the Secretary of the Army explaining why he was awarded the Army Commendation Medal with the V Device and the Bronze Star. Liszcz was only 21 years old when he died.

Sergeant Michael Lee Kubicki has been awarded the Bronze Star for heroism. Sgt. Kubicki was cited for his heroic actions, August 22, 1968, when, as commander of the self-propelled twin-engine gun, he came "under fire from heavy mortars and automatic weapons from an estimated two companies of North Vietnamese regulars. When the guns failed to function, after the fighting began, his crew left their post to fight from a nearby bunker, but Kubicki stayed on to repair his weapon. Although the fighting was very intense, Sgt. Kubicki, without regard for his personal safety, fixed his gun and was credited with knocking out four more of the enemy positions before the engagement was over." The citation concluded: "The coolness demonstrated by Sgt. Kubicki, under fire, was in the highest tradition of the service and certainly merits our great esteem."[23]

Specialist Four Mitchell Dubanewicz of Brooklyn, New York, is the recipient of two Purple Hearts, one in January and a second in August, both 1970. He also has three Bronze Stars (one with a V), and he holds the Combat Infantryman's Badge and the Army Commendation Medal.[24]

---

[22] "Army to Honor Young Hero Killed in Vietnam," *Polish American World* (June 23, 1967), p. 1.

[23] "Sergeant, 19, Gets Bronze Star Medal," *West Side Courier* (January 30, 1969), p. 1.

[24] "Dubanewicz Wins Army Medal for Vietnam Service," *Polish American World* (January 15, 1971), p. 1.

Army 1st Lt. Edward J. Nagorski, Army Chief Warrant Officer James J. Gersky, Jr., Spec. 5/c Anthony R. Rajca, Sgt. Richard W. Elinski, Major Wlodzimierz Pawlak, Army 1st Lt. Stanley D. Zelazny, Specialist Thomas Dziadosz, Army 1st Lt. James R. Dombrowski and John W. Kwiatkowski—also were awarded the Bronze Star for valor in Vietnam.

Pfc. Eugene Szweda considers it a miracle that he is alive. He was sent to Vietnam after training for jungle warfare. Although he was first assigned to be clerk-typist, Szweda volunteered for combat and was soon fighting for his life. He was singled out on March 31, 1967, by a lone Viet sniper who shot him in the arm and right side of the chest. A month later he returned to the United States.

The Navy Commendation Medal has been bestowed on Lance Corporal Michael V. Klimecki of Belleville, Michigan. The citation for the Commendation said:

> For heroic achievement while serving as a radio operator with Company F, Second Battalion, Fourth Marines, Third Marine Division in connection with combat operations against the enemy in the Republic of Vietnam. On 7 April 1969, Lance Corporal Klimecki's platoon was conducting a patrol near Hill 383 south of the Demilitarized Zone when the Marines came under sniper fire from the heavy underbush.
>
> With complete disregard for his own safety, Lance Corporal Klimecki remained at the side of his platoon commander throughout the entire fire fight, fearlessly moving with him from one position to another across the fire-swept terrain. During the engagement with the enemy, which lasted all afternoon. Lance Corporal Klimecki skillfully maintained reliable communications with higher headquarters, the artillery forward observer, gunships, air observers, and the medical evacuation helicopters, in addition to ably directing the marking of his unit's forward position to aid tactical aircraft as they provided close air support.
>
> By his courage, calm resourcefulness and steadfast devotion to duty in the face of great personal danger, Lance Corporal Klimecki upheld the finest traditions of the Marine Corps and of the United States Naval Service.[25]

---

[25] "Michael Klimecki Awarded Navy's Commendation Medal," *Belleville Enterprise* (September 3, 1969), p. 1.

No one can say that the Anthony Stozeski family, of Warren, Michigan, did not do their share in the Vietnam war. Six of Anthony Stozeski's sons (Fred, Joseph, James, Bernard, Eugene and Edward) participated in the war.[26]

Brigadier General Edwin R. Chess (Czeslowski), who joined as a Chaplain in 1942, was the chief of Air Force chaplains.

Edmund A. Rafalko—who completed 100 combat missions over Vietnam while vice-commander of a strategic unit of the Second Bomb Wing—was promoted to General while a base commander of Wright-Patterson AFB, Ohio.

The following Americans of Polish descent also hold the rank of General: Edward F. Wozenski, Lester S. Bork, Albin F. Irzyk, Harvey J. Joblonsky, Alvin L. Pachynski and Edward L. Rowny.

Corporal John J. Skalba was killed while on patrol near the big Marine air base, at Da Nang, on January 4, 1968. Before he died, he wrote his fiancee: "This is a job somebody has got to do, even if it means dying here, or someday we'll have to do it closer to home."

Lt. Richard J. Solczyk, who was killed in Vietnam, wrote the following letter to his parents:

> Though your hearts are full of grief and sorrow, I ask you please not to be bitter. My life is what I chose it to be and I fully realized the risk. I did it because I love you and I wanted to insure that your peace and happiness as well as everyone else's would not be disturbed by any enemy.
>
> Do not become hateful of anything for it is no one's fault; it was my choice. If I had it to do over again, I would; your freedom is more important than my life.
>
> Pray to God for me and everyone else, especially for those who will go after me and risk their lives for you.
>
> Some day this earth of ours will have peace and if I helped to get closer to that day, then I have done my part. That is what I wanted.[27]

---

[26] "Town Talk," *The Detroit News* (March 21, 1967), p. 15-A.
[27] "Solczyk's Last Letter Tells Love of Peace," *Polish-American Journal* (March 2, 1968), p. 6.

Twenty-year-old George J. Bojarski used poetry to express the feelings of a young man going to war as a troop ship carried him across the Pacific to Vietnam. He wrote:

> As the ship moves out under the cheers of a band,
> The men stare long at their native land.
> For most they will see it again in a year
> But for others there'll be nothing but loved ones' tears.

Bojarski mailed the poem to a former teacher upon arriving in Vietnam. His words proved prophetic. He was killed in action March 9, 1967.[28]

James Tomakowski was a poet, high school honor student, and world traveler, who believed in "taking life as it comes." His life ended abruptly on April 12, 1966, when an enemy device exploded in his face while he was on patrol near Da Nang, Vietnam. Tomakowski left a trunk full of his writings. Part of a poem entitled "Life of an Introvert," was quoted in the *Detroit News*.

> *Questions left unanswered, yes,*
> *All but one, the finall dress,*
> *The wooden kimono fits us all.*[29]

Lt. Frank Rybicki, Jr., was the second to die in West Point's class of 1966. Frank Rybicki, like most men of twenty-three, had little to leave in worldly goods or a formal biography describing his achievements. There is the yearbook photo in the 1966 issue of the *Howitzer*, a photo which catches a slender handsome face—most comfortable in a broad, flashing smile. Under the photo appears a catalog of extracurricular activities with an incomplete sketch:

> Frank Anthony Rybicki Jr, Balboa, Canal Zone. C-2. "Ask not what your country can do for you, but what you can do for your country." These are the words Frank lives by. . . . Frank's dedication

---

[28] Lawrence Gareau, "GI's Poetry Foretells Death," *The Detroit News* (March 13, 1967), p. 3-A.
[29] John J. Camper, "Takes Life as It Comes and Now Death, too," *The Detroit News* (April 14, 1966), p. 4-B.

to duty, together with his ceaseless wit, will always gain him respect and friendship. He will always be known as a leader of men as he proudly wears the crossed rifles down the trail of life chanting "Follow Me."

There is, now, a marker in the West Point Cemetery, one on a lengthening gray line of forty-one who sacrificed their lives in Vietnam. In addition, there are bright, scattered mosaic tiles which reflect the sparkles of fleeting memory.

Specialist Edward D. Dlugokinski, of Detroit, was troubled because he felt someone else had died in his place. As a medical corpsman stationed in Vietnam, he was overwhelmed when another soldier, with whom he had switched assignments, was killed in combat. The youth wrote his parents, expressing his remorse. "It should have been me," he believed. A few days later, Dlugokinski died of gunshot wounds while under fire in a small arms operation.[30]

Lance Corporal Edward C. Rozanski received posthumously the Silver Star medal for gallantry in action. Corporal Rozanski's final minutes are told in the citation that accompanied the posthumous award.

> Exercising complete disregard for his own safety, he rapidly moved forward some 50 meters across a fireswept paddy and destroyed the machinegun emplacement with a hand grenade, allowing his platoon to advance to his position.
> Mortally wounded during this encounter, Rozanski by his steadfast determination, bold initiative and selfless devotion to duty in the face of great danger, served to inspire all who observed him and upheld the finest tradition of the Marine Corps and the United States Naval Service.

Corporal Edward J. Lakwa was awarded posthumously the Bronze Star medal for meritorious service in connection with military operations against a hostile force, the Purple Heart for wounds received in action which resulted in his death; and the Good Conduct Medal. Prior to his death Corporal Lakwa had been awarded the Army Commendation Medal, National Defense

---

[30] Robert M. Pavich, "Pays Debt in Vietnam Fighting," *The Detroit News* (November 23, 1966), p. 13-A.

Medal, Service Medal, Vietnam Campaign Medal, Combat Infantryman Badge, Expert Badge with Automatic Rifle Bar, Sharpshooter Badge with Machine Gun and Mortar Bars, and the Marksman Badge with Rifle and Grenade Bars. The ribbons, medals and badges were presented to his parents. Corporal Lakwa died as a result of injuries received from an explosion of an enemy mine on September 24, 1970.

There are many other distinguished soldiers, sailors and marines—from Arizona,[31] California,[32] Connecticut,[33] Illinois,[34] Indiana,[35] Kentucky,[36] Maryland,[37] Massachusetts,[38] Michigan,[39] Minnesota[40] Nevada,[41] New Hampshire,[42] New Jersey,[43] New York,[44] North Carolina,[45] Ohio,[46] Pennsylvania,[47] Rhode Island,[48] Texas,[49] Washington,[50] Wisconsin,[51] Washington, D. C.[52]—who

---

[31] Seaman Joseph Kosik III (Tucson); Pfc. Carl Konopa (Tempe); Marine Pfc. John L. Czechowski, Jr. (Mesa).

[32] Sgt. J. G. Kasikowski (San Diego); George F. Lazar (San Francisco); and John D. Wyszomirski (Oceanside).

[33] Pfc. Joseph Baczalski (Wauregan); Spc. 4/c Edward J. Jurek (Meriden); Stephen S. Strycharz (Hartford); and Pfc. Charles J. Wisniewski Jr. (Unccasville).

[34] Airman 1/c Lawrence A. Berneski (Forest City); Sgt. John W. Bezecny (Riverside); Army Spec. 4/c Kerry M. Bugajski (Christopher); Sgt. Jeffrey Gurwitz (Skokie); Spec. 5/c Steve Klarik (East Chicago); Cpl. Richard Kosky (Cicero); Pfc. Louis Mucha (Elmhurst); Spc. 4/c Gerald F. Novak (Lombard); Sgt. Eugene A. Pastrowicz (Walshville); Sgt. Martin J. Rapczak (Kewanee); Ronald C. Rogowski (Norridge); Pfc. Leroy F. Schyska (Moline); Cpl. H. S. Turski (Oak Park); Cpl. Edwin R. Wierzba (Bridgeview); Cpl. Stanley Zalewski Sr. (Calumet); and Spc. 4/c Theodore L. Zawisza (Posen).

The following were from the city of Chicago: Spec. 4/c John E. Bobowski Jr.; Pfc. Stephn Z. Borczyk; Sgt. John C. Borowski; Lt. Richard Brazik; Sgt. James M. Ciupinski; Spc. Daniel P. Droszcz; Sgt. Joseph W. Dudek; Spc. 4/c John J. Hermanowicz; Cpl. Albert A. Kedroski; Walter Kisala Pfc. John S. Kmiec; Edward M. Kopec; Sgt. Gerald M. Krysztoszek; Spc. Leonard Kubiak; Lance Cpl. Richard J. Lis; Sgt. Stanley J. Michalowicz; Airman Raymond J. Michalowski; Robert S. Muller; Cpl. William A. Nosek; Pfc. Robert D. Nawrocki; Pfc. Kenneth B. Orszulak; Pfc. James A. Palenik; Pfc. Edward J. Pintowski; Leszek Puzyrewski; Spc. 4/c Mitchell F. Sek; Cpl. John P. Superczynski; Navy Hospitalman Zbigniew J. Tomaszewski; Gerald W. Warzecha; William Witek; Pfc. Lawrence A. Wojcik; Army Spc. 4/c James F. Wendolowski; and Pfc. Barry M. Wopinski.

[35] Spc. 4/c Robert J. Dorshak (Michigan City); Cpl. Robert A. Federowski (Lowell); Pfc. Cornel Gil (East Chicago); Cpl. Gustaw F. Gudleske (Griffith); Sgt. Larry E. Jankowski (South Bend); Bennie Ksiazek (East Gary); Pfc. Henry J. Markowski (Hammond); S1c. Wayne Michalak (Hammond); Pvt. 1/c George Straszewski (Gary).

[36] Spc. 4/c Stanley Jamrozy (Louisville); Lance Cpl. Joe R. Melczek (Insko).

[37] David J. Budka (Baltimore); Larry V. Chmiel (Glen Burnie); Pfc. David Wisniewski (Baltimore).

[38] Lt. Paul Cheslak (Wayland); Sgt. Robert E. Dudek (Ipswich); Cpl. John

Krawczyk (South Bridge); Lt. Paul S. Krzywonek (Houstanic); Pfc. David P. Kusy (Auburn); Cpl. John F. Lazarovich, Jr. (Scituate); Sgt. Robert R. Litwin (Chicopee); Pvt. Chester H. Seklecki (Holyoke); Cpl. Walter Staniszewski (Brockton); Spc. 4/c Edward P. Stefanik (Chicopee).

[39] Lance Cpl. Andrew Chmiel (Utica); R. Gronowski (Taylor Twp.); Gerald A. Huczek (Roseville); Pfc. Robert W. Jasura (Pincoming); Cpl. Roger E. Jozwiak (Warren); Pfc. Richard D. Kaminski (Lincoln Park); Sgt. Edward L. Kolka (Grosse Pointe); Pfc. Roger S. Kohut (Hamtramck); Gerald A. Kosakowski (Lincoln Park); Spc. 4/c James Kralowski (Hamtramck); Pfc. Arnold M. Marchlewicz (Warren); Pfc. Daniel Makarewicz (Grand Rapids); Spc. 4/c John M. Michalski (Hamtramck); Pfc. David M. Miszewski (North Muskegon); Spc. 4/c Paul F. Ruszkiewicz (Hamtramck); Cpl. Casimir Sylwanowicz (Flint); Army Spc. 4/c Donald D. Wilkoplan (Taylor); Captain Joseph C. Zamiara (Grand Rapids); and Spc. Michael R. Zurek (Filion).

The following were from the City of Detroit: Charles H. Batozynski; Spc. 4/c Thomas P. Ciecula; Lance Cpl. Richard Ginal; Cpl. Lawrence F. Jaworowicz; Lt. Jadwiga Orlowska (army nurse); Pfc. James W. Pawlak; Spc. 5/c Mark H. Pietrzyk; Sgt. Walter Przybylowicz; Spc. 4/c Frank B. Smyk; and Spc. G. R. Zywica.

[40] Lance Cpl. Richard O. Lozenski (Minneapolis); and Pfc. Dennis W. Pawlowicz (Duluth).

[41] Staff Sgt. John S. Szymanski (Babbitt).

[42] Glen A. Menowski (Nashua).

[43] Richard J. Anasiewicz (New Brunswick); Marine Cpl. Andrew Bucior (Perth Amboy); Pfc. Gregory T. Buczynski (Flemington); Pvt. Ronald Bukowski (Jersey City); Sgt. Paul J. Golembski (Camden); Sgt. Edward Kaminski (Rahway); Sgt. Stanley S. Klecz (Wildwood); Spc. 4/c Bohdan Kowal (Clifton); John J. Niemczyk (Trenton); Lt. (j.g.) Edward W. Pawlowski (Union); Spc. 4/c Casimir H. Slomiany (Wallington); Lt. Conrad A. Stybel (Plainfield); Pfc. George Szczepanczyk (Saddle Brook); Walter J. Weiss (Middlesex).

[44] John J. Bialkowski (West Seneca); Captain David A. Bujalski (Glen Cove); Thomas P. Ciborowski (Maspeth); Sgt. Alfred J. Dymerski (Brooklyn); G. G. Gierek (New York); Pfc. James A. Grzegorek (Buffalo); Cpl. Henry P. Jackowiak (Angola); Edward S. Kopik (Amsterdam); Sgt. Michael Kroll (New York City); Robert S. Liszcz (Hempstead); Sgt. Robert J. Kucinciak (Massapequa); Major Leonard E. Niski (Amsterdam); Pfc. Frank M. Pietras (Springfield Gardens); Pfc. Arthur T. Stachowski (Batavia); Pfc. Stanley R. Tomasovic (Hicksville); Lt. William A. Wilk (Utica); Sgt. Albert Wysocki (Brooklyn).

[45] Sgt. Raymond J. Borowski (Spring Lake); Sgt. 1/c George Ovask (Owsiak) (Fayetteville).

[46] Lance Cpl. Richard J. Cegielski (Cleveland); Staff Sgt. Robert C. Drewicz (Swanton); David A. Fialko (Springfield); Sgt. Walter Gawel (Cleveland); Michael S. Gozdan (Akron); Lance Cpl. Raymond Hodorowski (Lorraine); Robert M. Klevenowski (Cleveland); Capt. Eugene Korecki (Toledo); Lance Cpl. James A. Malecki (Cleveland); Sgt. Stefan A. Mika (Willoughby); Edward Malinowski (Cleveland); Spc. 4/c Howard Mucha (Plainville); Lance Cpl. Thomas E. Novak (Swanton); Cpl. Michael Pastva (Cleveland); Paul S. Sasinowski; Sgt. Elmer G. Sikorski (Cleveland); William M. Skowron (Warren); Spc. 4/c Joseph S. Sobczak (Peninsula); Pfc. Robert G. Stanko (Campbell); Pfc. Michael T. Sukara (Parma); Lance Cpl. Frank A. Szymanski (Cleveland).

[47] Lance Cpl. Michael A. Baranowski (Morristown); Andrew P. Chamaj (Scenery Hill); 1st Lt. Michael J. Ciesielska (Philadelphia); Spc. 4/c Frank A. Glowiak (Plymouth); Cpl. William A. Kuprevich (Philadelphia); Sgt. Francis M. Michonik (Coatesville); Pfc. Robert Nodolski (New Florence); Pfc. John M. Olszewski

were killed fighting an unpopular war in Vietnam. They exchanged youth for manhood on the battlefields of the rice paddies, and the jungles of Vietnam, but left their souls in the midst of vivid fighting on the battlefields signed with their honor. They were soldiers in an age, when being a soldier was sneered at or, worse, even held in contempt. The sight of a uniform back home was likely to elicit dirty stares, hatred—even rocks, or perhaps the pity of those among the "now" generation who see a man in uniform as the helpless victim of a cruel totalitarian system—pawns of the military industrial complex.

Lt. Carol Ann Drazba from Dunsmore, Pennsylvania, is the first American nurse to lose her life, in Vietnam, in the service of her country. She was killed on February 18, 1966, in a helicopter accident, in South Vietnam. She completed her nurses training in Scranton, Pennsylvania, in 1964. She was sent to Fort Sam Houston, Texas, to participate in the Nurse Corps basic orientation course. After serving at Fort Huachuca, Arkansas, she was sent to Vietnam.

Captain Teresa R. Buracheska, from Dickson City, Pennsylvania, was awarded the Bronze Star for her service in Vietnam.

Christine Gerych was awarded the American Spirit Honor Medal and Certificate. In a letter to her parents, Christine's com-

---

(Philadelphia); Pfc. Wayne A. Podlesnik (Clairton); Pfc. Stephen W. Sokalski (Allentown); Spc. 4/c Gerald J. Szoszorek (Erie); First Lt. John E. Tarantowicz (Dickson City); Spc. 4/c Joseph Torzok (Clairion); Sgt. Edward Zaczkowski (Philadelphia).

[48] Pfc. Richard A. Jurcak (Warwick); Capt. Edward C. Krawczyk (Riverside); Pfc. Thomas J. Szydlo (West Warwick).

[49] Pfc. John F. Barchak (San Antonio); Spc. 4/c Wallace S. Dworaczyk (Yorktown); Cpl. Bernie J. Noviski (New Waverly); Pfc. Billy J. Witzkoski (Houston).

[50] Pvt. Stanley J. Michalowicz; Major Raymond W. Visstsky; and Pfc John L. Wojcicky; Pfc. Rene L. Malarz (Winlock); and Cpl. William T. Grudzinski (Port Orchard).

[51] Spc. 4/c Dennis J. Adamski (Appleon); Pfc. Gregory J. Bartkowski (Milwaukee); Pfc. Leroy W. Cwikla (Lublin); Allen J. Kakuk (Two Rivers); Pfc. William R. Kuczewski (Milwaukee); Sgt. Donald C. Lepak (Amhert); Cpl. Theodore P. Lipinski (Milwaukee); John Mietus (Eagle River); Spc. 4/c John E. Milawnowski (Milwaukee); Pfc. Daniel J. Orlikowski (Athens); Staff Sgt. Robert E. Osuski (Milwaukee); Pfc. Donald Paskowicz (Greendale); Lt. Thomas Przybelski (Green Bay); Pfc. Kenneth W. Raronski (Milwaukee); Pfc. Robert P. Ruminski (Two Rivers); Sgt. Robert T. Szymanski (Milwaukee); James N. Tycz (Milwaukee); and Pfc. Richard T. Wucinski (West Allis)).

[52] Pfc. Leo S. Garalski; Sgt. Thomas G. Kolinski.

manding officer, Captain Mary Gore, commended the parents for raising such a fine daughter.

> This medal is given to only one recruit of the graduating companies who has, during her period of training, best exemplified the American spirit of honor, loyalty, initiative and comradeship.
> Christine is to be commended for her conscientious attention to duty which has led to this high honor. Young women with Christine's qualities are not created in a few short weeks of recruit training, as such success can grow only on a solid foundation established over many years in the home.
> Your contribution in bringing up this outstanding young American is of great value to this country's future.[53]

Pfc. Frank J. Antonowich, from Chicago, Illinois, expressed his viewpoint on an antiwar demonstration in the United States in a letter to Congressman Dan Rostenkowski. He stated: "Here, in Vietnam, we read about the anti-war demonstrations in hopeful disbelief. It grows harder for me to believe that demonstration is one of the freedoms I am here fighting to preserve."[54]

First Lt. Andrew Ladak was also concerned with the protests of bearded, long-haired, pot-smoking peace lovers. In his letter to his two sisters, in Detroit, he made the following comments:

> Don't talk to me about love, because I've had it. Don't talk to me about killing, because I've had to do it. Don't philosophize to me about death, because I've lived with it.
> Don't yell at me about work, because I've seen it. And don't preach to me about freedom, because, baby, I helped to buy it.[55]

Some Americans extended a hearty welcome to the prisoners of war, who for a long period of time maintained their faith in the American way of life despite indescribable difficulties and years of captivity, by the Viet Cong, in South Vietnamese prison camps. They were indeed true examples of the spirit of American

---

[53] Susan Fleming, "A bittersweet honor for Chris," *The Sunday News* (April 22, 1973), p. 17-A. Susan Fleming, "It's Christine's big day and parents are there," *The Detroit News* (April 7, 1973), p. 3-A.

[54] "Marine in Viet Nam Tells Scorn for Protestors," *Polish-American* (November 20, 1965), p. 1.

[55] "War has a purpose for this GI," *The Sunday News* (December 20, 1970), p. 3-A.

servicemen who chose to serve their nation in whatever way necessary.

Marine Sgt. Frank E. Cius, Jr. returned to his native Cheektowaga, New York, on April 19, 1973, after six years in captivity by the Viet Cong in a prison camp. The sentiments of the entire community were indeed reflected by over 500 persons who gathered at Buffalo International Airport to welcome back one of their most honored residents. James Harrigan, deputy director of the New York State Division of Veteran Affairs, was the host for the celebration, and introduced local dignitaries. Sister Mary Pachomia, president of Villa Maria College, presented a full scholarship to the co-ed college in the name of the Marine. Michael P. McKeating, representing County Executive Regan, gave Sgt. Cius a county memento. Cheektowaga Town Supervisor Weber introduced the sergeant's mother and father, and called the Marine "Cheektowaga's greatest son." Weber also echoed the bishop's comment, and assured Sgt. Cius that "a more sincere welcome was never rendered to any returning son in Cheektowaga." Rev. Edward D. Head, Bishop of the Diocese of Buffalo, was also among those present. Bishop Head called the day "a joyous occasion," and wished the family and Sgt. Cius the blessing of God in all future endeavors. Taking the microphone for about 30 seconds, Sgt. Cius said, "I am the most thankful person in the world to be back in my hometown and this is the most beautiful reception of my life."[56]

The following Polish-Americans were among the prisoners of war who were released by North Vietnam: Corporal Robert Babula; Ralph C. Bisz; Captain Richard Brazik; Captain Edward A. Budno (Air Force) of Harrison, New York (prisoner since 1965); Spec. 5/c Walter Cichon; Sergeant Raymond C. Czerwiec; Spec. 4/c Peter E. Drabic; Major Robert R. Dyczkowski; Captain Clifford W. Fieszel; Major Theodore E. Kryszak; Captain James Kula (Navy) of Manchester, New Hampshire, prisoner, since 1972; Major John C. Kwortnik; Lieut. Leonard J. Lewandowski, Jr.; Lieut. Louis F. Makowski (Air Force), of Midland, Texas; CWO2 Daniel F. Maslowski (Army); CWO2

---

[56] "Large Crowd Welcomes Home Sgt. Frank Cius," Am-Pol Eagle (April 26, 1973), p. 8.

James E. Nowicki (Army); Lieut. Dean A. Pogreba; Lieut. Bernard F. Rupinski; Pfc. Donald J. Trampski; Captain George K. Wanat, Jr. (Army) of Foxboro, Massachusetts; Lt. Commander Donald J. Woloszyk; Captain Frederick J. Wozniak (Air Force); Corporal Walter F. Wroblewski; Corporal Joseph S. Zatocki, Jr.; Lieut. Charles S. Zuhorski; Captain Robert J. Zulowski; Thomas W. Sima of Rivertown, New Jersey; John W. Brodak of Jennings, Missouri; Sgt. Joseph S. Sawlocki; and Major Ronald E. Storz.

Sgt. Joseph Zawtocki died a prisoner of war.[57]

News of peace in Vietnam came to the United States on Saturday, January 27, 1973, with the ringing of bells and the flying of flags as the nation turned to prayers, cheers, and silent contemplation to mark the end of its longest war. A ten-story bank of windows was lighted to spell the word "Peace" on the Allied Chemical Building in New York's Time Square.

On this day, ending the longest war in America's history went virtually unnoticed, in downtown Detroit, where throngs had gathered to celebrate the end of World War II. None of the churches had scheduled special services of thanksgiving for concluding the Vietnam war.[58] Had general apathy set in? Was the cease-fire a permanent one? What efforts and expenses would be required to reconstruct the country after the war? Defeat, embarrassment, the problem of saving the thousands of Americans now stranded in South Vietnam have all left its toll on the unusual peace after a cease-fire. There was also the problem of saving the thousands of Vietnamese orphans and other refugees who fought against the Viet Cong and their lives were left in jeopardy. The reaction in Detroit was probably repeated in countless cities throughout the United States, which was still concerned about its prisoners of war and a list of those persons unaccounted for to this day.

---

[57] "Hanoi lists 55 Americans who died as war prisoners," *The Detroit News* (January 9, 1973), p. 8-A.
[58] Jack Burdock, "Silent Detroit Streets Welcome the Signing of Viet Cease-fire," *The Sunday News* (January 23, 1973), p. 11-A.

CHAPTER 17

Polish-Black Relations in America

*This is the great abomination of slavery,
that it deprives a man of the common rights
of humanity, stamped upon him by his maker.*

—ERNESTINE POTOWSKI ROSE[1]

Before the Civil War, Negro slaves—regarded as chattel by plantation owners—were at the bottom of the social scale in the United States. Although liberating slaves was permitted in some states, the law held most of the slaves in permanent servitude. Whether they were free or bond, their color marked them off from the other classes of every rank. A high rate of illiteracy prevailed among them; their options for independent work was therefore curtailed by these circumstances.

With rare exceptions, the conditions of the slaves was pitiable, their labor excessively hard, their diet poor and scanty, their treatment cruel and oppressive. In certain instances, a minority of slaves who were fortunate in their masters often had a position superior to that of poor whites, but under the best conditions they were silent members of the social order, liable to punishment for the slightest disobedience and to terrible penalties for serious crime. Voiceless themselves, the slaves found but few spokesmen in the white race.

Among the pioneer white spokesmen for the Negro slaves was Brigadier General Thaddeus Kosciuszko, an American Revolutionary War hero, who was long disturbed by the plight of the

---
[1] Wytrwal, *Poles in American History and Tradition*, p. 126.

Negroes engaged in the routine of picking and cultivating cotton, tobacco, rice or indigo. General Kosciuszko regarded slavery as the darkest blot on the escutcheon of a free America. The toleration of bondage violated his concept of America as the land of the free and equal. Sixty-five years before the Civil War, Kosciuszko initiated procedures to abolish slavery in the United States. In his will and testament of May 5, 1798, Kosciuszko authorized Thomas Jefferson to sell his vast property in Indiana Territory and with the money purchase, liberate, educate, and train the slaves for worthy citizenship.[2]

> I, Thaddeus Kosciuszko, being just on my departure from America, do hereby declare and direct that, should I make no other testamentary disposition of my property in the United States, I hereby authorize my friend Thomas Jefferson to employ the whole thereof in purchasing negroes from among his own or any other and giving them liberty in my name; in giving them education in trade or otherwise; in having them instructed for their new condition in the duties of morality which may make them good neighbours, good fathers and mothers, husbands and wives, in their duty as citizens; teaching them to be defenders of their liberty and country, of the good order of society, and in whatsoever may make them happy and useful.[3]

Kosciuszko's humanitarian request helped found the "Colored School" at Newark, New Jersey, in 1826. This school is called by some as the first institution of higher learning for Blacks in the United States. The school is appropriately named after its benefactor, Thaddeus Kosciuszko. Knowing Jefferson's interest in seeing all men become free, Kosciuszko named him as executor of his will. In observance of Black History Week, each year the second week in February, the Polish American Congress, Illinois Division, presented a plaque of Kosciuszko's Last Will to the Dusable Museum of American History located in Chicago.

Kosciuszko was an ardent believer in liberty for all men, and felt deeply that Negroes should have a full opportunity to prove

---

[2] Philip S. Foner, *Thomas Jefferson Selection from His Writings* (New York: 1943), p. 69.

[3] Anthony O. Shallna, "Adjudication of General Kosciuszko's Wills," *The Massachusetts Law Society Journal* (December, 1949), XX, p. 123.

their merit. Kosciuszko had had some wartime contacts with Negroes.

> Perhaps as he drew up this will he recalled his once asking General Greene for permission to give two nearly naked Negro orderlies of John Laurens a part of the slain young colonel's clothing. Perhaps, too, he remembered Prince, who often served him as a messenger when he was in charge of the intelligence service between the patriots in Charleston and the American army command. Perhaps running through Kosciuszko's mind as he composed this will, was the recollection of a skirmish, at Port Johnston, in South Carolina, in November 1782, in which he led the American forces in the last skirmish of the war—one of the casualties was a mulatto who died of shoulder wounds.[4]

Agrippa Hull spent six years in the Revolutionary War and spent four of these as Thaddeus B. Kosciuszko's body servant. He was presented to Kosciuszko while at West Point by General John Paterson. Kosciuszko became quite attached to Agrippa Hull, and after his work was terminated at West Point, he wrote to General Washington the following letter, dated August 17, 1780:

> I beg your Excellency would grant me a request to carry my boy with me, who since three years wait on me. I have no other at present and I cannot get one to go with me so far off. Col. Sprout is willing if your Excellenncy will give order for it.[5]

Washington replied: "It is perfectly agreeable to me that you should carry your servant with you and so you will inform General Sprout." Thus Agrippa Hull, nicknamed "Grippy," served with Kosciuszko throughout the whole of the southern campaign, but not without some reward for on October 20, 1780, the Board of War of North Carolina issued an order for a pair of shoes "for Colonel Cusiasko's Servant. When Kosciuszko prepared to leave America for Paris, General Paterson was among the many comrades-in-arms, bidding Kosciuszko farewell from

---

[4] Benjamin Quarles, *The Negro in the American Revolution* (Chapel Hill: 1961), pp. 188-189.
[5] Miecislaus Haiman, *Kosciuszko in the American Revolution* (New York: 1943), p. 92.

New York. Gifts were exchanged and it was then that General Paterson gave Kosciuszko his faithful servant, Grippy. Since Agrippa Hull was fearful of the long ocean voyage, Kosciuszko gave him freedom. He settled on a farm in Stockbridge, Massachusetts, where he became a familiar and respected figure. Not only was Kosciuszko an emancipator, but he was also a benefactor of the first educational institution for Negroes in the United States.[6]

In 1802, there was a revolt in Santo Domingo, a French colony. To help suppress the rebellion, Napoleon sent three battalions of Polish Legions, in 1802, and a Polish brigade, in 1803. The French, supported by the Poles, who fought unwillingly, failed to suppress the rebellion.[7] The Poles—who were not taken into English captivity, or who did not perish in battle, or of tropical fever—went over to the Negroes and settled among them. Some native families in Haiti still bear Polish names.[8] When Olgierd Brudrewicz, editor of *Przekroj*, visted Haiti, he met a Negro, named Poniatowski, whose ancestor came to Haiti with General Leclerc.[9]

The Negro discovered other Poles who fought for the recognition of human dignity. They worked to abolish slavery through the use of petitions, lobbying individual political leaders and through public opinion exerted in certain areas.

Thomas G. Wengierski wrote of the American Negroes with compassion in 1783.

Julian Juzwikiewicz mentioned slavery in his *Polacy w Ameryce*. He considered slavery to be the only "deformity" of this country's social institutions, but hoped that it would gradually disappear through peaceful means.[10]

T. Lewinski, a prominent abolitionist writer, helped Cassius

---

[6] Frank Monaghan, "Tadeusz Andrzej Bonaventura Kosciuszko," *Dictionary of American Biography*, Dumas Malone, Editor (New York: 1933), X, p. 496.
[7] Of the 6,000 Polish Legionnaires sent to Haiti, only 300 returned.
[8] Jerzy Zubrzycki, *Polish Immigrants in Britain* (The Hague: 1956), pp. 4-5.
[9] The graves of the Poles who died in the French suppression of Haiti are located in Fond des Blancs. "Polskie Nazwiska na Haiti," *Dziennik Polski* (November 3, 1961), p. 16.
[10] Miecislaus Haiman, *Polish Past in America 1608-1865* (Chicago: 1939), p. 108.

M. Clay to edit *True American,* published first at Lexington, Kentucky, in 1845, and later at Cincinnati, Ohio, and in Louisville, Kentucky under a new title, *The Examiner*.[11] It was a dangerous job which might have cost him his life at any moment. The newspaper's office was transformed into a veritable fortress. Clay placed a keg of powder in the basement, ready to blow up the building and its occupants should the pro-slavery mob, which frequently attacked the newspaper, be victorious.[12]

Cyprian Norwid protested the death sentence of John Brown in his two poems entitled: "To Citizen John Brown" and "John Brown." After Brown's death, Norwid considered him a symbol of progress and a liberator equal to Washington.

Kalikst Wolski, a Polish traveler in America, relates in his book, *Do Ameryki i w Ameryce,* how a Polish exile, in New Orleans, liberated more than a score of slaves.

> Having come to America in 1845 or so, he quickly obtained a well-paid position in some city office. He had been an artillery officer and was very capable. It was his job to make plans and engrave new maps of the recently acquired southwestern states. With the money he was able to save, each year he would buy two Negro children and set them free, doing this over a period of years and always complying with every letter of the law. In this way, by the time I was in New Orleans, he had managed to free more than twenty children, some boys, some girls. All these were now grown up and completely free, working for a living, surrounding their benefactor with blessings. None of them would leave the city in which he lives, as they all vied with each other in showing him their gratitude.[13]

Holynski and Jacob Gordon also considered the subject of slavery and in their writings were sympathetic towards the slaves. They agreed with Lincoln, who reasoned: "if slavery is not wrong, nothing is wrong." So they sought to keep it from spreading so that it would one day die for lack of growth.

Inhabitants in partitioned Poland were also extremely inter-

---

[11] Edmund L. Kowalczyk, "Jottings from the Polish American Past," *Polish American Studies,* VII (July-December, 1950), p. 80.
[12] Haiman, *Polish Past in America 1608-1865,* p. 109.
[13] "New Orleans and the Mississippi in 1865," From the pages of *Do Ameryki i w Ameryce,* translated and edited by Marion Moore Coleman, *Polish-American Studies* (July-December, 1967), XXIV, p. 81.

ested in the slavery issue. Harriet Beecher Stowe's *Uncle Tom's Cabin* was published in four editions, in Poland. The first edition, *Chata Wuja Tomasza, czyli Zycie niewolnikow w Zjednoczonych Stanach Polnocnej Ameryki,* translated by Franciszek Dydacki, appeared in 1853. The second edition, *Chata Wuja Tomasza, przez Pania . . . opowiadania dzieciom przez Arabella Palmerowa,* translated by Wojciech Szymanowski, appeared in 1856. The third edition, *Chata Ojca Toma czyli Zycie Murzynow w Stanach niewolniczych Ameryki polnocnej,* translated by Waclaw Przybylski and Ignacy Iwicki, appeared in 1860. The fourth edition, with the text in Polish and French, was a Szymanowski translation.

Count Adam Gurowski was one of the most original minds of his age: a prolific writer, a powerful orator, and the anti-slavery movement's philosopher and theoretician. He gave the fledgling anti-slavery movement its moral thrust and many of its arguments. Count Gurowski—born in 1805—was a political refugee from Poland. He came to America, in 1849, disenchanted by the defeats in the struggle against the monarchial tyrannies, embittered at the petty rivalries and dissensions, and the lack of unity among the leaders of the Polish insurrection of 1830. Gurowski made a good adjustment to the American environment among the intellectuals of Boston and New England. For a number of years he was engaged in writing, teaching and lecturing. He found the American social life to his taste, and made friends among literary personalities of America.

The American Slave question caught Count Adam Gurowski's attention at the time of the Compromise of 1850. Count Gurowski denounced Senator Daniel Webster, before a Boston society, for supporting the Fugitive Slave Law of 1850. In the center of New England society, where many considered Daniel Webster's word law, Count Gurowski courageously declared, in rebellious phrases, that he could read and interpret the Constitution as well as Webster.

> I say that the Fugitive Slave Law is unconstitutional,—is an outrage and an imposition of which you will soon be ashamed. It is a disgrace to humanity and to your republicanism, and Mr. Webster should be hung for advocating it. He is a humbug or an ass, an ass if he believes

such an infamous law to be constitutional; and if he does not believe it, he is a humbug and a scoundrel for advocating it.[14]

From then on, Count Gurowski gave the subject constant observation, study and comment. His first printed opinion, on the slavery question, appeared in a chapter of *America and Europe*, published in 1857. In sixty pages Gurowski attacked not only the question of slavery, but much of the Southern culture. After briefly explaining his attitude toward the problem, he treated, point by point, pro-slavery reasoning and shattered each premise through an array of skillful arguments based on history and ethnology. His appeal to learning and reason proved popular with the intellectuals. The well-known Boston abolitionist, Edmund Quincy, declared in an anti-slavery speech that Gurowski's chapter did more to condemn slavery than any other publication.[15]

In 1860, Gurowski published *Slavery in History*, a 260-page volume, which was brought out by the small New York firm of A. B. Burdick. The book did well financially for the publisher and the author. When the book appeared, anti-slavery literature was at peak demand. Yet, similar publications must have outsold this volume, for its intellectual qualities limited its appeal. Count Gurowski himself considered his book a work of scholarship, with profit a remote possibility.

Count Gurowski did not believe slaves were better fed, clothed, and cared for than the free laborers in the North. To the argument that the American slave loved the institution which enmeshed him, Gurowski fired a barrage of questions. Why were there an ever increasing number of state laws to defend and strengthen slavery? Why did masters fear the slaves would escape? Why was there a need for the Fugitive Slave Law of 1850? Why did newspaper advertisements appear for runaway slaves? Why did owners of bloodhounds advertise to hunt fugitives? "Strange evidences of the felicity and satisfaction of the oppressed," Gurowski quipped.[16]

When the civil war broke out, Count Gurowski became one

---
[14] LeRoy H. Fisher, *Lincoln's Gadfly, Adam Gurowski* (Norman: 1964), p. 50.
[15] *Ibid.*, p. 227.
[16] *Ibid.*, p. 230.

of the most active supporters of the Northern States, and consistently urged Lincoln and his military staff to prosecute the military operations efficiently, swiftly, and with continued offensive. No one was more deeply concerned with the recruitment and use of Negro soldiers, in the Union armies, than Count Gurowski. Again and again, he urged Lincoln to issue a call for Negro troops. He referred to the fact that Negroes had been engaged in battle during the American War of Independence. The Negroes—who escaped from Confederate lines or were freed by the advancing military forces from the North—he concluded, could be recruited to fill the void as a result of heavy casualties. In addition, they would be able to prove their loyalty, ability, and courage. By this means, they also would win their birthright as free Americans and move toward racial equality. Because of prejudice and ignorance, Gurowski reasoned that a colored regiment would perhaps be left unsupported during a battle. To prevent this, he recommended that they be organized into larger units like brigades and divisions to withstand an overwhelming enemy onslaught until relief arrived. He also recommended to Secretary Stanton that the soldier's handbook of tactics and regulations be revised, or that a new book be written for their use. Gurowski also petitioned Secretary of War Stanton—while still employed in the State Department—to commission him colonel of a colored regiment, when the current events render it necessary. Twenty-six Radical Republican friends had "cordially" countersigned to recommend that his request be honored. No action was taken on the Count's request because many Union leaders in the party's Conservative wing believed that colored men should be used only as laborers. Lincoln also opposed the use of Negroes as soldiers. However, Gurowski's efforts began to bear fruit. In 1862, General Hunter organized a Negro regiment, and soon thereafter enlistment of Negroes into the Union forces increased considerably. In 1862, the three volume *Infantry Tactics* had been reduced to one. The title page designated the publication for "the use of colored troops of the United States Infantry."[17]

Closely associated with Count Gurowski's championing of the Negro soldier was his belief in the potential intellectual, psychological, and physiological equality of the races. Because the Negro had been almost always a slave, he had been kept in ignorance, and in a destitute condition, the Count reasoned; but provide him with freedom, education, and broad opportunity, and he would in time reach the status of the Caucasians. "The African speaks, thinks, loves, hates, reasons, comprehends," he explained, "and therefore he is capable of being initiated into a higher life. However distant the hour of initiation may be, strike it will for the African race."[18] The count viewed with disgust the widespread idea of Negro inferiority, which was voiced in the North—both in and out of Congress—even after the Emancipation Proclamation.

Count Gurowski was uncompromising on the question of racial and national equality. He called for the protection of the freed slave from his former master if the ideals of emancipation and racial equality are to be maintained. He believed that the Republicans must reform the South from the bottom to the top, and carry out a program that must have as a basis the broadest recognition of man as an intelligent self-governing being. He believed "that the loyal Africo-American ought to be the cornerstone of the reconstruction, and the disloyal white man should become an apprentice to loyalty, to human rights, and to intelligent liberty. The time is past and gone to force the loyal Africo-American to be tutored otherwise than by laws of equality with the whites, and whoever legislates differently is a traitor to humanity and his country.[19]

To keep the whites in the South from controlling that area and to keep it from the hands of the disloyal, he recommended giving the vote to the "always loyal Negro," so that the balance could be restored, and the political and legislative power would be retained by the honest and devoted white patriots. Count Gurowski had firmly asserted himself on the problem of racial equality and the role of the Northern and Southern Negro in the war.

> First, he insisted, they had won the right to equal status on a heroic pattern unprecedented in history. Second, they had been "true and

---

[17] *Ibid.*, p. 244.
[18] *Ibid.*, p. 246.
[19] *Ibid.*, p. 250.

loyal" to the Union. Finally, though "exposed to the most goading and cruel persecutions," they had remained loyal and devoted to the defenseless families of their deadly enemies.[20]

The abolitionist movement was not confined only to the male population of the Polish immigrants. An outstanding abolitionist was Ernestine S. Potowski-Rose; born in Piotrkow, Poland. Her emotional and intellectual involvement was genuine and devoid of adornment. Resourceful and obstinate, she brought her fine mind, ample energy, and personal views to bear on the movement. The anti-slavery leaders welcomed her assistance, and shared the platform with her on many important occasions. She addressed the American Anti-Slavery Society, in 1853. She spoke after Garrison, who delivered the main address. Her speech was saturated with wit, humor, and perceptive insights into every aspect of human life. As she related her experiences in Columbia, South Carolina, in the winter of 1847, she asked: "What is to be slave?" And she answered with an appealing foreign accent.

> Not to be your own, mentally, or morally—that is to be a slave. Ay, even if the slaveholders treated their slaves with the utmost kindness and charity; if I were told they kept them sitting on a sofa all day, and fed them with the best of the land, it is none the less slavery. For what does slavery mean? To work hard, to fare ill, to suffer hardships, that is not slavery; for many of us white men and women have to work hard, have to fare ill, to suffer hardship and yet we are not slaves. Slavery is, not to belong to yourself—to be robbed of yourself. . . . This is the great abomination of slavery, that it deprives a man of the common rights of humanity, stamped upon him by his maker. . . . But the great act of emancipation of 800,000 human beings as shown to the world that the African race are not only capable of taking care of themselves, but are capable of enjoying peacefully as much liberty and as much freedom as the white man.[21]

She travelled extensively. In May 1855, she addressed the anti-slavery convention, in New York, and later attended the New England Anti-Slavery Society where she shared the speak-

---

[20] Ibid., p. 250.
[21] Yuri Suhl, *Ernestine L. Rose and the Battle for Human Rights* (New York: 1959), p. 140.

ers' platform with the leaders of the abolitionist movement. When she delivered her address, Wendell Phillips, who followed her to the rostrum said:

> The speech, ladies and gentlemen, to which we have just listened, has Waldo Emerson's attribute of eloquence—it has a life behind it. What we have to do at the North is, to feel our souls our own—to dare think independently of institutions and majorities, and the old associations about us. The friend who has just taken her seat has taught us that lesson by a life that, before some of us had awakened to the duty of being free, was exerting its influences upon those about her. I am glad when she comes to the anti-slavery platform to give us the benefit of her clear insight, and her long example. They are the veteran troops of reform and free thought, that form the basis of every movement for the bettering of the race.[22]

During the same year, Ernestine Potowski-Rose also spoke at a convention of the Michigan Anti-Slavery Society, which was held in Battle Creek, Michigan.

Ernestine Potowski-Rose was also one of the main speakers at the meeting of "The Loyal Women of the Nation," in New York, on May 14, 1863. At this meeting the members of this organization pledged to collect a million signatures in order to petition Congress to pass the Thirteenth Amendment. One million signatures would have meant the names of one twentieth of the population of the northern states—an impossible goal; yet by the time "The Loyal Women of the Nation" disbanded, in August 1864, the League had gathered nearly 400,000 signatures. On February 9, 1864, two tall Negroes, symbolic figures, carried enormous bundles, made up of petition rolls, into the Senate chamber and placed them on the desk of the Senator from Massachusetts.[23]

Another voice heard around the land was that of Dr. Marie A. Zakrzewska. She became one of the leaders of the abolitionist movement, and was closely associated in this work with William Lloyd Garrison and Wendell Phillips. Her polemics against slavery did much to arouse New England sympathy for Negro

---

[22] Ibid., p. 170.
[23] Eleanor Flexner, Century of Struggle (Cambridge: 1959), pp. 109-111.

slaves, and to rally Northern support for the Anti-Slavery societies and the "Underground Railroad." Among the earliest Negro women to enter the field of medicine was Caroline V. Still, daughter of two famous "agents" on the Underground Railroad, William and Letitia Still of Philadelphia. Dr. Still interned at the New England Hospital for Women and Children which was founded by Dr. Marie A. Zakrzewska. It is also from this institution that the first Negro nurse, Mary Elizabeth Mahoney, graduated in 1879.[24]

The *Towarzystwo Demokratyczne Wygnancow Polskich u Ameryce* (Democratic Society of Polish Exiles in America)—though originally founded to support the effort of Polish independence—branched out to include the emancipation of the Negro in America as one more issue to champion.

Another exemplary Polish woman was Countess Maria Ledochowska (1863-1922) who gave up a life of luxury and leisure amid the aristocratic salons of Europe to minister to the spiritual and physical needs of Africa's impoverished downtrodden masses. At the age of 27, she founded a mission society known as the Sodality of St. Peter Claver. In addition to spreading the Christian gospel, Sister Maria Ledochowska was an outspoken foe of slavery, a major problem in Africa during the 19th century. She also sought to improve the material lot and hygienic standards of the natives. A major part of her efforts involved the creation of a publishing house which printed books in 19 different Negro dialects. After a life of total devotion to mission work and utter disregard for her own health and comfort, she died of sheer exhaustion in (what all who know her) "a state of sanctity." Recently Maria Teresa Ledochowska was beatified by Pope Paul VI.

During the Civil War, many Poles were appointed as officers of colored regiments. Ladislaus Zulawski organized, at Port Hudson, Louisiana, the Eighty-second Colored Regiment of which he was appointed colonel. In September 1863, it became the Tenth Infantry, called the "African Corps." When, during the Florida

---

[24] Flexner, *Century of Struggle*, p. 129. Sara W. Brown, "Colored Women Physicians, *Southern Workman*, LII (December, 1923), p. 584. Mary Ellen Chayer, "Mary E. Mahoney," *American Journal of Nursing*, LIV (April, 1954), pp. 429-431.

Expedition, General Alexander Asboth, commander, became mortally wounded at Marianna, Florida, on September 24, 1864, Colonel Zulawski took over the command and directed the expedition to Fort Pickens, a march of some 400 miles. Later, Zulawski commanded the First Brigade of the First Colored Division. In 1865 he was named commander of the garrison at Apalachicola, Florida.

Captain Peter Kiolbassa (1837-1905) was assigned as captain of the Sixth Colored Cavalry.

Lieutenant Julius S. Krzywoszynski resigned from the Third Pennsylvania Artillery Regiment to become a Second Lieutenant in the Colored Cavalry of the Twenty-Second Regiment which was added to the Signal Corps.

Artur Wrotnowski was appointed First Lieutenant and Adjutant of the First Louisiana Infantry in March 1863. On September 3, 1863, he was appointed Lieutenant Colonel, First Volunteers Engineers Corps d'Afrique; and finally, he became Colonel of the Ninety-Fifth United States Colored Volunteer Infantry, which was mustered out on November 26, 1864.[25]

After the Civil War, relations between the Blacks and the Polish-Americans continued to be cordial. Residents in Polish-American areas, adjacent to the black belt areas, did not organize to prevent Blacks from encroaching upon their neighborhoods. During World War I and World War II the migration of thousands of Southern Blacks to northern cities—many of which were inhabited by Polish-Americans—placed intolerable strains on housing, transportation, and recreational facilities. Still polarization between the two groups did not result.

American historians have all but ignored the newspaper reports and police records of arrest, injuries, and deaths which would indicate beyond a doubt that the Polish-Americans were not responsible for the race riots which accompanied the Black movement to northern cities. Polish-Americans and Blacks are still subject to manipulation by established power structures within the northern cities that are stifling the total development of Black and Polish-American well-being.

---

[25] Edmund L. Kowalczyk, "Jottings from the Polish American Past," *Polish American Studies*, VII (July-December, 1950), p. 87.

The Polish-Americans were receptive to practicing the American ideal and did not resist allowing Blacks into the mainstream of American life. There are many examples of concern and cooperation between the Blacks and Polish-Americans that dispel the myth that the Polish-Americans and Blacks are incompatible, do not work together, live together, and go to school together. Many Polish-Americans and Blacks work together for solutions to common problems involving transportation, law enforcement, drug traffic, unemployment, pollution, urban planning, education, and business ventures.

Ignacy Jan Paderewski often visited Andrew Carnegie at his home on Fifth Avenue, in New York City, and at his summer home in Massachusetts. One night after Paderewski played the piano for Andrew Carnegie and his guests, Paderewski retired to his room to write some music. All evening as he played and talked the melody had been whirling around in his head and he was anxious to set it down. Before beginning his work, he asked Joe, Carnegie's old Black servant for forty-five years, to bring him a pot of coffee. Paderewski always wrote music with a cup of black coffee near at hand.

In his mission to fulfill Paderewski's request, Joe missed the top step of the staircase and had fallen. The hot coffee poured over his face and into his eyes. He was a crumpled heap and his groans were deep and agonized when Paderewski lifted him in his arms and carried him to his bedroom. He put him down on his bed, and then ran for help. A doctor came and bandaged Joe's eyes, while Paderewski stood by whispering words of encouragement to the sufferer.

When the doctor was leaving, he informed Paderewski that Joe may be blind. After the doctor had gone, Paderewski went back to his room and sat on a sofa near Joe. He whispered a few words of regret to the old man, and told him the doctor had said he would be around soon. In a few months the Black man was as completely recovered as possible. One eye was gone, and the little sight that remained in the other was just enough to enable him to discern darkness from daylight.

But the color of the Black man's world was by no means gloomy. Something wonderful had happened to Joe while he was resting in a darkened room. He had been given a farm in his native Georgia, and he was to return there to live in comfort on his own land, for the remainder of his life. Every day he would be able to hear the laughter and chatter of his grandchildren, and when he wanted to walk through his garden, or to the sunny side of the house, their keen eyes and strong hands would be there to guide him.

All of his comfort and security had been given him by Ignacy Jan Paderewski. When Paderewski's friends protested that he was too generous with the old Negro, Paderewski answered them. "You recall that a Polish general fought with Washington, don't you?" Paderewski asked. "Yes," one friend replied. "Kosciuszko." Paderewski nodded and put a second question. "Then do you remember how he was compensated for his assistance?" he asked. The friend did. General Kosciuszko had been given a large tract of land by the American government, but, instead of using it himself, he had given it to Jefferson for the emancipation of Black slaves in America. "My countryman of long ago gave me a noble example to follow," Paderewski said.[26] After that there were no protests nor arguments about his gift to old Joe.

Dr. Haley Bell graduated from Meharry Medical College in Nashville, Tennessee, in 1922. Black people were leaving the South by the thousands to find jobs in Detroit's auto factories, and Dr. Bell—who had begun practicing dentistry in Lebanon, Tennessee—followed the crowd to Detroit. He had no money, no encouragement and little of anything except perseverance. While waiting to pass Michigan's state dental examination, he worked at Ford's for three weeks. Six months after he passed his examination, he opened his office, in Hamtramck, where several thousand black people lived. He sat back, waiting for the blacks to rush in. The rush never came.

> Bell worked for a downtown dentist for a few months then headed for Hamtramck where it turned out that his clientele would be 97 percent white and Polish. So he hired Estelle Grajek to be his interpreter and all-around aide. She still works for the Bell family, now assisting Bell's son-in-law, Dr. C. Robert Bass.[27]

---
[26] Antoni Gronowicz, *Paderewski, Pianist and Patriot* (New York: 1943), p. 94.
[27] Frank Angelo, "Black Broadcast Pioneer. He has Given 50 Years to Detroit," *Detroit Free Press* (March 9, 1973), p. 7-A.

Dr. Bell's first patient was a white fireman, who liked Dr. Bell's dental work so much that he sent several of his relatives back, who in turn, recommended more relatives and friends, and eventually Dr. Bell ended up with a practice that was 97 percent white. It remained that way from the time he opened, in January 1924, until he retired, in 1960.[28]

There are thousands of racially mixed children who are born out of wedlock in America. Significantly, these children were born of white mothers, who almost always give them up to welfare agencies. Neither black nor white, they are unclaimed by either race. In response to changing attitudes, many racially mixed children are adopted by Americans of Polish descent. Chris Borkowicz was only several months old and seriously ill when Mrs. Borkowicz accepted him as a foster child and nursed him back to health. Since she could not bear the thought of surrendering him, the Borkowicz family adopted him. Now, in the fourth grade, Chris has no problems adapting to life in a school on Milwaukee's predominantly white south side. Besides Chris, the Borkowicz family has four daughters, all older than Chris.[29]

Gene Krymkowski, an advertising executive, has also adopted Amy, a racially mixed child. He has also one son, Tommy.[30]

Tom and Jan Koby of Cuyahoga Falls, Ohio, adopted a biracial girl, Kristin, when she was thirteen months old, and a black boy, Douglas, when he was two years old. The Koby family have five children, two boys and three girls aged six to sixteen. Mrs. Koby explained that in adopting the two children they were not motivated by any benefits that would come to their children, but, "ironically, this has been one of our biggest rewards . . . seeing how the older children have taken them into the family so quickly."[31] Adoptions by the Koby family started a chain reaction.

---

[28] June Brown Garner, "The Dentist Who Put Detroit's Black Community on the Air," *Sunday News Magazine* (July 25, 1971), p. 10.

[29] Jerry Gnadt, "The Dawn of Acceptance," *The Sign* (January, 1971), p. 41.

[30] *Ibid.*, p. 44.

[31] "If you believe something—four adopt 'racial babies,'" *Catholic Chronicle* (March 19, 1971), p. 3.

Len and Pat Koby, Tom's brother and sister-in-law, adopted a bi-racial girl, Lea, when she was only eighteen months old.[32]

Father Paul Rybicki, associate pastor at St. Cecilia's Church, in northwest Detroit, and Father Bob Holmes, a teacher at St. Martin de Porres High School, are foster parents of four black boys. Both are members of the Basilian Order and had to gain the Basilian fathers' permission to start a foster family. The permission came through in 1969, and by the summer of 1970, Father Rybicki and Father Holmes had traded in rectory life for a small flat on Detroit's west side. The priests are foster parents, but they introduce each of the boys as "my son."

> And if it isn't so remarkable that the boys call both men "father," they also call Father Rybicki's parents, Mr. and Mrs. John Rybicki, of predominantly white Warren, "Grandpa and Grandma."[33]

Father Rybicki and Father Holmes also have a few joys other fathers may miss.

> "Once, when we were at a restaurant in an all-white neighborhood, the boys caught some flak from the other customers," Father Rybicki recalls.
> "Their reaction was, 'Father, how come white people and black people can't live together? They should come live with us.' "[34]

The priests say they have the normal headaches of fatherhood: brotherly squabbles, teachers' reports, and an occasional neighborhood fight. "When one of us has to chastize or punish the boys, the other does the comforting afterward," Father Rybicki says. "But we switch these roles."[35]

Frank and Joy Damaschke, of Port Huron, Michigan, experienced great difficulty in their adoption proceedings for Scott Damaschke. St. Clair County Judge Halford I. Streeter ruled that Frank Damaschke could not have custody of the boy. "Can't you see . . . if the child grows up with this family, when he gets to be

---
[32] *Ibid.*, p. 3.
[33] Cyndi Meagher, "Four Boys have two 'Fathers' to remember today," *The Sunday News* (June 17, 1973), p. 8-F.
[34] *Ibid.*, p. 8-F.
[35] *Ibid.*, p. 8-F.

fifteen or sixteen, who will he date?"—the judge asked during the proceedings.³⁶ Eventually, the judge waived jurisdiction to Probate Court. The Damaschkes have four sons and daughters. Robert Scott, a Black, had a moving experience during his visit to the Damaschke household.

> When the *Detroit News*' photographer Robert Scott, a Negro, arrived at the Damaschke home, Scott expressed interest and enthusiasm—first in his camera, then in the man whose color almost matched the child's.
> He touched Robert Scott's brown hand and then examined his own, smiling in a surprised sort of way. Then, he walked to a full length mirror on a closet door, took a long look at himself and then back at the photographer.
> He didn't say anything, but you could almost read his thoughts. He was quiet for a moment—and then returned to romping on the floor with his friends.
> Looking back, he asked incredulously: "Your name is Scott, too?"³⁷

Victoria Lukasik, who speaks little English, came to the United States from Lopczyce, Poland. She and her husband had three children and it had always been her wish to have "a priest of her own," according to her daughter, Leona. After her husband died, in 1940, Victoria Lukasik found work with Parke-Davis Company to help support her two daughters while her son, John, was in the service. Her interest in the mission was stimulated by contact with the Sisters of St. Peter Claver and two magazines *African Youth* and *Echo*.

In 1959, Victoria Lukasik wrote to the sisters and offered to help sponsor the baptism of African youngsters. She also offered to contribute to a seminarian's expense while she was still able to work. Her first donation of $250 was sent to the Diocese of Tororo, and Father Omodoi was selected by his bishop to receive the aid. Father Omodoi had always hoped to become a priest. Uganda is a nation that is predominantly Christian and one-third of these are Catholic. It was Father Omodoi's desire to do

---

³⁶ Luise Leismer, "Child's custody up to court. A tangle of race and love." *The Detroit News* (November 9, 1969), p. 1.
³⁷ *Ibid.*, p. 8-A.

pastoral work and teach in Uganda's school system, which since that nation's independence, in 1962, has been government controlled, including Catholic schools. Many priests are employed by the Ugandan government as administrators or teachers.

Father Omodoi might have had an easier time of it, but his father's death, in 1946, and his mother's death, in 1949, left him, at twenty, with a younger brother to support. An uncle was of some help, but for the time being thoughts of the seminary had to be put aside. It was Mrs. Lukasik's unexpected aid that returned Father Omodoi to the seminary and ordination, in 1960. As an ordination gift, Victoria Lukasik bought the new priest his chalice and paten and a sick call kit.[38]

Following his ordination, Father Omodoi taught at Mbale College. He also worked as the secretary of education, in the Catholic Department of Education, before the government assumed control. In 1970, Father Omodoi was sent to the United States by his superior, Bishop James Odongo, to further his studies in education and administration. During his three year stay in the United States—while attending Spalding College, in Louisville, Kentucky, and the University of Indiana—Father Omodoi had the opportunity to meet Victoria Lukasik for the first time, at her home, after a twelve-year correspondence. The introduction was arranged through Father James A. Maloney, director of the Detroit Archdiocesan office of the Society for the Propagation of the Faith. "It was a happy moment for me," Father Omodoi said. "I felt . . . great joy."[39]

Good, bad or indifferent, Polish-American families are taking racially mixed and black children into their homes in increasing numbers. The home and family life offer an attractive alternative to temporary foster homes and institutions.

Ron Marable, an artist whose paintings hang in many Detroit homes, finds a woman's face just as challenging as the canvas, and his talents are making him the nation's arbitrator of beauty for black women, just as George Masters and Vidal Sassoon are for white women. Marable has traveled to Europe, Hawaii, and

---

[38] Don Konrad, "A Widow Meets her 'Adopted' Priest," *The Michigan Catholic* (April 3, 1970), p. 1.
[39] *Ibid.*, p. 1.

throughout the United States demonstrating the proper make-up. He has been retained to do facial make-up for black actors in several films produced in Hollywood. Marable carefully studies musical and theatrical artists, and has made up many of them. A woman's aim should be to combine her face and her into a total picture of beauty, but many black stars don't succeed in making themselves as beautiful as they can be, Marable says. Ron Marable attributes his success to his mother—Dorothy Kowalski Marable.

> She's been my inspiration, and through the confidence, guidance and self-sacrifice of her and my father, Edward Marable, I was able to do something special with my life.[40]

In 1971, Cinema 1976 was established in Detroit. The principal officers of the new organization are Otto Wendt, president; Tom Walsh, board chairman; Richard Markowicz, executive vice-president for creative projects; and Tom Brank, vice-president in charge of finance. These four men have formed Cinema 1976 to produce pictures, recordings, television, industrial promotion films, and the entire spectrum of related works. They profess enthusiasm over the wealth of black and white talents in Detroit which go unnoticed and wasted for lack of proper recognition and exploitation. Cinema 1976 marks the beginning of a new Detroit spirit, a faith in the renaissance of Detroit which includes faith in the class of cultural elitism of Detroit. Since their establishment, they have had creative offers from New York and the West Coast. They have also declined financial offers from Chicago and Hollywood.[41]

Long before it became fashionable and financially feasible to invest in black artists, and long before Motown was established in Detroit, Leonard Chess, was the foremost exponent of black culture and black artists in America. Chess, who was born in Poland, had great faith, confidence and reliance in black talent. And many he recorded found fame and success. His recordings emphasized the black contribution to American culture and civi-

---

[40] June Brown Garner, "How a Black Beauty Expert Judges Women," *The Sunday News Magazine* (July 16, 1972), p. 8.
[41] Lawrence T. Carter, "New Film Company Offers Detroit Hope," *Detroit Sunday News* (May 2, 1971), p. 4-E.

lization. When Chess died of a heart attack, in 1969, at the age of 52, he left an estate of almost six million dollars. He also had 50 per cent of the L & P Broadcasting Corporation.[42]

Dan Wieczorek always lived in St. Clair Shores (a white neighborhood) and attended all white schools. Dan Carter lived fifteen years in an all black neighborhood, spent several years in mixed schools—like Henry Ford High School—and then transferred to Grosse Pointe University School. Wieczorek also selected Grosse Pointe University School. Dan Wieczorek co-captained the football team with Dan Carter, the first black to ever co-captain a Grosse Point University School football team. The black students—Wieczorek encountered and knew—were "really nice people, and all out to help you, and make friends with you."[43] Going to school with black students and friends, hasn't changed Dan's thinking. He formerly associated with some black friends of his father, who is a doctor. "The black students here only confirmed what I thought it would be like. I had a vague idea that there might be some problems and difficulties, but no major ones that couldn't be worked out. This has proved true."[44]

> He admires one of his black friends for his ability to mix with blacks and whites alike, and for his evident ability to handle whites. "He can be what he wants to be." This same friend spent two vacation days at Dan's house where, among other things, they talked about racial relations, and Dan feels they became able to see through their prejudices.
>
> He talked about, for example, the time Dan's band was due to play in downtown Detroit at the same time the Black Panthers planned to demonstrate. Dan said, smiling: There was no envy or question about it. My friend turned to me and said 'I'll keep my buddies off you in Detroit, if you'll keep your buddies off me in Grosse Pointe.' "[45]

---

[42] "Polski Emigrant Pozostawil Spadek Wartosci $5,406,323," *Ameryka Echo* (February 8, 1971), p. 7.
[43] Kathy Cosseboom, *Grosse Pointe Michigan: Race Against Race* (Lansing: 1972), p. 100.
[44] *Ibid.*, p. 101.
[45] *Ibid.*, p. 101.

After being transferred to Detroit, Mary Ann Piekosz and Connie Gilliard—who are employed by the Department of Housing and Urban Development (HUD)—helped start a federal college in Detroit. The two women had observed the success of a similar college in Chicago, and decided to try it in Detroit. They were appointed Federal Women Program Coordinators when the college was established. Federal-Metro College is geared primarily to public service employees on the national, state and local levels. The college enables federal agencies to train new employees, and increase the skills of others. Course offerings are based on a survey of employees' needs and skills. Its Detroit downtown location, in the First National Building, makes it readily accessible to an estimated 10,000 federal employees in the area. The program is implemented through Wayne State University's College of Lifelong Learning, which administers the courses and grants the credit. In a recent interview, Mary Piekosz made the following comments:

> In the beginning we had to do everything from pushing the furniture around to cleaning the ashtrays. We washed the blackboards, and when we complained because the walls in one room were not clean, we were told to get a can of cleaner and go to work. So we did.[46]

The efforts of Piekosz and Gilliard are purely voluntary. The two co-workers often spend evenings going over plans. "It's not a full-time job, but it requires a full time effort on our part," commented Mrs. Gilliard, who is black, in a recent interview.[47]

Vince Zuch was born, raised, and educated in an integrated neighborhood in southwest Detroit. Zuch has some outspoken ideas on how blacks and whites must work together if Detroit and other large cities are to remain integrated, and avoid the three kinds of neighborhoods, in existence, in the large cities: white, black, and changing. Zuch works at a blue-collar job and has spent nearly 5,000 hours of his own time, over the past two years, in a crusade against what Zuch says are the blockbusting

---

[46] Alice Hagerty, "They helped Start a Federal College," *The Detroit News* (December 4, 1974), p. 5-F.
[47] Ibid., p. 5-F.

tactics of some realtors.[48] Zuch claims that these real estate companies have preyed on black-white antagonisms to generate business artificially. Zuch also alleges that certain realtors drum up business through subtle racial-scare tactics, such as "compounded solicitation," which he describes as a bombardment of white homeowners with telephone and mail sales solicitation. The result of these tactics in other parts of the city, Zuch claims, has been to drive most whites out of their neighborhood and to draw blacks in.

Zuch is the outgoing president of the Emerson Community Homeowners Organization (ECHO).[49] The Detroit Emerson neighborhood is a square mile of about 3,400 houses and 15,000 residents bounded by W. Nichols, Seven Mile, Evergreen and the Southfield Freeway.

In 1972, with twenty-two white and black Emerson residents as plaintiffs, ECHO filed a (first-of-its-kind) class-action suit in U.S. District Court against fifteen white and black real estate firms, alleging that the firms "steered" home seekers on a racial basis. The suit was filed under the provisions of the 1968 Civil Rights Act in accordance with an opinion by Supreme Court Justice William O. Douglas that the impetus behind open-housing litigation must come from civil suits in which the complainants act as "private attorneys general."[50] Zuch hopes that the Emerson area will be the first area where integration will work, and not the last opportunity left to form an integrated neighborhood in Detroit.

Many Polish-Americans supported the "Open Housing" law. Many were convinced that the old Polish-American neighborhoods with their churches and meeting halls and schools will be a thing of the past unless "open housing" is implemented.

---

[48] Michael Graham, "Neighbors Unite to Stay Integrated," *Detroit Free Press* (June 4, 1973), p. 10-A.

[49] Residents and merchants who let their property deteriorate can expect visits from ECHO members, who strongly encourage remedial action. It usually is effective. Baby-sitting services are made available to working mothers by housewives and teen-agers, in ECHO, along with grass-cutting, leaf-raking, and snow removal services. To help keep the crime rate low, ECHO formed a radio patrol to keep an eye on the neighborhood at night.

[50] Graham, "Neighbors Unite to Stay Integrated," *Detroit Free Press* (June 4, 1973), p. 10-A.

The continual increase of the Negro population will force the Negro people to seek housing outside its present neighborhoods. Just as the younger Poles left the Polish neighborhoods and settled in north Detroit and the suburbs, so too, as the Negro population increases, housing must be provided for them. As of now, the only place that is open to them is the so-called "old neighborhood." The surge of the Negro population will gradually overrun our Polish neighborhoods. The only thing that can stop this is the passage of an "open housing" bill, whereby the Negro will be able to bypass the Polish Community and go into the suburbs.

For proof of this, all we have to do is look at our original Polish neighborhood around Canfield Avenue today. The Polish people have all but disappeared. The churches in that vicinity are almost empty and barely surviving. The reason is because all the other neighborhoods are closed to the Negro.[51]

Mayor Roman Gribbs (whose family name used to be Grzyb) was unequivocally committed to a policy of citizen involvement in city government. During his term of Office, Gribbs—in his attempts to reconcile differences, and reduce alienation in the City of Detroit—has appointed many Blacks to positions of responsibility.

"I have appointed more black persons to positions of authority than ever before in Detroit's history," Gribbs said.

As evidence of this, he cited his appointments of Greene, DPW Commissioner Clarence Russell and DSR Manager Ed Davis.

"Fully 40 percent of the city's employees are under the direct supervision of black department heads whom I have appointed," he said. "Before I took office, that figure was only 10 percent."[52]

When Senator Edmund S. Muskie came to California, on Labor Day, in 1971, to begin a four-month, 32-state campaign designed to take him directly to the Democratic nomination for President of the United States, at one point—in a private discussion with 30 or 35 Black leaders—he was asked if he would consider a black running mate, should he win the Democratic nomination.

Senator Muskie could have given a diplomatic answer to the

---

[51] "'Open Housing' Will Save Polonia," *Dziennik Polski* (December 18, 1967), p. 2.

[52] Clark Hallas, "Mayor Assails New Detroit Critics," *The Detroit News* (December 31, 1971), p. 6-A.

black-V.P. question for strictly political reasons. Senator Muskie could have talked of the many Blacks he knows who are "great, dedicated leaders" and "would be a credit to any ticket" without remotely pledging to pick a black running mate. Senator Muskie could easily have dodged the issue with the conventional type of political double talk.[53]

Senator Muskie who has adopted blunt honesty as a deliberate campaign policy, gave his, now famous, reply: "It is my judgment that such a ticket is not electable now."[54] He went on to say that he regretted it was so—it shouldn't be so, he said—but a ticket with a black man on it would be defeated and that would be a setback to the efforts of those who are committed to equality for Blacks.

Once the remark was transmitted to the American public, Senator Muskie insisted on carving the original version in stone, instead of making a simple and undoubtedly accurate clarification. What he undoubtedly meant to say was that the addition of a black, simply on the basis of his minority status, would be a losing proposition. This is patently correct, but it applies with equal force to Jews, Catholics, Greeks, Nisei or whatever minority group. The American electorate is far more sophisticated than many give it credit for being; above all, it resents manipulative cosmetics, or even the assumption that it is being toyed with.

Senator Muskie has stirred up all kinds of reactions: some hopeful, while others are discouraging, by his statement that a black man is "not electable" as vice-president at this time. "Senator Muskie was being super honest when he didn't need to be," said Rep. James R. Mann, South Carolina Democrat. "I think it was a serious mistake, and it definitely will be used against him in the campaign for the 1972 Democratic presidential nomination."[55]

---

[53] The four contemporary Democratic presidential contenders striving for support of the Black-Americans, at the Democratic Black Caucus, refused to say flatly that they would push for a black as a vice-presidential candidate. "Black V-P? Four Dems Sidestep it," *Detroit Free Press* (May 3, 1976), p. 4-A.

[54] James M. Perry, "How a Blooper Was Born at Ralph's Supermarket," *The National Observer* (October 2, 1971), p. 5.

[55] Louis Cassels, "Muskie's words on black veep stir strange reaction," *The Detroit News* (October 1, 1971), p. 5-B.

Black politicians in the south—who might have been expected to take umbrage, at least publicly, at Senator Muskie's remark—have responded in exactly the opposite way. They praised the Maine Democrat for "telling it like it is." Senator Muskie's statement has been recognized among them as a regretful observation about the present climate of the American public opinion rather than an expression of personal bigotry.

Rev. I. Dequincy Newman, a militant black leader of the NAACP, in South Carolina, made the following comments: "I think Muskie gave an honest answer to a difficult question. Others might have talked out of both sides of their mouth."[56] Newman personally agreed with Muskie's appraisal. "I wish a Black vice-president could be elected, but I very much doubt if it's possible with the amount of racism that now exists in this country."[57]

Because of Senator Muskie's statement—carefully and seriously exploring the possibility of a black man running for vice-president—he greatly advanced the black movement for equality. Today, it is generally accepted that a black presence on a Democratic ticket would pose a problem: things would be difficult, but they would not be impossible.

Senator Muskie's most attractive features as a presidential candidate: his candor and sincerity—did not agree with the politician's view as to what are the most essential characteristics of a candidate. His political peers wrecked his presidential hopes. However, he did advance the black cause. In the 1976 presidential campaign all four Democratic contenders: former governor of Georgia, Jimmy Carter; Senator Frank Church of Idaho; Rep. Morris Udall, of Arizona; and Governor Edmund G. Brown, of California; all agreed that America is ready for a black vice-president.[58] However, not one would make a flat commitment to select one as a running mate.

By speaking frankly, Muskie has prodded into action many blacks to take steps to convince the Democrats that they no longer can take black voters for granted. A third or fourth party "uprising" is always a possibility. However, the Democrats still did

---

[56] *Ibid.*, p. 5-b.
[57] *Ibid.*, p. 5-b.
[58] "Black V-P? Four Dems Sidestep it," *Detroit Free Press* (May 3, 1976), p. 1A.

not take drastic steps to appease Blacks and to bring their vital votes back into the fold.

Many members of the Polish-American clergy never grew disillusioned with the integration movement as a vehicle that would secure freedom and dignity for people whose ancestors had been slaves in America. Voicing a perfect faith that "all men are created equal," the fundamental thesis of the Constitution, many Polish-American priests believed that the church must offer vision and leadership to forming a coalition between all members of society, where all can unite in pursuing common social goals.

Monsignor Lucyan Bojnowski, of New Britain, Connecticut, was aware of prejudice against blacks in America. He proceeded to face the problem squarely as early as 1927.

> Indeed, at one point in 1927 he mildly admonished his parishioners for being excited because a marriage between a white and black person was reported in a nearby town. "They are both children of God," he proclaimed, "and if the cultural differences and the emotional maturity are not a problem, they should have a blessed marriage."[59]

Father Edward Popielarz became pastor of St. Joseph's Catholic Church, in Pontiac, Michigan, in 1969. The church was divided and in financial trouble. Father Popielarz immediately began breaking down the racial divisions of the church. During his early administration, someone kept sneaking onto the church grounds to paint black faces on all the white marble religious statues. And each time, on the very next night after it happened, another individual would appear and paint all the faces white again. Father Popielarz did the only logical thing he could think of under the circumstances. He painted all the statues himself in gold. He painted Christ and the angel who visited him in the Garden of Gethsemane in gold. He painted all the stations of the cross also in gold. "Gold is a neutral color that shines with love," Father Popielarz explained.[60] And inside the tiny red church he installed black, brown and white Madonnas, and established

---

[59] Daniel S. Buczek, *Immigrant Pastor. The Life of the Right Reverend Monsignor Lucyan Bojnowski of New Britain, Connecticut* (Waterbury: 1974), p. 146. See also *Przewodnik Katolicki* (March 27, 1927), p. 28.

[60] Rone Tempest, "Pontiac Church Survives. Priest Leads Mixed Flock," *Detroit Free Press* (September 16, 1973), p. 1.

separate festivals for the Poles, Blacks, Latins and "Gringos," who come to the church in this changing south Pontiac neighborhood.

As a result, the small parish—which was on the verge of closing four years ago—has nearly tripled in membership, with some sixty families as active members. Once, almost all Polish, the church has become one of the most racially mixed and active in the Detroit area, offering an unusual mixture of the old and new in Catholicism.

St. Casimir School, a Catholic elementary school, on Detroit's west side, in the last few years has become quite cosmopolitan. It is now attended by students from Polish, Black and Spanish backgrounds. Father Joseph Karasiewicz, the pastor, understood the change and developed a new curriculum which considers the language and culture of the Polish, Spanish and Black groups. Every student in the school is exposed to the culture and language of the three groups.[61] Not only did the curriculum bring a new dimension in learning, but it made the students grateful for the immeasurable contributions others have made to their lives. They no longer were blinded by arrogance and pride. In addition, the school became a very effective institution is uniting the community for more successful and cooperative living.[62] Father Karasiewicz clearly understood Mrs. Margaret Burroughs' dictum: "We should dig into our old cultures—Polish, Negro, Jewish alike—cling to them and learn to share them. This is the way to understanding."[63] Mrs. Burroughs is the founder and director of Chicago's DuSable Museum of African-American history.[64] When Father Karasiewicz was transferred to another parish, both white and black protested and picketed.[65] Leading the picketers was a Black, Moreland Loveland.

---

[61] "Polskie Koledy w Szkole Sw. Kazimierza," *Dziennik Polski* (December 10, 1969), p. 3.
[62] Joseph A. Wytrwal, "New Experiments in the Schools," *Ethnic Groups in the City*, Otto Feinstein, editor. (Lexington: 1971), p. 379.
[63] "History," *Tuesday Magazine* (December, 1969), p. 26.
[64] Organized more than ten years ago, the museum attracts some 5,000 visitors a month.
[65] "Picket Chancery Offices. West Siders Demonstrate Over Transfer of Priests," *West Side Courier* (February 13, 1970), p. 16.

Those working for improved human relations say the most heartening sign has been the courageous frankness of a number of younger Polish-American priests in Pittsburgh, appealing to the Christian conscience of their parishioners, and urging them to face the question of racism.[66]

Individual Polish-Americans were not the only ones working with the Blacks. The Polish Roman Catholic Union, the oldest Polish-American fraternal organization in America, was giving mortgages and loans to blacks long before any of the downtown Chicago banks assumed the risk.[67]

Although the Polish-Americans have known discrimination, they also have felt the weight of charges that they are prejudiced toward the Blacks. Since World War II many black and Polish communities in the large cities share the same neighborhoods, schools and places of employment. Nevertheless, many white liberals and wealthy civic leaders from the wealthy suburbs who have left the cities with a ruinous, eroded tax structure are outraged because the Poles are blocking black advancement. These liberals and leaders, who are not threatened, even believe the Polish-Americans to be racist. Their lack of understanding and lack of compassion is proof of their own racism and snobbery toward the Polish-American group. The desire of many Polish-American communities to remain intact have been misinterpreted.

> The *American Polonia Reporter* quarterly in its autumn 1968 issue under a headline "Slanderers of the Poles" reports and disputes an article by Rev. Andrew Greeley of the National Opinion Research Center in Chicago. Fr. Greeley said a national opinion showed that racism and anti-Semitism were highest among Polish Catholics (based on interviews with 361 Germans, 328 Irish, 370 Italians, 184 Poles and 177 French Canadians)."[68]

Many Polish-Americans resent these charges because some of their neighborhoods have been adjacent to the black communities.

---

[66] Clarke M. Thomas, "Pittsburgh Polonia. Living with Discrimination," *Pittsburgh Post-Gazette Daily Magazine* (April 26, 1973), p. 31.

[67] Lois Wille, "Black-Pole Coalition Forming," *Detroit Free Press* (November 30, 1969), p. 12-B.

[68] Thomas, "Pittsburgh's Polonia. Living With Discrimination," *Pittsburgh Post-Gazette Daily Magazine* (April 26, 1973), p. 31.

Father Leonard Chrobot, a young Polish-American priest, who is Dean at St. Mary's College, near Detroit, stated:

> It really annoys me to hear white liberals who have fled to the suburbs accuse my mother of being racist when she has lived next door to blacks in the inner city for years.[69]

Rev. Clifford Ruskowski of the Orchard Lake Schools, said it was irritating to hear himself lumped together with white racists.

> I'm a Polish racist. I'm not a total white racist. Look, my father worked as a janitor at the Plymouth plant for ten years until they found a black to take his place. The Pole is just one step ahead of the black.[70]

The Polish-American communities are tired of hearing the theme repeated over and over again, that 300 years of persecution of Blacks demand that present-day whites have to make restitution. The Polish-American communities do not accept the concept of guilt by inheritance, and they are not a bit influenced by the threats of "you must do this or we can't be responsible for what happens." Father Chrobot made this explicit.

> "You also don't impress these Poles with statements about how guilty white people are and how bad the blacks had it during slavery," adds Father Chrobot. "These people went through concentration camps in Europe, or they had relatives who did, so they know what suffering had meant to their own group, and they don't feel primarily responsible for the injustices that have been heaped upon blacks."[71]

It was not the Polish-Americans who had enslaved the Blacks. The first significant migration of Poles occurred after the Civil War. And unlike some other whites, the Polish-Americans have

---

[69] Frye Gaillard, "Poles in Detroit Ally with Blacks," *Race Relations Reporter*, Volume II (April 5, 1971), p. 9.
[70] Charles Nathanson, "Poles and Blacks try to 'get it together,'" *East Side Shopper* (October 6, 1971), p. 1.
[71] Gaillard, "Poles in Detroit Ally with Blacks," *Race Relations Reporter*, Volume II (April 5, 1971), p. 9.

not created institutions which have discriminated against and exploited Blacks in more recent years. The Polish-Americans have no guilt in that regard.

Enmity towards the Blacks was not the reason for the lure of the suburbs and the demise of the Detroit Polish communities. Many Polish-Americans were forced out when the Chrysler Freeway cut a broad swath through the houses between St. Josephat and Sweetest Heart of Mary Parish. Both churches lost scores of families.

> Not all moved because of enmity toward the blacks. Mrs. Pisarski, who moved to Sterling Heights, still returns to visit Emma McKinney, her black neighbor during her years in Poletown.
> Mrs. McKinney, 62, remembers Julia Pisarski fondly, as well as "Grandma" Selewski, another neighbor whose name she pronounced with great difficulty.
> She recalled giving Grandma Selewski rides to church and visiting with Julia on the front porches of the neighborhood.
> But her comments about the neighborhood's present condition are fraught with the same rhetoric of the "racist" Poles who moved out.
> "These damn welfare and ADC people is the ones got the damn neighborhood looking like it is," Mrs. McKinney said. "I blame the city, too. Dogs everywhere. Garbage everywhere. Hell, you afraid to go out of the house."
> "We don't have that much trouble with the neighborhood, it's just that they (the newer residents) aren't as nice as them Polak people that moved out. For my belief and for what I know, I wouldn't live in a neighborhood without them Polish people."[72]

Hamtramck, which is about two square miles, lacks room to grow, and that is the major factor in the population shift. Since the city limits are boxed in by Detroit and Highland Park, there is little land for more houses. Thus, many moved to Warren which is called "Little Hamtramck."

> "The Poles didn't leave Hamtramck because the blacks moved in," said Florence Cassidy, the International Institute's expert on the Polish community. "They moved to the suburbs to get more land—the

---

[72] Marco Trbovich, "Poletown: Its Joys, Its Sorrows, Its Fate," *Detroit Free Press* (March 25, 1973), p. 4-C.

houses in Hamtramck are very close together—and the blacks just bought the homes.

She said that the city has a very stable population, which is about twelve percent.

Fr. Fabian Slominski, priest at Detroit's integrated Corpus Christi parish, agreed. "Almost all of the high schools and grammar schools in Hamtramck are integrated," he said. "The neighborhoods are racially stable and there has been no panic and rapid sale of homes because people are closely tied to the community."[73]

Of course, the rise of crime drove many Polish-Americans out of Detroit's Polish neighborhoods, who might otherwise have preferred to remain.

"You went home at night and you stayed home," said one elderly emigrant to the suburbs.

"When they (the elderly) found that they couldn't sit on their porches any more," said a younger second-generation Polish housewife, "those that could afford to move, moved."[74]

The real tension between the Blacks and the Polish-Americans have been artificially created. There is evidence that the Polish-Americans (if they are racist) are less so than many of the established groups. According to a survey made public by the National Urban League, the white backlash is stronger among the native Anglo-Saxon Protestants, than among the Polish, Irish or Italian ethnic groups. The survey conducted by Louis Harris and Associates, also contradicted this popular concept, that the backlash against blacks is concentrated among the more recent immigrants to America. According to Whitney M. Young, executive director of the National Urban League, the study suggests that some Americans may be projecting their own prejudices to minorities of recent origin.

The Harris survey was based on a sample of 1,609 persons. Respondents were asked (1) if they felt the push for racial equality was too fast; (2 whether they disapproved the 1954 Supreme Court school desegregation decision; and (3) whether they favored racially separate schools.

---
[73] Andrea Anglin, "Detroit area Poles cut the generation gap," *The Detroit News* (June 1, 1970), p. 3.
[74] Marco Trbovich, "Crime Scatters Poletown's Oldsters," *Detroit Free Press* (March 27, 1973), p. 3-A.

About half of the Anglo-Saxon Americans questioned said the push for equality was too rapid, Harris reported, compared with 37 percent among Irish-Americans, 42 percent among Italian-Americans and 44 percent among Polish-Americans.

While 42 percent of the Anglo-Saxon Protestants disapproved the school decision, the 1954 ruling was opposed by 31 percent of the Irish and Italians, and 36 percent of Polish descent.

Twenty-two percent of Anglo-Saxon Americans favored separate schools, compared with 6 percent of the Irish, 5 percent of the Italians and 16 percent of the Poles.

A breakdown by religion showed that 51 percent of Protestants questioned felt racial progress was too fast, as against 47 percent of the Catholics and 2 percent of the Jews.[72]

As the Blacks moved into the surrounding areas in the large cities, many white families left the city for suburban life. They did not remain and help to rebuild the cities, and thus, they fostered the continuing decline of the cities. The Polish-Americans have not panicked. Although many Polish-Americans have shown a propensity not to make their houses available.

> The city's Polish population has shown the strongest inclination to hold onto its homes, its neighborhoods and its tradition of residential permanence.
> Chadsey High School, at 5335 Martin, on Detroit's southwest side, exemplifies this trend.
> The school has been roughly half Negro and half white for more than a decade, and most of the whites have been of Polish descent.
> There has been no radical white flight from the racially mixed Chadsey district even though surveys of racial attitudes rank the Polish highest of all immigrant groups in their prejudice against Negroes.[76]

The unwillingness to move out of established neighborhoods, away from traditional churches, schools, recreational areas and friends, created the impression of intransigence, unwillingness to make living room for the expanding black community, and of anti-black prejudice. Polish-American communities have remained remarkably stable. Driving through Detroit, one passes almost

---

[75] "White backlash found stronger among Protestants," *The Detroit News* (August 20, 1970), p. 18-A.
[76] "The Changes the City has Felt, the Problems That Change Has Brought," *Detroit Free Press* (March 9, 1969), p. 4-B.

imperceptibly from Polish to black neighborhoods with integrated buffer zones in between.

In the large metropolitan areas, both Polish-Americans and Blacks have common interests in the areas of crime-control, taxes, physical environment, city services and housing, health care, and the rights and needs of senior citizens. Both suffer from the at-large method of electing municipal citizens. Both suffer from the at-large method of electing municipal governing councils. The urban renewal and highway construction have had a devastating effects on both Black and Polish-American neighborhoods. And both ethnic groups could benefit from the inclusion of ethnic studies programs in the public schools, and in colleges and universities.

The main concern of Father Fabian Slominski and Father Daniel Bogus was to revitalize the wavering commitment of Detroit liberals, in general, and Polish-American liberals, in particular, to the cause of racial justice. In years past, Polish-American philantrophy, involvement in the civil rights movement, and general concern for the black's welfare, were welcomed enthusiastically. During the sixties the increasing mood of independence on the part of Blacks combined with Polish-American fears of black anti-Polishness tended to weaken Polish-American participation in the rights movement. The idea to focus on the well-meaning liberal Polish-American community, and to prod them to take a renewed interest in the struggle for human liberty, originated early in 1968 at a time when Detroit's newspapers were closed by a strike, and shortly after the city's riot of July 1967. The Black-Polish Conference grew out of a friendly overture made to the Black community, in 1968, by Rev. Bogus and Rev. Slominski, who were working in racially mixed parishes, and felt that the Polish-American community had an undeserved reputation for racism. Father Slominski was also concerned about his church, attended mostly by whites of Polish origin, while the school was attended mostly by Blacks.

Father Slominski arranged for a meeting at SS. Cyril & Methodius Seminary, on April 10, 1968, to ease tensions between the Polish-Americans and the Blacks. The meeting was sponsored by the Detroit Archdiocesan Priests Conference for Polish Affairs.⁷⁷ The Polish-American priests—led by Father Slominski and Father Bogus—expressed their support for open housing and for equal opportunity in employment, education, and the use of public facilities.

This extraordinary resolution caught the attention of Congressman John Conyers, Jr., who inserted it into the Congressional Record. He also invited the co-chairmen of the Conference, Father Bogus and Father Slominski, to Washington, D. C., for further discussion. Continued dialogue between the three led to the idea of an alliance of Blacks and Poles of greater Detroit to promote mutual trust and work towards common goals. The Priests' Conference endorsed this concept. Initial meetings between civic minded representatives of the two communities began, in December 1968, and the drive to move from crisis solving to the more positive role of seeking areas of agreement and common interests, led to the formation of the Black Polish Conference in Detroit.

Among the leaders who actively support the Black-Polish Conference are Polish-American priests and black ministers: the president of the Polish-American Chamber of Commerce; the head of the local black businessmen's association; university professors and administrators; political figures such as Congressmen John Conyers and Lucien Nedzi; Councilman Ernest Browne, Nicholas Hood and Robert Tindal; and Albert Zak, chairman of the County Board of Commissioners; journalists such as Stanley Krajewski of the *Polish Daily News,* Mitchell Lewandowski of the *Hamtramck Citizen* and Longworth Quinn, publisher of the the *Micigan Chronicle;* educators such as Dr. Joseph A. Wytrwal, principal of Wilson Middle School, in Detroit, and Edward Jagosz, teacher at Osborn High School; leaders of the traditionally conservative Polish American Congress; and Frank Ditto, the head of a militant black organization called the East Side Voice for Independent Detroit.

The conference has as its goals: (1) promoting increased knowledge of each other's history and culture, through meetings and educational programs; (2) developing and expanding avenues

---

⁷⁷ The Conference is an organization of Polish-American priests in the Archdiocese of Detroit. It has more than 100 Polish-American priests among its members.

of communications between the two communities; and (3) sponsoring programs of mutual benefit.

The Polish-Americans and Blacks bring different perspectives to many situations. The Polish-Americans—fearful of radicalism—are concerned about law and order. The Blacks are concerned about civil liberties and the advancement of their people. One of the biggest challenges to confront the Black-Polish Conference occurred in the spring of 1969.

> The Republic of New Africa, a black nationalist group that wants to set up a separate black nation in the southeastern part of the U.S. held a convention in Detroit, and two Polish policemen patrolling nearby were shot—one fatally. Police responded by arresting nearly everyone at the Republic of New Africa convention. There were charges by blacks of police brutality, and bitterness began to grow. Things became even more tense, however, when a black Recorder's Court judge, George W. Crockett, set up court in the jailhouse and, along with the local prosecutor, released all the black prisoners against whom there was no substantive evidence—which included nearly everyone arrested.[78]

The local newspapers accused Judge Crockett of wholesale, unjustified releases. The Polish-Americans were enraged by the death of the Polish policeman, and by what they saw as an obstruction of justice by a black judge. The Poles also believed that Judge Crocket had released people before they could be questioned, and that he had acted very irresponsibly. The Blacks were convinced that the incident was provoked, that the police overreacted and beat people, and that they nearly destroyed the church in which the Republic of North Africa was meeting.

The tension was resolved when Stanley Krajewski, the editor of the *Dziennik Polski,* an influential Polish-language newspaper in Detroit, concluded that Crockett was legally entitled to do what he had done, and he printed an editorial to that effect in his newspaper. Detroit's black newspaper, *The Michigan Chronicle,* printed a translation of the editorial, and a very dangerous situation had been effectively cooled.

---

[78] Gaillard, "Poles in Detroit Ally with Blacks," *Race Relations Reporter,* Volume II (April 5, 1971), p. 10.

One of the Black-Polish Conference's most successful projects was a dinner at the Polish Century Club attended by 300 blacks and Polish-Americans. It was held on October 9, 1969. The guests included middle-class businessmen, ministers, priests, politicians and other civic leaders, who ate fried chicken and Polish sausage, and mingled amiably with Austin and Gribbs, both of whom made a point of attending.

Another public event that was sponsored by the Black-Polish Conference was the "Workshop Program Number 1." The workshop was held at Wayne University's McGregor Memorial Conference Center. Polish-Black relations in metropolitan Detroit were the subject of a series of discussions between members of the Detroit's Black and Polish communities.[79] During the workshop many panelists and members of the audience spoke bluntly and did not wish to allow any momentary good feeling to obscure the real differences between the Blacks and the Polish-Americans. Many Polish-Americans disagreed with Blacks who talk generally of white racists as if all whites were racists in the same way and from similar motives. The workshop's objective was to thrash out ideas aimed at accentuating the positive and reducing the negative relations between Polish-Americans and Blacks. By reducing the negative relations between Polish-Americans and Blacks will result in the reduction of inevitable group conflict, racial isolation, and group polarization.

Many of the Conference leaders believe they are beginning to win friends among the two minorities who together comprise a majority of Detroit's 1.6 million residents.

> Father Daniel P. Bogus, a co-chairman of the conference, says a member of his bowling team told him not long ago about a black acquaintance who said: "I'm sure glad our people are finally working together, but I don't want you moving next door to me." Father Bogus laughs, "Can you imagine a black saying that to a Pole even a few years ago?" At one time, there would have been a fight over such a remark, Father Bogus says. Now, a black and a Pole can joke with each other.[80]

---

[79] Charles Nathanson, "Poles and blacks try to 'get it together,'" *Detroit East Side Shopper* (October 6, 1971), p. 1.

Father Bogus and Congressman Conyers have also engineered an editorial exchange between the black weekly the *Michigan Chronicle* and the *Dziennik Polski*. "If Detroit's two largest minority groups could co-operate, that could be one thing that would rescue Detroit from ever-increasing social chaos and might just turn this town around," the *Michigan Chronicle* stated in one of its editorials.[81] Another *Michigan Chronicle* was headlined "Blacks and Poles Are Now Working Together." This editorial was translated and reprinted in the *Dziennik Polski*. The *Michigan Chronicle* also reprinted two editorials of *Dziennik Polski*—one called for the election o fcouncilmen by districts, and the other took a restrained tone on controversial Black Recorder's Court Judge George Crockett.

In 1970, the Black Polish Conference has managed to raise approximately $50,000—more than $31,000 from New Detroit, $12,000 from the Archdiocese of Detroit, and $5,000 from the Polish Priests Conference. The Board of Directors consisted of the following: Rev. Daniel P. Bogus, Co-Chairman; Congressman John Conyers, Jr., Co-Chairman; Leon Atchison, Secretary; Dr. Joseph A. Wytrwal, Secretary; and Edward Jagosz, Treasurer.

Lansing, the capital of Michigan, also saw the efforts of the Black Polish coalition gain control of the Wayne County 26-member Board of Supervisors and push through legislation beneficial to the two minorities against the opposition of other groups in the city.[82]

The potential impact of the allegiance, in Detroit, between Polish-Americans and blacks has been a recurring theme at Chicago's first conference on ethnic groups. Father Bogus and Con-

---

[80] Clark Hoyt, "Blacks and Poles Look to the Future," *Detroit Free Press* (December 9, 1969), p. 6-B.

[81] Clark Hoyt, 'City's Blacks, Poles Form Uneasy, Powerful Alliance," *Detroit Free Press* (June 15, 1969), p. 1.

[82] The alliance between Blacks, Zak and other supervisors of Polish descent held together through the bitter fight over how much supervisors should be paid. Zak's forces at first pushed through a salary package that could have netted them more than $20,000. Later they backed down to a $10,000 wage. More recently, the blacks and Polish-Americans on the board united to help elect John Lesinski to the seat left vacant after Supervisor Frank Swapka resigned in the face of a recall threat. The supervisors, voting by secret ballot, passed over a labor-backed candidate to bring Lesinski into their fold. Clark Hoyt, "City's Blacks, Poles Form Uneasy, Powerful Alliance," *Detroit Free Press* (June 15, 1969), p. 2-A.

gressman Conyers were speakers at a session of the Chicago Consultation on Ethnicity at the University of Illinois, Chicago Circle Campus. Members of the conference also worked with Congressman Roman Pucinski and the Rev. Jesse Jackson of the Southern Christian Leadership Conference who were trying to establish a similar coalition of blacks and Polish-Americans in Chicago.

In May 1972, twenty Buffalo leaders, including Polish-Americans and black representatives, met in the Fronczak Library to lay the groundwork for what one leader called a political coalition for the "common good." Among the Polish-Americans convening were Stanley M. Makowski, the deputy mayor; Council President, Chester G. Gorski; State Senator, Frank J. Glinski, a vice-chairman of the Erie County Democratic Committee; Lovejoy Councilman Raymond Lewandowski; County Legislator Stanley H. Zagora (majority leader of the County Legislature); Councilman Richard F. Okoniewski; John C. Zielinski, Democratic leader of the Sixth Zone; and Stanley Franczyk, legislative assistant to the Common Council, and brother of Councilman-at-large Gus Franczyk. Among the black leaders were: Assemblyman, Arthur O. Eve; Council Majority Leader, Delmar L. Mitchell; Clifford Bell, vice-chairman of the Executive Committee of the Erie County Democratic Committee; Ellicott Councilman, George K. Arthur; William L. White, Democratic leader of the Fourth Zone; Leroy Jackson, Democratic leader of the 11th Zone; and County Legislator Alton Bowens. A member of the group explained the meeting in this fashion, "We just felt that the leaders of the two largest ethnic groups in the city, the Poles and the Blacks, should find ways and means of working together for the common good of Buffalo. Our objective is to find some common ground."[83]

The Black-Polish Conference goal is lopsided; it is not concerned with the welfare of the Polish-Americans, but for the advancement of Blacks and through lukewarm promises to stifle Polish-American criticism in Detroit or deplete existing tensions. Time and time again, in various projects, like low cost housing around St. Albertus' Church or Sweetest Heart of Mary Church,

---

[83] "Polish, Black Leaders Meet for Common Good," *Am-Pol Eagle* (June 1, 1972), p. 1.

the Polish-American population has been repeatedly betrayed and taken advantage of. So far the Blacks, in Detroit, have failed to deliver to the Polish-Americans on any issue. Mayor Young and the black ministers have failed to emulate the examples set by the former Mayor Roman S. Gribbs and the Polish-American clergy.

However, this was not true of all Blacks. Johnny Mathis was singing in 1956 with a group of young musicians in a jam session at San Francisco's Black Hawk nightclub, owned by Helen and John Noga, when Helen Noga—an aggressive talent manager—decided she wanted to manage his career. Deals were signed, and in practically no time at all, Johnny Mathis was earning $100,000 a year, then a million. Johnny Mathis was in demand on the Ed Sullivan and other TV shows, in nightclubs and at Columbia records. Over the next several years he became the most popular singer of the rich supperclub set, singing in a rich, romantic tenor that could caress a love lyric until the emotions trembled. As a result of Helen Noga's stewardship, after ten years, Johnny Mathis became one of the wealthiest singers in the world. His worth exceeded $1.6 million. In an *Ebony* article, Mathis acknowledged his appreciation: "She is the reason there is a Johnny Mathis today. I would never have had the fortitude to do the things she had to do for me."[84]

Today, many Blacks acknowledge their Polish heritage. Andrew Young is photogenic, personable, quotable and outspoken. He is the U.S. Ambassador to the United Nations. The son of a prosperous dentist, he was brought up in New Orleans. He has Indian as well as Black forebears. Among the ambassador's other ancestors was a mulatto woman slave who became the mistress of a New Orleans shipping magnate, a Pole named Czarnowski.[85] Many of their descendants were extremely light skinned and during the Depression some of Young's cousins crossed the racial line into the white world. Recently, in her search for roots, Ewa Czarnecka, editor of *Nowy Dziennik* in New York, discovered that Andrew Young is her cousin.[86]

---

[84] Johnny Mathis: His Own Man Now," *Ebony* (March, 1976), p. 48.
[85] Raymond Carroll and Eleanor Clift, "Outspoken Andy Young," *Newsweek* (March 28, 1977), p. 29.
[86] "Odnalazla sie polska kuzynka Amb. Younga!" *Dziennik Polski* (April 7, 1977), p. 3.

CHAPTER 18

Polish-Jewish Relations in America

> I was a Polish child, brought up in a Polish school. For us the Germans, like the Russians, were oppressors who robbed us of our independence for a century and a half, and against whom we had struggled in numerous insurrections. In school we sang the song of Maria Konopnicka, a great and celebrated poetess, with the following refrain: "The German will not spit in our faces, nor will he make Germans of our children."
> —Isaac Deutscher[1]

> I am a Pole and a Jew, and I wish to work for both, if God permits.
> —Maurycy Gottlieb

> *My fatherland is the Polish language,*
> *Words woven with verse.*
> *When I die, it does not matter where,*
> *When I die, they will bury me with it*
> *And in it will I remain.*
> —Marian Hemar

> If you save one life, it is as though you saved the entire world.
> —The Talmud

One of the ironies of history is that the Poles, who sacrificed more than any other people to assist their Jewish neighbors during World War II, have one of the worst reputations in this regard. Since World War II writers of the various Jewish histories have created a deliberate false stereotype of the Poles as raving anti-Semites. Also, a number of American scholars of Jewish

---

[1] Isaac Deutscher, *The Non-Jewish Jew and Other Essays* (London: 1968), p. 20.

descent have been the foremost exponents of ethnic discrimination against Poland and Americans of Polish descent. To spread this ethnic discrimination they have utilized the radio, TV, films, and the printed word to convey to the world that the Poles were just as guilty, if not more guilty, in the extermination of the Jews in Europe during World War II. Evidence of this belief are especially evident in various Jewish histories which appeared since World War II.

Solomon Grayzel was very explicit in his publication.

> People who, at great personal risk, came to the aid of the hunted, kept alive faith in the essential goodness of human nature. But there were others, far more numerous, in the invaded countries to the east who helped the Nazis in their destruction of the Jewish population. Poles, Romanians, Hungarians, and Ukrainians by the thousands, fawning upon their conquerors, outdid them in brutality.[2]

Max Wurmbrand and Cecil Roth also confirm this view.

> On September 1st, 1939, the Nazis irrupted into Poland, thus sparking off World War II, the most murderous struggle mankind has ever seen. Within less than a month Poland ceased to exist. All of western Poland was overrun by the Nazi military machine. Soviet Russia marched in and occupied the eastern part of the country. Out of Poland's three and a half million Jews, more than two million were now in the zone under German occupation, and for them disaster ensured immediately. Wherever the German army arrived, there were wide-spread outbreaks of violence, and brutal killings, in which the local Polish population often zealously co-operated with the German invader.[3]

Ed Grossman in a letter to *Time* Magazine made the following observation:

> Sir: As an ex-prisoner of Auschwitz-Birkenau I find it sad that John Cardinal Krol did not seize the opportunity of true ecumenism while at the beatification ceremony of his noble colleague, Friar Maximilian Kolbe (October 30). The fact remains that the overwhelming majority of those who lost their lives in Auschwitz were Jews, and among them many, many Polish Jews. Since many of the zealous Polish

---

[2] Solomon Grayzel, *A History of the Contemporary Jews* (New York: 1960), pp. 121-122.

[3] Max Wurmbrand and Cecil Roth, *The Jewish People 4000 Years of Survival* (Jerusalem: 1966), p. 411.

Catholics with the "emblazoned banners of their parishes" were equally zealous in helping the Nazis exterminate practically the entire Jewish population of Poland (more than 3 million dead), Cardinal Krol could have done a great service to humanity by reminding this zealous gathering and the world at large that hate and bigotry, racial or political, know no boundaries.[4]

Sidney du Broff in an article entitled "Poland Is Fascist Again But Not Most Poles" which was published in the *National Jewish Monthly* (July-August, 1969) made the following comment:

> In the Warsaw Ghetto Uprising the Jews received no help worth mentioning from the Poles. . . . Poles came to the Ghetto district and watched the destruction, not only with indifference, but with words of encouragement to the Germans. . . . Anti-Semitism was part of the fabric of Polish life and approved and sactioned and encouraged by the Church and States.[5]

Max I. Dimont also attacks the Poles:

> Poland's action was the most shameful. Without a protest she handed over 2,800,000 of her 3,300,000 Jews to the Germans. Poor Poland was to discover that Germans had even more contempt for her than for the Jews. The Germans slaughtered like cattle over 1,500,000 Poles.[6]

Thirsting for revenge, Dimont was pleased with the Germans who had solved Russia's "Polish problem" for her. In discussing the uprising in the Warsaw ghetto, in January 1943, Dimont made the following comment:

> The shelling of the ghetto was resumed. It became a hell of exploding shells, crumbling buildings, and moving walls of flame. In desperation the Jews appealed to the Polish underground for help, but in vain. The Poles hoped the Germans would solve their "Jewish problem" for them. Little did they realize the surprise that history had in store for them. When in July 1944, the Polish underground staged its own uprising against the Germans, the Poles begged the Russians to come to their aid. But just as the Poles had refused to come to the aid of the Jews, so the Russians refused to come to the

---

[4] "A Reminder," *Time* (November 27, 1972), p. 13.
[5] Eugene Kusielewicz, "B'Nai B'rith Slanders Poles," *Gwiazda Polarna* (December 6, 1969), p. 5.
[6] Max I. Dimont, *Jews, God and History* (New York: 1962), p. 387.

aid of the Poles. The well-armed Polish underground army of 150,000 men was annihilated. The Germans had solved Russia's "Polish problem" for her.[7]

Dimont completely ignores the fact that with the exception of the Polish Government in Exile, in London, the world took little note of the Jewish uprising in Warsaw, which includes the influential American Jewry.

A. N. Rosenthal in a *New York Times* Magazine entitled "Forgive Them Not—For They Know What They Did," blames the Poles as much as the Germans for the sufferings of the Jewish people during World War II.[8] For his title Rosenthal has taken the words of the gospel—words full of love and mercy—and has changed them into a litany of hatred against the Polish people. One leading Jewish publication went so far as to state that the reason Hitler established the death camps in Poland was to win the favor of the Poles.[9]

Teller made explicit his hatred of the Poles, in Poland, and in America.

> The Poles and Ukrainians formed a disreputable little enclave within the Austro-Hungarian district. Shuttling between mass and raucous saloons, they smelled of incense, vodka, and vomit. They brought these smells and habits with them across more than three thousand miles of ocean. In their native villages they had been sharecroppers and tenant farmers, who traded and bartered with the Jews, yet on a signal, when well soused, would pour into the *shtetl* to pillage, rape, and massacre the very Jew with whom they traded. In America, they became janitors and handymen on the Lower East Side, sweepers and porters in the garment center, too humbled and dependent on the Jew to erupt even when drunk.[10]

Harry Golden also singled out the Polish-Americans, in a foreword of a book.

---

[7] *Ibid.*, p. 385.
[8] Bruno S. Figura, "Charges Jewish Writers Wage Hate Campaign," *Polish American* (January 9, 1966), p. 5.
[9] "Polish Assisted Jews in World War II," *Garden Spot News* (October 14, 1970), p. 3.
[10] Judd L. Teller, *Strangers and Natives. The Evolution of the American Jew from 1921 to the Present* (New York: 1968), p. 6.

Scattered throughout the Lower East Side were small enclaves of Poles, whom we had always heard were the original anti-semites of Europe. Funny how the Poles, who had the entire American continent to drift about, settled cheek to jowl with Jewish immigrants.[11]

Most shocking of the recent publications are the so-called semi-autobiographical novels: *The Painted Bird* by the Jewish writer Jerzy Kosinski, *Mila 18* by Leon Uris, and *Forged in the Fury* by Elie Wiesel. Kosinski's *The Painted Bird* recounts the horrifying adventures of an abandoned boy (Jew or Gypsy) during the German occupation. The boy is chased from hut to hut, from village to village. The stupidity and cruelty of the local populace has no limit. They tried to drown the child in a pool of liquid waste, threw him beneath the ice on a lake and hanged him from the ceiling of a hut while encouraging a large dog to maul his body. Miraculously the boy survived all of these tortures. The lurid incidents in the novel sicken the reader with their horror and obscenity. The total picture the novel presents is that of a cruel, savagely ignorant and bestial race whose deeply felt Catholicism is more a matter of animal instinct than reasoned conviction.[12]

The novel, *The Painted Bird* was not accepted as fiction. *New York Herald Tribune* review stated: ". . . without a single important battle, the book tells us everything we need and more than we want to know about World War II."[13] Elie Wiesel, in his *New York Times* review of the same book says: ". . . a moving but frightening tale in which man is indicted and proven guilty."[14]

Leon Uris's *Mila 18* portrays the bulk of the Polish people in similar fashion: as uncivilized peasants who worship a black Madonna as foolishly as an African native practicing a form of fetishism. In *Mila 18* Uris uses such obnoxious phrases as "drunk

---

[11] *A Bintel Brief.* Sixty years of letters from the lower east side to the Jewish Daily *Forward.* Compiled, edited and with an introduction by Isaac Mezker. (New York: 1971), pp. 21-22.

[12] The Chicago *Sun Times* in connection with a review of Kosinski's book called the Polish people "the butcher's helpers." Bruno S. Figura, "Charges Jewish Writers Wage Hate Campaign," *Polish American* (January 29, 1966), p. 5.

[13] Joseph Modrzejewski, "Genocide of the National Character," *Gwiazda Polarna* (October 19, 1974), p. 5.

[14] *Ibid.*, p. 5.

as a Pole" and "violently Polish." His Polish characters are for the most part either ugly, villainous, or brutal, while in his references to Polish culture, he called Chopin a "wart" and makes a scurrilous reference to a "... pianist" playing Chopin in Chicago which could be taken as an oblique slur of Paderewski.

Michael Elkins' *Forged in the Fury* states that after the German-Polish campaign, Polish soldiers dropped their guns, grabbed sticks and used them for beating Jews.

The anniversary of the Warsaw Ghetto Uprising is always an occasion for a shockingly dishonest manipulation of the truth. On March 21, 1968, Congressman Jonathan Bingham of New York began a speech with the following words:

> Mr. Speaker, in the annals of the Jewish people, the persecution of the Jews in Poland has been one of the most dreadful chapters. The genocide perpetrated by Adolf Hitler was only the culmination of centuries of pogroms and persecution.[15]

On April 17, 1969, Congressman Farbstein of New York delivered a speech on the floor of the House of Representatives in commemoration of the 26th anniversary of the uprising. In his address Farbstein stated:

> During the uprising, the men and women of the ghetto asked for aid from their Polish neighbors and the underground. This was not given to them, Mr. Speaker. I must say that this was not out of the ordinary, for the Jews in Poland have and still are being persecuted to a degree which surpasses all standards of moral and simple human decency. Polish soil throughout the centuries has been literally soaked through with Jewish blood.[16]

Several other Congressmen besides Bingham and Farbstein have made statements which do credit neither to themselves nor to the legislative body which they represent. The anniversary of this tragic event is an excuse for slandering the Poles who according to Bingham, Farbstein and others, did nothing to assist the Jews. In fact, they actually affirm, that the Poles were actually delighted to see their countrymen exterminated.[17]

---

[15] "Polish Defamation and Congress," *Polish American* (April 13, 1968), p. 4.
[16] "Again, and Again, and ..." *Polish American* (April 26, 1969), p. 4.
[17] The *Polish American* in an editorial stated: "We suggest that April 19, the

A spate of anti-Polish movies and television plays have also contributed to the destruction of the Polish image in America. On November 6, 1967, Columbia Broadcasting System aired its weekly "The Carol Burnett Show." A comedy skit was performed presenting a situation on a "Slavic" airline. Background music for the skit was the Polish National Anthem. The captain of the plane named Kowalski was presented as something of an idiot. The stewardess was a dirty disordered witch, which in the minds of many Polish-Americans was a caricature taken out of the *It's Fun to Be a Polak* "jokebook."[18]

Perhaps the most flagrant example of ethnic defamation in history was the vile "QB VII" film based on a novel by Leon Uris. It was displayed by the American Broadcasting Company on April 22, 1975. It is saturated with hatred and disparagement of the Polish people. The TV version of Uris's novel portrays the villain, the surgeon Adam Kelno, as a liar and monster, a degenerate butcher who mutilates and murders those who fall prey to him. He is also clearly and emphatically identified as a Pole, a Christian and an anti-Communist.[19]

In the "Return From the Ashes" the leading male character is a Polish aristocrat named Stanislaw Pilgrin. He is portrayed as an atheist and degenerate killer. In one of the most revolting scenes ever projected onto a motion picture screen, Pilgrin is shown licking a woman's feet with pathological delight.

---

date of the beginning of the ghetto uprising, be proclaimed as "We Hate the Poles Day." This will give all those "twisters" of the truth an opportunity to expound their views on how anti-semitic Polish people are. By the same token, we also suggest that sometime in the remaining 364 days these same individuals acquaint themselves with the true historical facts of Polish-Jewish relations in Poland. We suggest that they enlighten themselves by reading the day-by-day account of the *Warsaw Ghetto Uprising*, written by Wladyslaw Bartoszewski. Or they could obtain a copy of an address by Dr. Joseph L. Lichten, director of the Department of Intercultural Affairs, Anti-Defamation League, entitled, "The Uprising of the Warsaw Ghetto: The Legend of Yesterday and the Reality of Today." Two books were recently translated into English which place the tragedy of 1943 in its proper historical context. The books are *Kto Ratuje Jedno Zycie* by Kazimierz Iranek-Osmecki and *Ten Jest z Ojczyzny Mojej* by Wladyslaw Bartoszewski and Zofia Lewinowa. "Again and Again, and . . ." *Polish American* (April 26, 1969), p. 4.

[18] "Pole-Americans Protest CBS 'Carol Burnett Show,'" *Polish American* (December 2, 1967), p. 1.

[19] "Americans of Polish Heritage Committee Blast QB VII," *Garden Spot News* (June 17, 1976), p. 3.

On the nationally broadcast David Susskind show, a leader of one Jewish group told millions of Americans that he still had not been able to find a single Pole who did anything to help the Jews in World War II.[20]

Steve Allen, host of the Dick Cavett Show on August 10, 1972, exhibited a most reprehensible anti-Polish routine.

Bob Einstein played the part of a representative of a Polish-American anti-defamation organization suing TV networks for airing "Polish Jokes." The whole plot was insidious and demeaning to ethnics, and particularly to Poles all over the world.

The concentrated venom of anti-Polish propaganda—packaged as art, entertainment, or scholarship—has elicited more than sporadic comment on numerous occasions. But no one has spoken more courageously on this subject than Father Henry Malak, O.F.M., who asserts that the Poles are the objects of a deliberate conspiracy to defame and denigrate their history, culture and traditions. Writing in the January (1966) issue of *Miesiecznik Franciszkanski,* Father Malak stated:

> In the last few months there have been repeated examples of similar, and sometimes even more defamatory, anti-Polish utterances by Jewish writers. At present it does not seem that we are dealing with isolated instances of individuals who have erred. It is apparent that the Jews in the United States have launched a conscious attack of mudslinging against everything Polish."[21]

Sigmund Gorson, from Wilmington, Delaware, made this observation.

> American Jews watched silently as six million Jews, among them my entire beloved family, were being killed by the Germans. If the American Jew who demonstrates now in sympathy with the Soviet Jews had only shown the same concern 30 years ago, six million of my innocent murdered people would be alive today. When reports of the brutal German death camps came before the American Jews they were busy with making money. Why bother with some East European Jews! And so the tragic reports from abroad were simply dismissed.

---

[20] "Polish Assisted Jews in World War II," *Garden Spot News* (October 14, 1970), p. 3.
[21] Quoted by Bruno S. Figura, "Charges Jewish Writers Wage Hate Campaign," *Polish American* (January 29, 1966), p. 5.

What a dramatic gesture to stir the conscience of the American Jews the suicide of the Polish-Jewish leader, Shmuel Zygielboim, a member of the Polish Council of National Unity (Polish Parliament in Exile) who had arrived in London illegally from the Warsaw ghetto, and did this as a protest against the indifference of the American Jews to the European Jewish tragedy. How dramatic is the text of the last message from the Jewish insurgents of the Warsaw ghetto, directed to the so-called American Jewish leaders: "Brothers. Answer. The remnants of the Jews in Poland live in the conviction that in the most horrible moments of our history, you gave us no help. Answer. This is our last appeal to you." No answer ever came.

I raise now the subject only to show that some of those who are today accusing the Polish nation and the Polish people of anti-Semitism during the holocaust, and those who know the truth but have kept silent and do not raise their voices to defend the honor of the heroic Poles, the only ones who did lend a helping hand to the condemned, bear direct or indirect responsibility for the scope of the Jewish tragedy. Both the accusations and the silence are even more shocking when, at the same time, they seem to forget about the real perpetrators of genocide, the German Herrenvolk.[22]

Despite the indictment of Jewish writers, who spread hate against Poland and the Poles, Father Malak asked for tolerance and understanding. His attitude is shared by all of the responsible leaders of the Polish-American community, who feel that there must be some peaceable avenue to rapprochement with the Jews. Most of these leaders are of the opinion that if the charges made in Father Malak's article are brought to the attention of the more mature members of the Jewish-American community— men and women of wisdom and strength of character—it is more than likely that they themselves will recognize the destructiveness of the course taken by some of their less well-intentioned co-religionists, and will adopt measures to curb these vindictive and rebellious spirits.

Responsible elements in the Polish-American and Jewish-American communities have tried to counter this stereotype. Now, as a result of this cooperation, the first authoritative reply to this stereotype has appeared in the English language. The book, *The Samaritans: Heroes of the Holocaust*, is an abridged version of the work edited by Wladyslaw Bartoszewski and Zofia Lewin, published originally in Polish under the title, *Ten Jest Z Ojczyzny*

---

[22] "Jews' Plea Was Ignored," *Gwiazda Polarna*, (June 29, 1974), p. 5.

Mojej. This work, whose editors are both Jewish, is a collection of statements by some of the 100,000 Jews whose lives were saved by Poles, who risked their lives and the lives of their wives and children, to assist their Jewish neighbors. "The stake they set for my life was high . . . their own lives," says one of the survivors of her saviours."[23]

Recently, there have been some meetings between representatives of B'nai B'rith and leaders of the Polish-American community.[24] In the course of these meetings, the leaders of B'nai B'rith dismissed defamation of Poles on the David Susskind show, and in a number of Jewish publications as the work of mavericks over whom they have no control. Some of the participants in those meetings are now interested in learning if the mavericks have gotten control of B'nai B'rith official publication *The National Jewish Monthly*.[25]

Alvin L. Kushner, Executive Director of the Jewish Community Council of Metropolitan Detroit, supported the ban on ethnic jokes.

> Recently your paper reported on the efforts of the Polish American Folk Theatre in its attempts to stop publication and distribution of "The Official Polish Joke Book."
>
> We share the concern of the Polish and Italian groups who found this book offensive. It is unfortunate there are still those who fail to distinguish between humor and insensitive and insulting representations.
>
> We concur with and support those who rightfully call for an end to this tasteless use of material and the quite unnecessary defamation of respected ethnic groups in our community.[26]

---

[23] The publication of this work has been the result of a cooperative effort of the Kosciuszko Foundation and the Polish Institute of Arts and Sciences. Despite the acknowledged importance of making this work available in America, it took almost two years to raise the necessary funds.

[24] "Poles, Jews hold meeting in Chicago," *Dziennik Polski*, (December 1, 1969), p. 2. "Stosunki Polsko-Zydowskie Tematem Konferencji," *Amerika Echo*, (December 6, 1970), p. 2. "Konferencja polsko-zydowska w Chicago," *Dziennik Polski*, (December 7, 1970), p. 6. "Rozmowy Polsko-Zydowskie w U.S.A.," *Pittsburczanin*, (December 5, 1969), p. 1.

[25] See article by Sidney du Broff entitled "Poland is Fascist Again But Not Most Poles," in the July-August 1969 issue of *The National Jewish Monthly*.

[26] "Ban on ethnic jokes supported," *The Sunday News*, (December 2, 1973), p. 3-E.

Rabbi J. Lelyveld, president of the American Jewish Congress, said a major sin of the television show "All in the Family" is that "children have come home from junior high school with "Polack jokes" that have been told them by their teachers.[27] Rabbi Lelyveld also made the following observations:

> If you think for a moment about applying the same technique of ridicule, of merciless satire, to other social evils of our time, you would think twice about applying lampooning and laughter to bigotry. Slums are not entertaining. War is not entertaining. There is no such thing as a harmless bigot any more than there is such a thing as a friendly cancer or a benign drug pusher or a lovable murderer or rapist.[28]

The Rabbi's comments appeared in the American Jewish Congress publication, *Congress Bi-Weekly*.

During his official visit to the United States, Isak Rabin, the Prime Minister of Israel met with several prominent political and public figures. The meeting was organized by the Consulate General of Israel and took place on February 1, 1976 at the Waldorf Astoria. After the prime minister's speech, the participants asked the minister a series of questions. Dr. Kusielewicz, President of the Kosciuszko Foundation, was the last one to speak, and after a brief introduction posed the following question:

> The overwhelming majority of the Polish-American community supports the cause of Israel. Polish-American Congressmen and Senator Muskie continually vote for appropriations to Israel. Unfortunately the Jewish American media continuously distorts Polish-Jewish relations to such a degree that in the hearts of most Jews, the words "Polish" and "Polish-American" are synonymous with anti-semite. Mr. Prime Minister what can you do to prevent alienation from the cause of Israel?[29]

Dr. Kusielewicz's question was met with a very strong applause from the gathered audience. Izak Rabin gave the following reply to the question: ". . . I don't represent the Jewish community in America. This is a problem for them rather than for me, but I

---

[27] "Archie Bunker blasted," *The Detroit News*, (April 23, 1972), p. 3-A.
[28] *Ibid.*, p. 3-A.
[29] Halina Kaminska, "Rev. L. Tolczyk and Dr. E. Kusielewicz Attend A Special Meeting With Israel's Prime Minister Izak Rabin," *Greenpoint Gazette*, (February 17, 1976), p. 9.

am sure that they will do everything possible to prevent Israel from losing its friends."[30] The question made a deep impression on the distinguished guests.

On a person-to-person basis, the Polish-Americans do not discriminate against the Jewish people. Marriage between Poles and Jews—although they are still rare—are occurring with ever greater frequency; and the Polish-Americans and Jews who live in such contiguous neighborhoods as Skokie, Morton Grove, and Niles, in the Chicago area, get along amicably with one another. Jewish commercial establishments have always thrived in Polish communities, and Polish-Americans have enjoyed doing business with their Jewish brethren since the days when the peddler who came to the kitchen door selling his wares was a familiar sight. Many Jewish doctors, lawyers and accountants, who serve as confidants and advisers, owe their success to the support they receive in the Polish-American communities.

Perhaps there were Poles who betrayed and blackmailed Jews. And also Poles who watched the murder of its Jews, if not with complacency, then at least in silence. But on the other hand, there were Poles who went into the ghettos, not only in Warsaw, but also in Krakow, Lodz, Lublin and Bialystok, and fought side by side with their fellow countrymen. There were Poles who took Jewish children into their homes, which was a crime when discovered—punishable by death. Others were secreted in convents and monasteries, sanctuaries of Catholicism where no Jew would enter except to save his life.

General Bor-Komorowski, the commander of the Home Army, in his book, the *Underground Army*, cites a horrifying case of repression by Nazis against those helping Jews. A Polish lady took a Jewish child into her family. In time, the Germans found out about her "criminal offense." The Gestapo agents entered her home, and shot two of the lady's own children, sparing the life of the Jewish child. Upon leaving the house, one of the Gestapo agents said to the Polish mother: "And now you can take care of the Jewish bastard."

Members of the Polish Home Army executed Poles who

---

[30] *Ibid.*, p. 9.

betrayed and blackmailed Jews. There were some who did even more.

> There were Christian nurses and maidservants who actually accompanied their Jewish households into the ghettoes and subsequently perished in the death camps. There was a family called Marczak who hid thirty-four fugitives in a dugout under their vegetable garden in Grojecka Street in Warsaw. More than fifty Jews passed through the Warsaw house of Janina Szandorowska. Seventeen Jews were given asylum in the house of a certain Jozef Kaleta-Pirowska. Lucja and Stefan Slominski hid ten Jews for more than two years.[31]

In other words, there were not only hundreds, but indeed tens of thousands of very brave people.

> Ludomir Marczak, mentioned above, was shot in Pawiak prison in March 1944. In fact, between September 1942 and May 1944, some two hundred peasants were executed by the Germans for harboring Jews. In at least two instances, the inhabitants of an entire village were burned alive by the Germans for this crime. For in some places, in a hamlet called Osiny, for example, the peasants deliberately assumed a collective responsibility and arranged that each should hide a Jewish girl for a certain period so that everyone would be guilty and no one could inform.[32]

These heroic people were faced with almost insuperable difficulties.

> There is a man called Bartoszewski, living in Warsaw, who saved several dozen lives, and is one of those who has had a tree dedicated to him in Jerusalem. Even today he often feels desperate (he is a devout Catholic) at not having been able to do more. "But one in four wore a caftan," he says. "It takes at least two men successfully to hide one, and half of them hardly spoke Polish. How do you hide a child who might unwittingly blurt out some phrase in Yiddish in front of a German?[33]

German anti-Semitic propaganda fell on stony ground, for the Poles were only too clearly aware that they and the Jews were in the same terrible predicament.

On December 16, 1942, during his visit to the United States,

---
[31] William Woods, *Poland: Eagle in the East*, (New York: 1968), pp. 27-8.
[32] *Ibid.*, p. 28.
[33] *Ibid.*, p. 29.

General Wladyslaw Sikorski was the guest of the Overseas Press Club of America. Speaking before an audience of more than 300 editors, correspondents, radio commentators and well known authorities on international affairs, General Sikorski made the following remarks:

> To realize the extent of the monstrous massacre of Jews, you must imagine the whole of Manhattan closed in by ghetto walls behind which all the Jews of the Western Hemisphere have been imprisoned, to be gradually and methodically exterminated in groups of several thousands daily by machine-gun fire, lethal gas or electrocution.
>
> Let us consider the reaction of our population. I will read you the text of a protest secretly circulated in Poznan, Warsaw, Wilno and Lwow: "The total number of Jews killed has reached one million, and this number is increasing daily. All perish: the rich and the poor, the infirm and the old, the women, the men, the youths and little children. Their only crime is that they were born into the Jewish people, and are condemned to extermination by Hitler. Therefore we, Catholics and Poles, desire to speak. We do not want to be Pontius Pilates. We cannot actively counteract the German crimes, we cannot help anything, we cannot save anybody, but we protest from the bottom of our hearts, filled with compassion, indignation and horror."
>
> On the day of victory the walls of the ghetto in Poland will fall. They will be destroyed by the Polish people. Now, however, means must be found to save the Polish Jews, victims of this bestial barbarism.[34]

At the height of the annihilation of the Jews of Europe, American officials were conspiring to prevent their rescue. When the Nazis began to mount their attacks on German Jewry, they were initially bent only on expulsion, not on murder. Josiah du Bois of the War Refugee Board wrote to his superior, John Pehle, in 1944, "To Hitler the failure of the United States to afford shelter to those who might be able to escape persecution has served as an excuse to continue his mad plan to exterminate the Jews of Europe."[35]

> A report to President Roosevelt in 1943, when the Nazi exterminations had peaked, said of some State Department officials, "They not only have failed to facilitate the obtaining of information con-

---

[34] *General Sikorski's Speeches During His Visit To the United States in December 1942*, (New York: Polish Information Center, 1942), pp. 18-19.

[35] David Polish, "Does the U.S. share guilt in murder of Jews?" *Chicago Sunday Sun-Times Book Week*, (February 11, 1968), p. 1.

cerning Hitler's plans to exterminate the Jews of Europe but in their official capacity have gone so far as to surreptitiously attempt to stop the obtaining of information concerning the murder of the Jewish population of Europe. . . . There is a growing number of responsible people who . . . see plain anti-Semitism motivating the actions of these State Department officials."[36]

Many individuals acted inhumanly, callously and inscrupulously in order to obstruct the rescue of the Jews. Breckinridge Long blocked any special efforts on behalf of the Jews. Carlton Hayes, ambassador to Spain, fought to keep Jews out of Spanish sanctuary. Robert Borden Reams prevented the flow of information about the Jewish plight. And Cordell Hull dismissed the reports of extermination as "exaggerated."

President Franklin Delano Roosevelt also lacked comprehension of the position of Polish Jewry. In the correspondence with Winston Churchill, President Roosevelt's position is revealed:

> The President asked His Majesty (Ibn Saud) for his advice regarding the problem of Jewish refugees driven from their homes in Europe. His Majesty replied that in his opinion the Jews should return to live in the lands from which they were driven.
> The President remarked that Poland might be considered a case in point. The Germans appear to have killed 3,000,000 Polish Jews, by which count there should be space in Poland for the resettlement of many homeless Jews."[37a]

All in all, there was probably more done by the Poles to help the Jews than by any other nation, and more than ever will be known, for we are less likely to hear about the heroes who were unfortunately caught and murdered. Nevertheless, some did receive world-wide attention, and some affection.

Abe Rothstein came to America in 1946. He has prospered, married and now owns two Brooklyn shoe stores. But in America, he has never forgotten Wojciech Konopczynski, his wife Anna, and their son John, who opened their farmhouse to him, when he was fleeing a Nazi raid on the village of Sokolov in Poland. For three years the Konopczynski family risked arrest

---

[37a] Philip Slomowitz, "The Roosevelt Record of Misjudging Jewish Needs," *The Detroit Jewish News*, (June 30, 1972), p. 2.
[36] Ibid., p. 1.

and death for sheltering Rothstein, a Pole of Jewish descent. In 1961, after four years of struggle to gain permission, Rothstein brought the Polish family of three to Brooklyn, New York, where he prepared an apartment already stocked with food and furniture. Here, they lived until they decided on a farm which Rothstein had purchased for them. Rothstein insists what he did for this Polish family is not repayment of a debt. "Life is much bigger than something which can be measured in payments or repayments. They shared their lives with us. Now it is time for us to share our lives with them."[37]

Kazimierz Korkuc is a Roman Catholic. His deeds of bravery on behalf of Polish Jewry have made him a legend to the families of those who survived because of what he did. After more than three decades, a group of them raised the money to fly him to Los Angeles, from Poland, to honor him for his courage. For the sixty-six year old farmer, it was his first trip out of Poland, his first flight in an airplane, and the first recognition for what he did so long ago.

One fall morning, in 1941, Korkuc had left mass, when he saw the Jewish people of the town lining up outside the town synagogue with all their valuables. The Nazi soldiers, who occupied the area, were taking them into custody. A short distance away he saw Miriam Kabacznik and her family trying to hide valuables in the garden beside their house. Korkuc had done business for years with the Kabaczniks, who owned a tannery and sold leather. He took them to his farm and hid them from the Germans. The Jews, who had turned themselves in to the Nazis, were executed. And in the years that followed, so were the Poles who hid Jews from the Nazis.

During the war Korkuc sheltered ninety-eight Jews. Many were caught but eighteen survived. Miriam Kabacznik, who was unmarried and twenty-two when the war began, survived. She welcomed him in Los Angeles, California.

A son of another survivor of those days, made the following comment:

---

[67] *The Detroit News,* (October 11, 1961), p. 3-4.

There is a Jewish legend that mankind will survive because thirty-six righteous men are born in every generation. My father thinks that Mr. Korkuc is one of those men.[38]

Korkuc was also at a yeshiva, in Brooklyn, New York, where he spoke to students at the assembly through a Polish translator. Of the five men and women he rescued, who attended the ceremonies, Mrs. Yaffa Eliach (now 36) a professor of Eastern European history and Judaic studies at Brooklyn College, said she was among the sixteen Jews who hid in or near Korkuc's home between 1942 and 1944.[39] Mrs. Eliach, whose husband is principal of the school where the Polish farmer was honored, said Korkuc "has been a symbol of goodness and kindness to me. He has told me that all people are created in the image of God and he just couldn't see why war should turn people into animals and enemies."[40] Asked why he saved Polish Jews, Korkuc said: "All people are told you are supposed to love your neighbor and I don't see why in time of trouble we should turn away."[41]

The Talmud states: "If you save one life, it is as though you saved the entire world." Romualda Ciesielska has saved the world many times. During World War II, she defied the Nazis again and again, to rescue Jews and other "non-Aryans." How many she saved is unknown, but the estimate goes as high as 100. Several who survived the war testified in her behalf when the Ciesielski's name was proposed for the Yad Vashem medal. Ciesielska's heroism and that of her martyred husband, Felix, have earned the coveted recognition of "Zadikei Umot Olam," the Righteous Among the Gentiles.

When the Germans took over Bydgoszcz, the townspeople were ordered to leave. Romualda Ciesielska, her husband—who was a Polish army officer—and their son fled in a cattle wagon. For three months, they moved from town to town. In December 1939, they took refuge in Krakow; their shelter consisted of two

---

[38] "Jews Recall Pole's Heroics in face of Nazi oppression," *The Detroit News*, (December 11, 1972), p. 3-B.
[39] "Honor Polish Catholic Who Saved Jews," *The New World*, (January 19, 1973), p. 20.
[40] *Ibid.*, p. 20.
[41] *Ibid.*, p. 20.

offices in a large apartment building in Kazimierz (a Jewish district). At the sight of Romualda Ciesielska's little boy, his legs chapped and bleeding from the cold, a young woman offered him a pair of stockings. It was this small gesture which influenced Romualda Ciesielska to make a moral decision that was to link her fate with the Jews, whom she had never met, yet would risk her life to save.

Suddenly, the Jewish Kazimierz district was completely cut off by the Gestapo. In their two small offices, the Ciesielski's were joined by twenty-three Jews. As the Gestapo neared the building, all Jewish eyes were riveted to Romualda Ciesielska. All knew that should she try to conceal them and be discovered as a collaborator, the Gestapo would kill her and her family first.

> There was a Catholic prayerbook in the corner of the room. Mrs. Ciesielska grabbed it, but not to pray. She tore it up, and with a paste from flour, mounted the holy pictures on the wall outside. Her work proclaimed, "This is an Aryan home," she had taken the step, and there was no turning back.
> The Gestapo entered the building, rounding up its inhabitants as they went from room to room. They approached the Ciesielski's door, its sign defying entry. In the frightening silence, two women behind the door fainted, but the sound was quickly muffled. The Gestapo moved on.[42]

When the street was opened again, the Jewish families left.

As the turmoil mounted, and the ghetto was being formed, in 1940, Romualda Ciesielska began to place Jews with peasant families outside of town.[43] A few days after finding shelter for a woman and her eleven-year old daughter, Romualda Ciesielska decided to visit them with some food. She packed a valise and set off for the neighboring town, only to discover, when she arrived, that the Nazis were rounding up Jews in the town square, and providing them with spades to dig their own graves in the forest. Ciesielska pretended the heavy valise was light and strolled away so as not to draw any undue attention. At the peasant home, she alerted the women that the Gestapo was coming.

---

[42] Charlotte Dubin, "Compassion in a World Gone Mad. Exploits of 'Righteous Gentile' Told," *The Detroit Jewish News*, (December 25, 1970), p. 8.

[43] *Ibid.*, p. 8.

> With what she describes today as God given inspiration, Mrs. Ciesielska ordered the older Jewish woman—who looked too Semitic to escape notice—into bed and told her to pretend she was dying. A towel was placed over head, a cross in her hands and candles at each side.
> Then Mrs. Ciesielska grabbed the peasant's apron and tied it on the little girl, who was commanded to kneel at the bed and start weeping. The peasant woman was sent outside to feed the chickens.
> When the Gestapo arrived, Mrs. Ciesielska told them in German, that they must be quiet; here was a dying woman. The Gestapo left.[44]

But her task was still not completed.

> Mrs. Ciecielska ran through the fields to another village where two Jewish women were being hidden. There was even less time to act here; and should she be found at a second house, the Gestapo would surely suspect her involvement.
> The women were concealed in the barn hay loft, and the peasant ordered to scatter barley on the floor for the chickens. As the Germans entered the barn, the chickens flew up into their faces. The Nazis bid a hasty retreat.[45]

Ciesielska is not certain how many Jews she saved by placing them with Gentiles; but thirteen cases have been verified, and she thinks that half of them did survive the war. When Ciesielska was in Israel, she met one of them whom she had rescued.

Toward the end of 1941 and into 1942, Romualda Ciesielska began to fabricate false identification papers, identifying Jews as Aryans. For such an undertaking she enlisted the cooperation of two Krakow priests: one Catholic, and the other Greek Orthodox, who issued birth certificates to make the documents credible. The Jews, who obtained such papers, acquired new names and new identities. A friend, working as a clerk in the Gestapo office, applied the official seal to each false identification. Although some Jews were apprehended, Ciesielska estimates that up to seventy were saved in this manner. In all her activities she had the assistance of her husband and an underground movement of Christians, called *Ruch Oporu*.

Early one morning, the Gestapo arrived at her office-apart-

---
[44] *Ibid.*, p. 8.
[45] *Ibid.*, p. 8

ment, in Krakow. She managed to hide the photographs of two Jews whose false identification papers were being prepared; however, two others who had come to the Ciesielski's for aid were not so fortunate. They were taken away, and the Gestapo settled down to wait for more. No other Jews arrived that day, but the Ciesielski's were already implicated. They were arrested for interrogation. It was the last time Ciesielska saw her husband. After four months of questioning and torture, whose scars remain, Ciesielska still had not provided the Gestapo with the information they needed about the false identification papers. She was removed from Krakow prison to Auschwitz, where she would remain for the next three years.

In 1967, Romualda Ciesielska was invited to Israel to accept the medal of the Righteous Among the Gentiles, and to witness the planting of a tree in her and her husband's name, on the Yad Vashem avenue. As a guest of the government, she was escorted throughout Israel, including the soldiers' home that is a counterpart of the one she had organized in Poland. There, Moshe Dayan greeted her with bread and salt—a Polish and Jewish custom upon entering a new home. One day, she was taken to a new building, from which three children emerged with a bouquet and a greeting in faltering Polish: "Welcome to the threshold of our new Ciesielski School."[46]

Four months later, after she arrived in Israel, she was ordered, with regret, to leave immediately. Dismayed that she might have done something wrong, Ciesielska left. One week later she learned why she had been sent home: the Six-Day War had commenced.[47]

There were two factors that motivated Ciesielska's heroism: "First, I suddenly realized, today they, tomorrow we. Second, I saw so many horrible things being done to the Jews. How could I not help? I suppose it was Christian conscience."[48] Ciesielska insists there were many Christians who laid their lives on the line to save Jews. She said she knows no Polish family that didn't have some member who tried to help, but she admits that there

---

[46] Ibid., p. 9
[47] Ibid., p. 9.
[48] Ibid., p. 9.

were "evil people in all nations" and some who had saved Jews, did so only for money.⁴⁹

In December 1970, Mrs. Zosia Irena Zajkowska-Jankie (Jankiewicz) invited Romualda Ciesielski to the United States, and extended hospitality and assistance to her. During her visit in the United States, Shaarit Haplaytah, an organization of the Holocaust, bestowed its Humanitarian Award upon Romualda Ciesielski. At a gathering of 300 members and guests, Dr. Mames, in presenting the plaque stated:

> Mrs. Ciesielska is one of the unsung heroes—hasidei umot haolam—who manifested an unusual greatness of a noble human spirit. This warm and compassionate person with a profound social conscience remained faithful to the deepest principles of humanity despite all the bloody blaze and raging terror of unspeakable brutalities.⁵⁰

Mrs. Leon Popowski, program chairman, presenting a special token of appreciation to Mrs. Ciesielska, remarked:

> No words can be strong enough, no expression sufficiently adequate to convey our warm affection. The entire Jewish community will remain eternally grateful for all your tireless efforts to save others from Nazi annihilation. You, like the other great heroes of the past, will be inscribed in the annals of our history.⁵¹

Without the help of Helena and Ignacy Chorazyczewski, Abe Kashtan, his brother, and at least two other young Jews could not have survived the Nazi Holocaust. Their paths crossed in peaceful days—when the Kashtan family arrived each week to trade at the Chorazyczewski farm in Perespa, a small town near Berezhnitsev, with its sizeable Jewish community.

With the invasion of Poland, the Kashtans sought shelter at the Chorazyczewski farm. On the day that the Kashtans had been staying in the Chorazyczewski home, 15,000 Jews were rounded up in Berezhnitsev and shot. Abe and his brother and two other young men managed to escape, swimming the river to the Chorazyczewski farm.

---
⁴⁹ Ibid., p. 9.
⁵⁰ "Survivors Cite Polish Heroine," *The Jewish News*, (February 5, 1971), p. 6.
⁵¹ Ibid., p. 6.

"Abe was the first to reach me," Helena recalls. "He fainted, and when he woke up he said, 'From now on, you're my parents and my whole family.'" During the day, the boys hid in the surrounding forests; at night, they came to the Chorazyczewski farm for food.[52]

After Chester had taken the others to safety, in a forest bunker with seventy other young Jews, Abe remained with the Chorazyczewskis for more than a year.

> During the early days of his stay with them, Abe was hidden in the attic, his presence unknown to the younger children for fear that they might even unwittingly reveal his whereabouts. Eventually, however, Ignacy and Helen felt they could let the youngsters in on the secret. They never betrayed it. Abe later made a safe departure, joining the partisans in the forests.[53]

Others came to the Chorazyczewskis for food and help, and they were never refused. As the police returned, again and again, looking for contraband humanity, one little boy, who had been separated from his family, was shunted back and forth among the neighbors. He was with the Chorazyczewskis when the Germans took them, in 1943, when they were rounded up and taken to camps in Germany. After several months of near-starvation at Neamark, the Chorazyczewskis were picked for the dubious honor of working for a Russian turncoat who had just acquired a farm in Germany and needed cheap labor. After their stay with the Russian farmer, the Chorazyczewskis were "employed" by Germans. It was here that their young Jewish ward ran away. If he survived it is not known.

A few years after liberation, the Chorazyczewskis were enabled to come to the United States by a Catholic relief organization. They settled first in Louisiana, and then, in 1950, came up to Detroit. While shopping one day in a neighborhood market, Helena recognized a face from Berezhnitsev—Oscar Bakalar, one of the few Jews who survived. In response to her excited questions, Bakalar said he didn't know what had become of Abe Kashtan, but he would try to find out. With the assistance of

---

[52] Charlotte Dubin, "Heroism of Polish Christian Family Emerges in Story of Local Woman," *The Detroit Jewish News*, (May 28, 1971), p. 16.
[53] Ibid., p. 16.

immigrant aid agencies, Kashtan was located in Silver Springs, a suburb of Washington, where he had opened a store.

Recollection of their reunion brought tears to Helena's eyes and to those of her listeners. "He came to my door, in Hamtramck, and he kissed me and called me mother. I can't tell you how wonderful it was." In 1954, when Abe married, five members of the Chorazyczewski family were sent tickets to attend the wedding in Silver Springs. They posed together—as a family. When Abe's two sons reached their Bar Mitzvah, Helena and Ignacy Chorazyczewski sat at the head table and blew out the candle on the cake reserved for grandparents. Even with Abe's death from a heart attack, four years ago, his wife and children still accept the Chorazyczewskis as family.

The Chorazyczewski family never sought recognition for their deeds of heroism. In fact, the story would not have come to light now, were it not for an element of chance. David Silver, who has a store in Hamtramck for many years, first met Helena when she came to him to translate some Hebrew letters sent by friends in Israel. With each letter he translated their friendship grew. An article in the *Detroit Jewish News*—which related the exploits of a Polish Righteous Gentile, Romualda Ciesielska—started Silver to thinking. Here was a Righteous Gentile right in his own vicinity.

When Silver was in Israel, in 1971, Silver met Mrs. Chorazyczewski's friends who corroborated her story. In answer to the same question asked of Romualda Ciesielska, Helena Chorazyckewska gave the same reply. Knowing what could happen to her and her family if caught by the Nazis, why did she do what she did? "My heart and my conscience told me to," she said. "And if there had been other boys like Abe who had come to me for help, I would have done the same thing for them." When it meant certain death to be discovered hiding Jews—Helena Chorazyczewsiki did so—"for God, for Abe and for me."[54]

Thirty-three years after World War II, the heroism of Franciszek Novak, of Manchester, New Hampshire was finally recognized for saving the life of a two-year old Jewish girl. Novak,

---

[54] *Ibid.*, p. 16.

then eighteen, was a farmer's helper in a small town in Poland. A young Jew, fleeing barefoot through deep snow from pursuing Nazi troops, stumbled to the farmhouse, with a small child, wrapped in an overcoat. Novak and his employer took the two, even though such an act of harboring Jews, was a serious "crime."

Despite Novak's twenty-four mile trek through the woods to obtain medicine, the young father, suffering from frostbite, perished. Novak's employer, also died—from a heart attack caused by the constant harassment of the searching Nazi troops. But Novak and his young charge did survive. He took care of the little girl for more than three years, begging, borrowing, and stealing food for her right "under the noses" of the Nazis. Finally, the little girl's uncle contacted the two and took the little girl out of Poland. That was the last time Novak ever saw her. Novak later married and raised a family. He came to America in 1967.

Rachel Auerbach, a director for the Yad Vashen Institute of Israel, documented Novak's story, traced him to Manchester and has put him in touch with that little Jewish girl he protected and defended so long ago. Little "Frieda," Novak's name for the child, is now living in Israel. She has grown into a beautiful young woman, is married, and has two children of her own. Novak, who had risked his life daily for three years, received international recognition for his deeds. Rabbi Joel T. Klein of Temple Israel, in Manchester, stated that the Roman Catholic Novak is memorialized with a tree and plaque in Tel Aviv.[55]

Thanks to Franciszek Siwek and Marie Kepa, David Heisler, his wife and three children, survived the horrors of the war. The Heislers, who stemmed from Krakow, Poland, had lived in Berlin. They were ordered to get out of Germany in 1938. They returned to Poland and settled in Podgrabiye, thirty kilometers from Krakow.

When the German roundup began, the Heislers were given shelter by Maria Kepa. With the aid of the Kepa family and Siwek, they dug an underground shelter under the Kepa home. Overnight, this task was accomplished. Then the Kepas, young

---

[55] "Polonian Saves Jewish Girl's Life in WW 2," *Post Eagle*, (July 25, 1973), p. 6.

and old, retaining the secret, helped them obtain the necessary food and other provisions, nightly by removing the pots that served their sanitary needs for lack of a toilet. During the entire ordeal, Siwek had possession of all their earthly means, sold items when it was necessary, brought them the money to pay for the food, and provided the Heislers with newspapers and information on what was going on in the outside world.

In 1947, David and his wife Antonia—along with their children, Alina, Pauline and Steven—came to New York, and in March 1949, they settled in Detroit. Working as a furrier until his retirement, in 1969, the Heislers corresponded with the Kepas and the Siweks. In appreciation for what Siwek has done, they brought him, in 1969, to Detroit for an American vacation.[56] The survival of the five Heislers is one of the dramatic tales during World War II, but also a tale of friendship which Christian Poles showed, in this instance, to a Jewish family.[57]

Among those who felt a surge of nobility, when the Jewish population was oppressed in Poland, was Wladyslaw Wojcik, who was recently honored by the Jewish Foundation with a diploma of recognition and appreciation. *Tydzien Polski* carried an extensive report of his activities.[58] Wojcik married Irena Zimmerman who was hidden during the war by Wojcik's friends.

For thirty-four years Tamara Rothbard Kotovich, an owner of a small coffee house in Tel Aviv, believed her son was dead. About a year and a half ago, she heard that her son, whom she threw from a lorry on the way from a concentration camp, when he was five, was picked up by a Polish farmer and was raised by him. The mother went to Poland to meet him. When she met him, immediately she started to fight the Polish authorities to let her son join her in Israel. After six weeks, her son Roman—now aged thirty-nine—returned with his mother to Israel.[59]

---

[56] "Pole Who Rescued Detroit Family of 5 from Nazis Ends Two-Month Vacation with them; Dramatic Humanitarian," *The Detroit Jewish News*, (November 28, 1969), p. 29.

[57] Alina is married to Irving Schurayts, an engineer who works for the city of Detroit. They have three children. Pauline is married to Dr. Albert Kaner. They have three children. Pauline's twin brother, Steven, also is married and has four children.

[58] "Niemalowany Ptak," *Tydzien Polski*, (April 8, 1972), pp. 6-7.

[59] "Finds Missing Son After 34 Years," *Jewish Press*, (August 20, 1976), p. 25.

Brotherhood is two Roman Catholic priests teaching a thirteen-year old retarded Jewish boy the Hebrew prayers he had to recite at his bar mitzvah. Stanley Wyczawski of Dearborn, Michigan, and John Larsen of Detroit, both students at St. John's Seminary in Plymouth learned Hebrew in their classrooms and from records. Mrs. Nathaniel Bookman went to the student priests after she had been unable to find a rabbi who had time to instruct her son. She asked them to deliver the instructions for two reasons: they were near the home and they were experienced in helping retarded children. The student priests had to teach Gary two prayers—the one he had to recite before and the one after the reading of the law. In addition, they also instructed the boy in the history of his culture. On August 16, 1970, Gary Bookman recited his prayers well, pleased Rabbi Jacob E. Segal of Congregation Ados Shalom, and in the Jewish tradition, became a man.[60]

Life was good to Professor Maurice Lakser in Poland. He was married, the father of a boy, with a good position in mathematics and physics in a state college located in his native city of Lwow, Poland. The good life was terminated when the Germans invaded Poland. In a short time, he was put into a concentration camp and his wife and son, his parents and his wife's parents were all put to death in the extermination camps. Professor Lakser worked in a stone quarry, at road work, and as an electrician in the concentration camp, where he suffered from hunger, cold and beatings. He escaped and found a haven with Polish friends in Lwow, living for a time in a secret room. After the war, Professor Lakser settled in America. He married the secretary and interpreter to one of the Displaced Camp directors. She had the same tragic background as his own. She too was saved by Poles from certain death in the concentration camps.[61]

There are many more untold stories of World War II, and how Poles befriended and protected many Jews at the risk of their own lives. No less than three books have been written on

---

[60] Ted Douglas, "Bar mitzvah hurdled. Seminarians aid youth." *The Detroit News*, (February 2, 1970), p. 13-A.
[61] Both Maurice and Elizabeth Lakser related their survival experience to Dr. Wytrwal. Both were personal friends of Dr. Wytrwal. Professor Lakser died in June, 1976.

this subject, based on authenticated research which was completed by the Yad Vashen Institute.

There are many brilliant pages in Polish-Jewish relations. There are many sad pages as well. Too many had stressed the sadness, in a malicious and bitter way. Regrettably, too many presentations of anti-Polishness will lead many Americans of Polish background to react in kind. Until they are corrected, much of America's future leadership will study and mature in an environment that serves to entrench, rather than dispel, irrational prejudices. To hasten its end, new approaches must be constantly devised. And the efforts of civic, religious and educational spokesmen, distinguished leaders in business and industry, real estate boards, Chambers of Commerce and women's clubs, must be enlisted to counter the false and malicious propaganda perpetrated by American Jews during the past decade.

The current wave of terrorism against the Jews—not only in Israel, but in other countries where they are established—seems to be the ultimate and periodic reaction to Jewry's hatred of the world's non-Jews. One cannot offend others perpetually, make them the scapegoats, treat them with impunity, and expect toleration or respect. One cannot infringe on their civil liberties by demanding an exaggerated interpretation of the Bill of Rights which endangers other human lives and shows no concern or care for others civil liberties. The Jew's selfish outlook at the world will continue to reap a harvest of bad seed until their egomaniacal concept "of the chosen people" is humanized into one for caring about others—especially non-Jews with as much passion and enthusiasm as they are about their own destiny and success. It is this relentless hatred which has inspired the phenomenon of anti-semitism all over the world wherever Jews have concentrated to become a social problem.

CHAPTER 19

Polish-Indian Relations

> Ye say they all have passed away,
> That noble race and brave;
> That their light canoes have vanished
> From off the crested wave;
> That mid the forest, where they roamed
> There rings no hunter's shout;
> But their names are on your waters,
> Ye may not wash them out.
>
> —SIGOURNEY

The American Indian probably numbered less than a million when the first foreigners touched the shores of America, a scant 500 years ago. But even then they had scattered across the breath of the continent. There were the Iroquois and Delawares of the Eastern Woodlands; the Sioux, Cheyenne, and Kiowa among the hunters of the Plains; the nomad Apaches; the Paiute and Shoshoni seed gatherers of the Far West; and the Chinook fishermen of the Northwest.

These native-born Americans made contributions to American civilization which are beginning to be better appreciated. They explored the continent ages before the Spanish Conquistadores entered upon the scene. They developed transportation which was ideally suited to America: the canoe by water and the snowshoe over deep snow in winter. They were past masters of woodcraft, and, most important, they introduced to the world a new diet which utilized native vegetables: white potatoes, tomatoes and peppers; also such luxuries as maple sugar, peanuts, chocolate and tobacco—all were "exported" by the New World to the Old.

"Succotash" and "hominy" are Indian words. So are "chipmunk" and "woodchuck." Half our states bear Indian names, from Connecticut to the Dakotas and Oregon. The Indian left his beauty on American art. He had a deep sense of human rights and democracy, which he defended from the Little Big Horn to Iwo Jima.

The Indian has written his own "Who's Who in America." High on the list are Samoset, the sagamore of the Pemaquids who welcomed the Pilgrims to Plymouth; Sequoya, the brilliant Cherokee who devised a system of writing for his people; Crazy Horse, the military genius who defeated the United States Cavalry; Geronimo, the Apache warrior who survived to ride in President Theodore Roosevelt's inaugural parade; and Maria Tallchief, the ballet dancer.

Long after the Indian the immigrants from Europe and Africa arrived on the American continent. Poles had contact with the American Indian from the very beginning of America's discovery. Many Polish books of the 17th century contain references to America, and some give curious descriptions from the new land: about the Indians and adventures of its explorers.

Francis Warnadowicz, a Pole, who settled in Cadiz, Spain (under the name of Francisco Fernandez) is said to have been a member of the motley crew of many nationalities who made the fateful voyage, in 1492, under Columbus, who discovered America and unfurled the flag of Spain in the New World. However, there is no documentary evidence to support this fact. It is known that a Fernandez was left at Hispaniola by Columbus. He later perished at the hands of the Indians, thus becoming the first European to claim such an unrewarding distinction.

The first instance of Polish bravery, in America, is recorded in 1609; when the Indians set an ambush to kill Captain John Smith during one of his visits to the glasshouse in Jamestown.

> Returning . . . from the glass-house alone hee incountered the king of Paspaheigh, a most stronge stout Savage whose perswasions not being able to perswade him to his ambush, seeing him only armed but with a fauchion, attempted to haue shot him, but the President prevented his shot by grapling with him, and the Savage as well prevented him from drawing his fauchion and perforce bore him into the river to haue drowned him; long they struggled in the water from whence the king perceiving two of the Poles upon the sandes

would have fled; but the President held him by the haire and throat till the Poles came in; then seeing howe pittifully the poore Savage begged his life, they conducted him prisoner to the fort.[1]

The Poles saved Captain Smith's life and captured an Indian chief. But their humane treatment of the Indian deserves another acknowledgement.

In 1616, during Governor George Yeardley's administration, we find another significant reference to a Polish soldier's gallantry. Yeardley—forced by a lack of provisions—organized an expedition against the Indians who broke the contract made by Governor Dale for the delivery of corn. In a battle, in which the Indians were routed, a "Robert a Polonian" took prisoner one of the red chieftains.[2]

Olbracht Zaborowski left Poland after 1659. After a brief stay in Holland, he came to America. Little is known of his early years on this continent. His later career shows that he must have been a man of truly American enterprise and energy.[3] He became an Indian interpreter, a trader, and owner of vast tracts of land in the present County of Bergen, New Jersey.[4] Zaborowski died on September 11, 1711, at Hackensack, where he settled permanently.[5]

It is said that Jacob, eldest son of Olbracht Zaborowski—when he was seven years old—was kidnapped by an Indian chief, who took a liking to the boy. The sachem afterwards disclosed his deed to the father with whom he lived on very friendly terms. At the disclosure, he also implored the father to let Jacob remain with the Indians. In that way he might acquire their language and learn their customs, and thus serve as arbitrator and interpreter between the Indians and the colonials, should disputes

---

[1] *A Map of Virginia, With a Description of the Countrey,* (Oxford: 1612), Oxford Tract CCXLV, pp. 80-81.
[2] Captain John Smith, *True Travels,* (Richmond: 1819), p. 28. Miecislaus Haiman, *Polish Pioneers of Virginia and Kentucky,* (Chicago: 1937), p. 50.
[3] Wytrwal, *Poles in American History and Tradition,* pp. 21-24.
[4] His signature as interpreter is found affixed to an Indian contract of purchase in 1679.
[5] In his day he was considered a very wealthy man. He was highly respected, not only for his liberality, but for his integrity, and above all for his fair dealings with the savages, who esteemed him highly. C. B. Harvey, *Genealogical History of Hudson and Bergen Counties, New Jersey,* (New York: 1900), p. 50.

arise in the future. The father agreed, and Jacob remained with the Indians for several years.

Anthony Sadowski, a Polish noble, appeared in Philadelphia in the very beginning of the 18th century. He became an Indian trader and interpreter, and attained some prominence in the colony. Governor Patrick Gordon employed him often as his envoy to the Indians. His trade took him far into the West, and he is said to have been one of the first whites to penetrate into Ohio and Kentucky as early as the fourth and fifth decades of the 18th century. Eventually, he settled in Virginia, and served as a surveyor in Augusta County, where he was insidiously killed by Indians, in 1774. He had several sons, typical backwoodsmen, who were skillful Indian fighters, and took part in many expeditions against them.

Reverend Frederick Post, born in Chojnice, Poland, in 1710, played an important part in the opening of the West to English settlement. One of the scattered members of the Polish Moravian Church, he came to America, in 1742. While in the service of the colonial authorities, as a Moravian missionary, he explored Pennsylvania, New York, Connecticut and Ohio. In the year 1743, he did religious work among the Iroquois Indians of upper New York. In 1759, he published, in London, a pamphlet entitled: *The Second Journal of Christian Frederick Post on a Message to the Governor of Pennsylvania on the Indians of Ohio.*[6] In the sixty-seven page pamphlet, he described his activities among the Indians of Ohio. Largely through his efforts, the British were able to arrange an alliance with the Indians, and to force the French to abandon Fort Duquesne. He was married three times; his first two wives were baptized Indian maidens. He died in Germantown, Pennsylvania, in 1785.

The Reverend Joseph Dabrowski also labored to convert Indians in Portage County (particularly those in the Chippewa village near Shantytown Lake), Wisconsin to the Catholic faith. He took great pains to learn the Chippewa dialect, and even began the compilation of a Chippewa-Polish dictionary for the use of

---

[6] The title page of Reverend Post's notes actually was added to the end of a work by Charles Thompson entitled, *An Enquiry into the Causes of the Alienation of the Delaware and Shawnee Indians.*

the Felician Sisters. Though the compilation has been lost, the parish baptismal register of the 1870's and 1880's carries the names of about 200 Indian converts baptized by Father Dabrowski. Older parishioners still recall a story about Dabrowski's attempt to help an Indian village near Shantytown Lake, Wisconsin. With his own funds he purchased seed potatoes, and showed the Indians how to plant the seedlings. Weeks later he returned to see how they were doing with the potato patch only to learn that the Indians had become hungry and eaten the seed.[7]

There is a growing possibility that the name Korczak Ziolkowski could become renowned in American history as the modern "Michelangelo of the Mountains." Since 1948, the Boston-born stone sculptor, Korczak Ziolkowski has been carving a monument of Indian Chief Crazy Horse and his pony out of the solid granite of Thunderhead Mountain, five miles north of Custer, South Dakota. The mountain is almost within sight of Mount Rushmore where Korczak Ziolkowski helped Gutzon Borglum put finishing touches on the faces of four presidents, in 1939.

The 563-foot, three-dimensional monument (ten times larger than Mount Rushmore) was approved by Crazy Horse's nephew, Chief Henry Standing Bear, who insisted on a monument that would commemorate the Indian: "We want the white man to know that Indians had heroes, too." The old chief discovered Korczak Ziolkowski through a newspaper account of a Paderewski bust, which had won a prize for Korczak Ziolkowski at the 1939 World's Fair

Korczak Ziolkowski accepted the commission without a fee. Unlike most builders, who wouldn't think of undertaking such an enormous project without dozens of men to help, Korczak Ziolkowski has labored almost alone, with only his family and a helper or two, now and then. During twenty-five years of work, Korczak Ziolkowski has almost single-handedly blasted away four million tons of rock—ten times as much as at Mount Rushmore. To complete the job, a total of six million tons of stone will have to be cut from the mountain.

[7] "Polish Ethnic Group in Portage County," *Gwiazda Polarna*, (January 20, 1973), p. 5. See also Malcolm Rosholt, *Our Country, Our Story*.

When the statue of Crazy Horse will be completed, it will be 641 feet long, and tower 563 feet—thirteen feet higher than the Washington Monument. According to Ziolkowski the four giant heads carved on Mount Rushmore, twenty miles away, would all fit into Crazy Horse's head, and that 1,000 people will be able to stand on the Indian's outstretched hand!

Boleslaw Cybis was born on July 23, 1895, in Wilno, Poland. His father was the chief architect of Peterhooff, the summer palace of Czarina Maria Fecdorowna. He graduated from the Warsaw Academy of Fine Arts, in 1925. After graduation he returned to the art of Rome and Florence to study the techniques of the Renaissance painters. In 1937, Cybis was appointed a professor at the Academy of Fine Arts in Warsaw. Two years later, he came to the United States when commissioned to paint two murals for the Hall of Fame at the New York World's Fair.

Following the completion of the murals, Cybis made a trip through the west, and sketched the American Indians in their native habitat. He found the American Indian a fascination equal to that of the peasants which he painted in his homeland, twenty years earlier. In these drawings, Cybis has captured the plight of the Indian. Their faces reflect the sadness, dignity and resignation of a proud people who mourn the passing of time, and the timelessness of their heritage.

It was these qualities that inspired the Cybis Studio to re-create, in limited edition, graphics of these nine portraits in folio one, "American Indian Portraits." So successfully had Cybis captured the essence of a vanishing people, and preserved a significant legacy of our country's history, that on May 31, 1972, President Nixon presented two of the original portraits as a gift of the United States People to the People of Poland.

In keeping with this reverence for the North American Indian, the Cybis firm recently started another series, this time in porcelain, instead of paper. Two of its Indian pieces have already been presented to the Red Chinese Premier Chou En-Lai and Chairman Mao-Tse-Tung by the U.S. Senators, Mike Mansfield and Hugh Scott. The Indian piece "Iroquois at the Council Fire" was presented to the People of the Soviet Union, by President Nixon, in 1973. Porcelain figures of Little Eagle, Cupid, and

Running Deer were among eleven handsome gifts President Ford had taken on his European trip to present to the heads of state. The remainder of the collection (there will be eighteen in all over the next ten years) are destined for Blair House, the President's guest house for visiting dignitaries to Washington, D.C.[8]

Wilma Janczynska-Bushewicz was commissioned to paint "Our Lady of the Ottawas" for a small northern Michigan Church of the Immaculate Conception, in Peshawbestown. To Janczynska-Bushewicz it seemed right and just that the native Americans of this continent should be singled out for special honors. She painted both virgin and child as Indians with Indian dress after researching extensively facial characteristics and dress of the American Indian. Despite the Indian characteristics, it is quite visible that the artist employed European techniques and characteristics in painting facial expressions.

Artist Janczynska-Bushewicz has successfully made the Indian people realize that this Madonna belongs to them. It was compared to "Our Lady of Guadalupe" (Spanish Madonna) and the "Virgin of Copper" (Cuban Madonna). The people of Peshawbestown are pleased, and the Indian congregation is delighted with the Madonna. It is a successful work as the comments from tourists and other Indian communities, have testified. The fame of the painting spread when it was reproduced on postcards. It attracts the notice of hundreds of persons annually, who visit the small northern church in order to view the painting. A few years ago, it was the subject of an article in *Diario Cadiz*, a daily newspaper in Cadiz, Spain.

Edward Oprinski, of Detroit, first became interested in Indian culture when he joined the Boy Scout Program, in 1932. Oprinski founded the "Help Michigan Indians Committee" because the American natives have been discriminated against and still continue to suffer. Besides making goodwill trip, Oprinski conducts lectures before interested groups, and also offers slide representations depicting Indian life.

Oprinski's gift giving is a year-round campaign. The last truck-

---

[8] Boleslaw Cybis died on May 30, 1957. Despite his untimely death, the Cybis Art Studio has carried on his work by taking his many designs and models of unfinished pieces and completing them in porcelain sculptures.

load brought to a total of more than 600 tons in food, clothing and miscellaneous articles which he delivered to the Indians personally. As head of the "Help Michigan Indians Committee," Oprinski is concerned about the state's four major settlements: Mount Pleasant, Bay Mills, Hannahville and L'Anse. Oprinski is aided in his efforts by members of Boy Scout Troop 586, where he serves as scoutmaster. For his significant efforts, Oprinski has been presented the National Good Samaritan Award.[9]

Gregg Markowski, from St. Louis, Missouri, read about the plight of the Sioux Indians in South Dakota. He decided to begin a campaign to ship the Indians clothing and food in time for Christmas. It was his project to earn the rank of Eagle in the Scouts. Markowski's campaign had rounded up enough material to fill "two or three tractor trailers." The project was a great success. The material collected was delivered by the Defense Department.[10]

Lynn Arends was married to Michael S. Milot, in 1970. Both attracted national attention when they asked for and received temporary custody of five Navajo brothers and sisters: Pam, Leonard, Gary, Peggy and Jimmy, who range in age from five to thirteen. The father was unemployed and unable to support them. Lynn Arends met the children and her husband while doing volunteer work at Mesa Vista Sanitarium in Boulder.[11]

Michael Przybylowicz defended the welfare of the Indians in the Kansas Legislature.

Dr. Felix Paul Wierzbicki, in his book *California As It Is and As It May Be,* considered Indian life, habits and culture.

Many Poles fought for Indian independence in other countries.

A Jan Sobieski, fought for Mexican independence under Juarez. He attained the rank of colonel.

Ludwig Flegel fought under General Bolivar to attain independence for Ecuador.

---

[9] "Never Forget Our Indians. West Sider Spreading Goodwill Year-round," *West Side Courier,* (January 3, 1974), p. 3.
[10] "Polish-American Scout Wanted to Help Indians," *Gwiazda Polarna,* (March 6, 1971), p. 5.
[11] *The Sunday News,* (January 18, 1970), p. 3.

Colonel Maurice Marcinkowski and Major Izydor Borowski served under General Simon Bolivar to attain Bolivian independence.

Ignacy Domeyko pleaded the cause of the Indians in his book *Araukania and Her Inhabitants,* which has been translated into English, French and German. It was widely read in Europe and South America. Domeyko also founded the University of Santiago and uncovered the rich mineral deposits of Chile.

The Pole has often displayed his concern for the welfare of other nationals, races or people who have suffered unjustly and unfairly the stigma and abuse of the majority people. As early as the 14th century with Paulus Vladimiri (Pawel Wlodkowicz) defending the pagan tribes of Lithuania to the present can be found a Polish hero brandishing his vective against the evils of the world. In this same spirit he champions unpopular causes, even when it is detrimental or not profitable to himself. However, the Pole also has an undaunted attitude that despite the greatest odds, the worst holocaust, he will not only survive, but endure and even succeed. Throughout the ravages of history this romantic spirit has benefited him, and it has been well illustrated in his deeds as an uncommon characteristic of man and nations.

CHAPTER 20

Poles and the American Labor Movement

> The man who goes into the depths of the mine and exchanges his day for night, that we may change the night into day; the man who faces the boiling caldron and draws ribbons of fire from the furnace for our safety and comfort . . . has justified his existence, and made ours easier, more beautiful, and safer.
>
> —PROFESSOR E. A. STEINER[1]

American histories could easily have given the readers the impression that Polish participation in the trade union movement was of recent development. Such impressions are anything but accurate. Skilled and unskilled Polish workers helped build the United States. They contributed to the growth of industries and resulting union movements throughout the country's history, though all too often the Polish worker was then denied his proportionate share of the rewards. As is the case with so many Polish traditions, the participation of the Poles in the labor movement can be traced to the very formative times of our nation—the period of the first colonization.

In 1619, during the second administration of Governor Yeardley, the London Company took another progressive step by giving the 1,000 men in the Virginia colony the right to share in their own government. Colonial records of Virginia reveal a group of Poles, somewhat offended and irritated during the brief, but extremely important session of the first Virginia assembly, which marked the first step toward representative government in

---

[1] Kenneth D. Miller, *Peasant Pioneers*, (New York: 1925), p. 180.

the New World. On the 30th day of July 1619, when the Virginia House of Burgesses—the first legislature assembled on the soil of America—had ushered in representative government, the Poles appeared upon the scene as political dissenters protesting an undemocratic slight being perpetrated in Jamestown, the cradle of democracy. Because they were not of English descent, they were disfranchised by the company authorities. In protest, the Poles refused to work until accorded the same voting privileges as those enjoyed by the English settlers; so they suspended operations in the glass factory, the tar distillery, and the soap establishments.

Thus it happened that those summer days of 1619 were to witness not only the first popular assembly in America, but also the first labor walkout. Governor Yeardley and the legislature were not long in undoing this political injustice; they quickly realized that if the colony sent empty ships to England, the consequences could be very unpleasant. Except for the few pounds of tobacco the English colonists were beginning to export, practically all of the profits realized by the London Company came from the re-sale of the products of the Polish industries. The governor gave the following account of the incident in the *Virginia County Court Book*.

> Upon some dispute of the Polonians resident in Virginia, it was now agreed (notwithstanding any former order to the contrary) that they shall be enfranchised and made as free as any inhabitants there whatsoever: and because their skill in making pitch and tar and soap ashes shall not die with them, it is agreed that some young men shall be put unto them to learn their skill and knowledge therein for the benefit of the country hereafter.[2]

From the excerpt, it is evident that this first strike in America was conducted not for higher wages and better working conditions, as is so often the objective today, but for democratic rights. These Polish immigrants to Jamestown were among the first champions of American civil liberties.

---

[2] Susan Myra Kingsbury, *An Introduction to the Records of the Virginia Company of London*, (Washington, D.C.: 1950), I, p. 251. Wytrwal, *Poles in American History and Tradition*, pp. 13-14.

Early in the twentieth century, the American labor movement was still in its infancy, uncoordinated and divided in strategy between those who favored the use of political methods, and those who believed the strike and boycott were the only roads to success. Union membership was also small; it leveled off at a mere one-tenth of the nonagricultural work force.[3] Labor's signal failure occurred in the mass production sector of the economy: motors, rubber, electrical equipment, food processing, and above all steel.

There are many reasons why the unionization of the mass-production industries in America was so long delayed. Most of the unskilled laborers in the mass-production industries were recent immigrants who had little experience with the labor organizations. Flocking to this country in the first decade of the century, the Poles, Croats, Serbs, Slovaks, Hungarians, and Italians filled the bottom ranks of the workers in the steel industry. They constituted, for example, nearly two-thirds of the common labor in a typical large steel plant, in 1910. Southern and Eastern Europeans, according to the U.S. Immigration Commission, made up 33.4 per cent of the total labor force in iron and steel, in 1907.[4]

Many employers followed the "balanced nationalities concept." This also delayed unionization. The Ford Motor Company classified its employees by ethnic origin. In 1916, of its 40,903 employees there were twenty-four nationalities with at least 100 employees. They are as follows: American 16,457; Polish 7,525; Italian 1,954; Canadian 1,819; Romanian 1,750; Jewish 1,437; German 1,360; Russian 1,160; English 1,159; Hungarian 690; Austrian 573; Syrian 555; Lithuanian 541; Scottish 480; Serbian 456; Armenian 437; Irish 399; Ruthenian 368; Greek 281; Bohemian 240; Swedish 166; Croatian 159; Finnish 106; Negro 106. In 1916, the Ford Motor Company listed fifty-eight different nationalities in its employment.[5]

---

[3] David Brody, *Labor in Crisis. The Steel Strike of 1919*, (Philadelphia: 1965), p. 39.
[4] *Ibid.*, p. 39.
[5] Jonathan Schwarz, "Henry Ford's Melting Pot," *Immigrants and Migrants: The Detroit Ethnic Experience*, (Detroit: 1974), p. 256.

Labor leaders had concluded that effective organization in the mass-production industries demanded the inclusion of all production workers in a single union regardless of their mechanical ability, their creed, color, or nationality. This was difficult. A deep social gap divided the recent immigrants and the English-speaking workmen in the mass production industries. Few skilled workers would move down to work among the immigrants, even temporarily, at the steel plants in Steeltown, Pennsylvania, in 1908; they preferred to be laid off. Anxious to disassociate himself from the immigrant, the American worker identified with the neighborhood shopkeeper and artisan, and with them tended to look up to the mill officials. Social tensions helped attach the skilled men to their employers. An anti-social environment encouraged race and ethnic prejudice.

> Race prejudice manifested in innumerable ways, was directed to keeping the Slav out of the mines. In 1889 and 1897 laws with this object in view were secured from the Pennsylvania Legislature, that of 1897, requiring one to have been a laborer in the mines of the Commonwealth for at least two years before he could become a miner, and making it necessary that one should pass an examination before a Miner's Examining Board. To do this the Slav had to possess a knowledge of the English language, which was not easy for him to acquire. Over these examining boards the English-speaking miner secured control, making their requirements operate to his advantage and to the disadvantage of the Slav. In a score of other ways he endeavored to ward off the competition of the Continental races, his resistance to the progress of the latter growing more and more pronounced as their numbers increased.[6]

A visitor to Scranton observed: "It goes against the grain in an English-speaking man to fetch and carry for a Slovak or a Pole."[7]

Ethnic background played a significant part in job assignment. Management did not wish all people (especially certain kinds of people) to be ambitious towards promotion. Hughes reports that one large American industrial concern has a breed known as the "Thank God for" people—the "unambitious people who can be

---

[6] Frank Julian Warne, *The Slav Invasion and the Mine Workers*, (Philadelphia: 1904), pp. 68-69.
[7] *Ibid.*, pp. 87-88.

counted on to stay where they are, and who keep things running while others are busy climbing the mobility ladder from one job to another."⁸ Those in the higher levels of an industrial hierarchy used their power to keep their own ranks ethnically and racially exclusive. Ethnic, national and class loyalty were undoubtedly factors in the original choice of people to be sponsored, and in their later rise.

> Some managers speak with nostalgia of the unambitious first generation of Poles, French-Canadians or peasant-workers of other ethnic groups; people who were content with their jobs, willing to work hard without hope of advancement. Of course, such people often had objectives outside industry to keep them at work and content; notably, the desire to have money for buying property. In spirit, they were not completely industrialized. A second or later generation which insists on advancement within industry is compared unfavorably with their fathers.⁹

To draw in the immigrants into the unions meant to alienate the native workingmen who were inclined to look upon the recent immigrants as that "pauper labor of Europe," likely to depress American standards of living. Thus, trade-union leadership accommodated itself to inclinations of the American native-born workmen, and made few attempts to organize or teach recent arrivals. Samuel Gompers saw the need to teach trade unionism to the immigrants: "untutored, born in the lands of oppression . . . reaching manhood without that full mental development which makes for independence and self-preservation." But labor leaders were blind to the equally important task of educating Americans in the kind of trade unionism that would offer a place for the immigrant workman."¹⁰ This omission would exact a heavy price.¹¹

---

⁸ Everett C. Hughes, "Queries Concerning Industry and Society Growing Out of Study of Ethnic Relations in Industry," *American Sociological Review*, (April, 1949), p. 219.

⁹ *Ibid.*, p. 218.

¹⁰ The AFL surely injured its cause, in the 1912 drive, by urging steelworkers to advise "your friends and relatives across the water . . . it would be to their advantage if they did not come to America for a year or two." David Brody, *Labor in Crisis. The Steel Strike of 1919*, p. 42.

¹¹ The Amalgamated Association—made up, as it was, of English-speaking men—lost enthusiasm for organizing work partly for this reason.

There are also other reasons for the long delay in unionization of the mass-production industries. Many contemporary Polish-American priests viewed trade unionism with mixed feelings. The labor movement offered obvious advantages, and just as clear disabilities, for many Polish-American priests assumed that the union movement had socialistic directions which were also atheistic. The unsympathetic attitude toward non-Polish organizations, an unwillingness toward high union dues which reduced their net wages, and the prejudice of native American workers—all of these elements had their effect on the ethnic minorities. In addition, immigrants from eastern Europe differed profoundly from the English-speaking men in the mass-production industries of America. They regarded their jobs only as a means of accumulating the wealth to purchase land, raise the mortgage in their native land in Europe, or place their hope in educating their children. Saving money was the one essential for the immigrants. Thriftiness and self-denial were two common virtues among the first generation Poles.

A dollar-seventy-five per day was not considered low wages by their standards, nor did they expect to live on the same level with Americans. The Immigration Commission discovered that one-third were unmarried; that of the married men who had been living in the United States less than five years, three-quarters of them had come alone.[12] Those with families, supplemented their incomes by lodging their countrymen.

> For a few dollars a month, a Polish steelworker could have a bed (which might have another occupant while he was at work) in the crowded rooms of the "boarding boss." At the end of each month, the bill for food, purchased and cooked by the wife, was divided among the adult males in the household. The boarding-boss arrangement permitted a common laborer to put aside as much as half of his earnings.[13]

The jobs were exhausting and dangerous. The accident rate much exceeded that of the English-speaking employees. Life in America was harsh and dismal, relieved only by the companionship of countrymen and the wild sprees on "pay night."

---

[12] Ibid., p. 39.
[13] Ibid., p. 40.

But the hard existence, in America, would come to an end when the hoard of dollars rose high enough, then the immigrant would go home. That seemed a fair exchange for whatever hardships the exile years extracted.

> The ruling criterion therefore was not the wage rate, the kind of work, or the outlandish way of American life, but employment itself. "It is a golden land so long as there is work," a Polish worker wrote, "but when there is none, then it is worth nothing."[14]

For the immigrant, the crucial necessity was that the work be uninterrupted, since unemployment insurance, seniority and other benefits were non-existent. During this period, lay-offs were common, and economic conditions fluctuated frequently and precipitantly.

The reception of the Polish immigrants was mixed. When labor was in short supply, their ready muscle and willing brain was vital to the progress of industrialization and the wealth of America; when it was not, they became undesirable aliens. After the close of the Civil War, Irish, German, and Welsh coal miners in Pennsylvania were complaining of "newer" immigrants, who took "bread from the lips of decent, law-abiding Americans."[15] In the 1870's, Irishmen repeatedly voiced their protests against the importation of "foreign labor" and "durrty furruners" into this grand and glorious country.

> In 1875, serious riots resulted when a Pennsylvania mine operator brought in Italians with breechloaders, and there were other occasions when Irishmen showed their antagonism toward Poles, Hungarians, Swedes and Negroes.[16]

Polish-American workers did not have an easy time during the early years of this century. Many Americans of Polish descent, in the Buffalo area, recall the entrance of the Poles on the labor scene.

> The third generation Poles recall a cherished image of their grandparents: It is of Father Pitass, stocky, protective, leading a group of

---
[14] Ibid., p. 40.
[15] Carl Wittke, *The Irish in America*, (New York: 1970), p. 225.
[16] Ibid., p. 225.

Polish workers down East Side streets to the plants, as scores of German-born workers—who had immigrated here before them—protested their intrusion on the labor market.

But the Poles got work. And ironically, in the plants, it was the Germans who taught them how to do it.[17]

The Polish immigrant succeeded in entering the labor market because they were needed, not only in the coal mines, but in the steel mines, shipyards and slaughter-packing houses. Hundreds of workers were needed in factories manufacturing railroad equipment; as well as in the construction and clothing industries. This movement was accelerated by the labor shortages of World War I. The vast expansion of American industry, that began in the 19th century, drew men and women from all over the world; Polish workers came with the rest, seeking work, and livelihood— what AFL President Samuel Gompers once termed "More."

When union leaders finally made attempts to organize the arrivals from Southern and Eastern Europe, they were successful.

When such attempts were made, as by the leaders of the United Mine Workers, the result was a large southern and Eastern European membership. In the clothing industry, meanwhile, the "new" immigrants organized their own unions. By 1910, the International Ladies Garment Workers' Union and the Amalgamated Clothing Workers of America, each of which was composed largely of Russian Jews, Italians, and Poles, were among the strongest labor unions in America.[18]

The trade union was perhaps the only institution in which immigrants mixed with others of different origin. For the rest, immigrant life was organized almost wholly along the lines of nationality. Each group exhibited strong tendencies to live in separate areas, and to move elsewhere when newcomers arrived.

Nonetheless, the New York Bureau of Labor could remark, in 1885, that, although immigrants might be prepared to work for low wages on arrival, in the United States, they soon became "sufficiently Americanized" to go on strike themselves. Indeed, Hungarians and Poles played a leading part in the bitter strikes

---

[17] Ellen Taussig, "The Polish Community Part I: 'We've Come A Long Way,'" *Buffalo Evening News*, (November 13, 1971), p. B-3.
[18] Maldwyn Allen Jones, *American Immigration*, (Chicago: 1960), p. 223.

which were held in the Pennsylvania coke region during the 1880's.[19]

In the early development of the American labor movement, immigrants participated significantly. In 1888, the well-known American economist, Francis A. Walker, remarked that ". . . the main impulse toward the formation of labor organizations, among us has been of foreign derivation, and . . . alien elements have contributed by far the greatest part of the membership."[20] This comment—reflecting as it did the contemporary tendency of the American-born to stigmatize trade unions as foreign importations —by no means overstated the case. Two years earlier, the Illinois Bureau of Labor had analyzed the ethnic composition of the state's trade unions and had found them to be twenty-one per cent native-born, thirty-three per cent German, nineteen per cent Irish, ten per cent British, twelve per cent Scandinavian, five per cent Polish, Bohemian and Italian.[21]

Poles presented a united front with other immigrant groups in organizing union locals or strike activities, as evidenced most clearly in the Hart, Schaffner and Marx strike (also called, more accurately, the Chicago Garment Workers' Strike), of 1910. Because of the intolerable working conditions at Hart, Schaffner and Marx Shop, strike activities began on September 29, 1910. The uprising spread rapidly, and within three weeks, most of the firm's 7,500 employees had joined the original group. Soon the greater part of the city's clothing workers—a total of nine nationalities, all foreign born—had united in support of the work stoppage. A. D. Marimpietri described the hectic, but exhilarating, early days of the strike.

> In sixteen halls in various parts of the city, the tailors met every day from early morning until late at night, listening to speakers and discussing among themselves the numerous complaints that had brought them together. In some of the halls the workers met in national or language groups: the Poles, the Bohemians, the Lithuanians, the Italians, the Jews. Such separate meetings were necessary because most of the workers did not understand the English language.[22]

[19] Jones, *American Immigration*, p. 222.
[20] *Ibid.*, p. 221.
[21] *Ibid.*, p. 221.
[22] Humbert S. Nellie, *Italians in Chicago 1880-1930. A Study in Ethnic Mobility*, (New York: 1970), pp. 81-82.

At the height of the strike an estimated 35,000 garment workers had stopped working. They rapidly won wide public sympathy, as well as financial and moral support from the Chicago Federation of Labor, the United Garment Workers (A.F.L.), the Women's Trade Union League, and various socialist and anarchist groups. The strike had lasted more than four months, and cost the lives of two laborers. It had not failed, however, because an agreement reached with Hart, Schaffner and Marx, on January 14, 1911, provided for the creation of an arbitration board that included workers as well as employers. This agreement opened the door for additional concessions benefiting workers in following years.

In mining towns, where the need for labor solidarity was great, Polish elements have joined other foreign groups to strengthen labor unions. In one area where they predominated, they formed a "singing union" and marched along the valleys, to and from work, singing Polish songs.[23]

In the memorable steel strike of 1919, the Polish immigrants played a significant role. For many steelworkers, the strike was a continuation of the war-time struggle for democracy. The caption, under the photograph of a young steelworker killed during the strike, underlined the main point.

> Casimir Mazurek, who fought on foreign soil to make the world free for Democracy, was shot to death by the hirelings and thugs of the Lackawanna Steel Co. because he fearlessly stood for industrial Democracy on American soil.[24]

The critical and agonizing issues of World War I affected especially the Poles whose lives touched two continents.

> "For why this war? For why we buy Liberty Bonds?" asked a Polish striker. "For mills? No, for freedom and America—for everybody. No more (work like) horse and wagon. For eight hour day."[25]

The unions made extensive use of Polish field workers in establishing new Polish locals. As they moved into organized

---

[23] R. A. Schermerhorn, *These Our People*, (Boston: 1949), pp. 284-285.
[24] Brody, *Labor in Crisis. The Steel Strike of 1919*, p. 155.
[25] *Ibid.*, p. 157.

labor, Poles tended to be influenced by economic factors and grievances, rather than philosophical considerations or intellectual panaceas. Thus, the primary goal in organizing locals was to obtain "bargaining power"; that is, some assurance that a union would achieve its stated objectives. Where such prospects existed, Polish immigrants organized rapidly and effectively.

Some leaders of American labor have feathered their own nests, and expanded their personal power at the expense of union members without giving anything substantial in return. Others have given their membership more service than money could every pay. Leon Krzycki was one of the latter. A great pioneer in the American labor movement, Leon Krzycki was born on August 10, 1881, in Milwaukee, Wisconsin. His parents came from Poznan, Poland. They had nine children.

At the age of fourteen, Krzycki started working in the printing trade, where, in 1904, he organized the strike of the apprentices. The strike was suppressed. The inhuman conditions of work, as well as the death of a few co-workers killed by bullets of the National Guard, during one of the strikes, had a decisive influence on the future activity of young Leon Krzycki.

In 1908, Krzycki joined the Socialist Party of the United States, thus combining political and union activity. In 1910, he cooperated with the tailors of Chicago, who were then organizing their own trade union. As a Socialist candidate, he was twice elected a member of the municipal council of Milwaukee, and in 1918-20, he held the office of Under Sheriff of the County. During this period he was elected secretary of the Socialist Party for the State of Wisconsin. The union of tailors (which became the Amalgamated Clothing Workers of America) entrusted Krzycki with various responsible tasks of the organizational work in Chicago, Buffalo, Philadelphia, Paterson and other cities.

In 1922, Krzycki was elected to the Governing Body of the Amalgamated Clothing Workers of America Union, then, later, was advanced to the position of National Vice-Chairman in which capacity he functioned until his retirement. Krzycki took an active part in many strikes, and workers' struggles in different parts of the United States. In 1919, he cooperated with the steel workers in their general strike; and in 1921, he participated in a strike of slaughterhouse workers of the meat packing industry, in Chicago. His ingenuity in successfully coping with labor problems brought him recognition as an exceptionally able organizer with the class struggle.

In 1930, Krzycki was elected a member of the Executive Committee of the Socialist Party of the United States; and, in 1933, became its Chairman due to his popularity and his ability to further socialist principles. He left the Socialist Party, in 1936, because of his disagreement with the majority of the Party authorities regarding the program of President Roosevelt's "New Deal." He expressed the opinion that the workers' movement should actively join in the action of bringing the proclaimed reforms into reality.

Toward the end of 1935, the Congress of Industrial Organization came into existence. Its aim was to organize trade unions in the main branches of industry; and Krzycki was one of its leading creators. He distinguished himself in the action of organizing trade unions in the automobile, steel, textile, manufacturing, as well as the electrical engineering, and other industries.

Leon Krzycki was a member of the American delegation of the Congress of Industrial Organization (C.I.O.) to the founding Congress of the World Federation of Trade Unions, in Paris, which was held from October 3 to October 10, 1945. In 1947, Krzycki went on the retired list, but continued his activities. In 1949, he was a delegate to the First World Peace Congress, in Paris, from whence he went to Warsaw for the Second Congress of Trade Unions. Krzycki died January 1, 1966, in Milwaukee.[26]

---

[26] Leon Krzycki was an inspired speaker and spoke Polish well. In 1919, he visited Poland, for the first time, and gave lectures in Poland on the situation of Polish workers in the United States.

In the field of politics, he condemned Hitler's and Mussolini's intervention in Spain. In 1939, he condemned Hitler's invasion of Poland and supported the developing struggle against the Nazi German invaders. At the first meeting of Americans of Slavic extraction—held in Detroit, on April 25th and 26th, 1942—he was elected chairman of the American Slav Congress, which office he held through 1950. At the Third American Slav Congress, which took place in New York City, September 21-23, 1946, he warmly received the chairman of the Polish delegation, General Karol Swierczewski (General Walter). At the conference of Polish union leaders, in Cleveland, April 16, 1944, he was elected chairman of the Polish American Workers' Council. He was enthusiastic when People's Poland—with her new western boundaries on the Odra and Nysa Rivers and on the Baltic Sea to the north—came into existence. In 1945, Krzycki attended the First Congress of

Joseph A. (Jock) Yablonski first went to work in the mines when he was fifteen to help his father support his family. The year after his father's death, as a result of a mine accident, Yablonski was elected to his first union post, as a local president. For more than a quarter of a century, in the coal mining district of Southwestern Pennsylvania, Yablonski led a full and vigorous political existence. He was fiercely loyal to the union leadership. In the 1930's, while other young rising young men of labor had their eyes on the total CIO picture, Yablonski focused on the United Mine Workers.

Yablonski supported John L. Lewis when he split with President Franklin D. Roosevelt on the issue of the war. Lewis also split with Murray over Roosevelt. Murray, a vice president of the United Mine Workers and head of the steel workers drive, accepted the presidency of the CIO at Lewis' urging. Yablonski was very important to Lewis because he beat Murray and Murray's men within their own district of the mine workers. Eventually Yablonski rose to entire control of that district, Number Five, and was placed on the national executive board.

Yablonski was loyal to Lewis even though Lewis, as he doffed the mantel of leadership, placed it on "Tony" Boyle. After Lewis died, Yablonski waited for the next national miners' election and entered the lists. He had a great deal of help. Ralph Nader, who despised the old leadership's neglect of the men and its wallowing in luxury, was impressed by Yablonski as affable as he was tough. Joseph L. Rauh, Jr., Washington D.C. lawyer and politician, and other liberal reformers stepped up to help him.

But the United Mine Workers had a system with traditions. The union is just a skeleton of its former self; old John Lewis' dictatorial way with banks, pension funds, and contracts could not continue to operate in the same way once the great organization was battered by the declining coal market and mechanization. Boyle's leadership was more of the same and with less

---

Trade Unions, in Warsaw. He received the invitation to attend from the Central Council of Trade Unions. At the Congress, he was greeted by the First President of the Polish People's Republic, President Boleslaw Bierut, who awarded him the Commander's Cross of the "Polonia Restituta" Order. As Chairman of the American Slav Congress, he also visited other Slavic countries, and was received by George Dimitrov, Joseph Tito, Edward Benes, and Joseph Stalin.

drive and strength; however, internal elections were still controllable. Yablonski knew that his chances were slim, but something stirred in him. While Lewis was living he would not even criticize, much less revolt. He had the loyalty to the great old man, probably even more than to the miners. But with Lewis gone, the miners and Yablonski's conscience remained.

On May 29, 1969, in a heavily-guarded press conference, in Washington's Mayflower Hotel, Yablonski—urged by Ralph Nader—announced he was a candidate for president of the United Mine Workers. It was doubly surprising, because not only was Yablonski the $26,000 a year chief lobbyist for the union, but he also appeared to be one of Boyle's more ardent supporters. But Yablonski discarded all that when he decided to challenge Boyle, which he disclosed at a press-conference.

> I have been part of this leadership. I participated in and tolerated the deteriorating performance of this leadership—but with increasingly troubled conscience. I will no longer be beholden to the past. I can no longer tolerate the low state to which our union has fallen.[27]

When he was asked why he thought such measures were necessary, Yablonski, a member of the union's executive board for the last twenty-nine years, replied: "I'm not naive enough to think that there won't be much difficulty, and I know the lengths they will go to."[28]

Yablonski's words were prophetic. Four days after his announcement, he met with a group of local union leaders in Springfield, Illinois. Talking to some of the men after the session, which had not been especially friendly, Yablonski was struck in the neck from behind and knocked unconscious. A doctor later told him that the karate chop narrowly missed a spinal nerve, which —if it had been injured—it could have killed or paralyzed him. A Yablonski rally a few days later, at Shenandoah, Pennsylvania, was broken up when a group of about 200 Boyle supporters created such a disturbance that it was impossible to continue.

The June 11, 1969, death of John L. Lewis provided Boyle

---

[27] Richard A. Ryan, "UMW fights stigma of feuds, Yablonski murders," *The Sunday Detroit News*, (June 25, 1972), p. 16-A.
[28] Ibid., p. 16-A.

with an unusual opportunity to ingratiate himself with retired miners, who made up nearly forty percent of the total union membership. A day after Boyle was named trustee of the rich welfare and retirement fund, Boyle convinced a second trustee, George Judy—who represented the coal industry on the fund—to agree to raise the monthly pension for retired miners from $115 to $150. The U.S. General Accounting Office conducted an audit and declared that the $35 per month increase would bankrupt the pension fund by 1975. But in any event, the attempt served its desired purpose. Boyle won ninety-three percent of the retired miners vote.

On several occasions during the long bitter campaign, Yablonski, through his attorney, Joseph Rauh, asked the U.S. Labor Department to supervise the election. Rauh cited to Labor Secretary, George Schultz, several instances in which he claimed the election was being stolen. Among the charges made by Rauh were that Boyle was using funds to finance the election; and that the *United Mine Workers Journal,* the official publication of the union, was being used as a campaign organ for Boyle. Schultz refused to intercede, claiming that the Labor Department "should not investigate and publicize the activities of one faction in the election in order to assist the campaign of another." On December 1, 1969, eight days before the election, Rauh again implored Schultz to step in. "The failure of the Department of Labor to take strong measures to insure a fair election may well bring in its trail ugly violence." Again, Schultz declined the request.

When the election count finally came in, Boyle had received more than 80,000 votes. Yablonski had received nearly 46,000. In locations where Yablonski had observers, he did well. But where he had no one present, he lost by as much as 50-1. Some locals reported more people voting for Boyle than were listed as members of the union. Yablonski forces wanted to station observers at each local. But they were unable to find out where the locals were located, or when they would vote. The union leadership refused to provide any information.

To the United Mine Workers Union it was a normal election. Justin McCarthy, editor of the *Mine Workers Journal* and union spokesman, said: "As I get it from here, it was a very clean election. Nobody got his head broken open. I'd say it was a real honest, clean election."[29]

Yablonski did not accept the verdict of the union counters, but vowed to keep on fighting and revealing. He was in a position to reveal, and had already revealed much during the campaign. Yablonski had been an administrator, the upper echelon of the miner's union, and performed the unthinkable act of running for the presidency while retaining his job in the union. When it was made official that Joseph Yablonski had lost his bid for the presidency of the United Mine Workers against the incumbent, W. A. (Tony) Boyle, Yablonski filed a complaint with the Labor Department alleging some 100 violations of the Landrum-Griffin act. He also told Boyle he would see him in court.

Sometimes, during the early morning hours on December 31, 1969, Joseph A. (Jock) Yablonski, his wife Margaret, and their daughter, Charlotte, were shot to death by three hired gunmen. Sudden death is no stranger to the coal fields. Miners and their families simply live with the prospect of men being crushed, burned or choked to death. But death came to the coal mining district of Southwestern Pennsylvania in an unfamiliar and more frightful manner. Men have been killed by other men in the coal fields, but it has been a long, long time since union politics motivated the killing of a man and his family.

At the funeral, in Washington, Pennsylvania, Kenneth Yablonski said that his father regretted not having done more for the miners and regarded the last few months of fighting for the miners, and against the entrenched leadership, as the greatest and best of his life.[30] Monsignor Charles Owen Rice, pastor of the parish from whose church Yablonski was buried, made the following observation:

> Yablonski, like many another man in his late 50's, wanted to give his life more significance, wanted to sacrifice and serve. His death may do what his life could not. A new deal may come to the miners and their way of life.[31]

---

[29] Ibid., p. 16-A.
[30] Msgr. Charles Owen Rice, "Late in life, something stirred," *National Catholic Reporter*, (January 21, 1970), p. 2.
[31] Ibid., p. 2.

His son stated that he had a two-fold dream: to see those responsible for the murders of his family arrested and convicted, and to see a "miners union run by miners for miners." The first dream was realized. The name of Yablonski can go down in history as that of a martyred labor leader, who fell victim by almost incredible circumstances in the nation's richest labor union, whose treasure coffers he dared to guard at the cost of his life.

The Polish-American leader is still a familiar figure on the labor scene. John J. Pilch was literally born into the labor movement. A native of Glassport, Pennsylvania, his father was born in Bochnia, Poland. Early in the century, the Pilch family moved to Aurora, Illinois. In 1925, he was initiated as a journeyman member of the Chicago Typographical Union, Number Sixteen. Pilch's early record in Chicago's Typographical Union, Number Sixteen, reveals that he was elected to office as an organizer and local bulletin editor for several terms. In 1947, he was elected president of Number Sixteen, an office which he held throughout the twenty-two month Chicago newspaper strike, from 1947-1949. He was re-elected president of the Chicago Typographical Union, in 1949, for another two year term. In 1952, then the ITU president appointed Pilch a representative of the president, travelling throughout the entire ITU jurisdiction servicing local unions in contract negotiations and other matters. Pilch was elected ITU first vice-president, in 1958, and upon the death of President Brown, in 1968, he assumed the presidency. In 1968, he was elected president receiving the largest vote with 50,087 votes cast in his favor. Pilch led his progressive party to victory in all contests by the 122,000 member union.

Clem Holewinski is president of the 20,000 members who belong to Local 12 of the United States Automobile, Aerospace, Agricultural Implement Workers of America. His leadership contributed to the fine labor-management relationship in the Toledo, Ohio area. John Grup serves as vice president of the local; John Plock is the financial secretary-treasurer; and Angie Zoldowski is a board member-at-large.

Edward Sadlowski is a director of the United States Steel Workers from District 31, which represents steel workers in 500 plants. Sadlowski is the third generation of his family to work in the steel mills. Sadlowski was bitterly opposed by I. W. Abel, the president of the steel workers union. It took Edward Sadlowski almost two years to get an honest election in the United Steel Workers District 31—the nation's largest regional claiming a membership of 140,000 members, and stretching from Chicago to Kankakee, Illinois, and from Waukegan to South Bend, Indiana. In the first election for directorship of District 31, Sadlowski lost by only 2,500 votes of the total 47,856 votes cast. Sadlowski appealed to the U.S. Department of Labor, which supported his claim that ballot-box stuffing and other irregularities did exist. In the new election—tightly supervised balloting by nearly 300 Federal Agents—Sadlowski received 39,637 votes to 20,158 for his opponent.[32]

One of the staunch supporters of Sadlowski was Kenneth Yablonski, the son of the late union rebel, Jock Yablonski. Yablonski saw the same rebel spirit in Sadlowski that he saw in his father.

Next, Edward Sadlowski challenged the powerful United Steelworkers leadership in his bid for the presidency of this 1.4 million member union. His slogan for the presidency to replace I. W. Abel (who is too old to run again) is "It's time to fight back." Sadlowski faced his share of violence as his campaign aides were shot or beaten.

Frank (Malin) Malinkiewicz, an employee of the Penn-Central Railroad, is president of Local 699, of the United Transportation Union. He is also president of the Polish-American Labor Leaders of Western, New York. Malinkiewicz is the immediate past president of the Professional and Businessmen's Association of Buffalo, New York. He also served as coordinator of the Pulaski Day parades, in Buffalo.

Roman C. Pucinski represented Illinois' 11th District in the House of Representatives since 1959. A member of the important House Education and Labor Committee, and House Committee on Veterans' Affairs, he has compiled an outstanding pro-labor record in the House of Representatives.[33]

---

[32] "Edward Sadlowski, Labor Reformer, Wins," *Polish American Journal*, (December, 1974), p. 1.

[33] Pucinski is a native of Chicago. He attended Northwestern University and

Walter Dorosz, Eddie Plawecki, and Stanley Nowak are very active in Local 600, UAW in Detroit.

Father Justin Figas, O.F.M., who gained an international reputation as an able organizer, superior, writer and orator, was also a champion of social justice.[34] In 1936, he was called to settle

---

John Marshall Law School. He was a staff reporter and writer for the *Chicago Sun Times* for twenty years.

[34] In 1926, Father Justin inaugurated, over a network of seventy stations, his radio program known to all as Father Justin's Rosary Hour (Godzina Rozancowa Justyna). He was not only fascinated by the invention of the radio, but saw in it a new providential medium through which the work of God could penetrate the mysterious regions of space and reach thousands, even millions, who never could have been assembled in any one place. He utilized this medium to fight the daily and hard battle of faith, to spread the evangelical truth, and to bring succor and spiritual nourishment to all the faithful. As a result of his avid reading and preaching, Father Justin became the author of lengthy serials, which described his travels to various countries, his impressions and personal experiences. Among these serials were those with the following titles: "On the Wings of the Hurricane," "What I Heard and Saw in the Old Country," "My Impressions of the Vatican," and "Hell Let Loose." As an orator, Father Justin was by no means limited to the pulpit and microphone, for on many memorable occasions he delivered speeches throughout the country in both the Polish and English language.

In 1923, the Franciscan Fathers assembled at a Provincial Chapter, in Buffalo, New York, electing Father Justin as their new provincial, to which post he was re-elected for five successive terms. His sixteen years as Provincial of a large community of Friars—scattered throughout the United States and Canada—were marked with a record of unique achievements in both ecclesiastical and secular fields.

During his regime, St. Anthony's province undertook the building of various institutions. In 1925, a high school for boys was erected at Athol Springs, New York. On June 28, 1927, St. Hyacinth Seminary, in Granby, Massachusetts, an institution of higher learning, was splendidly equipped with every facility for the thorough education of those who entered for the required study and training for the Catholic priesthood, was dedicated. On May 6, 1930, the cornerstone was laid for the new Novitiate at Ellicott City, Maryland, and the dedication for this magnificent new structure took place in 1931.

Father Justin's love for youth was always demonstrated in a practical manner. To meet the social needs among young people from the East Side living in Buffalo, New York, he had two large clubhouses erected: one for young women, and the other for young men of Corpus Christi parish. Father Justin also extended the missionary work of his Order by means of organizing two missionary bands, one ministering to the eastern States and Canada with headquarters in Ellicott City, Maryland, while the other for the western states, with headquarters in Harland, Wisconsin. At the request of Cardinal Stritch, he took over a daily newspaper, *Nowiny Polskie*, in Milwaukee, Wisconsin. Also a monthly magazine, *The Seraphic Chronicle*, began to be published during his administration.

Father Justin was a great champion in the cause of defending, supporting, and encouraging the American of Polish descent. For this trait he was always grateful to his parents, Jacob and Maryanna Szymanska. His knowledge and interest in the Polish language, he obtained gratefully from a parochial school in a small mining town of Everson, Pennsylvania, where he was born on June 24, 1886. He died on October 13, 1959. His constant aim was "A stronger America through a better individual."

a strike at the Duffy Silk Company, in Buffalo, New York. In January 1937, after considerable deliberation, the employees of the firm had adopted—by a vote of 450 to four—a collective bargaining and profit sharing plan proposed by the company. Under the agreement workers not only received wages equal to those paid by other firms, but also were given 75 per cent of the company's net profit. In addition to this, in 1937 and 1938, the company had waived $30,000—which it was entitled under the profit sharing provisions of the plan—thereby increasing by that amount each year the "net profit." The workers were satisfied and Father Justin was asked to remain as trustee and bargaining agent for the employees. So advantageous was the plan from the worker's standpoint that its adoption was also recommended by Rev. John P. Boland, then regional director for the NLRB at Buffalo, and by two departments of Labor Conciliators, Thomas Flinn and M. Williams.

Rev. Theophilus J. Wroblewski was also a champion of social justice. In a letter to the editor of the *National Catholic Register,* S. H. Ellner from Wilkes-Barre, Pennsylvania, made the following comments:

> There is a story that has been happening behind the scenes I think should be shared with the public. It concerns the Rev. Theophilus J. Wroblewski, pastor of St. Adelbert's Catholic Church at Glen Lyon, Pa., who has devoted a great deal of his time and money to helping the miners secure additional pension funds.
> As a result of his efforts, millions of dollars will be channeled in the coal fields in this and adjoining counties. His campaign involved trips to Harrisburg where the Governor and members of the General Assembly were contacted. He also visited Philadelphia and Washington where he enlisted other help for the cause.
> At no time was he compensated for the expense he incurred or the time and effort. I can assure you it takes money to travel these days. However, he financed his own trips. Nor has he ever, to my knowledge, received any recognition. His only reward is the satisfaction of doing a good deed for humanity in line with his calling. His unselfishness has been inspiring.
> To employ a man of his calibre would have cost a good deal of money, if his services were for sale, which they were not. He is eminently qualified.
> I think, in lieu of a testimonial, he should be saluted publicly for service to the public beyond the call of duty. I have been deeply impressed by his human understanding as well as his integrity and dedica-

tion to a worthy cause. We are very fortunate to have a neighbor of his qualities and ideals among us.

Nevertheless, I make these observations as a member of another faith, adding, I think, to the tribute he richly deserves.[35]

It requires a certain character with a valiant spirit who is also indignant about the corruption, hypocrisy, self-aggrandizement, ruthlessness or scheming immorality which has pervaded the administrative ranks of our unions in the United States. At times, this faith—as in the case of Jock Yablonski—required a life to be martyred defending a cause which would restore more honest representation of the laborers who depend on his trust. Polish-Americans have frequently pursued this idealistic role over the more common one of expediency or self-corruption for profit.

---

[35] "Voices of the People," *National Catholic Register*, October 10, 1970, p. 1.

CHAPTER 21

The Catholic Church vs. Polonia

> If Rome wants to salvage American Catholicism and the money which historically has come from it—it is going to have to retire a considerable number of mitered birdbrains.
> —FATHER ANDREW GREELEY[1]

For the most part, the Polish-American parish does not exist, even though ethnic identity was not replaced by religious identity. Polish-Americans are intermingled with other parishioners in "integrated" parishes. Although they have Polish-speaking priests, ceremonies and devotions in their traditional style—and occasionally Polish language societies—the parish is not "their parish" in the same sense that it was when it was founded and wholly supported by the Polish community.

The change is more noticeable in districts where the Polish-Americans comprise but a small minority of the entire community; but even in the large cities, the transition is gaining momentum. Where there are four or more Masses on Sunday, two of these are as a rule English Masses, and attendance at these is growing as it declines at the others. There is also a decline in attendance. In recent years the image of the typical Polish-American Catholic has disappeared. Today, it is difficult to tell where most Polish-Americans stand on any issue; doctrinal, moral or political. A characteristic of Polish-American Catholics is their unpredictability. Dr. Edward Tomasik, an optometrist from Cudahy, Wisconsin, made the following observation:

---

[1] Thomas C. Fox, "The company priest who discovered (and told) why half America's Catholics no longer attend mass," *Detroit Free Press*, (Detroit Magazine), (September 5, 1976), p. 15.

The Polish communities are indistinguishable from the Polish parishes, and when one dies the other dies too. At the Assumption of the Blessed Virgin Mary parish on Chicago's south side, all masses used to be said in Polish. Now, through intermarriage with other nationalities, only one mass is in Polish, attended primarily by the elderly, even though the parish still has 750 families on the rolls.[2]

Gone, at many of the parishes, are the Paschal Communion Cards, the blessing of food on Holy Saturday, and the breaking of the wafers (oplatki) at the Christmas evening meal. The Polish greetings and partings—graced with expressions imbued with the past traditions—are also gone. The blessing of the flowers on "Lady's Day"; or the uniquely Polish and poignant *Gorzkie Zale* (Bitter Lamentations) during the Lenten devotions; as well as the chanting of the "small hours" of Our Lady's Office before the Sunday High Mass—are gone also.

A parochial school system was developed largely within the Polish Roman Catholic parishes. Although the schools were originally designed to maintain and enrich the Polish culture, eventually there was a shift from a Polish emphasis to a curriculum resembling that of the public schools. As an example, in Detroit, with its estimated 200,000 to 350,000 first, second, and third generation residents of Polish descent, the Polish language is practically non-existent in the Catholic schools. St. Hyacinth School valiantly attempts to preserve the Polish language under the courageous direction of its pastor, Father Francis Skalski, as well as one of its dynamic young teachers, Michael Krolewski, who also organized the Galicja Song and Dance Ensemble as well as the Adam Mickiewicz Library. Michael Krolewski was formerly with St. Ladislaus School before the principal determined to de-emphasize Polish culture there. Even the Felician Order has lost its *raison d'etre* when they abdicated the fundamentals upon which the order was originally established.

> A few years ago it was possible to study the Polish language in virtually every one of the area's forty Polish parochial schools. Now language instruction is limited to Wayne State University, the Polish SS Cyril and Methodius Seminary at Orchard Lake and small classes

---

[2] Michael Sabiers, "Ethnicity is no joke. Polish Hope to Polish Image," *National Catholic Register*, (October 2, 1970), p. 5.

conducted by the organizations. This is one of the many indications of how the younger generation of Polish-Americans is being absorbed into the general life of the city.³

For many years Sister Hedwig taught all first grade subjects in two languages: English and Polish, at St. Francis of Assisi School, in Detroit.

> Every parent in the old days wanted his children to know Polish thoroughly. That is not true today, but except for a few children in the class. I still teach them a smattering, just enough to be able to read and write simple Polish words.⁴

There are significant differences in the degree to which Polish-American parochial schools are really "Polish." The Polzin study revealed evidence of the decline in the number of Polish language and history lessons taught.

> In 13.5 percent (of Polish parochial schools, in 1971) Polish reading was taught; in 20.4 percent Polish history and/or culture; and in 4.1 percent religious instruction was offered in the Polish language . . . from these data the decline in teaching of the Polish language (and culture) by the parochial school was therefore evident.⁵

The younger clergy, trained in diocesan seminaries, are becoming increasingly less proficient in the use of Polish. Furthermore, the content of these programs has lapsed considerably. There is little original material prepared for the Polish program. Also, unfortunately, many young Polish priests of Polish extraction view their cultural inheritance in respect to their religious ritual and vocation as a handicap which would destine them to minor roles in the American Catholic Church.⁶

---

³ James K. Anderson, "A Polonia in Transition," *Detroit News*, (September 15, 1957), p. 8a.
⁴ Harold Schachern, "Pupils Wiser, Less Ruly—Nun Compares Today's Crop of Children," *Detroit News*, (June 13, 1959), p. 14.
⁵ Theresita Polzin, *The Polish-Americans; Whence and Whither*, (Pulaski: 1973), pp. 148-149.
⁶ Father Gilbert L. Sheldon recently was consecrated auxiliary bishop of Cleveland, Ohio. He is the son of Ignatius and Mary Solinski. Recently Father Edwin R. Chess, who joined the armed forces as a chaplain, in 1942, was promoted to Brigadier General. His surname was Czeslowski. It is interesting to contemplate if Bishop Sheldon (Solinski) and Father Chess (Czeslowski) would have been singled out for promotion if they would have retained their Polish surnames. After consecration,

A total of 1,930 Polish Catholic missionaries, men and women, are serving in Africa, Latin America, Oceania, and Asia, according to Catholic Church officials in Warsaw, Poland.[7] When one considers the number of Polish parishes, schools, seminaries, convents, colleges, universities and hospitals founded or re-built throughout the United States, Poland and elsewhere in the world, the wealth of the Vatican has grown fantastically without adequate representation from the ranks of its Polish faithful. How would its history have been written if all of this real estate had never come to pass, or was withdrawn through a major schism? The Vatican has never seriously considered its blatant disloyalty to its Polish faithful either in Poland, the United States or anywhere else in the world. In fact, it's a wonder that not one Pole, throughout its long history, was elected to the papacy. It is also ironic that none of the nations ruled by the former Holy Roman Emperor (primarily Austria and Germany) are predominantly Catholic today. The percent of Catholics in Poland is much greater than in Italy (perhaps the most Catholic nation in the world), who have been taken for granted, their appeals dismissed and disregarded in order to continually weld their corrupting political power. The Vatican never considered how many millions of religious have dedicated their lives to a bare existence in the name of the Church to proselyte the faith that brought them no rewards or consideration in the end. The attitude of the Church has been disgraceful, not merely discriminating, but prejudicial and wholly underesrving of such support, or martyrdom throughout the centuries.

Even after the success of the Polish National Catholic Church, the Vatican refused to change its method of choosing the American episcopate, thereby approving the Irish influence in the church, who stressed early Americanization and assimilation.

Bishop Sheldon had chosen a coat of arms of red and white to commemorate his Polish heritage—a feeble attempt to compensate for altering his name.

According to Stanly Krajewski, Monsignor Wincenty Borkowicz was not promoted to bishop because of his attachment to Polish culture and civilization. S. Krajewski, "Pral. Borkowicz pasterzuje 35 lat na 'Stanislawowie,'" *Dziennik Polski*, (March 11, 1971), p. 6.

[7] "Polish Missionaries Number 1,930," *The Catholics News*, (August 26, 1976), p. 2.

Several lay and clerical congresses—sponsored by Polish-Americans—failed to improve the position of the Polish-American clergy in the American Roman Catholic hierarchy. The Catholic Church—in the appointment of Catholic bishops in the United States and its administration of the Polish-American parishes and schools—is guilty of gross discrimination. Today, the lack of representation of the Polish-Americans in the American hierarchy is one of the major complaints. Tokenism and discrimination are explicitly evident.

John Cardinal Krol, the present Archbishop of Philadelphia, was the first American of Polish ancestry elected to the College of Cardinals, in 1967, by Pope Paul VI. His fellow Bishops in the United States recognized his ability and appreciated his competency, and sense of leadership, when they elected him as the president of the National Conference of Catholic Bishops, in Washington D.C., on November 18, 1971. The reaction of the Detroit priest organization to his election was distasteful and biased.[8] Father William Keveney—associate pastor of Roseville's Sacred Heart Parish and president of the Detroit Priests' Senate—muttered feelings of disgust and said: "You should have sent a black-edged telegram.[9] In a voice which indicated disappointment before their sentences could be finished, Father Keveney explained that the Detroit Priests' Senate had submitted a list of acceptable candidates to the NCCB prior to the election. "It was a complete disregard of the recommendations of many Priests' Senates," said Fr. Jerome Fraser. "Krol was not on the list of many, if any at all."[10]

Monsignor Vincent V. Borkowicz was the only priest of Polish descent to comment on the bigotry of the Detroit Priests' Senate.

> The good Fathers are unnecessarily alarmed—and certainly poor losers and certainly poor sportsmen. You accept the defeat and congratulate the victor. Why don't you be men like you claim you are—

---

[8] Brian McNaught, "Detroit Reaction to Krol's Presidency: Disappointment," *The Michigan Catholic*, (November 24, 1971), p. 1.
[9] *Ibid.*, p. 1.
[10] *Ibid.*, p. 1.

the stalwart defenders of the right. What are your fears? Cardinal Dearden left a heritage of unfinished business. No chairman can discard or set aside *vox populi*.[11]

In making observations of the American Catholic hierarchy, many of the American clergy of Polish descent have become models of the religious vocation. They are committed to their calling.

James Michalski would not give up his chance to become a Jesuit priest for half a million dollars.

When Michalski takes his vow Thursday, in Milwaukee, Wisconsin, he will be giving up a family estate totaling almost that amount. His father Leon G. Michalski, who died in 1968, offered James the money in his will if he would leave the religious life.

"What's so surprising?" asked Michalski. "I don't see life in terms of money. I'm really very happy. I feel I can bring more love into the world in what I'm doing."[12]

Unfortunately, because of the hierarchial pressures, the Polish-American clergy has conformed. They don't wish to make waves. They are diligent and persevering. They have aspirations, but know that they cannot hope for great advancement—most of them remain local parish priests. They have become quite docile after a few sporadic attempts at self-assertion which were eventually quashed.[13] It is unusual to see any Polish-American priest initiate a project or organization for the dissemination or preservation of Polish culture in America. When this is attempted, he is aware that he incurs the wrath of his local bishop or cardinal.[14]

---

[11] Msgr. Vincent V. Borkowicz, "Cardinal Krol Qualified," *The Michigan Catholic*, (December 8, 1971), p. 4.
[12] "He Spurns $500,000," *Detroit Free Press*, (June 6, 1972), p. 8-D.
[13] The healthiest means of re-awakening a conscience in the Vatican towards its Polish faithful would be a second revival of the Polish National Catholic Church, or adopt the sect of Mariawici (a cloistered order of married priests and nuns who blatantly oppose celibacy on moral grounds as the cause of degeneracy in the church). The sect was spurned by the Church, but eventually its dogmas will be accepted by the Vatican, which has blatantly refused to make any concessions or modifications at self-improvement during its crises. None of the Protestant schism would have come to pass if the Vatican evils were corrected.
[14] Father Skalski, at St. Hyacinth Parish, in Detroit, valiantly attempts to keep the Polish language alive in the school, and Polish culture through exhibits, and a variety of cultural programs. There is no self-effacement here as far as his Polish heritage is concerned.

Catholic priests of Polish origin have never been blind to their minority status. Nevertheless, they did not react strongly to the intimation that eventually Polish parishes would be swallowed up, abolished, and replaced by territorial parishes. So sensitive has this issue remained among Polish-Americans that a report in April 1967, emanating from the National Conference of Catholic Bishops, disturbed many. It concerned a vote to request that the Holy See authorize the National Conference of Bishops to abolish national parishes. Charles Rozmarek, president of the Polish-American Congress in a petition sent by registered mail, in August 1967, to Pope Paul VI made the following observations:

> "In the past, this attitude of forced assimilation resulted in a schism among Polish Catholics here, through establishment of the 'Independent Polish National Church.' As dismaying as it is, this sad fact can be understood in the light of the previous study of the Polish national character, since for Poles the Church and the parish are both their religious and national home. And if the Church built by their sacrifice is threatened with 'expropriation' by the Church Authority, the tension resulting from this kind of injustice may prove to be too strong and lead to the breaking point."[15]

No commentator, on the American scene, has given adequate attention to this viewpoint of Polish-Americans. The problem, however, was extensively considered in the Polish-American press.[16]

In 1915, pastors of most of the Polish-language parishes, in Connecticut, formed a group to be known as the *Zjednoczenie Polskich Kaplanow* (Union of Polish Priests). The formation of the organization gave them a stronger vehicle to show concern over mutual parochial problems and over extra-parochial matters. They worked together to help newly arrived immigrants; they sparked efforts to bring aid to relatives of their parishioners in Polish territories; and they united efforts in contributing to the

---

[15] Reverend Theophil T. Mierzwinski, *The Association of Polish Priests in Connecticut: an interpretative history.* (Bloomfield: 1971), p. 26.

[16] "Prawo Do Zycia Parafii Polskich," *Dziennik Polski*, (May 3, 1967), p. 4. "O Co Biskupi Poprosili Rzym w Sprawie Parafii Ethnicznych?" *Dziennik Polski*, (June 13, 1967), p. 6. Ks. K. L. "Rzut Oka Na Likwidacje Duszpasterstwa Polskiego w USA," *Dziennik Polski*, (August 11, 1967), p. 6. *Dziennik Polski*, (August 14, 1967), p. 6.

support of the newly established independent Polish nation, in 1919. Additionally, they were interested in the welfare of Polish people who had settled in large groups in localities of the State where no Polish-language parish was available. They recommended that Church authorities establish new Polish-language parishes—frequently with the warning that failure to do so would result in the formation of schismatic parishes affiliated with the Polish National Catholic Church.[17]

During and after the First World War, George Cardinal Mundelein, Chicago's strong-willed bishop—little interested in Polish-Americans, and hostile to ethnic parishes in general—so irritated Chicago's Polish-American priests that, in 1917, they organized the Polish Clergy Association. Under Reverend Louis Grudzinski of St. John of God Parish, this association pushed for a greater consideration of Polish Catholic interests and an improvement or better rapport with the diocese.[18]

As late as 1953, the Polish-American clergy, in Detroit, saw no need to organize on an ethnic basis. It was Edward Cardinal Mooney, who personally suggested that the Polish-American clergy organize themselves into the Conference of Priests for Polish Affairs in order to work more effectively for their ethnic objectives in the Archdiocese of Detroit.[19]

By adopting the "melting pot" theory, the Polish-American clergy has not endeared themselves to many Polish-Americans for they have not exemplified any inspiring leadership.[20] Being too docile, and humble, they let clergymen of other ethnic backgrounds assume important posts of leadership by default or inheritance. They also allow other ethnic clergy to dictate policies which are not acceptable to the Polish faithful, even when it is abusive to them: the closing of Polish-American schools, the refusal of the diocese to repair the old historic parishes now abandoned to Black neighborhoods. To the Polish-Americans it is

---

[17] Mierzwinski, op. cit., p. 11.
[18] Edward R. Kantowicz, Polish-American Politics in Chicago 1888-1940, (Chicago: 1975), p. 174.
[19] Rev. Joseph Swastek, St. Albertus Centennial (1872-1973), (Detroit: n.d.), p. 197.
[20] Dr. Joseph A. Wytrwal, "Contemporary Polish American Clergy," Polish Daily News, English Edition, (December 28, 1974), p. 4.

unforgiveable that they had callously missed their ethnicity to thwart the aspirations of the Polish-American community. Polonia has pronounced them guilty of willingly becoming the "Polish Uncle Toms" of the Wasps and the Catholic (Irish dominated) establishment in their drive to implement Wasp values and the "melting pot" theory.[21] Edward Gorczyca states this frankly:

> As I go to my Polish church, I see statues and pictures of Polish kings as saints, Polish queens, Polish bishops, etc. Nowhere do I see a Polish housewife, coal miner or factory worker as a saint.
> Can you picture one of the above rulers interceding for a peasant whom he kept in slavery while he ruled? You may ask why our Polish parents were and kept in ignorance and poverty by their political, religious and business leaders. I don't know. Maybe it's a Polish tradition.
> May I suggest that at the next "Pulaski Day" parade, as you walk down Woodward toward the Detroit River, all you Polish leaders walk at least one block ahead of the throng and keep your heads high (as you usually do). Don't stop on Jefferson, just keep walking. The rest of you Polish peasants, I suggest you turn off on Jefferson.
> I take my hat off to the leaders of the black people. They have made more progress for their people in the last ten years than ours have since the creation of Poland.[22]

There are some Polish-American priests and nuns who are becoming confused, paralyzed and sometimes bitter because of this new turn of events in the Church. To Gorczyca's charges, one leader of the Polish-American clergy, a monsignor, summed up the basic tenet of the silent and ill-read and informed Polish-American clergy: "We don't believe we have enough information to know whether policies are right or wrong. We leave it to Cardinal Dearden." The Polish-American clergy concluded that the Polish-Americans have come a long way, and that "as patriotic Americans" it was time they stopped singing the blues and realized just how bright the future can be. These apologetic sentiments often are accompanied by a photograph of Cardinal Krol, or recently, by a photograph of Monsignor Edmund C. Szoka, who was appointed bishop of Gaylord. With a popula-

---

[21] Jan Siemienski in a letter made the following observation: ". . . Ale nasi religijni liderzy nie byli odważni i zdolni podolac zadaniu do jakiego byli powolani." Jan Sieminski, "Kogo Winic?" *Dziennik Polski*, (January 10, 1973), p. 3.
[22] Edward Gorczyca, "Questions Polish Tradition," *The Michigan Catholic*, (December 20, 1972), p. 4.

tion of 2,500 Gaylord is the smallest city in the United States to be the seat for a Catholic diocese.

Under Cardinal Dearden's leadership and administration the Polish-Americans received no recognition in the administration of the archdiocese. Bishop Thomas Gumbleton, who became Auxiliary Bishop of Detroit, in 1968, told Farley Clinton that forty per cent of the Catholics in the Archdiocese of Detroit have Polish names. "So I would suppose they are Polish, or at least a half or a quarter Polish," Gumbleton said.[23] In response to Bishop Gumbleton's observation Farley Clinton made the following observation:

> "How very strange that there is no Polish bishop in Detroit. Why would that be? Are forty percent of the priests here Polish?" "Oh, yes, I think the priests reflect the general composition of the Catholics," said Bishop Gumbleton. "Well, wouldn't it be natural, if half the people and the priests are Polish, to have at least a single Polish Bishop in the Archdiocese?" Bishop Gumbleton said it would be very natural. He coughed and said it might very well happen, sooner or later. I should think he would find it more democratic.[24]

Polish-Americans have been requesting a bishop to represent them since Bishop Zaleski left Detroit, in 1964, to become the Bishop of Lansing. Many individuals expressed their feelings in letters to the editor.

> Add my voice to that of E. T. K. who advises all Americans of Polish extraction to write to John Dearden and ask him to name a priest of Polish descent to be an Auxiliary in the Archdiocese.
> No ethnic group in the Archdiocese has done more for the Church than have the Poles and their sons and daughters. The number of churches, schools are evident proofs. So are the numbers of priests who served, serve and are to serve the Church and God here.
> And yet we do not have a Polish speaking Auxiliary! Now is the time to write, write and write to Cardinal Dearden and let him know what our desires are. Letter writing should be a "must" from all Polish-American organizations. The *Polish Daily* should have editorials as reminders. I am sending E. T. K.'s letter to the Cardinal. Who will join me?—J. W.[25]

---

[23] Farley Clinton, "Notes on a Schism in Michigan," *The Wanderer*, (October 12, 1972), pp. 1 and 7.
[24] *Ibid.*, pp. 1 and 7.
[25] *Dziennik Polski*, (June 27, 1969), p. 2.

P. Romski, in a letter to the *Michigan Catholic* editor voiced the same sentiment.

> It is interesting and amusing to read letters from people like Frederick MacNab who accuse Cardinal Krol of Philadelphia of being a racist.
> If Mr. MacNab is really interested in stopping racism why isn't he doing something about the racism in the Catholic Church in America against Polish-American Catholics?
> Polish-Americans in this country represent 25 percent of all the Catholics in America. Of the approximately 300 Catholic bishops in this country only a small handful are Poles. If we are represented by a fair ratio we would have 75 bishops of Polish descent.
> Frankly, friends and others we are tired of being treated as second class Catholics. We are tired of it! We are tired of it! We are tired of it![26]

When the Central Citizens' Committee petitioned Cardinal Dearden for representation in the administration of the archdiocese, he replied (in a letter dated March 28, 1967) that it is the Pope who nominates bishops under the inspiration of the Holy Ghost.[27] And for the next six years, the Cardinal was completely indifferent to the demands and needs of the Polish-American community—the largest ethnic group in the Archdiocese of Detroit.

> Yesterday Cardinal Dearden, who currently answers questions of Catholics on four weekly television shows, told vicars of the archdiocese that one of the most frequently asked questions is "When is a Polish bishop going to be named?"[28]

Kazimierz Olejarczyk proved without doubt the diminishing role of the Polish-American clergy in the Archdiocese of Detroit. In a letter to *Dziennik Polski,* he shared the following facts:

> I checked three Catholic Directories of 1949 (under Cardinal Mooney) of 1963 (4 years after the appointment of Archbishop Dearden) and the just published 1967 directory. I counted the names

---

[26] P. Romski, "Church Unfair to Poles," *Michigan Catholic,* (April 27, 1970), p. 6.

[27] Adam Robakowski, "Przypomnienie faktow," *Dziennik Polski,* (September 16, 1970), p. 6.

[28] Nancy Manser, "Archdiocese now has 4 auxiliaries. New Bishops called moderates," *The Detroit News,* (February 21, 1973), p. 23a.

of Polish-Americans appearing in the listing of the Archdiocesan Officials and Bureaus in relation to all such names.

In 1949, among the 122 names, 32 were of Polish-Americans, including one auxiliary bishop and the vice-chancellor. In 1963 out of 136 names, 22 were Polish-Americans including one auxiliary bishop. In 1967, out of 142 names, 21 are Polish and no auxiliary bishop or member of the closest staff of the Archbishop.

Thus it can not be denied that under Archbishop Dearden the importance of Polish-American clergy decreased both numerically (close to half of 1949) and in quality.

I also took a count of the number of prelates and monsignors in those years. The number of Polish-American monsignors stayed about the same: eight in 1949, eight in 1963 and eight active and one retired in 1967, while the total number of clergy thus honored climbed from 37 in 1949 to 70 in 1963 and to 85 in 1957.

Here again, the percentage of Polish-Americans decreased from 21.6 in 1949 to 11.4 in 1963 and to 10.5 in 1967.[29]

On May 2, 1967, Kazimierz Olejarczyk made the following comment.

> The pious platitude about the appointment of Bishops being an exclusive domain of the Holy Father belies paragraph 23 about the pastoral role of Bishops in Vatican II Constitution of the Church. It smacks rather of the pre-Council attitudes of the hierarchy. "Yours it is only to pray, to obey, and to pay."[30]

Six years later, Olejarczyk, as president of the Polish-American Congress, made the following observation: "There is absolutely no recognition except in collections. We are to pay. We are to feel guilty. And that's all."[31] To Olejarczyk, Cardinal Dearden's administration is an "Irish establishment in an anti-ethnic power structure."[32]

Casimer Kania in a letter to the *Detroit News* prepared the following resume of Cardinal Dearden's twelve year administration as Archbishop of Detroit:

---

[29] Kazimierz Olejarczyk, "Writer Aims to Prove Diminishing Role of Pol-Am Clergy in Archdiocese Here," *Dziennik Polski*, (September 27, 1967), p. 2.
[30] "Layman Adds Voice to Discussion on Appointment of Aux. Bishop Here," *Dziennik Polski*, (May 2, 1967), p. .
[31] Marco Trbovich, "Angry Poles Say Liberalized Church Ignored Ethnics," *Detroit Free Press*, (March 8, 1973), p. 11a.
[32] *Ibid.*, p. 11A.

Deficit spending leading to the brink of bankruptcy of the archdiocese. Threatened mass closings of the parochial schools. Polarization of black and white Catholics. Polarization of young and old clergy. Scandalous defections of clergy and religious.

Forced retirement of an internationally renowned pastor who put Royal Oak on the world map. Planned forced retirement of five eminently distinguished Polish-American pastors beloved by the over 600,000 Polish-American Catholics of the archdiocese who have served the church faithfully and loyally despite no representation in the diocesan hierarchy.

What's next on the cardinal's agenda? God help his successor—if there will be any need for one, except to preside over the administering of the last rites for the Catholic Church in Detroit.[33]

John Kudniewski made this observation:

If anyone is looking for those Catholics that have left the Church during the past year they don't have to look any further than to the Polish community in this country.

The 13 million Polish community in this country is (or rather was) 90 percent Catholic.

They just simply got tired of being treated as 2nd class Catholics.[34]

David Rambeau, black administrator of St. Theresa's Catholic School, also feels that Cardinal Dearden has not given enough "recognition to ethnic diversity" in the Detroit archdiocese.[35] Cardinal Dearden (and many other bishops with large Polish-American populations) do not send students to be educated and ordained at the only Polish seminary at Orchard Lake, Michigan, founded under Pope Leo XIII explicitly for that purpose. Three Detroit Monsignori: Maksimik, Szymanowski and Jasinski—have been forbidden by Cardinal Dearden from using their titles in Detroit. Cardinal Dearden—despite pressures from suburban parishes—demands that suburban parishes contribute to supporting Catholic inner-city schools, largely black and often attended by non-Catholics.[36]

---

[33] "Dearden's reign gets criticized," *Detroit News*, (April 1, 1971), p. 12-B.

[34] John Kudniewski, "Not Trying Harder," *Michigan Catholic*, (June 4, 1970), p. 5.

[35] Nancy Manser, "A look at the Dearden era in Detroit," *The Detroit News*, (May 19, 1973), p. 9-A.

[36] Thomas C. Fox, "Cardinal Dearden an Enigma to Many," *Detroit Free Press*, (October 6, 1975), p. 14-A.

In 1967, the Catholic Directory of the Archdiocese of Detroit listed only two parishes as Polish: Immaculate Conception and Assumption. The Directory also failed to list, among its organizations, the Priests' Conference for Polish Affairs. The *People's Mass Book* (new edition of the *People's Hymnal*) was published by the Archdiocese, in 1964, and used in the English language parishes and Masses. Among the 115 songs and hymns included in the hymnal over 30 were English or Anglo-Saxon, close to 40 German, over 20 in Latin, and a few Dutch, Bohemian, French and Flemish. There was not one Polish song translated into English, even though the Polish musical church literature is voluminous with notable examples for every occasion, even many not practiced here.

Nowhere is it being acknowledged that the Americans of Polish descent represent a thousand-year-old Catholic culture. The cultural values not only have been overlooked, but at times impugned. Instead, there has been an overriding concern for assimilation, and at best, a compromise with retaining ethnic parishes.

Some order of nuns (especially the Felician Order in Michigan) has been brainwashed with the "melting pot" theory, which they accepted with enthusiasm. The Felicians are not permitted any longer, by the Catholic Church, to maintain the tradition of accepting novitiates exclusively from among the Poles, Americans of Polish or Slavic ancestry. In responding to the most generous ideals of service and sacrifice, they moved away from the Polish-American communities. Mother Monica Sybilska, the founder of the American order, is reported once to have said to a young nun, "Sister, remember it was for the Polish language that I crossed the ocean."[37]

The demands of the church policy on universalism and its impact of *aggiornimento* turned out to be a very effective device for Americanization. Eager bishops attempt to regain Christian unity among all members in their diocese. To attain this objective, they break up ethnic boundaries. Thus, they insist upon the

---

[37] Artur Gorski, *Angela Truszkowska*, (Poznan: 1959), p. 375. See also Thaddeus C. Radzialkowski, "Reflections on the History of the Felicians in America," *Polish American Studies*, (Spring, 1975).

fullness of catholicity by assigning sisterhoods (among them the Felician Sisters) to evangelize in newly organized and obviously non-Polish schools. The Felicians are not only happy, but eager, to oblige. The whole premise for their establishment as a religious order has been invalidated.

There is a conspiracy of silence, at the *Michigan Catholic,* the church's weekly newspaper, when issues and events are raised regarding the Polish-American community. Cardinal Dearden with his urban cultural bag showed more concern for the Black and Latino minorities than for other ethnic groups.[38] When Black studies and Spanish-American studies were introduced to the parochial schools, the Polish-American Congress, as well as numerous individuals, requested the re-introduction of the Polish language instruction. The response was a form letter that thanked them for their interest in Spanish-American studies and assured them that their letters would be forwarded for consideration. The Polish-American community was deeply offended by what they considered this insensitive and bureaucratic response to their demands. Rev. Stanley F. Borucki commented, in his column in the *Polish Daily News,* on the decision of the Michigan Catholic Conference to introduce Spanish-American history in all grades of the more than 600 Catholic schools in Michigan. Rev. Borucki raised an important question: Why are the Spanish-Americans and Negroes favored, while the Polish-Americans and other ethnic groups are discriminated against? Arguing for the introduction of Polish-American studies in the Catholic schools, Rev. Borucki made the following observations:

> "The Poles have been in Michigan for more than a century and in the course of these 100 years at least 1 million Poles have lived and worked in this state. They have built three scores of parishes and also many schools. Presently, according to conservative figures, it is es-

---

[38] In 1968, the ADF allotted $1 million to Black and interracial inner-city projects, most of it going to inter-faith community projects, and in one case $20,000 for a revolving scholarship loan fund of the New Cavalry Baptist Church, 3975 Concord. It is interesting to note that not one scholarship for Polish-Americans has been established by Cardinal Dearden. The ADF, in 1970, allotted a large portion of the funds to "general needs of the Archdiocese, charities, or education for the disadvantaged in 21 inner-city schools." Again the Polish-American parochial schools received no aid or encouragement.

timated that there are 250,000 residents of Polish extraction in the Archdiocese of Detroit alone.

There are more Polish parishes in Michigan than of any other ethnic group. There are more priests of Polish extraction in our state than of any other national origin.

There is hardly a parochial school in this Archdiocese that does not have a number of children of Polish heritage. Often the names have been changed, but a study will show that one or both parents have Polish blood.

The Michigan Catholic Conference is willing to set up a program for 600 schools in which will be taught the Spanish American culture admitting that there are some 5,000 youngsters of Spanish origin.

We are sure that a survey will show that there are 50,000 youngsters of Polish extraction in those same schools. If 5,000 can have a program, can we logically deny a similar program for 50,000?"[39]

Eventually pressure began to be applied. On Sunday, May 3, 1970, the Polish American Congress, Michigan Division—a strong, unified voice for Americans of Polish descent—distributed 20,000 leaflets protesting ethnic discrimination when allocating Archdiocesan Development Funds, and encouraged Polish-Americans to boycott it. This is Cardinal Dearden's chief source of fund-raising revenues.[40] They urged Polish-Americans to donate to Polish-American organizations and institutions instead primarily to be earmarked for the Polish seminary at Orchard Lake, Michigan. Directed to the largely Polish-American parishes, the distribution coincided with the opening of the Archdiocesan-wide ADF campaign. Addressed to Catholics of Polish ancestry, the text of the letter read:

> The Polish American Congress has always maintained that when the rights of any group are threatened by discrimination, the rights of all are endangered. Since the beginning of the ADF, the Polish ethnic community has contributed generously their time, their effort, and their monetary resources to the success of the annual drive of the Archdiocesan Development Fund.
>
> Because ethnic discrimination existed and exists in the distribution and allocation of Archdiocesan Funds, the Polish American Con-

---

[39] "Pol-Ams Discriminated in History Courses. Father Borucki Reveals in P.A.J.," *Gwiazda Polarna*, (July 12, 1969), p. 5.

[40] The Polish American Congress is generally regarded as a major spokesman for Polish-Americans in the United States. Headquartered in Chicago (on the national as well as the local scene), it receives delegates from almost all Polish-American organizations, large or small. The Michigan Division of the Polish American Congress represents 54 Polish organizations, plus 16 Polish Roman Catholic parishes, and three parishes of the Protestant Polish National Catholic Church.

gress of the State of Michigan cannot endorse the present ADF campaign.[41]

Judge Don Binkowski of the 37th District Court at the Polish Constitution Day observance, on May 3, 1970, held at Belle Isle, charged that "prejudice exists in the American Catholic hierarchy, adding that . . . the hierarchy has betrayed the loyalty of the immigrants by destroying their heritage through processes of forced assimilation.[42] Judge Binkowski urged the large assembly and all Polish-Americans in the Detroit Archdiocese to contribute to the Polish Seminary at Orchard Lake, in lieu of the Archdiocesan contribution which was due Sunday. "Join me in making your check payable to Orchard Lake College because it is the only Polish seminary in the United States which supports Polish studies, culture and liturgical and historical associations."[43]

The appeal from the Polish-American Congress, Michigan Division, brought a backlash from Catholics (Polish and non-Polish) who simply stopped contributing to the annual drive. The archdiocese lost millions of dollars.[44]

A year later, Kazimierz Olejarczyk, president of the Michigan Division of the Polish-American Congress, wrote to Cardinal Dearden requesting a list of Polish-American organizations which have benefited from the ADF. When the information was not received, Olejarczyk announced that for the second successive year the Michigan Division of the Polish American Congress is not able to endorse the 1971 Roman Catholic Archdiocesan Fund Raising Drive. The reasons for the boycott were enumerated:

> In view of the existing discrimination in the allocation of archdiocesan funds, particularly towards the Polish Catholics who comprise one third of all the faithful.
> Ethnic discrimination continues to be an established fact in the operation of the ADF.

---

[41] "Polish Congress Seeking New Goals for ADF Drive," *The Michigan Catholic*, (May 7, 1970), p. 2.
[42] Mitch Kehetian, "Polish Anti-Defamation League Sought," *The Macomb Daily*, (May 4, 1970), p. 4.
[43] *Ibid.*, p. 4.
[44] Thomas C. Fox, "Cardinal Dearden an Enigma to Many," *Detroit Free Press*, (October 6, 1975), p. 14-A.

The PAC was not invited to participate in the planning of this year's ADF program as promised.⁴⁵

The published statement was similar in tone to the boycott leaflet of the previous year.⁴⁶ Within a week Olejarczyk was contacted by a representative of the archdiocese and asked to discuss the matter. Not long afterward Olejarczyk was appointed to a vacancy on the Michigan Catholic Conference.

Discrimination was not terminated. Five years later Olejarczyk made the following observations:

> Why are we (of the Polish background) left out from participating in important decision-making conferences in this Archdiocese?
> It was five years ago when a delegation of the Polish-American laity presented Bishop Gumbleton, as vicar-general, with serious concerns from our community. Among them was a demand for "a rightful representation of ethnic groups in Archdiocesan offices and positions, particularly from the Polish community which comprises one third of all the faithful."
> A few days later, in a statement concerning the ADF, the Polish American Congress pointed out that we, of the Polish laity, were not invited to participate in planning the annual ADF campaigns. To this day, it is still a fact.
> I understand that each parish has now a definite quota for ADF, which it has to make up from general parish funds if voluntary contributions fall short of the set goal.
> This is indeed taxation without representation. In this bicentennial year I ask you, in all liberty and justice, how more un-American, in this respect, can our Archdiocesan administration become?⁴⁷

---

⁴⁵ "PAC Boycott Diocesan Fund," *Gwiazda Polarna*, (June 19, 1971), p. 5.

⁴⁶ Members of the Polish-American community applauded with enthusiasm the position of the Polish American Congress, Michigan Division. Tomasz Ubik, member of the Central Citizens Committee, stated: "Dzis nalezy nam wszystkim, przyklasnac tej akcji." (Today we can applaud ourselves for this action.) He further stated: "Tylko ludzie swieccy z komitetu wyznaniowego Kongresu i Centralnego Komitetu, beda mowic za Polonie, a nie zaden ksiadz." (Only lay people from the committee appointed and the Central Committee of the PAC will speak for Polonia and not any priest.) "Oswiadczenie przez. Komit. Wyznaniowego KPA i CKO," *Dziennik Polski*, (May 19, 1970), p. 5. "Od Wladz Koscielnych — Domagac sie, a nie ustepowac — sprawozdanie T. Ubika," *Dziennik Polski*, (March 12, 1970), p. 3. See also "Postawa Wydz. Stan. Kongr. Polonii w sprawie ADF," *Dziennik Polski*, (May 19, 1970), p. 3. "Na Obchodzie 3 Maja — Silne Tony przemowien Nedziego i Binkowskiego," *Dziennik Polski*, (May 4, 1970), p. 1.

⁴⁷ "Empty-handed?" *Michigan Catholic*, (July 7, 1976), p. 4.

Today the objectives of the ADF are achieved through compulsion, not with sincerity and conviction. Dissatisfaction with Cardinal Dearden's administration also continues.

> Furthermore I say that if Cardinal Dearden is going to continue to ignore the needs of Polonia while continuing to tacitly support those who would degrade her, and if he is going to continue his raids on Polonia's treasuries while refusing to give her proper representation at the decision making levels of the church, then I say that it is time that Polonia began to seek his removal.[48]

Bishop Thomas J. Gumbleton, vicar representing the parishes of the archdiocese, now admits that there has been an insensitivity practiced in regards for the cultural values of the Poles during the last decade. "I would have to say, frankly, that I didn't have the sensitivity to their (the Poles) needs that I should have had," he said. "It's obvious that within the last few years we have failed to recognize that nationality was an important factor."[49]

Cardinal Dearden assumed the leadership of the archdiocese on January 29, 1959, replacing Edward Cardinal Mooney, under whom the Polish-American community enjoyed status, recognition and opportunity for leadership. Dearden was elevated to cardinal, in 1969; admired by some Catholics, he was despised by others. One priest says of him:

> He runs the archdiocese on a neither here nor there basis. It's like a guy drowning in water. They throw him enough rope to pull out his head, but not enough to take him out of the water.[50]

Other criticisms focus on two things: the cardinal's apparent reluctance to speak on issues which are considered important; and his view of authority, some regard as ignoring serious matters. To hold all the divergent views together in an archdiocese "requires a very strong person," said Bishop Gumbleton.[51]

---

[48] Alex Jendryka, "Cardinal Dearden?" *Post Eagle*, (November 10, 1976), p. 17.

[49] Marco Trbovich, "Angry Poles Say Liberalized Church Ignored Ethnics," *Detroit Free Press*, (March 8, 1973), p. 11a.

[50] Thomas C. Fox, "Cardinal Dearden an Enigma to Many," *Detroit Free Press*, (October 6, 1975), p. 14-A.

[51] Nancy Manser, "A look at the Dearden era in Detroit," *The Detroit News*, (May 19, 1973), p. 9-A.

Perhaps, more pertinent criteria would be fairness, and consideration for the faithful Cardinal Dearden represents and leads as a shepherd of the church—which should mean always to have a moral posture, and be without reproach. His image of self-piety is a true facade of hypocrisy. Eighteen years have elapsed since he took office. His prejudice towards Polish people has not changed. The toleration of his biased administration should be nearing an end. Many Polish-American leaders are considering a direct appeal to the Vatican for his ousting since he cannot appreciate what the Polish people have done for the Church, and if wishes to disenchant and lose thousands more by his ineptness. If Cardinal Dearden refuses to recognize the needs of this major ethnic group in Detroit, he is obviously in the wrong diocese. Perhaps removal to a rural community or forced retirement would serve the faithful better in the Detroit Archdiocese.

Discrimination of Polish-Americans, in the Catholic Church, is not confined only to Michigan. On June 1, 1974, a delegation of leaders from various Polish-American organizations, under the auspices of the Polish American Congress, met with Bishop Mugavero, of the Brooklyn Diocese, in order to discuss the relations between the Polish-American community and the Catholic Church.[52] The delegation raised the following points:

1. The status of immigrant priests from Poland. Many parishes with a large Polish congregation are staffed by clergy unfamiliar with the Polish language and culture. Others have priests of Polish extraction, but with a limited knowledge of the language and culture of Poland. At the same time, there are numerous priests from Poland, men of the highest caliber, who are denied incardination and kept outside the sphere of pastoral work. The use of such priests—tested in the fire of communist repression—could revitalize the Polish parishes spiritually, while, at the same time bringing into the churches many recent immigrants now kept away by the absence of a Polish language and atmosphere.

---

[52] The delegation—headed by Steve Markowski, vice-president of the Polish American Congress for downstate New York also included: Dr. Kleban, executive director of the Polish Institute of Arts and Sciences; Frank Gacek, president of the Polish and Slavic Center; Z. Konikowski, adjutant general of the Polish Veterans' Association; J. Mierzwa, representing the Konopnicka Educational Society; A. T. Jordan, writer and journalist; J. Panciewicz, editor of Polish Center Newsletter; and J. Dubicki, of the *Polish Dziennik*.

2. The use of the Polish language in parochial schools. The era of abandonment of ethnic identity is over. Bi-lingual instruction is promoted even in public schools, and there is no reason why Polish children should be denied a knowledge of the language of their parents, while receiving instruction in English. A Polish catechism should be published by the Brooklyn Diocese so that parents could assist their children in its study.

3. Assistance by the Catholic Charities for the needs of the Polish community, which has not been so far a beneficiary of grants by the Catholic Charities of the diocese, although the revenues are contributed by Polish as well as other parishioners.

4. Liaison between the Diocese and the Polish community. There has been, so far, little or no contact through the parishes. It would be highly desirable to have a senior member of the Chancery in charge of relations with the Polish community. Virtually all Poles are Catholics, consequently, organizations could be mutually beneficial. Had such liaison existed in the past, some of the problems mentioned above might have been solved earlier. The Catholic community is second to none in its dedication to the Catholic Faith, but it expects the Church to recognize and respect its ethnic identity, rather than ignore it in the interest of an obsolete "melting pot" concept.[53]

Recently, many Americans are beginning to recognize the danger of losing their ethnic identity. Dr. Lawrence J. McCaffery, chairman of the history department at Loyola University in Chicago, said "the loss of Irish identity might be a disaster not yet fully-recognized or appreciated."[54] In a speech to a meeting of the American Catholic Historical Association, Dr. McCaffery said that "in suburbia, the Irish exist as frustrated, confused, displaced persons who seem to have gone from Someplace to Noplace. . . ."[55] Perhaps, Dr. McCaffery speculated, many of the current problems in the Church can be traced to the fact that "for many people, when they cease to be ethnic, it may no longer be important for them to be Catholic."[56]

Delivering the keynote address of the 25th annual Diocesan Teachers' Convention in Worcester, Massachusetts, Monsignor

---

[53] "Polish Catholics Demand Fair Treatment," *Greenpoint Gazette and Advertiser*, (July 9, 1974), p. 1.
[54] "Warns U.S. Irish Losing Identity," *The Michigan Catholic*, (May 24, 1972), p. 5.
[55] *Ibid.*, p. 5.
[56] *Ibid.*, p. 5.

Geno C. Baroni, founder and president of the National Center of Urban Ethnic Affairs, in Washington, D.C., said:

> American society is guilty of cultural injustice toward the American Catholic. Our idea of a "melting pot" has been to melt away the distinct Catholic ethnic and cultural values that are part of us.
> It is time for us to educate Catholics to share our diverse traditions, to teach that it is legitimate in a pluralistic society, such as ours, to be both Catholic and American.
> This search for our identity, for a respect for pluralism, should lead us to question the image of the "melting pot" which has long dominated the rhetoric of educational and social philosophy. It is tolerable, if not openly desirable, for a nation to be united and diverse.
> We live, whether we accept it or not, in a global village where racial, cultural and ethnic traditions should not be snuffed out, but shared and developed.[57]

Monsignor Baroni also stated that ethnic diversity and pluralism in the church should help Catholics recognize and accept such diversity in the rest of American society.

Recently, in an address, in Chicago, Bishop Jean Jadot, the apostolic delegate to the United States, stated:

> There is a realization that there are important values in one's own racial and ethnic and cultural traditions, and in the traditions of others which should not be submerged or snuffed out, but rather cherished and preserved.[58]

Catholics—at the 41st International Eucharistic Congress held in August 1976—celebrated the wide variety of ethnic heritages which makes the U.S. Roman Catholic church, the church of immigrants. There were twenty-seven different ethnic liturgies delivered in their native tongues: Korean, Lithuanian, Polish, German, Italian, Gaelic, Croatian, Chinese besides a host of others. The tone of the Congress was set by Sergio Cardinal Pignedoli of the Vatican, who told worshippers at an Italian-American service that such gatherings were important so as to "not forget your origins and the traditions of your country."

---

[57] Richard Higgins, "Educators Told to Respect Cultural, Ethnic Differences," *The Michigan Catholic*, (October 1, 1975), p. 9.
[58] Richard Orley, "Immigrants made it America," *Catholic Universe Bulletin*, (September 26, 1975), p. 3.

Yet, the cardinal said, the services also represented "people who have decided to take part in fullest cooperation with a second country which unites you all." And he concluded: "This fact, to aspire to a great union between the most diverse peoples, is a fundamentally Christian idea."[59]

The Polish cultural ties in the Polish Catholic parishes had been deliberately eroded by the policies set by the local dioceses. Neither the priests or nuns of Polish descent are capable nor allowed to develop projects which would enable the third generation to develop a strong sense of identity to the community. Since the third generation must find positive strength and value in their Polish culture, which gives them identity, many have turned to cultural values and ethnic organizations which have helped them to define their place in American society. In this way, they have found it possible to sustain their Americanism and yet confirm the relationship which bound them to their forebears, whom they no longer wished to reject.

The Roman Catholic leaders, of the Polish-American community were very much impressed with the leadership of Bishop A. Slowakiewicz, former pastor of Our Savior of Golgotha Church in Dearborn Heighths, Michigan.[60] On March 18, 1971, more than 500 of the most prominent Polish-Americans attended a testimonial dinner in his honor.[61] He was elevated to the bishopric of the Polish National Catholic Church in 1962. He has been an advocate of the equal treatment of Poles as well as a leader in community affairs. In his address he admonished: "Our feelings as people should always take precedence over our membership in organizations."[62]

On rare occasions members of the Roman Catholic Clergy,

---

[59] "Catholics honor ethnic heritages," *The Sunday News,* (August 8, 1976), p. 6-A.

[60] The headquarters of the Polish National Catholic Church is in Scranton, Pennsylvania where in 1897 they broke away from the Catholic Church because Polish-American clergy were not given proportionate representation to their membership in the Church and not elevated to higher offices. The doctrine of papal infallibility and his primacy were successfully challenged. A new synod was formed where laymen outnumber the clergy to form the chief authority of the church.

[61] Arthur W. O'Shea, "Religious spirit forgotten. Poles will honor Bishop Slowakiewicz," *The Detroit News,* (March 18, 1971), p. 21-A.

[62] *Ibid.,* p. 21-A.

THE CATHOLIC CHURCH VS. POLONIA

among them even bishops, have addressed themselves to the moral and social issues of the day with courage. At a recent (October 1976) Polish-American Heritage Awards Dinner, in Chicago, where Jimmy Carter was the honored guest, Auxiliary Bishop Alfred L. Abramowicz stunned the assembled audience when he jibed Carter's pro-abortion sentiments. The occasion was a rare one at which to make a point—especially since the presidential candidate already assumed that the entire Polish vote from Chicago would be in support of him. It was a rude awakening. Perhaps if at more occasions Poles would express their honest feelings so articulately, the Polish-Americans would not be taken for granted.[63]

Not only are the clergymen, but all professional and successful Polish-Americans responsible for the negative Polish-American image—mostly by default. We hope for all others to understand the Polish-Americans, their aspirations, and appreciate their good works, so that the Polish-American future would be less fraught with indignity and prejudice. Polish-Americans hope that opportunities would come to them as freely as they do to the chosen Blacks, Latinos and Jews living in America with the same considerations with whom they daily exchange services and experience life together. Polish-Americans want the same assurances that any abuse of the Polish-Americans living in the United States would be dealt with summarily (such as anti-Polish jokes) as would any racial slur or implied anti-semitism. Polish-Americans should arrive at a level where their greater numbers should be recognized as a body of people with an ancient heritage that has respected others more than other nationalities have respected the Poles, despite the Polish sacrifice and service to them. It is not a time where Polish-Americans have to prove their worth; that has been achieved countless times on various levels of human contact and association: whether at war or peace.

It must be the apex of our evolution and understanding of world humanity to act assertively, even though this is so foreign to Polish nature and traditional behavior. The Polonia in the United States, as well as in other countries, must be better organ-

---

[63] Mike Royko, "Did the Bishop Start a Trend?" *Detroit Free Press* (October 17, 1976), p. 3-D.

ized and self-reliant, especially in this respect that Polish-Americans do not have to align themselves with institutions or religions that receive their loyalty, but take them for granted. Polish-Americans should act for their own self-approval, which requires the recognition naturally accorded it once it is comprehended that their support is desirable. Becoming independent and self-reliant of the church, unions, political parties, etc. can build a positive image in addition to the Polish enduring character. Others will then seek Polish-Americans out and their favors and Polish-Americans shall no longer suffer the humiliation, indignities, slights, lack of appreciation, injustices that so long has been meted out to them. It is not an advocation of isolation, but one which will reveal the strength and power that a noble people have borne through the ages.

CHAPTER 22

The Third Generation

The men of any generation are like dwarfs seated on the shoulders of giants. In developing knowledge men must collaborate with their ancestors. Otherwise they must begin, not where their ancestors arrived, but where their ancestors began.

—BERNARD OF CHARTRES

*One generation passeth away,
and another commeth;
And the earth abideth forever.*

—ECCL. 1:4

The United States is, by ideal and expressed definition, an open class society with equal opportunity for everyone to advance to that position to which his ability and effort entitle him. As a result, one central characteristic of American society is the phenomenon of upward mobility: of advancement through education, business success, and political power to social and economic positions higher than the one at which the person began. Opportunity, upward mobility, personal fulfillment, and advancement are considered measures of success in American culture. The interaction of the members of American society is constantly related to the effort of individuals to find their place in the range of positions available. As a result, the problem of identity and the problem of status, especially for the third generation, which no longer is a product of a foreign culture, is complicated by the relationship between ethnic identity and class identity.

The ethnic identity is based on generations or centuries in which a group has existed in a given geographical location which now constitutes its history, traditions and progress, or lack of it. An individual's relationship to earlier history gives historical identity, e.g. those who have been able to trace their genealogy to American Revolutionary War soldiers, or earlier ancestors from Europe, or other continents. Here, the individual feels he is somebody because he belongs somewhere and acquires the prestige accorded to that ethnic group. Until recently, immigrants were accepted on a quota system which did arbitrarily rate the immigrant's national origin, not his skills, education or character. Under ethnic identity, individuals are labeled and therefore, not recognized for their worth as individuals. This they must prove, and in most respects, the struggle for success is affected by the degree of acceptability of the ethnic group the individual is most identified with. Achievement is a personal matter, but does not indicate how much effort had to be expended in order to arrive at success.

In class identity, time, the span of years, generations, or centuries in which a group of prestigious families have existed forms its elite history, or progress economically and socially. In class identity an individual is a member of a social group in which achievement of any objective or the fulfillment of any function has been attained by distinguished predecessors and is recognized as an asset apart from what the individual attains independently. His identity in terms of class tends to depend on his birth, and rearing in a privileged environment. The class identity has developed its own standard of living, with a specific code of values and relationships within the group and outside of it. It takes on the characteristics of a culture of its own. In class identity the person is known, accepted, and esteemed as a member of a distinguished family of wealth and privilege. There is an aura of glamour and resplendence associated with the surname, for these prior family achievements. Class identity is aligned to the prominence of family dynasties, distinguished American families whose surnames are instantly recognizable as prestigious, notable, and associated with great wealth.

Poles—in most instances, outside of a few titled noblemen—did not receive the recognition or grace of class distinction. If they were successful, they were able to rise economically by means of a fine education or entering the political arena. The aspiration of many Polish parents was to have their children become lawyers, physicians and especially to have one son to be dedicated to the priesthood. The religious (whether priest or nun) received a certain reverence and high respect in the community. Economic status also has a significance in identifying people. Here, one's profession becomes an indicator to his earning as his style of living, the ability to entertain, to travel, the acquisition of prestige symbols: expensive home, cars, fine clothes—the visible measures of success.

At the middle economic level the member finds his identity in the experience of the immediate community whose function is psycho-social: providing for the individual the satisfaction of belonging to a group of fellow men, of being recognized and appreciated for himself. The group supports and perpetuates its own values, and exercises a spontaneous, informal social control over its members. At the middle economic level an American of Polish descent feels a closer identity with a middle-class American of German or other Slavic descent, than he feels with Polish-Americans from a lower economic class. Barring the factor of language, middle class people of various cultures share similar values and attitudes which are distinct from the ones they share with poor people of their own ethnic group.

The ethnic and class identity, including the economic level, does not always exhaust a person's social experience. In many cases, societal structures develop outside of the above-mentioned factors. There are political, religious and cultural groups: neighborhoods, school districts and divisions, educational and recreational clubs; all sharing various expressed interests in common. Each identity provides the potential for organized, planned and co-ordinated action.[1]

---

[1] Without organization, however, these categories would consist merely of loosely aligned collections of individuals who would choose an informal organizational strategy, that is, they would organize friends and neighbors, get them to write letters, and sign petitions. They would not act alone, that is, they can contact political leaders, writing them letters directly or writing to a newspaper. As such, they would be vulnerable to outside threats or incursions, and they would also be unable to intervene successfully in larger political affairs to influence policies that would benefit their interests.

To achieve their political, social, community or cultural goals, they need representation. It is necessary for like-minded individuals to organize in order to exert influence, to be heard, to obtain results, or to veto solutions. These various communal settings are responsible for the development of more or less permanent formal associations.

The ethnic groups have organized mutual aid societies, and improvement associations, as well as a local unit of a political party. The occupations organize trade unions, or business, or professional associations. There will be community clubs, neighborhood associations, conservation leagues, prohibition societies, and many others. Where there is a felt need, an "organizational weapon" for the defense of and pursuit of the groups' interest will be developed.

The various groups support parties and candidates, and between elections, they exert pressure to influence policies. Policy is regarded as an outcome, a compromise of the various demands coming from these organizations. In the course of negotiations between the contending organizations, compromises will be worked out so that every contender receives some benefit, and no candidate is left out. The net result is that the participants learn the processes and benefits of compromise. They learn, in short, the advantage of avoiding direct, open, and destructive conflict. A major consequence of the negotiations process is that conflict is moderated.

The fundamental axiom is the theory and practice of American pluralism: instead of a single center of sovereign power there must be multiple centers of power, none of which are or can be wholly sovereign. The constant negotiations among different centers of power will allow individuals and leaders to perfect the precious art of dealing peacefully with their conflict.

Multiple involvements and commitments provide another moderating influence. Most individuals will not be located in a single communal grouping. They will have, for example, a neighborhood linkage, a separate occupational involvement, and still another tie with an ethnic group. This means that individuals will feel the pressures or constraints of these alternative commitments, and also will be in a position to know and understand the significance of the resulting compromise. The multiple involvements then serve to educate people, and also lead them to check or restrain their own demands.

The life of the third generation of Polish-Americans is marked by a continuing process of acculturation and assimilation. Acculturation is concerned with the giving up of the ethnic culture in favor of main-stream American culture. It has proceeded at such a rapid pace that the majority of Polish-Americans have already adopted American ways of life by the second generation (the first native-born generation), reflecting ethnic customs, arts, dances, and music to ceremonial occasions, and even giving up many ethnic food habits and religious practices.[2]

Assimilation—which refers to social and other relationships with people of non-ethnic background—has also proceeded, but far more slowly, because people change their social structures and relationships more slowly than their cultures and attitudes. Now, assimilation is no longer the name-changing and rejection of origins necessary for mobility that was associated with the first and second generation, but it becomes a spontaneous and almost unconscious process of discovering that the people one finds compatible as neighbors, friends, and spouses do not necessarily have to come from one's own ethnic group.

Today, the dominant patterns and institutions of Polish-Americans have been established for over a century. What now remains to be explored is, what do Polish-Americans, now, do because they are Americans of Polish descent? What do they think, how do they respond to their religious traditions?

The search for community and identity among most Polish-Americans is a very practical undertaking. The genius of the Polish-American community is organization. To be an active American of Polish descent is to belong to an organization. To manifest Polish culture is to carry out, individually or collectively, the program of an organization. Of course, there is a perfectly good sense in which this claim is false; there are many less public and less formal individual manifestations of Polish culture. Nevertheless, the activity which overwhelmingly dominates the

---

[2] Joseph A. Wytrwal, *America's Polish Heritage. A Social History of the Poles in America*, (Detroit: 1961), pp. xv-xxii.

Polish-American life is organizational, and the ways in which Polish-Americans are Polish are the institutional ways of the fraternals, cultural clubs, and the Polish-American Congress, a national organization.

There is a steady erosion in the use of the Polish language: in the church (by intent), in the street, in the school, on the radio, and even in the home, as the Polish communities, or ghettoes, are disappearing. For reasons of mobility, the Polish language had eroded slowly among the Americans of Polish descent. Although, in 1960, a three-generation total of 2,184,936 persons claimed Polish as the mother tongue, the Polish language is an echo of the past, not the sound of the future. This statistic will remain so for some time, for as the older generation dies out, new immigrants arrive and fill the void. It is hard to really estimate the number of Poles there are in America. Because they become assimilated, that should not decrease their number. Blacks are considered Black even though they may be octoroons or even less, which is not discernable. It is true that racial differences are harder to erase.

The Polish-language content of the Polish radio programs has been reduced appreciably. At one time in the Detroit area, they broadcasted seven daily radio programs in the Polish language, over four stations. Today, only one station broadcasts in the Polish language. From 1910 to 1929, there were, in Detroit, five theaters where Polish plays were given exclusively. Today, the Polish theater is being kept alive by one organization, the "Polish Artists' Guild."[3] As a rule, the original local Polish theaters have been replaced by Polish musical revues, plays, films and folk dance companies directly from Poland. They are so popular that they are sold-out to capacity audiences.

In 1930, there were a total of 88 Polish publications, with 84 printed exclusively in the Polish language, two bi-lingual, and two in English; by 1960, this sum had dropped to a total of 43 publications: 37 in the Polish language, two bi-lingual, and four in English. In terms of circulation, in 1930 there were 1,037,000 Polish newspapers printed with 999,000 in the Polish language,

---

[3] "Polish Theater in Detroit," *Polish American Historical Association Bulletin*, Dr. Joseph A. Wytrwal, Editor, Bulletin No. 176, (March, 1959).

23,000 bi-lingual, and 15,000 in English. By 1960, the total had decreased to 717,000: 690,000 in the mother tongue, 9,000 bi-lingual, and 18,000 in English.[4]

At the beginning of the twentieth century, there were several all-Polish newspapers published in Detroit. Today, there is only one daily, the *Dziennik Polski* and a weekly, *Glos Ludowy*. *Dziennik Dla Wszystkich*—one of the largest Polish newspapers in the United States—was declared bankrupt on August 10, 1957. In recent years, it had a circulation of about 30,000. In 1971, the daily, *Dziennik Chicagoski,* and the weeklies, *Polish-American* and *Ameryka Echo,* ceased publication.[5] On June 10, 1972, Henry Dende, publisher of the finest Polish-American newspaper in the English language, announced that the *Polish American Journal* would become a monthly instead of continuing as a bi-weekly newspaper.[6] At present, Polish culture in the United States, is mainly relegated to what Polish-Americans do under the auspices of the Polish American Congress and other Polish cultural and fraternal organizations. The character of the Polish-American community is the program of its organizations. And it is this which directly leads to the identification of organizational tasks and responsibilities with "the Polish way of life." The organizations provide ideology which one may assume when he becomes a member of its program. One cannot join the Polish-American community in the United States; but one can join the Polish-American organizations, which function as a quasi-community.

Active Polish-American communal identification is no longer sneered at. It is part of the preferred pattern of Americans—in regard to leisure, consumption, status, class and living—to join ethnic organizations, and to be active in the community. Most of the conditions which have contributed to the widespread hostility toward Polish identification have disappeared. Polish cul-

---

[4] Neil C. Sandberg, *Ethnic Identity and Assimilation: The Polish-American Community. Case Study of Metropolitan Los Angeles,* (New York: 1974), p. 28.

[5] Jozef F. Bialasiewicz, "Dramat 3 Polskich Pism i Ksiegarni w Chicago," *Pittsburczanin,* (June 18, 1971), p. 5.

[6] Henry Dende has always considered his newspaper as the model for all American Polish newspapers. It is well written by a journalist with a command of English that is difficult to excel.

ture is not identified with the former poor immigrant culture, and most Polish-Americans can now economically afford to participate in a community life which is more than socially acceptable.

The intellectual and emotional demands of the cultural organizations are not burdensome. They are precisely what appeals to those orientated towards leisure, consumption, and status. There is no agony, turmoil, or anguish. People in communities seek to overcome doubt through activity, and escape from loneliness by means of organizations. Despair, even inconclusiveness, are not part of the ideology of the community. Participation in the organization usually involves doing something for others. Many Polish-American organizations are purely philanthropic, or service organizations. Service to others is central to the organization's purposes. This is a commendable direction.

Often individuals join organizations for ulterior motives: single women to meet available men, and vice versa. If the organization has snob appeal, or status, that will also attract people. It is not the good work or what one can benefit from it culturally that attracts them as members. Another factor is the age of the organization. If an organization is old and established, it gives credence to its members that the fee will not go to waste. Other cultural organizations are avocationally or hobby-oriented: choirs, dancing groups, stamp-collectors, coin-collectors. Only highly cultural people join groups where philosophy, profound literature, and history are discussed.

Polish-American cultural life, in the United States, is whatever is accomplished under the auspices of Polish-American organizations. Even though some organizational service is cultural, as well as philanthropic, the fact remains that involvement in the organization encourages what may be called a "philanthropic attitude." And this is precisely what may make it so attractive to third generation Americans of Polish descent. The activity of the organization provides satisfaction in doing something for others, and this may well be what the essence of contemporary Polish-Americanism is all about.

John Stuart Mill observed that "one person with a belief is a social power equal to ninety-nine who have only an interest." It is rare to find, among the contemporary leadership of the large

Polish-American fraternal organizations, individuals who have the charisma, dedication, sense of direction, articulation, perseverance, and time necessary to maintain and lead fraternal organizations as a vibrant force.[7] Rarely is there a leader in the Polish-American fraternals who is fluently bi-lingual, well-educated, skillful in public relations, and imaginative in creating programs and fine exhibits. Many who assumed important posts of leadership by default, or inheritance in the fraternals, will not work with the same zeal for the goals that the fraternals have been founded. The fraternals ceased to be viable when they became plagued by lack of leadership, personality clashes, not to mention mismanagement of funds. Failure to attract new members should have indicated to them that the fraternals were losing their mass following, and are a sad disappointment to the Polish-American communities.[8]

Not one of the leaders among the large fraternals has motivated or directed the mass of Polish-Americans to take bold, meaningful steps in the interest of their heritage and welfare. Only recently, a few individuals (Benedict Markowski, Blanka Rosenstiel, Dr. Charles Allen Baretski, J. Irene Jankie, A. Noreen Smialek-Sinclair, Gregory Rej, Dr. Edward J. Tomasik, Dr. Edward C. Rozanski, Jan Szulec, Chester Grabowski, Sister Mary Ellen Kuznicki, Michael Krolewski) began to get busy asking the hard, perhaps embarrassing questions, about how to restore and re-invigorate the fraternal organizations so that they could

---

[7] Dr. Joseph A. Wytrwal, "Polish American Leadership," *Polish Daily News*, English Edition, (March 29, 1975), p. 4. Wytrwal, "Leadership to forge ahead," *Polish Daily News*, (June 8, 1975), p. 4. Wytrwal, "Low-keyed American leaders," *Polish Daily News*, (July 26, 1975), p. 4. Wytrwal, "Creative Leadership in Fraternals," *Polish Daily News*, (August 23, 1975), p. 4. Wytrwal, "Our fraternal leaders—naive or cynical?" *Polish Daily News*, (September 6, 1975), p. 4. Wytrwal, "Polish-American fraternal leadership," *Polish Daily News*, (September 13, 1975), p. 4. Wytrwal, "Unity and leadership—ingredients for success," *Polish Daily News* (September 17, 1975), p. 4. Wytrwal, "Courage in leadership," *Polish Daily News*, (October 11, 1975), p. 4. Wytrwal, "Leadership concepts for Polish-Americans," *Polish Daily News*, (November 1, 1975), p. 4.

[8] Wytrwal, "Polish American fraternals," *Polish Daily News*, (May 3, 1975), p. 4. Wytrwal, "Polish American fraternal organizations," *Polish Daily News*, (October 4, 1975), p. 1975), p. 4. Wytrwal, "Guidelines for Pol-Am fraternal members," *Polish Daily News*, (November 9, 1975), p. 4.

continue the long, hard march toward the objective for which they were originally established.[9]

The presidents of the national Polish-American fraternal organizations enjoy delivering and publishing proclamations pledging support for everything good and the well-being of the Polish-American cause. At every convention, during the banquets, the newly elected national officers are apt to wax grandiloquent on ceremonial occasions and sing *"nie damy pogrzesc mowy"* or *"mowa ojcow naszych, mowa naszych dzieci."*[10] Such sentiments are no doubt beautiful and commendable, but the problem lies in the fact that they are purely declaratory, and that the most stirring resolutions are forgotten almost as soon as they are pronounced. Unfortunately the pledge from Maria Konopnicka's *Rota*—that they will forever preserve the Polish language—at this stage of Polish-American history—appears to have lost any ring of truth for some time.

These ungenuine assurances and pledges mean very little. In most instances they are shallow promises. For example, millions of words have been uttered on the needs of showing greater interest towards the Polish-American youth, of helping some deserving young men and women to achieve prominence in their chosen field—not only through financial aid, but through moral support. And while words of praise and promise keep echoing at almost every gathering, Polish-American youth are compelled to seek recognition and support among people indifferent to their ethnic heritage, and must compete with others with more favorable racial or ethnic origins.[11]

---

[9] Michael Krolewski, of Detroit, has made the propagation of Polish culture and heritage a full-time career. He is founder and director of the Polish-American Folk Theater, the editor of a monthly periodical, *Pokój*, and a teacher of Polish culture at St. Hyacinth's School. His theater group project included study of folklore courses in Poland. He is truly making an effort to close the "generation gap" in the Polish-American communities. At the convention of the Polish-American Congress, Krolewski laid heavy emphasis on youth and the necessity to stimulate cultural awareness of young Polish-Americans. Krolewski should seriously be considered for leadership in the national Polish-American fraternals. Nothing but a renaissance would be the result of his administration.

[10] Translations: "We will not allow to bury our language." "The language of our fathers is the language of our children."

[11] In contrast to the loud and empty oratories of pompous fraternal leaders, there are some individuals whose deeds often are unpublished. These individuals do, what fraternal leaders promise. One such individual is Michael Paszyn, an artist

THE THIRD GENERATION

To absolve themselves of any responsibility, the fraternal presidents of organizations with large resources, have shifted the responsibility of preserving and expanding the Polish heritage to the Polish-American Congress whose resources are inadequate and insignificant. Thus, the preservation of the Polish heritage, in America, is not carried on by those salaried and elected to accomplish it—but by volunteers. Like all of the volunteer organizations to be found in the Polish-American communities, the Polish cause is still in evidence, and carried on only because of the intense activity of the few volunteers.[12]

The average Polish-American has been content to exercise no more control over the fraternal organizations that the typical citizen over the national, state, or local government. He has been unaware of what these organizations were saying and doing in his name as a non-participating member. He is usually a member, because of gregariousness, group insurance, or other benefits. The typical member does not attend chapter meetings. He is content to mail his check once a year, serenely confident that the

---

of international fame, who has studios in New York and Italy. While in the United States, in 1965, in conjunction with the unveiling of his monument—erected in memory of John F. Kennedy at Fontanna, California—Paszyn disclosed that before leaving Italy, he arranged that two Polish artists: viz., Stefan Mrozewski (recently deceased) to have an exhibit of woodcuts in the Galleria Uffici at Florence, Italy; and Bronislaw Bak, a graphic artist and designer of stained-glass windows—to exhibit his designs and projects in the Galleria Nazionale, in Rome. Artist Bak is known as the designer of the largest-glass window in the United States, in St. John the Baptist Church, at Collegeville, Minnesota, as well as other stained-glass windows in Wilmette, Waukegan and Fargo, North Dakota. Both exhibits opened in world renowned galleries which made possible wider opportunities for fame and further recognition for both artists. This was possible because Paszyn does not believe in empty phraseology, but deeds where they count the most.

[12] Michael Labowski wanted an organization that would unite the Civil Service employees of Polish-American descent. In 1956, he was successful in forming the Pulaski Association of the Police Department. He served as President until 1962, and then went to other New York City Civil Service employees to encourage their cooperation. Subsequently, Pulaski Associations started in Fire, Correction, Sanitation, New Jersey Police & Fire, Transit, Highway, U.S. Post Office, Parks, Transit Police and Nassau County Police. All are affiliated with the Grand Council of Pulaski Associations.

Sgt. Labowski was elected president of the Grand Council serving in that capacity through 1960-1964. He was re-elected for the term 1967-1968, again re-elected 1968-1970, and 1971-1972.

The Polish-American community in Metropolitan New York appreciated the leadership of Sgt. Labowski by honoring him with a testimonial dinner in 1972.

organization is doing something for Polish-Americans and Polish culture.

The ambitious individuals, who succeed to the upper echelon of such organizations, are often less interested in Polish-Americans than in performing a pirouette on a larger stage. They are essentially conservatives fighting an issue defeated thirty years ago and supporting an imaginary government in exile, residing in London. They use the Polish organizations to unify the support for their political cause and gain funds to pursue this end relentlessly without faltering. That is why the Polish American Congress behaves as if it were under the delusion that it is really the conscience of Polish-Americans. It is a secular organization established to protect the interests of Polish-American people. Long ago, it decided to seek new purposes to defend, which altered its effectiveness, for it was no longer able to be effective. Its present function seems to be to produce a steady stream of press releases. Like most other Polish-American organizations, its success is measured not only by solid accomplishments, but by the column inches it receives in the American press. The Polish-American Congress may be neither a Congress, nor typically American; but in all fairness, its role and effectiveness does not seem to appear any worse than that made by most other Polish-American organizations of national scope and membership. It is conscious of Polish issues, but in a myopic sense, rather than the total breadth of the matter, and how to resolve it. Unfortunately, many organizations and individual members have also lost their faith in the Polish American Congress which they once had.

The individuals who have gained control of Polish-American organizations cannot focus on helping their members—whether it is because their position will not open the door of opportunity to other political or financial successes, or they have become jaded with remaining too long at the helm of the organization—resting on past laurels. Polish-American organizations see Americans of Polish descent as a source of money, and non-Poles as a group that must be influenced. The critical issues of the early Poles brought popularity and wealth to the organizations which decided that greater wealth was necessary for its effectiveness in leadership. In time, it appears that there is a tendency to reduce the ordinary people to a mere member status—ignoring the individual and removing the individual from the decision-making process.

How does one enter the echelon among the power elite? The most common way is by means of vertical mobility, so that a young man begins his career of community service in fund-raising, then assumes a committee assignment, progresses to the presidency of a local lodge, and finally achieves a high ranking position in one of the national organizations. It is at this last stage where the individual either achieves the stability of power, or falls out of favor in the struggle.

Horizontal mobility means entering the power structure near the top administrative level without advancing through the ranks. Because this is not the usual way of entering the power structure, it is usually reserved for several special individuals. They are persons of high-prestige, persons who can be used for attracting publicity; but it must be remarked: these people do not achieve bona fide power; they remain subservient to the interests and directions of the true members of the power structure. The second type of individual who achieves power by horizontal mobility is the large (or potentially large) donor who feels that power and prestige are due him by virtue of his wealth and status. Finally, horizontal mobility may be used to induce an older individual who has money, prestige, and capability to become active in community work. Such an individual cannot obviously, be asked to start at the lowest level; he must begin nearer the top echelon. Leaders of the power structure are reluctant to appoint someone to the top position without previously testing him in positions of lesser responsibility. Select candidates who move horizontally have an unknown quantity. As the need for additional funds in the Polish-American community increases in Polish-American enterprises, one may expect to see an increased concentration of power in the hands of the very wealthy, whose gifts alone will determine the success or failure of many communal projects.

Like the preceding generation, the third generation—a good majority was born since World War II, reared in the shadow of the bomb, alienated from the life of their parents, and nurtured on television—responds to the only world it knows: the world of their fathers. The children of the immigrants, who fled from the ghettos, rejected in their entirety the ideals of the first generation. For the second generation, a Polish identity was synonymous with the Polish ghetto, including the thick foreign accent, and struggling poverty. By turning ethnic identity into a poisonous source of self-contempt, society had instilled in the children of the immigrants a sense of shame, at times flaring into self-pity and self-hatred for being hyphenated-Americans.

The second generation lived uneventfully in their own middle-class communities. In search of better homes with larger backyards, young second generation Polish-Americans discovered the added boon of non-Polish neighbors. Their children—literally worlds away from their unhappy and ill-adjusted grandparents—are no longer caught between mutually exclusive worlds. The third generation of Polish-Americans had little reason to feel inferior. They were American-born and comparatively prosperous. Their parents, for the most part English-speaking, were integrated into American life. Few, if any experienced a sense of alienation.

The ideals available to the third generation demand neither rejection nor total acceptance. Their life situation is different, requiring selective and more varied responses. The third generation responds to the ideals of its fathers by: (1) accepting some without change, (2) accepting others with modification, or (3) rejecting still others.

Secure in their middle-class American background, members of the third generation can afford to be discriminating about their fathers' ideals. They feel no urgency to escape the world of their fathers. Some aspects of this world are quite acceptable; while others require little adaptation. Sentiment exceeds commitment with the third generation; it is sufficient to assuage their conscience without isolating them from the general community. What the son of the immigrant wishes to forget, the grandson often wishes to remember. While recollections of the Old World arouse deep emotions—among the first and second generations, which stemmed from the European environment—many of the third generation are equally aroused by the tales that come from there, the photos they often see in their parents' albums, the incidents recorded in literature, the traveling dance companies, orchestras, or Polish films which they are able to see, even any information in the news may evoke interest to a great emotion when confronted with it.

The grandsons acknowledge their Polish heritage without embarrassment or apology. The magnitude of their grandparents' choice to emigrate dawned upon them with full force. They appreciated the fact that their grandparents possessed the restlessness and the courage to part with the homeland in order to find a more meaningful life in America. The spirit of adventure of their forebears is in contrast to what Americans had always taken for granted: birth and life in America. However, even though they were raised on another continent, this did not mean that the Polish heritage of their grandparents should be hidden in a thick mist of ignorance.

Quite often, they were rather curious about the folk mores and quaint old customs of their grandparents. Many of them felt the need to establish roots, and a sense of origin—if only because respectability had become a cherished value in American life. While the need for respectability had frequently led to a deliberate rejection of Polish cultural values a generation earlier, most Americans recognized that assimilation was not the answer. One's origins, whatever they are, would have to be re-examined and, if possible, invested with respectability. And this was exactly what many thousands of third-generation Polish-Americans set about to do. Greater leisure and earnings allow many third generation persons to visit Poland where they can study their grandparents' language, culture and history, but, also, to discover and became acquainted with their Polish relatives, their family origins and geographical region where their family hailed from. Poles are quite a diversified group of people with individual characteristics often attributed to such persons: a person from Poznan is considered dependable, hard-working, thrifty and stolid—slower in reaction; a native of Warsaw is cosmopolitan, witty, sharp; from Krakow where they are imbued with history and culture they are considered conservative and cultivated; other parts of what was once considered Austrian Poland (Galicia) natives were denigrated because of their outlandish taste in mixing bright colors, etc.

Edward R. Kantowicz, despite his Polish name, considers himself an outsider to the Polish-American community.

> My grandfather came from Poland and worked in the Chicago stockyards; and my grandmother, until the day of her death, when she was almost 90 years old, never learned English. But my parents left the old neighborhood, discarded the Polish newspapers, and even became Republicans in their politics! They made a point of not teaching Polish to my sister and me. We were going to be Americans! Like a great part of the third generation of Poles in America, I am now an outsider to Polonia.
>
> This cutting off from my roots is a part of the now famous generation gap. Yet it is not an unbridgeable gap. As a student of history at the University of Chicago, I have begun to go back to find out where I came from. I have taught myself at least the rudiments of Polish and have started to study the activities, especially the political activities, of the Polish-Americans in Chicago. Some day I hope to publish my research as a book on American politics in Polonia's capital.[13]

Mary B. Sudwoj is also proud of her Polish heritage.

> I am 25 years old, and even though I was for the most of my life reared in America and went to schools here, I never stopped being proud of my Polish heritage in spite of the fact that some of my teachers told me to forget my Polish and stick to the English.
>
> I did not give up, and thanks to my parents I learned both languages in reading, writing and speaking. It is a shame that for many years our Polish immigrants in America let themselves down and felt ashamed of admitting in public their Polish ancestry, while at the same time the Irish, German, Italian and other publicized their nationality and no one stepped on their toes. It is time indeed to raise our heads and say that we are proud of our Polish heritage and of the land of our fathers as there is much to be proud of.
>
> Last year for the first time in my life I spent six weeks in Poland. The impression this visit left on me could not be matched with any other experience I have ever had. I sincerely hope that many other Polish young people will have the opportunity to see Poland as I had, and then they would be able to see why there is so much to be proud of being a Pole. Poland has much to show for itself in history, in its land, its people of yesteryears, and even more today. It's time for us,

---

[13] Edward R. Kantowicz, "Reflections of a Polish-American 'Outsider,'" *Polish American*, (February 5, 1969), p. 7.

young Polish people, to support this movement in this country, and contribute all we can to show others that we have much to our name in culture, education, arts and sciences, and erase the ignorant images of the past that were false, and based on prejudice.[14]

Father Chrobot, a Polish-American educator, made this observation:

> "I'm not Polish, I'm American. But I'm not just any kind of American. I'm an American of Polish descent, and my background has colored my values. And I think some of those values are better than the ones the mainstream culture presents."[15]

Tom Korzeniowski is one of Detroit's most popular TV newscasters. But only two years ago, he was known as Tom Conrad, the name his parents chose upon arriving from Poland, in place of the "foreign-sounding" original surname.

Recently, a Mary Martins legally restored her Polish surname Strzyzewska. According to her own admission, it was her deep pride in her cultural heritage that prompted her to change. And throughout the country, it seems that more and more younger Polish-Americans, free of any complexes—third and fourth generations in school and at work—are beginning to insist on the correct pronunciation of their names.

No longer apologetic about the members of a minority, nor eager to discard their past, the third generation acknowledges their Polish attributes without hesitation or explanation. First of all, the new wave of ethnicity has made it popular, and secondly, it has made these members wiser about themselves. Songs about Polish-Americans and their romantic feelings, which reveal their pride and self-awareness, have become increasingly evident all across the country. Badges proclaiming "I am Proud to Be a Polish-American," T-shirts espousing "Polish Power," and bumper stickers boasting "Polish and Proud"—have become a part of the current scene. In addition, ethnic festivals are increasing in both size, frequency, and popularity as well as in smaller

---

[14] Mary B. Sudwoj, "Proud of Polish Heritage," *Gwiazda Polarna*, (May 26, 1973), p. 5.
[15] John Askins, "Ethnicity: Diluting the Power of WASP Values?" *Detroit Free Press*, (March 3, 1975), p. 1-C.

communities where they are often better organized than those featured in cities, especially Detroit. It is the young who are leading the movement for a more visible Polish-American community. The Polish-American youth have learned well from the one fundamental mistake made by their parents, which contributed to the Polish-American inability to gain recognition, or status, in society.

This was due to an unwillingness on the part of their parents to expand interests and activities, not only outside the Polish-American community, but also by denying their heritage and source in order to realize their pride and self-awareness.

Polish-American youth are not plagued by the same insecurities that promoted insularism among our older community leaders. Instead, they are prideful and speak of their Polish heritage wherever they travel. They wear their "Polish and Proud" T-shirts on Main Street, as well as on Broadway. They are not afraid to compete with non-Poles because of self-imposed inadequacies. They allow their abilities, not their heritage, to determine their position in the communty. This awareness of heritage is therapeutic for the chronic problem of schizophrenic identity with which their parents have been struggling vainlessly.

If the burden of pressure were not put upon all ethnics by the Anglo-Saxon community to compel all Americans to conform to their identity as the model, much of this disorientation, alienation, disharmony and unhappiness could have been avoided. The recent militancy of the French, in Canada, and the Latinos, in southwestern United States, has finally brought the Anglo-Saxon to his senses: either they desist, or the result will be another Civil War that could diminish the union by secession.

Perhaps in the days of metropolitan ghettoes, Polish identity was absorbed passively, but in the modern more sophisticated suburbs, where increasing numbers of third-generation Poles live today, a large percent of their neighbors are likely to be non-Poles. Polish identity had to be cultivated actively if it was to survive, especially if it was to have any meaning for children growing up once more—minority members among many in a mixed society. By returning to the heritage of their ancestors, whole new horizons were revealed—opening up a world of an Eastern European past that gave a three-dimensional perspective on life: American, Polish and Polish-American, as well as a confrontation with all of the other national and racial origins.

Rejecting uniqueness in social behavior, the third generation rejects a social life based solely on ethnic ties. The communities of the third generation are not ethnic, but status communities in which there are usually more non-Poles than Poles. The third generation accepts the values of their status communities, conforming in a way that renders them indistinguishable from their non-Polish neighbors. Almost convinced that there really are no differences between Poles and non-Poles, the third generation vigorously sets about eliminating any differences that remain to make a difference in the way the third generation is treated socially.

The third generation cannot afford to be content with mere superficial emulation of Polish-American patterns. They have broadened their status audience, and now must acquire the refinements for approbation. The significant status judgments are made by the general society, rather than the minority group, and all the factors that enter these judgments, now, become important to the third generation. The status community of the third generation imposes non-Polish values unknown to their predecessors. The changes in the structure of the minority community, from one generation to the next, have been the consequence of an increasing incorporation of the values of the dominant society. Each generation has experienced conflict between Polish and non-Polish values, and anxiety about which community offers the most promise. The conflict between the generations has characteristically been a conflict of values in which each generation has redefined its values in ways relevant to its own life situation; the resolutions of conflict have been in the direction of greater acceptance of the dominant values. The isolating and protecting values of the ghetto have collapsed under the impact of American life with the opportunity for mobility in the general class structure. Those of the gilded ghetto gave way with increasing social contact with non-Poles. The conflict between the first and second generation was a conflict between the values of the traditional ghetto and the values of an acculturated ethnic community. The conflict between the second and third generation is a conflict between the values of an acculturated, but separate ethnic community, and the values of the general status community.

Of course, one cannot ignore the fact that there are many third, fourth and fifth generation ethnics who remain militantly ethnically oriented and reject wholly the majority point of view. American Indians and Blacks stress being different to the point of flaunting it. There are also many Poles who emulate this posture. Well educated Polish-Americans who are familiar with their heritage are more cosmopolitan and appreciate all other languages and cultures more readily and make a deliberate effort to do so.

Ethnic life in the past depended upon the existence of ethnic districts which have largely disappeared. Self-help societies—once so important to the first generation—are less important. Many individuals today have first loyalties to their professions or specialized vocations rather than to ethnic and familial traditions.

By returning to the heritage of their ancestors, whole new horizons were revealed, opening up a world of an Eastern European past that gave their perspective on life three-dimensional fullness, American, Polish, and Polish-American, where the story of their grandparents' immigration began. The struggle to be recognized as a "normal" American, at the expense of suppressing the Polish identity in their grandsons, diminished after the grandsons accepted the fact that they are Americans of Polish descent. They no longer feel any less American because of their ethnic heritage. With the option of learning about, and perhaps accepting, the rich Polish legacy that is theirs to inherit, they need not feel apologetic—as their parents have for most of their lives—for their dual identity. In looking ahead, there could very well be similar problems of identity for their children, perhaps further compounded by the actual mixing of their ethnic backgrounds.

In the process of assimilation, identity on the basis of national origin tends to weaken; it is no longer feasible for people to identify themselves by language, culture or custom. Identification tends to rest more on common interests, which become related to ethnic backgrounds, rather than constituting an ethnic background. The third generation—confident now of their identity as Americans—look for some symbol which would give them a specific identity. The two features of the old world culture which they can revive, and which can be legitimately manifested in American life, is the ethnic identity of their forebears, and the utilization of the Polish language, if not mastering it to perfection. Thus, they not only revive their interest in the ethnic identity of their grandparents but also communicate and use their ethnic heritage as the basis for their specific identity in America.

Also very little in our experience has prepared us to deal with our present problems, for they differ fundamentally, from those we have faced or overcome in the past. To begin with, for the first time in our history as a nation we are no longer masters of our own destiny. Every major problem that confronts us now is global and to be solved only through cooperation with other nations. Second, we can no longer fall back on the comforting assumption that our resources are infinite. Now we must face that fact that these resources are finite. Third, we who heretofore have not been able to face even the possibility of defeat are now required to take the possibility of annihilation into our calculations. All of our most fateful decisions are made under the shadow of the atomic weapon.

Nevertheless—one year after the bicentennial, and 200 years of one of the great success stories of history—we can still count on our natural resources, on our resourceful people and on a leadership with vision, courage, intelligence and determination to cope with the problems that glare upon us from every quarter of the horizon.

CHAPTER 23

America in the Bicentennial

> It has been the policy of mine—and the policy of my Administration—to listen carefully to the voice of Polish America. When it comes to sacrifice and achievement, you have given more, far more, than your share in making this the greatest country in the history of mankind.
>
> —President Gerald Ford

> Our ethnic heritage is the living fiber that holds America together. I intend to see it preserved.
>
> —Jimmy Carter

Nineteen seventy-six: The year America elected a president, went to the Olympics, fired a landing craft to Mars, hosted the first trans-Atlantic supersonic airliner, pulled out of a recession, gained a clean sweep of Nobel prizes in each category from literature to physics, and celebrated the American Revolution Bicentennial. Also, the Liberty Bell was rung in Philadelphia; an armada of tall ships in New York Harbor sailed into the sunset of history; fireworks bursted over the capitol in Washington and other cities throughout the land; a cornucopia of Bicentennial art shows flourished, and parades and speeches were delivered before throngs of people. Across the land the people manifested themselves in a thousand original, spectacular or homespun ways; every red, white and blue sentiment dazzled the eyes of the world as America wished itself a happy 200th birthday!—but not without incidents also.

Individuals might be oblivious to the epic quality of the long journey which their forebears had made, but as a group Polish-Americans understood its real significance. It was a time to look back along the road their forefathers and fathers have traveled to remember their sacrifices, deeds and vitality that drove them to seek a new life across the Atlantic. It was a time to honor and remember Polish-Americans who fought in American wars to preserve the country and its heritage. Also, it was a time to put into proper perspective many things that have been out of focus while they were actually experiencing them.

The events of history generally move exceedingly slow. For the most part, individuals are not even aware of movement until years, decades or even centuries later. Horace Kallen made the following observation: "Men may change their clothes, their politics, their wives, their religion, their philosophies, to a greater or lesser extent; they cannot change their grandfathers."[1] Not only is the individual related to his ethnic group involuntarily and indissolubly, but in a positive sense the individual realizes himself and his potentialities through membership in this group. Nevertheless, in the perspective of history, Polish-Americans understood that physical separation inevitably results in cultural separation. The general movement of our society—and of technological society, in general—is away from ethnic exclusivity and toward national uniformity. Language, dress, separate ethnic churches, the ethnic press, even gestures and food preferences are on the decline. The rate of inter-marriage—the barometer of the extent of ethnic solidarity—is also on the rise for all groups.

The Polish-American, under seventy years of age, is either American born, or so firmly rooted in American soil, that it would provoke a smile were one to suggest a return to Poland. Sixty years ago, a Polish-American orator was heard exclaiming: "We love Poland as our mother, and America as our bride." Today, it would be truer to say: "We love America as our mother and Poland as our grandmother, of whom, for a fast growing number there will be soon little remaining but fond tradition." However, the opportunity to travel to Poland inexpensively and comfortably has removed a barrier from knowing Poland, her culture, and their ancestral family residing there.

---

[1] Horace Kallen, *Culture and Democracy in the United States*, p. 60.

The Polish language—so vigorously guarded and preserved by their grandparents and parents within living memory—faded into the background. Because of increased mobility and also because many resided in unsophisticated communities with little exposure to culture, or where the beautiful Polish language could be heard or expressed eloquently, the Polish immigrant—usually of peasant stock—found himself limited in vocabulary so that his language was frequently sprinkled with corruptions of English words. The Polish language fell into disuse, or became garbled, or interspersed with macaronic Americanisms among Americans of Polish descent.

Polish customs and traditions were affected and changed by American environment, culture and civilization. Still, Polish-Americans cannot help feeling that Poland, Polish heritage, as well as their stalwart character and industriousness, did much to enable them to reach the goal they set for themselves. Poland was a country that once extended from Sweden and the Baltic Sea to the Black Sea, and from the Oder River to the environs of Moscow; not by conquest, but by a peaceful confederation. Poland was a country that protected western civilization from the invaders from the east. Poland was a country that saved Vienna from the Turks without any remuneration or compensation. Poland was also the only country in the world that offered a haven to Jews for more than a thousand years.

Because of their history and culture, Polish-Americans have a mutual ethnic pride—not a racist pride, not a prejudiced or chauvinistic pride—but a natural human pride in what their ancestors accomplished for Poland, America and the rest of the world! And when Polish-Americans serve America, they do so proudly as Americans of Polish descent with malice toward none, and compassion for all, and with the courage to face what they have to face, as did their ancestors. As a people they are highly evolved.

The Polish immigrants, who would have given their lives for the maintenance of the Polish language—could they have only stood at the end of the long road—might have felt not merely reconciled, but happy at the way things had developed. For an America, dominated by a single nationality or race, would have been culturally a poor country; that composite of cultures that has become the real America is richer, more exciting and more alive, since each dilutes and enriches the other. And at the end of the long road, it is possible to see that the most remarkable fact about America is its diversity which reaches every corner of the earth, crossing national and ideological boundaries. It is from this diversity of people that the greatness of the nation probably springs, and it is the triumph of America, that in the midst of such diversity, there is also unity; the mingling of traditions, temperaments, and cultures. These account for its health and rejuvenation.

A retrospective view helped Polish-Americans gain a perspective of their own history and achievements for a true appreciation of things as they are. The Polish-Americans realized that they were different from what they had been in the beginning: each touched and changed by the alchemy of the American environment, and by living and mingling with Americans of other backgrounds. The descendants of the Polish immigrants realized that the Polish pioneers had achieved a kind of biological immortality. From the beginning, America has been for all the world a great experiment, a moral force, a dream. "To be an American," said the philosopher, George Santayana, "is of itself almost a moral condition, an education, and a career."

We are, it has been said, a nation of immigrants. For generations, the people of America have come from all corners of the earth, bringing to America different languages, cultures, religions and historical experiences: Poles and Anglo-Saxons, Jews and Lithuanians, Blacks and Serbians, Italians and Germans, the Dutch and the Orientals, Irish and Mexicans—they and many more from lands far away have peopled America, wrestled with the resources of this vast land, and brought ingenuity to bear on developing the most decent and economically stable society in the world's history. The United States succeeded—as only Rome had done before—in opening opportunities to an extraordinary variety of peoples on the basis of common citizenship and a single civic ideal. "We are the Romans of the modern world," observed Oliver Wendell Holmes, "the great assimilating people."

Assimilation is not synonymous with elimination in the evolution of a cosmopolitan nation, for much of the foreign flavor, introduced by thousands of immigrants, is fortunately of a lasting nature. The people from faraway lands alter a nation, even as the nation alters them. Once the two elements are joined, nothing ever remains the same—neither the people, nor the nation. It is part of the mystery of America that there still is no such person as the "typical American," nor is there, truly a "typical American city." This metamorphosis continues with fickle disregard for the calculations and predictions of the experts.

The great old families of pre-Colonial America arrived here with the same uncertainty, fear and hope that many of the later immigrants experienced. These earlier generations of immigrants found land and opportunity in the unsettled West. Since 1870, when Polish immigrants arrived in large numbers, the United States, as a nation, stretched from coast to coast. During that period, square miles of forest had been cleared for grain fields. America was nowhere near finished. They had come at the height of the age of railroads, and at the beginning of the age of steel. The frontier in the west was closed. However, another frontier of unskilled labor, remained open almost until World War II. Thousands of immigrants found jobs as workers on railroads, digging canals, building highways, and at factory tasks which required little special skill. As laborers they were able to support families, educate their children to enjoy the diversity of culture, place and people. They also found the opportunity to choose one's own religion, and many did.

Individuals are both inner and outer beings. They must have some sense of their own worth and human identity. They also must find some meaningful place in their society. If they are denied and rejected by the world around them, they have two basic choices: they can sink into despair and passivity, that resigned acceptance we often mistake for devotion to peace and order; or they can create their own world and their own society —a Polish-American society.

Polish immigrants were true subscribers of cultural pluralism. Maybe they could not define it, but they practiced it. They never denounced the American way of life. They hurried to become a part of that life, but at the same time they endeavored to retain as much of the old culture as seemed practical in their new environment. It is true, their press preserved the Polish language, but at the same time, its timely advice and explanation eased the transition into the American culture. Because they had organized themselves into some 800 communities, the Polish immigrants, and their descendants, were able to give the Polish tradition a continuity which would have been shattered at the foot of the Statue of Liberty and in the Labyrintian halls of Castle Garden. "Be American, but do not lose the Polish touch. Be two individuals of two cultures rather than one individual." That could well have been the motto and the theme of Polish-American history. Their quest for identity, freedom and opportunity was a voyage that had to survive shoals and rapids. They had two cultures, rather than only one, with which somehow they had to make their peace: identifying themselves with segments of both as they grew older, while sifting both of them through their fears and insecurities, their hopes and strengths; accepting and rejecting; and finally out of this process they discovered who they were. Many who managed to survive these challenging experiences were developed into sturdier personalities.

It is true, that the Polish immigrants of the 1870's, and later, accepted the most menial jobs, worked long hours for low wages, and suffered ridicule for their different manner of speech and dress. Often they were greeted with suspicion, if not open hostility. It is also true that in self-defense the Polish immigrants huddled together in cities, and created an aspect of clannishness. This was so partly because amongst their own they could maintain cultural identity. Their organized communities served as a bridge spanning the gap between countries and cultures. The organized "Polonians" provided a cushion which absorbed the shocks of acculturation; they also served as bases from which the Polish immigrants and their descendants could penetrate deeper and deeper into the American culture. This was true especially of the second and third generation (the native born and children of native-born respectively). Though the Polish immigrants had many common characteristics, they cannot be labeled with a collective name. Like other contemporary minorities, they found themselves subdivided into numerous social classes, disinterested groups, and conflicting factions. This was true for the foreign-born generation, but it was truer for the others that were the native-born. By the time the second generation was old enough to assume responsibility in the many societies and fraternals, interest groups definitely supplanted ethnic divisions, and cultural pluralism found itself rapidly surrendering to the dominant culture.

There have been and there will be peaks and valleys in the American experience, in the quest for a better society. All this the Polish-Americans can see in better perspective. The Bicentennial crystalized the magnitude of the moment, and spelled out the challenge of the future. Whatever Americans wish to do, so long as it can be logically conceived, they can accomplish it. But these goals cannot be met with mere money and good intentions, nor even with skills and machinery. They require the selfless dedication to perform the jobs, acquire the self-discipline of a people who can explore the problem logically, then create solutions imaginatively, and execute them effectively.

Polish-Americans have a passion for achievement, and a passion for family, and those are rare and valuable assets. As they contemplate the bright side of their American experience—past, present, and future—they pour their energies and talents into America's intellectual, artistic and scientific life. They also perform the hard labor of the mines, factories and farms. And they always find fulfillment in maintaining, through participation in both civil and military services, America's freedom and honor. Some history has been altered because of them, and millions of Americans have been affected in special ways through their contributions. As president Johnson, on the occasion of the Polish Millenium celebration, so aptly stated: "Our National Heritage is rich with the gifts of the Polish people."

The Bicentennial did mark a solid historical milestone in American history. In America, there is much to build a life with: opportunity, tradition, stability, ideals and strength. Such blessings are probably the most that any people ever had the right to ask of history and their forebears as they approach the third century of nationhood. But the reverse of the coin is also true, that there could be a better American society if its laws gave protection and encouraged good citizenry instead of the social problems and difficulties which offers special privileges to criminals and all those who participate in it for profit. Swift justice is a rare occurrence in America today, based on its legal system which lacks an ethical code. It is concerned more with the techniques and ritual of court procedures than discovering guilt and punishing the criminals. The immigrants' European judicial tradition has retained this so that rampant and wantom crime is not apparent in the countries of origin, which does provide the security for a given society so much needed in America today. There must be sanity to its existence, an expected code of behavior without selfishness or malice. Eliminate this and we will have the best society. The last line or common denominator will be either opportunity or jeopardy to life and property. Let it be the former rather than the latter.

Bibliography

Abrahams, Israel. *Jewish Life in the Middle Ages.* New York: Meridian Books, 1958.

Adamic, Louis. *Two-Way Passage.* New York: Harper & Brothers Publishers, 1941.

Anderson, James K. "A Polonia in Transition," *Detroit News* (September 15, 1957).

Angelo, Frank. "Black Broadcast Pioneer. He Has Given 50 Years to Detroit," *Detroit Free Press* (March 9, 1973).

Anglin, Andrea. "Detroit Area Poles Cut the Generation Gap," *The Detroit News* (June 1, 1970).

Askins, John. "Ethnicity: Diluting of Power of WASP Values?" *Detroit Free Press* (March 3, 1975).

Austin, H. Russel. *The Milwaukee Story. The Making of An American City.* Milwaukee: The Milwaukee Journal, 1946.

Balch, Emily Greene. *Our Slavic Fellow Citizens.* New York: Charities Publications Committee, 1910.

Balch, Emily Greene. "Our Slavic Fellow Citizens, History or Settlement Previous to 1880," *Charities and the Commons* (April 20, 1907).

Beitzell, Robert. *The Uneasy Alliance, America, Britain and Russia 1941-1943.* New York: Knopf Publishers, 1972.

Bercovici, Konrad. *On New Shores.* New York: D. Appleton Century Company, Inc., 1925.

Bernault, Elsa. *Polish Peasant Autobiographies.* Unpublished Ph.D. dissertation, Columbia University, 1950.

Bialasiewicz, Jozef F. "Dramat 3 Polskich Pism i Ksiegarni w Chicago," *Pittsburczanin* (June 18, 1971).

Blejwas, Stanislaw A. "The Origins and Practice of 'Organic Work' in Poland: 1795-1863," *The Polish Review* (Autumn, 1970).

Bochenski, Aleksander. "Polish Bibliophiles," *Poland* (December, 1972).

Bolek, Rev. F. "Zycie Kulturalne Polakow w Ameryce," *Przeglad Katolicki* (March, 1928).

Borejsza Jerzy W. *Emigracja Polska Po Powstaniu Styczniowym.* Warszawa: Panstwowe Wydawnictwo Naukowe, 1966.

Borkowicz, Monsignor Vincent V. "Cardinal Krol Qualified," *The Michigan Catholic* (December 8, 1971).

Boswell, Bruce. *Poland and the Poles*. London: Methuen & Company Ltd., 1919.

Brandes, George. *Poland, A Study of the Land, People and Literature*. London: William Hainemann, 1904.

Brody, David. *Labor in Crisis. The Steel Strike of 1919*. Philadelphia: Lippincott, 1965.

Brown, Sara W. "Colored Women Physicians," *Southern Workman*, LII (December, 1940).

Bryan, Julien. *Siege*. New York: Doubleday, Doran & Company, 1940.

Buczek, Daniel S. *Immigrant Pastor. The Life of the Right Reverend Monsignor Lucyan Bojnowski of New Britain, Connecticut*. Waterbury: Hemingway Corporation, 1974.

Buczynski, Theodore Joseph. *Ignace Jan Paderewski as an Orator*. Unpublished Master's thesis, De Paul University, 1949.

Burant, Rt. Rev. Msgr. *Statement to the Subcommittee on Immigration and Naturalization*. New York: Polish Immigration Committee, 1953.

Burdock, Jack. "Silent Detroit Streets Welcome the Signing of Viet Ceasefire," *The Sunday News* (January 23, 1973).

Burke, Karol. *Jedziemy do Polski*. Chicago: Drukiem Dziennika Zwiazkowego, 1936.

Burns, James MacGregor. *Roosevelt: Soldier of Freedom*. New York: Harcourt Brace Jovanovich, 1970.

Cady, Richard. "Courage Braces Legless Viet Hero," *The Detroit News* (July 3, 1967).

Camper, John J. "Takes Life as It Comes and Now Death, too," *The Detroit News* (April 14, 1966).

Carpenter, Niles and Daniel Katz. "The Cultural Adjustment of the Polish Group in the City of Buffalo: An Experiment in the Technique of Social Investigation," *Social Forces* (September, 1927).

Carr, Jay. "Polish Dancers Dazzle Audience," *The Detroit News* (March 6, 1971).

Carter, Lawrence T. "New Film Company Offers Detroit Hope," *Detroit Sunday News* (May 2, 1971).

Cassels, Louis. "Muskie's words on black veep stir strange reaction," *The Detroit News* (October 1, 1971).

Chayer, Mary Ellen. "Mary E. Mahoney," *American Journal of Nursing*, LIV (April, 1954).

Ciechanowski, Jan. *Defeat in Victory*. New York: Doubleday & Company, Inc., 1947.

Clinton, Farley. "Notes on a Schism in Michigan," *The Wanderer* (October 12, 1972).

Coleman, Marion Moore. "New Orleans and the Mississippi in 1865," *Polish American Studies* (July-December, 1967).

Cosseboom, Kathy. *Grosse Pointe, Michigan: Race Against Race*. Lansing: Michigan State University Press, 1972.

Cuneo, Ernest. "No Joking Matter," *The Polish American World* (June 1, 1968).

Dallin, Alexander. "Future of Poland," *Russian Diplomacy and Eastern Europe*. New York: King's Crown Press, 1963.

Daniels, John. *America via the Neighborhood*. New York: Harper and Brothers Publishers, 1920.

Daniels, Josephus. *The Wilson Era: Years of War and After 1917-1923*. Chapel Hill: The University of North Carolina Press, 1946.

Dec, Jan. "The Polish Army Veterans Association of America," *The Polish American Journal* (April 29, 1967).

Deutscher, Isaac. *The Non-Polish Jew and Other Essays*. London: Oxford University Press, 1968.

Dimont, Max. *Jew, God and History*. New York: Simon and Schuster, 1962.

Doubnow, S. *An Outline of Jewish History*. New York: M. N. Maisel, 1929.

Dyboski, Roman. *Poland in World Civilization*. Ludwig Krzyzanowski (Ed.). New York: J. M. Barrett Corporation, 1950.

Dybowski, Zygmunt. *Protokol 3cej Krajowej Konwecji Kongresu Polonji Amerykanskiej*. Chicago: Alliance Printers, 1952.

Elliott, J. H. *The Old World and the New 1492-1650*. Cambridge: Cambridge University Press, 1970.

Elliot, John P. "The Decapitalization of a Nation," *Gwiazda Polarna* (January 6, 1972).

Ellis, John Tracy. *The Life of James Cardinal Gibbons Archbishop of Baltimore 1834-1921*. Milwaukee: The Bruce Publishing Company, 1951. Two Volumes.

Figura, Bruno S. "Zygmunt Stojowski, Father of the ACPCC," *Polish American* (August 16, 1969).

Fisher, LeRoy H. *Lincoln's Gadfly, Adam Gurowski*. Norman: University of Oklahoma Press, 1964.

Fleming, Susan. "It's Christine's big day and parents are there," *The Detroit News* (April 7, 1973).

Fleming, Susan. "A bittersweet honor for Chris," *The Sunday News* (April 22, 1973).

Flexner, Eleanor. *Century of Struggle: The Women's Rights Movement in the United States.* Cambridge: Harvard University Press, 1959.

Foner, Philip S. *Thomas Jefferson Selection from His Writings.* New York: Wiley Book Company, 1944.

Fox, Paul. *The Polish National Catholic Church.* Scranton: School of Christian Living (n.d.).

Fox, Thomas C. "Cardinal Dearden an Enigma to Many," *Detroit Free Press* (October 6, 1975).

Fox, Thomas C. "The company priest who discovered (and told) why half America's Catholics no longer attend mass," *Detroit Free Press,* Detroit Magazine (September 5, 1976).

Furlong, William Barry. "Wisconsin: State of Insurgents," *The New York Times Magazine* (April 3, 1960).

Gaillard, Frye. "Poles in Detroit Ally with Blacks," *Race Relations Reporter,* II (April 5, 1971).

Gareau, Lawrence. "GI's Poetry Foretells Death," *The Detroit News* (March 13, 1967).

Garner, June Brown. "How a Black Beauty Expert Judges Women," *The Sunday News Magazine* (July 16, 1972).

Garner, June Brown. "The Dentist Who Put Detroit's Black Community on the Air," *Sunday News Magazine* (July 25, 1971).

Gilboa, John Murray. *Canadian Mosaic.* New York: Dodd, Mead & Company, 1939.

Gilboa, Jehoshua A. *The Black Years of Soviet Jewry 1939-1953.* Boston: Little, Brown & Company, 1971.

Gnadt, Jerry. "The Dawn of Acceptance," *The Sign* (January, 1971).

Golden, Harry. "Poles and Italians Had Classy Funerals," *Detroit Free Press* (September 13, 1969).

Gorski, Artur. *Angela Truszkowska.* Poznan: 1959.

Graff, George P. "Michigan's Polish and Lithuanian Immigrants—Settlers of City and Countryside," *The People of Michigan* (Lansing: 1974).

Graham, Michael. "Neighbors United to Stay Integrated," *Detroit Free Press* (June 4, 1973).

Grayzel, Solomon. *A History of Contemporary Jews.* New York: Meridian Books, 1960.

Greenberg, Louis. *The Jews in Russia. The Struggle for Emancipation.* New Haven: Yale University Press, 1944.

Gronowicz, Antoni. *Paderewski, Pianist and Patriot.* New York: Nelson, 1943.

Gunther, John. *Procession.* New York: Harper and Row, 1965.

Hagerty, Alice. "They Helped Start a Federal College," *The Detroit News* (December, 1974)

Haiman, Miecislaus. "The Poles in Chicago," *Poles of Chicago 1837-1937*. Chicago: Polish Pageant, Inc., 1937.

Haiman, Miecislaus. *Polish Pioneers of Virginia and Kentucky*. Chicago: Archives and Museum of the Polish Roman Catholic Union, 1937.

Haiman, Miecislaus. *Polish Past in America, 1608-1865*. Chicago: Archives and Museum of the Polish Roman Catholic Union, 1939.

Haiman, Miecislaus. *Kosciuszko in the American Revolution*. New York: Polish Institute of Arts and Sciences in America, 1943.

Haiman, Mieczyslaw. *Polacy Wsrod Pionierow Ameryki*. Chicago: Drukiem Dziennika Zjednoczenia, 1930.

Haiman, Mieczyslaw. *Slady Polskie w Ameryce*. Chicago: Drukiem Dziennika Zjednoczenia, 1938.

Haiman, Mieczyslaw. *Z Przeszlosci Polskiej w Ameryce*. Buffalo: Drukiem Telegramu, 1927.

Haiman, Mieczyslaw. *Zjednoczenie Polskie Rzymsko-Katolickie w Ameryce 1873-1948*. Chicago: Alliance Press, 1948.

Hallas, Clark. "Mayor Assails New Detroit Critics," *The Detroit News* (December 31, 1971).

Harvey, C. B. *Genealogical History of Hudson and Bergen Counties, New Jersey*. New York: The New Jersey Genealogical Publishing Company, 1900.

Hess, William N. *The American Aces of World War II and Korea*. New York: Arco Publishing Company, 1968.

Hewins, Jack. *Borleske, Never Far from Hope*. Seattle: Superior Publishing Company, 1966.

Higgins, Richard. "Educators Told to Respect Cultural, Ethnic Differences," *The Michigan Catholic* (October 1, 1975).

Holden, W. Sprague. "A Crime Without Parallel," *The Sunday News* (October 24, 1971).

Hoover, Herbert. *The Memoirs of Herbert Hoover. Years of Adventure 1874-1920*. New York: The Macmillan Company, 1951.

Horne, Alistair. *To Lose A Battle: France 1940*. Boston: Little, Brown & Company, 1969.

Hoyt, Clark. "Blacks and Poles Look to the Future," *Detroit Free Press* (December 9, 1969).

Hoyt, Clark. "City's Blacks, Poles Form Uneasy, Powerful Alliance," *Detroit Free Press* (June 15, 1969).

Hughes, Everett C. "Queries Concerning Industry and Society Growing

Out of Study of Ethnic Relations in Industry," *American Sociological Review* (April, 1949).

Humphrey, Grace. *Poland the Unexplored.* Indianapolis: The Bobbs-Merrill Company, 1931.

Iorizzo, Luciana J. and Salvatore Mondello. *The Italian-Americans.* New York: Twayne Publishers, 1971.

Janta, Alexander. "Barriers into bridges: Polish Culture in America," *The Polish Review,* II (Spring-Summer, 1957).

Jasinski, Rev. Walery, Ph.D. *Po Co Uczyc Jezyka Polskiego i Kultury Polskiej w Ameryce.* Plymouth: Felician Sisters, 1941.

Jasinski, Walery J. *Teksty Dotyczace Asymilacji Polakow w Ameryce.* Detroit: Fireside Printing Company, 1944.

Jendryka, Alex. "Cardinal Dearden," *Post Eagle* (November 10, 1976).

Jones, Maldwyn Allen. *American Immigration.* Chicago: University of Chicago Press, 1960.

Kallen, Horace Meyer. *Culture and Democracy in the United States.* New York: Boni and Liveright, 1924.

Kallen, Horace M. "Democracy Versus the Melting Pot," *The New Immigration.* New York: 1971.

Kantowicz, Edward R. "Reflections of a Polish-American 'Outsider,'" *Polish American* (February 5, 1969).

Kantowicz, Edward R. *Polish American Politics in Chicago 1888-1940.* Chicago: The University of Chicago Press, 1975.

Karlowiczowa, Jadwiga. *Historia Zwiazku Polek w Ameryce.* Chicago: Zwiazek Polek w Ameryce, 1938.

Kehetian, Mitch. "Polish Anti-Defamation League Sought," *The Macomb Daily* (May 4, 1970).

Keller, Werner. *Diaspora; the Post-Biblical History of the Jews.* Translated from the German by Richard and Clara Winston. New York: Harcourt, Brace and World, 1969.

Kesselring, Albert. *Kesselring A Soldier's Record.* New York: William Morrow and Company, 1954.

Kinel, Lola. "Jozefa Kudlicka," *Common Ground,* I (Winter, 1940).

Kirkconnell, Watson. *Canadian Overtones.* Winnipeg: Columbia Press, 1935.

Kmiec, Helen Kwiecien. "The Polish Legion of American Veterans, Chicago, Illinois," *Polish American Encyclopedia.* Buffalo: Polish-American Encyclopedia Committee, 1954.

Konrad, Don. "A Widow Meets her 'Adopted' Priest," *The Michigan Catholic* (April 3, 1970).

Kotula, Stanley. "On the Fiftieth Anniversary of the Polish National

Union of America," *Pamietnik Zlotego Jubileuszu Polsko Narodowej Spojni 1908-1958*. Scranton: 1958.
Kowalczyk, Edmund L. "Jottings From the Polish American Past," *Polish American Studies*, VII (July-December, 1950).
Kozakiewicz, Kasimir. "The President's Pad," *Narod Polski* (May 19, 1955).
Krajewski, S. "Pral. Borkowicz pastèrzuje 35 lat na 'Stanislawowie,' " *Dziennik Polski* (March 11, 1971).
Krajewski, Stanislaw. "W Ameryce Brak Polskich Intelektualistow—Mowil Brat E. Stanislaw, w Orchard Lake," *Dziennik Polski* (June 3, 1958).
Kridl, Manfred. *A Survey of Polish Literature and Culture*. New York: Columbia University Press, 1956.
Kruszka, Ks. Waclaw. *Historja Polska w Ameryce*. Milwaukee: Drukiem Spolki Wydawniczej Kuryera, 1905. 13 Volumes.
Kruszka, Ks. Waclaw. *Siedm Siedmioleci Czyli Pol Wieku Zycia*. Poznan: Czcionkami Drukarni Sw. Wojciecha w Poznaniu, 1924. Two Volumes.
Kryniewicz, Thaddeus Theodore. *The Polish Immigration Committee in the United States—An Historical Study of the American Committee for the Relief of Polish Immigrants: 1947-1952*. Unpublished Master's thesis, Fordham University, 1953.
Kudniewski, John. "Not trying Harder," *Michigan Catholic* (June 4, 1970).
Kudniewski, Eugene. "The Tatra Mountaineers' Alliance," *The Polish American World* (June 15, 1962).
Kuzniewski, Anthony J., S.J. "Polish Catholics in America," *The Catholic Weekly* (April 9, 1976).
Landau, Rom. *Ignace Paderewski, Musician and Statesman*. New York: Thomas Y. Crowell Company, 1936.
Learsi, Rufus. *A History of the Jewish People*. Cleveland: World Publishing Company, 1949.
Leismer, Luise. "Child's custody up to court. A tangle of race and love," *The Detroit News* (November 9, 1969).
Lenart, Dr. F. "Potrzeba Zorganizowania Intelligencji Zawodowej Na Wychodztwie," *Kongres Wychodztwa Polskiego w Ameryce, Odezwy, Mowy, Referaty, Uchwaly, oraz Urzedowy Protokol*. Detroit: No imprint, 1925.
Lerski, Jerzy Jan. *A Polish Chapter in Jacksonian America*. Madison: The University of Wisconsin Press, 1958.
Levine, Edward M. *The Irish and Irish Politicians*. Notre Dame: University of Notre Dame Press, 1966.

Lippman, Theo. Jr. and Donald C. Hansen. *Muskie*. New York: W. W. Norton Company, 1971.

Lopata, Helena Znaniecki. *The Function of Voluntary Association in an Ethnic Community: Polonia*. Unpublished Ph.D. dissertation, University of Chicago, 1954.

Lukaszewicz, W. *Targowica i powstanie kosciuszkowskie*. Warszawa: Wydawnictwo Ministerstwa Obrony Narodowej, 1953.

MacKinder, Sir Halford John. *Democratic Ideals and Reality*. New York: Norton, 1962.

Maisel, Albert Q. "The Poles Among Us," *Zgoda* (May 15, 1958).

Maisel, Albert Q. "The Poles Among Us," *Zgoda* (June 15, 1958).

Maisky, Ivan. *Memoirs of a Soviet Ambassador*. New York: Charles Scribner's Sons, 1968.

Manly, Claude C. *History of Company K, 127th Infantry, 32nd Division (Kosciuszko Guard) Wisconsin National Guard 1874-1924*. Milwaukee: 1924.

Manning, Clarence A. *A History of Slavic Studies in the United States*. Milwaukee: The Marquette University Press, 1957.

Manser, Nancy. "Archdiocese now has 4 auxiliaries. New Bishops called moderates," *The Detroit News* (February 23, 1973).

Manser, Nancy. "A look at the Dearden era in Detroit," *The Detroit News* (May 19, 1973).

Markowski, Benedict. *Kopernik the Great Humanist*. Detroit: Endurance Press, 1973.

Mastalski, Joseph. "Bishop Francis Hodur," *Pamietnik Jubileuszu Polsko Narodowej Spojni, 1908-1958*. Scranton: 1958.

May, Arthur J. *The Passing of the Hapsburg Monarchy 1914-1918*. Philadelphia: University of Pennsylvania Press, 1966.

McNaught, Brian. "Detroit Reaction to Krol's Presidency: Disappointment," *The Michigan Catholic* (November 24, 1971).

Meagher, Cyndi. "Four Boys have two 'Fathers' to remember today," *The Sunday News* (June 17, 1973).

Miaso, Jozef. *Dzieje Oswiaty Polonijnej w Stanach Zjednoczonych*. Warszawa: Panstwowe Wydawnictwo Naukowe, 1970.

Midowicz, Casimir E. "The Polish National Alliance," *Poland, Journal of Commerce and Industry* (August, 1927).

Mielcarek, Sister Mary Georgiana, F.O.S.F. *The Recreation of Poland, 1914-1920*. Unpublished Master's Thesis. University of Detroit, 1937.

Mierzwinski, Rev. Theophil T. *The Association of Polish Priests in Connecticut: An interpretative history*. Bloomfield, Connecticut. Unpublished typescript, 1971.

Miller, Kenneth D. *Peasant Pioneers*. New York: Council of Women for home missions and Missionary education movement, 1925.
Mizwa, Stephen P. "Polish-American Cultural Relationships," *Poland*, Bernadotte E. Schmitt, Editor. Los Angeles: University of California Press, 1945.
Monaghan, Frank. "Tadeusz Andrzej Bonaventura Kosciuszko," *Dictionary of American Biography*, Dumas Malone, Editor. New York: Charles Scribner's Sons, 1933.
Morray, Joseph P. *From Yalta to Disarmament; cold war debate*. New York: Monthly Review Press, 1961.
Moynihan, James H. *The Life of Archbishop John Ireland*. New York: Harper & Brothers Publishers, 1953.
Murawski, Ladislaus Francis. *The History and Development of St. Joseph's Home for Polish Immigrants of 425 West Forty-Fourth Street, New York*. Unpublished project, Fordham University, 1941.
Murzynowska, Krystyna. "Henryk Korwin-Kalussowski (1806-1894) *Problemy Polonii Zagranicznej*, V (Warszawa: 1964-1965).
Nathanson, Charles. "Poles and Blacks try to 'get it together,'" *East Side Shopper* (October 6, 1971).
Nelli, Humbert S. *Italians in Chicago 1880-1930. A Study in Ethnic Mobility*. New York: Oxford University Press, 1970.
Offner, Arnold A. *The Origins of the Second World War. American Foreign Policy and World Politics 1917-1941*. New York: Praeger Publishers, 1975.
Olejarczyk, Kazimierz. "Writer Aims to Prove Diminishing Role of Pol-Am Clergy in Archdiocese Here," *Dziennik Polski* (September 27, 1967).
Olejniczak, J. "Oredzie na Sejm Zjednoczenia Polskiego," *Polacy Zagranica* (February, 1931).
Olszyk, Edmund G. *The Polish Press in America*. Milwaukee: Marquette University Press, 1940.
Orley, Richard. "Immigrants made it America," *Catholic Universe Bulletin* (September 26, 1975).
Osada, Stanislaw. *Historja Zwiazku Narodowego Polskiego*. Chicago: Zwiazek Narodowy Polski, 1905.
Osada, Stanislaw. *Jak Sie Ksztaltowala Polska Dusza Wychodztwa w Ameryce*. Pittsburgh: Nakladem i drukiem "Sokola Polskiego," 1930.
O'Shea, Arthur W. "Religious spirit forgotten. Poles will honor Bishop Slowakiewicz," *The Detroit News* (March 18, 1971).
Ostafin, Peter A. *The Polish Peasant in Transition: A Study of Group Integration as a Function of Symbiosis and Common Definitions*. Unpublished Ph.D. dissertation, University of Michigan, 1948.

Paderewski, I. J. "Helping Poland," *Independent Magazine,* 83 (August, 1915).
Paderewski, I. J. "Plea for Poles," *Free Poland,* I (April 16, 1915).
Pare, George. *The Catholic Church in Detroit 1701-1888.* Detroit: The Gabriel Richard Press, 1951.
Park, Robert Ezra and Herbert A. Miller. *Old World Traits Transplanted.* New York: Harper & Brothers, 1921.
Pavich, Robert M. "Pays Debt to Death in Vietnam Fighting," *The Detroit News* (November 23, 1966).
Pawelek, Anne Josepha. *An American in Poland.* Detroit: Endurance Press, 1967.
Perry, James M. "How a Blooper Was Born at Ralph's Supermarket," *The National Observer* (October 2, 1971).
Phillips, Charles. *Paderewski: the Story of a Modern Immortal.* New York: The Macmillan Company, 1934.
Pilarski, Laura. *They Came From Poland. The Stories of Famous Polish Americans.* New York: Dodd, Mead & Company, 1969.
Pliska, Stanley H. *Polish Independence and the Polish Americans.* Unpublished Ph.D. dissertation, Teachers College, Columbia University, 1955.
Pliska, Stanley R. "The 'Polish-American Army' 1917-1921," *The Polish Review,* X (Summer, 1965).
Poliakov, Leon. *The History of Anti-Semitism. From the Time of Christ to the Court Jews.* New York: Schoken Books, 1965.
Poliakov, Leon. *The History of Anti-Semitism.* Translated from the French by Richard Howard. New York: Vanguard Publishers, 1965.
Polzin, Theresita. *The Polish-Americans: Whence and Whither.* Pulaski: Franciscan Publishers, 1973.
Quarles, Benjamin. *The Negro in the American Revolution.* Chapel Hill: University of North Carolina Press, 1961.
Quigley, Caroll. *Tragedy and Hope. A History of the World of Our Times.* New York: Macmillan Company, 1966.
Rabinowicz, Harry M. *The Legacy of Polish Jewry. A History of the Jews in the Inter-War Years 1919-1939.* New York: T. Yozeloff, 1965.
Radzialkowski, C. "Reflections on the History of the Felicians in America," *Polish American Studies* (Spring, 1975).
Reymont, Ladislaus. *The Peasants.* New York: Alfred A. Knopf, 1925.
Rice, Msgr. Charles Owen. "Late in life, something stirred," *National Catholic Reporter* (January 21, 1970).
Robakowski, Adam. "Przypomnienie faktow," *Dziennik Polski* (September 16, 1970).

Romski, P. "Church Unfair to Poles," *The Michigan Catholic* (April 27, 1970).

Rose, William John. *Poland Old and New*. London: G. Bell & Sons, Ltd., 1948.

Rose, William John. *The Rise of Polish Democracy*. London: G. Bell & Sons, Ltd., 1944.

Roth, Cecil. *A Short History of the Jewish People*. London: East and West Library, 1948.

Roucek, Joseph S. "Polish Americans," *One America*. Francis J. Brown and Joseph Slabey Roucek (Eds.). New York: Prentice-Hall, Inc., 1946.

Rozek, Edward J. *Allied Wartime Diplomacy a Pattern in Poland*. New York: John Wiley & Sons, Inc., 1958.

Rozmarek, Charles. "Poland and the Atlantic Charter," *Polish American Congress Bulletin* (February, 1944).

Ryan, Richard A. "UMW fights stigma of feuds, Yablonski murders," *The Sunday Detroit News* (June 25, 1972).

Sabiers, Michael. "Ethnicity is no joke. Polish Hope to Polish Image," *National Catholic Register* (October 2, 1970).

Saloutos, Theodore. *They Remember America: The Story of the Repatriated Greek-Americans*. Berkeley: University of California Press, 1956.

Sandberg, Neil C. *Ethnic Identity and Assimilation. The Polish American Community. Case Study of Metropolitan Los Angeles*. New York: Praeger Publishers, 1974.

Schachern, Harold. "Pupils Wiser, Less Ruly—Nun Compares Today's Crop of Children," *Detroit News* (June 13, 1959).

Schemerhorn, Robert S. *These Our People: Minorities in American Culture*. Boston: D. C. Heath and Company, 1949.

Schickel, Richard. *The World of Carnegie Hall*. New York: Julian Messner, Inc., 1960.

Schneiweis, Joseph A. *Certain Aspects of Polish Assimilation in the State of New York*. Unpublished Master's thesis, Columbia University, 1930.

Schwarz, Jonathan. "Henry Ford's Melting Pot," *Immigrants and Migrants: The Detroit Ethnic Experience*. Detroit: Journal of University Studies, 1974.

Schweitzer, Frederick M. *A History of the Jews Since the First Century A.D.* New York: Macmillan Company, 1971.

Seroczynski, Felix Thomas. "Poles in the United States," *The Catholic Encyclopedia*. New York: The Encyclopedia Press, Inc., 1914.

Shallna, Anthony O. "Adjudication of General Kosciuszko's Wills," *The Massachusetts Law Society Journal*, XX (December, 1949).

Shearer, Lloyd. "Who Really Invented the H-Bomb?/Now It Should Be Told." *Parade the Sunday Newspaper Magazine* (February 23, 1964).

Shepperson, Wilbur S. *Restless Strangers; Nevada's Immigrants and Their Interpreters.* Reno: University of Nevada Press, 1970.

Siedlak, Jan. " 'Gzibas' and 'Rybas' in Stevens Point," *Gwiazda Polarna* (January 1, 1972).

Sierocinski, Joseph. *Armia Polska we Francji.* Warszawa: 1929.

Slesinski, Thaddeus. "Past, Present, Future Report Given to Polish Cultural Clubs," *Dziennik Polski* (August 7, 1959).

Slesinski, Thaddeus. "The Development of Cultural Activities in Polish American Communities," *Polish American Studies*, V (July-December, 1948).

Slesinski, Thaddeus. "The Second Generation of Immigrants in the Assimilative Process," *The Annals of the American Academy of Political and Social Science* (January, 1921).

Smith, Captain John. *True Travels.* Richmond: Franklin Press, 1819.

Smith, William Carson. *Americans in the Making.* New York: D. Appleton Century Company, 1939.

Smolczynski, Wincenty. *Historya Osady i Parafij Polskich w Detroit, Michigan. Ksiazka Pamiatkowa z zycia Polakow na obczyznie.* Detroit: Marcin J. Burzynski, 1907.

Smulski, John F. "Poland's Role during the World War," *Poland*, X (April, 1927).

Solzhenitzyn, Alexander I. "Stalin: Weaken the Will to Strengthen the State," *The Cincinnati Enquirer* (December 30, 1973).

Sorrell, Richard S. "Life, Work and Acculturation Patterns of Eastern European Immigrants in Lackawanna, New York: 1900-1922," *The Polish Review*, XIV (Autumn, 1969).

Speek, Peter A. *A Stake in the Land.* New York: Harper & Brothers Publishers, 1921.

Stahl, Zdzislaw. "Byly Oficer 'Smerszu' o Katyniu," *Nowy Dziennik* (July 3, 1975).

Stark, Al. "Sandra Severo—the fiery lady who makes Detroit Dance," *The Sunday News Magazine* (December 3, 1972).

Starzynski, F. "Polish Americans," *Polish Medical and Dental Bulletin* (November, 1938).

Stefan, Stanley Bruno. *The Preparation of the American Poles for Polish Independence 1880-1918.* Unpublished Master's thesis, University of Detroit, 1939.

Straszewska, Maria. *Zycie Literackie Wielkiej Emigracji we Francji 1831-1840*. Warszawa: 1970.
Strawson, John. *Hitler's Battles for Europe*. New York: Scribner, 1971.
Strzelczyk, Marian. "Contributions to Polish Culture," *Ksiega Pamiatkowa Diamentowego Jubilieuszu Kola Dramatycznego i Czytelni Im. Adama Mickiewicza* (Buffalo, 1970).
Sudwoj, Mary B. "Proud of Polish Heritage," *Gwiazda Polarna* (May 26, 1973).
Suhl, Yuri. *Ernestine L. Rose and the Battle for Human Rights*. New York: Reynal & Company, 1959.
Super, Paul. *Events and Personalities in Polish History*. Bombay: The Indo-Polish Library, 1944.
Super, Paul. *Twenty-Five Years with the Poles*. Trenton: Paul Super Memorial Fund, Inc., 1947.
Szczepanski, Jan. *Polish Society*. New York: Random House, 1970.
Szopinski, Rev. D. "Od Redakcji," *Przeglad Katolicki* (January, 1926).
Targosz, Rev. S. *Polonja Katolicka w Stanach Zjednoczonych w Przekroju*. Detroit: Naklad Autora, 1943.
Taussig, Ellen. "The Polish Community Part I . . . We've Come a Long Way . . ." *Buffalo Evening News* (November 13, 1973).
Taylor, Graham. *Pioneering on Social Frontiers*. Chicago: The University of Chicago Press, 1930.
Teller, Judd L. *Strangers and Natives. The Evolution of the American Jew from 1921 to the Present*. New York: Delacorte Press, 1968.
Tempest, Rone. "Pontiac Church Survives. Priest Leads Mixed Flock," *Detroit Free Press* (September 16, 1973).
Theodosetta, Sister M., H.F.N. "The Polish Immigrants in Philadelphia to 1914," *Records of the American Catholic Historical Society in Philadelphia*, LXV (June, 1954).
Thomas, Clark M. "Pittsburgh Polonia Living with Discrimination," *Pittsburgh Post-Gazette Magazine* (April 26, 1973).
Thomas, Clark M. "Pittsburgh Polonia—Weddings, Yes, and Much More," *Pittsburgh Post Gazette* (April 25, 1973).
Tomaszkiewicz, M. "Na Fundusz Ratunkowy," *Zgoda* (April 15, 1971).
Townsend, Peter. *Duel of Eagles*. New York: Simon and Schuster, 1970.
Trbovich, Marco. "Angry Poles Say Liberalized Church Ignored Ethnics," *Detroit Free Press* (March 8, 1973).
Trbovich, Marco. "Poletown: Its Joys, Its Sorrows, Its Fate," *Detroit Free Press* (March 25, 1973).
Trbovich, Marco. "Crime Scatters Poletown's Oldsters," *Detroit Free Press* (March 27, 1973).

Tremaine, Anna G. *The Effect of Polish Immigration on Buffalo Politics.* Unpublished Master's thesis, Columbia University, 1928.

Tyner, Howard A. "Church-State tensions appear easing in Communist Poland," *Long Island Press* (August 20, 1972).

Uminski, Sigmund H. "Individual Polish Americans and World War II," *Polish American Studies,* III (January-June, 1946).

Valentin, Hugo. *Antisemitism Historically and Critically Examined.* London: Viking Press, 1936.

Wachtl, Dr. Karol. *Dzieje Zjednoczenia P.R. Katolickiego w Ameryce.* Chicago: L. J. Winiecki, 1913.

Wachtl, Dr. Karol. *Polonja w Ameryce.* Philadelphia: Polish Star Publishing Company, 1944.

Warne, Frank Julian. *The Slav Invasion and the Mine Workers.* Philadelphia: J. B. Lippincott Company, 1904.

Warner, W. Lloyd and Leo Srole. *The Social Systems of American Ethnic Groups.* New Haven: Yale University Press, 1947.

Wassell, F. F. *Attitudes of the Various Polish-American Organizations Toward American Foreign Policy Affecting Poland: 1939-1945.* Unpublished Master's thesis, Columbia University, 1945.

Weintraub, Wiktor. "Czy Ameryka byla dla Norwida infernem?" *Kultura* (April, 1963).

Weld, Ralph Foster. *Brooklyn in America.* New York: Columbia University Press, 1950.

Wilczynska, Marja. *Unforgotten Heroes.* Baltimore: No Imprint, 1947.

Wille, Lois. "Black-Pole Coalition Forming," *Detroit Free Press* (November 30, 1969).

Winter, Nevin O. *The New Poland.* Boston: L. C. Page & Company, 1923.

Winterbotham, F. W. *The Ultra Secret.* New York: Harper and Row, 1974.

Wittke, Carl. *The Irish in America.* Baton Rouge: Louisiana State University Press, 1956.

Woodward, Llewellyn. *British Foreign Policy in the Second World War.* London: 1962.

Woolsey, L. H. "Poland at Yalta and Dumbarton Oaks," *The American Journal of International Law,* XXXIX, 1945.

Wright, Herbert. "Poland and the Crimea Conference," *The American Journal of International Law,* XXXIX, 1945.

Wronski, Casimir J. B. "The Polish Alma Mater of America," *Poles of Chicago 1937-1937.* Leon Zglenicki (Ed.). Chicago: Polish Pageant Inc., 1937.

Wronski, Stanislaw and Maria Zwolakowa. *Polacy Zydzi 1939-1945*. Warszawa: Ksiazka i Wiedza, 1971.

Wurmbrand, Max and Cecil Roth. *The Jewish People 4000 Years of Survival*. Jerusalem: Shengold Publishers, 1966.

Wytrwal, Joseph A. "Memorials to General Casimir Pulaski in the United States," *The Georgia Historical Quarterly*, XLIV (September, 1960), Number 3.

Wytrwal, Joseph A. *America's Polish Heritage. A Social History of the Poles in America*. Detroit: Endurance Press, 1961.

Wytrwal, Joseph A. *Poles in American History and Tradition*. Detroit: Endurance Press, 1969.

Wytrwal, Joseph A. *Poles in America*. Minneapolis: Lerner Publications, 1969.

Wytrwal, Joseph A. "The Polish National Alliance," *Dziennik Polski* (October 3, 1970).

Wytrwal, Joseph A. "New Experiments in the Schools," *Ethnic Groups in the City*. Otto Feinstein, Editor. Lexington, D. C. Heath and Company, 1971.

Wytrwal, Joseph A. "Why Ethnic Studies?" *Teachers Guide for Senior High School Ethnic Studies Course*. Detroit: Detroit Public Schools, 1972.

Wytrwal, Dr. Joseph A. "Contemporary Polish American Clergy," *Dziennik Polski*, English Edition (December 28, 1974).

Wytrwal, Dr. Joseph A. "Dred Scott . . . Alfred Dreyfus . . . now Benedict Markowski," *Dziennik Polski*, English Edition (January 4, 1975).

Wytrwal, Jozef A. "Towarzystwo Laur Zespol Tancow i Spiewu w Detroit," *Bialy Orzel* (July, 1951).

Znaniecki, Florian. "The Significance of Cultural Associations in the Modern World," *American Council of Polish Cultural Clubs Convention Bulletin* (August, 1955).

Zubrzycki, Jerzy. *Polish Immigrants in Britain*. The Hague: Martinus Nijhoff, 1956.

Index

Aachen, 348
Abel, I. W., 550
Aberdeen Proving Ground, 388
Abhez, E., 422
Abraham, I., 71
Abrahams, 81
Abramowicz, A. L., Bishop, 426, 577
Academy of the Holy Family of Nazareth (Chicago), 124
acculturation, 53
Adam Mickiewicz Library, 306, 307, 555
Adamczak, F. S., 385
Adamczaks, 42
Adamic, 233
Adamic, L., 353, 354
Adamski, D. J., 453
Adamskis, 42
Addams, Jane, 95
Adelaida, 6
ADF, 568-572
AFL, 537
Africa, 2, 198, 341, 356, 368, 370, 383, 397, 399, 557
Africans, 254
African Corp, 468
African Youth, 474
Afro-Americans, 180
Aisne, Marne, 226
Akron, Ohio, 452
Alabama, 40, 43
Albanians, 254
Albosta, M. G., 328
Alfred Jurzykowski Foundation, 330
Algeria, 381
Allen, Julian, 47
Allen, S., 504
Allentown, Pa., 453
Alliance College (Cambridge Springs, Pa.), 124, 153, 204, 242, 310, 427
Alliance Daily, 358
Alliance Ladies' Guild, 156
Alliance of American Veterans of Polish Extraction, 260

Alliance of Poles in America, 156
Alliance of Poles in Ohio, 156
Alliance of Polish Priests in America, 131-133
Alliance of Polish Turners of the U.S. of America, 161
Alliance of Polish Women of America, 243
Alliancer, 156
Alobr, R., 357
Alpena Michigan, 370, 385
Alps, 198
Alsace, 225
Alski, W. L., 277, 278
Alter, V., 360
Amada Turner's Company, 44
Amalgamated Association, 537
Amalgamated Clothing Workers of America, 540, 543
Ambridge, Pa., 163
American Aid Committee, 45
American Anti-Slavery Society, 466
American Broadcasting Company, 503
American Catholic Historical Association, 574
American Council of Polish Cultural Clubs, 325, 326, 327
American Institute of Polish Culture (Miami), 331, 332
American Jewish Congress, 507
American Journal of International Law, 413
American Mathematical Society, 315
American Polonia Reporter, 485
American Relief for Poland, 397
American Slav Congress, 544, 545
Ameherst, Wisconsin, 453
Ameryka-Echo, 135, 282, 477, 506, 585
Amish, 252, 254
Amoraim, 79
Am-Pol Eagle, 120, 127, 443, 455, 495
Amsterdam, New York, 452
Andes Mountains, 27

Andes Railway, 27
Anasiewicz, R. J., 452
Anders, W., General, 356
Anderson, C. P., 389
Anderson, J. K., 556
Anderson, L., 431
Andruszkiewicz, S. A., 381
Andrzejewski, 392
Andrzejkowicz, J., 143, 144, 145
Angelo, F., 472
Anglin, A., 488
Angola, N. Y., 452
Anglo-Saxons, 237, 238, 244, 245, 246, 253, 603
Annunciation of the Blessed Virgin Church (Polonia, Wis.), 108
Ansonia, Conn., 163
Anti-semitism, 74, 80, 82, 90, 495, 499, 501, 505, 509, 511, 577
Antonowicz, F. J., 454
Anuszkiewicz, B. T., 384, 393
Anuszkiewicz, William, 383
Anzio, 385
Apaches, 524, 525
Apalachicola, Florida, 469
Appel, J. J., 251
Appleton, Wis., 452
Arabs, 194, 198, 254
Archdiocesan Development Fund (Detroit), 569-572
Archdiocese of Detroit, 491, 494, 561, 563, 564, 567, 569, 573
Archduke Ferdinand, 197
Archibald, 212
Arends, L., 531
Arians, 13, 64
Arizona, 163, 441, 451, 482
Arizona (battleship), 365
Armenians, 254, 343, 535
Armia Krajowa, 343
Arthur, G. K., 495
Asboth, A., General, 469
Asia, 2, 393, 397, 442, 557
Askenazy, S., 65, 66
Askins, J., 595
Asnyk, A., 90
Assimilation, 253, 583
Association of National Defense, 359
Association of Polish Doctors and Dentists, 286
Association of Polish Exiles in America, 49
Association of Sons of Poland, 164-167
Assumption of the Blessed Virgin Mary Church (Chicago), 555
Atchison, L., 494
Athens, Wis., 453
Athol Springs, N. Y., 551
Atlantic Charter, 359-361, 408, 409, 413, 416
Attu, 380
Auburn, Mass., 452
Auburn, N. Y., 163
Auerbach, R., 520
August I, 19, 20, 63
August II, 20, 63
August, Zygmunt, 16, 19
August County (Virginia), 527
Augustynski, F., 163
Aurora, Ill., 549
Auschwitz, 515, 516
Auschwitz-Birkenau, 498
Austin, H. Russell, 113
Austin, H. R., 310
Austin, R., 386, 493
Austin, Stephen, 44
Austin, W. R., 432
Australians, 254, 433
Austria, 2, 16, 24, 25, 36, 58, 60-64, 66, 69, 72, 82, 143, 198, 201, 232, 322, 343, 535, 557
Austria-Hungary 197, 200-202
Austrian Poland, 34, 37, 38, 45, 56, 58, 68, 85, 86, 87
Austrians, 82, 98, 178, 199, 221
Austro-Germans, 199
Azarjew, A., 330

Babbitt, Nevada, 452
Babula, R., 455
Babylonia, 78, 79
Bach, 299
Baczalski, J., 451
Baden, 26
Badricout, 225
Baginski, M., 304
Baginski, M. W., 376, 377
Bagrowski, A., 385
Bak, B., 589
Bakalar, C., 518
Baker, N. D., 218, 230
Balbaud, R., 347
Balboa, 449
Balch, E. G., 34
Baldwin, Locomotive Works, 310
Balicki, Z., 85
Balkans, 72
Ballagh, J., 39

INDEX

Baltic Sea, 1, 3, 4, 6, 10, 11, 12, 62, 235, 360, 594
Baltimore, Maryland, 163, 184, 186, 258, 259, 260, 284, 387, 391, 394, 451
Baltimore Council, 196
Banachs, 42
Baptists, 96
Barabasz, M., Rev., 131
Baraga, J., 365
Baran, F., OFM, Rev., 113
Baranowski, M. A., 452
Baranowski, P., 390
Barc, 284, 285
Barc, F., 258-260
Barchak, J. F., 453
Baretski, C. A., Dr., 587
Barlin, see Berlin
Baroni, G., Rev., 575
Bartek, J., 384
Bartkowski, G. J., 453
Bartolome de las Casas, 14
Barton, J. R., 252
Bartosz, A., 331
Bartoszewski, W., 503, 505, 509
Barylski, B., 386
Barzynski, John, 140
Barzynski, J., 394
Barzynski, V., Rev., 110, 125, 140, 142, 148, 149, 170, 171
Bashau, E., 357
Basilian Order, 473
Basle, 348
Bass, Robert, Dr., 471
Batavia, N. Y., 357, 452
Batoczynski, C. H., 452
Baton Rouge, La., 247
Batory, Stefan, 19, 20, 63, 80
Batowski, S., 159
Battery Park (New York), 13
Battle Creek, Michigan, 467
Battle of Argonne, 227
Battle of Britain, 263
Battle of Cape Matapan, 391
Battle of Juvigny, 226, 227
Battle of Leyte Gulf, 375
Battle of Raclawice, 114
Battle of Vienna, 69
Bauer, 432
Bay City, Michigan, 117, 380, 385, 386
Bay Mills, Michigan, 531
Beck, J. M., 212
Beczkiewicz, P., 143

Bedford, Mass., 440
Bedford-Stuyvesant, 40
Beethoven, 219
Beitzell, R., 400, 401
Belgians, 26, 55, 254
Belgium, 54, 55, 198, 200, 206, 207, 219, 221, 262, 379
Bell, C., 495
Bell, H., Dr., 471, 472
Belle Isle (Detroit), 570
Belleville Enterprise, 447
Belleville, Michigan, 442, 447
Beltrand, G., 391
Belza, S., 307
Belzowski, F. J., 381
Bem, 65
Bem, J., General, 26
Benda, W., 324
Benedict V, Pope, 5
Benedictines, 5
Benes, E., 545
Bercovici, K., 246
Berezhnitsev, 517, 518
Bergen County, 526
Berle, M., 432
Berlin, 3, 8, 219, 300, 348, 364, 420, 520
Bernard of Chartres, 579
Bernadine Sisters of St. Joseph, 117
Bernault, E., 36
Berneski, L. A., 451
Bernstorff, Count, 213
Berra, 432
Bessarabia, 400
Bethe, H., 387
Bethmann-Hollweg, 213
Bezecny, J. W., 451
Biachowski, J., 143
Biadynski, J., 143
Bialasiewicz, J. F., 585
Bialkowski, J. J., 452
Bialy Orzel, 251
Bialystok, 508
Bibliotheque National, 333
Bielawski, A., 304
Bierut, B., 545
Bigos, A., 317
bi-lingual instruction, 574
Bilski, C., 307
Bingham, J., 502
Binkowski, D., Judge, 570, 571
Bismarck, 41, 195
Biasz, R. C., 455
Bizerte, 368

Blacks, 127, 249, 422, 457-496, 568, 577, 603
Black History Week, 458
Black Panthers, 477
Black-Polish Conference, 490-495
Black Sea, 2, 10, 12, 602
Blair House, 530
Blawatek, 263
Blejwas, Stanislaw, 23
Bletchley, 391
blitzkrieg, 338, 340, 341, 352
Blue Army, 205, 219
Bober River, 7
Bobolewski, J., Rev., 125
Bobowski, J. E., 451
Bobrzynski, M., 64, 65
Bochenski, Aleksander, 17
Bochnia, Poland, 549
Bochta, B., 163
Bodnar, J., 112
Boeck, L. J., 49
Bogacki, G. J., 370
Bogus, D., Rev., 490-494
Bohemia, 6, 13, 74, 75
Bohemians, 5, 535, 541, 567
Bojanowski, F. J., 41, 42
Bojarski, G. J., 449
Bojko, J., 86
Bojnowski, L., Monsignor, 134, 483
Bok, E., 212
Boland, J. P., Rev., 552
Bolek, Rev. F., 282
Boleslaw II, 6, 7
Boleslaw III, 7
Boleslaw IV, 8
Boleslaw V, 8
Boleslaw Chrobry, 6
Boleslaw the Brave, 62
Boleslaw the Pious, 70
Boleslaw the Wrymouth, 8
Bolinski, T. R., 390
Bolivar, S., General, 531, 532
Bolivia, 532
Bolshevik, 262
Bonaparte, Napoleon, 23, 43
Bonaventure College (Pulaski, Wis.), 124
Bonzano, Archbishop, 184
Bookman, Gary, 522
Bookman, N., 522
Bork, J., 110
Borczyk, S. Z., 451
Borejsza, J. W., 50, 52
Borglum, G., 528

Bor-Komorowski, General, 403, 508
Bork, L. S., 448
Borkowicz, C., 472
Borkowicz, V. J., Monsignor, 557-559
Borleske, Herman, 41
Borowski, I., Major, 532
Borowski, J. C., 451
Borowski, R. J., 452
Borszcz, Rev., 186
Borucki, S. F., Rev., 568, 569
Boston, 39, 47, 272, 327, 462
Boswell, A. B., 197
Bougainville, 379
Boulder, Colorado, 531
Bourdell, 306
Bourne, R., 251
Bourskaya, Ina, 324
Bowman, N. L., 52
Bowens, Alton, 495
Boyle, Tony, 545-548
Brach, S. C., 392
Bradbury, N., 389
Brahe River, 352
Brahms, 219
Brand, Premier, 165
Brandes, G., 119
Brandenburg, 8
Brandt, J., 314
Branibor, 8
Brank, T., 476
Brazik, R., Capt., 455
Brazik, R., 451
Bremerhaven, 423
Breslau, 75
Brest, 341
Brewer, T., 431
Bridesburg, Pa., 163
Bridgeview, Illinois, 451
Brillowski, 42
Britain, 43, 340-345, 348, 363, 399, 416, 417
British, 43, 54, 341, 343, 346, 349, 364, 390, 391, 399, 402, 403, 541
British Broadcasting Corporation, 418
Broadway, 422
Brocktown, Mass., 452
Brodak, J. W., 456
Brody, D., 535, 537, 542
Bronars, J., Lt. Col., 439, 440
Brook Farm, 51
Brooklyn College, 513
Brooklyn Diocese, 573, 574
Brooklyn, New York, 40, 112, 130,

132, 357, 383, 384, 442, 446, 452, 511-513
Brooklyn Star, 443
Brown, 549
Brown, E. C., Governor, 482
Brown, J., 461
Browne, E., Councilman, 491
Brownson, O. A., 192
Brudrewicz, O., 460
Brunswick, Germany, 370
Bryan, J., 352, 353
Brylowski, 42
Brysk, T., 304
Bucior, A., Cpl., 452
Buczek, D. S., 483
Buczynski, B., Rev., 107
Buczynski, G. T., 452
Buczynski, T. J., 207-209
Buda Synod, 76
Budarz, J. M., 328
Budka, D., 451
Budno, E. A., Capt., 455
Buffalo, 35, 109, 111, 116-118, 120, 121, 127, 154, 155, 186, 217, 239, 261, 306, 308, 325, 327, 330, 353, 357, 363, 377, 378, 380, 409, 416, 443, 452, 455, 495, 539, 543, 550-552
Buffalo Evening News, 120, 126, 127, 110, 540
Buffalo River, 44
Bug River, 342
Bugajski, K. M., 451
Bugelski, B. R., Dr., 308
Bujalski, D. A., Capt., 452
Bukovina, 400
Bukowinski, 200
Bukowski, F., 163
Bukowski, R., 452
Bulas, K., 313
Bulewski, L., 50
Bulgarians, 417
Buna, New Guinea, 378
Buracheska, T. R., 453
Burant, F., Msgr., 425
Burdick, A. B., 463
Burdock, J., 456
Burke, K., 238
Burnett, C., 503
Burns, M. J., 404
Burroughs, M., 484
Burton, R., 418
Burzynski, E. S., 386
Bushaw, E., 357

Bydgoszcz, 513
Byelorussians, 342, 343
Byron, 306
Byzantine, 4, 65

Cadiz, Spain, 525, 530
Cady, Richard, 445
Cagliani, Sardinia, 368
Cajetan, Sister (Felician), 117
California, 51, 145, 327, 330, 392, 394, 439, 451, 480, 482, 512, 589
Calisia, see Kalisz
Calumet City, Ill., 163, 451
Cambridge Springs, Pa., 153, 204, 327
Camden, N. J., 452
Camp Douglas, 224
Camp Evans, Vietnam, 443
Camp McArthur, 224
Camp Pendleton, 439
Camp Quinton, 204
Campbell, M., 387
Campbell, Ohio, 452
Campter, J. J., 449
Canada, 203, 204, 216, 262, 327, 333, 551, 596
Canadian Officers Training Corp, 204
Canadian War Office, 203
Canadians, 190, 254, 535
Canal Zone, 449
Canisius College, 120
Canisius High School, 120
Cannonsburg, Pa., 394
Canute, 6
Capistrano, J., 76
Cardwell, Ann Su, 414
Carnap, R., 59
Carnegie, A., 470
Carnegie, D., 364
Carnegie Hall, 312
Carnegie-Mellon University, 327-328
Carolingian Empire, 70
Carpathian Mts., 3, 4
Carpenter, 271
Carpenter, N., 239
Carr, J., 308
Carson City, 52
Carter, D., 477
Carter, Jimmie, President, 482, 577, 600
Carter, L. T., 476
Casimir the Great, 70
Cassels, L., 481
Cassidy, F., 487
Catherine the Great, 22, 62

Catholics, 96, 119, 481, 489, 499, 510
Catholic Chronicle, 472
Catholic Church (Poland), 68-83, 402
Catholic League for Religious Assistance to Poland, 425, 426
Catholic News, 557
Catholic Universe Bulletin, 575
Catholic University of Lublin, 159, 430
Catholic World, 413
Catholicism, 60, 63, 75
Cavett, D., 504
Cavour, 144
Cegielski, R. J., Cpl., 452
Celtes, Konrad, 10
Central Citizens Committee (Detroit), 564
Central-Verein, 196
Cetlinski, W. A., 381
Chadsey High School (Detroit), 369, 372, 381, 489
Chalcarz, F., Rev., 189
Chalubinski, T., Dr., 316
Chamaj, A. P., 452
Chamberlain, N., 337
Champ D'Asile, 43
Charleston, S. C., 459
Chase, M. E., 52
Chayer, M. E., 468
Cheektowaga, N. Y., 111, 455
Chelmonski, J., 314
Chelsea, Mass., 357
Cherokee, 525
Cherwack, L., Cpl., 445
Cheslak, P., 451
Chess, E. R., General, 448
Chess, R., General, 556
Chess, L., 476, 477
Cheyenne, 524
Chwalek, L., 383
Chateau-Thierry, 226
Chicago, 35, 41, 50, 102, 109, 110, 116, 117, 124, 125, 140, 142, 144, 145, 153, 154, 155, 156-163, 175, 185, 186, 194, 195, 205, 216, 218, 222, 228, 231, 237, 238, 241, 256-261, 264, 272, 282, 309, 323, 325, 327, 330, 333, 353, 357, 364, 392, 393, 395, 410, 427, 439, 441-443, 444, 451, 454, 458, 476, 478, 484, 485, 494, 495, 502, 506, 508, 543, 544, 549, 550, 555, 561, 574, 575, 577, 594
Chicago Arts Club, 323
Chicago (East), 451

Chicago Federation of Labor, 542
Chicago Garment Workers' Strike, 541
Chicago Polish Arts Club, 324, 325
Chicago Sun Times, 551
Chicago Typographical Union, 549
Chicopee, Massachusetts, 395, 452
Chile, 26, 532
China, 2, 403
Chinese, 42, 403, 433, 575
Chinook, 524
Chippewa, 527
Chledowski, E., 357
Chmiel, Andrew, 452
Chmiel, L. V., 451
Chmielewska, S., 157
Chmielewski, P., 60
Choate, J., 212
Chodzko, L., 53
Chojnacki, C., 386
Chojnacki, F. S., 328
Chojnice, 40
Chojnice, Poland, 527
Chopin, F., 26, 208, 209, 213, 219, 299, 300, 312, 313, 328, 502
Chopin Fine Arts Club (South Bend), 327
Chopin Scholarships, 311, 313, 315, 316
Chorazyczewski, H., 517-519
Chorazyczewski, I., 517-519
Chou-En-Lai, Premier, 529
Christopher, Ill., 451
Chrobot, L., Rev., 485, 595
Chrostowski, H., 385
Chrysler Freeway, 487
Chrzanowski, General, 26, 54
Church, F., Senator, 482
Church of the Immaculate Conception (Peshawbestown), 530
Churchill, Winston, 341, 345, 346, 359, 401-409, 411, 415-419, 511
Chwieroch, F., 163
Ciaglo, J. A., 261
Ciborowski, T. P., 452
Cicero, Ill., 261, 451, 452
Ciechanowski, J., 411
Cichon, E., 131
Cichon, W., 455
Cichy, V., 331
Ciecula, T. P., 452
Cierges, 226
Ciesielska, M. J., Lt., 452
Ciesielska, R., 513-517, 519
Ciesielski, F., 513

INDEX

Ciesielski School (Israel), 516
Cieszkowski, A., 335
Cincinnati, Ohio, 179, 460
Cincinnati Ohio Enquirer, 179, 402, 418
Cinema 1976, 476
CIO, 544, 545
Ciolkowski, Konstantin, 27
Ciseski, 42
Cisewski, 42
Cistercians, 5, 10
Ciszewskis, 42
Ciupinski, J. M., 451
Cius, F. E., 455
Clarion, 83
Clairion, Pa., 453
Clairton, Pa., 453
Clay, C. M., 460, 461
Cleveland, 156, 162, 183, 184, 186, 260-262, 286, 328, 330, 452, 544, 556
Cliburn, Van, 311, 315
Clifton, N. J., 452
Clinton, F., 563
Clooney, R., 431
Club Polonaise (Passaic), 327
Coatesville, Pa., 452
Cocteau, Jean, 26
Colbert, C., 336
Cole Nat (King), 422
Coleman, Dr., 242
Coleman, M. M., 461
College de France, 53, 306
Collegeville, Minn., 589
Colorado, 229, 328
Colton, Bishop, 111
Columbia Broadcasting System, 503
Columbia, S. C., 466
Columbia University, 18, 237, 320, 428
Columbus, C., 119, 525
Command and General Staff College (Ft. Leavenworth), 434
Commendori, 7
Committee of National Defense, 359
Common Schools, 90
Common Schools Society Endowment Fund, 100
Communists, 433
Community Homeowners Organization, 479
Como, Perry, 432
Company K, 224-228, 386, 393
Conference of Priests for Polish Affairs, 561

Congregation Ados Shalom, 522
Congress Bi-Weekly, 507
Congress Kingdom, 38, 89, 90
Congress of Industrial Organization, 544
Congregation of the Fathers of the Divine Love, 125
Congress of World Federation of Trade Unions, 544
Congressional Medal of Honor, 366, 377, 384
Congressmen, 304
Conklin, E. M., 390
Connecticut, 46, 163, 167, 217, 304, 387, 392, 451, 483, 525, 527, 560
Conrad, J., 252
Conrad, T., 595
Conyers, John, Congressman, 491, 494, 495
Cooper, James F., 45
Copernican Observatory, 315
Copernicus, see Kopernik
Copernicus Society of America, 332, 333
Copernicus Symposium (Miami), 332
Cornflower, 263
Corpus Christi Church (Buffalo), 551
Corpus Christi Church (Detroit), 488
Cossacks, 20, 63, 80, 81
Cosseboom, K., 477
Cotes du Nord, 204
Council for Polish Relief, **355**
Council of Clermont, 74
Council of Constance, 14
Council of the Four Lands, 73, 74
Courland River, 33
Courlanders, 33
Cracow, 79
Crazy Horse, Chief, 525, 528
Crazy Horse Monument, 529
Crimea, 404, 405, 415
Croatians, 535, 575
Crockett, D., 432
Crockett, G. W., Judge, 492, 494
Crusades, 74
Cudahy, Wisconsin, 554
Cultural Pluralism, 278
Curie, Eve, 158
Curie, Sklodowska Marie, 129, 252
Curie Radium Institute, 129
Currie, M. S., 59
Curtis, C., 212
Curzon Line, 343, 400, 402, 404, 408, 411, 413, 417
Custer, South Dakota, 528

Cuyahoga Falls, Ohio, 472
Cwikla, L. W., 453
Cybis, B., 529, 530
Cylkowski, E., 385
Czajka, J., 228
Czar Alexander II, 87
Czarina, Catherine II, 82, 83
Czarina, Maria Fedorowna, 529
Czarnecka, E., 496
Czarnecki, Hetman, 21
Czarnecki, S., 163, 365
Czarnomski, I., 45
Czarnowski, 496
Czartoryski, 14, 313
Czartoryski, A. J., Prince, 23, 54, 56, 65
Czas, 52, 58, 168
Czech Legion, 217
Czechoslovakia, 2, 64, 316, 337, 343
Czechowski, J. L., 451
Czechs, 6, 176, 199, 217, 300, 417
Czekajski, T., 365
Czerwiec, R. C., 455
Czerwiec, S., 308
Czeslowski see Chess

Dabrowka, 5
Dabrowski, 307
Dabrowski, J., Rev., 107, 108, 117, 124, 140, 195, 527, 528
Dakota 43
Dakotas, 35, 525
D'Alfonse, E., 49
Dale, Governor, 526
Dallin, Alexander, 201
Damaschkes, 474
Damaschke, F., 473, 474
Damaschke, J., 473, 474
Damaschke, S., 474
DaNang, AB, 442
DaNang, 448, 449
Danes, 252
Daniels, J., 130, 213, 214, 220, 221
Dante, 306
Danube River, 6
Dardas, L. R., 379, 380
Daszynski, I., 85
David, J., 319
Davis, E., 480
Dayan, M., 516
Dearborn, Michigan, 368, 373, 385, 522
Dearden, Cardinal, 559, 562-566, 568- 570, 572, 573

Debicki, M., 44
Debkowska, B., 393
Dec, Jan, 263
DeLaSalle College, 374
Delaware, 39, 163, 164, 395, 504
Delawares, 524
Del Mar, Vina, see Stack
Democratic Society of Polish Exiles, 49, 50
Democratic Society of Polish Exiles in America, 568
Dende, Henry, 585
Denmark, 6
Denver, Colorado, 328
Denver Park, 328
Denver Polish Club, 328
DePaul University, 207
Derby, Conn., 163
Detroit American, 443
Detroit Archdiocesan Priests Conference, 490, 494
Detroit Free Press, 299, 368, 370, 372, 374, 377, 378, 402, 404, 406, 418, 472, 479, 481, 482, 484, 485, 488, 489, 494, 554, 559, 565, 566, 570, 572, 595
Detroit Historical Society, 109
Detroit Jewish News, 511, 514, 518, 519, 521
Detroit, Michigan, 35, 108, 109, 117, 118, 139, 140, 163, 175, 186, 238, 241, 244, 245, 251, 259, 260, 261, 267, 282, 285, 303, 304, 309, 327, 329, 330, 333, 353, 359, 370, 372- 376, 379-387, 394, 396, 404, 408, 450, 452, 454, 456, 471, 473, 477- 470, 487, 489-496, 521, 522, 530, 551, 555, 556, 558, 559, 562, 565, 573, 583, 584, 585, 588, 595, 596
Detroit News, 282, 368-372, 374-376, 379-382, 384, 394, 402, 404, 407, 418, 434, 445, 448, 449, 450, 454, 456, 474, 478, 488, 489, 507, 512, 513, 556, 564-566, 572, 576
Detroit Priests' Senate, 558
Detroit Public Library, 105
Detroit Seamless Tube Company, 374
Detroit Sunday News, 476
Detroit Urban League, 496
Deutsche Schnellpost, 49
Deutscher, I., 497
DeWaterville Regiment, 43
Dewey, J., 312
Dewey, T. E., 410, 411
Diaspora, 78

INDEX 633

Dickson City, Pa., 188, 441, 453
Dilcher, H. S., 376
Dimaggio, 432
Dimitrov, G., 545
Dimont, M., 499, 500
Dingus Day, 294
Diocese of Tororo, 474
Disney, W. E., 213
Disney, W., 336
Displaced Persons, 423, 424, 429
Disraeli, B., 85
Ditto, F., 491
Dlugokinski, E. D., 450
Dlugosz, Jan, 10
Dmowski, Roman, 27, 60, 63, 80, 241
Dnieper River, 4
Dniester River, 4, 12
Dobosz, J., 329
Domanski, V., 143
Dombrowski, 217
Dombrowski, J. R., 447
Domeyko, I., 27, 532
Dominicans, 5
Don Bosco College (New Jersey), 427
Dondero, G. A., 401
Donne, J., 103
Dorosz, W., 551
Dorsey, 337
Dorshak, R. J., 451
Doubnow, 76-79
Dougherty, D. J., 185
Douglas, T., 522
Douglas, W. O., Justice, 479
Dowagiac, Michigan, 373
Drabic, P. E., 455
Drabik, A. A., 382
Drachsler, J., 119
Drazba, C. A., Lt., 453
Dred Scott, 287
Drewicz, R. C., 452
Dreyfus, A., 287
Droszcz, D. P., 451
Drwal, J., 169
Drzewieniecki, Dr., 308
Dubanewicz, M., 446
Dubicki, J., 573
Dubin, C., 514, 518
DuBois, J., 510
duBroff, S., 499, 506
Duc Duc, 443
Duchess of Hohenberg, 197
Duchy of Warsaw, 2
Duchy of Muscovy, 16, 20
Dudek, J. W., 451
Dudek, R. E., 451

Dudley, Lord, 49
Dudzik, R., 163
Duffy Silk Company, 552
Duke of Anjou, 19
Duke of Lorraine, 20
Duluth, Minn., 179, 452
Dunsmore, Pa., 453
Duquesne University, 327, 328
Duryea, Pa., 188
Dusable Museum, 458, 484
Dutch, 33, 178, 247, 252, 303, 567, 603
Dworaczyk, W. S., 453
Dyboski, R., 223
Dybowski, Prof., 325
Dybowski, Z., 426
Dyczkowski, R. R., 455
Dydacki, F., 462
Dyke, F., 392
Dykta, 394
Dymerski, A. J., Sgt., 452
Dyniewicz, W., 135, 144
Dziadosz, T., 447
Dzienkowski, J. S., Sgt., 443, 444
Dziennik Chicagoski, 135, 148, 330, 585
Dziennik Dla Wszystkich, 135, 357, 358, 585
Dziennik Polski, 135, 138, 252, 439, 480, 484, 492, 494, 506, 557 560-565, 571, 573, 585
Dzierzynski, F., 85
Dzikowski, E., 443
Dziob, F., 163
Dziuban, S., 394
Dziulikowski, W. H., 357
Dzwoniecki, see Maxwell

Eagle River, Wis., 453
Earl of Beaconsfield, 85
East Chicago, Indiana, 451
East Gary, Indiana, 451
East Germany, 2
East Prussia, 13
East Side Shopper, 486, 493
Ebony, 496
Echo, 474
ECHO (Detroit Organization), 479
Echo z Polski, 52, 135
Ecorse, Michigan, 385
Ecuador, 42
Edelweiss Restaurant, 328
Eden, A., 404, 406
Edison, T., 212
Egypt, T., 212, 229

Eichelberger, R. L., 378
Eichler, B. A., 135
Eiffel Tower, 370
Eighty-Second Colored Regiment, 468
Einstein, A., 312, 390
Einstein, B., 504
Eis, Bishop, 151
Eisenhower, D., President, 382, 392, 396, 414, 415, 428
Elbe River, 4, 6, 8
Eliach, Y., 513
Elinski, R. W., 447
Eliot, J. P., 402
Elizabeth I, 16
Elizabeth, N. J., 163
Elkins, M., 502
Ellicott City, Maryland, 551
Elliott, J. H., 38
Ellis Island, 132, 174, 179, 181, 196, 233, 238
Ellner, S. H., 552
Elmhurst, Illinois, 451
Elster River, 6
Emerson, 247
Emerson, R. W., 306
Emerson, W., 467
Emigration Congress, 241
Empire State Building, 423
Engels, 85
England, 2, 6, 16, 23, 46, 49, 63, 72-75, 144, 178 194, 241, 252, 300, 307, 310, 330, 343, 358, 360, 361, 367, 368, 371, 390, 534
English, 63, 94, 95, 98, 121, 122, 147, 209, 247, 248, 252, 303, 535
ENIAC, 388
Enigma, 390, 391
Eniwetok, 389
Episcopalians, 96
Erie County Democratic Committee, 495
Erie County, New York, 127
Erie, Pennsylvania, 111, 124, 240, 453
Erlich, H., 360
Essen, 345
Estonia, 360, 400
Eve, A. O., 495
Everett, C., 388
Everett, E. E., Governor, 39
Everson, Pa., 551

Falat, J., 314
Falcon Order in America, 160-163, 197, 203, 204, 205, 217, 223, 238
Falkaviges, 42

Falkiewicz, 42
Falkowski, J. J., Pvt., 443
Fannin, J., 44
Farbstein, Congressman, 502
Fargo, N. Daxota, 589
Farley, Cardinal, 212
Fascism, 343
Fayetteville, N.C., 452
Federal-Metro College, 478
Federowski, R. A., 451
Felician Sisters, Order of St. Felix, 117, 118, 132-134, 195, 303, 528, 555, 567, 568
Fernandez, F., 525
Fialko, D. A., 452
Fibich, M., 383
Fieszel, C. W., 455
Fighting Fund, 205
Figura, B. S., 326, 500, 501, 504
Filion, Michigan, 452
Finn, M., 337
Finnish, 535
Firkuses, 42
Fisher, L. H., 463
Flaczek, T., Rev., 111
Flegel, L., 531
Fleming, S., 454
Flensburg, 368
Flexner, E., 467, 468
Flinn, T., 552
Flint, Michigan, 374, 386, 452
Florence, Italy, 529, 589
Florida, 43, 331, 468, 469
Fond des Blancs, 461
Foner, P. S., 458
Fontana, California, 589
Ford, G., President, 530, 600
Ford, Henry, 312
Ford Motor Company, 451, 471, 535
Fort Barrie, 43
Fort Benning (Georgia), 434
Fort Duquesne, 527
Fort Hancock, 395
Fort Huachuca, Arkansas, 453
Fort Leavenworth, Kansas,
Fort McNair, 434
Fort Meade, 395
Fort Niagara, 217
Fort Pickens, 469
Fort Sam Houston, 453
Fortuna, S. F., 385
Forward (Jewish Daily), 501
Foster, R., 393
Fourth Luteran Council, 75
Fox, 42

INDEX

Fox, P., 135, 174, 187, 189, 190
Fox, T. C., 554, 566, 570, 572
Foxboro, Massachusetts, 456
France, 2, 14-16, 20, 23, 24, 43, 46, 52-55, 58, 69, 72, 73, 75, 159, 163, 165, 218, 219, 224, 228, 231, 241, 252, 261-263, 340, 342-345, 347, 348, 366, 368, 370, 377, 379, 382, 393, 416
Franciscans, 5, 551
Franczyk, Gus, 495
Franczyk, Stanley, 495
Frankfurt, 367
Fraser, J., Rev., 558
Fraternal of Slavs, 50
Frederick the Great, 62
Freeland, Pa., 186
French, 23, 24, 26, 39, 41, 43, 52, 105, 107, 147, 178, 194, 216, 222, 248, 252, 254, 303, 306, 307, 341, 346, 347, 348, 349, 391, 460, 462, 527, 567, 596
French Canadians, 180, 485, 537
Friedel, F., 135
Friends of Polish Art (Detroit), 327
Friesenhahn, K., 382
Fronczak, F. E., Dr., 119, 120, 121, 307
Fronczak Library, 495
Frydrychowicz, Rev., 186
Fudyja, E., 390
Fugitive Slave Law, 462, 463
Fuller-Ossoli, M., 306
Fullerton Hall, 324
Fundusz Bojowy (see Fighting Fund)
Fundusz Niepodleglosciowy (see Independence Fund)
Funerals, 299
Furlong, W. B., 252
Futema, Okinawa, 443

Gabreski, F., 366, 367, 433, 434
Gacek, F., 573
Gaelic, 575
Gaillard, F., 486, 492
Gajewska, Janina, 131
Galek, A., 372
Galicia, 68, 85, 199
Galicja Song and Dance Ensemble, 555
Gallatin, A., 47
Galleria Nazionale, 589
Galleria Uffici, 589
Gallus Anonymous, 5
Gamelin, G., General, 346, 347, 348
Garalski, L. S., 453

Garden Spot News, 500, 503, 504
Gareau, L., 449
Garibaldi, 26, 144
Garner, J. B., 472, 476
Garrison, W. L., 466, 467
Gartner, I., Rev. 109
Gary, Indiana, 451
Gasiorowski, W., 135
Gasparri, P., Cardinal, 185
Gawel, W., Sgt., 452
Gawell, F. J., Capt., 441
Gawronski, W., 135
Gaylord, Michigan, 562, 563
Gazeta Katolicka, 148
Gazeta Narodowa, 52
Gazeta Polska, 48, 135, 142, 144
Gdansk, 9, 11, 12, 13, 17, 20, 349
Gdynia, 235, 369
Geary, M., 331
General Motor Corporation, 421
General Pulaski Day, 277
General Pulaski Day Banquet, 328
Geneva, 415
George Washington University, 434
Georgia, 40, 471, 482
Georgia Historical Quarterly, 40
Germans, 6, 9, 10, 12, 13, 23, 38, 50, 75, 81, 94, 95, 98, 105, 107, 120, 132, 147, 165, 176, 178, 185, 191, 193, 194, 198, 199, 200, 221, 224-228, 247, 248, 252, 254, 300, 307, 338-341, 343, 349, 350, 357, 361, 400-405, 416, 485, 497, 499, 500, 504, 508, 509, 512-514, 518, 535, 539-541, 567, 575, 581, 594, 603
German Jews, 76
Germantown, Pa., 527
Germany, 2, 14, 27, 55, 60, 72, 73, 76, 77, 198-202, 228, 248, 262, 263, 336, 337, 340-342, 344, 345, 347-349, 351, 355, 358, 360, 368, 370, 382, 383, 394, 400, 402, 404, 416, 417, 425, 557
Geronimo, 525
Gersky, J. J., 447
Gerych, Christine, 453, 454
Gerycz, S., Sgt., 374
Gesnes, 227
Gestapo, 356
Geza, 6
Ghetto, 82
GI Bill, 422
Gibbon, J. M., 20, 217
Gibbons, J., Cardinal, 178, 180-185, 195, 196, 212, 273

Gierek, Edward, 31
Gierek, G. G., 452
Gieryk, T., Rev., 139, 140
Gil, C., 451
Gilboa, Y. A., 360
Gilder, F. W., Mrs., 212
Giller, A., 142, 143
Gilliard, C., 478
Ginal, R., 452
Glassport, Pa., 549
Glen Burnie, Maryland, 451
Glen Cove, N.Y., 452
Glen Martin Company, 387
Glenski, F., Sgt., 373
Glinski, F. J., 495
Gliwice, 110
Glod, M., 261
Glogow, 7
Glos Ludowy, 585
Glos Narodu, 444
Glos Polek, 159, 160
Gloskowski, J., 140
Glowacki, A., 58
Glowiak, F. A., 452
Gmernicki, M., 135
Gnadt, J., 472
Gniezno, A., 3, 4, 5, 40
Gobi Desert, 332
Goda, W., 261
Godlewski, B., 364
Godrych, J. A., Rev., 125
Goebbels, J., 410
Gold Hill Daily News, 51
Golden, H., 298, 299, 500
Golembski, P. J., 452
Goleto, 44
Goliad, 44
Gompers, S., 537, 540
Gomulka, W., 31
Gontarek, J., 163
Gontko, J., 329
Good Shepherd Parish (Plymouth, Pa.), 125
Goodman, 337
Goral, B. E., Rev., 135
Gorale, 316, 317
Gorczyca, E., 562
Gordon, F., Rev., 170, 171
Gordon, F., 135, 337
Gordon, J., 461
Gordon, P., Governor, 527
Gore, Mary, Captain, 454
Gormier, Rev., 188
Gornik, 135
Gorski, A., 567

Gorski, C., 309
Gorski, C. G., 495
Gorson, S., 504
Gorzkie Zale, 555
Gottlieb, M.. 497
Gozdan, M. S., 452
Grabiarz, W., 377
Grabiarz Expressway, 378
Grabowski, A., 163
Grabowski, B. J., Sgt., 373
Grabowski, C., 324, 587
Grabowski, F., 329
Grabowski, H., 372
Graff, G. P., 272
Graham, M., 479
Grajek, Estelle, 471
Grajewski, M., 304
Grand Council of Pulaski Associations, 589
Grand Rapids, Michigan, 325, 327, 365, 373, 376, 385, 386, 452
Grapczynski, W. R., 385
Grayzel, S., 498
Great Britain, 2, 14, 16, 33, 63, 262, 343, 359, 360, 400, 404
Great Courland, 33
Great Lakes, 35
Great Neck, L.I., 366
Greboszow, 349
Greece, 420
Greeks, 94, 96, 194, 249, 481, 535
Greeley, A., Rev., 485, 554
Green, V. R., 36
Green Bay, Wisconsin, 107, 453
Green Lake, Wisconsin, 385
Greenberg, L., 89
Greendale, Wis., 453
Greene, 480
Greene, W., General, 439, 459
Greenpoint Gazette & Advertiser, 574
Greenpointe Gazette, 507
Greenwood, 346
Gregory, J. J., 377, 378
Gribbs, R., Mayor, 480, 493, 496
Griffith, Indiana, 451
Grodzicki, A. P., Lt., 373
Gromada, Jan., 317, 318
Gromada, T. V., 318
Gronek, Leo J., 382
Gronowicz, A., 471
Gronowski, R., 452
Gronski, P., 331
Grosheks, 42
Grosse Pointe, Michigan, 368, 452
Grosse Pointe University School, 477

INDEX

Grossman, E., 498
Grosz, N. H., Capt., 445
Grosz Polski, 154
Grudnicki, C., 372
Grudzinski, L., Rev., 561
Grudzinski, W. T., Cpl., 453
Grunwald, 12, 14, 16, 128
Grup, J., 549
Grutza, W., Rev., 112, 113
Grzeworek J. A., 452
Grzyb, see Gribbs
Guadalcanal, 369, 373-376, 384, 387
Guderian, H., General, 341, 352
Gudleske, G. F., 451
Gulcz, J., Rev., 131
Gumbleton, T., Bishop, 563, 571, 573
Gunther, Blair F., 424
Gunther, J., 346, 417, 418
Gurda, L. M., 225, 226
Gurowski, A., Count, 462-465
Gurwitz, J., 451
Gutowski, I., 329
Gutowski, P., Rev., 109
Guzicki, A., Rev., 109
Gwiazda Polarna, 42, 135, 402, 429, 499, 501, 505, 528, 531, 569, 571
Gwidz, W., 385
Gypsies, 13, 254, 501

Hackensack, N.J., 526
Hadacz, H. J., 385
Haduch, L., 135
Hagenbach, 225
Hagerty, A., 478
Hague, 14
Haiman, 39, 43, 45, 46, 111, 135, 145, 229, 241-243, 459, 461
Haiti, 460, 461
Hajduk, J., 325
Hale, E., 247
Halecki, O., Dr., 319
Halick, S. A., 260, 261
Halicz, 8
Halka, 309
Hallas, C., 481
Haller, J., General, 205, 218, 219, 263
Halsey, W. F., Admiral, 373, 374
Hamerski, F. D., 387
Hamilton, Bermuda, 381
Hammerstein, 422
Hammond, Indiana, 381
Hamtramck Citizen, 491
Hamtramck High School, 373, 378
Hamtramck, Michigan, 305, 372-375, 380, 85, 452, 471, 487, 488, 519

Hamtramck Philharmonic, 329
Handlin, O., 33
Handzlik, E. R., 328
Hannahville, Michigan, 531
Hanseatic League, 11
Hansen, D. C., 98
Hanson, H., Dr., 312
Hapgood, Hutchins, 95
Hapsburgs, 63, 65, 67, 199
Harbut, C., 387
Hardas, J., 163
Harding, W., President, 165
Hardyniec, A. S., 385
Harland, Wisconsin, 551
Harrigan, Jr., 455
Harris, L., 488, 489
Harrison, N.Y., 455
Harsch, J., 348
Hart, 541, 542
Hartford, Conn., 40, 451
Harvard College, 47
Harvard University, 312, 315, 387
Harvey, C. B., 526
Hawaiian Islands, 365, 475
Hayes, C., 511
Hayes Elementary School (Milwaukee), 439
Head, E. D., Bishop, 455
Heatter, G., 337
H-Bomb, 387-390
Hecker, I., Rev., 192
Hedwig, Sister, 556
Heike, E., 304
Heinzen, K., 49
Heisler, 520, 521
Heisler, Alina, 521
Heisler, Antonia, 521
Heisler, Steven, 521
Helena Modjeska Memorial Scholarship, 315
Helena Modrzejewska Polish Cultural Club (Los Angeles), 327
Heller, B., 360
Hemar, 308, 497
Hemingway, E., 422
Hempstead, L.I., 445
Hempstead, N.Y., 452
Henderson Field, 369
Henri, J., Bishop, 107
Henri de Valois, 19, 63
Henry II, Emperor, 6
Henry, P., 221
Henry Ford High School (Detroit), 477
Henry the Pious, 108

Henryk IV, 9
Herder, 89
Hermann, H., 351
Hermanowicz, J. J., 451
Hess, W. N., 434
Hewins, J., 42
Hicksville, N.Y., 452
Higgins, R., 575
Highland Park, Michigan, 487
Hill, J. S., 59
Hiller, H. A., 246
Hillman Library, 327
Himmler, 344
Hindenburg Line, 227, 228
Hispaniola, 525
historians, 65-66
Hitler, Adolf, 335, 337, 338, 339, 342, 353, 391, 400, 402, 409, 423, 425, 500, 502, 510, 511, 544
Hoban, Bishop, 189
Hodorowski, R., Cpl., 452
Hodur, F., Bishop, 125, 168, 169, 187, 191, 194
Hoffman, F., 389
Hohenzollerns, 67
Hojnacki, S. A., see S. A. Hoyle
Holden, W. S., 401
Holewinski, C., 549
Holewinski, S., Lt., 373
Holland, 33, 526
Hollywood, Calif., 396, 476
Holmes, B., Rev., 473
Holmes, O. W., 603
Holowezke, W. J., 382
Holy Apostolic See, 146, 154, 183, 184, 185, 188, 196
Holy Mother of the Rosary Church (Buffalo), 110
Holynski, 461
Holyoke, Mass., 163, 452
Holz Bay, 380
Home Army, 508
Hong Kong, 403
Hood, N., 491
Hood, Robin, 316
Hoover, Colonel, 213
Hoover, H., President, 236, 312, 354, 411, 412
Hope, Bob, 396
Hordynski, J., Major, 47
Horne, A., 347, 348
Hornet Carrier, 375, 376
Horst, W., 307
Horzewski, A. S., 385
Hotel Lambert, 56

House of Anjou, 12
House of Burgesses, 534
House, Colonel, 213-215, 221
Houstanic, Mass., 452
Houston, S., General, 44
Houston, Texas, 314, 453
Howitzer, 449
Hoyle, S. A., 282
Hoyt, C., 494
Hruska, V., 328
Huczek, G. A., 452
Hue, 443, 444
Huerta, President of Mexico, 162
Hughes, E. C., 536, 537
Hugo, V., 53
Huguenots, 13
Hull, Agrippa, 459, 460
Hull, Cordell, 511
Humboldt Park, 159
Humphrey, Grace, 160, 201
Hungarians, 10, 94, 96, 417, 498, 535, 539, 540
Hungary, 5, 12, 13, 21, 26, 74, 76, 344, 346
Hunter, General 464
Huntsville (Alabama) Volunteers, 44
Hussars, 10
Hussites, 13

Iceland, 252
Iciek, S., Rev., 135
Idaho, 482
Ignasiak, A., Rev., 240
Ignasiak, S. J., 383
Ignatius Paderewski Society, 156
Ignatowski, A., Lt., 371
Illinois, 34, 40, 116, 145, 153, 156, 163, 260, 261, 304, 327, 385, 443, 451, 454, 541, 546, 549, 550
Illowiecki, J., 135
Imlay City, Michigan, 375
Inchon, 433
Independence Fund, 205
India, 10, 16
Indian-Americans, 180
Indiana, 40, 118, 223, 327, 451, 458, 550
Indians, 14, 52, 524-532, 598
Innocent III, 75
Insko, Kentucky, 451
Institute for the Blind (Laski, Poland), 168
Institute of Research on Poles in America, 323

Instytut Wiedzy o Polonii Amerykanskiej, 323
International Alliance of Poles, 242
International Court of Justice, 14
International Eucharistic Congress, 575
International Institute (Detroit), 487
International Ladies Garment Workers Union, 540
International Red Cross, 401
Iorizzo, L. J., 179
Iowa, 40
Ipswich, Mass., 451
Iranek-Osmecki, K., 503
Iraq, 229
Ireland, 6, 63, 181
Ireland, J., Archbishop, 174, 178, 179, 182, 196, 273
Irish, 94, 132, 141, 142, 149, 150, 175-177, 179, 181, 185, 191-194, 216, 247, 248, 249, 257, 269, 279, 485, 488, 489, 535, 539, 541, 562, 574, 594, 603
Irish-American Clergy, 175-183, 186, 191-193, 196
Irish-Americans, 180, 191, 192
Iron Curtain, 420
Iroquois, 524, 527
Irzyk, A. F., 448
Irzyk, F., 304
Island of St. Andrew, 33
Island of Tobago, 33
Israel, 7, 254, 507, 508, 515, 516, 519, 520, 521
Israelites, 150
Isserles, M., Rabbi, 71
Italians, 41, 50, 94-96, 176, 177, 179, 180, 185, 194, 249, 254, 485, 488, 489, 535, 539, 540, 541, 575, 603
Italy, 5, 54, 55, 70, 72, 144, 159, 218, 262, 306, 336, 343, 383, 378, 384, 390, 399, 403, 557, 558, 589, 594
Ivan the Terrible, 20, 63
Iwanczyk, M., 328
Iwanowski, O. K., 328
Iwicki, I., 462
Iwo Jima, 374, 525

Jablonowski, F. C., 43
Jablonski, F. H., 135
Jacinski, J., 163
Jackowiak, H. P., Cpl., 452
Jackson, J., Rev., 495
Jackson, Leroy, 495
Jackson, Michigan, 163
Jacob, Duke of Courland, 33
Jadot, J., Bishop, 575
Jadwiga, Queen, 12, 114
Jaffa, M., Rabbi, 78
Jagiello, 12
Jagiello, Wladyslaw, 13
Jagiellonczyk, K., King, 79
Jagiellonian Dynasty, 3, 13, 16
Jagiellonian University, 10, 61, 307, 325, 332, 408
Jagiellon, Katarzyna, 63
Jagiellons, 61
Jagosz, E., 491, 494
Jakicic, J. J., 135
Jakubiak, E. A., 371
Jakubowski, H. J., 366
Jakuszes, 42
Jamrozy, S., 451
Jamestown, 308, 525, 534
Jan, Bishop of Wroclaw, 5
Janczynska-Bushewicz, W., 530
Jankie, J. I., 587
Jankowski, L. E., 451
Janocki, 22
Janosik, 316
Janowski, H., 171
Janta, A., 286, 308
Januszewski, F., 135
Japan, 2, 343, 403, 419
Japanese, 365-367, 373-376, 378, 380, 382, 384, 386, 398
Jaresz, W. J., 383
Jarkowski, J., 163
Jarosz, S., Dr., 316, 317
Jaroszynski, B., 45
Jasinski, V., Monsignor, 123, 124, 566
Jasiorkowski, T., 135
Jaskolski, T., 357
Jaskowiak, F., 163
Jaslow, E., 332
Jastrzemski, E. C., 365
Jasura, R. W., 452
Jaszynski, B., 163
Jaworowski, L. F., 452
Jaworowski, R. I., 135
Jaworowski, R. J., 52
Jeffries, E. J., 394
Jefferson, T., President, 47, 458, 471
Jelonek, D. B., Sgt., 443
Jendrewski, C., 385
Jendryka, A., 572
Jendrzejewicz, W., 323
Jennnigs, Missouri, 456
Jenorog, 307
Jersey City, N.J., 166, 183, 452
Jerusalem, 74, 75, 509

Jerzykiewicz, L., Rev., 45
Jesuit College, 22
Jesuits, 21, 62, 79, 80, 81, 114, 559
Jewish Foundation, 521
Jewish Legion, 82
Jewish News, 517
Jewish Pale, 83
Jews, 9, 13, 29, 35, 69-83, 85, 90, 94, 95, 96, 127, 194, 248, 252, 254, 257, 268, 300, 339, 360, 422, 481, 484, 489, 497-523, 535, 540, 541, 577, 602-603
Jewish Socialist Bund, 360
Jewish Press, 521
Jezalowicz, K. A., Sgt., 373
Joachim, J., 219
Joblonsky, H. J., 448
Jodl, 348
John Marshall Law School, 551
Johnson, L., President, 438, 439, 606
Jones, M. A., 540, 541
Jordan, A. T., 573
Josefiak, W. J., 374
Joselevitch, Berek, 82
Jozef Pilsudski Institute of America, 322, 323
Jozefowicz, B., Sgt., 373
Jozefowicz, R. J., Lt., 372
Jozwiak, R. E., 452
Jozwikowski, W., 135
Judaism, 79
Judy, G., 547
Juilliard School of Music, 311
Jurcak, R. A., 453
Jurek, E. J., 451
Jurkiewicz, H. J., 385
Justin, F., Rev. 551, 552
Juszczyk, C., Sgt., 373
Juzwikiewicz, J., 460
Jurzykowski Foundation, 330

Kabacznik, M., 512
Kaczmarczyk, A., 384, 387
Kakuk, A. J., 453
Kalamazoo, Michigan, 385
Kaleta-Pirowska, J., 509
Kalinka, Father, 57
Kalisz, 4, 200
Kalisz, W. F., 261
Kallen, Horace, 94, 251, 601
Kaluch, L., 444
Kalussowski, H., 45-47, 138
Kaluza, J., 163
Kaminska, H., 507
Kaminski, 41

Kaminski, E., Sgt., 452
Kaminski, E. J., 382
Kaminski, G., 163
Kaminski, L. J., 373
Kaminski, R. D., 452
Kaner, A., Dr., 521
Kania, C., 565
Kankakee, Illinois, 550
Kansas, 434, 531
Kantowicz, E. R., 561, 594
Kaptur, S., 331
Kapustin, M., Dr., 248
Karasiewicz, 392
Karasiewicz, R., Rev., 484
Karge, J., 49
Karlewska, A., 171
Karlowiczowa, J., 160, 243
Karpinski, John J., Monsignor, 425
Karsh, J., 326
Kashtan, A., 517-519
Kasikowski, J. G., 451
Kasprowicz, I., 163
Kaszubians, 108
Katyn Forest, 401, 413
Katyn Massacre, 401, 402
Katz, 271
Katzer, F., Archbishop, 178
Kawa, W. J., 385
Kawajalein, 380
Kazimierski, 20
Kazimierz (Krakow), 514
Kazimierz I, 6
Kazimierz Jagiellonczyk, 11
Kazimierz the Great, 10, 11, 12, 62, 70
Kazimierz the Just, 8
Kazmierczak, 226
Kazmierczak, G., 331
Keane, Bishop, 184
Keczmerski, P., 163
Kedron, J., 318
Kedroski, A. A., 451
Kehetian, M., 570
Keller, Werner, 75
Kelly, Mayor, 410
Kelly, E. P., 310, 313
Kelno, A., 503
Kendzior, H. A., 386
Kennedy, John F., President, 589
Kenny, B., 337
Kentucky, 40, 451, 527, 460, 475
Kepa, M., 520, 521
Kesselring, Field Marshal, 351
Keveney, W., Rev.,, 558
Kewanee, Illinois, 451

INDEX

Kiel, 368
Kieliszewskis, 42
Kieran-Jaworowski, Z., 332
Kiev, 6, 12, 80
Kij, J., Dr., 121
Kinel, L., 251
King, 42
King Casimir the Great Polish Citizens Club, 129
King Sigismund, 79
Kings County, New York, 392
Kingsbury, S. M., 534
Kiolbassa, P., 140
Kiolbassa, P., Capt., 469
Kiowa, 524
Kirkconnel, W., Dr., 243, 244
Kisala, W., 451
Kiska, 380
Klarik, S., 451
Klaudyna, Countess, 23
Klawiter, A., Rev., 111, 186
Kleban, Dr., 573
Klecha, J. J., 386
Klecz, S. S., 452
Kleczka, J., 304
Klein, J. T., Rabbi, 520
Klemba, S., 163
Klevenowski, R. M., 452
Klimaszefski, T., Sgt., 370
Klimaszewski, S., 163
Klimczak, W. E., 386
Klimecki, H., 132
Klimecki, M. V., Corporal, 447
Klimowicz, F. C., 386
Klimowicz, G., 385
Klucks, 42
Kluczkowski, 42
Kluczynski, 42
Klug-Iwanowski, O., 327
Klukowski, 42
Kluz, B., 331
Kluz, M., 328
Kmiec, H. K., 261
Kmiec, J. S., 451
Knieja, E. J., 369
Knowland, W., Senator, 415
Knox, F., 373
Koby, J., 472
Koby, K., 472
Koby, L., 473
Koby, P., 473
Koby, T., 472
Kochanek, A., 108
Koczan, R. J., Sgt., 444
Kogut, J., 163

Kohut, R. S., 452
Kolakowski, H., 163
Kolar, J. V., 386
Kolasinski, D., Rev., 109, 186
Kolaszewski, F., Rev., 186
Kolbe, M., Friar, 498
Kolendy, 291, 299
Kolinski, T. G., Sgt., 453
Kolka, E. L., Sgt., 452
Komarnicki, T., 323
Komitet Narodu Polskiego, 55
Komitet Obrony Narodowy (see National Defense Committee)
Komorowski, 318
Komosa, A. A., Lt., 434, 435
Koniegska, W. F., 373
Konikowski, Z., 573
Konitz, 52
Konopa, C., 451
Konopczynski, A., 511
Konopczynski, W., 511
Konopinski, E., 390
Konopnicka, M., 158, 328, 497, 588
Konopnicka Polish Educational Society, 131, 573
Konrad, D., 475
Kopacz, R. J., 385
Kopczynski, J., 295
Kopczynski, O., 22
Kopec, E. M., 451
Kopernik, Mikolaj, 10, 312, 314, 328, 332, 333
Kopernik Quadricentennial, 312
Kopiel, J., 385
Kopik, E. S., 452
Kopytkiewicz, M., Rev., 164
Koraleski, W. J., Capt., 370, 371
Korea, 432-436, 575
Korean War, 433, 435
Korecki, E., 452
Korkuc, K., 512, 513
Kornicky, J., 44
Korzeniewski, E., 373
Korzeniowski, T., 595
Korzon, T., 66
Kosakowski, G. A., 452
Koscielny, L. S., Sgt., 373
Kosciuszko Army, 223
Kosciuszko Association, 319, 320
Kosciuszko (cities), 41
Kosciuszko Club, 105
Kosciuszko Division, 408
Kosciuszko Foundation, 168, 214, 238, 285, 310-316, 320, 325, 427, 430, 506, 507

Kosciuszko Fund, 205
Kosciuszko League, 408
Kosciuszko Monuments, 159
Kosciuszko (surname), 41
Kosciuszko, T., General, 23, 39, 41, 48, 53, 65, 82, 94, 97, 114, 118, 154, 159, 205, 209, 215, 310, 314, 394, 426, 457-460, 471
Kosciuszko Year, 147
Kosciuszko's Will, 458
Kosierowski, R. J., Sgt., 442, 443
Kosik, J., 451
Kosinski, J., 501
Koska, E., Sgt., 373
Kosky, R., Cpl., 451
Koslowski, E., 375
Kossak, J., 314
Kossak, W., 314
Kot, S., 360
Kotkowski, J., 163
Kotovich, T. R., 521
Kotowski, E. A., 386
Kotula, S., 169
Koussevitsky, S., 219
Kovaleski, J., Sgt., 373
Kowal, B., 452
Kowal, M., 386
Kowalczyk, E., 469
Kowalczyk, E. L., 461
Kowalewski, J. T., 386
Kowalik, W., 333
Kowallske, 42
Kowalski, 41
Kowalski, B. S., 386
Kowalski, J. W., 184
Kowalski, W. J., 385
Kozak, Dr., 308
Kozak, E. J., Rev., 391
Kozakiewicz, K. I., 120, 121
Koziarski, E. F., Lt., 370
Kozlowski, A., Rev., 186
Kozlowski, E., Bishop, 194
Kozmian, J., 48
Kozminski, Jerzy, 22
Krajewski, S., 286, 491, 492, 557
Krakow, 4, 8, 9, 11, 12, 17, 29, 49, 61, 67, 76, 79, 113, 117, 158, 294, 306, 308, 310, 311, 332, 340, 341, 344, 354, 408, 508, 513, 515, 516, 520, 593
Krakow (cities), 40
Krakow Historical School, 58, 61, 64, 65, 66
Krakowiak Polish Dancers, 327
Krakowski, W., 385

Krakus, 96
Kralowski, J., 452
Kranowski, D., 331
Krasicki, Zygmunt, 23
Krasinski, 205
Krasinski, Zygmunt, 29
Kraszewski, J. I., 60
Krawczyk, E. C., Capt., 453
Krawczyk, J., Cpl., 451, 452
Krawiec, L., 158
Krezel, M., 317
Kridl, Manfred, 20
Kriniak, R., 385
Krol, 42
Krol, J., Cardinal, 498, 499, 562, 564, 558
Krol, P., 163
Krolewski, M., 555, 587, 588
Kroll, M., Sgt., 452
Krukar, A. S., 393
Krukar, C., 393
Krukar, E. J., 393
Krukar, J., 393
Krukar, M. A., 393
Krukar, R. A., 393
Krukar, Raymond, 393
Krupinski, C. J., 396
Krupp Factories, 345
Kruszewski, E. J., 385
Kruszka, W., Rev., 151, 152, 192-194
Kruszwica, 5
Kryczynski, J. N., 47
Krygier, 394
Krymkowski, A., 472
Krymkowski, G., 472
Krymkowski, T., 472
Kryniewicz, T. T., 425
Kryszak, T. E., 455
Krysztoszek, G. M., 451
Krzycki, L., 543, 544
Krzynowek, Claudia, 440
Krzynowek, P. S., Lt., 440
Krzysztofiak, W. P., 385
Krzywonek, P. S., Lt., 452
Krzywoszynski, J. S., 469
Krzyzanowski, 394
Krzyzanowski Garrison, 366
Krzyzanowski, V., 49
Krzyzowski, E. C., Capt., 434
Ksiazek, B., 451
Kubiak, L., 451
Kubicki, M. L., 446
Kubik, S., 375
Kubinski, H., Sgt., 373
Kucharski, I., 163

INDEX

Kucharski, J., 386
Kucielski, T., 143
Kucinciak, R. J., Sgt., 452
Kucinski, H., 383
Kucyk, M. J., 373
Kuczewski, W. R., 453
Kudella, J., 385
Kudlicka, J., 251
Kudniewski, J., 566
Kuibyshev, 360
Kujawa, M., 393
Kujawinski, A. E., 376
Kukiel, M., 313
Kukurowski, A. A., Lt., 373
Kula, J., 455
Kulakowski, E. W., 386
Kulchesky, H., Sgt., 374
Kulski, W. W., 410
Kumencki, W. J., 378
Kuncewicz, M., 330
Kunz, H., 304
Kupiszewska, 394
Kuprevich, W. A., 452
Kurek, Adam, 47
Kurek, J., 357
Kurier Bostonski, 135
Kurier Nowojorski, 135
Kurjer Polski, 135
Kuryer Polski, 119
Kushner, A. L., 506
Kusielewicz, E., 318, 499, 507
Kusowski, M., 163
Kusowski, T., 370
Kusper, S. T., 397
Kusy, D. P., 452
Kutno, 341
Kuwait, 229
Kuznicki, M. E., Sister, 587
Kuzniewski, A.. Rev., 191
Kwasnik, J., 386
Kwiatkowski, 44
Kwiatkowski, J. W., 447
Kwortnik, J. C., 455

Labowski, M., 589
Lackawanna, New York, 121
Lackawanna Steel Company, 542
Ladak, A., Lt., 454
Lafayette, General, 53
Laine, F., 431
Lakser, E., 522
Lakser, M., 522
Lakwa, E. J., Cpl., 450, 451
Lallemand, C., General, 43
L'Anse Michigan, 531

Landau, R., 205
Landers, A., 41
Landrum-Griffin Act, 548
Lane, F., 233, 246
Lange, O., 408
Lange, W., 45
Langley, AFB (Virginia), 441
Langres, 225
Lansing, Michigan, 272, 494, 563
Lanza, Mario, 431
Lapacinski, L., 384
Lapinska, 394
Lapinski, C. W., 376
Lapinski, L. J., 376
LaPorte, Indiana, 434
Larsen, J., 522
LaSalle College, 286
LaSalle, Illinois, 117
Lateran Councils, 76
Latinos, 254, 568, 577, 596
Latkowski, H. J., 386
La Tribuna Italiana Transatlantica, 180
Latvia, 344, 360, 400
Latvians, 9
Laudon, G., 157
Laur Dancing Society, 244, 329
Laurens, John, 459
Lazar, G. F., 451
Lazarovich, J. F., 451
Lazienki Palace, 272
Lazonski, J., 386
League of Nations, 14
Learsi, Rufus, 76, 80, 81
Lebanon, Tenn., 471
Lech I, King, 3
Leclerc, General, 460
LeComte, Auguste, 59
Leczyca, 8, 16
Lednicki, W., Dr., 319
Ledochowska, J., 200
Ledochowska, M., Countess, 468
Ledochowski, M., Cardinal, 187, 188, 195, 196
Lehard, J., Rev., 125
Leismer, L., 474
Leiter, J., 212
Lelewel, J., 54, 55, 66, 89
Lelyveld, J., Rabbi, 507
Lemanski, B., 386
Lemanski, R. L., Sgt., 374
Lenart, F., 282, 283, 285
Lenox, Michigan, 385
Lenski, A. J., Major, 442
Leoniak, Z., 131
Lepak, D. C., Sgt., 453

Lerski, J. J., 47
Lesinski, J., 375, 494
Lesinski, W. U., 386
Lesnieski, K., 390
Lesniewski, J. F., 385
Leszczynska, Marie, Queen of France, 20
Leszczynski, S., 62
Leszczynski, S., King, 19, 20, 22
Leszek, Prince, 8
Levine, E., 176, 177 179
Lexington Kentucky, 460
Lewandowski, B., 163
Lewandowski J. M., 261
Lewandowski, Judge, 329
Lewandowski, L. J., 455
Lewandowski, M., 491
Lewandowski, R., Councilman, 495
Lewicki, S. A., 386
Lewin, Z., 503, 505
Lewinski, T., 460
Lewis, John L., 545, 546
Leyte, 380
Libau, 33
Liberty, Texas, 43
liberum veto, 61, 64
libraries, 50, 105, 153, 163, 307, 320, 322
Library of Congress, 427
Lichten, J., Dr., 503
Lille, 368
Limanowski, B., 84
Lincoln, A., President, 366, 461, 464
Lincoln Park, Michigan, 452
Linden, New Jersey, 440
Lipinski, J., 143
Lipinski, T. P., 453
Lipke, C. W., 365
Lipke Park, 379
Lippman, T., 98
Lipski, C., Lt., 366
Lis, 42
Lis, Jan, 163
Lis, R. J., Cpl., 451
Liske, X., Prof., 65
Liss, 42
Liscz, R. S., 452, 445, 446
Liszt, 219
Literary Association of Friends of Poland, 49
Lithuania, 12, 16, 63, 77, 79, 80, 128, 319, 360, 400, 532
Lithuanians, 9, 13, 16, 63, 254, 272, 343, 535, 541, 575, 603
Little Big Horn, 525

Litwin, R. R., Sgt., 452
Liverpool, England, 50, 412
Livonia, 16, 20
Lodz, 219, 340, 508
Lombard, Illinois, 451
London, 33, 300, 333, 356, 357, 360, 361, 391, 399, 401-404, 415, 416, 500, 505, 527, 589
London Company, 308, 533, 534
Long, B., 511
Long Island, 387
Lopata, H. Z., 324, 424
Lopczyce, Poland, 474
Lopez, A., General, 44
Lorraine, Ohio, 452
Los Alamos, 387-390
Los Angeles, California, 327, 294, 512
Louis XIV, King of France, 33
Louis XV, King of France, 20
Louis, J., 422
Louisiana, 43, 468, 469, 518
Louisville, Kentucky, 451, 460, 475
Louvain, 200
Loveland, Moreland, 484
Lovelock, 52
Lowell, Indiana, 451
Loyola University (Chicago), 574
Lozenski, R. O., 452
L & P Broadcasting Corp., 477
Lublin, 16, 79, 201, 351, 405, 508
Lublin Committee, 402, 403
Lublin, Wisconsin, 453
Lubomirski, M., 50
Ludendorff Bridge, 382
Ludwik I, King, 12
Luftwaffe, 338-340, 345, 348, 349, 351, 353
Lukasavige, 42
Lukasik, J. L., Major, 441
Lukasik, M., 357
Lukasik, W. S., 372
Lukasik, V., 474, 475
Lukaszewicz, W., 68
Luke AFB (Arizona), 441
Luria, S., Rabbi, 78
Lusatians, 6
Lusienski, E., 304
Luther, Martin, 189
Lutherans, 96
Lutnia Singing Society, 329
Luxemborg, Rosa, 60, 85
Luzon, 382
Lwow, 6, 12, 86, 87, 113, 158, 167, 207, 387, 416, 510, 522
Lwow University, 65, 66

INDEX

Lwowski, S., 357
Lyceum (Krzemieniec), 54
Lyczakow Cemetery, 158
Lysogorski, S., 386

MacArthur, Douglas, General, 377, 380, 382, 431
MacCracken, H. C., Dr., 310, 313
Macek, J., 16
Machrowicz, T., 401
Maciejewski, J., 307
Maciejewski, S. T., 372
Macierz Polska, see Polish Alma Mater of America
MacKinder, H. J., 399
MacLean's Magazine, 216
MacNab, F., 564
Macomb Daily, 570
Madej, S. C., 386
Madonna College, 427
Mafia, 414
Maginot Line, 346-348
Mahoney, M. E., 468
Maimolski, L. C., Sgt., 374
Maine, 98, 482
Maino, Monsignor A., 192
Maisel, A., 223, 392
Maisky, I., 345, 346
Majer, D., Rev., 155
Majewski, L. J., Lt., 372, 373
Makarewicz, D., 452
Makowiecki, J., 265
Makowski, L. F., Lt., 455
Makowski, S. M., Mayor, 495
Maksimik, Monsignor, 566
Maksymowicz, T., 354
Malachowski, C., General, 43
Malak, H., Rev., 504, 505
Malarz, R. L., 453
Malcuzynski, W., 332
Malczewski, A., 43
Malczewski, C., 43
Malczewski, J., 314
Mlecki, J. A., Cpl., 452
Malinkiewicz, A., 383
Malinkowski, A., 383
Malinowski, B., Dr., 319
Malinowski, E., 452
Malinowski, E. J., Lt., 374
Malinowski, Ernest, 27
Malinowski, J., 314
Malinowski, J. S., 365
Malinowski, T., 163
Maliszewski, C. J., 385
Maliszewski, E. P., Lt., 368

Malkowski, F., 163
Maloney, J. A., Rev., 475
Mames, Dr., 517
Manchester, N. H., 455
Manila, 377
Manly, C., 225
Mann, J. R., Congressman, 481
Manning, C. A., 319
Manru, 317, 327
Mansavage, 42
Manser, N., 564-566, 572
Mansfield M., Senator, 529
Mao-Tse-Tung, 529
Marable, D. K., 476
Marable, E., 476
Marable, Ron, 475, 476
Marchlewicz, A. M., 452
Marchlewski, J., 85
Marcinkowski, A., 386
Marcinkowski M., Col., 532
Marczak, L., 508, 509
Marianna, Florida, 469
Marimpietri, A. D., 541
Markowicz, R., 476
Markowski, B., 85, 265, 287, 312, 321, 587
Markowski, Gregg, 531
Markowski, H. J., 451
Markowski, S., 573
Marquette, Michigan, 151
Mars, 337
Marshall Islands, 389
Marshall, J. M., 452
Marshall Plan, 420
Martin, 432
Martin, Mary, 42
Martinelli, S., Archbishop, 113
Marusiak, J., Capt., 372, 374
Marx, Karl, 85, 541, 542
Maryland, 163, 164, 388, 391, 394, 395, 451
Maslowski, D. F., 455
Masons, 40
Maspeth, N. Y., 261, 452
Massachusetts, 52, 163, 175, 180, 259, 304, 327, 440, 451, 560, 567, 470
Massachusetts Institute of Technology, 434
Massapequa, N.Y., 452
Mastalski, J., 169
Masters, G., 475
Masztakowski, C. M., 385
Matejko, 26, 89
Matejko, J., 314
Matewicz, S. J., Sgt., 443

Matla, A., Rev., 331
Mathis, Johnny, 496
Matula, S. J., 328
Matuszewski, I., 362
Matyka, 394
Maxwell, W. S., 229
May, A. J., 199
Mazovians, 4
Mazowia, 8, 9
Mazowsze, 307, 430
Mazur, C., 385
Mazur, J., 163
Mazur, Joseph, 111
Mazur, Wladyslaw, 131
Mazurek, C., 542
Mazzini, 50, 143, 306
Mbale College, 475
McAdoo, 231
McCaffery, L. J., Dr., 574
McCarthy, J., Senator, 433, 547
McCrossen, S., 357
McGee, F., 337
McGreer, H., 108
McKeating, M. P., 455
McKinley, President, 120
McKinney, E., 487
McNaught, B., 558
McNichols, J. T., 179
McQuaid, Bishop, 184
Meagher, C., 473
Medal of Honor, 366
Meharry Medical College, 471
Melcher, Bishop, 107, 108
Melczek, J. R., 451
Melting Pot, 245-254, 275, 278
Menominee, Michigan, 380
Menowski, G. A., 452
Mercury, 330
Meriden, Conn., 163, 451
Merkuriusz, 330
Mesa, Arizona, 451
Mesa Vista Sanitorium, 531
Messner, Archbishop, 119, 184, 196
Methodists, 96
Metropolitan Opera House, 312
Meuse River, 228
Mexicans, 43, 44, 603
Mexico, 14, 43, 44, 384
Miami, Florida, 331, 332
Mianowski, Dr., 308
Miara, W., 386
Miaso, Jozef, 116
Michalak, W., 451
Michalowicz, S. J., 451, 453
Michalowski, R. J., 451

Michalski, J., 559
Michalski, J. M., 452
Michalski, L. G., 559
Michalski, T. J., Lt., 373
Michelet, 306
Michigan, 34, 40, 108, 109, 116, 118, 139, 145, 151, 153, 156, 163, 186, 225, 259, 260, 261, 272, 285, 286, 304, 324, 325, 327, 333, 365, 373, 376, 378, 379, 380, 381, 385, 386, 394, 442, 447, 451, 452, 467, 471, 473, 477, 483, 484, 487, 488, 498, 494, 522, 530, 566-569, 573
Michigan Anti-Slavery Society, 467
Michigan Catholic, 474, 558, 559, 562, 564, 566, 568, 570, 571, 574, 575
Michigan Catholic Conference, 569, 571
Michigan Chronicle, 491, 492, 494
Michigan City, Indiana, 451
Michonik, F. M., Sgt., 452
Mickiewicz, Adam, 26, 55, 97, 205, 306, 326, 328
Mickiewicz Centennial, 326
Mickiewicz Hall, 308
Mickiewicz Library, 306, 307
Mickiewicz Library (Detroit), 555
Mickiewicz Monument, 306
Mickiewicz Society, 309
Middlesex, N.J., 452
Middletown, Conn., 163
Midland, Texas, 455
Midowicz, C., 145, 146
Midway, 373
Mielcarek, M. C., Sister, 199, 200
Mierowslawski, Ludwik, 26
Mierzwa, J., 573
Mierzwa, Jan, 131
Mierzwinski, T. J., Rev. 560, 561
Miesiecznik Franciszkanski, 504
Miesiewiczes, 42
Mieszko I, King, 5, 6, 70, 109
Mieszko II, King, 6, 22
Mietus, J., 453
Mika, S. A., 452
Mikolajczyk, S., 30, 356, 562
Mikusek, L., 163
Milanowski, H. D., 375, 385
Milanowski, J. E., 453
Milche, 348
Mill Creek, Pa., 189
Mill, J. S., 586
Milland, R., 336
Miller, 337
Miller, K. D., 533

INDEX

Milosz, C., 330
Milot, M. S., 531
Milton, 233
Milwaukee, 35, 107-109, 112, 114, 119, 144, 156, 163, 175, 178, 184, 223, 224, 228, 261, 304, 309, 327, 330, 333, 386, 393, 420, 439, 441, 453, 472, 543, 544, 551, 559
Minneapolis, Minn., 327, 452
Minnesota, 154, 155, 304, 589
Minsk, 12, 401
Misiaszek, J., Rev., 125
Mississippi, 41
Missouri, 34, 40, 51
Miszewski, D. M., 452
Mitana, T., Dr., 325
Mitau, 33
Mitchell, D. L., 495
Mitkiewicz, Count, 51
Mizwa, S., 168, 310, 311, 314, 315, 319
Mlynarski, A., 219
Mlynarski, E., 219
Modjeska, Helena, 51, 315, 327, 328
Modjeska Memorial Scholarship, 315
Modrzejewska, H. ,158, 328
Modrzejewska Polish Cultural Club (Los Angeles), 327
Modrzejewski, E. A., 378
Modrzejewski, J., 501
Modrzejewski, R. J., Major, 438, 439
Modzelewski, 392
Mogilno, 307
Moline, Illinois, 451
Molotov,, M., 342, 360, 406
Monaghan, F., 460
Mondello, S., 179
Mongolians, 14
Monica, Sister, 117
Moniuszko, 26, 89
Monroe, V., 431
Monte Cassino, 263
Montgomery, B. L., 390
Mooney, E., Cardinal, 561, 564, 572
Moore, Garry, 432
Moravia, 6
Morawski, A. R., 393
Morgan, A., 212
Morizet, J. R., 41
Moronczyk, T., 385
Morray, J. P., 405-407
Morris, P., 337
Morristown, Pa., 452
Morton Grove, 508
Moscicki, I., President, 338

Moscow, 12, 342, 360, 402, 403, 404, 406, 416, 602
Moselle River, 346
Mosinee, Wisconsin, 331
Moslems, 14
Mostwin, Danuta, 429
Motown, 476
Motyka, S. L., Sgt., 374
Mount Carmel Church (Bayonne, N.J.), 392
Mount Horeb, 252
Mount Pleasant, Mich., 531
Mount Rushmore, 528, 529
Moynihan, J. H., 196
Mozejewski, Rev., 111
Mroczkowski, S. G., 376
Mrozewski, S., 589
Mrozinski, S., 163
Mrozowski, Dr., 308
Mrs. Paul's Kitchens, 332
Mt. Everest, 423
Mucha, F., 380
Mucha, Howard, 452
Mucha, L., 451
Mugavero, Bishop, 573
Muhlembau Aircraft Plant, 370
Muller, R. S., 451
Munda, 385
Mundelein, G. W., 185, 561
Murawski, L. F., 132
Murray, 545
Musical America, 210
Muske, P. H., 385
Muskegon, Michigan, 385
Murawski, S., 307
Murielles, France, 382
Murzynowska, K., 46
Muscowy, 81
Muskie, E. S., Senator, 98, 480-482, 507
Muskiewicz, T. J., 385
Mussolini, 544
Muszynski, J. T., 386

NAACP, 287, 482
Nabozna, 394
Nabywaniec, C., 366
Nader, R., 545, 546
Nagorski, L. C., Sgt., 374
Nakonieczny, W. E., Sgt., 374
Nanticoke, Pa., 187, 188
Napieralski, S., 307
Napoleon Bonaparte, 1, 23, 219, 460
Narew River, 342
Narkon, S., 387

Narkun, W. J., 385
Narod Polski, 121, 287, 333
Narvick, 263
Nashua, N.H., 452
Nashville, Tenn., 471
Nassau, 387, 589
Nastal, C. A., Sgt., 372
Nastal, T., Sgt., 372
Natanson Family, 90
Nathanson, C., 486, 493
National Association of Polish Cultural Clubs, 325
National Catholic Almanac, 190
National Catholic Register, 552, 553, 555
National Catholic Reporter, 548
National Center of Urban Ethnic Affairs, 575
National Committee of Americans of Polish Descent, 361-363
National Conference of Catholic Bishops, 558, 560
National Defense Committee, 241
National Democratic Direction, 86
National Intelligencer, 46
National Jewish Monthly, 499, 506
National Lancers, 39
National League, 86
National Observer, 481
National Treasury, 205
National Urban League, 488
NATO, 420
Navajo Indians, 531
Nawrocki, R. D., 451
Nazis, 83, 343, 346, 354, 360, 498, 499, 508, 510, 512, 513, 514, 519, 520
Neamark, Germany, 518
Nebraska, 40, 304
Nedzi, L., Congressman, 491, 571
Negroes, 43, 62, 194, 254, 457-496, 535, 539, 568
Neisse River, 2, 7, 400
Nellie, H. S., 180, 541
Neuman, J., von., 387
Nevada, 51, 451
Nevada Morning Appeal, 52
Nevadans, 51
New Boston, Michigan, 385
New Britain, Conn., 134, 163, 483
New Brunswick, N.J., 452
New Cavalry Baptist Church (Detroit), 568
New Detroit, 494
New England Anti-Slavery Society, 466

New England Hospital for Women and Children, 468
New Florence, Pa., 452
New Georgia, 385
New Glarus, 252
New Guinea, 376, 378
New Hampshire, 46, 451, 455, 519
New Harmony, 51
New Haven, Conn., 163, 392
New Holland, 39
New Jersey, 163, 164, 166-168, 260, 304, 318, 327, 384, 392, 395, 445, 451, 452, 456, 458, 526, 589
New Kensington, Pa., 163
New Mexico, 2, 389
New Orleans, 303, 461
New Waverly, Texas, 453
New World, 38, 43, 48
New York, 35, 45-50, 52, 116, 118, 127, 133, 144, 145, 153, 162, 163, 166, 167, 203, 210, 212, 221, 233, 236, 246, 251, 252, 260, 261, 304, 312, 327, 356, 357, 366, 367, 387, 392, 422, 443, 451, 452, 455, 460, 466, 467, 476, 521, 527, 540, 544, 550-552, 573, 589
New York City, 131, 132, 203, 208, 222, 298, 313, 322, 330, 331, 333, 359, 361, 362, 404, 411, 470
New York Daily Tribune, 49
New York Herald Tribune, 501
New York Legislature, 47
New York Weekly News, 50
New York Welfare and Health Council, 425
New York Times, 181, 413, 414, 500, 501, 502
New York Times Magazine, 252
Newark, N.J., 163, 327, 392, 458
Newberry Medal, 311
Newman, I. D., Rev., 482
newspapers, 134, 135, 584, 585
Niagara Falls, 43, 321
Niagara-on-the-Lake, 216, 217
Niagara University, 109
Nicholas I, Czar, 25
Nicholas, Grand Duke, 200
Niedbala, C. J., 386
Niedzwiecki, P., 365
Niedzwiecki, R., 365, 386
Niemczyk, J. J., 452
Niemiec, B., 379
Niemiec, J. J., Sgt., 373
Niemiec, W., 373
Niepodleglosc, 52

INDEX

Niles, 508
Nisei, 481
Niski, L. E., Major, 452
Niszczak, J. J., 381
Nixon, Richard, President, 386, 394, 529
Nobel Prize, 51, 600
Nodolski, R., 452
Noga, Helen, 496
Noga, John, 496
Noga, S., 163
Normandy, 377, 379, 383, 391
Norridge, Illinois, 451
North Carolina, 451, 459
North Dakota, 589
North Muskegon, Michigan, 452
Northwestern University, 550
Norway, 6, 341, 343
Norwegians, 252
Norwid, Cyprian K., 26, 50, 461
Norwid Literary Contest, 326
Nosek, E., 383
Nosek, W. A., 451
Notre Dame University, 367
Novak, A. H., 386
Novak, C. B., 386
Novak, F., 519, 520
Novak, T. E., 451
Novak, T. E., 452
Noviski, B. J., Cpl., 453
Nowacki, Z. E., 444, 445
Nowak, 41
Nowak, B. G., 304
Nowak, S., 304, 551
Nowakowski, A. D., Sgt., 373
Nowakowski, C. F., Sgt., 374
Nowe Drogi, 330
Nowicki, B. F., 385
Nowicki, J. E., 456
Nowicki, S. S., 307
Nowicki, W., Lt., 374
Nowosad, F., 385
Nowiny Polskie, 135, 551
Nowy Dziennik, 496
Nowy Swiat, 361, 362
Nuremberg, 348
Nykiel, R. J., 372
Nysa River, 544

Oak Park, Illinois, 451
Oak Ridge, N.J., 168
Obertynska, B., 330
Oceana, 557
Oceanside, California, 451
Ochmanski, F. G., 386

O'Connell, Cardinal, 212
Odongo, J., Bishop, 475
Oder River, 2, 4, 7, 8, 602
Odra River, 544
Offner, A. A., 338
Ogden, G., Judge, 42
Ogorek, W., 329
O'Hara, Bishop, 189
Ohio, 116, 156, 186, 260, 261, 282, 325, 327, 328, 382, 448, 451, 452, 472, 527
Oil City, Pennsylvania, 366
Oise-Aisne, 226
Okinawa, 376, 380, 443
Okoniewski, R. F., 495
O'Konski, A. E., 410
Okulicki, General, 407
Olejarczyk, K., 564, 565, 570, 571
Olejniczak, J., 257, 258
Oleszkowicz, W. J., 385
Olfier, J., 163
Olkowski, L. J., Lt., 373
Olowniuk, W. V., Sgt., 373
Olszanski, J., 163
Olszewski, J. M., 452
Olszowski, Primate, 22
Olszyk, A. J., 393
Olszyk, E. G., 152, 393
Olszyk, H. A., 393
Olszyk, L. M., 393
Olszyk, M., 393
Olszyk, S. R., 393
Omaha, 186
Omodoi, Rev., 474, 475
Ontario, 216
Opanowski, E. A., 380
open housing, 479, 480, 491
Oplatek, 289, 290, 293
Opoka, C. F., 386
Opole, 40
Oprinski, E., 530, 531
Orchard Lake, Michigan, 153, 286, 555, 566
Orchard Lake Schools, 153, 286, 486, 555, 566
Oregon, 52, 525
organic work, 57, 59, 60
Orientals, 603
Orley, R., 575
Orlikowski, D. J., 453
Orlowska, Jadwiga, Lt., 452
Orszulak, K. B., 451
Orzechowski, H., 331
Orzel Bialy, 52
Orzeszkowa, E., 60, 158

Osada, S., 142, 144, 255
Osborn High School (Detroit), 491
O'Shea, A., 576
Osiny, 509
Osservatore Romano, 159
Osowski, E., 380, 386
Ostafin, P., 186, 285, 286
Ostopowicz, J., 390
Ostrowski, A. A., 386
Ostrowski, J. F., 366
Osuch, J., Rev., 329
Osuski, R. E., Sgt., 453
Ottawa, Canada, 333
Ottoman Empire, 1
Our Lady of Czestochowa, 158, 289
Our Lady of Czestochowa (Brooklyn), 112
Our Savior of Golgotha Church (Dearborn, Michigan), 576
Ovask, G., 452
Overseas Press Club, 510
Owen Sound, Canada, 357
Owsiak, 452

Pachomia, Mary, Sister, 455
Pachynski, A. L., 448
Pacta Conventa, 19
Paderewska, Helena, 158, 159, 171
Paderewski Foundation, 426, 427
Paderewski, Ignacy, 197, 205-215, 218-221, 229, 230, 241, 262, 263, 312, 313, 317, 327, 328, 335, 427, 470, 471, 502, 528
Paderewski Invalid Fund, 263
Paderewski Society, 156
Paderewski University Club (Scranton), 327
Paderewski's Relief Fund, 213
Page, Patti, 431
Paiute, 524
Palenik, J. A., 451
Palestine, 73
Palmer, F., 227
Pan Slavism, 60
Pancewicz, J., 573
Pancho Villa, 384
Pankowski, B. J., Col., J 434
Panmujom, 433
Panna Maria, Texas, 41
Papacy, 10
Papiak, R. J., 386
Papielinski, J. N., 143
Papua, 378
Pare, G., 186
Paris, 1, 19, 53, 54, 56, 84, 85, 220, 221, 300, 306, 333, 355, 370, 415, 426, 459, 544
Parma, Ohio, 452
Park, R. E., 246
Parke-Davis Company, 474
Parsons, F., 337
Partyka, M. J., 386
Parylak, J., 385
Paryski, I. J., 282
Parz, T. A., Capt., 394
Paskiewicz, P. I., Lt., 374
Paskowicz, D., 453
Paspaheigh, King, 525
Passic, N.J., 317, 327, 357
Pastoralki, 299
Pastrowicz, E. A., 451
Pastva, M., Cpl., 452
Paszyn, M., 588, 589
Paterson, 543
Paterson, J., General, 459, 560
Patrzycki, J., Rev., 131
Patton, G. S., General, 379, 380, 387, 396
PAVAA, 262
Pavich, R. M., 450
Pawelek, A. J., 238
Pawelski, H. J., 374
Pawlak, D. F., 127
Pawlak, J. W., 452
Pawlak, W., Major, 447
Pawlick, F. J., 374
Pawlicki, G. S., 390
Pawlowicz, B., 308
Pawlowicz, D. W., 452
Pawlowski, C., 163
Pawlowski, E. W., 452
Pawlowski, J., 386
Pawlowski, S. J., 380
Pazuchowski, E. L., 386
Pearl Harbor, 365-367, 386, 394, 397
Peczynski, J. A., 380, 381
Pehle, J., 510
Pelech, S., 373
Peleliu, 374
Pelka, J., 304
Pemaquids, 525
Peninsula, Ohio, 452
Penn, William, 39
Penn-Central Railroad, 550
Pennsylvania, 34, 35, 112, 116, 118, 145, 153, 162-164, 171, 186, 188, 204, 230, 240, 327, 392-396, 441, 451, 452, 453, 485, 527, 536, 539, 541, 545, 548, 549
Perejslaw Treaty, 20

Perespa, Poland, 517
Perry, J. M., 481
Pershing, General, 225, 228, 384
Perth Amboy, N. J., 384, 392, 452
Pesko, A., 373
Peter I, 82
Peter Yolles Dissertation Fund, 311
Peterhoff, 529
Petrussewicz, A., 44
Petrussewicz, F., 44
Pezda, Edwin F., Capt., 373
Philadelphia, 43, 105, 125, 143, 144, 163, 164, 171, 172, 185, 219, 327, 333, 387, 395, 452, 453, 527, 543, 552, 558, 564
Philbrick, H., 433
Philippines, 373, 382, 393
Phillips, C., 212, 213, 215, 218, 222
Phillips, W., 467, 468
Phoenix, Arizona, 163
Phoenix, Illinois, 357
Phouc Long Province, 444
Phu Cat AB, 442
physicians (Polish-American), 127
Piarist Fathers, 54
Piasecki, D., 386
Piasecki, F. N., 387
Piasecki, P. F., 224
Piaseczny, W. L., 373, 374
Piast Dynasty, 5, 7, 9, 12
Piasts, 6, 61, 302
Piekary, Poland, 110
Piekosz, M. A., 478
Pieprzak, W. F., 385
Pieprzny, G., 163
Pietras, Frank M., 452
Pietrowicz, F., 161
Pietruszka, L., 357
Pietrzak, E., 357
Pietrzyk, M. H., 452
Pietrzykowski, E., 331
Pignedoli, Cardinal, 575, 576
Pilarski, L., 45
Pilch, J. J., 549
Pilgrin, S., 503
Pilsudski, Jozef, Marshal, 27, 28, 85, 201, 308, 323, 359
Pincoming, Michigan 452
Pinsk, 113
Pintowski, E. J., 451
Piotrkow, Poland, 16, 466
Piotrowska, I., Dr., 319
Piotrowski, E. A., Sgt., 368, 369
Pisa River, 342
Pisanki, 291, 292

Pisarski, E. P., 374
Pisarski, Mrs., 487
Piszek, E. J., 332
Pitass, A., Rev. Dr., 307
Pitass, John, Rev., 109, 110, 307, 539
Pittsburczanin, 135, 506, 585
Pittsburgh 35, 111, 154, 162, 163, 204, 215, 255, 268, 295, 327, 395, 485
Pittsburgh Post Gazette, 112
Pitula, S., 131
Piwinski L. J.. 386
Piwok, S. J., 385
Plainfield, N.J., 357, 452
Plainville, 452
Plater, Emily Countess, 23, 48
Plawecki, E., 551
Pliny, 4
Pliska, S. R., 88, 203, 204, 216-218, 237, 240, 256
Plock, J., 549
Plotkowski, G. S., 386
Plotkowski, R. L., 386
pluralism, 248-254, 575, 605
Plymouth, Pa., 125, 188, 233, 452
Pniewska, B., 332
Pniewski, A. L., 386
Podczaszynski, M., 53
Podgrabiye, 520
Podhale, 38, 318
Podlesie, 4
Podlesnik, W. A., 453
Podolia, 73
Pogreba, D. A., 456
Pogroms, 77
Poincare, President, 197, 216, 219
Point Four, 420
Pokorny, R. B., Lt., 373
Polak, J., Rev., 107
Polanie, 4
Polanie Club, 327
Polanki (Milwaukee), 327
Polanski, A. L., 386
Polena, W., 331
Polewski, Anton, 393
Polewski, F., 393
Polewski, J., 393
Polewski, L., 393
Polewski, Steve, 393
Polewski, Sylvester, 393
Polewski, W., Capt., 393
Poliakov, L., 71-73
Polish, D., 510
Polish Air Force, 364, 357
Polish Alma Mater of America, 170

Polish American, 440-446, 454, 500, 502, 504, 585, 594
Polish American Academic Association, 329
Polish American Arts Association (Washington, D.C.), 327
Polish American bishops, 154
Polish American Chamber of Commerce, 491
Polish American Clergy, 97, 126, 131, 149, 193-195, 240, 483, 485, 486, 488, 490, 491, 496, 538, 556, 558, 559, 560-565, 570, 573, 576
Polish American Congress, 154, 184, 287, 363, 397, 408, 409, 415, 424, 426, 427, 428, 458, 491, 560, 565, 568, 573, 584, 588, 590
Polish American Congress (Michigan Division), 333, 569, 570, 571, 590
Polish American Congress (New York Division), 573
Polish American Council, 356
Polish American Cultural Club (Mosinee), 331
Polish American Encyclopedia, 261
Polish American Historical Association, 40, 323
Polish American Immigration and Relief Committee, 425
Polish American Journal, 41, 42, 161, 282, 439, 440, 445, 446, 448, 550, 585
Polish American National Guard, 163
Polish American newspapers, 134, 135
Polish American Numismatic Association (Chicago), 333
Polish American parishes, 192
Polish American Studies, 323, 461, 469, 567
Polish American Union in America, 167
Polish American Workers' Council, 544
Polish American World, 318, 446
Polish and Slavic Center (Brooklyn), 573
Polish Army, 216-220
Polish Army Veterans Association, 261, 262
Polish Army Veterans of America, 359
Polish Artists Guild, 584
Polish Arts and Culture Foundation (San Francisco), 330, 331
Polish Arts and Science Institute, 426
Polish Arts Club (Buffalo), 327
Polish Arts Club (Chicago), 327
Polish Arts Club (Newark), 327
Polish Arts Club (Rochester), 327
Polish Arts Club (Youngstown), 327
Polish Arts League (Pittsburgh), 327, 328
Polish Arts League (Syracuse), 327
Polish Association of America, 156
Polish Beneficial Society, 164
Polish Brethren, 13
Polish Buiro Szyfrow, 391
Polish Catholic Congress, 110, 184, 191
Polish Catholic League, 397
Polish Clergy, 274, 286, 430, 561
Polish Clergy Association, 561
Polish Club of Alliance College, 327
Polish College (Rome), 426
Polish Combatants Association, 131
Polish Committee, 44, 45
Polish Commonwealth, 19
Polish Constitution Day, 570
Polish Cultural Garden (Cleveland), 328
Polish Daily News, 491, 492, 561, 563, 568, 586
Polish Dances, 300
Polish Falcons of America, 131, 161, 162, 163, 203, 205, 223, 395
Polish Franciscan Sisters, 117
Polish Fraternals, 586, 588, 589
Polish Government-in-Exile (London), 163, 356-358, 360-362, 400, 403, 405, 409, 500
Polish Heritage Society (Grand Rapids), 327
Polish Heritage Society (Philadelphia), 327
Polish Highlanders Club, 317
Polish Home of Greenpoint, 130
Polish Immigration Committee, 424, 425
Polish Institute (Rome), 426
Polish Institute of Arts and Sciences in America, 319, 323, 424, 427, 473
Polish Lancers, 162
Polish language, 59, 123, 124, 129, 252, 257, 264, 555, 556, 559-561, 567, 584, 588, 602-603, 605
Polish League, 59, 85, 86
Polish Legion, 201, 206
Polish Legion of the American Army, 261
Polish Legions, 460
Polish Military Alliance of the East, 165

INDEX

Polish missionaries abroad, 557
Polish Moravian Church, 527
Polish Museum of America, 153, 154, 159
Polish National Alliance of Brooklyn, 131, 168
Polish National Alliance of Chicago, 124, 131, 144-155, 161, 168, 205, 236-240, 242, 255-260, 263, 283-285, 287, 359, 397, 409, 424, 427
Polish National Catholic Church, 111, 125, 126, 168-170, 182, 190, 191, 557, 559, 560, 561, 569, 576
Polish National Committee, 204, 220
Polish National Congress, 282
Polish National Liberation Committee, 402
Polish National Union, 125
Polish National Union of America, 168-170
Polish Opera Club, 3, 9
Polish People's Direction, 86
Polish People's Republic, 545
Polish Rebellion (1830), 50
Polish Relief, 426
Polish Review, 320, 321, 356, 357
Polish Riflemen's Societies, 201
Polish Roman Catholic Union, 120, 140, 141, 148-154, 205, 239, 242, 243, 255, 257-260, 283-286, 359, 395, 427, 485
Polish Seminary (Orchard Lake), 324, 566, 569, 570
Polish Seminary (Paris), 426
Polish Singers 'Alliance, 428
Polish Sisters of St. Joseph, 117
Polish Slavonic Literary Assn., 47
Polish Squadrons, 367
Polish Student's Association (London), 330
Polish surnames, 41
Polish Tatra Mountaineers Alliance of America, 317, 318
Polish Union of U.S. of North America, 154, 155
Polish Veterans' Association, 573
Polish Victims' Relief Fund, 210, 212
Polish War Relief Fund, 359, 397
Polish Women's Alliance in America, 156-161, 205
Polish Youth Association, 131
Polishville, 40
Pollack, J., Rabbi, 78
Polack, 20
Polonaise Arts Club, 328

Polonia Greenpoint Soccer Team, 131
Polonia Restituta, 166
Polonia, Wisconsin, 107, 108, 117, 118, 186
Polonians, 4
Polonium, 308
Polonus Philatelic Society, 333
Polska, Partia Socijalistyczna, 84
Polski Instytut Naukowy, 426
Polskie Stowarzyszenie Kasy p.o. Sw. Jana Kantego, see Polish Beneficial Society.
Polskie Towarzystwo Tatrzanskie, 316
Polsko Narodowa Spojnia w Ameryca, see Polish National Union of America
Polud Club (Detroit), 328, 329
Polzin, T., 556
Pomerania, 9, 13, 339, 352
Poniatowski, Stanislaw August (King), 19, 20, 21, 62
Poniatowski (Polish-Black), 460
Poniewierski, T., Sgt., 373
Pontiac, Michigan, 484
Popatowski, A., 131
Pope Benedict XV, 159
Pope Innocent 55, 75
Pope Leo XIII, 188, 189, 192, 566
Pope Paul VI, 468, 558, 560
Pope Pius X, 111
Pope Pius XI, 113
Pope Pius XII, 355
Pope Urban II, 74
Popielarz, E., Rev., 468
Poplawski, J., 86
Popowski, L., Mrs., 517
population (Polish), 3
Pork Chop Hill, 433
Port Hudson, La., 468
Port Johnston, S.C., 459
Port Orchard, Washington, 453
Portage County, Wis., 107, 527
Portugal, 55, 72, 343
Portuguese, 41, 254
Posen, 40, 80
Posen, Illinois, 451
Posen, Michigan, 121, 122
Positivists, 58, 59, 60, 66
Posner, 36
Post Eagle, 520, 572
Post, F., Rev., 527
Postep, 135
Postula, T., 384
Potocka Countess, (Dzialynski), 23
Potocki, A., Count, 56, 65

Potocki, Ignacy (Count), 22
Potocki, J., Count, 199
Potocki, R., Count, 199
Potocki, Stanislaw Szczesny, 23
Potrzeba, J. J., 386
Potsdam, 414, 415
Poughkeepsie, N.Y., 203
Powalski, W., 393
Poznan, Illinois, 40
Poznan, Poland, 4, 12, 31, 40, 41, 67, 70, 76, 85, 195, 340, 510, 543, 567, 593
Poznania, 37
Prado, P., 431
Prague, 74
Pranica, 287
Presbyterians, 96
Pretelat, General, 347
Princeton, N.J., 387
Princeton University Press, 313
Prokop, F. P., Lt., 374
Prus, A., 60
Prussia, 2, 5, 9, 16, 23-25, 36, 58, 60-63, 69, 82, 143, 154, 199, 322, 400
Prussia (East), 339
Prussian Poland, 34, 37, 38, 56, 60, 68, 69
Prussians, 16, 27, 104
Przeglad Polski, 61
Przemysl II, 9
Przewodnik Katolicki, 483
Przybelski, T., Lt., 453
Przyborski, E. T., 385
Przybyl, C. R., 386
Przybylowicz, M., 531
Przybylowicz, W., 452
Przybylski, W., 462
Prywara, J., 387
Ptolemy, 4
Pucilowski, G. A., 367, 368
Pucinski, R., 495, 550
Pudlo, W., Sgt., 373
Pulaski Association (Police Dept.), 589
Pulaski, Casimir, General, 39, 40, 94, 97, 118, 154, 159, 166, 209, 298, 328, 394
Pulaski (cities), 40
Pulaski Day Banquet, 328
Pulaski Hall (Chicago), 157
Pulaski High School (Milwaukee), 439
Pulaski (Masonic Lodges), 40
Pulaski Monuments, 40
Pulaski Parades, 298, 329, 354, 411, 550, 562
Pulaski Park (Denver), 328

Pulaski Plaza (Hartford, Conn.), 40
Pulaski School (New York City), 40
Pulaski, Wisconsin, 124, 252
Pusan, 433
Pustelnik, G. H., 374
Puzyrewski, L., 451
PV Engineering Forum, 387
Pybik, H. J., 374
Pyle, E., 370
Pyongang, 433
Pyry, Poland, 391
Pyszczynski, P., 304
Quarles, B., 459
Quels River, 7
Quigley, C., 345
Quigly, Bishop, 110
Quincy, E., 463
Quincy, Josiah, 47
Quinet, 306
Quinn, L., 491
Quota Law, 238

Rabi, I. I., 389
Rabin, I., 507
Rabinowicz, H. M., 70, 71, 79
Racibor, 110
Racinowski, J., 357
Racki, Z., 307
Radom, 31
Radzialkowski, T. C., 567
Radziminska, Rose, 392
Radziwill, Antoni, Prince, 56
Rafalko, E. A., 448
Rahway, N. J., 452
Rajca, A. R., 447
Rambeau, D., 566
Rapala, M., 163
Rapczak, M. J., Sgt., 451
Raphael, Sister, 117
Rappersville Fund, 159, 165
Rappersville, Switzerland, 164
Raronski, K. W., 453
Rataj, J., 394
Raugh, J. L., 545
Rauh, J., 547
Ravinia Park, 324
Rawlowski, J., 386
Rawski, J., 386
Ray, J., 431
Reading, Pa., 117, 393, 394
Reams, R. B., 511
Red Army, 341, 360, 402, 407, 413, 416
Red Arrow Division, 224, 386
Red Ruthenia, 6

Redzinski, R., 394
Regensburg, 370
Reichsrath, 87
Reichswehr, 391
Rej, G., 587
Rejewski, M., 391
Rejtan, 65
Remagen, 382
Rembowski, R., 66
Republicans, 304, 414
Resettlement Committee, 424, 425
Resurrectionist Fathers, 148, 149
Retzweiler, 225, 226
Reymont, L. A., 36, 307, 324
Rhee, S., 435
Rhine River, 1, 228, 346, 348, 382
Rhode Island, 451
Rhode, Paul, Bishop, 194, 243
Riabov, 332
Ribbentrop-Molotov Pact, 337
Rice, C. O., Monsignor, 548
Rice Institute, 313-314
Rickenbacker, E., 384, 387
Riga, 12
Riis, J., 95
Rindfleish, 76
Riond Bosson, 205
Riveredge, New Jersey, 445
Riverside, Illinois, 451
Riverside, R.I., 453
Riverton, New Jersey, 456
Rizzuto, 432
Robak, J. C., Sgt., 373
Robakowski, A., 564
Robinson, Jackie, 422
Rockefeller Foundation, 221
Rochester, New York, 51, 184, 327
Rockets (V-2's), 343
Rodgers, 422
Rodziewicz, M., 158, 159
Rogalski, J., 163
Rogawski, J. J., 386
Roginski, R. S., 385
Rogowski, E., Sgt., 374
Rogowski, R. C., 451
ROK's, 433
Rokosz, M., 157
Rolak, J. J., 386
Romagne, 227
Roman Legions, 4
Romania, 319, 344, 355
Romanians, 498, 535
Romanov, 68
Romans, 3, 4, 166
Romanticism, 89

Rome, 6, 68, 75, 82, 109-111, 149, 150, 183, 186-191, 195, 306, 529, 589
Rommel, E., General, 390
Romney, G., 396
Romski, P., 564
Romulus, Michigan, 373, 442
Roncheres, 226
Roosevelt, Eleanor, 418
Roosevelt, F. D., President, 120, 193, 313, 338, 341, 359-361, 366, 384, 400-406, 409-411, 415-418, 510, 511, 525, 544, 545
Rosary Hour, 551
Rose, E. P., 457, 466, 467
Rose, M., 394
Rose, W. J., 57, 68
Rosenthal, A. N., 500
Rosentiel, Blanka, 331, 587
Roseville, Michigan, 378, 452, 558
Rosholt, M., 528
Rosochacki, E., 386
Ross, B., 385
Rostenkowski, D., Congressman, 454
Rotary Club, 390
Roth, C., 70, 498
Rothstein, A., 511, 512
Rotterdam, 368
Roucek, J. S., 233, 401
Rouen, 368
Rowinski, Z., 163
Rowny, E. L., 448
Royal Oak, Michigan, 372, 566
Rozanski, E. C., Corporal, 450
Rozanski, E. C., 587
Rozek, E., Dr., 410-412
Rozman, J. C., 386
Rozmarek, C., 560
Rozmarek, K., 256, 287, 363, 409-411, 415, 424
Roztworowski, J., 308
Rozycki, J., 391
Rubinstein, A., 219, 220, 312, 313
Ruch Oporu, 515
Ruczaja, J., 307
Rudnicki, 308
Rudzinski, August, 140
Ruhr Region, 345
Rumanians, 417
Ruminski, R. P., 453
Runstedt, 348
Rupinski, C., Rev., 486
Ruskowski, C., Rev., 486
Russell, C., 480
Russia, 2, 4, 21, 23, 25, 27, 35, 36,

Ryan, R. A., 546
Ryan, S., Bishop, 110 111
Rybarczyk, E., 357
Rybicki, E. C., 231
Rybicki, F., Lt., 449, 450
Rybicki, J., 473
Rybicki, P., Rev., 473
Rykulski, S. J., 386
Ryzowicz, J., 163
Rzadkowolski, A. J., 386
Rzepka, J. J., Sgt., 374

Saar River, 228
Sabiers, M., 555
Sacred Heart Parish (Roseville, Mich.), 558
Saddle Brook, N.J., 452
Sadlowski, E., 549, 550
Sadowski, A., 527
Sadowski, Anthony, 381
Sadowski, A. J., 381
Sadowski, J. J., 384
Saginaw, Michigan, 163, 373, 374, 385
Saint Albertus Church (Detroit), 139
Saint Anthony of Padua (Jersey City), 183
Saint Hyacinth Church (Chicago), 156
Saint John Cantius, 164
Saint John Cantius College (Erie, Pa.), 124
Saint Mary's College (Orchard Lake, Michigan), 127
Saint Paul, Minn., 154, 155
Saint Stanislaus Church (Chicago), 156, 170
Saint Stanislaus Church (New York), 208
Saint Stanislaus Church (Scranton), 187, 188, 189
Saint Stanislaus College, 148
Saints Cyril & Methodius Seminary (Orchard Lake), 124, 140
Saipan, 383
46, 57, 58, 60-64, 66, 69, 81, 82, 89, 143, 165, 198-202, 219, 232, 316, 322, 340, 342, 343, 360, 361, 400-402, 405, 410, 413, 420
Russian Poland, 34, 37, 52, 54, 56, 59, 60, 68, 83, 85
Russians, 21, 23, 25-28, 46, 64, 98, 104, 207, 248, 252, 342, 349, 400, 402, 403, 416, 697, 499, 535
Roszkiewicz, P. F., 452
Ruthenia, 12
Ruthenians, 13, 63, 300, 535

Salamaua, 371
Salmonski, J. K., 47
Saloutos, T., 94
Samoset, 525
San Antonio, Texas, 453
San Diego, California, 451
San Francisco, 42, 144, 206, 330, 451
San Jacinto, 44
San Pietro, 278
San River, 342
Sanchez, C. E., 42
Sand, George, 306
Sandberg, N. C., 585
Sandomierz, 8
Sanguszko, Prince, 23
Sanocki, F. J., 386
Sanok, A. H., 385
Santa Anna, 44
Santa Cruz Islands, 376
Santa Fe *New Mexican*, 380
Santayana, G., 603
Santo Domingo, 43, 460
Sapiehas, Princes, 23
Saratoga, 311
Sarmatians, 4
Sasinowski, P. S., 452
Sasson, S., 431
Sasson, V., 475
Satterlee, H. L., 212
Saturday Evening Post, 387, 414
Savannah, Georgia, 40, 94, 298
Savatski, K. D., 42
Savonarola Theological Seminary, 125
Saucinas, E., 357
Saud, Ibn, 511
Saudi Arabia, 229
Saxons, 21, 22
Sawicki, J., Sgt., 369, 370
Sawlocki, J. S., 456
Scajaquada Creek Expressway, 378
Scandinavians, 254, 303, 541
Scenery Hill, Pa., 452
Schachern, H., 556
Schaefer Scholarships, 315
Schaffner, 541, 542
Schenectady, New York, 125
Schermerhorn, R. A., 272, 358, 542
Schleck, M., 59
Schlesinger, A. M., 192
Schmidt, Germany, 383
Schmidt, Hans-Thilo, 391
Schneiweis, J. S., 118
Schnickel, R., 210
scholarships, 284, 310, 315
Schollatta, F., 51, 52

INDEX

schools, 80, 87, 116-122, 127, 194, 268, 269, 271, 272, 303, 428, 484, 555, 556, 574
Schreiber, A., 307
Schriftgiesser, 52
Schrusnecki, J., 44
Schultz, G., 547
Schultz, J., 535
Schumaker, G., 357
Schurayts, I., 521
Schwab, R., 131
Schwarz, J., 535
Schweitzer, F. M., 74, 78
Schyska, L. F., 451
Scituate, Mass., 452
Scotch Calvinists, 13
Scotland, 63
Scots, 178, 198, 247, 535
Scott, Hugh, 529
Scott, P. D., 331
Scott, R., 474
Scout Movement, 259
scouting programs, 154
Scranton, Pa., 125, 169, 186, 188, 189, 257, 258, 327, 393, 453, 536, 576
Scranton, Diocese, 189
Sea League of America, 131
Sedita, F. A., 309
Sedrowski, E., 386
Sefranski, L., 390
Segal, J. E., Rabbi, 522
Sek, M. F., 451
Seklecki, C. H., 452
Selewski, 487
Sembrich-Kochanski, M., 326
Seneski, B. V., 385
Seoul, 433, 434
Sequoya, 525
Seraphic Chronicle, 551
Serbians, 197, 254, 535, 603
Seroczynski, F. T., 147
Severo, S., 267
Seward, W. H., 47
Sexton, J. H., 282
Seymour, C., 214
Shaarit Haplytah, 517
Shachna, S., Rabbi, 78
Shaffer, G. K., 385
Shallna, A. O., 458
Shamokin, Pa., 118, 392
Shannon, W. V., 178
Shantytown Lake, Wis., 528
Shapley, H., Dr., 312, 315
Shearer, L., 388
Sheldon, G. L., Bishop, 556, 557

Shenandoah Pa., 546
Shepperson, W. S., 52
Sherwood Forest, 316
Shikoski, D. P., 385
Shore, D., 337
Shoshoni, 524
Siberia, 26, 59, 100
Sicily, 26, 379, 384, 385, 392
Sidzina, J. A., 381
Siedlak, Jan, 41, 42
Siedlarczyk, M., 317
Siegfried Line, 346, 348, 349
Siekierski, J., 381
Siemienski, J., 562
Siemovit IV, 12
Sienkiewicz, C., 395
Sienkiewicz, Henryk, 26, 51, 97, 199, 205, 209, 308, 328
Sierocinski, J., 223
Sigismund III, King, 21, 80
Sigismund of Luxemburg, 14
Signal Battery, 420
Sigourney, 524
Sikorski, E. G., 452
Sikorski, W., General, 308, 356-358, 362, 399-402, 510
Silesia, 7, 8, 12, 85, 110, 143, 165, 199, 235
Silver, D., 519
Sima, T. W., 456
Sioux Indians, 524, 531
Sisters of Notre Dame, 117
Sisters of St. Peter Claver, 474
Sisters of the Holy Family of Nazareth, 117, 195
Sisters of the Immaculate Conception, 134
Sisters of the Resurrection., 117
Sisters of the Third Order of St. Francis, 117
Sitko, J., 163
Sitko, M., 331
Siwek, M. J., 373
Siwiak, J., 308
Siwek, F., 520, 521
Sixth Colored Cavalry, 469
Skalba, J. J., Cpl., 448
Skalski, F., Rev., 555, 559
Skarb Narodowy, see National Treasury
Skarga, P., Rev., 144
Skiba, J., 357
Skibinski, C., 304
Sklodowska-Curie, M., 158, 308, 328
Skokie, Illinois, 451, 508
Skorupski, H. J., 373

Skowron, W. M., 452
Skrobanki, 291
Skrzynecki, Jan, General, 26
Skupienski, E., 357
Slask, 165, 430
Slaski, Corporal, 226
Slavonic Tribes, 4, 10
Slavophilism, 60
Slavs, 3, 6, 62, 254, 581
Slawisz, J. S., 366
Slesinski, T., 252, 270, 324-326
Slonina, A. J., 395
Slisz, J., 306, 307
Slisza, J., 307
Slikinski, A., S., 386
Slomiany, C. H., 452
Slominski, F., Rev., 488, 490, 491
Slominski, L., 509
Slominski, S., 509
Slomowitz, P., 511
Slovaks, 6, 417, 535
Slowacki, Juliusz, 26, 55, 97, 205
Slowakiewicz, A., Bishop, 576
Slowik, R. A., Capt., 442
Smagowicz, F., 163
Smalec, S. J., 386
Smialek-Sinclair, A. N., 587
Smith, J., Captain, 525, 526
Smith, Kate, 337
Smith, W. C., 233, 246, 247
Smithsonian Institute, 332, 333
Smithsonian Magazine, 332
Smolczynski, W., 108
Smolensk, 12, 401
Smolenski, W., 66
Smulski, J., 205, 211
Smyk, F. B., 452
Sobanski, B. W., 384, 386
Sobczak, J. S., 452
Sobieniowski, S. Rev. Dr., 307
Sobieski, A., 51, 63
Sobieski, Jan III, King, 1, 2, 14, 19-22, 40, 51, 69, 128, 147, 311, 531
Sobieski, T. J., Capt., 373
Sobkowiak, W., 393
Sobolewski, Paul, 48
Social Democratic Party, 85
Socialist Parties, 83-86
Socialist Party of the U.S., 543-544
Society for Polish Immigrants of New York, 131
Society of Polish Arts & Letters (Chicago), 327
Society of the Remagen Bridgehead, 382

Society of St. Peter Claver, 468
Sokalski, S., 453
Sokolov, Poland, 511
Solczyk, R. J., Lt., 448
Solinski, I., 556
Solinski, M., 556
Solzhenitsyn, A. E., 417, 418
Sons of Poland, 131, 238
Sophia, Duchess of Hohenberg, 197
Sorbonne University, 12
Sorrell, Richard S., 121, 122
Sosnowski, J. B., 304
South America, 2
South Bend, Indiana, 223, 327, 451, 550
South Bridge, Mass., 452
South Carolina, 459, 466, 481, 482
South Dakota, 528, 531
Southeastern High School (Detroit), 371
Southern Christian Leadership Conference, 495
Southhampton, L.I., 184
Soviet Union, 342, 343, 356, 360, 400-405, 408, 412, 413, 529
Soviets, 361
Spain, 2, 6, 55, 72, 73, 77, 78, 219, 220, 343, 511, 525, 530, 544
Spalding College, 475
Spalding, J., 182
Spanish, 38, 39, 178, 194, 254, 303, 484, 569
Spanish American War 112
Spanish Jews, 78
Sparks, J., 47
Speek, P. A., 121, 122
Spellman, F., Cardinal, 354
Spencer, Herbert, 59, 85
Spender, S., 436
Spring Lake, N.C., 452
Springfield Gardens, N.Y., 452
Springfield, Illinois, 546
Springfield, Ohio, 542
Sprout, Col., 459
Srole, L., 180
SS Cyril & Methodius Seminary, 490, 555
St. Adalbert, 5
St. Adalbert's Church (Buffalo), 111
St. Adalbert's Church (Glen Lyon, Pa.), 552
St. Adalbert's Church (Pittsburgh), 112
St. Albertus Church (Detroit), 108, 109, 496

INDEX

St. Barbara's School (Lackawanna), 121
St. Bonaventure College, 124
St. Casimir Church (Brooklyn), 112
St. Casimir Church (Detroit), 109, 112, 114, 484
St. Cecelia Church (Detroit), 473
St. Clair, Michigan, 385
St. Clair Shores, Michigan, 477
St. Cloud, Minn., 393
St. Francis of Assisi School (Detroit), 556
St. Hedwig Church (Detroit), 108
St. Hyacinth School (Detroit), 555, 559, 588
St. Hyacinth Seminary (Granby, Mass.), 551
St. John Cantius, 114
St. John Cantius College (Erie, Pa.), 124
St. John de Crevecoeur, 247
St. John Kanty College, 427
St. John's College (Philadelphia), 125
St. John's College (Washington, D.C.), 125
St. John's Michigan, 385
St. John of God Parish (Chicago), 561
St. John's Seminary (Plymouth, Mich.), 522
St. John the Baptist Church (Collegeville, Minn.), 589
St. Josaphat (Detroit), 267
St. Josaphat's Basilica (Milwaukee), 112-114
St. Joseph, Michigan, 373
St. Josephat Church (Detroit), 487
St. Joseph's Charity Organization, 131
St. Joseph's Church (Pontiac), 483, 484
St. Joseph's Church (Polonia, Mich.), 107
St. Joseph's Home for Polish Immigrants, 131-134
St. Joseph's Polish Church (Denver), 328
St. Ladislaus School (Detroit), 555
St. Lo, 377
St. Louis, Missouri, 117, 531
St. Martin Church (Polonia, Wis.), 107
St. Martin de Porres High School, 473
St. Mary of Czestochowa Church (Pittsburgh), 112
St. Mary's College (Orchard Lake, Mich.), 124, 427, 486
St. Michael's Church (Buffalo), 109, 110
St. Patrick's Cathedral (New York City), 354
St. Paul, Minn., 196, 327
St. Peter's Basilica (Rome), 111, 113
St. Petersburgh, 22, 82
St. Stanislaus, 108, 110, 111, 114, 120
St. Stanislaus Church (Buffalo), 110
St. Stanislaus Church (Chicago), 10
St. Stanislaus Church (Pittsburgh), 111
St. Stanislaus Kostka Church (Brooklyn), 112
St. Stanislaus Kostka Church (Milwaukee), 108
St. Stanislaus Kostka College (Chicago), 125
St. Stanislaus Kostka Society of Chicago, 102
St. Stanislaus Society, 109
St. Theresa Catholic School (Detroit), 566
Stachowiak, C., 304
Stachowski, A. T., 452
Stack, V. S., 396
Stahl, Z., 401
Stalin, J., 342, 353, 400-407, 409-411, 413, 415, 416, 417, 545
Stalingrad 412
Stan Lesny Scholarships, 315
Stanczyks, 58, 65
Standard Oil Company, 212
Standing Bear, Chief, 528
Stanislaw, E., Brother, 286
Staniszewski, A., 163
Staniszewski, E., Cpl., 452
Stankevich, J. J., Sgt., 373
Stankiewicz, E. H., 386
Stanko, R. G., 452
Stansbury, E. A., 50
Stanton, Sec. of War, 464
Stark, A., 267, 331
Starzynski, P., 243
Stasiewicz, F. H., 381
Statute of Kalisz, 70
Stec, A., 386
Steeltown, Pa., 536
Stefan, B., 231
Stefanik, E. P., 452
Steinbeck, John, 337
Steiner, E. A., 533
Stelmach, J., Monsignor, 111
Stepanski, J. S., Lt., 373
Stephanowski, M., 109

Sterling Heights, Mich., 487
Stevens Point, Wis., 41, 107, 117, 385
Still, C. V., 468
Still, L., 468
Still, W., 468
Stockbridge, Mass., 460
Stockette, 225
Stojowski, Z., Dr., 325, 326
Stoklosa, J. S., 375, 376
Stoklosa, P., 376
Stone, M., 212
Stopa, L. A., 374
Storz, R. E., 456
Stowarzyszenie Polakow w Ameryce, see Polish Association in America
Stowarzyszenie Synow Polski, see Association of Sons of Poland
Stowe, H. B., 462
Stozeski, A., 448
Stozeski, Bernard, 448
Stozeski, Edward, 448
Stozeski, Eugene, 448
Stozeski, Fred, 448
Stozeski, James, 448
Stozeski, Joseph, 448
Straka, C. C., 386
Strasbourg, 347
Straszewska, M., 53
Straszewski, G., 451
Stravinsky's Sonata, 219
Strawson, J., 352
Straz, 125
Streeter, H. I. (Judge), 473
Stremplewski, J., 440, 441
Stritch, Cardinal, 551
Strycharz, S. S., 451
Styniaski, J. F., 386
Strzelczyk, M., 309
Strzelka, W. A., 385
Strzyzewski, M., 42
Stuart, James, 63
Stuka Squadrons, 351, 353
Stuyvesant, P., 39
Stybel, C. A., 452
Styka, J., 314
Stypula, M., 163
Sucharski, H., 349
Sudwoj, M. B., 594, 595
Suhl, Y., 466
Sukara, M. T., 452
Sulewski, R. J., 373
Sullivan, Ed., 496
Summit, Illinois, 385
Sun Times (Chicago), 501

Sunday News (Detroit), 454, 456, 473, 506, 531, 546, 576
Sunday News Magazine, 476
Super, P., 199, 412
Superczynski, J. P., 451
Surowiec, E. S., 386
Susskind, D., 504, 506
Suszek, L. C., Sgt. 374
Sven, 6
Swanton, Ohio, 452
Swapka, F., 494
Swastek, J., Rev., 561
Sweden, 2, 16, 20, 21, 63, 81, 300, 602
Swedes, 41, 80, 128, 247, 535, 539
Sweetest Heart of Mary Church (Detroit), 109, 487, 496
Swieconka, 292, 293
Swierczewski, K., General, 344
Swierz, N. F., Sgt., 373
Swietchowski, A., 60
Swietlik, F. X., 397
Swiss, 10, 178, 252
Swiss Guard, 39
Switanowski, H. H., Sgt., 371
Switzerland, 85, 142, 159, 165, 205, 225, 346
Swoboda, 135
Sybilska, Monica, Mother, 567
Sylwanowicz, C., 452
Symfonia Choir, 131
Symons, A., Archbishop, 192
Synod of Baltimore, 188
Syracuse, New York, 327
Syracuse University, 410
Syrians, 535
Sytkowski, H. A., 386
Szablowski, W., 131
Szajnert, J., 143
Szandorowska, J., 509
Szatkowski, L. S., 366
Szawlewski, Dr., 235
Szczechowski, S., 366
Szczepanczyk, G., 452
Szczepanski, J., 344
Szczepanski, P., 163
Szczewski, R. S., 386
Szczygiel, J. F., 386
Szczyglinski, M., 189
Szczypinski, W. J., 386
Szegen, A., 163
Szemplewski, E., Sgt., 374
Szkodzinski, E., Lt., 374
Szoka, E. C., Monsignor, 562
Szopinski, D., Rev., 282

Szostakowski, C., 386
Szoszorek, G. J., 453
Szrajfer, K., 343
Szujkowski, F. A., 385
Szujski, J., 61, 64
Szulczynski, J., 163
Szulec, J., 587
Szumusiak, W. B., 386
Szwed, J. C., 386
Szweda, E., Pfc., 447
Szwedowa, F., 171
Szwejkowski, B., 386
Szydlo, T. J., 453
Szymanowski, Monsignor, 566
Szymanowski, W., 462
Szymanska, M., 551
Szymanski, F. A., 452
Szymanski, J., 551
Szymanski, J. S., 452
Szymanski, R. T., 453
Szymanski, V., 385

Tabak, A., 328
Taft, President, 212
Tallchief, Maria, 525
Talleyrand, 205
Talmud, 78, 79, 83, 497, 513
Tannenberg, 12, 14
Tarantowicz, J. E., Lt., 453
Tarawa, 383
Targosz, S., Rev., 117
Tarkowski, J., 163
Tarnapowicz, F. P., 395
Tarnopol, 344
Tarnow, 40
Tarnowski, E. J., 376
Tartars, 9, 13, 14, 20
Tatarkiewicz, Dr. 308
Tatra Mountains, 62, 316, 317
Tatrzanski Orzel, 318
Taussif, Ellen, 110, 120, 126, 127, 377, 540
Taylor, G., 232
Taylor, Michigan, 452
Tazbir, J., 38
Teheran, 407, 408, 411, 414
Teheran Conference, 407
Tel Aviv, 520, 521
Telemann, G. P., 299
Teller, E., Dr., 387-389
Teller, J. L., 500
Tempe, Arizona, 451
Tempest, R., 484
Tennant, A. E., 198
Tennessee, 471

Terryville, Conn., 357
Testem Benevolentiae, 195
Tetmajer, K. P., 317
Tetmajer, W., 314
Teutonic Knights, 8, 12, 128
Teutonic Order, 12, 13, 16
Texas, 34, 41, 43, 44, 224, 451, 453, 455
Texas Hall of State, 44
Texas Revolution, 44
The Examiner, 460
Theodosetta, Sister, 105
Third Armored Division, 394
Third Penn. Artillery Regiment, 469
Thomas, C. M., 112, 268, 295, 485
Thomas, William, 302
threefold loyalty, 58
Thunderhead Mountain, 528
Time Weekly Magazine, 415, 416, 498
Tindal, R., 491
Ting, Sam, 42
Tito, J., 545
Tobruk, 263
Tochman, K., Major, 46, 47
Tokyo, 364
Tolczyk, L., Rev., 507
Toledo, Ohio, 109, 282, 382, 452, 549
Tomaczykowska, W., 331
Tomakowski, J. T., 449
Tomasik, E., Dr., 554, 587
Tomasovic, S. R., 452
Tomaszewski, Z. J., 451
Tomaszkiewicz, M., 359, 397
Topolski, J., 329, 304
Torah, 78
Torrecremata, Cardinal, 17
Torrington, Conn., 387
Torun, 11, 12, 17
Torzok, J., 453
Toton, J., Dr., 329
Towarzystwo Demokratyczne Wygnacow Polskich w Ameryce, 468
Towarzystwo Patriotyczne, 55
Townsend, P., 351
Trampski, D. J., 456
Transylvania, 20
Trbovich, M., 488, 565, 572
Treaty of Lublin, 63
Treaty of Riga, 400, 413
Trebnik, A. C., Sgt., 374
Tremaine, A. G., 121
Trenton, N.J., 452
Trombka, S., 386
Troyanowski, J., Lt., 373
Truchan, G., 385

Truman Doctrine, 420
Truman H., President, 374, 389, 413, 415, 419, 432, 433
Tucson, Arizona, 451
Tulagi, 384
Turek, J. A., 386
Turkey, 10, 73
Turks, 1, 14, 20, 21, 63, 69, 80, 104, 128, 299, 311, 433, 602
Turner, A., Captain, 44
Turowska, F., 325
Turski, H. S., Cpl., 451
Tuszynski, J. F., 386
Two Rivers, Wis., 453
Twork, J., 385
Tworki, 202
Tyckowski, B. J., 374
Tycz, J. N., 453
Tyczowski, J., 163
Tydzien Polski, 521
Tyndall, 442
Tyssowski, J., 49

UAW-CIO, 421
Ubik, T., 571
Udall, M., 482
Uganda, 474, 475
Ukraine, 20, 21, 63, 343, 344
Ukrainians, 254, 342, 343, 498, 500
Ulam, S., Dr., 366, 387-390
Ultra, 390, 391
Uminski, S. H., 392
Uncasville, Conn., 451
Underground Railroad, 468
Unia Polek w Ameryce, see Union of Polish Women in America
Union City, 163
Union, N.J., 452
Union of Hadziacz, 21
Union of Horodlo, 16
Union of Lublin, 50
Union of Polish Falcons, 215
Union of Polish Priests, 560
Union of Polish Socialists Abroad, 84
Union of Polish Women in America, 171
Unitarianism, 13
United Garment Workers, 542
United Mine Workers, 540, 545-548
United Mine Workers Journal, 547
United Nations, 433
United Nations Conference, 415
United Polish Women of America, 172
United Transportation Union, 550
University of Brussels, 55

University of Buffalo, 120
University of Buffalo Dental School, 127
University of California (Berkeley), 314
University of Chicago, 390, 594
University of Detroit, 199, 231, 328, 329
University of Illinois, 495
University of Indiana, 475
University of Miami, 332
University of Michigan, 286, 379, 390
University of Pittsburgh, 327, 328
University of Santiago, 532
University of Toledo, 282
University of Toronto, 204
University of Torun, 315
University of Warsaw, 54, 65
University of Wilno, 54
University of Wisconsin, 252, 439
UNRRA, 423
Urban, M. A., Sgt., 374
Urbanek, E., 386
Urbanik, C., 385
Urbas, J., 317
Uris, L., 501, 503
U.S. Atomic Energy Commission, 390
U.S. Military Academy, 434
U.S. National Guard, 162
U.S. Naval Academy, 229
U.S. Navy Department, 213
USSR, 342, 343, 360
Uszynski, J., 163
Utica, Michigan, 452
Utica, New York, 452

Valentin, Hugo, 72, 80
Vanderbilt, F. A., 212
Vanderlip, F. A., 212
Vanutelli, Cardinals, 188
Varus, 4
Vasa, Zymgund III, 19
Vasas, 63
Vassar College, 310, 313
Vatican, 39, 54, 67, 69, 111, 177, 184, 185, 241, 557, 559, 573, 575
Vauclain, S. M., 310
Venedi, 6
Versailles Conference, 214
Vesle River, 226
Vienna, 2, 14, 21, 59, 63, 69, 128, 147, 311, 602
Vietnam, 436-450, 453, 454
Vietcong, 437, 440, 442, 443, 445, 454, 455, 456

INDEX

Villa Maria College, 55
Vince River, 44
Vincent, Sister, 117
Virginia, 40, 308, 527, 533, 534
Virginia City, Nevada, 51
Visstsky, R. W., 453
Vistula River, 4, 5, 11, 28, 154, 352, 403
Viznicki, C., 386
Vladimiri, Paulus, 532
Voice of America, 420
Voltaire, 23
Von Besseler, 201, 202
Von Bock, F., General, 339
Von Ribbentrop, 342
Von Runstedt, G., General, 339
Vratislaw II, Prince, 74

Wachtel, K., 139, 141
Wachtl, K., Dr., 151, 358
Waco, Texas, 225
Wahol, L. G., 386
Kahoo Chief, 337
Wake, 373
Walczak, L. J., 383
Walczak, N. F., 435
Waldo, F. E., 385
Waldorf-Astoria Hotel, 313, 507, 509
Walenczak, W., 386
Wales, 63
Walker, F. A., 541
Walkowiak, A. J., 307
Walkowski, L. M., 386
Wallington, N. J., 452
Walsh, T., 476
Walshville, Illinois, 451
Walter, General, 544
Wanamaker, Mrs. J., 212
Wanat, G. K., Capt., 456
Wansart, R., 357
Ward, R. F., 384
Wardzinski, F., 44
Warholak, H., 386
Warwinski, Z. C., 373
Warnadowicz, F., 525
Warne, F. J., 536
Warner, W. L., 180
Warren, Michigan, 448, 452, 473, 487
Warren, Ohio, 542
Warsaw Academy of Fine Arts, 529
Warsaw Ghetto, 499, 502, 503, 505
Warsaw Poland, 12, 22, 24, 25, 28, 40, 54, 58, 59, 66, 67, 81, 82, 124, 129, 201, 202, 219, 242, 272, 308, 322, 339, 340, 341, 349, 350-355, 341, 391, 402, 403, 405, 406, 500, 508, 509, 510, 545, 557, 593
Warwick, R. I., 453
Warynski, Ludwik, 84
Warzecha, G. W., 451
Washington, 49, 241, 451, 519
Washington, D.C., 125, 144, 154, 211, 214, 230, 360, 451, 453, 491, 530, 545, 552, 558, 575, 600
Washington, G., President, 39, 49, 319, 327, 459, 461, 471
Washington Island, Wis., 252
Washington, Missouri, 52
Washington, Pa., 548
Wasilewski, A., 47
Waskewicz, H. J., 374
Wasowicz, B., Lt., 374
Wassell, F. F., 359, 414, 415
Waszkiewicz, 394
Waterville Regiment, 43
Waukegan, 550
Waukegan, N. Dakota, 589
Wauregan, Conn., 451
Wawel Castle, 272
Wawel Hill, 306
Wawrzawszek, A., 163
Wawrzynek, W. C., 374
Wawrzyniak, P., Rev., Msgr., 307
Wayland, Mass., 451
Waymart, Pa., 170
Wayne State University, 555
Wayne State University College of Lifelong Learning, 478
Wazyk, A., 399
Wdowicki, B. J., Sgt., 373
Weber High School (Chicago), 125
Weber, Supervisor, 455
Webster, D., 462, 463
Wegrzynek, M. F., 360-363
Weintraub, Wiktor, 49
Weiss, W. J., 452
Weld, R. F., 112, 393
Wells, O., 337
Welsh, 539
Wenceslaus, Sister, 11
Wendolowski, J. F., 451
Wendt, O., 476
Wengierski, T. G., 460
Wends, 6
Werwinski, I., 223
Wesolowski, E. A., 374
Wesolowski, J. W., 380
Wessel, J., 163
West Allis, Wis., 453
West Germany, 2

West Point Academy, 94, 394, 427, 449, 459
West Seneca, N.Y., 452
West Side Courier, 442, 443, 446, 484, 531
West Warwick, 453
Westerplatte, 349, 350, 355
Westphal, General, 348
Weyer, H., 331
Whisner, B., Major, 434
White House, 213, 382, 438
White, J., 230
White Russians, 13
White, W. L., 495
Whitfield, F., 314
Whitman, Walt, 247
Wiadomosci, 445
Wiadomosci Codzienne, 135
Widelski, R. J., 386
Wieczorek, D., 477
Wielbik, H., 329
Wielkopolanin, 135
Wielopolski, M. A., 56
Wiercinski, T. I., 385
Wierusz-Kowalski, A., 314
Wierzba, E. R., Cpl., 451
Wierzbicki, F. P., Dr., 531
Wierzynski, K., 329
Wiesel, E., 501
Wigilia, 289, 290, 329
Wilczynska, M., 394
Wildwood, N.J., 452
Wilk, F. E., Sgt., 373
Wilk, F. J., Sgt., 373
Wilk, W. A., Lt., 452
Wilkes-Barre, Pa., 155, 188, 552
Wilkoplan, D. D., 452
Williams, M., 552
Williams, W., 485
Willie, L., 485
Willoughby, Ohio, 452
Wilmette, N. Dakota, 589
Wilmington, Del., 163, 504
Wilno, 12, 20, 40, 54, 85, 167, 344, 510, 529
Wilski, 384
Wilson Bishop, 212
Wilson Middle School (Detroit), 491
Wilson, Mrs. W., 213
Wilson, Woodrow, President, 162, 165, 203, 212-215, 220
Winiarski, E. T., 386
Winkowski, J. R., Commander, 441
Winlock, Washington, 453
Winnemucca, 52

Winnipeg, 244
Winston, R. and C., 75
Winter, N. O., 223, 224
Winterbothan, F. W., 391
Wisconsin, 34, 35, 40-42, 107, 108, 116, 118, 145, 156, 163, 186, 223, 224, 225, 252, 260, 261, 304, 327, 331, 385, 387, 410, 439, 441, 451, 453, 527, 528, 543, 551, 559
Wisinski, N. J., 386
Wisla, A., 163
Wisniewski, 41
Wisniewski, C. J., 451
Wisniewski, D., 451
Wisniewski, D. E., Pvt., 444
Wisniewski, J., 394
Wisniewski, Z., 163
Wisniowiecki, M., 20
Witek, W., 451
Witos, M., 406
Witos, Wincenty, 86, 87
Wittke, C., 192, 247, 539
Witzkoski, B. J., 453
Wiznak, George, 394
Wiznak, John, 394
Wiznak, M., 394
Wiznak, Michael, 394
Wiznak, Raymond, 394
Wiznak, Thomas, 394
Wladyslaw IV, 63, 64, 81
Wladyslaw Herman, 7
Wladyslaw the Short, 9
Wloch, K. J., 307, 308
Wlodkowicz, Pawel, 13, 14
Wlodkowicz, P., 532
Wloszczewski, S., Dr., 324
Wodzinski, F. T., 373
Wojcicky, J. L., 453
Wojciechowski, M., 386
Wojciechowski, W. A., 376
Wojcik, L. A., 451
Wojcik, J., Rev., 131
Wojcik, W., 521
Wojczynski, A., 143
Wojewodzic, E. T., 380
Wojnar, W. J., 386
Wojnarowski, L., 390
Wojnarowski, S., 386
Wojnarski, S., 385
Wojtal, F., 261
Wojtalewicz, P., 228
Wojtanek, Maria, 317
Wojtkowiak, S., 304
Wojtonowski, L., 390
Wojtowicz, F., 163

INDEX 665

Wojtusik, S., 163
Wolak, A., 383
Wolfe, Thomas, 419
Woloszyk, D. J., 456
Wolowska, L., 157
Wolski, K., 461
Wolynia, 8, 73
Women's Trade Union League, 542
Wondolowski, J. J., 395
Wonsan, 433
Wonsart, R., 357
Wood, K., 345
Woods, W., 509
Woodward, L., 400
Woolsey, L. H., 413
Wopinski, B. M., 451
Worcester, Mass., 378, 574
World Almanac, 140
Wozniak, F. J., Capt., 456
Wozenski, E. F., General, 379, 435, 448
Woznicki, S., Bishop, 425
Wozniak, T. F., 386
Wright, H., 413
Wright, Orville, 312
Wright-Patterson AFB, 448
Wroblewski, T. J., Rev., 552
Wroblewski, W. F., Cpl., 456
Wroclaw, 5, 7, 9
Wronki, 70
Wronki, C. J. B., 171
Wronski, S., 29
Wrotnowski, A., 469
Wucinski, R. T., 453
Wudarski, R. B., 386
Wujcicki, W., 383
Wurmbrand, M., 498
Wyandotte, Michigan, 373, 384, 385
Wyatt, P. S., 44
Wycinanki, 291
Wyczawski, S., 522
Wyczolkowski, L., 314
Wydra, C. S., 374
Wydrzynski, C. S., 385
Wydzial Narodowy, 241
Wykowski, E. S., 386
Wysocki, A., 452
Wysocki, R., 331
Wyspianski, S., 26, 89, 308
Wyszomirski, J. D., 451
Wyszynski, Eustachy, 48
Wyszynski, R. J., 386
Wyszynski, Stefan, Cardinal, 31, 426
Wytrwal, Joseph A., Dr., 36, 39, 40, 43, 46, 47, 51, 65, 90, 120, 124, 138, 147, 152, 158, 175, 197, 212, 244, 245, 248, 251, 287, 308, 321, 329, 398, 424, 457, 484, 491, 494, 522, 526, 534, 561, 583, 584, 587

Yablonski, 545-550, 553
Yablonski, C., 548
Yablonski, K., 548 49,, 50
Yablonski, M., 548
Yad Vashem Avenue, 516
Yad Vashem Institute, 520, 523
Yad Vashem Medal, 513
Yalta, 404, 412-418
Yalta Conference, 405, 406, 409, 410, 415, 416
Yalta Treaty, 411
Yalu River, 433
Yeardley, Governor, 308, 326, 533, 534
Yiddish, 73, 78, 96
Yorktown, Texas, 453
Young, C., Mayor, 496
Young, Andrew, 496
Young, W. M., 488
Youngstown, Ohio, 325, 327
Yugoslavia, 64, 346

Zabinski, E. J., 383
Zaborowski, J., 526, 527
Zaborowski, O., 526
Zaborowski, S., Sgt., 373
Zaczek, S., 131
Zaczkowski, E., Sgt., 453
Zagora, S. H., 495
Zagorski, W., 57
Zajac, S. J., 373
Zajkowska-Jankie, Z. I., 516
Zak, A., 491, 494
Zakopane, 316
Zakrzewska, A., 467, 468
Zakrzeski, A., Capt., 440
Zakrzewski Memorial Scholarships, 315
Zalenka, S. A., 386
Zaleski, A., Bishop, 563
Zaleski, Bohdan, 48
Zaleski, M. J., 373
Zaleski, Oleg, 386
Zalewski, L., 376
Zalewski, S., Cpl., 451
Zaluski, J. A., Bishop, 22
Zamek, 201, 202
Zamiara, J. C., 452
Zamojski, A., 56
Zamojski, J., Chancellor, 19
Zamojski, W., 49

Zamosc, 19
Zangwill, I., 247, 248, 275
Zanussi, K., 332
Zapytowska, I., 163
Zaraza, P., General, 26
Zatocki, J. S., 456
Zawacki, H., 385
Zawisza, T. L., 451
Zawtocki, J., Sgt., 456
Zbikowski, E. J., 386
Zbikowski, M. G., 373
Zdanowski, J. T., 385
Zelazny, S. D., Lt., 447
Zelenski, B. S., 386
Zeleszovska, Catherine, 79
Zempolno. 352
Zemsta, M. J., 385, 386
Zeromski, 97, 324
Zew Mlodych, 330
Zgoda, 135, 146, 287, 359
Zielinski, Edward, 379
Zielinski, Eugene A., Lt., 371
Zielinski, F., 163
Zielinski, J. C., 495
Zielinski, P., 379
Ziemovit, 4
Zimmerman, I., 521
Ziolkowski, K., 528, 529
Zion, 82
Zglenicki, L., 171
Zjednoczenie Emigracji Polski, 55
Zjednoczenie Polskich Kaplanow, 560
Zjednoczenie Polskie Narodowe, see Polish National Alliance of Brooklyn
Zjednoczenie Polskie Rzymsko—Katolickie w Ameryce, see Polish Roman Catholic Union
Zmuda, H. J., 386
Zmuda, S. A., 386
Znaniecki, F., Dr., 302, 333
Zoldowski, A., 549
Zolkowska, G., 157

Zubrzycki, J., 37, 460
Zuch, Vince, 478, 479
Zuexano, D., 247
Zuhorski, C. S., Lt., 456
Zuk, M., Sgt., 371, 374
Zukowski, C. F., 386
Zulawski, L., 468, 469
Zulowski R. J., 456
Zurek,, M. R., 452
Zuzga, W. L., 383
Zwiazek Ludu Polskiego, 52
Zwiazek Narodowy Polski, see Polish National Alliance
Zwiazek Podhalan, 316
Zwiazek Polakow w Ameryce, see Alliance of Poles in America
Zwiazek Polek, 243
Zwiazek Polek w Ameryce, see Polish Women's Ailliance in America
Zwiazek Polskich Ksiezy w Ameryce, 131
Zwiazkowiec, see Alliancer
Zwolakowa, Maria, 29
Zychlinski, T., 161
Zygalski, H., 391
Zygielboim, S., 505
Zygmunt I, 63, 71, 79
Zygmunt II, 63, 79
Zygmunt III, Vasa, 63, 300
Zygmunt August, 73, 80, 81
Zygmunt, H. J., 328
Zygmunt, J. J., 385
Zygmunt, M., 393
Zyszkiewicz, B., 393
Zyszkiewicz, Ervin, 393
Zyszkiewicz, Henry, 393
Zyszkiewicz, John, 393
Zyszkiewicz, Joseph, 393
Zyszkiewicz, Leo, 393
Zyszkiewicz, Stanley, 393
Zywiec, G. R., 452

THE SLAVS IN 1950[a]

Nationality	Number	Religion	Citizenship
Eastern Slavs			
Great Russians	95,000,000	Greek Orthodox	USSR
Ukrainians	36,000,000	Greek Orthodox & Greek Catholic	USSR
Byelo-Russians	8,000,000	Greek Orthodox	USSR
Western Slavs			
Poles	24,000,000	Roman Catholic	Poland
Czechs	8,000,000	Roman Catholic	Czechoslovakia
Slovaks	3,000,000	Roman Catholic	Czechoslovakia
Lusatians	100,000	Protestant and Catholic	Eastern Germany
Southern Slavs			
Serbs	7,500,000	Greek Orthodox	Yugoslavia
Croats	4,500,000	Roman Catholic	Yugoslavia
Slovenes	1,400,000	Roman Catholic	Yugoslavia
Macedonians	1,100,000	Greek Orthodox	Yugoslavia
Bulgarians	6,500,000	Greek Orthodox	Bulgaria

---

[a] Hans Kohn, *Pan-Slavism, Its History and Ideology* (Notre Dame: Univesrity of Notre Dame Press, 1953), p. 337.